EZEKIEL
21–37

VOLUME 22A

The Anchor Bible is a fresh approach to the world's greatest classic. Its object is to make the Bible accessible to the modern reader; its method is to arrive at the meaning of biblical literature through exact translation and extended exposition, and to reconstruct the ancient setting of the biblical story, as well as the circumstances of its transcription and the characteristics of its transcribers.

The Anchor Bible is a project of international and interfaith scope: Protestant, Catholic, and Jewish scholars from many countries contribute individual volumes. The project is not sponsored by any ecclesiastical organization and is not intended to reflect any particular theological doctrine. Prepared under our joint supervision, The Anchor Bible is an effort to make available all the significant historical and linguistic knowledge which bears on the interpretation of the biblical record.

The Anchor Bible is aimed at the general reader with no special formal training in biblical studies; yet, it is written with the most exacting standards of scholarship, reflecting the highest technical accomplishment.

This project marks the beginning of a new era of cooperation among scholars in biblical research, thus forming a common body of knowledge to be shared by all.

William Foxwell Albright
David Noel Freedman
GENERAL EDITORS

THE ANCHOR BIBLE

EZEKIEL
21–37

◆

A New Translation
with Introduction and Commentary

MOSHE GREENBERG

THE ANCHOR BIBLE
Doubleday
New York London Toronto Sydney Auckland

The Anchor Bible
Published by Doubleday
a division of Bantam Doubleday Dell Publishing Group, Inc.
1540 Broadway, New York, New York 10036

Library of Congress Cataloging-in-Publication Data
Bible. O. T. Ezekiel XXI–XXXVII. English. Greenberg. 1997.
Ezekiel 21–37 : a new translation with introduction and commentary / Moshe Greenberg.
p. cm. — (The Anchor Bible ; 22A)
Includes bibliographical references and index.
1. Bible. O. T. Ezekiel XXI–XXXVII — Commentaries.
I. Greenberg, Moshe. II. Title. III. Series: Bible. English.
Anchor Bible.
1964 ; v. 22A.
BS192.2.A1 1964.G3 Vol. 22a
[BS1543]
224'.4077 — dc21 97-24287
CIP

ISBN 0-385-18200-7

Printed in the United States of America
September 1997

10 9 8 7 6 5 4 3 2 1

First Edition

Contents

◆

PREFACE

◆

Here by the grace of God is the second installment of my commentary to the Book of Ezekiel. That it has been so long in the making is largely owing to the extraordinary difficulties standing in the way of one who would understand the Book.

One set of difficulties stems from the encyclopedic range of Ezekiel's references. Since he was a priest, and therefore trained in the traditions and literature of his people, we may suppose that in principle everything contained under the rubrics "literature" and "traditions" in the sixth century B.C.E. kingdom of Judah was accessible to him. And in fact he does allude to almost every genre of Israelite literature known from the Bible:

(a) narrative (e.g., creation stories, the Flood, the promises to the Patriarchs, the Egyptian sojourn and the Exodus, the lawgiving and the rebellions in the wilderness, the illicit worship in the land, the political and military events of the kingdoms)
(b) poetry (e.g., echoes of Moses' Song [Deut 32])
(c) law—especially the substance and style of the priestly laws of the Pentateuch
(d) covenant blessings and curses
(e) prophecy (influence of, e.g., Amos, Hosea, Isaiah, but especially of Jeremiah's restoration prophecies)

While these allusions are illuminated by their antecedents and parallels elsewhere in the Bible, there are always divergences between the two, challenging the interpreter to ascertain whether Ezekiel reflects a different version or is reshaping (or distorting) for his purpose the version known to us from elsewhere.

Beside the literary allusions, the prophet's familiarity with a wide range of realia (not mentioned elsewhere in the Bible) appears repeatedly: e.g., the events attending childbirth, smelting processes, brothel argot, the construction and crew of a Tyrian ship, Tyre's trade, the ethnic components of Egypt's army, and Egypt's main cities.

Especially difficult to assess is the extent of the prophet's use of non-Israelite culture material. Was he familiar, e.g., with Mesopotamian iconography (in connection with the chariot vision); with Assyrian royal inscriptions (in connection with depictions of battlefield corpses); with native mythical representation of Egypt's king?

Ideally, one who aspires to be an interpreter to another age of such a polymath in his historical setting should possess a correspondingly wide range of antiquarian knowledge. In the real world one must settle for something less. The gain in ripeness from the delay in the completion of this commentary has, I hope, narrowed the gap between the ideal and the reality.

To these intrinsic difficulties must be added the ever-increasing body of conjecture challenging the integrity, authorship, and authenticity of the Book. It is doubtful that there can be found five consecutive verses on which all critics agree that they stem from the sixth-century exilic prophet. I have stated my position on the method of such criticism as an answer to the question "What are Valid Criteria for Determining Inauthentic Matter in Ezekiel?" (in J. Lust, ed., *Ezekiel and His Book*, pp. 123–35; see bibliography). Clearly MT contains a good deal of variant readings (conflated passages) and explanatory increments not present in the Hebrew *Vorlage* of the Greek translators. The provenience of such additional matter is unknown. E. Tov, in his study "Recensional Differences between the MT and LXX of Ezekiel" (see bibliography), regards them as an added layer in the literary history of the Book; this leaves open the question of origin of this matter (could not the prophet have been his own [first?] editor?).

The common assumption of an "Ezekiel school" that went on for generations updating the original oracles fails to appreciate the essentially static (merely explanatory or synonymous or stereotypical-formulaic) character of the so-called updating. There are, to be sure, a few manifest instances of updating, the most important of which is the amendment to the Tyre prophecy in 29:17–21; but it is expressly attributed to the prophet, and its chronological-historical frame is demonstrably limited to the reign of Nebuchadnezzar II or the presumed lifetime of the prophet.

I have not found the hypothesis of an Ezekiel school necessary to account for the present text; on the contrary, the attribution of extensive parts of the text to the "school" impoverishes, when it does not actually deform, the text (as it does, e.g., by denying the originality of 36:23b$^{\beta}$–38). The art and design of the present text yield its secrets to the critic who works with the ("holistic") hypothesis of its integrity as far as it will go (its limits are discussed in my "Valid Criteria" and in "Reflections on Interpretation," in M. Greenberg, *Studies in the Bible and Jewish Thought* [see bibliography]). Nevertheless, the fragmentation of the text produced by advocates of the "school" hypothesis can serve the holistic critic valuably as a heuristic foil.

Since the art and design of the oracles in the Book of Ezekiel show a characteristic configuration of features (e.g., the "halving" pattern and other hallmarks described in *Ezekiel 1–20*, pp. 25ff., which continue to appear in the present portion of the Book), it does not seem naive or implausible to suggest that an individual authorial mind and hand are responsible for them.

Ezekiel 21–37 accumulates more evidence in support of this interpretational stance.

I gladly acknowledge the help I have received in preparing this volume. During my sabbatical stay at Yale in 1987 Brevard Childs generously gave me the freedom of his library, thus enabling me to stock my study with all essential books. During the late eighties my then research assistant, Ilana Goldberg, critically annotated portions of my draft; her name appears repeatedly in the earlier chapters of this volume. The unhampered stretch of time that made it possible to finish and revise the draft was given to me in 1994–95 through a fellowship in the Center for Judaic Studies of the University of Pennsylvania, under the benevolent directorship of David Ruderman. The entire manuscript underwent the careful scrutiny of the general editor of this series, David Noel Freedman, whose contribution to the substance of the book and to the morale of its author is incalculable. My wife, Evelyn, was always ready to respond to my drafts as a representative "intelligent reader" and to help in such tasks as only such a reader can.

ABBREVIATIONS

SUPPLEMENT TO LIST IN *EZEKIEL 1–20*

◆

ABD	*Anchor Bible Dictionary*
AHw	W. von Soden, *Akkadisches Handwörterbuch,* 3 vols. Wiesbaden: Harrassowitz, 1965–81
AV	*The Authorized (King James) Version,* 1611
BHSyn	B. K. Waltke and M. O'Connor, *An Introduction to Biblical Hebrew Syntax,* Winona Lake, Ind.: Eisenbrauns, 1990
CBQ	*Catholic Biblical Quarterly*
DJD I	*Qumran Cave I,* Discoveries in the Judaean Desert—1, ed. D. Barthelemy et al., Oxford: Clarendon Press, 1955
DNF	David Noel Freedman (editorial comment)
EI	*Eretz-Israel*
G^L	The Lucianic revision of the Greek text (fourth century C.E.), as presented in G (Ziegler's edition of the Septuagint)
I	*Ezekiel 1–20,* Anchor Bible (followed by page number)
JSOTSup	Journal for the Study of the Old Testament Supplement Series
MenbSh	Menaḥem bar Shim'on (see bibliography in *Ezekiel 1–20*)
NRSV	*The New Revised Standard Version,* 1989
OTS	*Oudtestamentische Studiën*
PEQ	*Palestine Exploration Quarterly*
REB	*Revised English Bible,* 1989
SBLDS	Society of Biblical Literature Dissertation Series
T^O	Targum Onkelos, according to A. Sperber, ed., *The Bible in Aramaic,* I. Leiden: E. J. Brill, 1959

Location of tractates in Mishnaic and related literature

b.	Babylonian Talmud, e.g., *b. Sotah*
j.	"Jerusalem" (= Palestinian) Talmud, e.g., *j. Sanhedrin*
m.	Mishnah, e.g., *m. 'Abot*
t.	Tosefta, e.g., *t. Baba Qamma*

Bibliography

Works Cited for the First Time in This Volume or Missing from the Bibliography of *Ezekiel 1–20*

◆

Allen, L. C. "Ezekiel 24:3–14: A Rhetorical Perspective." *CBQ* 49 (1987), 404–14.

———. "The Rejected Sceptre in Ezekiel XXI 15b, 18a." *VT* 39 (1989), 67–71.

———. *Ezekiel 20–48*. Word Biblical Commentary 29. Dallas: Word Books, 1990. Cited as "Allen."

Anbar, M. "Une nouvelle allusion à une tradition babylonienne dans Ézéchiel (XXII 24)." *VT* 9 (1979), 352–53.

Astour, M. C. "The Origin of the Terms 'Canaan,' 'Phoenician,' and 'Purple.'" *JNES* 24 (1965), 346–50.

Avigad, N., and J. C. Greenfield. "A Bronze *phiale* with a Phoenician Dedicatory Inscription." *IEJ* 32 (1982), 118–28.

———. *Discovering Jerusalem*. Nashville: Th. Nelson, 1983.

Avishur, Y. "bṣlm dmwt tbnytw." *Lešonenu* 51 (5647 [1987]), 231–34.

Baker, D. W. "Further Examples of the *waw explicativum*." *VT* 30 (1980), 129–36.

Barnett, R. D. "Ezekiel and Tyre." In *W. F. Albright Volume*, ed. A Malamat. *EI* 9, 6–13 (English section). Jerusalem: Israel Exploration Society, 1969.

Barr, J. "Some Notes on *ben* 'between' in Classical Hebrew." *JSS* 23 (1978), 1–22.

Bartelmus, R. "Ez 37:1–14, die Verbform *weqatal* und die Anfänge der Auferstehungshoffnung." ZAW 97 (1985), 366–89.

Bartlett, J. R. "Edom and the Fall of Jerusalem, 587 B.C." *PEQ* 114 (1982), 13–24.

———. *Edom and the Edomites*. JSOTSup 77 (1989).

Bass, G. F. "Oldest Known Shipwreck Reveals Splendors of the Bronze Age." *National Geographic* 172/6 (December 1987), 693–733.

Berlin, A. "Jeremiah 29:5–7: A Deuteronomic Allusion." *Hebrew Annual Review* 8 (1984), 3–11.

———. *The Dynamics of Biblical Parallelism*. Bloomington: Indiana University Press, 1985.

Bewer, J. "Beiträge zur Exegese des Buches Ezechiel." ZAW 63 (1951), 193–201.

———. *The Book of Ezekiel*. 2 vols. Harper's Annotated Bible Series. New York: Harper and Brothers, 1954. Cited as "Bewer."

BIRKELAND, H. "The Belief in the Resurrection of the Dead in the Old Testament." *Studia Theologica* 3 (1949), 60–78.

BLANK, S. H. "Isaiah 52.5 and the Profanation of the Name." *HUCA* 25 (1954), 1–8.

BLAU, J. "On the Repetition of the Predicate in the Bible" (Hebrew). In *The Bible and Jewish History* (Memorial Volume for J. Liver), ed. B. Uffenheimer, pp. 234–40. Tel Aviv: Tel Aviv University, 1971.

BOADT, L. *Ezekiel's Oracles against Egypt.* Biblica et Orientalia 37. Rome: Pontifical Biblical Institute, 1980.

BODI, D. *The Book of Ezekiel and the Poem of Erra.* Orbis Biblicus et Orientalis 104. Freiburg Schweiz: Universitätsverlag; Göttingen: Vandenhoeck and Ruprecht, 1991.

BOGAERT, M. "Montaigne sainte, jardin d'Eden et sanctuaire (hiérosolymitain) dans un Oracle d'Ézéchiel contre le Prince de Tyr [Ez 28:11–19]." In *Le Myth, son Langage et son Message,* eds. H. Limet and J. Reis, pp. 131–53. Homo Religiosus 9. Louvain-la-Neuve: Centre d'Histoire des Religions, 1983.

BONNET-TZAVELLAS, C. "Le dieu Melqart en Phénicia et dans le bassin Méditerranéen: un culte national et official." *Studia Phoenicia,* I–II, ed. F. Gubel et al. Orientalia Lovaniensia Analecta 15 (1983), pp. 195–208.

BREASTED, J. H. *Ancient Records of Egypt.* 5 vols. 1906. Reprint, New York: Russell and Russell, 1962.

BRONGERS, H. A. "Some Remarks on the Biblical Particle *h^{a}lo'.*" *OTS* 21 (1981), 177–89.

BROSHI, M. "The Expansion of Jerusalem in the Reigns of Hezekiah and Manasseh." *IEJ* 24 (1974), 21–26.

BROWN, M. L. "'Is It Not?' or 'Indeed!': *HL* in Northwest Semitic." *Maarav* 4 (1987), 201–19.

BUNNENS, G. *L'expansion phénicienne en Méditerranée.* Rome and Brussels: Institut Historique Belge de Rome, 1979.

CARROLL, R. P. *When Prophecy Failed.* London: SCM Press, 1979.

CASSON, L. *Ships and Seamanship in the Ancient World.* Princeton: Princeton University Press, 1971.

CASSUTO, U. *Biblical and Oriental Studies,* II. Jerusalem: Magnes Press, 1975.

COHEN, H. R. *Biblical Hapaxlegomena in the Light of Akkadian and Ugaritic.* SBLDS 37. Missoula: Scholars Press, 1978.

DHORME, E. *L'emploi métaphorique des noms de parties du corps en hébreu et en akkadien.* Paris: P. Geuthner, 1963.

DIAKONOFF, I. M. "The Naval Power and Trade of Tyre." *IEJ* 42 (1992), 168–93.

DICOU, B. *Edom, Israel's Brother and Antagonist: The Role of Edom in Biblical Prophecy and Story.* JSOTSup 169 (1994).

DONNER, H. "The Separate States of Israel and Judah." In *Israelite and Judaean History,* eds. S. H. Hayes and J. M. Miller, pp. 381–434. London: SCM Press, 1977.

DOTAN, A. "*Swb'ym* — a Methodological Trait of the Tiberian Punctuation System" (in Hebrew). In *The Bible and Jewish History* (Memorial Volume for J. Liver), ed. B. Uffenheimer, pp. 241–47. Tel Aviv: Tel Aviv University, 1971.

DRIVER, G. R. "Linguistic and Textual Problems: Ezekiel." *Biblica* 19 (1938), 60–69, 175–87.

———. *Aramaic Documents of the Fifth Century* B.C. Abr. and rev. ed. Oxford: Clarendon Press, 1965.

DUS, J. "Melek Ṣor—Melqart?" *Archiv Orientální* 26 (1958), 179–85.

EDEL, E. "Amasis und Nebukadrezar II." *Göttinger Miscellenen* 29 (1978), 13–20.

EISSFELDT, O. "Schwerterschlagene bei Hesekiel." In *Studies in Old Testament Prophecy* (Festschrift T. H. Robinson), ed. H. H. Rowley, pp. 73–81. New York: Charles Scribner's Sons, 1950.

ELAT, M. *Economic Relations in the Lands of the Bible* (in Hebrew). Jerusalem: Bialik Institute, 1977.

———. "Trade and Commerce." In *The Age of the Monarchies: Culture and Society*. Vol. V of *The World History of the Jewish People*, ed. A. Malamat, pp. 173–80. Jerusalem: Massada, 1979.

———. "Tarshish and the Problem of Phoenician Colonization in the Western Mediterranean." *Orientalia Lovanensia Periodica* 13 (1982), 55–61.

———. "The Iron Export from Uzal (Ezekiel xxvii 19)." *VT* 33 (1983), 323–26.

EPH'AL, I. "Israel: Fall and Exile." In *The Age of the Monarchies: Political History*. Vol. IV/1 of *The World History of the Jewish People*, ed. A. Malamat, pp. 180–92. Jerusalem: Massada, 1979.

———. *The Ancient Arabs*. Jerusalem: Magnes Press, 1982.

FELDMAN, E. *Biblical and Post-Biblical Defilement and Mourning: Law as Theology*. New York: Yeshiva University Press, 1977.

FENSHAM, F. C. "The Curse of the Dry Bones in Ezekiel 37:1–14 Changed to a Blessing of Resurrection." *Journal of Northwest Semitic Languages* 13 (1987), 59–60.

FITZGERALD, A. "The Mythological Background for the Representation of Jerusalem as a Queen and False Worship as Adultery in the O.T." *CBQ* 34 (1972), 403–16.

FLEMING, W. B. *The History of Tyre*. New York: Columbia University Press, 1915.

FLUSSER, D., AND SH. SAFRAI. "bṣlm dmwt tbnytw." In *Sefer Yiṣḥaq 'Arye Seeligmann*, ed. A. Rofé and Y. Zakovitch, pp. 453–61 (Hebrew section). Jerusalem: E. Rubinstein, 1983.

FOX, M. V. "The Rhetoric of Ezekiel's Vision of the Valley of the Bones." *HUCA* 51 (1980), 1–15.

FRANKFORT, H. *Kingship and the Gods*. Chicago: University of Chicago Press, 1948.

———. *Ancient Egyptian Religion*. New York: Harper Brothers, 1961.

FRIEDMAN, R. E. "The Biblical Expression *mastir panim*." *Hebrew Annual Review* 1 (1977), 139–47.

GADD, C. J. "Some Babylonian Divinatory Methods and Their Inter-relations." In *La divination en Mésopotamie ancienne*, XIVe Rencontre Assyriologique Internationale, pp. 21–34. Paris: Presses Universitaires de France, 1966.

GALAMBUSH, J. *Jerusalem in the Book of Ezekiel: The City as Yahweh's Wife*. SBLDS 130. Atlanta: Scholars Press, 1992.

GESE, H. *Die Religionen Altsyriens, Altarabiens und der Mandäer.* Stuttgart: Kohlhammer, 1970.

GEYER, J. B. "Mythology and Culture in the Oracles against the Nations." *VT* 36 (1986), 129–45.

GIBSON, J. C. L. *Canaanite Myths and Legends.* Edinburgh: T. & T. Clark, 1978.

GOLDBERG, I. "The Poetic Structure of the Dirge over the King of Tyre" (in Hebrew). *Tarbiz* 58/2 (1989), 277–81.

[GOSHEN-]GOTTSTEIN, M. "Remedying the Failures of History in Ezekiel's Consolations" (in Hebrew). In *Sefer Auerbach,* ed. A. Biram, pp. 175–78. Jerusalem: Kiryat Sepher, 1955.

GOSSE, B. "Le recueil d'oracles contre les nations d'Ézéchiel xxv–xxxii dans la redaction du livre d'Ézéchiel." *RB* 93 (1986), 535–62.

GRAESSER, C. F. "Standing Stones in Ancient Palestine." *BA* 35 (1972), 34–63.

GRAFFY, A. *A Prophet Confronts His People.* Analecta Biblica 104. Rome: Biblical Institute Press, 1984.

GRASSI, J. "Ezekiel xxxvii 1–14 and the New Testament." *New Testament Studies* 11 (1964–65), 162–64.

GREEN, A. R. W. "The Identity of King So of Egypt—an Alternative Interpretation." *JNES* 52 (1993), 99–108.

GREENBERG, M. "What Are Valid Criteria for Determining Inauthentic Matter in Ezekiel." In *Ezekiel and His Book,* ed. J. Lust, pp. 123–35. See ahead at Lust, J., ed.

———. "Nebuchadnezzar at the Parting of the Ways: Ezek. 21:26–27." In *Ah, Assyria . . .* (Festschrift Ḥayim Tadmor), ed. M. Cogan and I. Eph'al. Scripta Hierosolymitana 33, 267–71. Jerusalem: Magnes Press, 1991.

———. "Is There a Mari Parallel to the Israelite Enemy-*ḥerem?*" (in Hebrew). In *Avraham Malamat Volume,* ed. S. Ahituv et al. *EI* 24, 49–53. Jerusalem: Israel Exploration Society, 1993.

———. "Reflections on Interpretation." In M. Greenberg, *Studies in the Bible and Jewish Thought,* pp. 227–34. Philadelphia: Jewish Publication Society, 1995. (Reprint of first part of Greenberg, M., "The Vision of Jerusalem . . . ," in bibliography of *Ezekiel 1–20.*)

GREENBERG, S. *The Relation between God and Israel in the Bible.* Ph.D. diss., Dropsie College, Philadelphia, 1933.

GREENFIELD, J. C. "A Touch of Eden." In *Orientalia J. Duchesne-Guillemin emerito oblata.* Acta Iranica 23, 219–24. Leiden: E. J. Brill, 1984.

———. See above at Avigad, N., and J. C. Greenfield.

GRINTZ, Y. M. "Don't Eat on the Blood." *Annual of the Swedish Theological Institute* 8 (1970–71), 78–105.

HALLO, W. W. "Biblical Abominations and Sumerian Taboos." *JQR* 76 (1985), 21–40.

HARDEN, D. *The Phoenicians.* Harmondsworth: Penguin, 1971.

HELD, M. "Studies in Comparative Semitic Lexicography." In *Studies in Honor of B. Landsberger.* Assyriological Studies 16, 395–406. Chicago: Oriental Institute of the University of Chicago, 1965.

HILLERS, D. R. *Treaty-Curses and the Old Testament Prophets.* Rome: Pontifical Biblical Institute, 1964.

———. "A Convention in Hebrew Literature: The Reaction to Bad News." ZAW 77 (1965), 86–90.

———. "Delocutive Verbs in Biblical Hebrew." *JBL* 86 (1967), 320–44.

———. "*Hôy* and *Hôy*-Oracles: A Neglected Syntactic Aspect." In *The Word of the Lord Shall Go Forth* (Festschrift D. N. Freedman), ed. C. L. Meyers et al., pp. 185–88. Winona Lake: Eisenbrauns, 1983.

HOFFMANN, Y. *The Prophecies Against Foreign Nations in the Bible* (in Hebrew). Tel Aviv: Tel Aviv University, 1977.

HOFFNER, H. A. "Second Millennium Antecedents to the Hebrew *'ÔB*." *JBL* 86 (1967), 385–401.

HONEYMAN, A. M. "*Merismus* in Biblical Hebrew." *JBL* 71 (1952), 11–18.

HULST, A. R. "*Kol baśar* in der Priestlichen Fluterzählung." *OTS* 12 (1958), 28–68.

HURVITZ, A. "The Usage of *šš* and *bwṣ* in the Bible and Its Implications for the Date of P." *HTR* 60 (1967), 117–21.

———. "'Diachronic Chiasm' in Biblical Hebrew" (in Hebrew). In *The Bible and Jewish History* (Memorial Volume for J. Liver), ed. B. Uffenheimer. pp. 248–55. Tel Aviv: Tel Aviv University, 1971.

———. *The Transition Period in Biblical Hebrew* (in Hebrew). Jerusalem: Bialik Institute, 1972.

———. "The Evidence of Language in Dating the Priestly Code." *Revue Biblique* 81 (1974), 24–56.

———. *A Linguistic Study of the Relationship between the Priestly Source and the Book of Ezekiel.* Cahiers de la Revue Biblique 20. Paris: Gabalda, 1982.

IWRY, S. "New Evidence for Belomancy in Ancient Palestine and Phoenicia." *JAOS* 81 (1961), 27–33.

IZRE'EL, S. "*'t* = *'l* in Biblical Hebrew" (in Hebrew). *Shnaton* 3 (1978), 204–12.

JAHN, G. *Das Buch Ezechiel.* Leipzig: E. Pfeiffer, 1905.

JASTROW, M. *Die Religion Babyloniens und Assyriens.* 3 vols. Giessen: A. Töpelmann, 1905–12.

JENNI, E. "Das Wort *'ōlām* im AT." ZAW 64 (1952), 197–248; 65 (1953), 1–35.

JOÜON-MURAOKA, P. JOÜON, *A Grammar of Biblical Hebrew,* trans. and rev. T. Muraoka. 2 vols. Rome: Pontifical Biblical Institute, 1991.

KATZENSTEIN, J. *The History of Tyre.* Jerusalem: Schocken Institute, 1973.

KNOHL, I. "The Priestly Torah versus the Holiness Code: Sabbath and the Festivals." *HUCA* 58 (1987), 65–118.

KRAELING, C. H. *The Synagogue,* The Excavations at Dura-Europos: Final Report, VIII/1. New Haven: Yale University Press, 1956.

KRANTZ, E. S. *Des Schiffes Weg mitten im Meer.* Lund: CWK Gleerup, 1982.

KRAŠOVEC, J. *Der Merismus im Biblisch-Hebräischen und Nordwestsemitischen.* Biblica et Orientalia 33. Rome: Biblical Institute Press, 1977.

KUTLER, L. "A Structural Semantic Approach to Israelite Communal Terminology." *JANES* 14 (1982), 69–77.

KUTSCHER, E. Y. *A History of the Hebrew Language.* Jerusalem: Magnes Press, 1982.

KUTSCHER, R. "*mahl^ekim* (Zech 3:7) and Its Sisters" (in Hebrew). *Lešonenu* 26 (5722 [1962]), 93–96.

LAMBDIN, T. O. "Egyptian Loanwords in the Old Testament." *JAOS* 73 (1953), 145–55.

LAMBERT, W. G. "The Theology of Death." In *Death in Mesopotamia,* ed. B. Alster, pp. 53–66. Copenhagen: Akademisk Forlag, 1980.

LANG, B. "Street Theater, Raising the Dead, and the Zoroastrian Connection in Ezekiel's Prophecy." In *Ezekiel and His Book,* ed. J. Lust, pp. 298–307. See ahead at Lust, J., ed.

LANGDON, S. *Die Neubabylonischen Königsinschriften.* Leipzig: J. C. Hinrich, 1912.

LEVEY, S. H. *The Targum of Ezekiel.* The Aramaic Bible 13. Wilmington: M. Glazier, 1987.

LEVI, J. *Die Inkongruenz im Biblischen Hebräisch.* Wiesbaden: Harrassowitz, 1987.

LEVINE, B. "Silence, Sound, and the Phenomenology of Mourning in Biblical Israel." *JANES* 22 (1993), 89–106.

LIVERANI, M. "The Trade Network of Tyre according to Ezek. 27." In *Ah, Assyria . . .* (Festschrift Ḥayim Tadmor), ed. M. Cogan and I. Ephʿal. Scripta Hierosolymitana 33, 54–79. Jerusalem: Magnes Press, 1991.

LODS, A. "La 'mort des incirconcis.'" *Comptes rendus de l'Académie des Inscriptions et Belle-Lettres,* pp. 271–83, 1943.

LOHFINK, N. "Enthielten die im AT bezeugten Klageriten eine Phase des Schweigens." *VT* 12 (1962), 260–77.

LORETZ, O. "Der Sturz des Fürsten von Tyrus (Ez 28:1–19)." *Ugarit-Forschungen* 8 (1976), 455–458.

———. *Ugarit und die Bibel.* Darmstadt: Wissenschaftliche Buchgesellschaft, 1990.

LUCKENBILL, D. D. *The Annals of Sennacherib.* Chicago: University of Chicago Press, 1924.

LUST, J. "Ezekiel 36–40 in the Oldest Greek Manuscript." *Catholic Biblical Quarterly* 43 (1981), 517–33.

———, ed. *Ezekiel and His Book.* Bibliotheca Ephemeridum Theologicarum Lovaniensium 74. Leuven: Peeters, 1986.

MALAMAT, A. *Israel in Biblical Times* (in Hebrew). Jerusalem: Bialik Institute, 1983.

MARGULIES, S. H. *Das "Schwertlied" Ezechiels.* Scripta Universitatis atque bibliothecae Hierosolymitanarum. Orientalia et Judaica, I/8. Jerusalem, 1923.

MAZAR, B. *The Early Biblical Period.* Jerusalem: Israel Exploration Society, 1986.

MCKANE, W. "Poison, Trial by Ordeal, and the Cup of Wrath." *VT* 30 (1980), 487–92.

MELAMED, E. Z. "Break-Up of Stereotype Phrases as an Artistic Device in Biblical Poetry." In *Studies in the Bible,* ed. C. Rabin. Scripta Hierosolymitana 8, 115–44. Jerusalem: Magnes Press, 1961.

MENAḤEM BEN SARUQ. *Maḥberet Menaḥem*, ed. Z. Filipowski. Edinburgh: Filipowski, 1854.

MENDENHALL, G. E. *The Tenth Generation*. Baltimore: Johns Hopkins University Press, 1973.

METTINGER, T. N. D. *King and Messiah*. Coniectanea Biblica OT 8. Lund: GWK Gleerup, 1976.

MEYER, E. *Geschichte des Altertums* II/1 ("Die Zeit der Ägyptischen Grossmacht"). Stuttgart and Berlin: J. G. Cotta'sche Buchhandlung Nachfolger, 1928.

MILLARD, A. R. "Ezekiel xxvii 19: The Wine Trade of Damascus." *JSS* 7 (1962), 201–3.

———. "The Etymology of Eden." *VT* 34 (1984), 103–6.

MIRSKY, A. "Stylistic Device for Conclusion in Hebrew." *Semitics* 5 (1977), 9–23.

MORAN, W. L. "Gen 49:10 and Its Use in Ez 21:32." *Biblica* 39 (1958), 405–25.

MORIARTY, F. L. "The Lament over Tyre." *Gregorianum* 46 (1965), 83–88.

MOWINCKEL, S. "Drive and/or Ride in O.T." *VT* 12 (1962), 278–94.

MUFFS, Y. *Love and Joy*. New York: Jewish Theological Seminary, 1992.

MÜLLER, D. H. "Der Prophet Ezechiel entlehnt eine Stelle des Propheten Zephanja und glossiert sie." In *Komposition und Strophenbau*, XIV, pp. 30–36. (Jahresbericht der israelitisch-theologisch Lehranstalt in Wien.) Wien, 1907.

MÜLLER, H.-P. "Mantische Weisheit und Apokalyptik." SVT 22 (1972), 268–93.

MURAOKA, T. "The Status Constructus of Adjectives in Biblical Hebrew." *VT* 27 (1977), 375–80.

———. *Emphatic Words and Structures in Biblical Hebrew*. Jerusalem: Magnes Press; Leiden: E. J. Brill, 1985.

NEUSS, W. *Das Buch Ezechiel in Theologie und Kunst bis zum Ende des XII. Jahrhunderts*. Münster: Aschendorff, 1912.

NIELSON, K. *There Is Hope for a Tree*. JSOTSup 65 (1989).

ODED, B. "Judah and the Exile." In *Israelite and Judaean History*, ed. J. H. Hayes and J. M. Miller, pp. 435–88. London: SCM Press, 1977.

OLMSTEAD, A. T. *History of Assyria*. New York: Charles Scribner's Sons, 1923.

OPPENHEIM, A. L. "The Golden Garments of the Gods." *JNES* 8 (1949), 172–93.

———. *Ancient Mesopotamia*. Rev. ed. completed by E. Reiner. Chicago: University of Chicago Press, 1977.

OREN, E. "Migdol: A New Fortress on the Edge of the Eastern Nile Delta." *BASOR* 256 (1984), 7–44.

ORLINSKY, H. M. "The Hebrew Root *škb*." *JBL* 63 (1944), 19–44.

PAGE, S. "Joash and Samaria in a New Stela Excavated at Tell Al Rimah, Iraq." *VT* 19 (1969), 483–84.

PARAN, M. *Forms of the Priestly Style in the Pentateuch* (in Hebrew). Jerusalem: Magnes Press, 1989.

PARROT, A. *Nineveh and Babylon*. London: Thames and Hudson, 1961.

PATAI, R. *Man and Temple*. London: Nelson, 1947.

PAUL, S. M. "Hosea 8:10 *mś' mlk śrym* and Ancient Near Eastern Royal Epithets." In *Studies in the Bible and the Ancient Near East* (in honor of S.

Loewenstamm) (Hebrew volume), ed. J. Blau and Y. Avishur, pp. 309–18. Jerusalem: Rubinstein, 1978.

PEELS, H. G. L. "The Vengeance of God: The Meaning of the Root NQM and the Function of the NQM Texts in the Context of Divine Revelation in the OT." *OTS* 31. Leiden: E. J. Brill, 1995.

PERLES, F. "*nwl* = 'Gewebe' im Alten Testament." *Orientalische Literaturzeitung* 12 (1909), 251–52.

POLZIN, R. *Late Biblical Hebrew: Toward an Historical Typology of Biblical Hebrew Prose.* Harvard Semitic Monographs 12. Missoula: Scholars Press, 1976.

POPE, M. *'El in the Ugaritic Texts.* SVT 2. Leiden: E. J. Brill, 1955.

PORADA, E. "The Iconography of Death in Mesopotamia in the Early Second Millennium B.C." In *Death in Mesopotamia,* ed. B. Alster. Copenhagen: Akademisk Forlag, 1980.

PROPP, W. H. "The Origins of Infant Circumcision in Israel." *Hebrew Annual Review* 11 (1987), 355–70.

QIMRON, E. *The Hebrew of the Dead Sea Scrolls.* Harvard Semitic Studies 29. Atlanta: Scholars Press, 1986.

RAINEY, A. F. *A Social Structure of Ugarit* (in Hebrew). Jerusalem: Bialik Institute, 1967.

REIDER, J. "Etymological Studies in Biblical Hebrew." *VT* 4 (1954), 276–95.

ROFÉ, A. *Introduction to the Prophetic Literature* (in Hebrew). Jerusalem: Academon, 5752 (1991).

ROOKER, M. F. *Biblical Hebrew in Transition.* JSOTSup 90 (1990).

RUMMEL, S., ed. *Ras Shamra Parallels,* III. Rome: Pontificium Institutum Biblicum, 1981.

SAGGS, H. W. F. *The Encounter with the Divine in Mesopotamia and Israel.* London: Athlone Press, 1978.

SASSON, J. "Circumcision in the Ancient Near East." *JBL* 85 (1966), 473–76.

SEELIGMANN, I. L. "Zur Terminologie für das Gerichtsverfahren im Wortschatz des biblischen Hebräisch." In *Hebräische Wortforschung* (Festschrift W. Baumgartner). SVT 16 (1967), 251–78.

SEUX, M.-J. *Épithètes royales akkadiennes et sumériennes.* Paris: Letouzey et Ane, 1967.

SHALIT, A. "ḥbšym 'rzym bmrkltk." *Lešonenu* 7 (1935–36), 131–35.

SINGER, C., et al. *A History of Technology,* I. Oxford: Clarendon Press, 1958.

SKINNER, J. *The Book of Ezekiel.* The Expositor's Bible. London: Hodder and Stoughton, 1895.

SMITH, G. A. *The Historical Geography of the Holy Land.* 25th ed. London: Hodder and Stoughton, 1931.

SMITH, S. "The Ship Tyre." *PEQ* 85 (1953), 97–110.

STOLZ, F. "Die Bäume des Gottesgartens auf dem Libanon." ZAW 84 (1972), 141–56.

SYMMACHUS. Author of a Greek translation produced toward the end of the second century C.E., as presented in G (Ziegler's edition of the Septuagint).

TADMOR, H. "Assyria and the West in the Ninth Century and Its Aftermath." In

Unity and Diversity, ed. H. Goedicke and J. J. M. Roberts, pp. 36–40. Baltimore: Johns Hopkins University Press, 1975.

TALMON, S. "Double Readings in the Massoretic Text." *Textus* 1 (1960), 144–84.

THACKERAY, H. ST. JOHN. *The Septuagint and Jewish Worship*. London: Oxford University Press, 1921.

TOV, E. "Did the Septuagint Translators Always Understand Their Hebrew Text?" In *De Septuaginta: Studies in Honour of J. W. Wevers*, ed. A. Pietersma and C. Cox, pp. 53–70. Mississauga: Benben Publications, 1984.

———. "Recensional Differences between the MT and LXX of Ezekiel." *Ephemerides Theologicae Lovanienses* 62 (1986), 89–101.

TROMP, N. J. *Primitive Conceptions of Death and the Nether World in the Old Testament*. Biblica et Orientalia 21. Rome: Pontifical Biblical Institute, 1969.

TSIRKIN, Y. B. "Japheth's Progeny and the Phoenicians." In *Phoenicia and the Bible*, ed. E. Lipinski, pp. 117–31. Leuven: Peeters, 1991.

TUR-SINAI, N. H. *Pešuṭo šel Miqra*, III/2. (On Ezekiel and the Twelve.) Jerusalem: Kiryat Sepher, 1967.

VAN BEEK, G. "Frankincense and Myrrh." *Biblical Archeologist Reader*, II, pp. 99–126. Garden City: Doubleday, 1965.

VAN DIJK, H. J. *Ezekiel's Prophecy on Tyre*. Biblica et Orientalia 20. Rome: Pontifical Biblical Institute, 1968.

VAN DIJK-HEMMES, F. "The Metaphorization of Woman in Prophetic Speech: An Analysis of Ezekiel xxiii." *VT* 43 (1993), 162–70.

VAN SETERS, J. *Prologue to History: The Yahwist as Historian in Genesis*. Louisville: Westminster/John Knox Press, 1992.

VOGELS, W. "Restauration de l'Égypte et universalisme en Ez 29:13–16." *Biblica* 53 (1972), 473–94.

WACHSMANN, S. "On the Syro-Canaanite Sea Trade in the Late Bronze Age." In *Commerce in Palestine Throughout the Ages* (in Hebrew), ed. B. Z. Kedar et al., pp. 42–66. Jerusalem: Yad Izhak ben Zvi/Israel Exploration Society, 1990.

WEINFELD, M. "The Covenant of Grant in the Old Testament and in the Ancient Near East." *JAOS* 90 (1970), 184–203.

WIDENGREN, G. "The Gathering of the Dispersed." *Svensk Exegetisk Aarsbok* 41/42 (1976–77), 224–34.

WILLIAMS, A. J. "The Mythological Background of Ezekiel 28:12–19?" *Biblical Theology Bulletin* 6 (1976), 49–61.

WILLIAMS, R. J. *Hebrew Syntax*. 2d ed. Toronto: University of Toronto Press, 1976.

WILSON, R. R. "The Death of the King of Tyre: The Editorial History of Ezekiel 28." In *Love and Death in the Ancient Near East* (Festschrift M. H. Pope), ed. J. H. Marks and R. M. Good, pp. 211–18. Guilford, Conn.: Four Quarters Publishing Co., 1987.

WINNETT, F. V., AND W. L. REED. *Ancient Records from North Arabia*. Toronto: University of Toronto Press, 1970.

WISEMAN, D. J. *Nebuchadrezzar and Babylon*. Oxford: British Academy, 1985.

YADIN, Y. *The Art of Warfare in Biblical Lands.* 2 vols. Jerusalem and Ramat Gan: International Publishing Co., 1963.

YARON, K. "The Dirge over the King of Tyre." *Annual of the Swedish Theological Institute* 3 (1964), 28–57.

ZIMMERN, H. *Akkadische Fremdwörter als ein Beweis für babylonischen Kultureinfluss.* Leipzig: Hinrichs, 1917.

TRADITIONAL HEBREW COMMENTATORS CITED

◆

For bibliographic information, see bibliography in *Ezekiel 1–20*.

Abarbanel = Don Isaac Abarbanel (Abravanel). Iberian Peninsula–Italy, 1437–1508.

Eliezer of Beaugency. North France, twelfth century.

Kara = Joseph Kara. North France, eleventh century.

Kimḥi = David Kimḥi. Provence (South France), ca. 1160–1235.

Malbim. Acronym of Rabbi Meir Loeb ben Jehiel Michael. Eastern-Central Europe, 1809–79.

Menaḥem bar Shim'on of Posquières. Provence (South France), twelfth to thirteenth centuries.

Meṣudot (comprising *Meṣudat David*; *Meṣudat Ṣiyyon*). A two-tiered Bible commentary by David and Jeḥiel (son of David) Altschul(er). Galicia (Eastern Europe), eighteenth century.

Minḥat Shay. Critical Notes on MT by Jedidiah Solomon Norzi. Italy, 1560–1616.

Moshe ben Sheshet. Spain, twelfth(?) century.

Rashi. Acronym of Rabbi Solomon ben Isaac. North France, 1040–1105.

When a commentator offers more than one explanation of a passage, a raised number after his name indicates the order of appearance of the cited explanation. Thus "Rashi[1]" means: the first of several explanations offered by Rashi ad loc.

TRANSLATION, COMMENT, STRUCTURE AND THEMES

XX. God's Sword
(21:1–37)

21 [1]The word of YHWH came to me:
[2]Man, set your face toward Teman,
and proclaim against Darom,
and prophesy against the scrub country,[a] the Negeb.

[3]And say to the scrub of the Negeb: Hear the word of YHWH! Thus said Lord YHWH: I am kindling a fire in you that shall consume every green tree and every dry tree in you. The blazing flame shall not go out, and all faces shall be scorched by it from south to north. [4]All flesh shall see[b] that I, YHWH, ignited it; it shall not go out. [5]Then I said: Ah Lord YHWH, they are saying about me, "He is certainly a master of figurative speech!"

[6]The word of YHWH came to me:
[7]Man, set your face toward Jerusalem,
and proclaim against [c]the sanctums,[c]
and prophesy against the soil of Israel.

[8]And say to the soil of Israel: Thus said YHWH: I am coming at you! I will take my sword out of its sheath and cut off righteous and wicked from you. [9]Because I am cutting off righteous and wicked from you, therefore my sword shall come out of its sheath against all flesh from south to north. [10]All flesh shall know that I YHWH have taken my sword out of its sheath; it shall never be returned.

[11]And you, man, sigh! With body collapsed and in bitterness you shall sigh before their eyes. [12]When they say to you, "Why are you sighing," say:
Because of news that is coming,
at which every heart shall melt,
and all hands go slack,
and every spirit shall faint,
and all knees run with water.
It is coming and it shall happen, declares Lord YHWH.

[13]The word of YHWH came to me: [14]Man, prophesy and say: Thus said the Lord: Say:

[a]G "the chief forest" (*y‘r hśr*?); S does not reflect *hśdh*.
[b]G "know."
[c–c]G S "their sanctuary."

A sword, a sword has been whetted, even burnished.
[15]It has been whetted to make a slaughter;
it has been burnished in order to flash.
Or shall we rejoice, rod of my son, despising every tree.
[16]It was given to burnish, to be grasped in the hand.
It was whetted, the sword, and it was burnished,
to be put into the hand of a killer.
[17]Shriek and wail, man,
for it has come against my people,
it, against all the chiefs of Israel.
Victims of the sword have my people been;
therefore slap your thigh.
[18]For [it is] a trial; and what, if even a rod it despises, shall not be, declares
Lord YHWH.
[19]And you, man, prophesy,
and clap your hands.
The sword shall be redoubled [d]a third time[d] —
it is a sword of the slain,
a [e]sword of the great mass of slain, that besets[e] them —
[20]in order that hearts may melt
and falterings[f] be many.
I will station the terror[g] of the sword at all their gates —
ah! made for lightning,
polished for slaughter.
[21]Focus on the right;
attack[h] on the left,
wherever your blade has been assigned!
[22]I too will clap my hands and assuage my fury;
I YHWH have spoken.

[23]The word of YHWH came to me: [24]And you, man, make two ways by which
the sword of the king of Babylon may come; let the two issue from one country.
[i]And clear a place; at the beginning of the way to [each] city clear it. [25]A way
make[i] for the sword to come to Rabbah of the Ammonites and to Judah in fortified Jerusalem. [26]For the king of Babylon halts at the parting of the ways, at the
beginning of the two ways, to perform divination. He shakes arrows, he consults
the teraphim, he examines the liver. [27]In its right [side] is the divination-omen
"Jerusalem" — for placing rams, for opening mouths with shouting,[j] for raising

d–d G "the third (one)"; V "and also tripled."
e–e G "the great sword of the slain (plural) and it will amaze"; S "sword of the slain (plural) of the great one that frightens"; T also represents *hḥdrt* by "that frightens."
f G S "feeble ones."
g G "slaughter."
h Not in G.
i–i G "and a hand in the head of the road of a city at the head of a road you shall put" (as from *wyd br'š drk 'yr br'š drk tśym*).
j So G; see comment.

voices in war cries; for placing rams against gates, for throwing up ramps, for building a circumvallation. 28They will regard it as idle divining—[k]solemn oaths have they.[k] And that will bring iniquity to mind [for which] to be seized.

29Surely thus said Lord YHWH: Because you have brought your iniquity to mind, since your transgressions have been disclosed so that your sins in all your misdeeds are exposed; because you have been brought to mind you will be seized in the hand.

30As for you, you wicked corpse, chief of Israel, whose day has come at the time of terminal iniquity, 31thus said Lord YHWH:

Remove the turban!
Take off the crown!
This, not this.
Lift the lowly!
Lower the lofty!

32Awry, awry, awry, I will make it. Nor will this come about until he to whom punishing belongs comes and I entrust [it] to him.

33And you, man, prophesy and say: Thus said Lord YHWH concerning the Ammonites and concerning their taunts: Say:

Sword, sword unsheathed,
  for slaughter burnished [l]to the utmost,[l]
  in order to flash,
  34when idle visions were uttered about you,
  when falsehood was divined about you,
  to set you against the necks of corpses of wicked men
    whose day had come at the time of terminal iniquity—
35Back to its sheath!
In the place where you were created,
  in the land of your origin
  I will judge you.
36I will pour out my rage on you;
  I will blow on you the fire of my wrath,
  and I will put you into the hands of brutish men,
    craftsmen of destruction.
37You will be fuel for fire;
  your blood will be in the midst of the land;
  you will not be remembered,
  for I YHWH have spoken.

COMMENT

21:2. *Set* (śim) . . . *toward* (derek) *Teman*. The transcribed Hebrew words recur in vs. 24 in a different sense ("Make . . . ways"); see Structure and Themes. Each one of the words *teman, darom, negeb* is both a term meaning "south" and the

[k–k]Not in G S.
[l–l]G T "for destruction."

name of a locality. Teman is an unidentified place in Edom; the Negeb is the wilderness country south of the Judean hills; in Mishnaic Hebrew Darom is a region of Judea north of Beersheba and south of Beth-Gubrin (M. Avi-Yonah, *The Holy Land, from the Persian to the Arab Conquests* [Grand Rapids: Baker Book House, 1966], pp. 160f.); here it may also serve as a region and thus be ambiguous. Modern renderings vacillate; e.g., OJPS, Moffatt, *RSV* ". . . south . . . south . . . Negeb"; *NAB* "southward . . . south . . . southern land"; *NEB* "Teman . . . south . . . Negeb." I follow G and NJPS in taking them all as localities: since vss. 2–4 are explicitly a parable (vs. 5), it seems fitting to regard the three terms as localities standing for other localities (vs. 7); so, e.g., Canaan in 17:4 signifies Babylonia.

proclaim. Lit. "cause (words) to drip (*nṭp*, from the mouth)." For the figure, cf. "My words dropped (dripped) upon them," Job 29:22 (and note vs. 23; Prov 5:3; Deut 32:2). This verb regularly denotes elevated prophetic speech (Amos 7:16; Mic 2:6). The metaphor is related to Mishnaic "drink thirstily [the sages'] words" (*m. 'Abot* 1.4).

scrub country (ya'ar haśśade). *ya'ar* "forest" also may mean uncultivated wasteland, scrub (Hos 2:14; Isa 29:17)—here the wild south of the land of Israel (see also vs. 3); cf. the Judahite town Kiriath Jearim "city of scrublands." *śade* here means "(open) country, region," and the pair is perhaps equivalent to *śᵉde ya'ar* "region of scrub"—a poetic epithet of Kiriath Jearim in Ps 132:6. (On invertible constructs, see comment to 20:28.) Cf. D. Baly, *Geography of the Bible* (London: Lutterworth, 1964), p. 93.

Negeb is equivalent to *negbah* (a form found in some Hebrew mss.) as *ṣapon* in vs. 9 is to *ṣaponah* (found there in some mss.); GKC, § 118 d–g.

S renders only *ya'ar hannegeb* (as MT in vs. 3), but the strange rendition of G (see text note) suggests that its *Vorlage* had *hśr*, very like MT's *hśdh.* S may be a simplified reading. MT not only is more difficult (and therefore more likely to be original) but evokes Micah's doom prophecy: "Zion shall be plowed into a field (*śade,* i.e., open country), . . . and the Temple mount into a height of scrub (*ya'ar*)" (3:12).

3. *every green . . . dry tree.* = "all trees alike" (Cooke). Wevers recognized this—without naming it—as a merism: a figure representing a whole by two (often polar) parts. Other examples are: plowing and reaping (Gen 45:6) = the annual agricultural cycle; man and beast (Ezek 25:13) = all living creatures; old and young (Jer 16:6) = people of all ages (A. M. Honeyman, "*Merismus* in Biblical Hebrew," *JBL* 71 [1952], 11–18; J. Krašovec, *Der Merismus im Biblisch-Hebräischen und Nordwestsemitischen,* Biblica et Orientalia 33 [Rome: Biblical Institute Press, 1977]; neither author noted this example). Cf. comment on *ṣaddiq-raša'* "innocent-guilty" in vss. 8f.

blazing flame (lhbt šlhbt). Lit. "flame of flame," the second word an augmented form of the first, with preformative *š* found in Aramaic (borrowed from Ugaritic and Akkadian, where it serves as the *h* of Hebrew hif'il); considered an Aramaism by Wagner (p. 113, Aramaic *šlh(y)b(t)'*). "A genitival group of two synonymous or semantically close substantives can sometimes express a superlative nuance" (Joüon-Muraoka, § 141 m). The absence of the expected article (on the second term) is a feature of high style; see Structure and Themes.

lahebet and the alternate form *lahab* (properly "flame") denote the flashing metal head of a spear (I Sam 17:7; Job 39:23), the latter also the flashing blade of a sword (Judg 3:22). Nahum 3:3 speaks of "the flash of the sword and the lightning (*baraq*) of the spear." This suffices to suggest that *lahebet* here anticipates its referent, the sword, as disclosed in vss. 8ff. Even the more distant "lightning" of vss. 13ff. is prepared for in this term.

all faces. Indiscriminately; see the language of vss. 9f.

4. *See.* With their eyes, related to "faces" in vs. 3, and so preferable to G "know"—as in the interpretative vs. 10.

5. *"He is certainly a master of figurative speech!"* For *hl'* "certainly" see H. A. Brongers, "Some Remarks on the Biblical Particle *hªlo*," *OTS* 21 (1981), 177–89, esp. 181ff. The pi'el of *mšl* (only here) serves to express repetition, the making of many and varied figures of speech (*mešalim*); GKC, § 52 f; Joüon-Muraoka, § 52 d; Ehrlich, *Randglossen,* to Gen 29:13 *wynšq,* with reference to Num 22:4 (*yelaḥªku*—pi'el, many subjects, contrasted with *kileḥok*—qal, a single subject). Is the prophet's complaint that he cannot be understood because he speaks in riddles (Luzzatto, Smend, Fohrer, Zimmerli)? But Ezekiel's parables are regularly explained—and when not, are hardly unintelligible. Or is it that his parables seemed to be a display of virtuosity rather than God's word (Kara, Kimḥi)? But that implies that it was unusual for prophets to speak in parables—which is not the case (e.g., Nathan, II Sam 12:1–4; Isaiah, Isa 5:1–6; 28:23–26). However, it is the case that no prophet rivals, or even approaches, Ezekiel in the richness of his repertoire; hence it may be that his complaint concerned his popular image as an artist, an entertainer. People came to hear him for his artistry; they directed toward him not so much "contemptuous mockery" (Eichrodt; cf. NJPS: "He is just a riddle-monger") as a curiosity bereft of seriousness that neutralized the impact of his reproofs (so 33:30–33).

7. The three southern locations are interpreted as allusions to Israel's soil, its sanctuary, and the city Jerusalem—precisely the same triad as in the lament, Ps 79:1, "your inheritance (the land), your holy temple, Jerusalem." These are all "south" of Babylon, not in latitude (they lie on the same latitude), but with reference to the approach to them from Babylon, which, skirting the intervening Arabian desert, is from the north.

miqdašim, alluding to the Jerusalem Temple, is a plural of extension, indicating that the referent of the noun is inherently large or complex (*BHSyn* 7.4.lc; König III, § 260 f). Other instances denoting the Temple are Ps 68:36; 73:17; 132:5.

8. *YHWH.* Instead of the usual "Lord YHWH," while in the next occurrence of the formula, in vs. 14, "Lord" alone appears, without YHWH (S and other witnesses normalize both). The variation is characteristic of Ezekiel.

take . . . out (whwṣ'ty). Cf. *teṣe* "come out" in vs. 9. The hif'il of *yṣ'* replaces the usual *šalap* (e.g., I Sam 17:51) or *heriq* (e.g., Ezek 5:2) to mean (only here) "unsheathe"—perhaps for its assonance with *mṣyt* "kindle" in vs. 3. The qal *teṣe* can also go with fire (5:4), which in vs. 3 stood for the sword of this verse. Similarly *'akal* "consume"—with the subject "fire" in vs. 3—is a normal usage with sword, e.g., Deut 32:42. In our passage, metaphoric *'akal* of vs. 3 is replaced by nonmetaphoric *hikrit* "cut off" in vs. 8; in Nahum 3:15 both verbs are predicated of the sword.

righteous and wicked. Or: innocent and guilty; a merism for "everybody." Yet the choice of these terms rather than, say, "young and old" implies that punishment will not discriminate between those who do and those who do not deserve to die. G "unjust and wicked"; T "I will exile your righteous from your midst in order to destroy your wicked"; and such elaborations of T as Kara (Jehoiachin's generation of righteous were exiled eleven years before Zedekiah's wicked generation so that the latter might be wiped out) and Abarbanel (the righteous Josiah died untimely so as not to undergo the disaster) are evidence of embarrassment. Bar Hebraeus varies the G: righteous means not the genuinely so, but one who thought himself so. See Structure and Themes for a discussion of the thought of this verse.

9. This interprets the "scorching of all faces from south to north" of vs. 3. It seems to mean that, in his transport of fury, God will keep striking at the fugitive Israelites as they stream northward to exile (cf. 5:2, 12); but, just as he cut down the Israelites indiscriminately, so all who happen to be in the path of his merciless sword will be promiscuously killed, gentiles as well. Once the floodgates of divine wrath are opened, the torrent will sweep all away: having destroyed his own people, God will be reckless with the rest of mankind.

Perfect *hikratti* expresses "a fixed resolve" (Cooke; this instance is listed by S. R. Driver, *Tenses*, § 13, among uses of the perfect to announce a resolution, promise, or decree).

10. *All flesh.* The world at large, who will witness the carnage; evidently more extensive than "all flesh" of vs. 9, who will be cut down. Yet we cannot be certain: in Ezekiel's prophecies against the nations it is said repeatedly that they are to be annihilated "that they may know that I am YHWH" (25:7, 11, 17; 26:6; 39:6). The same paradox occurs in the Exodus story: Exod 14:4 has God declaring he will destroy Pharaoh and his army so that they may know that he is YHWH ("Egypt" in vs. 4 means Pharaoh and his army as throughout this passage—vss. 9, 10, 13, 17, etc.). Are we to understand that just before expiring, the gentiles will recognize YHWH, or that there will be some survivors who will recognize him? In any event this logical difficulty (which, as we have seen, is recurrent) gives no ground for impugning the authenticity of vs. 9 (Cooke, followed by A. R. Hulst, "*Kol baśar* in der priesterlichen Fluterzählung," *OTS* 12 [1958], 28–68). See further on the ideas of this passage in Structure and Themes.

it shall never be returned. Spoken in the heat of passion, this assertion can hardly be God's last word; indeed vs. 35 contradicts it.

11. This command to behave dramatically, anticipating the future conduct of the people, recalls such earlier commands as 4:9ff.; 12:3ff., 17ff.; cf. also 24:15ff. It is meant to arouse an inquiry.

with body collapsed (bšbrwn mtnym). Lit. "with rupture of tendons"; *mtnym* denotes the strong musculature that links the upper part of the body with the lower—traditionally "loins" (M. Held, "Studies in Comparative Semitic Lexicography," in *Studies in Honor of B. Landsberger*, Assyriological Studies 16 [Chicago: Oriental Institute of the University of Chicago, 1965] 405). The decisive blow against an enemy is figured as shattering his *mtnym* (Deut 33:11); quaking fills or seizes them and they are "loosed" in terror (Nahum 2:11; Isa 21:3; 45:1; Dan 5:6). Strength, on the other hand, has its seat in them: Nahum 2:2.

The translation parses the verse according to the accents, which set the caesura after "sigh!"; the first clause is thus structurally identical with vs. 19a$^{\alpha}$: "And you, man, prophesy." Both clauses are unusual in that they close with an imperative instead of isolating the address ("[and you] man") and initiating the next clause with the imperative (as, e.g., vss. 2, 7, 14, 24, 33). But while the structure in vs. 19a$^{\alpha}$ is assured by the balance it gives to the verset, in vs. 11 it destroys the balance, unpleasantly shortening the pre-caesura and lengthening the post-caesura. Disregarding the accents, the portion of the verse after the address falls into a chiastic bicolon (3:3):

Sigh with body collapsed,
  and in bitterness sigh before their eyes

This accords with the poetic quality of the next verse (12b).

12. *Because of news that is coming.* This parsing of the first component of the verse follows the accents: the disjunctive *pazer* is on *bʾh* "coming"; hence not, "Because of tidings. When it comes, etc." as *RSV*. Moreover, the final stress of *bʾh* shows it to be a participle, not a perfect ("that have come," NJPS). My translation of the ambiguous closure of this clause (*ky bʾh*) is modeled after *ʿl hr ṣywn ššmm* "because of Mount Zion that is desolate," in Lam 5:18 (*ky* = *š*). But the clause may with equal cogency be taken as comprising two causal phrases: "because of news, for it is coming" (so G). One might even construe the sequence *šmwʿh ky bʾh* as a rhetorical transposition of (*ʿl*) *ky bʾh šmwʿh*, lit. "(because) that news is coming" (much as the sequence "God saw the light that it was good [*ʾt hʾwr ky ṭwb*]," Gen 1:4 = "God saw that the light was good" [*ky ṭwb hʾwr*])." However construed, the pattern emphasizes the noun after *ʿl* by giving it priority and a phrase of its own; then by introducing the second phrase with a particle of its own (*ky*) the two elements of the clause are equalized.

The same ambiguous construction occurs in 25:3.

at which every heart shall melt . . . These four versets are an artistic expansion of 7:17: the external organs mentioned there (hands, knees) are supplemented here by internal (heart, spirit), thus (echo of 7:17 is in boldface):

α	wnms kl lb	γ	wkhth kl rwḥ
β	**wrpw kl ydym**	δ	**wkl brkym tlknh mym**

New matter (α γ) alternates with old; synonymous verbs (____ ____) are chiastically arranged (α δ β γ); verb precedes subject in versets α β γ; the last verset effects closure by reversal of elements and change (increase) of quantity. On reversal as a means of closure, see A. Mirsky, "Stylistic Device for Conclusion in

Hebrew," *Semitics* 5 (1977), 9–23. That "all knees shall run with water" means to urinate from fear was argued at 7:17. That the preceding metaphoric "melting (heart)" and "fainting (spirit)" may be linked with such a literal expression is shown by *Genesis Rabba* 65.1 (on Jacob's terror at being asked by Isaac to draw near, Gen 27:21): "water poured onto his shanks (*nšpkw mym ʿl šwqyw*) and his heart grew soft as wax."

D. R. Hillers has shown that the images of this passage follow (to use the title of his study) "A Convention in Hebrew Literature: The Reaction to Bad News," ZAW 77 (1965), 86–90. Among other examples, he cites Isa 13:7f.; Jer 6:24. He regards Ezek 7:17 as showing the influence of this commonplace (88).

14. *Say.* Turgidity characteristic of Ezekiel (and not found here in some ancient versions); cf. the repeated "and say" of vs. 33 (which is found in the ancient versions).

A sword, a sword. The repetition bespeaks excitement, as with the threefold "awry" in vs. 32 (cf. "My head, my head," II Kings 4:19; "My guts, my guts," Jer 4:19). The same is conveyed by the succession of short lines, with considerable repetition, that sets in here and continues to vs. 22. Eichrodt perceives the passage as a magical spell, but it has none of the monotony and the legalistic accumulation of clauses typical of spells (see, e.g., *ANET*[3], pp. 328–29, 658–59).

even burnished (mrwṭh). A passive participle, though the subsequent mates of *huḥadda* "has been whetted" (hofʿal perfect) in vss. 15–16 are the qal passive perfect *moraṭṭa* (anomalous doubling of *ṭ* influenced by the doubled *d* of *huḥadda*; contrast the normal *korata*, Judg 6:28). Since all early translations render the three cases identically (as pasts), *BHS* directs to read here *moraṭṭa*. In vs. 33 *mrwṭh* recurs, but there it is paired with another passive participle, *ptwḥh* "unsheathed." Burnishing the blade of the sword made it flash, terrorizing the enemy (Kimḥi); cf. *m. Soṭah* 8.1: "'Let not your heart faint' (Deut 20:3) because of the neighing of the [war-]horses and the flashing (*ṣiḥṣuᵃḥ*, lit. "polish") of the swords"; Kara at vs. 15: "When the sword is sharpened and polished well it shines like a lightning flash (*'wr mbryq*)."

15. *in order to flash* (lmʿn hyh lh brq). Lit. "so that it might have lightning" (see citation from Kara in the previous comment). The imperative vocalization of *hᵉye* (we expect the infinitive construct form *hᵉyot*) may be a colloquialism on the analogy of the strong verb, where imperative and infinitive construct are identical; so, too, *harbe* (for *harbot*) in vs. 20. More such in texts with supralinear (Babylonian) vocalization are adduced in Bergsträsser, § 30 c [a]. For the locution *hyh l-X Y*, where Y is a feature of X, compare *wgbh lhm wyr'h lhm* "they had height and they had dread" in 1:18 (see I, 47); this is a stylistic trait of Ezekiel.

Or shall we rejoice . . . "This verse is both unintelligible and unimprovable" (Rothstein). The ancient versions do not reflect a better text but an inability to make sense of what was before them; e.g., S: "and it was made ready to make the scepter of my son droop, and I shall despise every tree." Typical of the futile efforts that moderns have spent on these words is S. H. Margulies, *Das "Schwertlied" Ezechiels*, Scripta Universitatis atque bibliothecae Hierosolymitanarum, Orientalia et Judaica, I/8 (Jerusalem, 1923): This is a second response to the people's question in vs. 12 ("Why are you sighing?"), and is to be translated,

"Should we [God and I] then rejoice? It [the sword] despises [does not spare, Jer 14:19; Isa 33:8] even the scepter of my son [David, cf. 19:11, 14], every piece of wood [*'ṣ* as in vs. 3]." Margulies juggles similarly with the related expressions in vs. 18. There have been many proposals to emend, none more convincing than Kaufmann's (*Toldot* III, p. 515 n. 46): annex the last word of the preceding line and read, *mrṭh kšyš / šbṭ m'st / bdy kl 'ṣ* "[the sword] polished like marble / boughs it ruins / the branches of every tree" (parallelism of *šbṭ* and *bdy* as in 19:14). But how likely is the notion of a whetted sword being wielded against a tree, not to speak of the inapplicability of this proposal to vs. 18 (Kaufmann ignores that problem)? Disconnection with its context suggests that vs. 15b$^{\alpha}$, and its echo in vs. 18, are extraneous bodies. According to L. C. Allen, they are out of place, having originated as annotations to vs. 3 and vs. 32 respectively, alluding to the Davidic dynasty as a "rejected scepter" ("The Rejected Sceptre in Ezekiel XXI 15b, 18a," *VT* 39 [1989], 67–71; cf. Margulies's conjecture mentioned above). Allen's reading of 15b$^{\alpha}$ is: "Every tree [a lemma to words in vs. 3]: or the ruler(s) of Israel [*nś yś*—abbreviations for *nśy'* [*y*] *yśr'l*], the rejected sceptre [read *nm'st*, but why feminine?]." This would seem to be creating a text rather than interpreting it.

16. *It was given.* Lit. "one gave it"—indefinite subject to express the passive (GKC, § 144 d; Joüon-Muraoka, § 155 e). The form of *lmrṭh* is, like *lrḥqh* (8:6) and *lḥmlh* (16:5), a feminine qal infinitive construct.

It was whetted . . . A variation on vs. 14b, with the emotion there expressed by repeating "sword" effected here by twofold *hy'* "it" and the redundant post-verbal "the sword."

17. *Shriek and wail.* A poetic pair appearing only in the prophets (Hos 7:14; Zeph 1:10 [cognate nouns]; Isa 65:14), particularly in oracles against the nations (Isa 14:31; Jer 25:34, 36 [cognate nouns]; 47:2; 48:20, 31; 49:3); note the clustering in late texts.

has come against. For the hostile sense of *hyh b-*, see I Sam 14:20 (of a sword); Gen 37:27 (hand); Deut 2:15 (God's hand). Kimḥi and Moshe ben Sheshet understand *hyth* "has come (lit. 'been')" as a prophetic perfect, depicting the future as present.

victims. Following Skinner (see ahead); the exact sense of *mgwry 'l* is uncertain. The verb appears to be a qal passive participle of *mgr* "cast down" otherwise attested, only in pi'el, in Ps 89:45: "You have cast his throne to (*miggarta l-*) the ground." The participle is in construct with a prepositional phrase (Joüon-Muraoka, § 129 m); the resultant sense "thrown to the sword" (Cooke) is not convincing. Others compare Ezek 35:5 *wattager 'al y^{e}de ḥereb* "you felled (*ngr* hif'il) . . . by the sword," revocalizing to *muggare* (hof'al participle) "felled." The subject *'my* "my people" is preceded by *'t* reflecting its real (rather than its grammatical) object status, as the victim of the sword (similar use of *'t* in, e.g., II Kings 18:30; Jer 36:22, on which see Blau, pp. 13f.). Others take *'t* as "with," e.g., Skinner: "Victims of the sword are they [the chiefs], they and [= with] my people."

slap your thigh. In grief, as in Jer 31:19, where the gesture stands between "I am remorseful" and "I am ashamed."

18. The verse, like the related vs. 15b, is unintelligible. Margulies (see comment on vs. 15b) rendered: "For it [= my people] has been tested; to what end? [They're still corrupt!] (I swear that) it shall be; (the sword) shall even despise [= not spare] the scepter!" The English is not more tortuous than the Hebrew, and is as likely. Allen (see same comment) takes the verse to be a marginal note to vs. 32b, and construes it: "For investigation has been made, and what (if it means that) also the rejected scepter will not continue?" This strains the Hebrew and stretches it to fit an extraneous conception of its meaning.

19. Unlike all other occurrences of "prophesy," this one is not followed by a statement explicitly marked as the content of the prophecy (for the normal sequel, see vs. 14a); perhaps the next line ("The sword shall be redoubled . . .") is to be so understood.

Hand-clapping here (unlike 6:11) is a gesture of vexation — being fed up and about to take action, as in 22:13.

a third time. As *šlyšyt* in I Sam 3:8; final unstressed *a(h)* may be meaningless, "a poetic appendage" (GKC, § 90 f). But the whole clause is obscure, and the versions, like the medievals, seem to be guessing on the basis of our text: G resembles Kara and Rashi, who think of a third, climactic calamity; Kimḥi speaks of a doubling and tripling of calamities — like V, preferred by moderns, who emend to *wᵉšullᵉša*(!); (cf. Rothstein's comment on "the ever-increasing activity of the sword, not soon to diminish, but rather to continue to the bitter end of annihilating the people"). MT recalls the "third" to be struck down by the sword (5:2, 12), on the basis of which Zimmerli wonders whether it means that the sword will double its portion (i.e., consume two-thirds). In view of the doubled (= repeated) "sword" of vs. 14b, and the second doubling of the word in vss. 16–17, perhaps we have here an allusion to yet a third iteration of "sword" or an iteration "up to a third time" (*a*[*h*] expressing goal), viz., the threefold mention of sword in vss. 19–20.

of the great mass of slain. Taking *ḥll hgdwl* as a collective term (cf. 6:7; 11:6; 30:4) = *rb ḥll* of Nahum 3:3, "a mass of slain." *ḥll* lacks an article (so as to agree with its adjective), a lack characteristic of late usage (e.g., *š'r h'lywn* [9:2]; *gb'wt hgbhwt* [Jer 17:2]). A contrastive treatment of early and late Hebrew on this point may be found in A. Bendavid, *Lᵉšon miqra u-lᵉšon ḥᵃkamim*, II (Tel Aviv: Dvir, 1971), pp. 638f. The variously distorted renderings of G S (see text note) apparently derive from the graphs in MT.

that besets them. The sword is the subject, as is shown by the feminine verb. Most moderns understand the verb (a hapax) so, according to the meaning of *ḥdr* in Syriac — "surround, beset" — and the description of the sword's activity in vss. 20–21 and 28:23aᵞ. Medievals link our verb with *ḥeder* "inner chamber" (8:12) and interpret it as "pursue you into innermost chambers" (Rashi), whence AV "which entereth into their privy chambers" — approved by Bewer ("Beiträge zur Exegese des Buches Ezechiel," ZAW 63 [1951], 198). G S T translate the verb as though it were *ḥrdt* "trembling, anxious" but making it, against usage, transitive — viz., "frighten."

20. *In order that hearts may melt.* The doubled expression of purpose, here

through both *lmʿn* and *l-*, is characteristic of late Biblical Hebrew; e.g., *bʿbwr lḥqr* I Chron 19:3 as opposed to *bʿbwr ḥqr* "in order to explore" in II Sam 10:3.

hearts may melt. A restatement in different (for us more obscure) terms of the incapacitation described in vs. 12. As Rashi observed, *mwg* means both "be agitated, waver" (|| "quake" in Nahum 1:5, and cf. Arabic *mawj* "wave") and "melt" (cf. the conjunction in Josh 2:9 of *nm[w]gw* with *wyms lbbnw* in vs. 11); perhaps the basic sense is "liquefy." Here the meaning "melt" is supported by *nms* "melt" of vs. 12. G renders the verbs used with "heart" (*nms, mwg*) identically in both verses—"be broken"; V renders them both by "melt." For the connection of vss. 12 and 20, compare further the combination of their terms in Isa 35:3 and Job 4:4.

and falterings be many. harbe is an infinitive (see comment to *hᵉye* in vs. 15), parallel to *lmwg*, and *mikšol* functions as a verbal noun "fall, failure, collapse." In view of the combination with *lb* "heart, courage" in *mkšl lb* "failure of courage" in I Sam 25:31 (NJPS: "faltering courage") perhaps we are to understand *mkšlym* as implicitly complemented by *lb*, carried over from the preceding *lmwg lb*.

G S translate *mkšlym* as "feeble ones," perhaps concrete for abstract. Moderns take this as reflecting a reading *mukšalim* "felled," but the sole occurrence of that word in Jer 18:23 (NJPS: "made to stumble") is not translated thus in G or S.

terror of (ʾbḥt) *the sword.* The meaning of *ʾbḥt*—a hapax legomenon, etymology unknown—is guessed variously: G "slaughter" = *ṭbḥt*—cf. vs. 15a (so many moderns emend, e.g., *BHS*); V "confusion"; T "killers"; Moshe ben Sheshet and Menaḥem ben Saruq "terror"—adopted here for contextual fitness (e.g., cf. I Chron 21:30), though Ibn Janaḥ's suggestion, "blade," is equally suitable.

ah! As in 6:11, but somewhat strange.

polished (mʿṭh). Cognate with Arabic *mʿṭ* "pluck clean" = Hebrew *mrṭ* (as in Ezra 9:3), and supposing that, like *mrṭ*, Hebrew *mʿṭ* ("be few") had a semantic range including "rub clean, polish" (so Smend, B-Y). For the adjectival noun pattern, cf., e.g., *ʿagol, ʿᵃgulla*. Most moderns emend to a passive form of *mrṭ*.

21. Vs. 21a comprises two verb clauses, in each of which the first verb is an action qualified adverbially by the second (for this unusual order, cf. Jer 4:5 *qirʾu malᵉʾu* "cry fill! = cry in a full voice"; GKC, § 120 h end). The conjectured meaning of *htʾḥdy* "focus, concentrate" (Smend) derives it from *ʾḥd* "one, single." G "be sharpened" (the preferred reading in T also), as though related to or derived from *ḥdd* (the verb in vss. 14, 16), underlies Cooke's "cut sharply to the right." For *hśymy* "attack!" cf. *śymw* "attack!" in I Kings 20:12 (Luzzatto; hifʿil here under the influence of the adjacent *hymny* and *hśmyly* "head right, left!" but see also comment to 14:8 on pseudo-hifʿil of *śim*). We ought probably to understand the two clauses as mutually complementary—thus, "focus your attack on the right, ditto on the left"—and as leading to the next clause: "wherever your blade has been assigned." The meaning of the whole verse will then be: in whatever quarter you are set, attack with all your force! On the combination "left"/"right" meaning "on every side," see E. Z. Melamed, "Break-Up of Stereotype Phrases as an Artistic Device in Biblical Poetry," in *Studies in the Bible*, ed.

C. Rabin, Scripta Hierosolymitana 8 (Jerusalem: Magnes Press, 1961), 146f. The principle that in poetic parallelism terms of the a-colon are often to be combined with those of the b-colon is found in Saadya's tenth-century commentary to Prov 1:8–9 (ed. Y. Kafaḥ [Jerusalem: Committee for the Publication of the Works of Saadya Gaon, 1976], pp. 26f.). Saadya illustrated the principle from Prov 1:8: "Heed, my son, the discipline of your father, / and do not forsake the instruction of your mother," which he paraphrased: "My son, heed the discipline of your father and mother, and do not forsake their instruction."

G's omission of *hśymy* disrupts the balance of the clauses; it may reflect an error of haplography in G's *Vorlage*, due to similarity with the following *hśmyly*.

wherever your blade (pnyk) *has been assigned* (m'dwt). For the idea, cf. the sword in Jer 47:7 that God has assigned (*yeʿdah;* qal) to attack cities. With *pnyk* (lit. "your face") cf. the *pnym* of an axe in Eccl 10:10, apparently its cutting edge, or blade. Jer 24:1 speaks of "baskets situated (*mwʿdym;* hofʿal participle, like our *mʿdwt*) before the Temple" (see W. McKane, *Jeremiah I*, ICC, pp. 605ff.). *pnym* is feminine as in Mishnaic Hebrew; e.g., *panim meʾirot, ḥašekot* "glowing, dark faces" (*Mekilta, Wayyassaʿ* 2, to Exod 16:7).

22. *I too.* Like you (cf. vs. 19); "that God himself will clap his hands [in vexation; see comment at vs. 19] is one of the strongest turns of language ventured by Ezekiel" (Herrmann). It is a fitting climax to the excited speech of this section.

24–25. The main sentence runs: "Make two ways by which the sword of the king of Babylon may come (vs. $24a^{\alpha}$) to Rabbah . . . and to . . . Jerusalem" (vs. $25a^{\gamma}$–b). But at vs. $24a^{\beta}$ the narrator backtracks to fill in details: start with a single road issuing from one country, and where it forks into two, clear a space. In vs. 25a the unfinished main sentence is recapitulated, with inversion of verb and object to indicate reference (*śym . . . drkym* [24]; *drk tśym* [25]). The halting manner draws out (for the sake of suspense) the presentation of the two alternatives open to the Babylonian king and the necessity of his deciding between them. The cleared spot at the fork is the stage for the dramatic ceremony described in vss. 26–27. Only at the end of vs. 25 is the dread alternative "Jerusalem" named as the object of his campaign.

Though *śym drk* would normally mean "make a real road" (Isa 43:19), here it must refer to a representation—"to trace in the sand, we may imagine" (Cooke). Masculine *ʾḥd* is unusual with *ʾrṣ* (*BHS* notes that two medieval mss. have feminine *ʾḥt*, probably a correction), but *ʾrṣ* is exceptionally construed as a masculine in Gen 13:6 also (Samaritan Pentateuch, feminine) and Isa 18:1f.; assonance with *htʾḥdy* of vs. 21 is thereby achieved (on the place of assonance in this oracle, see Structure and Themes). It seems preferable to admit a minor grammatical irregularity (as with *dmwt ʾḥd* in 1:16) than to resort to such shifts as are proposed by Ehrlich (read: *mhʾrṣ ʾḥd* "[on issuing] from the land, [let the two be] one") or G. R. Driver (1954, p. 145: "the same land," according to Driver a wrong extension of an elliptical idiom, properly illustrated by *dmwt ʾḥd*, which he translates, lit. "the likeness of one [wheel]" = all alike).

clear a place (wyd brʾ). The verb is attested by S *gby* "choose" (as from Hebrew *brh* [I Sam 17:8] = *brr*) and T "prepare." It means "hew down" (a forest, Josh

17:15, 18), and in Ezek 23:47 "cleave" (with a sword). The noun *yd* means "place" in Deut 23:13; Num 2:17; Jer 6:3. The phrase *r'š drk,* lit. "head of a way" (in 16:25, 31, "crossroad") gets specificity here by the addition of *ʿyr* "(of/to a [= each]) city." Where the road forks to continue to each city, the prophet is to clear a space ("of thorns and thistles," Rashi), where he will act out what the king of Babylonia is described as doing in vss. 26f. (so Kaufmann, *Toldot* III, p. 513).

The unusual expressions in vs. 24b and the repetition of consonantal sequences (*br' br'š*) make G's shorter text attractive (see text note i–i). G, which attaches to the end of vs. 24b the first words of vs. 25 (*drk tśym*), favors the interpretation of *yd* as "sign" (in I Sam 15:12 it means "monument," and Ehrlich compares the phrase *hṣyb yd* "set up a monument" [ibid.] with *hṣyb ṣywn, śym tmrwr* "set up signposts" [Jer 31:21]). Moderns emend the text variously to arrive at the meaning: "a sign at the head of each road set up." G or the emendations based thereon yield a passable text, without the halting, resumptive style of MT (explicable as erroneous dittographs) and the strange *yd br'*. Yet piʿel *br'* does occur in Ezek 23:47; and the strange phrase evokes the image of the destroyed forest at the beginning of the oracle, as the words *śym, drk, ymyn* (vss. 25–27) evoke *śym, drk, tymn* of vs. 2; and the alliterative, resumptive style is quite Ezekielian. In Ezekiel the presumption of original simplicity is not strong.

25. *to come to.* The construction *bw'* with *'t* (instead of the usual *'l*) is supported by the usage of its antonym *yṣ' 't* "come out of" (e.g., Gen 44:4; Exod 9:29) and is probably inferable from the suffixed pronouns in Ezek 32:11; Ps 119:41, 77; and the construction in Ps 100:4. (For *'t* = *'l,* Ibn Janaḥ [*Haschoraschim,* p. 52] cites, among other examples, *hlk 't* "go to" in Judg 19:18, and *ngš 't* "come up to" in I Sam 30:21. See further, S. Izre'el, *Shnaton* 3 [1978], 204–12.)

Rabbah of the Ammonites. Lit. "the great (or: chief) [city]" qualified by "of the Ammonites" to distinguish it from others so named (e.g., of Judah, Josh 15:60; Rabbat Moab of Hellenistic texts [M. Avi-Yonah, *The Holy Land* (Grand Rapids: Baker Book House, 1966), p. 117; B. Oded, *EM* 7.315]). On the part played by the Ammonites in the rebellion against Nebuchadnezzar, see Structure and Themes to ch. 25.

Judah . . . Jerusalem. The population of Judah concentrated in fortified Jerusalem so as to withstand the assault; cf. Jer 4:5f.: ". . . Gather yourselves and let us come into the fortified cities! Raise a signpost to Zion! Take refuge [in her], do not delay!" We expect an article with *bṣwrh,* but note that it is sometimes omitted with qualifiers of proper nouns (e.g., Beth-horon *ʿelyon, taḥton* "upper, lower B." [Josh 16:3, 5]; GKC, § 126 y; König III, § 334 m). The word order of the preceding phrase is inverted, so that here the city (Jerusalem) follows the ethnopolitical name, evidently for climax. G "against Judah and against Jerusalem in the midst of her" (as reading *btwkh* for MT *bṣwrh*) is simpler and grammatically neater but is not on that account to be preferred; Jer 4:5 (cited above) supports MT.

26. *halts.* G "will stand"; V "stood" (so AV; NJPS "has stood"); *RSV, NAB* "stands"; *NEB* "halts." The Hebrew verb form here and in the next verse is perfect, which allows all these interpretations. The question is whether the events

related in vss. 26–27 are depicted as having occurred or as about to occur, or is the presentation the main thing and the time indifferent? Most critics regard the scene of vss. 26–27 as evidencing the actual start of Nebuchadnezzar's campaign to the west, as if the prophet could not imagine the scene beforehand. But the incidents of these and the next verses are not so realistic as to make this interpretation compelling: e.g., the mixture of divination procedures cannot be verified (see ahead), not to speak of the improbability that the object of the campaign—which city to attack—was not plotted in advance. The Judahites' reaction to Nebuchadnezzar's divination described in vs. 28 (how did they hear of it?) is surely not a past or confirmed event. It seems most likely, then, that the scene is imaginary, reflecting the conviction (expressed already in ch. 17) that the rebellion in the west would be crushed by Nebuchadnezzar, and perhaps, though not necessarily, inspired by rumor that the campaign was being prepared or had begun. The presentation of the scene was the main thing—a piece of threatening rhetoric independent of events; hence we render the verbs as presents.

parting of the ways. Lit. "mother of the way"; this unique idiom is explained by the next phrase, "the beginning (*r'š* "head") of the two ways." An Aramaic equivalent appears in *Lamentations Rabba, Petiḥta* 23: *'m' dbṣlyh* "mother of branching ones."

shakes (qlql) *arrows.* Cf. the parallelism in Jer 4:24 of *htqlql* with *r'š* "quake" (hills). Jerome explains Nebuchadnezzar's procedure: ". . . placing the arrows in a quiver and shuffling them, after having inscribed or marked them with the names of his various enemies, to see which would emerge, and, thereby, which town he must attack" (commentary to Ezekiel, cited and translated by G. Contenau, *La divination chez les Assyriens et les Babyloniens* [Paris: Payot, 1940], p. 184). This is strikingly like the procedure known from pre-Islamic Arabia, carried out before the image of the god Hubal in the Ka'ba at Mecca:

> [In the course of digging the well Zamzam, 'Abdu'l-Muṭṭalib, Muḥammad's grandfather, uncovered valuables that were claimed by the Quraysh tribe.] 'Abdu'l-Muṭṭalib denied [their claim], but was willing to submit the matter to the sacred lot. He said that he would make two arrows for the Ka'ba, two for them, and two for himself. The two arrows which came out from the quiver would determine to whom the property belonged. This was agreed, and accordingly he made two yellow arrows for the Ka'ba, two black ones for himself, and two white ones for Quraysh. They were then given to the priest in charge of the divinatory arrows, which were thrown beside Hubal. . . . 'Abdu'l-Muṭṭalib began to pray to God, and when the priests threw the arrows the two yellow ones for the [gold] gazelles came out in favour of the Ka'ba. The two black ones allotted the swords and coats of mail to 'Abdu'l-Muṭṭalib, and the two arrows of Quraysh remained behind. (*The Life of Muḥammad*, a translation of Ibn Isḥāq's *Sīrat rasūl allāh*, introduction and notes by A. Guillaume [1955; reprint, Lahore: Oxford University Press, Pakistan Branch, 1967], p. 64)

See further, S. Iwry, "New Evidence for Belomancy in Ancient Palestine and Phoenicia," *JAOS* 81 (1961), 27–33. (The shooting of arrows in I Sam 20:20ff.

and II Kings 13:17ff., though compared by some moderns, has little in common with this divinatory practice.) There is, however, no native documentation of arrow-divination in Babylonia.

consults the teraphim. In ancient Israel, teraphim were "figurines, sometimes, at least, in human shape (I Sam xix 13, 16) which were in popular use for purposes of divination" (Speiser, *Genesis,* AB, p. 245, explaining Gen 31:34); cf. Zech 10:2. Again, native Babylonian sources are silent concerning this device. H. A. Hoffner, "Hittite *Tarpiš* and Hebrew *Terāphīm,*" *JNES* 27 [1968], 61–68, suggests an Anatolian etymology—Hittite *tarpiš* "evil demon"; he cannot show Mesopotamian borrowing of the term.

examines the liver. Contrary to the two previous procedures, examination of the liver of a sacrificed animal is a common form of Mesopotamian divination; for liver models marked for divinatory use, see *ANEP*², ##594, 595, 844, and for discussion, H. W. F. Saggs, *The Encounter with the Divine in Mesopotamia and Israel* (London: Athlone Press, 1978), pp. 128ff. Either the prophet had information we lack that Nebuchadnezzar adopted western (Israelite, Arab) techniques of divination (in his western campaigns?), or else he created a visionary montage of diverse techniques (cf. the montage of pagan rites in ch. 8, and the remarks thereon in I, 201f.). In either case, the threefold consultation is true to life: "In the extispicium [the divination from internal organs of sacrificed animals] . . . the custom was to repeat, and even treble the test, [moreover] . . . the question was normally put again another day, when a different answer might be returned" (C. J. Gadd, in *La divination en Mésopotamie ancienne,* XIVe Rencontre Assyriologique Internationale [Paris: Presses Universitaires de France, 1966], pp. 27f.). Capping the series with liver-divination may reflect awareness of the high regard in which that method was held in Mesopotamia.

The point of this scene at the crossroad is dramatic (if unrealistic): well along in the campaign, the first object of attack still undetermined, Nebuchadnezzar paused, when decision could no longer be postponed, to consult "all" available means of divination, one after the other. The upshot is related in the next verse.

27. *In its right* [*side*] . . . H. Cohen (*EJ* 14.179, s.v. "Right and Left") sees an implication here "that omens that appear on the right side are lucky . . . on the left unlucky." He refers to the principle common in Babylonian liver-divination that phenomena of the right side in the liver were lucky and/or about "us," while those of the left were unlucky and/or about the enemy (B. Meissner, *Babylonien und Assyrien,* II [Heidelberg: Carl Winter, 1925], p. 247; for details, see M. Jastrow, *Die Religion Babyloniens und Assyriens* [Giessen: A. Töpelmann, 1905–12], II/1, pp. 244, 340, 349, 359, etc.). *bymynw* then will refer to the right part of the liver (the immediately preceding antecedent of the possessive suffix): "In its right part was the divinatory sign of Jerusalem"; i.e., an attack on Jerusalem was signaled as auspicious. If this clause is not taken as summarizing the results of all the preceding techniques (Rashi, Kara), but is referred to but one of them, it is surely more apt linguistically and culturally to attach it to the immediately preceding one (liver) than to follow those moderns who fix on the arrows as the decisive mode of divination: "In his right hand is the divining arrow marked 'Jerusalem'" (*NAB*); "The augur's arrow marked 'Jerusalem' falls at his right hand"

(*NEB*). See further, my article "Nebuchadnezzar at the Parting of the Ways: Ezek. 21:26–27," in M. Cogan and I. Ephʿal, eds., *Ah, Assyria . . .* (Festschrift Ḥayim Tadmor), Scripta Hierosolymitana 33 (Jerusalem: Magnes Press, 1991), 267–71.

Although the scene at the crossroad may be a figment, Nebuchadnezzar did in fact attack Judah before Ammon, apparently to forestall the entrenchment of the Egyptian army in Palestine. "That Apries [Hophra] indeed sent an Egyptian army to Palestine (Jer 37:5ff.) justifies Nebuchadnezzar's decision. The capture of Judah and severance of communication between Egypt and Palestine might have eased the later subjugation of Ammon" (I. Ephʿal, *The Ancient Arabs* [Jerusalem: Magnes Press, 1982], p. 177 n. 599).

On rams, ramps, and circumvallation, see comment on 4:2 (I, 103).

with shouting. Treating *reṣaḥ* as metathesized **ṣeraḥ*, an otherwise unattested cognate of the verb *ṣrḥ* "shout," in Isa 42:13 parallel to *hryʿ*—whose cognate *trwʿh* "war cry" appears here in the next clause; cf. G. To render it "slaughter" as derived from *rṣḥ* "murder" (V, AV, OJPS) ignores the fact that that verb is not used of slaying in war (Luzzatto). On metathesis, see the collection of examples in Ibn Janaḥ, *Riqma*, ch. 32 (31), p. 352.

for placing rams. Since this clause appears below in a longer version, critics delete it here (e.g., *BHS*), though to be sure all ancient versions have the repetition. Emendation is justified, and it ought to start from the observation that—excepting the clauses in question and their parallel in 4:2—there is an inverse relation between our series and that of 4:2 (a sign of reference); thus:

	4:2		21:27
a	*wbnyt ʿlyh dyq*	c′	*lptḥ ph brṣḥ*
			lhrym qwl btrwʿh
b	*wšpkt ʿlyh sllh*	b′	*lšpk sllh*
c	*wntth ʿlyh mḥnwt*	a′	*lbnwt dyq*

The "armies" of c and the "shouts" and "war cries" of c′ are linked through "a sound of tumult (*hmlh*) like the sound of an army (*mḥnh*)" of 1:24; cf. the Targumic paraphrase of *hmlh* in Jer 11:16 (the only recurrence) by "armies of nations." According to this scheme, the last item (d) of the series in 4:2, "rams" (*wśym ʿlyh krym sbyb*), ought to have its equivalent at the head of ours (d′)—where, indeed, *lśwm krym* appears. But the second, "repeated" version (*lśwm krym ʿl šʿrym*) is preferable as the head of our series because its three stresses better suit the following two clauses, each of which has three stresses. Presumably the "repetition"—the better reading—was once a marginal correction of the erroneous, truncated first term in our series. Early on it was copied into the text at the end of the three-stress clauses where it now is in MT (and was already in G's *Vorlage*). In both series closure is effected by a change in the structure: Whereas 4:2 adds a stress to the last line, our passage ends the series with two two-stress lines (a variation of 4:2's four-stress ending). See the following stress pattern:

4:2	21:27
/ / /	/ / /
/ / /	/ / /
/ / /	/ / /
/ / / /	/ / *lšpk sllh*
wśym ʿlyh krym sbyb	/ / *lbnwt dyq*

Gates were the weak spots in a city wall; battering rams could be wheeled up the path leading to the gate without requiring a specially built ramp; see Y. Yadin, *The Art of Warfare in Biblical Lands*, 2 vols. (Jerusalem and Ramat Gan: International Publishing Co., 1963), p. 315; the picture on p. 424 shows two rams, one on a ramp, the other attacking the gate from the path.

28. A difficult verse. "They" who discount the omens can hardly be the Babylonians; since they have good cause to mount a campaign against the rebels (Jerusalem and Rabbah), they cannot be depicted as scoffing at their oracles that unanimously favor an attack against Jerusalem. "They" must, then, be Judahites—in Jerusalem or the prophet's audience—who on hearing (from the prophet) about Nebuchadnezzar's divination will discount it (the terms are similar to those of 12:24; 13:6, 8, 23). The next clause, which functions, perhaps, as the ground of the discounting, is even more obscure; that may be why G and S omit it. The unusual *š^{e}buʿe* has been taken as qal passive participle = *nišbaʿe* "ones who have sworn"; the full phrase *š^{e}buʿe š^{e}buʿot lahem* is translated accordingly, "they have persons under oath (to them)." M. Tsevat plausibly interprets the construct pair as an elative, "solemn oaths," on the analogy of, e.g., post-biblical *qole qolot* "loud sounds/voices" (*JBL* 78 [1959], 202). In either case, the reference is apparently to an ally (cf. *bʿly šbwʿh lw* "were his confederates" [lit. "oath-takers"], Neh 6:18), who inspired in the Judahites such confidence as to allow them to scoff at the omens. The ally may be God, whose covenant with Israel is referred to as an oath in 16:8, or the Egyptians, to whom King Zedekiah turned for help against the Babylonians (17:15; so Davidson); the second possibility seems preferable in the light of the next clause.

And that. That very insouciant belittling of the omens out of misplaced confidence—

will bring iniquity to mind [for which] to be seized. I.e., captured by Nebuchadnezzar. The obscure phrase *mzkyr ʿwn* recurs in 29:16, alluding to Egypt's inspiring Judah with false confidence: in time to come Egypt will be reduced to a small power, so as not to constitute for Israel "a source of trust, bringing iniquity to mind" (*mbtḥ mzkyr ʿwn*). That passage tends to confirm the second interpretation of the preceding "they have solemn oaths" as alluding to the alliance with Egypt, an offense that the prophet has denounced in 16:26 (see discussion in I, 299).

The tribunal before whom "iniquity is brought to mind" is God, as emerges from I Kings 17:18, where the Phoenician woman blames Elijah for the death of her child, in that he has "brought her iniquity to mind" by the mere fact of taking up lodgings in her home ("Seemingly, she believes that the presence of the man of God in her house has directed God's attention to her and that she is being punished for some past sin which would otherwise have been overlooked" [L. Honor, *Book of Kings I* (New York: Union of American Hebrew Congregations, 1955), p. 252]). H. von Reventlow's idea that *mzkyr ʿwn* means "public prosecutor," here referring to Nebuchadnezzar, who will act as God's agent to punish Judah, though adopted by Zimmerli, Wevers, and Eichrodt, calls into being a functionary unknown in Israel or elsewhere in the ancient east (I. L. Seeligmann, "Zur Terminologie für das Gerichtsverfahren im Wortschatz des biblischen Hebräisch," *Hebräische Wortforschung* [Festschrift W. Baumgartner], SVT 16 [Leiden: E. J. Brill, 1967], 260f.).

Some medievals and most moderns understand the "iniquity" and the preceding reference to "oaths" as allusions to Zedekiah's "sinful" breach of his vassal oath taken (it is supposed) in YHWH's name (17:19–21, according to the Chronicler-Tsevat view; see I, 320ff.). Tsevat translates our verse: "It (the divination) may appear to them (the Judeans) as hocus-pocus, and yet they are bound by the most solemn oaths, which brings (their) guilt to remembrance so that they will be captured" (ibid.). I have already stated my strictures concerning that view and offered an alternative to it. Here I may add: Why should the Judeans regard as hocus-pocus the omen specifying Jerusalem as Nebuchadnezzar's target? If (as Tsevat interprets) "they are bound by the most solemn oaths" to the Babylonian king, which they have broken, report of the outcome of the omen-taking can only arouse gravest concern among the Judeans, who cannot have the slightest excuse for brushing them aside carelessly.

Luzzatto's interpretation of our verse, though straining the meaning of "oath-takers," does justice to its general import: "The Israelites won't believe that the Babylonian king will come against Jerusalem, and this divining of Nebuchadnezzar will therefore seem to them idle; for they have oath-takers, i.e., false prophets who swear to them that N. will not attack them. That in itself calls their iniquity to God's mind, so that they will be seized and caught in it, never to recover."

to be seized. See comment on *tpś* at 14:5.

29. An address to the Jerusalemites: the iniquity just referred to is just the "tip of the iceberg"; notice of it triggers recall of the whole accumulation of guilt, on account of which they shall be delivered into the hand of Nebuchadnezzar. "It is like a servant who offended his master time and again. Had he not repeated his offense, the master would have put it out of mind; but his second offense recalled the first, and the third the second" (Kara).

30. *you wicked corpse* (ḥalal). I.e., wicked man as good as dead; cf. T *ḥyb qtlʾ* "condemned to death." Ehrlich aptly compares the heavenly declaration that, according to the Talmud, snatched triumph from the Babylonian conqueror: *ʿmʾ qtylʾ qtlt hyklʾ qlyʾ qlyt* "a slain (= already condemned [Rashi]) people you have slain, a burnt temple you have burned" (*b. Sanhedrin* 96b). *ḥalal* means "corpse" in vs. 19 (cf. vs. 34) and throughout Ezekiel. On the other hand, G S translate "defiled" (NJPS: "dishonored"; cf. *ḥᵃlala* "defiled woman" in Lev 21:7, 14), evoking the concept of the king's sanctity (Ps 89:21 — the king is anointed with God's holy oil; cf. vs. 40: "You have desecrated [*ḥllt*] his diadem [lowering it] to the earth"; Lam 2:2: "He has lowered to the earth, he has desecrated [*ḥll*] the kingdom and its officers." Tones of "desecration" are struck from, or at least retrospec-

tively lent to, this word by the description given in the next verse of the degradation of royal dignity. Cf. comment to 22:16, and the wordplay on the noun and verb *ḥll* in 28:7ff.

The appositional/adjectival construction of *ḥalal rašaʿ*, lit. "a corpse, a wicked one," is normal—cf. *ʾadam rašaʿ* "wicked person" (Prov 11:7), *malʾak rašaʿ* "wicked messenger" (Prov 13:17)—and is not to be conformed to the syntactically different pluralization of it in vs. 34. There the first term is in construct with the second, *ḥalᵉle rᵉšaʿim*, lit. "corpses of the wicked"—meaning, again, wicked persons as good as dead. Pursuing conformity, KB³ reads here *ḥᵃlal* (construct) *rešaʿ*, the plural of which in vs. 34 it translates "dishonorable evildoers."

chief of Israel. D. N. Freedman observes (by letter) that this epithet may reflect the traditional title of Davidic kings, kept long after they lost control of the northern kingdom, and even after it disappeared.

day has come . . . terminal iniquity (ʿᵃwon qeṣ). For the first expression, see 7:7, 10, 12, and I Sam 26:10, "his day (of doom) will come." The second, an invention of Ezekiel, reflects the idea of a set measure or term (*qṣ*, cf. I, 147, top) of iniquity which when filled will trigger punishment: "At *the time* when the bushel is filled, when the final iniquity that fills the measure arrives" (Rashi). The phrase recurs in 35:5 "at the time of their disaster (*ʾydm*), at the time of their terminal iniquity (*ʿwn qṣ*)," where Rashi glosses more exactly "when the measure (*qṣ*) of their iniquity is complete and their bushel is filled." The origin of the conception appears to be Gen 15:16 (on which see I, 368, 384).

Here, as in 19:14 and 34:5f., ultimate responsibility for the guilt that caused Israel's collapse is laid on the king.

31. *turban . . . crown. mṣnpt* occurs only as the high priest's headgear (Exod 28:4, etc.), but its cognate *ṣnyp* (*mlwkh*) "(royal) turban" appears in Isa 62:3 as a parallel to *ʿṭrt* "crown." The removal of these signs of dignity signifies degradation, as in Job 19:9, Lam 5:16.

The imperative verbs are not consistently vocalized: first (*hsyr*), second (*hrym*), and fourth (*hšpyl*), containing the vowel-letter *y*, are given *i* as their second vowel—the normal pattern of infinitive constructs. The third verb (*hgbh*), without *y*, has *e* as its second vowel—as is normal for the imperative or infinitive absolute (the latter often serving as an imperative). To "correct" the three forms in conformity with the fourth (so moderns; see *BHS*) is sheer pedantry—especially in view of the occasional evidence outside Ezekiel that the infinitive construct did serve as an imperative (Jer 17:18; Ps 94:1; GKC, § 53 m). Evidently these forms, so close in vocalization and meaning, were not always distinguished.

This, not this. Cooke paraphrases this obscure expression, "This is no more this; all is topsy-turvy." Perhaps = "This, not that." In any case, seemingly an introduction to the reversals stated in the sequel. J. Bewer ("Textual and Exegetical Notes on the Book of Ezekiel," *JBL* 72 [1953], 162) showed the G "Woe to her, such shall be" to be secondary, and Ziegler's text does not have it; yet *BHS* offers a Hebrew "retroversion" of this as a proposed emendation!

Lift . . . lower. As in 17:24, and, as there, mistakenly interpreted by some medievals and moderns in specific personal terms (e.g., lift the lowly Jehoiachin and his exiles, lower the high Zedekiah and the homelanders—Kimḥi; Fohrer). See comment to 17:24 (I, 317), and add Ps 75:8 ("For God it is who judges: he lowers one, he lifts another") and lines 192ff. of the "vassal treaty" of Esarhaddon ("abase the mighty, lift up the lowly"; *ANET*³, p. 536b) — expressions of absolute sovereign power in terms of reversing fortunes at will.

The unstressed *a(h)* ending of *hšplh* "the lowly," not a feminine marker, recalls *hḥšmlh* (8:2; see comment there); it may serve a rhythmic function (Joüon-Muraoka, § 93 i).

32. *Awry* (ʿawwa) . . . This hapax is connected by Kimḥi to Isa 24:1: "YHWH will strip the earth bare . . . and twist (*wᵉʿiwwa*) its surface" — signifying agitation and overturning (Eliezer of Beaugency, *Commentary to Isaiah*, ed. J. W. Nutt [(London, etc.): J. Baer & Co., 1879], ad loc.), apt terms for characterizing the preceding lines. BDB and Moran (see next comment) render "distortion." Alternatively, a connection with *ʿy* "ruin" has been proposed, but the reference is hardly to "worldwide chaos" as in Jer 4:23–26 (Eichrodt). The threefold repetition is "a periphrasis for the superlative" (GKC, § 133 l), as in Isa 6:3: "Holy, holy, holy."

Nor will this come about. An allusion to "This, not this" in vs. 31, apparently meaning: the aforesaid reversals also have their appointed time, viz., when "he to whom punishing belongs comes." The verb *hyh* disagrees in gender with *zʾt* (fem.), on which see König III, § 345 d; its time aspect is equivalent to English future perfect ("will have come to be"); S. R. Driver, *Tenses*, § 17.

punishing (mišpaṭ) . . . *entrust [it] to him* (unᵉtattiw). *mišpaṭ* (usually "judgment") here, as in 16:38 (plural); 5:8 (plural); 23:45; 39:21, means "punishment, punishing." Combination with the verb *ntn* recurs in 23:24: "I will entrust judgment/punishing to them (*wntty lpnyhm mšpṭ*) and they will judge/punish you." As G saw, the object verbal suffix (*-w*) is to be taken as indirect object (cf. *nttny* "you have given to me," Josh 15:19; Kimḥi, *Mikhlol*, § 83 b; Dahood, *Psalms III*, AB, pp. 377f. [use with caution!]), with the direct object unstated. Eliezer of Beaugency gives the sense: "Until Nebuchadnezzar, into whose hand I have committed my punishing, comes to punish him (Zedekiah)." Rashi couches his gloss in the idiom of 25:14: "I will commit (*wntty*) my retribution (*nqmty*; Rashi here: *nqmty wmšpṭy*) against Edom into the hands of my people . . ." Deut 32:41 associates *mšpṭ* with God's sword, and contains other similarities to our oracle: "If I whet my flashing sword (*brq ḥrby*) and my hand seize upon judgment/punishment (*mšpṭ*)"; cf. also Isa 34:5; 66:16. The final clause of this section thus harks back to the earlier themes of the sword and the agency of Nebuchadnezzar.

Many moderns, however, take *mšpṭ* to mean "due, right" (as in "the firstborn right," *mšpṭ hbkrh*, Deut 21:17) and render "until he comes whose right it is" or the like (*RSV*; cf. OJPS, NJPS, *NEB*). Several commentators hear an echo of the obscure phrase *ʿd ky ybw šlh* of Gen 49:10 interpreted messianically as "until he to whom it (the kingdom, the right to rule, reading *šello* for MT *šilo* "Shiloh") is, comes" — a notion that may have inspired G here: "until he comes to whom it is proper" (but at Gen 49:10 G translates otherwise); see Smend, Cooke, Fohrer, Eichrodt. Bar Hebraeus comments: "Literally, Zerubbabel [is alluded to], spiritually, our Lord [Jesus]." W. L. Moran ("Gen 49:10 and Its Use in Ez 21:32,"

Biblica 39 [1958], 405–25) connects our passage with Gen 49:10, but sees the blessing of Genesis transformed here into a curse: instead of a savior, a destroyer will come in this topsy-turvy time. Such a parody would befit Ezekiel.

Whether or not there is an echo here of Gen 49:10, only a menacing sense of *mšpṭ* suits the context. A messianic or any other hope (e.g., Moffatt: "till the rightful man arrives—and I will give him everything") is an incongruous conclusion of the verse.

33. The formulas introducing the oracular words "Sword, sword" resemble those introducing the same words in vs. 14, even to the resumptive "and say" (*'ᵉmor/wᵉ'amarta*) at the start of the *b* clause. Here again the prophecy is not directed to anyone in particular.

concerning ('l) *the Ammonites and concerning* (w'l) *their taunts.* The coordinate object "their taunts" makes it plain that *'mr . . . 'l* here cannot mean "said . . . to" (as in, e.g., 34:20) but "said . . . concerning"—unusual in Ezekiel (cf. *'mr l-* in 12:19) but found in contemporary literature: II Kings 19:32; Jer 22:18; 27:19—all in the prophetic message formula, as here. This sequence of five Hebrew words has sown confusion in the interpretation of vss. 33–37; only by ignoring them can sense be made out of what follows. The taunts of the Ammonites are specified and denounced in 25:3–6; they express malicious glee over the fall of Judah and its exile, but are not accompanied by armed attack, to which the sequel here refers. On the other hand, the present passage does not specify taunts but (preparations for) armed attack. Most exegetes understand the oracle as a doom pronounced over the Ammonites, but divide on its specific referents. The anonymous sword addressed throughout is said by some to allude to an otherwise unattested Ammonite attack on Judah (Eliezer; Smend; Herrmann; Cooke). Others take it to refer to Nebuchadnezzar's attack on Ammon after conquering Judah (Rashi[1]; Kara). Yet others divide the passage, taking vss. 34–35 as a prophecy against the Ammonites, and vss. 35–37 as against Babylon (Bewer; Zimmerli; Allen). But the terms of vss. 33b–34 are so similar to those employed in the immediately preceding sections predicting Nebuchadnezzar's attack on Judah that a continuation of that theme seems to be the most plausible line of interpretation (Rashi[2]; Luzzatto; Ehrlich [Hebrew]). Here is Ehrlich's paraphrase of the section:

> It was said before that when King Nebuchadnezzar decided by lot whom to attack, whether Jerusalem or the Ammonites, the lot fell on Jerusalem. In the nature of things, the Ammonites jeered at Jerusalem and taunted it at its fall. This oracle is accordingly intended to throw their taunts back in their faces, and to tell them that God has not permanently abandoned his people. Babylon conquered them, and its sword devoured them, but that was God's punishment for their sins. In the end, when Israel will have suffered at God's hand for all their sins he would have pity on them. Then he would call to account the sword of Babylon for having shed his people's blood. This oracle says nothing about punishing the Ammonites (as most scholars think), for that is the subject of the first section of ch. 25. This speech, from start to finish, addresses the sword of Babylon, the Ammonites being only an audience.

Kaufmann (*Toldot* III, p. 516) follows Ehrlich, adding that the reference to the Ammonites arises out of their previous mention (vs. 25), though the intent of the oracle is to include all Judah's neighbors who prematurely rejoiced over Babylon's victory—prematurely, since in the end Babylon itself would be destroyed.

While this construction of these verses is plausible, the role of audience that is given to the Ammonites (and other neighbors of Judah) is not in the text. The Ammonites and their taunts are said to be rather the occasion of an oracle addressed to an anonymous sword; what are we to make of that? When Rashi became convinced that these verses continued the previous theme (Rashi²), he inserted Nebuchadnezzar into vs. 33a alongside the Ammonites, thus: "concerning Nebuchadnezzar whose destruction of Israel caused the Ammonites to taunt them." Modern critics, contrariwise, excise or emend in order to obtain coherence. For example, Lang, *Kein Aufstand*, pp. 120f., regards the reference to the Ammonites as an editorial deflection to Ammon of an originally anti-Judean prophecy. B. Gosse takes vss. 33–37 to have originally concerned Jerusalem; see "Le recueil d'oracles contre les nations d'Ézéchiel xxv–xxxii dans la redaction du livre d'Ézéchiel," *RB* 93 (1986), 535–62. Ehrlich, *Randglossen*, alters *bny ʿmwn* "Ammonites" to *šobe ʿammi* "captors of my people," i.e., the Babylonians. Still others delete all allusions in the following verse to the sword of the Babylonians (e.g., Wevers).

Since the least strained interpretation of the following verses applies them to Babylon, perhaps the solution to the puzzle is to understand the title "concerning the Ammonites and concerning their taunts" to be purposely misleading. It was dangerous to speak explicitly of Babylonia's ultimate destruction at the height of its power; we recall the threatened fates of the two exilic prophets whose weal-prophecy was subversive to the foreign empire (Jer 29:21ff.). Cf. the use of the code name "Sheshach" for Babylon in Jer 25:26 and Bright's comment thereto (*Jeremiah*, AB, p. 161). By entitling this prophecy "concerning the Ammonites and their taunts" it was related to the post-fall setting of 25:3–6 on the one hand, and to its present context (vss. 25ff.) on the other. "It is inserted very cleverly here where it would not arouse the suspicion of the Babylonians" (Bewer, on vss. 35–37).

Sword, sword . . . flash. A condensed, typically Ezekielian variation on vss. 14b–15a. The language of the sequel (vs. 34)—an address in the second person—shows "sword" here to be vocative (not as in vs. 14b).

unsheathed. So T; lit. "opened, exposed" (cf. 25:9) as in Ps 37:14; cf. Ps 55:22, where *ptḥwt* apparently = "drawn swords," lit. "openings" = "unsheathings."

to the utmost. So Smend and Ehrlich guess at *lhkyl*, lit. "to contain"—i.e., as much as it can tolerate. This difficult expression is translated in G T "to destruction"—based either on another reading (*lklh?*, *lklwt*) or on a loose interpretation of our reading (Kara indeed paraphrases our term by *lklwt* "to destroy"). Rashi's gloss "to fell [*lhpyl*] many corpses" indicates that he read the first radical of our infinitive as *p* instead of *k* (cf. Ps 37:14).

Ignoring MT's accents, the line falls into four versets of two stresses each: "Sword, sword / unsheathed for slaughter / burnished *lhkyl* ("to be adequate [for slaughter]"—Kimḥi, Eliezer) / in order to flash."

34. The terms of vss. 28a$^{\alpha}$ and 30 are combined and augmented: *qs(w)m* "divine" and *šw'* "idle" of vs. 28a$^{\alpha}$ are separated, and each is provided with a mate to form independent clauses (*ḥzwt šw'* "utter idle visions," *qsm kzb* "divine falsehood"), modeled on 13:6–9. Words formerly in the singular (*ḥll* "corpse," *rš'* "wicked," and *ywmw* "his day") are here pluralized. The meaning of vs. 34a is uncertain; the referent of these idle visions and false divination is ambiguous (like the almost identical terms in 12:24; see I, 228, comment on vs. 24). One may say that Nebuchadnezzar's omens are false in that their instruction to attack Jerusalem hides from him its aftermath—as vs. 35 explains, his ruination. Or perhaps the disparaging terms applied to the omens merely echo (ironically?) the popular Judahite assessment of the Babylonian's divination (as in vs. 28a$^{\alpha}$), which, paradoxically, despite its formal emptiness (being heathen) reveals a truth concerning Jerusalem's condemned status (Kaufmann, *Toldot* III, p. 516). The plural victims of vs. 34b are presumably the ruling classes mentioned, e.g., in 22:25ff.

35. *Back* (lit. "return [it]") *to its sheath!* The verbal form *hašab* "return" is imperative (or infinitive absolute, used imperatively); the second syllable is irregularly vocalized *a* instead of *e* (*a* occurs only in pause, as in Isa 42:22 end; GKC, § 29 q; B-L, p. 405). The remarkable shift to third person ("its sheath") implies a momentary address to others; cf. the call to an undefined hearer in 7:23: "Forge the chain!"

the place where you were created . . . land of your origin. As Bar Hebraeus saw, the land of the Babylonians is referred to—as in the "one land" of vs. 24. After its bloody work is done, the sword (Nebuchadnezzar['s forces]) will be sheathed—in stark contrast to the threat of vss. 9f. ("I have unsheathed . . . it shall never be returned")—to be judged and destroyed in its home country. "The fate of Sennacherib, the Lord's agent against Jerusalem in 701 B.C. [who was killed on his return home from his campaign in Judah] (cf. II Kings 19:36f.; Isa. 37:37f.) appears to have been the pattern for this oracle against Nebuchadnezzar" (Bewer).

36. The dominant image seems to be of the sword being melted down and consumed in a fire God has blown upon in order to intensify it (vss. 36a, 37a$^{\alpha}$), like the similar language in 22:20. Vs. 36b can be harmonized with this image: God will ruin his instrument by delivering it into the hands of brutish—and hence destructive—craftsmen (*bo'ᵃrim*, as in Ps 94:8 connected with *b'yr* "brute, animal"; the word also means "burning" and evokes *bi'artiha* "I have ignited it" in vs. 4 of our oracle). On the other hand, *ḥaraše mašḥit* "craftsmen of destruction" may signify expert destroyers, and vs. 36b may abandon the image of melting down, replacing it with nonfigurative language: God will transfer his weapon to the hands of newly chosen executioners, brutish men who will (so it is implied) devastate Babylon. The destroyers are not named, but prior to Babylon's fall it appears that (among Judah's prophets at least) the Medes and other northern "barbarians" were considered the most likely candidates for the role (Jer 51:11, 27f.). With our passage the description in Isa 13:17f. of the Medes as ruthless murderers who despise the values of civilized peoples in their bloodlust may be compared.

37. If vs. 37a$^{\alpha}$ continues the image of melting (at the hands of brutish craftsmen), the shift to bloodiness in vs. 37a$^{\beta}$ intrudes the human referent into the image. Alternatively, the entire verse may continue the allusion to savage experts at devastation: the fire will then be a real conflagration in which Babylon will be destroyed, and the blood, that of its slaughtered inhabitants (but see ahead, comment on "your blood").

you will be fuel (l'klh, lit. "for consuming"). The clause recalls 15:4, 6. The verb *thyh* (normally second person masculine or third person feminine) seems to be a slip for or an equivalent of *thyy* (second person feminine); the same in 23:32; cf. 16:34 (*wthy* for *wthyy*); 22:4 (*wtbw'* for *wtbw'y*); Jer 3:5 (*wtwkl* for *wtwkly*).

your blood will be in the midst of the land. An unclear expression: Fohrer and Eichrodt translate the verb "will flow," ascribing the blood to the subject of the verb (as in 16:22), here the culprit (human—in our interpretation, the Babylonians). But "your blood" in 22:4 (note "blood in its midst" in vs. 3), "your blood in your midst" in 22:13, and "her blood" in 24:7 refer to the blood of victims, whence Ehrlich compares 7:4, "your abominations shall fester within you" (see comment there, I, 147), and explains our phrase: the iniquity of blood(shed) will be amidst Babylon (entailing punishment). The latter agrees better with Ezekiel's attested usage of *dam- b^{e}tok-* "blood in the midst of."

you will not be remembered. Said of the Ammonites in 25:10, hence appealed to by proponents of the view that the sword of Ammon is addressed in these verses. But the expression is a commonplace: Jer 11:19; Zech 13:2; Ps 83:5; cf. Ps 9:7; 34:17 (where a noun phrase with *zeker* "memorial, appellation" replaces the verb).

STRUCTURE AND THEMES

Skinner placed ch. 21 "by the side of ch. vii as the most agitated utterance in the whole book . . . a series of rhapsodies . . . where differing aspects of the impending doom are set forth by the help of vivid images which pass in quick succession through the prophet's mind" (pp. 160, 162). As in ch. 7, the agitation survived the transposition of what presumably was an oral statement into written form, resulting in one of the most difficult texts in the book.

The chapter consists of a sequence of pieces united and set apart from their environment (chs. 20, 22) by the pervasive theme "sword." Formulaic guides to structure—e.g., the revelation formula (vss. 1, 6, 13, 23)—are not wholly reliable. The revelation formula of vs. 6, rather than marking an absolutely new beginning, introduces a nonfigurative recasting of the preceding oracle (cf. the use of the formula in 12:8; 17:11). The form of address initiating a major division, "Man" (vss. 2, 7, 14), is expected in vs. 24, where, however, the subdivisional "And you, man" appears instead. Vs. 33, with its new theme, also opens with the subdivisional formula of address.

Combining formulaic, thematic, and stylistic criteria, the pieces may be grouped in three large divisions: A, vss. 1–12; B, vss. 13–22; and C, vss. 23–37. Each begins with a revelation formula (that of vs. 6—like that of 12:8—marks a stage in a complex event) and ends with a familiar closing formula. Each has a distinctive texture: A is mostly prosaic, B is poetic (repetition, short lines, etc.), C is half and half. Each depicts the sword under a distinct aspect, and each is associated terminologically with its fellow.

A (vss. 1–12): God's sword unsheathed and its effects. This piece, opening with a revelation formula, consists of:

A1 (vss. 2–4): an allegorical forest fire, kindled by God, will work a general destruction; formulas of opening ("Man") and closing ("all flesh shall see, etc.," a variation of the familiar recognition formula, "X shall know, etc."). Ezekiel's protest (vs. 5) forms a transition to A2.

A2 (vss. 6–10): God recasts his message in plain language; Jerusalem is to be told that God's unsheathed sword will work a general destruction. This subsection, too, is marked off by formulas of opening ("Man") and closing ("All flesh shall know, etc.").

A3 (vss. 11–12): Ezekiel is to enact despondency, the effect of the coming news of Jerusalem's doom. Subdivisional formulas mark the beginning ("And you, man") and the end ("declares Lord YHWH"). The poetic structure of these verses has been discussed in the comments. A3 is not closely linked with A1–A2 (for a topical parallel, see 12:17–20—unlike A3, marked off as a distinct revelation event), but the sequence "proclamation of doom"–"enactment of agitated reaction" recurs in B, in vss. 14–16 (doom), 17ff. (reaction). It may be a feature of this series of oracles, deriving ultimately from the actual sequence of revelations. Cf., e.g., the sequence of Micah 1:3–8.

A is mostly prosaic, clearly well structured, and, in its prose parts (A1, A2), rather abstracted from reality: God is the actor, "the soil of Israel" and "all flesh" the objects on which he acts.

B (vss. 13–22): a sword (not God's but unattributed) sows dismay and death. A revelation formula (vs. 13) is followed by an address ("Man") and a command to prophesy (to nobody in particular; vs. 14a). Midway between this beginning and the concluding formula, "I YHWH have spoken" (vs. 22), subdivisional concluding and opening formulas appear ("declares Lord YHWH [18b]. And you man" [19a]), dividing this section into B1 and B2.

B1 (vss. 14b–17) falls into two parts: B1a, the sword readied for slaughter (vss. 14b–16), and B1b (vs. 17; note that the address, "Man" is postpositional), its work bewailed. Leaving out of account the two unintelligible lines (vss. 15b, 18, obviously related), we note diverse patterning. In B1a the poet parcels into bits the impersonal preparation of the sword for its terrible work, only at the very end mentioning the killer who would wield it. Vs. 14b is a segmented line, factual (a sword is whetted and burnished). The facts are motivated in vs. 15: the α segment of vs. 14b is elaborated in vs. $15a^{\alpha}$ (whetted for slaughter), its β segment in vs. $15a^{\beta}$ (burnished to flash; for this pattern of elaboration, see I, 158). Vs. 16a picks up burnishing and carries it forward with allusion to a human agent—"the hand." Vs. 16b returns (with variation) to the opening line (14b) and brings the passage to a climax by explicit naming of the human agent, no longer a disembodied "hand" but "the hand of a killer."

B1b (vs. 17), several commands to show dismay, takes a concentric form: $17a^{\alpha}$

and b^{β}—the extremes—contain imperatives, dictating the action; 17a^{β} and b^{α} speak tenderly of "my people" as victims, while the center (a^{γ}) speaks so of "the chiefs of Israel." At the same time, B1b is linked to the immediately preceding lines through the repeated pronoun "it" (lit. "she") and the referent, "sword." The last line ("slap your thigh") anticipates the opening of B2.

B2 (vss. 19–22), dismay over the bloody work of the sword, expands B1b, with echoes of A3 (cf. the demoralization described in vs. 20a with vs. 11) and B1a as well. A vestige of concentricity is the climactic correspondence of the closure ("I [God] too will clap my hands," vs. 22a) to the opening ("You . . . clap your hands," 19). The body of B2 (vss. 19b–21) details the extent of the slaughter and its terror, compacted together by repetition and alliteration of plosives (*k/q, p/b, t/d*), laryngeals (*h/ḥʿ*), and liquids (*l/m/r*).

vs. 19: HK KP ʾL KP
wTKPL ḤRB šLyšTh
ḤRB ḤLL HGDwL
HḤDRT LHM
vs. 20: LMʿn LMwG LB
wHRBh HMKsLYM

These sounds reverberate in the sequel, too: ʾBḤT ḤRB ʾḤ . . . ṬBḤ HTʾḤDy MʿDT. The last two words echo *hwḥdh* of B1a, as all of vs. 20b echoes B1 (*brq, mʿṭh* [= *mrṭh*], *ṭbh*). The climax of the body of B2 is the apostrophe to the sword personified in vs. 21, whose suggestion of uncertainty as to direction of action foreshadows the scene at the crossroad in the next division.

B as a whole is more concrete and vivid than A. Its central figure, the sword, is elaborated in detail from two aspects: its preparation and its victims. Yet, like A, a measure of abstraction governs the piece: the sword is nobody's; indeed it is so independent, it can finally be addressed as a person in its own right. In B1b a remarkable tenderness expresses itself in identification of the victims as "my people" (twice) and the "chiefs [plural, no one in particular] of Israel"; otherwise, however, the victims and their location are anonymous. God and the prophet are as it were onlookers on horrifying nameless tableaux: all verbs in the description of the sword and its work are impersonal or passive, save one ("I have set," vs. 20).

C (vss. 23–37): Nebuchadnezzar's sword. This disjointed series of scenes opens with a fresh revelation formula (vs. 23), followed, surprisingly, by the subdivisional formula, "And you, man"; the effect is to suggest that this oracle is more closely connected with the preceding one than it would appear to be. Although vs. 32 does not end with any formula of closure, vs. 33 opens a new topic with the subdivisional formula ("And you, man"). Vs. 37 ends with a familiar closure, "I YHWH have spoken"—precisely as B ended (vs. 22). Vss. 24–32 consist of C1, C2, and C3.

C1 (vss. 24–29): Nebuchadnezzar's omen and the Israelites' vexing misapprehension of it. The prophet is to draw a road forking (vss. 24–25); then, instead of a proclamation, an imaginary narrative of Nebuchadnezzar's omen-taking follows, by which he decides to attack Jerusalem (vss. 26–27). The people's disbelief, grounded on misplaced confidence in an ally, will lead to recollection of all their sins, resulting in their capture (vss. 28, 29). Vs. 29, opening with *laken* and a message formula, surprisingly addresses the Israelites directly, although no order to prophesy intervenes between the relation of vss. 26–27 and the prophetic message drawing the consequence (*laken*) of their misdeeds. Through "objective" depiction of the Babylonian's action and the Israelite reaction, the ambiguous value of the pagan divination is brought out: it is essentially hocus-pocus, but the Israelites' judging it so is in this instance both erroneous and self-condemning. This is the first in a series of surprises (paradoxes, reversals).

C2 (vss. 30–32): the overthrow of the political order in Israel. A new address ("And you . . .") opens an oracle to Israel's chief; after a long descriptive clause the divine proclamation to him is introduced by a message formula (vss. 30b, 31a$^{\alpha}$). Next, formulas of reversal are climaxed by a solemn threefold assertion of "awriness" and a cryptic allusion to a judgment on the Judahite king couched perhaps paradoxically in messianic terms (vss. 31–32).

C1 and C2 are prose, in contrast to B, which is poetic; moreover, their subjects are specific and localized: Nebuchadnezzar, the land of Babylon, Jerusalem in Judah, Rabbah of the Ammonites; divination techniques, siege works, confidence in alliance oaths; the chief (singular, specific); the royal crown and turban. God enters only in vs. 32 ("I will make it") in a final burst of cryptic language.

C3 (vss. 33–37), coda: the punishment of the sword. The subdivisional opening formula ("And you, man") is followed by a command to prophesy (to an undefined audience) and a message formula (as in vs. 14). This latter is unexpectedly complemented by the problematic "concerning the Ammonites, etc.," on which see comment. A complex "pendant" expression follows, consisting of an apostrophe ("sword, sword") qualified by passive participle phrases ("unsheathed . . . burnished . . .") to which temporal phrases are attached ("when . . ."). These qualifying phrases review the career of the sword in terms drawn from B and C1–C2; they are followed by the main line of the apostrophe, which they have interrupted, viz., God's doom against the sword (vss. 35–37). The subdivisional opening formula ("And you, man") points to a connection with the preceding section, and indeed the theme of reversal pervades this section as well. On the other hand, its abstract, inexplicit, poetic style recalls B and its figurative language and fire imagery, A1. In short, C3 concentrates reminiscences of all the previous sections in a concluding piece that is the grandest reversal of all: the sword of judgment will itself be judged and destroyed! The cryptical nature of the coda evokes the opening section of this series—the allegory that elicited the prophet's protest of being taken for a skilled maker of verbal figures.

While each of the three divisions is structurally self-contained and stylistically distinct, there is a cumulative relation among them: the unattributed sword of B is charged with meaning lent it by A's explicit talk of God's sword; C (1–2) reveals the earthly referent (Nebuchadnezzar) of the allegoric heavenly sword.

The cumulative lexical and phraseological relation of the divisions is striking: see table.

The table yields the following observations:

1. *ḥrb* "sword," appearing in A three times, in B eight times, and in C four

Table 1

A raised digit tells the number of occurrences, if more than one, of a word and other derivatives of its root in a given section; the digit is attached to the first occurrence. Thus in vs. 8 *hwṣ'ty*^{2} tells that in A2 two derivatives of **yṣ'* occur (*hwṣ'ty* in vs. 8 and *tṣ'* in vs. 9).

A bracketed word is a reminder of an earlier word—semantic (e.g., *z'q* and *hyll* [vs. 17] = *h'nḥ* [vs. 11]) or phonic (*ht'ḥdy* [vs. 21] recalls *hwḥdh* [vs. 14]).

§		A1	A2	A3	B1	B2	C1	C2	CODA
vs. 1									
2		שים *śym*							
		פניך *pnyk*							
		דרך *drk*							
3	A1	מצית *msyt*							
		אש *'š*							
		אכלה *'klh*							
		עץ *'ṣ*^{2}							
4		בערתיה *b'rtyh*							
5									
6									
7		שים *śym*							
		פניך *pnyk*							
8	A2	הרצאתי *hwṣ'ty*^{2}							
			חרבי *ḥrby*^{3}						
			תערה *t'rh*^{2}						
9			רשע *rš'*^{2}						
10			תשוב *tšwb*						
11				האנח *h'nḥ*^{2}					
12				באה *b'h*^{2}					
	A3			נמס *nms*					
				לב *lb*					
				ידים *ydym*					
13									
14			חרב *ḥrb*^{3}		הוחדה *hwḥdh*^{3}				
15					מרוטה *mrwṭh*^{4}				
					למען *lm'n*^{2}				
		עץ *'ṣ*^{2}			טבח *ṭbḥ*^{2}				
					ברק *brq*				
					ויתן *wytn*^{2}				
16	B1			יד *yd*	לתפש *ltpś*				
			חרב *ḥrb*		כף *kp*				
17				[זעק *z'q*]					
					נשיאי *nśy'y*				
				[הילל *hyll*]	ספק *spq*				
18									

19			חרב ḥrb[4]		[הך hk][2]	חללים ḥllym[4]			
					כף kp[4]				
20				[למוג lmwg]	למען lm'n				
				לב lb	נתתי ntty	שעריהם š'ryhm			
	B2				ברק brq				
					[מעטה m'ṭh]				
					טבח ṭbḥ				
21		השימי hśymy			[התאחדי ht'ḥdy]				
		פניך pnyk				הימני hymny			
22						חמתי ḥmty			
23									
24		שים śym[4]	חרב ḥrb[2]	לבוא lbw'[2]	[אחד 'ḥd]		ארץ 'rṣ		
		דרכים drkym[5]		יד yd			ברא br'		
		יצאו yṣ'w							
25									
26							לקסם lqsm[4]		
27	C1					ימינו ymynw	לפתח lptḥ		
							להרים lhrym		
						שערים š'rym	לשפך lšpk		
28					להתפש lhtpś[2]		שוא šw'		
							מזכיר mzkyr[3]		
29					כף kp		עון 'wn[2]		
30			רשע rš'	בא b'[2]	נשיא nśy'	חלל ḥll	עון 'wn	קץ qṣ	
								יומו ywmw	
	C2							עת 't	
31							הרים hrym		
32		אשימנה 'śymnh			נתתיו nttyw		[עוה 'wh][3]	משפט mšpṭ	
33			חרב ḥrb[2]		טבח ṭbḥ		פתוחה ptwḥh		
					מרוטה mrwṭh				
					למען lm'n				
					ברק brq				להכיל lhkyl
34			רשעים rš'ym	בא b'		חללי ḥlly	שוא šw'	יומם ywmm	בחזות bḥzwt
							בקסם bqsm	עת 't	כזב kzb
					לתת ltt[2]		עון 'wn	קץ qṣ	צוארי ṣw'ry
35	CODA		השב hšb				נבראת nbr't		מקום mqwm
			תערה t'rh				ארץ 'rṣ	אשפט 'špṭ	מכרות mkrwt
36		אש 'š		יד yd		[ועמי z'my]	שפכתי špkty		אפיח 'pyḥ
		בערים b'rym				[עברתי 'brty]			חרשי ḥršy
									משחית mšḥyt
37		לאכלה l'klh					תזכרי tzkry		דם dm

times, serves as the major terminological and thematic link among all the sections.

2. Each section has a "growing edge" of new terms, but it also incorporates (from A2 onward) vocabulary drawn from all preceding sections. A3 is the sole exception; its language is stereotypical, the conventional formulation of reaction to bad news (Hillers, cited in comment to vs. 12). Functionally it parallels vs. 17 (B1b). Related to *ḥrb*, the following terms recur: the synonyms *kp* "palm/hand" and *yd* "hand"; the verbs *ntn* "give, put" and *tpś* "seize"; and the combinations *ntn byd* "put into the hand" and *tpś* / *ntpś bkp* "seize / be seized in the hand."

3. At the beginning of C1, many terms found in A1–A2 recur—albeit often with different meanings (e.g., *śym, drk, yṣ'*), and the rare *br'* evokes the destruction of forest trees in the allegory of A1 (see comment to "clear a place," vs. 24). It is as though an echo of A1–A2 were intended, with a skewing of its terms.

4. In B2 echoes of A occur in sufficient strength to tie the two sections together in accord with the familiar "halving" pattern.

5. Putting items 3 and 4 together, an overall "halving" pattern appears: Vss. 1–22 (A, B) speak of a sword of God or of an unattributed, ultimately personified sword—an abstract or unearthly concept; beside the sword only God and the prophet are active. Vss. 23–32 (C1–C2) on the other hand speak of the concrete sword of Nebuchadnezzar, and the actors are earthly (agents and victims). These two major sections are followed, in accord with a familiar pattern, by a coda (C3) that fuses terms drawn from both with characteristic Ezekielian virtuosity. No other section exhibits the "growing edge" terms of the others in such profusion and density. The coda is four and a half verses long (33b–37) and comprises sixty-two words. Of these only ten are new, while the remaining fifty-two words include twenty-nine "growing edge" terms—of A, nine (out of seventeen); of B, eight (out of fourteen); of C, twelve (out of thirteen). Particularly subtle is the relation of two clauses from the end of the two "halves": *whnḥty ḥmty* "I will assuage my fury" in vs. 22 (end of B) is answered by *wšpkty . . . z'my b'š 'brty 'pyḥ* "I will pour out my rage, I will blow the fire of my anger" in vs. 36 (toward the end of the coda). The antithesis between God's satisfaction over the punishment executed by his sword and his final wrath against his erstwhile instrument is highlighted by the verbal correspondence. Although the sword of the coda is most likely Nebuchadnezzar's (as argued in the comments), and so connected conceptually with the immediately preceding sections, the style of the coda is poetic and figurative, thus reverting at the very end to the allegorical cast of the opening section. Reversion to the beginning is a widely used closure device (see, e.g., ch. 17).

Features of poetic "high" style, such as alliteration and chiasm, occur throughout. Repetition is both literal (*ḥrb* in vss. 14, 33; *'wh* in vs. 32) and varying (*r'h/yd'*, vss. 4, 10; *nms lb / lmwg lb*, vss. 12, 20; *mᵉruṭa / moraṭṭa / mᵉ'uṭṭa*, vss. 14ff., 20). Undetermined nouns appear where in ordinary prose some determining elements (article, suffixes) would be expected (König III, § 292; Brockelmann, *Syntax*, § 20). Critics (cf. *BHS*) have (inconsistently) normalized such nouns, appealing to the (inconsistent) evidence of G. For example:

		MT	G	*BHS*
vs. 7	*mqdšym*	"sanctums"	"their sanctums"	=G
vs. 11	*mtnym*	"loins"	"your loins"	=MT
vs. 12	*šmwʿh*	"news"	"the news"	=MT
vs. 20	*lb*	"heart"	G^L "their hearts"	=G
vs. 27	*šʿrym*	"gates"	"her gates"	=MT
(but vs. 20	*šʿryhm*	"their gates"	"gates"	=MT)

Final unstressed—decorative?—*a(h)* occurs twice (vss. 19, 31; *BHS* does away with both). Rare and unique terms connected with swords occur throughout: *hḥd* "be whetted," *mrṭ* "burnish," *ḥdr* "surround(?)," *pnym* "blade(?)," *ptḥ* "draw (out of scabbard)," *mʿṭ* "polish(?)," and the obscure *ʾbḥh* (vs. 20) and *lhkyl* (vs. 33), which critics have not failed to "emend." Ezekiel shows himself again (as in ch. 16) to have expert knowledge of special terminology (cf. also the three techniques of divination listed in vs. 26); our ignorance should cause neither surprise nor recourse to emendation.

Despite the apparent disjointedness of these pieces, their collocation shows a clear progress and development of theme. Section A speaks of God's sword and its victims from a "celestial" viewpoint; B speaks of an "anonymous" earthly sword, a fairly abstract entity, in the end apostrophized. Only C gives full earthly concreteness to the sword, identifying it as Nebuchadnezzar's, whose work is described realistically. The coda, predicting the destruction of the sword, a figure for the Babylonian's army, ties the end of the series to its beginning.

The terminological interconnection of the parts is most readily explained by temporal proximity of composition. Like the cases of chs. 16 and 17, ordered complexity seems to have arisen out of the joining of pieces probably composed separately, but clearly in conjunction with and dependence on one another.

The characteristic feature of these oracles is the reuse and intensification of motifs found in previous oracles. Ezekiel's penchant for combining and repeating with variation his favorite themes is strikingly illustrated here.

God's sword—the central theme of this chapter—is a figure well documented in poetry and prophecy. The kernel of Ezekiel's inspiration may have been these lines in the poem of Deut 32 (God is speaking):

Once I have whetted my flashing sword (*brq ḥrby*)
And my hand (*ydy*) seizes judgment (*mšpṭ*) . . .
My sword shall consume flesh (*bśr*). (vss. 41f.)

The flash ("lightning") of the sword is mentioned only here and in Deut 32.

God's punishing sword has a prominent place in the warnings of Lev 26: "I will bring upon you a sword exacting retribution for the [breach of the] covenant" (vs. 25; see also vss. 33, 36f.). Jer 47:6f. speaks of God punishing gentiles in terms similar to Ezekiel's:

O sword of YHWH!
Till when will you not be quiet?

Withdraw into your sheath (*tʿrk*) . . .
How can it be quiet
When YHWH has ordered it—
Against Ashkelon and the sea-coast,
There he has assigned it (*yʿdh*).

The language of our chapter may reverberate in Isa 66:16.

For with fire (*bʾš*) YHWH enters into judgment (*nšpṭ*),
And by his sword with all flesh (*kl bśr*);
The corpses of (*ḥlly*) YHWH will be many.

Ezekiel equated fire with sword in the symbolic action of 5:1–4; unattributed sword appears in 6:3 (11:8, etc.) and in the deadly trio sword, famine, and plague (6:11f.). The sword of God makes its first appearance in Ezekiel here (for subsequent occurrences, see 30:24f.; 32:10). The image of a forest fire is a manifold intensification of the metaphoric charred vinestock of ch. 15 and the burning vine of ch. 19. The extent of the catastrophe—in 7:2 "the four corners of the earth"—is here said to include "all flesh." New and astonishing is the motive given in vs. 9 for this scope: since, in his rage, God will not discriminate among the victims within Israel, he will surely not pick and choose among the rest of humanity.

The singularity of Ezekiel's view is underlined by comparison with an analogous passage in Jeremiah. In Jer 25 the prophet is ordered to give all nations "the cup of YHWH's fury" to drink (25:15–28); if they refuse, he must say to them (vs. 29):

> See, I am starting my evil work in the city called by my name; do you, then, expect to get off scot-free? Indeed I am summoning a sword against all the inhabitants of the earth, declares YHWH of hosts.

In an adjacent passage (vs. 31) YHWH declares he has a quarrel with the nations and is "entering into judgment with all flesh: the wicked—he has delivered them to the sword." The general slaughter of vs. 29 is specifically limited to the wicked. Ezekiel's emphasis on indiscriminateness ("righteous and wicked") has no parallel and indeed contradicts his own teachings elsewhere: in 9:4 he described the exemption from destruction of "those who moan and groan over all Jerusalem's abominations"; in 14:13–20 and in ch. 18 he elaborated a theory of individualized, discriminating retribution. Those positions cannot be harmonized with the one taken here. Herrmann's conjecture that this prophecy came before those is an unpersuasive makeshift (especially in the light of the evidence that this is a later prophecy that builds on preceding ones). Cooke says rightly, "but he is not now working out a theory as in ch. 18 . . . he is in a passionate mood [and] can think of one thing only—the sword and its victims." For all that Ezekiel loves system and scheme, these do not extend beyond the case in point. As in the conception of the remnant (see I, 140f.) or the relation of repentance to restoration (see at ch. 36), the various pronouncements of the prophet cannot always be brought into agreement. He speaks for a given occasion and his message is tailored to it. Here the occasion is epitomized in his coinage "the time of terminal iniquity" (vss. 30, 34): the measure of iniquity is full, God's patience is at an end; his pent-up fury will explode in a storm that will carry all before it, precisely the mode of conduct that Abraham challenged in his debate with God before the overthrow of Sodom and Gommorah, "Will you indeed sweep away the righteous with the wicked?" (Gen 18:23).

Of great interest for the history—and persistence—of ideas is the aptness of certain midrashic epigrams (a millennium after Ezekiel) recognizing the grim reality of indiscriminateness in collective visitations. *Genesis Rabba* 49.8 (end) compares such visitations "to a she-bear killing animals; when she runs out of animals to kill, she kills her own cubs . . . to a sickle cutting down brambles—if it found none, it cuts down lilies." On the astonishing house arrest imposed on the Israelites the night of the firstborn plague in Egypt, lest "the Destroyer" strike them down with the Egyptians (Exod 12:23), the Mechilta (*Pisḥa* 11) remarks, "This shows that once the angel is licensed to strike he does not discriminate between the innocent and the guilty," and compares further Isa 26:20 and Exod 33:22. Needless to say, many other passages in midrashic literature propound the romantic, theologically more acceptable view that God deals out just deserts to all men. With these latter we may class the following assertion of Heschel: "The divine pathos . . . was never thought of as an impulsive act . . . It is neither irrational nor irresistible . . . It comes about in the light of moral judgment rather than in the darkness of passion" (*The Prophets*, p. 298). Ezekiel and his midrashic disciples had (at times) more realistic, tough-minded visions of God's sovereign conduct.

To this intense divine rage corresponds the heightened reaction that must be playacted by the prophet (vss. 11–12). His previously commanded reaction to a doom oracle was to eat in trembling (12:17ff.); now he is to present a picture of physical collapse, explained in terms doubling the expressions of demoralization of 7:17 (vs. 11; see comment). Within this chapter, his second commanded reaction (21:17) augments "Sigh" (vs. 11) to "Shriek and wail."

The two-tiered presentation of events—first from a celestial or figurative viewpoint, then from a terrestrial, concrete one—so effective in ch. 17 (the fable of the two eagles), is reused here to bond vss. 1–22 (A–B) and 23–37 (C). Once again (as in ch. 17) God('s sword) and Nebuchadnezzar stand in parallelism. The scene of Nebuchadnezzar at the fork in the road is a dramatic device to bring home the quirkiness and inevitability of Jerusalem's fate. Israel cannot bank on the falsity of heathen omen-taking; in God's plan even liver-omens speak "truth." On this occasion, the terminology of false prophecy (12:24; 13:7f.) is called back into play—with a twist: not in reference to Israelite prophecy, but to pagan hocus-pocus, paradoxically true despite the Israelites. The counterpart to the pagan false divination is Israel's false confidence in the "solemn oaths" of their ally (an echo of 17:7, 15). Israel thus resists the verdict of God, and this theopolitical error calls to mind its ages-long apostasy; it has repeatedly turned from God to rely on other gods and earthly powers (see the indictment of 16:15–

29). This would seem to be the "iniquity called to mind" by Israel's present miscalculation.

Israel's "chief(s)" first appeared in 7:27 ("clothed in desolation"); in ch. 12 the reigning chief is portrayed as a pitiful refugee-captive; ch. 19 first describes him with negative features. Here he is derogated with the vilest epithet: "wicked corpse" (overtone: "profaned one"). When next mentioned (22:25, corrected reading), the epithet will be justified.

How the coda resumes the terminology of all the preceding sections, and how it resembles the allegorical opening in its cryptic nature, have been described above. It remains to comment on the theme of the piece: God's turning upon his instrument and destroying it. Whether the intention of vs. 34a is straightforward or ironical, at bottom it correctly describes the pagan divination (from the prophet's viewpoint): it is indeed idle and false.

That is why it cannot represent the last word concerning Nebuchadnezzar's sword. Though it was commissioned to punish "wicked corpses," since its fundamental drive was heathen and bloodthirsty, it cannot be allowed a final triumph. So the coda closes the ring of oracles with the imagery of the opening one: God's sword was drawn "not to be sheathed again"—i.e., before having completed its task (vs. 10). Now, having completed it, the sword must "return to its sheath"—in other words, to "the land in which it was created"—and there be destroyed. The reuse of the sheath image necessarily precludes the concept of Isa 14:25 (Assyria will be broken in the land of Israel) and requires the alternative mode of disposing of the enemy described in II Kings 19:36f.; Isa 37:37f. (Sennacherib will return to his land and there be killed).

It is generally supposed that this collection of oracles reflects the onset of the rebellion in the west and the start of Nebuchadnezzar's march to quell it; this suits its location between the dates in 20:1 (August 591) and 24:1 (January 588). But in view of Ezekiel's long-standing insistence that Judah's rebellious mood (since 594), part of a general western resistance to Babylonian rule, would surely result in its destruction, it does not seem necessary to suppose actual military movement as the stimulus of this oracle. We have argued in the comments that the scene at the crossroad is more likely to be a fantasy than a reflection of an actual event.

Most critics have understood vss. 33–37 (the coda) to be an oracle against Ammon and as such to be dated, with the anti-Ammon oracle of ch. 25, after the fall of Jerusalem. (Another result of this interpretation is to deny Ezekiel's authorship on the ground that terms repeated in it from preceding sections have been "misunderstood"; e.g., the application to Ammon in vs. 34a of the Babylonian "idle oracle" of vs. 28: see Zimmerli and Wevers.) Even on our understanding of the coda as a veiled anti-Babylonian oracle, however, the title "concerning the Ammonites and concerning their taunts" is best connected to the gloating ascribed to the Ammonites in ch. 25—hence from after the fall of Jerusalem. Assuming that the title is original and not a later addition, dependence on ch. 25 (not any intrinsic improbability of a consolatory ending to a doom oracle) points to the possibility that the coda is a post-fall complement to a series of pre-fall dooms. At the time of composition Babylon's collapse was still in the future, and its power was such as to recommend circumlocution in entitling a prophecy predicting it.

How much time elapsed between the creation of the coda (if it is later than the preceding sections) and the last-composed part of ch. 21 cannot be known. But the literary integration of the coda with the body of ch. 21 suggests it originated with the same poet.

XXI. JERUSALEM ALL DEFILED AND CORRUPT (22:1–31)

22 [1]The word of YHWH came to me: [2]And you, man, will you arraign, will you
arraign the bloody city? then declare to her all her abominations! [3]And say: Thus
said Lord YHWH:

City shedding blood in her midst, so that her time has come;
that makes idols all over her, becoming defiled—
[4]Through the blood that you shed, you have become guilty,
and through the idols that you made, you have become defiled.
[a]You have brought near your [last] days,
you have arrived at [the end of] your years.[a]
For that I am subjecting you to the taunts of nations,
to the derision of all lands.
[5]Those near and far from you deride you—
"Impure of name, rife with tumult!"

[6]See, the chiefs of Israel have each resorted to force in you,
in order to shed blood.
[7]Father and mother they have dishonored in you;
The alien they have cheated of his due in your midst;
Orphan and widow they have wronged in you.
[8]My holy things you have despised,
And my sabbaths you have desecrated.
[9]Slanderers have been in you, in order to shed blood.
People have eaten on the mountains in you.
They have acted depravedly in your midst.
[10]One has uncovered [his] father's nakedness in you;
they have forced the menstrually impure woman in you;
[11]and one has committed abomination with his fellow's wife,
and one has depravedly defiled his daughter-in-law,
and one has forced his paternal sister in you.

[a–a]G V "You have brought near your days and brought (as from *wtby'y*) the time (as from *'t*) of your years"; S "Your days have come near, the time of your years has arrived"; T "The day of your ruin nears, the time of your misfortune has arrived. Oriental mss. show *'t* K, *'d* Q (*Minḥat Shay*).

[12]They have taken bribes in you, in order to shed blood.
You have taken interest and increase,
 and have profited your friends through cheating;
Me you have forgotten, declares Lord YHWH.
[13]Now see, I clap my hand over the profit you have made,
 and over the [b]bloodshed that is[b] in your midst.
[14]Will your heart be stout, will your hands be firm
 on the days [to come] when I deal with you?
I am YHWH; what I have spoken I will do!
[15]I will scatter you among the nations,
 disperse you among the lands,
 and purge your impurity out of you.
[16]You will be dishonored in you in the sight of the nations,
And you shall know that I am YHWH.

[17]The word of YHWH came to me: [18]Man, for me the house of Israel have
become dross: all of them are copper, tin, iron and lead in a crucible; dross of
silver are they. [19]So then, thus said Lord YHWH: because you have all become
dross, therefore I am gathering you into Jerusalem. [20]As one gathers silver and
copper and iron and lead and tin into a crucible to blow fire on it to melt it, so
will I, in my anger and in my fury, gather and throw and melt you. [21]I will collect
you and blow on you the fire of my wrath, and you shall melt within her. [22]As
silver is melted in a crucible so you shall be melted in her midst; and you shall
know that I, YHWH, have poured out my fury on you.

[23]The word of YHWH came to me: [24]Man, say to her: A land not purged are
you, not rained on in the day of rage.

[25] [c]Her conspiracy of prophets[c] in her midst were like a roaring lion, tearing
prey; they ate people, they took treasure and precious things; they made many
widows in her midst.

[26]Her priests did violence to my instruction and desecrated my holy things:
they did not distinguish between the sacred and the profane, or teach the difference between the impure and the pure. My sabbaths they disregarded, and I have
been desecrated among them.

[27]Her officers within her were like wolves who tear prey—shedding blood, destroying lives, in order to make profit.

[28]And her prophets daubed for them untempered plaster, having idle visions
and divining for them falsehood, saying, "Thus said Lord YHWH," when YHWH
did not speak.

[29]The people of the land withheld what was due and committed robbery; the
poor and needy they wronged, and [d]deprived the alien of [his] due unjustly.[d]

[30]I sought among them a man who would build a fence and stand in the

[b–b] MT singular noun, plural verb; G plural noun, plural verb; S T singular noun, singular verb.

[c–c] G "whose chiefs" (as from *'šr nśy'yh*).

[d–d] G "toward the proselyte they have not behaved (same verb as in vs. 7a[β]) with justice."

breach before me on behalf of the land, so that I should not destroy it, but I found none. [31]So I poured out my rage on them, in my fiery wrath I made an end of them; I brought their conduct down on their heads, declares Lord YHWH.

COMMENT

22:2. *And you, man.* For this opening formula, see at 7:2.

will you arraign, will you arraign . . . declare. See comments at 16:2 and 20:4. The repetition of "arraign" bespeaks excitement, as elsewhere; e.g., 33:11 (*šwbw šwbw*). G balks at repetition: in 21:32 it reduces to two MT's threefold *ʿwh;* in 20:4 and 33:11 it replaces MT's verb-verb sequence by a verb-noun one; in 24:6 and here it represents only one of MT's repeated words. Hence G is a shaky basis for conjecturing that an originally simple Hebrew here was secondarily doubled under the influence of 20:4 (*BHS*).

bloody city. Lit. "city of blood[shed/guilt]," earlier applied by the prophet Nahum (3:1) to Nineveh, capital of Assyria, the destroyer of Israel. Ezekiel repeats the shocking epithet in 24:6, 10; cf. his accusations in 9:9; 11:6; 16:38 (referring to 16:20f.). As described below in vss. 6, 9, and 27, the primary reference is to "judicial murder"—killing as an exercise of administrative power (Peels, "The Vengeance of God," pp. 123f.).

3. *City.* G "O City" correctly understood this to be an address, but that does not indicate that it read here an exclamatory particle, such as *h-* or *hoy* (*BHS*). At Prov 6:6 G renders "O lazybones" and at 8:4 "O men," though the Hebrew lacks an equivalent for "O."

in her midst. Repeated in vss. 7 and 13, and together with reiterated "in you" (vss. 6–7, 9–12, 16), these expressions convey the impression of the city as a receptacle, a sink, of impurity; foul deeds fester within it calling down punishment (see comment at 7:4). Cf. Amos 3:9, with its doubling of "in her midst" in an indictment of Samaria (further contact with the Amos passage appears in vs. 5 below).

so that her time has come. "X's time" = "the time of X's doom" as in Jer 27:7; Eccl 9:12. The phraseology is repeated from 7:7, 12.

that makes (wʿśth). The perfect consecutive following the participle (*špkt* "shedding") carries on the participle's denotation of indefinitely repeated (frequent, continuous) action; cf. 33:30 ("they [repeatedly] speak"); Jer 21:9 ("whoever . . . deserts"). See S. R. Driver, *Tenses,* § 117; GKC, § 112 k.

idols all over her (glwlym ʿlyh). An unusual use of *ʿl* "upon," found again in Ps 110:6, "over a wide country." In the light of the subsequent list of wrongdoings, Abarbanel interprets *glwlym* here as foul deeds, social rather than cultic offenses (see Structure and Themes). This view is strengthened if the closing summary of the list in vs. 13 consisting of two phrases, "make [ill-gotten] profit" and "blood that is in you," is taken as the inverted equivalent of the terms "shed blood" and "make *glwlym*" of the opening summary in vss. 3f.

4. *the* (lit. "your") *blood.* I.e., of your victims; see comment to 21:37 "your blood."

your [last] days . . . your years. "Days"—of judgment—is plural, as in 12:23 ("the days draw near" [Zimmerli]); the plural of years is due to attraction.

have arrived at (wtbʾ ʿd). The third person feminine (= second person masculine) verb serves for second person feminine, as in 21:37 (*wthyh* for *wthyy* = 23:32; 26:14) and 26:14 (*tbnh* for *tbny*)—a scribal slip or a local peculiarity? Each of the parallel lines *c* and *d* has its own syntax:

c	*wtqryby* (transitive verb) "you have brought near"	*ymyk* (direct object) "your days"
d	*wtbwʾ* (intransitive) "you have arrived"	*ʾd šnwtyk* (adverbial noun phrase) "at your years"

The ancient versions cited in text note a–a have in common the syntactic leveling of the two parallel lines—G and V making the complementing noun in both clauses direct object, S and T making the nouns in both clauses the subjects of the verb. Such leveling is likely to be secondary to MT's syntactic divergence.

The Oriental K variant *ʿt* "time" for the received text *ʿd* "at" (so Leningrad and Aleppo mss.) appears to underlie the versional renderings. It is the subject of the third person feminine verb *wtbwʾ* as *ʿth* is of the infinitive *lbwʾ* in vs. 3; it is also commonly paired with *ywm* "day" (21:30, 34; 30:3; reverse order in 7:7, 12). Against these considerations is the awkwardness of "time of your years," an unparalleled expression, whereas *bwʾ ʿd* "arrive at" is common. Each reading has advantages that are canceled by disadvantages (which may account for the alternative); a decision between them is not possible.

With "you have brought near your [last] days" compare 12:23, in which the same idiom is used for the predicted, and hence predetermined, time of Jerusalem's doom. Here the thought seems to be that by excess of sinning, she has shortened the remaining span of time allotted to her.

5. *"Impure of name."* In S this is preceded by "and they shall say," showing that, like Rashi, it interpreted the following two epithets as hurled at Jerusalem by the deriding gentiles—an attractive idea. Eliezer's gloss, "murderess, adulteress"—the impure names of the bloody city—accords with the predominance of sexual and social offenses in the following list (vss. 6–12; see Structure and Themes); these and not religious offenses would excite gentile reproach. For Ezekiel the name of Jerusalem was so bound to impurity that in his vision of the restoration the city is renamed (assonantly) *YHWH-šamma* "YHWH is there" (48:35—the last words of the book).

"rife with tumult (mhwmh)." In 7:7 *mhwmh* occurs in the context of the confusion of doomsday; here the relevant parallel is Amos 3:9f.: Samaria is full of *mhwmt*—lawless disorder, as explained by the following *ʿšwqym* "deprivation of right/due." In Prov 15:16 the term contrasts with "God-fearing."

6. *the chiefs of Israel have each resorted to force.* Hebrew *ʾiš lizroʿo hayu*, lit. "each (according) to his arm were"; cf. *ʾiš zᵉroaʿ* "strong-armed, violent man" (Job 22:8). BDB (p. 516, def. j [b]) defines this use of *l-* as "denoting the principle with regard to which an act is done"; here the personal power one has at his disposal. Kimḥi's specification of its source—"based on wealth or relatives"—

sheds light on G's "each associated with his kinsman" (or as reading *zarʿo* "his offspring"; so, too, S). Ehrlich [Hebrew] paraphrases, "each in accord with the law of his fist."

The "chiefs of Israel" — the Davidic kings whose seat was Jerusalem — head a list of offenses that are not parceled out among distinct ranks, as is the list of vss. 25ff. This would be suspicious (indeed, Smend disconnects our verse from the sequel and joins it to vss. 25ff.) were it not the duty of kings to maintain a just social order. Jer 22:2–3 attaches court and people to the king ("your courtiers, your people"), hence the injunctions to preserve justice (e.g., "rescue from the cheat him who is robbed"), though couched in the plural, are ultimately for the king to execute, as chief of state. The particular responsibility of the king to prevent the abuse of parents and the helpless (vs. 7) is illuminated by two Sumerian passages (translation by S. N. Kramer, *The Sumerians* [Chicago: University of Chicago Press, 1963], pp. 336f., 319). In the prologue to his laws, King Lipit Ishtar of Isin (early second millennium B.C.E.) records how he rectified social wrongs in his city, in the course of which:

> I made the father support his children, (and) I made the children support their father; I made the father stand by his children, (and) I made the children stand by their father.

An item of the reforms instituted by Urukagina of Lagash (mid-third millennium B.C.E.) reads, "Urukagina made a covenant with [the god] Ningirsu that a man of power must not commit an (injustice) against an orphan or widow." The violence of Israel's kings, seated in Jerusalem, heads the prophet's bill of indictment because far from maintaining justice they set an example that undermined the norms of their society, as described in the following verses.

7. *they have dishonored.* While it is possible to take the preceding "chiefs of Israel" (vs. 6) as the antecedent of "they" (so, e.g., Wevers) — for, as explained in the previous note, the kings might be held responsible for all social wrongdoing — it is more likely that "they" signifies undefined persons, just as in vs. 9b the third plural subject of "they ate" is not necessarily the preceding "slanderers" — to whom the idolatrous rite in question is not especially appropriate.

dishonored. This is the sense of *heqal* (*qll* hifʿil) in II Sam 19:44; Isa 23:9. But in view of Deut 27:16, "Cursed be one who dishonors *maqle* (*qlh* hifʿil) his father or his mother," this might be a deliberate variation. The following offenses are all formulated with slight deviations from their cognates in the laws of the Torah.

alien . . . orphan and widow. This triad of the easily victimized occurs first in Exod 22:20f. (the last two terms transposed), and, in the present order, it is a Deuteronomic commonplace (e.g., Deut 14:29; 16:11, 14; 24:17, 19–21; 27:19; cf. Jer 7:6; 22:3). On *ʿšq* "withholding what is due, depriving of a right," see comment at 18:18; on *hona* "wrong," see at 18:7. Ezekiel's mark is evident in the circumlocution *l-X ʿsw bʿšq* "toward . . . they acted with deprivation of right" instead of the simple *(ʾt)* X *ʿšqw* (as below in vs. 29b); cf. *ʿśwt bnqmh* in 25:15 "acting with vengeance" instead of the simple *(h)nqm mn/b-*.

8. The offenses attributed here to the city are ascribed to the priests in vs. 26; see comment there. If the city = the people at large, such laic offenses as consuming sacrificial meat in an impure state (Lev 7:20), or beyond the time allowed for it (Lev 7:15–18; 19:6–8), or violation of the sabbaths as described in Jer 17:21f., may be intended. The pair *qdšy-šbtty* "holy things-sabbaths" recalls *šbtty-mqdšy* "sabbaths-sanctuary" in Lev 19:30; cf. Kara's detailed comparison with that chapter cited in Structure and Themes. This passage is echoed in *m. 'Abot* 3.11 (note the inversion): "He who desecrates the holy things (*mḥll qdšym*) and despises the holydays (*mbzh mw'dwt*) . . . has no share in the world to come."

9. *Slanderers* ('nšy rkyl). In such constructions as *'nšy lṣwn* "scoffers" (lit. "men of scoffing," Prov 29:8), *'nšy tmyd* "men of regular duty" (lit. "men of continuity," Ezek 39:14), the second word is a noun; accordingly *rkyl* (on the pattern of action nouns, like *ḥryš* "plowing") is "retailing" (information, gossip, presumably connected with *rkl* "to trade"; hence S "traders"). With *hlk* "go about," *rkyl* serves adverbially ("retailingly"), as in Lev 19:16, always in an evil sense (König III, § 329 k; GKC, § 118 q). G renders *rkyl* by expressions of treachery, deceit, and crookedness (Lev 19:16; Prov 11:13; Jer 6:28) — here "robbers." But in post-Biblical Hebrew it is uniformly understood to mean "slander/er" (so T here). The connection with slaying here and in Lev 19:16 is "to get rid of persons obnoxious to their [the slanderers'] power by false accusation" (Cooke).

eaten on the mountains. See comment at 18:6.

They have acted depravedly. "A generality covering all forbidden sexual unions, followed by some particulars" (Kimḥi). Ezekiel's use of *zimma* "depravity" to denote unchastity (16:27, 58; 22:9, 11; 23:21, 27, 35, 44, 48f.) follows priestly usage in the Torah: Lev 18:17; 19:29; 20:14.

10. *uncovered . . . father's nakedness.* I.e., cohabited with his father's wife. The expression occurs in Lev 18:7 (explicated by "the nakedness of your mother"), where Ehrlich correctly explains it as the nakedness that is lawfully accessible (uncoverable) solely to your father. See the explanation of Deut 23:1 given in the comment to 16:8.

forced. The sexual use of *'nh* "humiliate, oppress" occurs in Deut 21:14; 22:24, 29; here and in vs. 11 it signifies unwillingness of the woman to acquiesce in the illegal union. The prohibition is in Lev 18:19 (cf. comment at 18:6). The description of the woman is, literally, "impure (by reason) of menstrual impurity" (cf. 18:6), a construction identical with that of "impure of name" in vs. 5.

11. *with* ('t) *his fellow's wife.* "His fellow's wife" cannot be the direct object, like the females in the following clauses, each of which is preceded by the object marker *'t,* since that function is served by "abomination." We are forced (with *Meṣudot* and moderns) to take *'t* as the preposition "with," though there is no other instance of *'śh tw'bh 't* "commit abominations with." Strictly speaking, the expression suggests complicity of the woman, which, as the following clauses show, cannot be intended. G S render *'śh tw'bh* by a transitive verb, with "wife" as direct object. The Hebrew is a syntactically loose combination of such formulations as *'yš 'šr yn'p 't 'št r'hw* "a man who violates (usually: commits adultery with) his fellow's wife" (Lev 20:10 — "with" is not in the Hebrew, and in the En-

glish means here "on the person of") and the self-contained clause *'śh tw'bh* "commit abomination" (Lev 20:13; Ezek 18:12). A closer approximation to the sense of *'t* in this hybrid expression is "on the person of (the wife)."

paternal sister. Laxness with respect to this union is suggested by the iterated ban on it in Lev 18:9 and 11. See the discussion in P. K. McCarter, *II Samuel*, AB, pp. 323f. (to II Sam 13:13).

12. *bribes . . . shed blood.* Cf. Deut 27:25: "Cursed be one who takes a bribe to strike down the life of an innocent person."

interest and increase. See comment to 18:8 (I, 330).

profited your friends. Taking *bṣ'* (pi'el) as a causative of *beṣa'* "gain, profit" (usually ill-gotten), and *re'im* "friends" as in Jer 3:1 and Lam 1:2 ("paramours" / political allies); so T, explicated by Kimḥi: "You profited your allies, giving them monetary gain from that which you wrongfully withheld from your own people . . . 'Friends' are Assyria and Egypt, from whom they used to buy aid." Accordingly, the following censure will mean: by turning for help to foreign nations you showed that you forgot me. That is the meaning of forgetting YHWH in 23:35 (cf. Hos 13:6 in context; Jer 2:32; 3:21). But the interpretation of S, "they defrauded their friends unjustly," is followed by most moderns; e.g., "[you] make gain of your neighbors by extortion" (*RSV*); "you have defrauded your countrymen to your profit" (NJPS). *biṣṣa'* = "violently make gain of" (BDB); "friends" = fellow countrymen (a strain on the metaphor of Dame Jerusalem); forgetting YHWH = forgetting that he forbade all the foregoing evil practices.

13. *I clap my hand.* In vexation; see comment to 21:19. The verb is an instantaneous or performative perfect, denoting an act performed as the verb is spoken (Joüon-Muraoka, § 112 f; *BHSyn* 30.5.1d). G adds "to my hand" (as from *'l kpy*), somewhat like 21:19 *kp 'l kp* "hand to hand." Evidently there were several ways of saying this in Biblical Hebrew; MT is an abbreviated way (like 6:11 *hkh bkpk* "clap your hand!"), not a wrong one.

the bloodshed that is. See text note b–b: Kimḥi explained the MT plural verb as a collective conception of the subject *dm* "blood[shed]," but *dm* is nowhere else treated so (24:7 *dmh hyh*, 21:37 *dmk yhyh*—verbs singular). However, with second person feminine singular suffixes both singular and plural noun forms occur: *bdmyk/bdmk* (16:6, 22), and similarly with the third masculine singular suffix: *dmyw/dmw* (18:13; 33:4f.)—the verb in both cases being singular (*yhyh*). Scribes exchanged the plural forms with the singular perhaps because in later Hebrew the two were pronounced alike. In Aramaic the second person feminine suffix is the same with singular or plural nouns; in Qumran Hebrew apparently the third person masculine suffixes with singular and plural nouns were pronounced alike; see E. Qimron, *The Hebrew of the Dead Sea Scrolls* (Atlanta: Scholars Press, 1986), § 322 (4).

14. *your heart be stout* (y'md, lit. "stand fast, endure"). The meaning of this unusual expression is clarified by its opposite in 21:12 "heart will melt" *nms;* cf. Ps 147:17–18, where *my y'md* is a double entendre: "who can stand fast / water becomes firm (= freezes, opposite of *ymsm* "he melts them"). Similarly, in the next clause *ḥzq* "be strong" (hands) is the opposite of *rph* "be slack" (hands) in

21:12. Alternatively, *ʿmd lb* "heart stands fast" may be the contrary of *npl lb* "heart falls" (= courage fails) in I Sam 17:32.

on the days. For the plural, see above comment to vs. 4. *l-* "at, on" (BDB, p. 516, def. 6a) recurs in the similar Mal 3:17; in Isa 10:3 it occurs with the explicit "day of punishment" (*ywm pqdh*).

deal. Hostilely; see I, 315, top.

I am YHWH; what I have spoken I will do (dbrty wʿśyty). This attribute of YHWH first appeared in 17:24 (in a closing recognition formula) and will be repeated in 36:36 and 37:14 in similar contexts. In our passage the clause appears to reinforce the foregoing *ʾny ʿśh:* "I say that I am going to deal hostilely with you and you may believe me, for I am YHWH who can be relied upon to carry out what he says." By adding one word (*wʿśyty*) to the signature phrase, "(for) I, YHWH, have spoken" (e.g., 5:15, 17; 17:21 [a recognition clause]), it becomes a self-description (altering the syntactic relation of *ʾny* to *YHWH*). The speech of YHWH is a sure presage of things to come, for that is YHWH's character: what he says he will do, he does; see the variant formulation 24:14: "I YHWH have spoken (*dbrty*): it is coming and I will do it (*wʿśyty*)." The same words but without the formula appear in 12:21–28, where the (non-)relation of God's oracles to events is at issue. The single occurrence of this signature outside of Ezekiel shows its oath-like function, and its association with *ʿśh* foreshadows Ezekiel; thus Num 14:35: "I, YHWH, have spoken; surely, this will I do (*ʿśh*) to this evil congregation . . ."

These formulas expand the brief, open-ended "I am YHWH" so dear to Ezekiel (see comment to 6:7 [I, 133]). They interpret the tetragram specifically as implying the fulfillment of promises and declarations; see W. Randall Garr, "The Grammar and Interpretation of Exodus 6:3," *JBL* 3 (1992), 385–408. (Is this a reading of the tetragram as causative of *hyh* with the sense "he brings to pass"?)

15. The reference has shifted: "you" is now the inhabitants rather than the city, causing uncertainty about the sense of the last clause, lit. "I will put an end to your impurity," translated "I will purge your impurity" so as to imitate the assonance of *whtmty ṭmʾtk*. Luzzatto's paraphrase glosses over the shift: "When its inhabitants, whose wicked conduct defiled it, will be exiled [the first two "you's"], the city will be purged of its ["your"] impurity." Others maintain the shift through the verse — "you" refers always to the inhabitants: they will be dispersed, and the troubles of the exile will chasten and purge them (Eliezer; cf. Kimḥi). This makes for consistency in this verse, but for inconsistency with the next, in which the referent is once again the city.

16. *You will be dishonored in you. ḥillel* "desecrate," for which *niḥal* (nifʿal of *ḥll*) regularly serves as passive, may also express degradation and dishonor, as in 28:7, 9, where its object is Tyre's royal splendor (cf. Isa 23:9; Lam 2:2 [Judah's royalty and nobility]). "In you" would be intolerable in any other context, but here it caps a series of scandals contained "in (the midst of)" Jerusalem; the culminating scandal will be Jerusalem's disgrace in the sight of the nations (cf. 5:8, 14f.). This clause is illuminated retrospectively by God's accusation in vs. 26, "I have been desecrated in their midst": as they dishonored me so they shall be dishonored.

MT vocalizes the verb *wnḥlt* as second person, but the versions translate it, in line with the previous verbs, as first person: G S, unintelligently, "I will inherit" (as from *nḥl*; cf. similar confusion in 7:24; see comment there); T "I will be sanctified"—a bold euphemistic reversal described by M. L. Klein, "Converse Translation: A Targumic Technique," *Biblica* 57 (1976), 515ff., esp. 529ff. Although some moderns prefer first person (*BHS*), it is out of place as the last item in a series of punishments. Furthermore, the following recognition clause best attaches itself to the immediately preceding, which should tell of some calamity that has befallen people—not God—with the result that they recognize YHWH's authority. The versional translations may indicate their inability to comprehend an unusual expression (see E. Tov, "Did the Septuagint Translators Always Understand Their Hebrew Text?" in A. Pietersma and C. Cox, eds., *De Septuaginta: Studies in Honour of J. W. Wevers* [Mississauga: Benben Publications, 1984], pp. 53–70, esp. pp. 61ff., 67ff.).

18–19. The meaning of the key term in these verses, *sig(im)*, is uncertain. Some have taken it to mean litharge (KB^3)—a stage in the processing of the mineral alloy of lead and silver, perhaps equivalent to "rejected silver" (Jer 6:30), silver whose impurities remain. S. Abramsky, "'Slag' and 'Tin' in the First Chapter of Isaiah," *EI* 5 (1958), 105–7 (Hebrew section), cites Isa 1:22, "Your silver has turned to *sigim*" paralleling "your wine is cut with water," whence *sigim* must be a mixture of worthy and base (so already S. D. Luzzatto in his Isaiah commentary, 1855), and Isa 1:25, "I will refine your *sigim*," implying that silver is present in the alloy. More commonly the word is taken to denote dross or slag—the impurities alone—as in Prov 25:4–5:

The *sigim* having been separated from the silver,
  a vessel emerged for the smith;
Remove the wicked from the king's presence
  and his throne will be established in justice.

In the final clause of our vs. 18 the uncertainty is aggravated by syntactical difficulty. S. R. Driver (*Tenses*, § 188) construed *sgym ksp hyw* as "dross of silver have they become"—*ksp* being appositional and defining, like the second word in *mṣltym nḥšt* "cymbals of bronze" (I Chron 15:19). G. R. Driver (1938, p. 69) emends to *syg mksp*, which he translates "dross (separated) from, without silver," probably to be deleted as a gloss. As an alternative to deleting it, *BHS* proposes transferring "silver" to the beginning of the list, after *klm* "all of them (are)"—cf. vs. 20 (tacitly assuming that *sgym* is a mixture including silver). NJPS includes the preceding two words in its novel rendering: "But in a crucible, the dross shall turn into silver" (labeled "uncertain")—not at all suitable to the context. We have followed T (= S. R. Driver) with misgivings.

Since silver-bearing ores are not found in the land of Israel, knowledge of their processing was presumably restricted to secondary stages (e.g., processing of imported partially processed ingots [E. Stern, *EM* 5.669]) or was transmitted from abroad. This may account for the elusiveness of the term *sgym*, or our difficulty in identifying it with processes known from elsewhere.

copper . . . in a crucible. In which, in the course of smelting, the elements of the alloy are separated; for these elements, see Charles Singer et al., *A History of Technology*, I (Oxford: Clarendon Press, 1958), pp. 581, 584. Abarbanel paraphrases vs. 18 thus: "I once regarded the house of Israel as choice silver, but when I put it into a crucible to refine it it turned out to be all dross; nothing remained in the crucible but copper, tin, etc. In the crucible they appeared as dross, though they were [as] silver at first" (for the last clause, cf. Kimḥi: "dross, but once they had been silver"). Cf. Ps 53:4: "Everyone is dross, altogether foul; there is none who does good, not even one"—a notion that straddles this and the following oracle.

19. Metaphor and referent are confused: since you, Israel, have proved to be nothing but dross (metaphor), I will collect you all into Jerusalem (referent)—an allusion to the flight of Judahites into the city for refuge; see Jer 4:5f. In vs. $20b^{\beta}$ "and throw," etc., metaphoric language is resumed.

Vss. 19ff. present a different aspect of the metallurgical figure: a smith collects in a crucible ores in which silver is alloyed with baser elements in order to melt them down. As used here, the point of the figure is not the refining process out of which silver comes—for God has no hope of finding a worthy residue (vs. 18)—but the liquefying of the elements, regarded as their obliteration. Thus vs. 18 states the outcome of God's "refining"—the realization that Israel is all dross—while vs. 19 states the consequence: they will be gathered into crucible-Jerusalem to be liquefied (liquidated). Since the prophet uses the metallurgical figure to express both the discovery that Israel is all dross and the punishment entailed thereby (the correct order of events in the referent), he must reverse the true order of events in the figure. What in the smith's reality begins the refining process—the melting down of the ores—here takes second place as a metaphor for the punishment of Jerusalem (vss. 19–21). What in the smith's reality is a result of smelting—the discovery that the ores are all dross—here takes first place as a metaphor for the ground of punishment (vs. 18).

20. *As one gathers* (lit. "the gathering of") . . . *so will I . . . gather.* The simile is expressed in a mixed construction: it begins like a cognate accusative construction, **qbwṣt ksp . . . 'qbṣ*, lit. "the gathering of silver . . . I will gather" = "I will gather you as silver is gathered" (cf. Jer 22:19 *qbwrt ḥmwr yqbr* "he will be buried as an ass is buried [lit. 'the burial of an ass']"). The comparative function of the noun phrase is implicit and requires no explicit expression (such as *k-* before the noun phrase and *kn* before the verb, as in vs. 22). But here, the length of the cognate accusative phrase (the whole of vs. 20a) was felt to obscure its comparative function, hence *kn* ("pleonastic-explanatory," König III, § 371 l) introduces the main clause, thus establishing the comparative function of what precedes it. The versions start the cognate accusative phrase (as I do) with "as," though from that one cannot surely infer that they had an explicit Hebrew equivalent in their *Vorlage* (T at Jer 22:19 starts off with *km'* "as" and precedes the verb with *kn* "so," though neither appears in MT, which it closely follows as a rule).

to melt it (lhntyk). Implicit object is common (GKC, § 117 f); nonassimilation of first radical *n* is less so, but when it occurs it is, as here, in the pause (GKC, § 66 f), where slowing allows the preservation of sounds ordinarily elided.

and throw. You into the crucible. For the rare use of *hnyḥ* as "throw," see Amos 5:7; Isa 28:2, where the expression *hnyḥ l'rṣ* = *hšlyk l'rṣ* "throw to the ground" in Dan 8:12; and cf. *hšlyk b'š* "throw into fire" (metal objects in order to melt them down, for making the golden calf), Exod 32:24. T paraphrases "I will annihilate"; G S do not represent *whnḥty*, nor does G represent the preceding pair "in my anger and in my fury" (*wbḥmty*) by more than one word. Is G a shortened text, based on a *Vorlage* in which one of the two similar adjacent graphs *wbḥmty whnḥty* was mistakenly omitted? Or is MT's longer text inflated by dittography (generating the verb with the rare meaning)?

21. *I will collect*. The verb *kinnes*—again in 39:28—is found only in exilic and post-exilic literature; see A. Hurvitz, *The Transition Period in Biblical Hebrew* (in Hebrew) (Jerusalem: Bialik Institute, 1972), p. 175.

22. *As silver is melted*. Lit. "like the melting of silver." *hittuk* is in form a pi'el verbal noun of **htk*, which is a back-formation of *hittik* (hif'il of *ntk*), some of whose perfect forms (e.g., *hittakty*, vs. 21) look like pi'el forms of a nonexistent **htk* (B-L, p. 481 n. 3). Further variety is lent to iterated forms of *ntk* in this verse by using hof'al *tuttᵉku* "you will be melted" instead of repeating nif'al *nittaktem* of the previous verse. Liquefaction again represents liquidation. Note the strong alliteration of plosive consonants echoing the last two words of vs. 21 (*wntktm btwkh*): *KhTwK KsP BTwK Kwr Kn TTKw BTwKh*.

24. *not purged*. Echoes "impure of name" of vs. 5. The passive construction *lo mᵉṭohara* instead of the adjectival (cf. Gen 7:2 *lo ṭᵉhora* "not [ritually] clean") implies failure, or lack, of efforts to purify. Cf. 24:13: "I tried to purge (lit. 'purged') you but you would not be clean"; see comment there for possible meanings. The expression looks backward to the preceding figure of unrefinable metallic impurities and forward—since purging is by water (36:25)—to the following clause.

not rained on (gušmah). Pu'al with middle radical not doubled, as often when it is a vowelless sibilant (as in *yiś'u* [34:29] for **yiśśᵉ'u*; GKC, § 20 m), and with "euphonic *mappiq*" in the *h* (Kimḥi, second explanation, see his *Mikhlol*, § 59 c; moderns simply delete the *mappiq* in all such cases—see *BHS* here). The alternative construction of *gšmh* as a noun **gošem* = *gešem* "rain" with third feminine suffix (so, e.g., GKC, § 93 q, Kimḥi's first explanation) entails the assumption of a harsh elision: "whose rain [fell] not"—acceptable, however, to G ("nor rain was upon you") and S ("and rain fell not on you"). If rain here is not, uniquely in Scripture, a metaphor for purgation (cf. T's paraphrase: "no good deeds were performed in it that would protect it"), the reference may be to drought—regularly the punishment for forsaking YHWH: Deut 11:16f.; I Kings 17–18; Amos 4:7. Ezek 34:26 associates seasonable rain with just administration of the state; here drought is connected with lawlessness.

G has "wetted, rained upon" for MT's "purged"—presumably reading *mmṭrh* (from *mṭr* "rain") for MT's *mṭhrh;* as paralleling the following clause this is preferred by moderns (e.g., *BHS*), though it impoverishes the text by removing its Janus-faced element. Eliezer regards the two parts of the verse as cross-referential: "Just as you refrained from purging yourself with water so I will withhold water from you to extinguish my fiery rage" (Eliezer shows how MT's "purged" might have been taken as "wetted" by G without implying a different text reading.)

The third person pronoun *hy'* following the predicate "land not purged" serves as a copula ("are")—like the third person pronoun in such sentences as *'th hw' YHWH h'lwhym* (Neh 9:7) "You are God YHWH" (F. Andersen, *The Hebrew Verbless Clause in the Pentateuch* [Nashville: Abingdon, 1970], pp. 36, 42; R. J. Williams, *Syntax*, § 113; GKC, § 141 f–h). A similar post-predicate pronoun-copula occurs in Zeph 2:12 *gm 'tm . . . ḥlly ḥrby hmh* "You too . . . are slain by my sword." See König III, § 338 g. The post-predicate location facilitates the shift from second to third person in the sequel.

day of rage. In vs. 31 God's rage and fiery wrath motivate his destruction of the land; the day of rage is therefore doomsday. Our verse describes the state of irremediable pollution (and, perhaps, drought) that the land was in at the time ("on the day") judgment was rendered on it. Malbim understands it to say that even "the day of rage" failed to cleanse the land—a possible reading (cf. 11:18 and comment, I, 190) that posits a post-fall perspective. And indeed the sequel describes the degeneracy of the people and their punishment in the perfect (past tense). This may indicate that the passage is post-fall, but not necessarily, since prophecy often speaks of the future in past terms, as having occurred (the "prophetic perfect").

A tradition that Jerusalem or the entire land of Israel was untouched by the Flood was fancifully connected with this verse by various talmudic sages (*Genesis Rabba* 32.10; 33.6; *b. Zebaḥim* 113a). M. Anbar, "Une nouvelle allusion à une tradition babylonienne dans Ézéchiel (XXII 24)," *VT* 9 (1979), 352–53, connects this tradition—attached by the Samaritans to their sacred mountain Gerizim—with a Babylonian parallel in the Erra Epic according to which the "eternal city" Sippar was not inundated by the Flood. (See now D. Bodi, *The Book of Ezekiel and the Poem of Erra*, pp. 113–16.) Interesting as the Babylonian-Jewish analogy is, it can hardly have anything to do with our passage, in which lack of rain is not a blessing but a blemish (|| "not purged").

25. *Her conspiracy of prophets.* Compare such expressions as "a pride of lions," "a gaggle of geese," in which a group is denoted by an attribute—though nowhere else is *qešer* "conspiracy" (lit. "tie") so used (but cf. *ḥebel nebi'im* "band of prophets" [Ilana Goldberg]). The real difficulty is "prophets": the violent offenses ascribed to them in the sequel are inappropriate; moreover, "prophets" recurs in vs. 28 with appropriate offenses. Kimḥi lamely explains that murder and looting are here laid at the prophets' door because by encouraging complacency they brought on the enemy who inflicted these on the people, and as the cause of all trouble they are named again in vs. 28. The similar denunciation of Zeph 3:3f. reads (in the NJPS):

Her officers in her midst are roaring lions,
Her judges are wolves of the steppe;
They leave no bone until morning.
Her prophets are reckless, faithless fellows,

Her priests desecrate what is holy;
  they do violence to instruction.

Zephaniah's description of the "officers and judges" recalls that of the "chiefs of" (*nśy'y*) Israel in Ezek 19:6—which shares terms with our verse ("roaring lion," "tear prey," "eat people," "widows")—and resembles that of the faithless "shepherds" of Israel in ch. 34. Elsewhere, too, civil rulers appear at the head of prophetic denunciation; e.g., Mic 3:11 ("heads, priests, prophets"), Jer 1:18 ("kings, officers, priests, people of the land"). Hence the irresistible appeal of the retroverted *Vorlage* of G "whose chiefs" (see text note c–c), which is unanimously preferred by moderns. How MT became corrupted from the *Vorlage* is unclear, since the letters in question (' > *q* and *ś* > *b*) are not similar in any stage of their development.

they took treasure and precious things. The two object nouns (the second, *yqr*, an Aramaism; Wagner, #121) recur together only in Jer 20:5—in a prediction of the Babylonian looting of Jerusalem. The enemy, Ezekiel implies, has been anticipated by Judah's own kings. With the shifting tenses of the verbs in this verse (perfect, imperfect, perfect) Zimmerli compares the tenses in 18:5–9 and rejects a proposal to adopt a ms. reading *lqḥw* for MT *yqḥw* merely for the sake of leveling all the forms. (On the interchangeability of the tenses in statements of general truths, see comment to 18:2 [I, 327]).

they made many widows. = "They killed many men"; cf. Ps 109:9: "and [may] his wife [be] a widow" = may he die. Cornill, basing himself on S (which curiously distorts the last clause), takes *'lmnwt-* "widows" as a variant of *'rmnwt-* "palaces" (as in Isa 13:22), rendering it: "they increase their palaces in her." But our translation is supported by Jer 15:8, "its widows are more numerous than the sands of the sea." Cf. Shakespeare's *King John* 5.2.15–17: ". . . Oh, it grieves my soul / That I must draw this metal [= weapon] from my side / To be a widow maker . . ."

26. *did violence to my instruction.* Evidently borrowed from Zeph 3:4, the sense may be: perverted the divine ordinances entrusted to them (see end of comment to 7:26 [I, 156]). Cf. the accusation of Mal 2:8: "You [priests] have made many stumble in [matters of] instruction" (i.e., through your rulings on what is permitted and what prohibited). The following clauses illustrate this accusation.

desecrated my holy things. E.g., by consuming sacred offerings in a state of impurity (Lev 22:1–9).

did not distinguish (hbdylw). Lev 10:10 states the priestly duty to distinguish (*lhbdyl*) between sacred and profane, pure and impure, and to teach the distinction to the people. Ezek 44:23 lays this obligation on the restored priesthood of the future. The sequence of determinate (*hṭm'*) and indeterminate (*ṭhwr*) recurs in 42:20 (*hqdš . . . ḥl*), "suggesting that this was an idiom accepted by Ezekiel and support[ing] the genuineness of both texts" (J. Barr, "Some Notes on *ben* 'between' in Classical Hebrew," *JSS* 23 [1978], 5).

they disregarded. Lit. "hid their eyes from," i.e., "turned a blind eye to"; in Lev 20:4 the phrase expresses the citizenry's deliberate refusal to prosecute a Molech-worshiper. On the analogy of that passage, medievals take this one to refer to the priesthood's indifference toward sabbath violation on the part of the public (cf. the expostulation of Jer 17:21ff.). In Ezek 44:24, however, the restored priesthood is enjoined to "sanctify" the sabbath, the term used in Jer 17:24 for abstaining from work thereon; whence it is inferable that priests are here blamed for working on the sabbath. Does this reflect a difference between the prophet and the Jerusalem priesthood about the applicability to the temple service of the ban on labor on the sabbath? On the difference between the Holiness Code and the Priestly Code regarding the ban on labor, see I. Knohl, "The Priestly Torah versus the Holiness Code: Sabbath and the Festivals," *HUCA* 58 (1987), 72–77.

I have been desecrated among them. Among those who are charged with guarding my holiness (Smend; cf. Lev 21:6; 22:2).

27. *wolves.* Predators next in rank after lions, in Zeph 3:3 as in Gen 49:27 (cf. vs. 9).

28. *daubed for them . . . divining for them.* The pronoun refers to the preceding leading classes, whose malfeasance the prophets encouraged by their complaisant oracles. The offenses of these prophets are couched in the terms of 13:10, 6, 5 — in that inverse order. Alternatively, the pronouns express the ethical dative, referring to the prophets themselves: their oracles were self-serving.

29. The citizenry at large (7:27; 12:19) is described in terms reminiscent of the wicked son of 18:12, 18. In the last clause, "unjustly" strikes most moderns as redundant after the verb *'šqw.* Since G translates the verb by "deal with," its translation of *'św* in vs. 7a, they infer that its *Vorlage* read *'św* "they treated" here as well, which, as it obviates the redundancy, is judged preferable. But G deals rather freely with the last clause ("toward the proselyte not dealing with judgment"), patterning it on vs. 7a, whereas MT shows Ezekiel's typical varying repetition, as well as his penchant for combining synonymous expressions (e.g., 5:13, see comment; 6:11, see comment to "the evil abominations"). Ehrlich [Hebrew] cleverly interprets the MT's redundance: "they deprived the alien of his due without [even the semblance of] justice" — but this reads too much into a stylistic habit of the prophet.

30. God sought among all classes a man who could intervene on behalf of the people to ward off God's assault, but found none. The language recalls 13:5, where prophets are blamed for not "going up into the breaches and making a fence about the house of Israel"; see comment there. Here the idea is carried further: had anyone worthy been found among the people — G paraphrases Hebrew "a man who would build a fence" by "one behaving uprightly"; similarly T, "a man who has good deeds" — they might have been saved. On the basis of the parallel in Ps 106:23 ("He would have destroyed them / had not Moses his chosen one / confronted him in the breach / to avert his destructive wrath") it is plausible to suppose that this worthy, like Moses (Exod 32:1–14), would have saved the people by intercessory prayer (T explicitly inserts "and pray" before "on behalf of"). But since the text does not say so, the idea may be that the mere presence of the righteous would have been enough to save the city; on the contradiction of 14:12–20, see Structure and Themes.

31. God's acts, expressed in verbs imperfect consecutive and perfect, appear as already accomplished; the viewpoint is therefore post-fall. But Abarbanel, *Meṣu-*

dot, Davidson, and NJPS understand the punishment to be in the future. Indeed the imperfect consecutive may express an event that has not yet occurred "as flowing naturally out of, being an immediate consequence of, the situation described in the preceding sentences" (S. R. Driver, *Tenses*, § 82 [pp. 93f.]). Driver compares 28:16, where the still unaccomplished punishment of Tyre's king is described through imperfect consecutive verbs (in vss. 17ff. perfects are used). Similarly in 31:12–17 Pharaoh's fall and descent into Sheol (still in the future) are portrayed in imperfect consecutives and perfects. (The expression "I have brought their conduct down on their heads" regularly climaxes threats of future punishment: 9:10; 11:21; 16:43.)

Moderns, however, generally regard vs. 31—and the entire section that it closes—as looking back on the destruction of Jerusalem as an accomplished fact; see Structure and Themes.

STRUCTURE AND THEMES

The chapter contains three discrete oracles, each with its introductory formula (vss. 1, 17, 23); the three are so closely related as to suggest that from the first they formed a complementary sequence.

A (vss. 1–16): judgment of the bloody city. The oracle opens with what is usually a subdivisional formula ("And you, man," vs. 2), bidding the prophet to address a judgment to the bloody city. A message formula ("Thus said Lord YHWH," vs. 3) introduces a bill of indictment that runs through vs. 12. "Now see" (*whnh*, vs. 13) opens the consequential part of the oracle (instead of the usual *laken; hnh* "see!" served in vs. 6 to mark a section in the indictment; see ahead), which ends with the recognition formula ("and you shall know . . . ," vs. 16).

This oracle may be further divided into three subsections:

Al (vss. 1–5): a general indictment and presage of doom, whose consequence (introduced in vs. 4b by "therefore") is public disgrace.

A2 (vss. 6–12): a detailed indictment, introduced by *hnh*, whose items are grouped in three clusters, each beginning with a social offense calculated "to shed blood" (vss. 6–8, 9–11, 12). Within and among the clusters a change in person or number of the verbs occurs: in the first and last cluster, third person plural shifts to second feminine singular; in the middle cluster third plural shifts to third masculine singular, then back to third plural (*'nw*, vs. 10). Ezekiel will have variety in his repetition. The listing closes with "declares Lord YHWH."

A3 (vss. 13–16): the consequence, consisting of God's agitated reaction (clapping hands, threatening rhetorical question, resolve to execute threat) with a rare closure (see comment to vs. 14, "I will do"), followed by a solemn, cadenced sentencing—a procession of first person verbs, ending in the recognition formula.

A is knit together by iterated key terms—"(shedding) blood" (vss. 3, 4, 6, 9, 12, 13), "impurity" (3, 4, 5, 10, 15) and associated concepts "abominations" (2, 11), "depravity" (9, 11), "dishonor/degradation" (8, 16). The resumption of Al's notions of impurity and public disgrace (vss. 3–5) in the concluding lines of A3 (vss. 15b–16) is a characteristic closure device.

B (vss. 17–22): a metallurgical figure: Israel, all dross, will be melted down in God's annihilating fire. "Man" introduces a declaration that, when tested in a crucible, Israel proved to be nothing but (four) base metals usually alloyed with silver (vs. 18). Consequently (*laken . . . ya'an . . . laken*) it will be gathered into crucible-Jerusalem and liquefied. The concluding recognition formula is expanded with an appropriately liquid metaphor: "I . . . poured out my fury on you" (vs. 22). The complication in the stages of the imagery has been explained in the comments. Though short, the oracle is intensely compact and impactful by reason of its sustained metallurgical figure, the repetitions (list of base metals, acts of smelting), and alliteration.

C (vss. 23–31): the land of Israel defiled through the corruption of all ranks of its population. "Man" opens an address to the prophet to declare to the land its impurity (vs. 24). The subject shifts in vss. 25–29 to the classes of the population, all dissolute; the topic "land" reverberates in the title of the last class, "the people of the land." Since no worthy person can be (or was) found to avert God's punishment, God will annihilate (or annihilated) the people in outpoured rage (a closing echo of "day of rage" at the oracle's start). The oracle closes with the formula "declares Lord YHWH."

There are strong links among the oracles. The objects of God's wrath complement one another: in A the city, bloody and impure; in B "the house of Israel," all dross; in C the land unpurged of the corruption of its inhabitants. A ends with God's threat to "purge the impurity" of Jerusalem, anticipating as it were the figure of smelting in the next oracles. The smelting crucible of B is identified with Jerusalem—the bloody city of A—while the base elements gathered into it for fiery liquefaction ("in the fire of my wrath" and outpoured fury, vss. 21f.) foreshadow the corrupt ranks of C, destined to destruction in outpoured rage, "in the fire of my wrath" (vs. 31). C, though longer than B, and an independent oracle, resembles an Ezekielian coda in that it resumes the idiom of A, combining with it, at the conclusion, the idiom of B (vss. 21f. echoed in vs. 31). A's leading concept of impurity reappears at the start of C (vs. 23). A's "chiefs of Israel" whose violence is the first item of its indictment reappears in C (after the text is emended) at the head of offending ranks. A's desecration recurs in vs. 26. Several of the offenses listed in A, or terms connected with them, recur in C: "widow" (vss. 7, 25), "sabbaths, holy things" (vss. 8, 26), "shed blood" (pervades A, vs. 27), "make profit" (vss. 12f., 27), and "deprive right / withhold due of, wrong, rob" (vss. 7, 12, 29).

Over against these unifying features lie discrepancies. The punishment with which the bloody city is threatened in A is dispersal (of its population) among the nations; but in B the house of Israel will be collected into Jerusalem and there liquefied. (C's terms—"destroy, annihilate"—are vague enough to suit either conception.) Moreover, while A and B explicitly place the punishment in the future, C views it as accomplished. Whether or not C is really a post-fall prophecy, this viewpoint justifies placing it after A and B.

The pervasive theme of Jerusalem (or the land) as a receptacle of impurity and bloodguilt is an elaboration of previously undeveloped suggestions: 7:4, 9 (note *btwkk* "in your midst"); 11:7–9, 11 (*b/mtkh* "in/from her midst")—indeed the present crucible is a transformation of the pot of ch. 11. Bloodguilt for sacrificial child-killing is a motif of ch. 16 (e.g., vs. 38); here bloodguilt is generalized and attached to a variety of moral offenses, as though they aimed at (or were equivalent to?) murder. The concept of "impurity" is similarly maximized. In the priestly laws of the Torah concerning purgations, impurity is caused only by material objects and physical states—leprosy, discharges, cadavers, certain foods. Defilement of the land by the gross offenses of homicide and unchastity is also recognized; its threat to YHWH's presence is suggested. "For blood(shed) pollutes (*yḥnyp*) the land . . . You shall not defile (*tṭm'*) the land in which you live, in which I myself dwell, for I YHWH dwell among the people of Israel" (Num 35:33f.). Exile is the punishment for defiling the land: "Do not defile yourselves (*tṭm'w*) in any of those ways [of unchastity aforementioned], for it was by such that the nations that I am casting out before you defiled themselves. Thus the land became defiled . . . and the land spewed out its inhabitants. So let the land not spew you out for defiling it" (Lev 18:24–28). A prophetic, not a priestly, concept is the impurity of idolatry: "You will treat as impure the silver overlay of your images" (Isa 30:22; for this meaning of pi'el *wṭm'tm*, see D. R. Hillers, "Delocutive Verbs in Biblical Hebrew," *JBL* 86 [1967], 320–24); cf. Ezek 7:20b.

The idea that idolatry defiles the people and the Temple is a commonplace of the priest-prophets Jeremiah and Ezekiel (Jer 2:23; 7:30; Ezek 5:11; 20:7, 18, 31). On all the above, see D. P. Wright, "Unclean and Clean," *ABD* VI, pp. 729–47. Here in oracles A and C the concept is further extended, as all of Israel's offenses, moral and cultic, are accounted as defiling: Jerusalem is "impure of name" (vs. 5), so God will "purge her impurity" (vs. 15); the land is "not purged" (vs. 24). This extension of the concept of impurity appears also in 36:17: "When the house of Israel lived in their land they defiled it by their way and their deeds: like the impurity of menstruation was their way in my sight." Impurity incurred for moral offenses has a parallel here in bloodguilt for such nonhomicidal offenses as slander and bribe taking; it reflects a heightened sensitivity to the heinousness of these offenses. (Abarbanel, alert to the broadening of traditional terms in this oracle, understood *gillulim* in vs. 3 as a generality covering all the iniquities listed in the following verses.) Another indication of this is the implicit equation of (ill-gotten) profit and bloodshed in the summary of vs. 13 in which God gives vent to his vexation ("I clap my hand"). The mention of a social, rather than a religious, offense in this summary statement was played up by Rabbi Yoḥanan (Palestine, third century C.E.): "Ezekiel set forth a list of twenty-four sins and of them all he singled out robbery to seal (= close, cap) it with; [prooftext:] 'See, I clap my hand over the [ill-gotten] profit you have made!'" (*Leviticus Rabba* 33.3).

After once again portraying the gentiles as scandalized by Jerusalem's corruption (vs. 5; see I, 76), the prophet proceeds to arraign the bloody city. Vss. 6–12 are formulated in terms of laws found in the Torah—mainly in Lev 18–20 (Holiness Code) and in Deuteronomy—almost as counts charging violation of these specific statutes. Kara paraphrases dramatically:

> I wrote in my Torah, "You shall not murder," but they shed blood, and blood defiles the land, as it says, "You must not pollute the land . . . you must not defile the land" (Num 35:33f.).
>
> I wrote in my Torah, "Honor your father and your mother," but they—"father and mother they dishonored in you."
>
> I wrote in my Torah, "You must not cheat the poor and needy hireling of his due" (Deut 24:14), but they cheated, and the widow they afflicted.
>
> I wrote in my Torah, "You must keep my sabbaths" (Lev 19:3), but they despised the holy things and desecrated the holy days.
>
> I wrote in my Torah, "You must not go about as a slanderer" (Lev 19:16), but they went about slandering even in order to shed blood.
>
> I wrote in my Torah, "You must not uncover the nakedness of your father—that is, the nakedness of your mother" (Lev 18:7), but they—"one has uncovered [his] father's nakedness in you."
>
> I wrote in my Torah, "A man who lies with a woman in her infirmity," etc. (Lev 20:18), but they "have forced the menstrually impure woman in you."
>
> I wrote in my Torah, "A man who commits adultery with a married woman . . . with his fellow's wife," etc. (Lev 20:10), but they committed adultery with married women.
>
> I wrote in my Torah, "A man who lies with his daughter-in-law," etc. (Lev 20:12), but they—"one has depravedly defiled his daughter-in-law."
>
> I wrote in my Torah, "A man who takes his paternal sister," etc. (Lev 20:17), but they—"one has forced his paternal sister in you."
>
> I wrote in my Torah, "You must not accept a ransom for the life of a murderer" (Num 35:31), but they "have taken bribes in you in order to shed blood."
>
> I wrote in my Torah, "Do not take from him interest or increase" (Lev 25:36), but they—"you have taken interest and increase."
>
> . . . It has thus been demonstrated that they transgressed everything written [in Lev 19–20]; hence they are called, at the beginning of this prophecy, "Impure of name."

Comparison of these items with those of ch. 18 (I, 343) reveals that our list adds desecration of sacred objects and times, and enlarges on sins of unchastity. The former reflects a view similar to Jer 17 that violation of the sabbath entails exile; the latter also threaten national well-being—cf. the epilogues of Lev 18 and 20. Nevertheless even here social offenses predominate:

cultic offenses—three:
holy things (8), sabbaths (8), eating on mountains (9)
unchastity—five:
father's wife (10), menstruant (10), adultery (11), daughter-in-law (11), paternal sister (11)

social offenses—eight:
bloodshed (6), parents (7), alien (7), orphan and widow (7), slanderer (9), bribes (12), interest (12), ill-gotten profit (12)

Eight social offenses equal the other two categories combined; once again the prophetic evaluation asserts itself (see I, 347, end).

The metallurgical image of oracle B occurs in the three major prophets in a distinct progression. The first occurrence is in Isa 1:22, 25; however unclear vs. 22 is, vs. 25 postulates a kernel of worth in the people that will be freed of base adherents by God's impending punishment:

I will smelt away your dross as with lye,
and remove all your slag.

Successful refining recurs in Zech 13:9; Mal 3:2f.

Isaiah's wording *śryk swrrym* (Isa 1:23: "your officers are defiant") reverberates in Jeremiah's formulation of the image:

All of them are excessively defiant (*sry swrrym*),
peddling slander.
Copper and iron, all of them act corruptly.
The bellows are scorched with fire,
The lead is consumed;
In vain the refiner refines:
The base elements are not separated.
"Refuse silver" they are called,
For YHWH has refused them. (Jer 6:28–30)

For Jeremiah there is no hope; unlike Isa 1:25, the impurities—"copper and iron"—cannot be separated from the silver (for the process, using lead, see Bright's comment in *Jeremiah*, AB, p. 49); hence the ore is rejected as "refuse silver." There is a trace of silver, but it is not extricable. Ezekiel's use of the image is characteristically drastic: Israel, once having been regarded as silver, turns out in the smelting crucible to be all dross. The two base elements mentioned in Jeremiah, copper and iron, have become four in Ezekiel (foreshadowing the breakdown into classes of oracle C). Moreover, in Jeremiah the lead is annihilated as a normal part of the smelting process; Ezekiel weirdly transforms the entire process into a symbol of obliteration. Here, as elsewhere in Ezekiel, fire is not a purifying but a destructive force.

D. H. Müller pointed out the relation of oracle C to Zeph 3:1–8; he called it "glossed borrowing" ("Der Prophet Ezechiel entlehnt eine Stelle . . ."), and Allen, too, regards the Zephaniah passage as its source. The resemblance is indeed striking (see comment to vs. 25). Both passages begin with an address to the maleficent city (Zeph: *hywnh:* cf. *hwnh/w* "wrong" in Ezek 22:7, 29), described as impure (Zeph: "sullied and polluted"). Both characterize its classes pejoratively. In the sequel, both threaten destruction in a fiery outpouring of divine rage (*-špk*

ʿlyhm zʿmy, bʾš qnʾty/ʿbrty). Zephaniah couples the two civil authorities, "officers and judges" (Exod 2:14; Mic 7:3; Ps 148:11), characterized in metaphors, and follows with the two religious authorities ("prophets and priests") described nonmetaphorically. Ezekiel puts royalty ("chiefs") at the head, according to contemporary custom (Jer 1:18; 8:1; 44:21), followed by priest, the highest-ranking religious authority; cf. "king and priest" in Lam 2:6. In Ezekiel's list as in Zephaniah's the equivalent civil classes are described figuratively (here the figures are similes), but the changed order of classes results in an alternation of figurative and nonfigurative language. In taking over Zephaniah's passage Ezekiel suited it to his usage and concerns — the terms "tear prey, consume persons" (cf. 19:3, 6), the priestly distinctions between sacred and profane, pure and impure. Terms from oracle A reappear: "shed blood," "profit." The description of prophet and intercessor in vss. 28 and 30 recalls 13:5–16.

(In her commentary to Zephaniah [AB, p. 138] A. Berlin refrains from committing herself on the relation of the two passages, allowing the possibility that both drew on a "common tradition." Such a possibility cannot be denied, but is it more likely than the assumption of borrowing? How much lost "background" creativity can plausibly be assumed to have existed in the little kingdom of ancient Judah?)

The portrait of Jerusalem as corrupt from top to bottom is hyperbole reminiscent of Jer 5:1–9; had a single righteous person been found in the city, Jeremiah says, it would have been spared (cf. 6:13; 8:6, 10). Ezekiel all but explicitly says the same here, with the result that he appears to contradict his teaching in 14:12–20 that in a general visitation the righteous can save only themselves, not others, not even their own sons and daughters. But each proposition is a rhetorical necessity in its context. In ch. 14 it is first established that only the righteous can survive a general disaster, in order to highlight the ironic exception to the rule: in Jerusalem's case, corrupt "sons and daughters" will escape in order to "console" the exiles by proving that God had good reason to destroy the city (see at ch. 14, Structure and Themes). Here the prophet's purpose is to underline God's frustration: though he would have seized upon the slightest pretext to spare the city, Jerusalem's total corruption left him no alternative but to destroy her. (For a superb exposition of God's two minds regarding punishment, and the intercessor's exploitation of his dilemma, see Y. Muffs, *Love and Joy* [New York: Jewish Theological Seminary, 1992], pp. 9–48.) Rhetoric that serves a given context may contradict that of another context, as has already been discussed in connection with 21:8 above. For all his love of rules Ezekiel was not a systematic theologian.

Taking the hyperbolic, wholesale condemnation for sober fact raises other questions. Torrey wondered that Ezekiel ignored his contemporary, Jeremiah, surely a Jerusalemite worthy of averting God's wrath; he concluded, logically, that Ezekiel must be represented as belonging to another age (*Pseudo-Ezekiel*, p. 70). And what of the contrary implication of 9:4, 11, that indeed there were right-minded people in Jerusalem? Prophetic argument cannot sustain such a rigorous critique. One might as well wonder at the contradiction between Jeremiah's blanket derogation of all Jerusalem's classes in 5:1–9 and the story of ch. 26, where some God-fearing nobles rescue him from death (so Bright, *Jeremiah*, AB, p.

172); or at his ignoring of such true prophets as are alluded to in 5:13 in his wholesale denunciations of 5:31; 14:13ff.; 23:13ff. Again, Lam 2:14, in which Judah's prophets are blamed (in the very words used by Ezekiel) for failing to correct the people, similarly "ignores" Jeremiah and Ezekiel. Comparable is Elijah's cry (I Kings 19:10, 14) that he alone remains a prophet of YHWH, when the preceding story (18:13) tells of a hundred others who survived Jezebel's persecution. "What [Elijah] complains of is the entire suppression of the religion of Yahweh, which is, historically considered, an exaggeration, though one that is natural in an emotional outburst" (J. Skinner, *Kings*, The Century Bible [Edinburgh: Clark, n.d.], p. 240). Poets and prophets, intent on making a point, are not the best source of sober facts and balanced judgments; to treat them as such is naive.

A literary-historical assessment of these three oracles must weigh their progressive interconnection (e.g., B carrying forward and illumined by A, C echoing A and B) against the divergence among them (especially in punishments and, possibly, in the post-fall perspective of C). The divergence reinforces the suggestion of the distinct oracle headings that the three originated separately. A natural inference from these facts is that B was composed with A in mind, and C composed with a vivid awareness of A and B—whatever intervals of time and circumstances separated them.

The location of this integrated series of oracles may have been determined by the verbal and figural links between it and the immediately preceding section (Smend): "I will pour out my rage on you, blow on you with my fiery wrath . . . your blood will be in the midst of the land" (21:36f.; cf. 22:3f., 20f., 31). Note further "heart . . . hands" in 21:12 and 22:14; "chiefs of Israel" in 21:17 and 22:6 (cf. vs. 25, emended); "clap hand(s)" in 21:19, 22, and 22:13; "idle divination" in 21:28 and 22:28.

XXII. The Wanton Sisters
(23:1–49)

23 1The word of YHWH came to me: 2Man, there were two women, daughters
of the same mother. 3They harloted in Egypt, in their youth [a]they harloted;[a] there
their breasts were squeezed, there they pressed their virgin nipples. 4As for their
names: Oholah was the bigger one and Oholibah her sister. They became mine,
and they gave birth to sons and daughters. (As for their names: Samaria was Oholah and Jerusalem, Oholibah.)

5Oholah harloted while married to me, and lusted after her lovers, after Assyrians — guardsmen 6dressed in blue, governors and prefects, desirable young men
all of them, cavalrymen riding horses. 7She bestowed her harlotry on them, the
elite of Assyria all of them. And with all that she lusted, she defiled herself with
all their idols. 8Nor did she quit her harlotry from [of old with] Egypt, since they
had bedded her in her youth, they had pressed her virgin nipples and poured
their fornication on her. 9So I handed her over to her lovers, to the Assyrians after
whom she lusted. 10They exposed her nakedness; her sons and daughters they
took, and her they killed by the sword. She became a byword among women,
and the punishments [that] they inflicted on her.

11Her sister, Oholibah, saw it and lusted more viciously than she, and harloted
more [viciously] than her sister's harloting. 12She lusted after the Assyrians, governors and prefects, guardsmen dressed to perfection, cavalrymen riding horses,
desirable young men all. 13I saw that she defiled herself, [that] the course of both
women was the same. 14But then she added to her harlotry: she saw [figures of]
men engraved on the wall, figures of Chaldeans incised in red, 15their hips girt
with waistbands, with trailing turbans on their heads, all having the appearance
of officers, the image of Babylonians whose native land was Chaldea. 16At the
mere sight, she lusted after them, and sent messengers for them to Chaldea.
17The Babylonians came to her for lovemaking and defiled her with their fornication. Becoming defiled by them, her soul recoiled from them. 18She displayed
her harlotry and displayed her nakedness, and my soul recoiled from her as it had
recoiled from her sister. 19Then she increased her harlotry, remembering the days
of her youth, how she had harloted in the land of Egypt. 20She lusted after concubinage to them, whose members were like those of asses and whose discharge

[a–a] Not in G S.

was like that of horses. [21]You reverted to the depravity of your youth, when your nipples were pressed in Egypt [b]on account of[b] your young breasts.

[22]So, Oholibah, thus said Lord YHWH: I will incite your lovers against you, from whom your soul recoiled, and bring them against you from all sides: [23]men of Babylon and all the Chaldeans, Pekod, Shoa, and Koa, with them all the Assyrians, desirable young men, governors and prefects all of them, officers and notables, all of them riding horses. [24]They shall come against you with arms,[c] chariot, and wheel, and with an assemblage of armies. With shield, buckler, and helmet they shall attack you on all sides. I will commit judgment to them and they shall judge you by their laws. [25]I will inflict my passion on you, and they shall treat you with fury: your nose and your ears they shall take off and the rest of you shall fall by the sword. They shall take your sons and your daughters, and the rest of you shall be consumed in fire. [26]They shall strip you of your clothes and take your glorious articles. [27]Thus will I put an end to your depravity and your harlotry from [the time you were in] Egypt. You shall not cast your eyes on them or remember Egypt any more.

[28]Indeed, thus said Lord YHWH: See, I am handing you over to those you hate, to those from whom your soul recoils. [29]They shall treat you with hatred and take away all you have toiled for and leave you stark naked. Your harloting nakedness shall be exposed and[d] your depravity and [e]your harlotry. [30]These things shall be done to you[e] for your harloting after nations, because you defiled yourself with their idols. [31]You followed the course of your sister, so I will put her cup into your hand.

[32]Thus said Lord YHWH:
You shall drink the cup of your sister,
the [cup] deep and wide;
[f]It[g] shall be for derision and scorn,[f]
amply capacious.
[33]You shall be filled with drunkenness and grief.
The cup of appallment and desolation,
the cup of your sister Samaria—
[34]You shall drink it and drain it;
You shall gnaw its shards,
[f]And you shall tear out your breasts,[f]
For I have spoken, declares Lord YHWH.

[35]So thus said Lord YHWH: Because you forgot me and cast me behind your back, then suffer for your depravity and your harlotry!

[36]YHWH said to me: Man, will you arraign Ohola and Oholibah? Then tell them their abominations! [37]For they have committed adultery, and blood is on their

[b–b]S V "were crushed."
[c]G "from the north."
[d]Not in V.
[e–e]G "your harlotry did these to you"; S "for your harlotry were these done to you."
[f–f]Not in G.
[g]S T "you" (feminine singular).

hands; namely, they have committed adultery with their idols and also have delivered up to them as food the children whom they bore to me. [38]This too they did to me: they defiled my sanctuary [f]on that day[f] and they desecrated my sabbaths; [39]namely, when they slaughtered their children to their idols they entered my sanctuary [f]on that day[f] to desecrate it. See, that is what they did inside my house! [40]Furthermore, they[h] sent for men to come from afar, to whom a messenger was sent, and see, they came; [men] for whom you[i] bathed, you[i] painted your[j] eyes and you[i] put on ornaments. [41]You[i] sat on an opulent bed, with a set table before it, and you[i] laid my oil and my incense on it.[k] [42][l]And the noise of a careless throng was there;[l] and to [the] men—so numerous the people—were brought wines from the desert; and they set bracelets on their arms and a glorious crown on their heads. [43]I said: [m]The jade [still] has adultery [in her]; now she and her harlotry harlot on.[m] [44]They[n] came in to her as one comes in to a harlot; so they came in to Oholah and Oholibah, [o]the depraved women.[o] [45]Righteous men will condemn them to be punished as adulterers and murderers, for they are adulterers, and blood is on their hands. [46]Indeed, thus said Lord YHWH: I will summon a crowd against them[p] and make them a horror and an object of plunder! [47]They shall pelt them with crowd-stones and cleave them with their swords. Their[q] sons and daughters they shall kill and their houses they shall burn with fire. [48]Thus will I put an end to depravity on the earth, and all women shall be admonished and not imitate your[r] depravity. [49]They[s] shall lay your depravity on you, and you shall bear the sins of your idolatry. Then you[t] shall know that I am Lord YHWH.

COMMENT

23:2. *the same mother.* The common origin of the "sister" kingdoms of Judah and Israel is alluded to; this accounts for their similar natures. In contrast to 16:44 the character of the mother is not invoked to explain the viciousness of the daughters.

3. *They harloted in Egypt.* This does not entail breach of faith, since the girls are as yet unmarried. Before marriage (vs. 4) the Egyptians introduced the girls to the pleasures of the flesh, and the two kept coming back to them for more for the rest of their lives (vss. 8, 19ff.). In 20:7f. addiction to Egyptian gods is spoken

[h] T editions: "you" (feminine singular).
[i] S "they" (feminine plural).
[j] S "their."
[k] G T "them" (masculine); S "them" (feminine).
[l–l] G "they struck up a song in unison."
[m–m] G "not in these (as from *l' b'lh*) do they commit adultery? and the work of a harlot and she fornicated"; S "in these they commit adultery and in works of a harlot they harlot"; T "to the congregation of Israel whose people were worn out with sin: now she will desist from her sins and turn back to my worship but she did not turn back."
[n] For the singular form of the verb, see text note a to 14:1 (I, 247).
[o–o] G "to commit (as from *'ś[w]t*) lawlessness."
[p] *'lyhm;* G S translate suffix as feminine; some mss. read *-hn.*
[q] All suffixes in this verse are *-hm;* S translates as feminine, and some mss. read *-hn.*
[r] G "their."
[s] S and mss. "I."
[t] S T feminine verb form (as from *wyd'tn*).

of, but here, as in the case of the later Mesopotamian paramours, attraction to political power is no less involved.

The second "they harloted" is not rendered in G S; but such repetition of the predicate is a feature of priestly style (Gen 1:27; Lev 4:12). See M. Paran, *Forms of the Priestly Style in the Pentateuch* (in Hebrew) (Jerusalem: Magnes Press, 1989), pp. 49–97, who cites our passage on p. 75.

In the parallel clauses of vs. 3b a good example of variety in repetition appears: in b^{α} *šmh* "there" and passive verb, in b^{β} *šm* "there" and active verb. In the present context, *šmh* = *šm* semantically, but the lengthened form prevents fusion of the two *m* consonants in the sequence *šm m'kw*); cf. comment to 15:3 (I, 265).

they pressed. *'śh* II in KB^3 appears in Talmudic Hebrew as "coerce" (a man to grant a divorce, *j. Giṭṭin* 50d); it is cognate with Jewish Aramaic *'sy* "press" (grapes, Targum Esther [*Mikra'ot Gedolot*] 1:10) and is related to Hebrew *'ss* "crush, trample" (Mal 3:21); cf. *'sys* "(pressed-out) juice" (Amos 9:13).

nipples. In Biblical as in post-Biblical Hebrew *dad* may refer to the entire breast as well (cf. BDB; similarly Syriac *td'*).

Handling the girls' breasts awakened and seduced them to venery. In vs. 8 sexual intercourse is ascribed to the girls' Egyptian period, but here the beginning of their corruption is described. Ultimately the ensnaring members will suffer a terrible penalty (vs. 34). G S, paraphrasing the last clause (about "virgin nipples") as "there they were deflowered," miss the gradation. In Mishnaic Hebrew a similar expression explicitly excludes sexual intercourse: a priest's daughter who was captured by raiders and then returned is not presumed to have been violated so as to disqualify her from consuming sacred donations: "What did that Arab do to her? Did his giving her breasts a squeeze disqualify her from priestly perquisites?" (*mi'ek lah ben dadeha*, lit. "he squeezed her between her breasts," *b. Ketubbot* 36b).

4. *bigger one.* As in 16:46 (comment I, 288) rather than "elder" (so, e.g., RSV, NJPS).

Oholah has usually been interpreted as "her tent" (= sanctuary, as in Ps 15:1; 61:5)—as though the final *h* were the feminine possessive suffix—in contrast with Oholibah, taken to mean "my tent [is] in her" (again, as though the final *h* were the suffix). These putatively symbolic names are supposed to refer respectively to the illegitimate, unauthorized sanctuaries of the northern, Samarian kingdom (I Kings 12:28ff.; "the calf of Samaria," Hos 8:6) and to the authorized Jerusalem Temple. Comparable is the explicitly symbolic name of the future Zion, Hephzibah "my delight is in her," as explained in Isa 62:4. Because "tent" is not used in this sense in Ezekiel, Zimmerli prefers to regard these names as evocative of tent-dwelling shepherds (as opposed to the Egyptians), comparing Oholibama, the name of Esau's wife (Gen 36:2) and of an Edomite tribe (Gen 36:5), and Oholiab, a Danite (Exod 31:6), and as such a reminiscence of Israelite origins. With the assonance of the two names he compares that of the two sons of the Caliph Ali, Hasan and Husayn.

They became mine. In marriage, as in 16:8. The women were already profligate when taken by God (unlike the foundling of 16:8)—recalling the command to

Hosea that he take in marriage "a woman of harlotry" (Hos 1:2) in order to enact God's relations with Israel.

Vs. 4b, translated in parentheses, appears to be a gloss to vs. 4a$^{\alpha}$, repeating the beginning of the verse as a lemma ("As for their names") and identifying the nicknames. For the technique, see comment to 1:2 (I, 41). The extraneous character of the gloss is indicated by the continued use of the nicknames throughout the oracle (against an older view that Samaria and Jerusalem were the married names of the women [Smend, Ehrlich]).

5–7. Israel's "liaison" with Assyria started with tribute King Jehu paid to Shalmaneser III (841), perhaps to gain Assyrian support for his new regime. Jehu's grandson Joash paid tribute to Adad-Nirari III (796)—supposed by some to be the "savior" from Aramean depredations alluded to in II Kings 13:5. After Tiglath-Pileser III conquered Hamath (738), "Menahem of Samaria" (so titled in the Assyrian annals) was among the western kinglets who paid him tribute—again, perhaps, in the hope of confirming his shaky throne (II Kings 15:19). See *ANET*^{3}, pp. 280, 281, 283; S. Page, "Joash and Samaria in a New Stela . . . ," *VT* 19 (1969), 483–84; H. Tadmor, "Assyria and the West in the Ninth Century and Its Aftermath," in H. Goedicke and J. J. M. Roberts, eds., *Unity and Diversity* (Baltimore: Johns Hopkins University Press, 1975), pp. 36–40; H. Donner, "The Separate States of Israel and Judah," in S. H. Hayes and J. M. Miller, eds., *Israelite and Judaean History* (London: SCM Press, 1977), pp. 412f., 414, 423f.

5. *while married to me.* Lit. "under me"; see comment to 16:32 (I, 284).

lusted after. Derivatives of *'gb* "love, desire carnally" occur only in this oracle, in 33:31f., and in the thematically related Jer 4:30 ("Lovers despise you; they seek [to take] your life!"). The irregular vocalization of the verbal preformative in the Leningrad ms. (*BHS*), *ta-*, is not shared by the Aleppo codex, which has the normal form *te'gab* (known also to *Minḥat Shay*). *ta-* appears here by analogy with the lengthened form *ta'agba* in vss. 16 (Q) and 20, where the forward movement of the stress commonly correlates with a change of the preformative vowel from *e* to *a* (B-L, § 49 q).

guardsmen (qrwbym). The term (whose singular would be *qarob* "someone near") hebraizes Akkadian *qurbu, qur(u)būtu* "(body-)guard," lit. "one close [to the king]" (von Soden, *AHw* II, p. 929, col. i). How the term came into Hebrew is suggested by the title *qurubūtu* given to a man with an Israelite name in an Assyrian document from shortly after the fall of the northern kingdom of Israel; Israelites were integrated into the Assyrian military forces (I. Eph'al in A. Malamat, ed., *The World History of the Jewish People* IV/1, *The Age of the Monarchies: Political History* [Jerusalem: Massada, 1979], p. 191). As the listing in vs. 12 shows, the word should be conjoined to what follows.

blue. That is, fabric dyed blue. Assyrian soldiery, colorfully attired, are pictured in A. Parrot, *Nineveh and Babylon* (London: Thames and Hudson, 1961), pp. 106–7 (plates 115–17). The blue dye was produced from a mollusk and was used for expensive, decorative fabrics, as those in the Tabernacle (e.g., Exod 26:1) and in the royal palace of Persia (Est 8:15). The exact hue is uncertain—purple-blue in one view (C. L. Wickwire, *IDB*, s.v. "Blue"), blue-green in another (J. Felix,

EJ 15.913–14, s.v. "Tekhelet," citing *j. Berakot* 1.5 [3a]: "*Tekhelet* resembles the sea, the sea resembles grass, and grass resembles the heavens").

governors and prefects. The Hebrew *paḥot* and *s^e^ganim* are loanwords from Assyrian administrative vocabulary: [*bēl*] *pā/īḫāti* and *šaknu* respectively.

cavalrymen. "Organized cavalry are first met with in the time of Assurnaṣirpal II (883–859); thereafter cavalry is very important as the chief assault force of the Assyrian army" (A. Kempinsky, *EM* 5.1005–8, s.v. *sus*). What an imposing figure the Assyrian horseman struck can be seen in Parrot, *Nineveh*, p. 47 (plate 57); cf. also ANEP², #375.

7. *with all that she lusted, she defiled herself with all their idols.* That is: in all cases of her lusting, with whomever she lusted after, she defiled herself. The antecedent of the pronoun in "their idols" is the aforementioned "choice men of Assyria."

Vs. 7b combines religious with political promiscuity (just as 16:26ff. adds political to the foregoing religious; see I, 299, for antecedents). The Assyrians attract by their power, but connection with them leads to adopting their idolatry. The historical reference is obscure. Moderns have pointed to the supposed reproof of north Israel's paganism in Amos 5:26 (reading "Sakkut" and "Kaiwan," Mesopotamian stellar deities) and II Kings 17:16 (worship of the host of heaven) as evidence for adoption of Assyrian cults (J. Gray, *I & II Kings, 2d ed., Old Testament Library [Philadelphia: Westminster Press, 1970], p. 648). M. Cogan doubts the Assyrian origin of these cults (Imperialism, pp. 103ff.).*

8. Nor did she quit her harlotry from [of old with] Egypt. When temporal m(n) "from (a time)" is prefixed to a place-name, the place-name represents time spent at that place; thus: "The Israelites remained stripped of their ornaments from [the time they were at] Mount Horeb [on]" (Exod 33:6); "Only I have been your God from [the time you were in] Egypt [on]" (Hos 13:4). So here: during her affair with Assyria Israel kept whoring with Egypt, as she had been doing since her sojourn there.

The reference is to the application by King Hoshea of Israel to Egypt for help in his rebellion against Assyria — a rebellion that eventuated in the fall of Samaria (722), a great deportation of Israelites, and the introduction of a mixed eastern population into their territory (cf. the next verse, the comment to 16:26–29 [I, 282f.], and II Kings 17:1–6, 24).

had bedded her (*'wth škbw*)*. Rather than "correct" what looks like a suffixed direct object marker to the prepositional 'ittah "(had lain) with her" (Zimmerli, BHS, and others; so already BHS at Gen 34:2), and thus invent a usage (*šakab 'itt-) never attested in MT, it would be better to explain the repeated occurrences of šakab 'ot- in one of two ways:*

*(1) (Adopted in my translation.) 'ot- marks the direct object of the verb šakab, which in this sexual sense is transitive, equivalent in meaning but not of so vulgar a register as "lay" in its sexual sense ("they had laid her"). That the euphemism šakab 'im "lie with" exists (Gen 39:14 [cf. vs. 12, "lie alongside"]; Lev 15:33; Deut 22:22–29; II Sam 11:4) does not prove that šakab 'et means the same, and hence that šakab 'ot- is a Masoretic misvocalization of an original *šakab 'itt- "lie with" ("falsche Tradition," KB³, p. 1378b; BHS here and at Gen 34:2). The*

fact that the inflected particle always takes the ʾot- form (Gen 34:2; Lev 15:18, 24; Num 5:13, 19; II Sam 13:14), which is normally that of the direct object marker, indicates that the uninflected ʾet is that marker, not the preposition "with." Moreover, the substitution of Q šakab for the—evidently indecorous—transitive K šagal in Deut 28:30 (with direct object suffix) and in passives (Isa 13:16; Jer 3:2; Zech 14:2) indicates that to the ancient Hebrew ear, šakab admitted a transitive construction when serving for "cohabit" (in disagreement with S. R. Driver, Notes on the Hebrew Text and the Topography of the Books of Samuel, 2d ed. (Oxford: Clarendon Press, 1913), p. 298, who regards Q šakab as "proving nothing regarding the living language." Contrary also to Driver, ibid., footnote, ʾitt- in Ezekiel is not constantly written ʾot- [see 16:62; 17:13, 16, 20; 20:35; 30:11; etc.]). Cf. GKC, § 117 u, and correct Ehrlich, Randglossen I, p. 172.

(2) ʾot- = ʾitt-. H. M. Orlinsky, "The Hebrew Root škb," JBL 63 (1944), 19–44, argues that šakab ʾet is the equivalent (favored in priestly writings) of the elsewhere attested šakab ʿim "lie with, cohabit"; the ʾet is therefore the preposition "with." As for the inflected form ʾot-, it is simply an alternative to ʾitt-, as stated in BDB (p. 85, col. b), ʾot- = ʾitt- "first in Josh 10:25; 14:12; next in II Sam 24:24, then repeatedly . . . in Jer [and] Ez[ek]" (e.g., Ezek 2:1; 23:23). To be sure, the versions regularly render šakab ʾot- as "lie with," but this does not prove that they read ʾitt-. Some Targumic renderings of this ʾot- by the accusative marker yat point to a pre-Masoretic vocalization ʾot-. Hence šakab ʾot- "lie with, cohabit" is not a late invention of the Masoretes.

P. K. McCarter alleges that the 4QSam[a] reading (wyškb) ʾth in II Sam 13:14 indicates a vocalization ʾittah according to the scroll's orthography (II Samuel, AB, ad loc.). To evaluate that allegation we await the scroll's publication; in the meantime that vocalization is unattested in MT.

However one takes the *ʾt(-)* of sexual *škb ʾt*, what is denoted by the expression is illicit, unsanctioned, or disapproved intercourse, e.g.: incestuous (Gen 19:33f.; Lev 20:11f.), out of wedlock (Gen 26:10), adulterous (Num 5:13, 19)—as opposed to *škb ʿm*, which serves as a euphemism for licit intercourse (Gen 30:15f.; II Sam 11:11) as well as illicit (Gen 19:35; II Sam 11:4). But alone *škb ʾt* never means rape; for that, it is necessary to add the verb *ʿinna* "humiliate, afflict" (Gen 34:2; II Sam 13:14 [contrast the opinion of F. Van Dijk-Hemmes, cited below in the Note following Structure and Themes]).

poured their fornication. The same expression as in 16:15 ("poured your harlotry"), evoking genital emissions.

9–10. For a narrative of the history of Samaria's last days, see H. Donner's essay "The Separate States of Israel and Judah," pp. 432f., and I. Ephʿal, "Israel: Fall and Exile."

exposed her nakedness. Punished and humiliated her; see comment to 16:37 (I, 286).

She became a byword. Lit. "a name"; so the name of the regicide Zimri was applied by Jezebel to Jehu: "You Zimri, slayer of his lord" (II Kings 9:31, alluding to I Kings 16:9–10). The name of a person who came to a bad end might be invoked in a curse: "You shall leave behind a name by which my elect shall curse, '[So] may Lord YHWH slay you!'" (Isa 65:15; cf. Jer 29:22: "a curse shall be taken [= derived] from them, etc."). Rashi interprets the phrase in the light of vs. 48b below to mean that Oholah became a horrible example, warning women away from adultery.

This conclusion to the allegory of Ohola imagines the repercussions among the gentiles ("women") of Samaria's conduct and fate. Such attributions are common in Ezekiel (e.g., 16:27b; in many of the prophecies against the nations) and serve to aggravate Israel's disgrace.

and the punishments [*that*] *they inflicted on her.* They, too, became "a name"—a byword. The parataxis (juxtaposition of the clauses: "She became a byword, and the punishments . . .") perhaps implies causal subordination: "She became a byword because of the punishments . . ." since she became exemplary only through her terrible end.

šᵉpuṭim "punishments" is plural of *šᵉpoṭ*, II Chron 20:9, with unstressed *o* becoming *u* (GKC, § 27 n). The commoner *šᵉpaṭim* (5:10, etc.) may derive from **šᵉpaṭ* (long *a*), an alternative of *šᵉpoṭ* (GKC, § 84 a, note; Joüon-Muraoka, § 88E d–f) rather than from **šepeṭ* (BDB).

For the asyndetic relative clause ("that" omitted), found especially in elevated prose, see Joüon-Muraoka, § 158 a*, a.

12. Jerusalem's "affairs" with Assyria, Babylonia (vss. 14–17), and Egypt (vss. 19–21) are set out in the comment to 16:26–29 (I, 282f.).

dressed to perfection (miklol). An assonant variation on "dressed in blue (*tᵉkelet*)" of vs. 6. S obliterates the sound-play by rendering both words "purple." *miklol* recurs in 38:4 in a similar martial context; G vacillates, translating here "fine purple-bordered robes," there, "breastplates." T and medievals derive it from *kll* "be complete, perfect," and this is supported by the usage in the Dead Sea Scrolls, DJD I, p. 124, line 25: *mklwl hdr* "perfection of beauty" (a play on *mkll ypy* of Ps 50:2). Is it related to *maklul* "choice fabric" in 27:24?

14–15. The colored wall engravings alluded to can be illustrated by colored animal figures carved on the Ishtar gate of seventh-to-sixth-century Babylon (A. Parrot, *Nineveh*, p. 174, plate 221). A mural with large human figures, red, blue, and white its predominant colors, has been restored from Neo-Assyrian Khorsabad (Parrot, p. 99, plate 108). The paintings of Til Barsip (Neo-Assyrian) make lavish use of reds (Parrot, plates 109–20). The waistbands and "trailing turbans" appear on a boundary stone showing the Babylonian rebel Merodach-baladan wearing a turban with a streamer, while both he and his officer (opposite) wear waistbands (Parrot, p. 169, plate 216; *ANEP*², #454; for the turbans, see also the Babylonian tribute bearers in the sixth-to-fifth-century engravings from Persepolis, Parrot, p. 189, plate 238). Ezekiel may have seen Babylonians in gorgeous dress; he may even have seen them pictured on local buildings and monuments, but that does not account for the bizarre scene he depicts here: Oholibah-Jerusalem gazing at painted engravings of Babylonian officers—located where?—and being aroused to lust for them. Apparently the prophet escalates his wanton's lewdness: if at first she lusted for the Assyrians in the flesh, the next stage of her degeneracy is conceiving a passion for Babylonians from mere pictures of them, and inviting them to an orgy from afar.

[*figures of*] *men engraved.* Lit. "men of engravings," *m*^{e}*ḥuqqe* (here and in 8:10) a substantival adjective (GKC, § 128 w), a passive puʿal participle of *ḥqh* = *ḥqq* (cf. *ḥ*^{a}*quqim* "incised" at verse-end). In I Kings 6:35 *hammeḥuqqe* means "the carvings."

red (šāšar). Borrowed from Neo-Assyrian *šaššeru* (*AHw*, p. 1191) "red paste."

15. *girt with waistbands* (ḥ^{a}agore ʾezor). "Some copies have *ḥ*^{a}*gure*" (*Minḥat Shay*)—the expected form of the passive participle. Perhaps vowel assimilation has occurred (-ORe -OR) in order to create an assonant pair like the pair following—*s*^{e}*rUḥe ṭ*^{e}*bUlim.*

with trailing turbans. Kimḥi explains: "Trailing" (*s*^{e}*ruḥe*) qualifies the men: they were trailing with reference to their headgear, the turbans, which properly speaking did the trailing. Cf. "like a terebinth wilted of leaf" (Isa 1:30)—the tree is said to be wilted with reference to its leaves, which properly speaking were wilted. Similarly "shaved-off of beard / torn of clothing" (Jer 41:5); GKC, § 116 k; Joüon-Muraoka, § 121 o; see the refined analysis of T. Muraoka, "The Status Constructus of Adjectives in Biblical Hebrew," *VT* 27 (1977), 375–80.

16. *she lusted.* K *wtʿgb* (as in vs. 5) to be read (Q) *wattaʿg*^{e}*ba* (as written out in vs. 20, *wtʿgbh*)—doubly anomalous: a very rare voluntative form of the third person (first person forms ending in *-ah*—cohortatives—are the rule), serving uniquely with *waw-* consecutive as a narrative past.

sent messengers for them to Chaldea. Possibly a reference to an otherwise unrecorded Judahite mission sent by King Hezekiah to the Babylonian Merodach-baladan, soliciting an alliance with him against Assyria, prior to the Babylonian embassy to Jerusalem whose cordial reception by Hezekiah incensed Isaiah (II Kings 20:12–21). Zimmerli conjectures a mission sent by Josiah to coordinate war against the tottering Assyrian empire almost a century later.

17. *lovemaking.* Lit. "a l(a)ying (or: a bed) of lovemaking"; on *dodim*, see comment to 16:8 (I, 277). On the underlying reality of this figure, see the previous note.

her soul recoiled from them. The expression "soul recoils" (*y/nqʿ*) occurs only in this oracle (here and vss. 18 and 28) and in Jer 6:8. The verb alone occurs in Gen 32:26, with the subject Jacob's hip socket ("put out of joint"); the basic sense seems to be "separate, fall apart." The Arabic cognate (*wqʿ*) "fall" when construed with *mn* or *ʿn* "from" means "deviate, stray from." Judah's change of policy from alliance with Babylonia (under Hezekiah and Josiah) to rebellion against it (under Jehoiakim and Zedekiah) is metaphorized as the wanton's disgust with herself projected against her lovers.

18. A definite direct object (*tznwtyh*) not marked by the accusative sign *ʾt* followed by another that is so marked (*ʾt ʿrwth*) is a sequence occurring twice more in this oracle: vss. 27, 35.

19–21. The alliance with Egypt in Ezekiel's time (see 17:15) is depicted under the figure of stirring the embers of an old love. In contrast with the conquering Assyrians and Babylonians, the ineffective Egyptians are depicted not as virile and warlike but as voluptuaries.

19. In this and the next verse the verbs in MT are third person feminine,

changing in vs. 21 to second person. G in all three verses (19–21) shows second person, thus giving the subsection (see Structure and Themes) a uniformity—hardly original—absent in MT.

20. *She lusted.* On the form of the verb, see comment to vs. 16.

after concubinage to them. So Rashi, Kara, taking the plural noun (lit. "after their concubines") as an abstract, but this is hardly admissible. Others stretch "concubines"—elsewhere always feminine—to be masculine, "their servants" (T; Symmachus; Menaḥem bar Shim'on: she was so wanton she harloted with the servants of the Egyptians, to her shame). No solution is satisfactory.

whose members . . . Lit. "flesh"—a euphemism, as in 16:26; see comment there. The oversize genitals of Egyptians figure as well in 16:26 (evidently a commonplace, expressing a popular notion of their lewdness), and are here compared in size and seminal discharge to those of equines, proverbially lascivious, Jer 5:8.

discharge. The hapax *zirma* "effusion (of semen)" is related to *zerem* "fluid, stream (of rain)" (so medievals, *NEB*). G S "genitals" (NJPS: "organs"), which KB^3 prefers ("phallus") and connects with *z*^{e}*mora* "(vine-)branch," were better supported by the semantic analogue *šopka* "penis" from *špk* "pour out."

21. *You reverted to.* The verb *pqd* "attend to, call to mind" can have the specific connotation of turning back to something after having left it (Ehrlich): Samson's revisiting his wife (Judg 15:1); God's finally taking up the cause of his enslaved people (Exod 4:31). NJPS renders "you reverted to," which expresses the meaning nicely.

The shift from third person (heretofore) to second person anticipates the direct address in the next verses—the sentencing of the harlot to punishment. Such shifts of person are not uncommon: cf. ahead vss. 40–42 (third-second-third person); 46–49 (third-second); 26:3–4 (second-third), 7–8 (third-second), 14 (second-third); 28:22–23 (second-third); 35:8 (third-second). (Some of these are explicable otherwise; see comments.)

when . . . were pressed. The irregularly vocalized infinitive *ba'śot* (so Leningrad, Aleppo mss.; printings normalize to the form of qal, *ba'*^{a}*śot*) is to be understood as pi'el (like *'iśśu* of vs. 3), contracted from **b*^{e}*'aśśot.* The initial shewa, colored by the vowel of the following laryngeal *'ayin* (Kimḥi: "When shewa is followed by a laryngeal . . . its quality is that of the vowel of the laryngeal," *Mikhlol*, § 4 b, p. 16), became a full vowel, the vowel of the laryngeal was correspondingly reduced, and the following *ś*, now at the head of its syllable, lost its doubling. Cf. *bohšamma* < **b*^{e}*hoššamma* (Lev 26:43); *yaḥl*^{e}*qu* (Josh 14:5) < *y*^{e}*ḥall*^{e}*qu* (I Kings 18:6); R. Kutscher, "*mahl*^{e}*kim* (Zech 3:7) and Its Sisters" (in Hebrew), *Lešonenu* 26 (5722 [1962]), 93–96, describes the phenomenon but does not note our case. On the passive sense of an active infinitive, see comment to 20:12 "that it might be known" (I, 366).

on account of your young breasts. "On account of your young breasts, which were pressed for you in Egypt back then, you remembered with affection their old love and took up harloting with them again" (MenbSh). This cannot obviate the strangeness of *lm'n* "for the sake / on account of" in this context. In the light of the sequence of *m'kw* (were squeezed)–*'św* (were pressed) in vs. 3, and of the rendering here of S and V—"(and the breasts of your youth) were crushed"—the emendation of *lm'n* to *lm'k* (qal or pi'el) "squeezing" is compelling. More precisely: "(your young breasts) being squeezed," the active infinitive serving as a passive (see previous note) and the infinitive rendered as a gerund; see comment to 16:31 "in that you scorned hire" (I, 284).

With this emendation, the sequence of the verbs *'śh* and *m'k* here reverses that of vs. 3, marking a closure of this section.

23. "The order of [these] ethnic groups conforms in principle with the scheme of the ethnic and political entities in the prism of Nebuchadnezzar II published by Ungar (pp. 290f.). 'Men of Babylon' equals 'the great men of Akkad' on the prism. The prism lists next all the Chaldean tribal units [= "all the Chaldeans"], while Puqudu is mentioned after them among the Aramean tribes, as being evidently the most important of them. Qoa and Shoa, perhaps neither Chaldean nor Aramean tribes, are not known from any other source" (R. Zadok, *EM* 7.103). "All the Assyrians" can refer to military units of the defeated Assyrians pressed into service of the Babylonian conqueror.

notables. Zimmerli rightly observes that *qrw'ym* is a free variant of *qrwbym* ("guardsmen," vss. 5, 12) and is not to be "corrected" into it (as *BHS*). For the sense, lit. "summoned men," cf. *qrw'y(Q) h'dh* "men called to the assembly" (Num 1:16). My translation is inspired by G "(men) of note."

24. *with arms* (hoṣen). An obscure hapax, whose initial consonant is *h* not *ḥ* "according to the best texts" (*Minḥat Shay*). My translation follows T, whose guess is close to that of S, "armed (with)." G "from the north" is influenced by 26:7 and the motif of an enemy from the north (Jeremiah). The similar series of "horseman and wheel and chariot" in 26:10 suggests that *hoṣen* = "horseman"; on the other hand "stallions, chariots, wheels" in Jer 47:3 suggests "horses"—whence B-Y's conjecture that our word is cognate with Arabic *ḥiṣan* "horse, stallion." Others compare Jer 47:3's threefold reference to the noise of an army, and emend our hapax to *hm(w)n* "tumult, rumbling" (in Ezek 26:10, *qol* "noise" of an army).

The preposition *b-* "with" (arms, chariot, wheel, shield, etc.) is implicitly present with the two triads of undetermined nouns denoting the means of the attack, on the analogy of "with an assemblage of (*bqhl*) armies," which is located between the triads, where alone it is explicit. In 26:7 the situation is reversed: the triad denoting the means of attack—"horse, chariot, horsemen"—has the preposition (*b-*), and only "a great assemblage" that follows them lacks it. The predominating lack of prepositions in our case is unusual.

shield (ṣinna), *buckler* (magen). The former gave total body cover and might have another man designated to carry it (as in Goliath's case, I Sam 17:7); the latter was a smaller shield. For illustrations of both, see *ANEP*², ##372, 373, 368.

attack (yaśimu) *you.* Lit. "set upon you"; a military term that "covers every device which could be used to secure the downfall of the city, and it is therefore incorrect to postulate the ellipse of any special object after the verb" (Burney, *Notes to . . . Kings*, p. 234, on I Kings 20:12: "'Attack! [*śimu*]'; and they attacked [*wayyaśimu 'al*] the city"). In Ps 3:7 the synonymous *šyt 'l* "beset," lit. "set upon," occurs.

judge you by their laws. Apparently an allusion to the mutilations mentioned in the next verse, penalties unknown to biblical law. Rashi detects a reference to the blinding of Zedekiah, a penalty "I did not prescribe in my Torah."

25. *my passion*. See comment to 5:13 "in my passion" (I, 115).

your nose and your ears they shall take off. Subordinates who broke faith were punished thus in the ancient Near East: Egyptian officials who were false to their commission (*ANET*³, p. 215); slaves who receive stolen goods from their master's wife (Middle Assyrian laws, A 4; *ANET*³, p. 180), while the thieving wife's nose or ears may be cut off (Middle Assyrian laws, A 4–5; ibid.); an adulteress's nose may be cut off at her husband's wish (Middle Assyrian laws, A 15; p. 181). Among the Hittites, the nose, eyes, or ears of a slave who angered his master might be "injured" (*ANET*³, p. 207).

and the rest of you (ʾḥrytk). Lit. "the after-part of you," what is left after the mutilation. This unusual meaning of *ʾḥryt* seems to imply a contrast with *roš* "head" (in which nose and ears are located), as in (the somewhat unclear) Amos 9:1: "and cut them in the head (*roš*), all of them; and their after-part (*ʾḥrytm*) I will kill by the sword"—alluding perhaps to the leaders on the one hand and to the rest of the people on the other.

This is the punishment inflicted on Oholibah's person and is the equivalent of the personal punishment of Oholah described in vs. 10a$^{\gamma}$: "her they killed by the sword."

They shall take your sons and your daughters. Into captivity; the same happened to Oholah's children in vs. 10a$^{\beta}$.

and the rest of you shall be consumed in fire. Unclear; there seems to be a contrast between the aforementioned children who will be taken captive (= the exiles) and what will be left behind to be consumed in fire, whether figuratively (i.e., humans, as 5:2; see comment thereto [I, 108]) or literally (as 23:47, "burn their houses with fire"). The shift in meaning of *ʾḥryt* is facilitated by the connotation "posterity" that clings to the word in some contexts (Jer 31:17; Ps 109:13; Dan 11:4), and that glimmers in both occurrences of the word in this verse.

26. Echoes 16:39a$^{\gamma}$; see comment thereto (I, 287).

27. *cast your eyes on them*. Amorously, as in Gen 39:7 (Potiphar's wife); but since the phrase means also "look for help to" (18:6; see comment), it serves both the metaphorical and the referential (political-military) sense.

28. *Indeed, thus said Lord YHWH*. This formula using the Hebrew phrase *ky kh ʾmr ʾdny* introduces matter closely linked to what precedes. Here the matter is supplemental to vss. 22, 26 (see Structure and Themes, A.4b); below, in vss. 46ff., the allusion to judgment in vs. 45 is carried forward (just as 16:59 carries forward vs. 55b). In the same way 25:6 and 32:11 elaborate what immediately precedes them. On the other hand, the link may be contrastive, and the sense of *ky* is "notwithstanding, however"; so in 14:21 and 29:13 where the matter introduced reverses the purport of what came before.

hate . . . recoils. Vs. 17b.

29. *all you have toiled for*. All that you have acquired by toil; cf. the curse of Deut 28:33: foreigners shall consume "the yield of your soil and all you have toiled for." The expression hardly suits the property of a regal courtesan, as Oholi-

bah is portrayed; it is rather another instance of the referent—the Judahites—intruding into the metaphor.

shall be exposed. The context demands a feminine perfect consecutive (*wnglth*); what appears is *wnglh*, a masculine perfect form, whose identity with the feminine participle, however, masks its disagreement.

30. *These things shall be done to you.* The infinitive absolute *'aśo* has here the force of a future passive (GKC, § 113 ff; Joüon-Muraoka, § 123 w). *Minḥat Shay* notes an alternative spelling, *'św*, as in Jer 4:18, where, except for the verb that is vocalized as a perfect, the identical phrase occurs. Guided by Jeremiah ("Your course and your deeds have done these [things] to [= brought these upon] you"), most critics take the last two words of vs. 29 to be the subject of the verb: "Your depravity (omitting *w-*, with V) and your harlotry have done these [things] to you" (G S: "your harlotry has done"). The last two words of vs. 29 encumber the verse, and their transfer to the following sentence is surely a gain in elegance.

defiled yourself with their idols. Oholah's offense (vs. 7b), only now ascribed to her sister.

31. On the image of the cup, see Structure and Themes.

32. *It shall be for derision and scorn.* The cup, whose contents will devastate the one who drinks it, will provoke the taunts of Jerusalem's enemies at her fall (Kimḥi). Drinking the cup and becoming the object of abuse are cause and effect also in Jer 49:12–13. Understanding *thyh* as third person, with *kws* "cup" as subject, makes the entire verse a description of the cup. S T render the verb *thyh* as second person (*thyy*), "You shall become [the object of] derision and scorn," a familiar locution; cf. Ps 44:14, "You make us the butt of our neighbors, the [object of] scorn and derision of those around us." For a similar versional treatment of MT *whyth*, see 5:15, text note and comment, and 26:14, where *thyh* and *tbnh* stand for second person verbs. But if the versional understanding here is correct, the sequel, "amply capacious," awkwardly goes back to the cup. T circumvents the awkwardness by a free translation of this sequel, "due to the multitude of troubles that will come upon you." G omits "it shall be for derision and scorn," and is followed by critics, who thus connect "amply capacious" directly to the description of the cup in the *a* clause of the verse. However, the relief offered by G's omission must be weighed against the unlikelihood of a late invention of such a complicating "gloss" (for so critics term our clause) on the one hand, and on the other, the reinforcement of this clause in vs. 33b (*šamma*) "appallment" (see ahead).

amply capacious. Lit. "doing much containing"—*mirba* an unusual variant of *marba* (hif'il feminine participle); cf. *mirša'at* "wicked, evildoing" (II Chron 24:7; from *lhršy'* "to do evil"), for regular *marša'at* (GKC, § 53 o).

33. *appallment and desolation* (šamma uš^{e}mamma). Though *šamma* does not occur otherwise in Ezekiel, it does in Jeremiah, where it is coupled with such reactions of witnesses to the devastated state of Judah as *š^{e}reqa* "whistling" and *ḥerpa* "taunting" (Jer 18:16; 19:8; 25:9; 29:18; 49:13)—recalling "derision and scorn" in our passage (vs. 32b). The pair *šamma uš^{e}mamma* is therefore unlike the assonant pairs discussed at 6:14 (see comment), whose effect is emphasis. This pair tends to a hendiadys effect: appallment over desolation—in the spirit

of Lev 26:32: "I will desolate (*whšmty*) the land, so that your enemies who dwell in it shall be appalled (*w*^{e}*šam*^{e}*mu*) by it." G renders the pair by one word, as it does the commoner pair *š*^{e}*mama um*^{e}*šamma* in 33:28, apparently a simplification.

34. *and drain it.* Against your will, compelled to do so by me; Isa 51:17; Ps 75:9. V: "drain it all the way to the dregs," inspired by the parallel picture in Ps 75:9.

gnaw its shards. The verb *grm* is obscure. Rashi defines it: "Scraping around the bone (*gerem* "bone") — or the shard — with one's teeth to remove from it what flesh sticks to it" (he comments similarly at Num 24:8, where *grm* is paralleled by *ʾkl* "eat"). Of the ancient versions only V translated our clause: "its fragments you shall devour." (In Num 24:8 V translates *grm* "crush"; so, e.g., Ibn Ezra there. The remaining occurrence of the verb, Zeph 3:3, is altogether unclear.) The sense here will be: deranged by the contents of the cup, you will greedily smash the earthenware vessel in order to squeeze or suck out (as it were) the liquid absorbed in the clay. This grotesque image is outdone by what follows.

Modern emendations (see *BHS*) tame the text, conforming it to Ps 75:9; e.g., *šmryh tgmʾy/tgmry* "you shall gulp (Cornill) / finish (Ehrlich) its dregs."

And . . . tear out your breasts. In a paroxysm of self-loathing (cf. 20:43b; 36:31b) you will destroy "the peccant members" (G. R. Driver, 1954, p. 155), around which erotic memories lingered that caused you to reject your Mesopotamian lovers for Egyptians, to your misfortune. Such self-mutilation in an extreme of passion has a literary analogue in the Egyptian story of the Two Brothers: falsely accused of violating his older brother's wife, the younger, saved by a miracle from his pursuing sib, cuts off his own penis as a gesture of abjuration and purgation (*ANET*^{3}, p. 24). That G does not show this shocking line, so typical of Ezekiel's extravagance, is hardly evidence that it is secondary.

For I have spoken, declares Lord YHWH. A closure that recurs in 28:10, and as the first of a double closure in 26:5 and 39:5.

35. *cast . . . behind your back.* A metaphor found in the speeches of I Kings 14:9 and Neh 9:26, and, in a positive context, in the psalm of Isa 38:17.

36. *YHWH said to me.* A unique phrase in Ezekiel, it replaces the regular revelation formula (see vs. 1); hence it is not comparable to "He said to me" (e.g., 2:3; 3:1, 4; 4:15, 16), "Said YHWH" (4:13), or "Said to me YHWH" (44:2, 5) occurring in the course of a narrative. Such a formula is common in Moses' speech in Deuteronomy and in the (related) speeches of Jeremiah. Here it is an irregular introduction to an erratic passage, which has the attributes of a pastiche.

The verse recalls 20:4; 22:2. That both Oholah and Oholibah are addressed indicates an unreal time; see Structure and Themes.

37. Recalls 16:17, 20–21.

namely. The *waw* of *wʾt* is explicative, each of the two clauses that follow it explaining each that precedes it. For a discussion of this usage, see D. W. Baker, "Further Examples of the *waw explicativum*," *VT* 30 (1980), 129–36.

38. The verse combines elements of 20:27a ("this too/besides"), 5:11 (sanctuary defiled), and 22:8 (sabbaths desecrated). For the juxtaposition of sanctuary

and sabbath, see Lev 19:30: "My sabbaths you shall keep and my sanctuary you shall revere." Both consist of delimited sanctity, the one in space, the other in time.

"On that day" both in this and the next verse is not in G. Here it connects child sacrifice (vs. 37) temporally with defilement of the sanctuary and desecration of the sabbath; see the next verse.

39. The initial *waw* is again explicative: the additional outrage referred to in vs. 38 consisted in the child-slayers' coming to God's Temple, defiled as they were by bloodshed and idolatry, and thus desecrating it. Repeated "on that day" in MT intensifies the offenses by underlining their contiguity; the mention of sabbaths at the end of vs. 38 further aggravates them by suggesting they were committed on, and thus desecrated, sacred time. Such concentration of sin recalls the cluster of Temple abominations in ch. 8.

The suffixes and pronouns of this verse, though referring to the women, are all masculine plural, either as a feature of later Biblical Hebrew (M. F. Rooker, *Biblical Hebrew in Transition*, JSOTSup 90 [1990], 78–81) or as an intrusion of the real referents of the allegorical women — the Israelites.

40. *Furthermore* (w'p ky). Julie Galambush, *Jerusalem in the Book of Ezekiel*, p. 119, translates vs. 39b "For here is what they did inside my temple," as pointing forward to what she calls "defiling religious observances" described in vss. 40–42. But the sequence *hnh . . . 'p ky* that she cites for support (p. 77 n. gg, attached to a different rendering of vss. 39b–40: "Not only thus did they do . . . but they even . . .") is the form of an *a minori ad majus* (Mishnaic Hebrew *qal waḥomer*) argument. If it occurs here (and the *w* of *whnh* and *w'p* makes it doubtful), then the sense of our passage would be: "Thus (as we have just said) they behaved in my Temple; how much worse their behavior apart from it" — for there is not a hint that the harloting of vss. 40–44 takes place in the Temple. But in fact the harloting is not worse than the murder and idolatry of the previous verses, so there is no room here for the aforesaid argument. Hence *whnh* is not bound to *w'p ky*, but looks back in anger, while *w'p ky* only introduces another lurid episode in the lives of the wantons — "furthermore" — with political rather than religious reference.

they sent (tišlaḥna). The imperfect form represents an old preterite, frequent in poetry (e.g., *tiblaʿemo* "swallowed them," Exod 15:12), less so in prose (yet more than generally supposed; e.g., Gen 37:7 *tᵉsubbena* "came around"; Judg 2:1 *'aʿᵃle* "I brought up"); see R. J. Williams, *Hebrew Syntax*, 2d ed., §§ 176–77; *BHSyn* 31.1.

With the sending of a messenger, cf. vs. 16.

The preparations for the love feast in vss. 40–41 enlarge upon what is called lovemaking (lit. "a bed of love") in vs. 17. They recall 16:11–12, 18, in particular and Prov 7:15–16 in general.

for whom you (singular) *bathed.* The shift from third person plural to second person singular is jarring. S seeks to impose a measure of regularity (see text note), but the raw state of MT has an original, unedited appearance; see Structure and Themes.

painted (kaḥalt) *your eyes.* With kohl, Mishnaic Hebrew *koḥal,* on which see H. R. Cohen, *Biblical Hapaxlegomena,* pp. 117–18 (he doubts the identification with antimony).

41. *an opulent bed.* The unique adjective *kᵉbudda* (short *u* despite plene writing; see GKC, § 9 o) from **kabod* (short *o*; after the pattern *ʿarom, ʿᵃrumma* "naked") presumably corresponds to the meanings of the noun *kabod* (long *o*) "riches" (e.g., Gen 31:1) and "glory"—the usual sense. In this context "opulent" must mean something like "covered with glorious cushions" (T), or "glorified and adorned with beautiful spreads" (Kara). These explanations of *kᵉbudda* raise the possibility that G S "(out)spread" are renditions of MT rather than of a *Vorlage* **rebuda* "bespread" (*BHS*)—conjectured on the basis of Prov 7:16 "I have bespread with spreads (*marbaddim rabadti*) my bed." Indeed, the later Greek versions of Aquila and Theodotion translate the verb in Proverbs with words of the same base as that of G here.

laid my oil and my incense on it. Aromatic oil, as in Prov 27:9; Song 1:3, to perfume the bed; thus the seductress of Prov 7:17 says: "I have sprinkled my bed with myrrh, aloes, and cinnamon." The versions go astray.

42. *And the noise of a careless throng was there* (lit. "in it/her"). A difficult sequence. G "they struck up a song in unison" is a guess from context; see Menaḥem bar Shimʿon cited in the next comment.

and to [the] men . . . were brought wines from the desert. A hard passage whose conjectural translation follows A. Dotan, "*Swbʾym.*" He explains *sobaʾim* (plene writing [*sw-* for short qameṣ]) on the pattern of *qodašim* as plural of **sobe* (|| *qodeš*) "wine" (cf. *sobʾek* "your wine" in Isa 1:22). "[Wines] are brought from afar, from the desert. Perhaps the guests themselves brought them the drinks, as their part in the orgy, just as they brought gifts and other harlots' hire."

The most coherent medieval interpretation of our verse, that of Menaḥem bar Shimʿon, merits citation, if only for the light it sheds on G's paraphrase (noted in the first comment to this verse):

> *On account of* (ʾl = ʿl) *men—so numerous were the people* who came to her to eat, drink, and make merry with her—was that noise, and on no other account; compare "the noise of carousing I hear" (Exod 32:18). *Brought* to her, since she sent for them to bring them there. *Drunk* (*sobᵉʾim*)—cognate with "glutton and drunkard (*sobe*)" (Deut 21:20) . . . the meaning is that they were so drunk from the wine-feast that they broke into song (*natᵉnu qol nᵉginot*).

The passage may well be corrupt.

bracelets . . . glorious crown. Recalls 16:11, 12. Here harlots' hire is meant.

43. Any rendering is guesswork. "Jade" renders *bala,* feminine participle of *blh* "wear out"—said of clothing (e.g., Josh 9:13) or an aged woman (Gen 18:12). *Leviticus Rabba* 33.6 records a Greek translation (not extant) *palaia pornē,* which means "old (= worn-out) whore." The rest of the verse is probably corrupt; lit. "now they will fornicate her fornications and she"; the versions (see text note m–m) look like makeshift paraphrases of MT.

44. Clause *a* seems to mean: she was as accessible as a harlot; one had no

apprehensions about approaching her as one had in the case of a married woman, concerned over concealing her infidelity. For the structure of the verse as a whole, see J. Blau, "On the Repetition of the Predicate in the Bible," pp. 234–40.

the depraved women (ʾiššot hazzimma). G. R. Driver (1938) explains the unusual plural of *ʾišša* "woman" as influenced by the corresponding Akkadian plural *aššātu*. G appears to have read *(l)ʿśt hzmh* (16:43; 22:9; Hos 6:9; Prov 10:23) "to commit depravity," an attractive emendation of MT.

45. *Righteous men* (ṣaddiqim). T adds "in comparison with them," in the spirit of 16:51–52, since the foreigners of vs. 23 — either they or their likes are undoubtedly intended — can hardly be righteous in an absolute sense. Moshe ben Sheshet suggests as a plausible alternative: they are called *ṣaddiqim*, just men, because they will execute a just (*ṣedeq*) judgment against her, befitting her deeds (so, e.g., Fohrer).

them (ʾothem). The occurrence of masculine suffixes where feminines are due (see last comment to vs. 39) peaks in vss. 45–49, with regular alternation in vss. 46–47. The author of this confusion seems not to have distinguished the two forms in pronunciation. In all these cases some mss. and versions replace with regular feminine forms. Retention of *o* in the first syllable with biconsonantal suffix (*-hm*) is unique (*BHS* records mss. variants tending to regularize: *ʾwthn*, *ʾthn*). In the next verse, the regular *ʾethen* occurs, and in the next (47) *ʾothen* — likewise unique. It is as though the copyist preserved maximal variants in a text tradition that vacillated on such fine points.

The terms of this verse recall 16:38 and vs. 37 above.

How the simultaneous punishment of the two sisters can be adjusted to the fact that Samaria fell over a century before Jerusalem has troubled commentators. Menaḥem bar Shimʿon surmised that the Assyrian depopulation of the northern kingdom was not complete, but left a considerable population that were later deported by Nebuchadnezzar. Fohrer regards the entire passage (from vs. 36 on) as a late afterthought; the sisters are not the pre-exilic kingdoms but later political entities unknown to us. For another, literary, explanation, see Structure and Themes.

46. *I will summon* (haʿale) . . . *and make* (wenaton). The verbs are infinitives absolute, and so can serve as any form of finite verb (see the fine treatment in *BHSyn* 35.5.2). The sequential verbs in vss. 47–49 represent future acts, hence the choice of future for those in this verse. No person is indicated; Kimḥi specifies first person ("the infinitive is tantamount to 'I will summon' and 'I will make'") — cf. the infinitives in I Kings 22:30 (G T "I will disguise myself and go"). This would create an alternating person-pattern with the immediately following verbs — 1-3-1-3. On the other hand, the similar expression in 16:40 ("they shall summon a crowd against you") justifies the third person: "They shall summon . . . and make." Many moderns (e.g., *RSV*, *NEB*, NJPS) construe the verbs in our verse as imperative and infinitive respectively; this is possible but entails needless shifts in mood from imperative (vs. 46) to jussive (vs. 47) to future (vs. 48), and incidentally opens the door to misinterpreting vs. 46 as "initiating the woman's punishment, rather than merely threatening it" (Galambush, p. 90).

The "crowd" (*qhl*) refers to "the crowd of armies" (*qhl ʿmym*) of vs. 24, an invading army rather than a judicial assembly (see comment to 16:40; I, 287), as indicated also by "make them an object of plunder" at the end of the verse. Against the concept of a judicial assembly Cooke notes the absence of the article, in contrast to the judicial *hqhl* of Ezra 10:12, 14; Neh 8:2, 17.

47. *crowd-stones.* The means of execution used by a crowd—a strange and suspect expression. But to construe "crowd" as the subject of "they shall pelt" as S does is stranger.

and cleave them. The unusual verb used in 21:24, on which see comment (to "clear a place"). The form is piʿel infinitive absolute, continuing the perfect consecutive (*wrgmw*); GKC, § 113 z. This verse thus uses three verbal modes of expressing futurity: perfect consecutive, infinitive absolute, and imperfect (*yhrgw* "they shall kill," *yśrpw* "they shall burn")—variation characteristic of Ezekiel.

Vs. 47 radicalizes vs. 25: double death to the women; death to the children; fire to the houses. With vs. 48a it echoes 16:40–41.

48. *be admonished* (w^{e}niwwass^{e}ru). The unusual form (from root *y/wsr*) resembles Mishnaic nitpaʿel, with the preformative *t* assimilated to the first radical (*w*); similarly *w^{e}nikkapper* "shall be atoned for" (< **wntkpr*) in Deut 21:8.

Vs. 48b stays within the allegory: Oholibah's terrible fate will be an object lesson to all women (cf. vs. 10) who will take it to heart and eschew her profligacy. As before (5:7; 16:27, 34), Ezekiel portrays Israel as more corrupt than the gentiles.

your depravity. Note the transition to second person; cf. vs. 21 and comment.

49. *They shall lay.* The crowd of executioners of vs. 47; S and mss. "I will lay," agreeing with vs. 48—probably a smoothing. For "lay [the penalty]" and "bear [the punishment]" of evildoing, see comment to 7:13 (I, 147).

Then you (masculine) *shall know.* This may refer to the women, as do the masculine suffix pronouns in vss. 45–47; or "the prophet is thinking of the people, not in an allegory, but as they are" (Cooke). In S T the verb form is feminine.

I am Lord YHWH. Only here and in 13:9; 24:24; 28:24; 29:16, does "Lord" precede the tetragram in the concluding recognition formula. Ezekiel (or his copyist) was not a machine.

STRUCTURE AND THEMES

Ch. 23 contains a main oracle, vss. 1–34, and a subordinate oracle dependent upon it, vss. 36–49 (on vs. 35, see ahead). The main oracle (A) is an allegory about two nymphomaniacal sisters, representing Samaria and Jerusalem, whose excesses and bad ends are set out in chronological sequence. The subordinate oracle (B) ignores the real time sequence, depicting the careers of the women as contemporaneous and their punishment as still to come. But defiance of historical reality is not confined to B; A, too, ignores it when it represents the Egyptian sojourn, the time of Israel's youth, as shared in by the two sisters—as though Samaria and Jerusalem existed from the beginning of national history. As often in Ezekiel, reality is subordinated to an ideal: Israel, in the prophet's mind, is a single nation, whose monarchic components, represented by Samaria and Jerusalem, were present at its birth (oracle A) as at its destruction (oracle B).

The main oracle (A) opens with the sexual awakening of the sisters at the hands of the Egyptians (vs. 3), and this is referred to toward, or at, the end of each of the subsections: vs. 8 (while carrying on with Assyrians, Oholah did not forsake the Egyptians); vss. 19–21 (recoiling from the Babylonians, Oholibah reverted to her Egyptian lovers); vs. 27 (God will put an end to her calling on Egypt). The horrifying finale of the oracle (vs. 34) is Oholibah's tearing off her breasts — the organs by which she was originally seduced in Egypt. Even the orphan vs. 35 evokes the sister's constant recourse to Egypt through God's antithetic censure, "Because you forgot me and cast me behind your back." Thus while the oracle lists all the partners to the sisters' harloting, what rankles YHWH most is their reversion time and again to their "original sin," the affair with Egypt.

Oracle A falls into two main divisions: God tells the prophet the story of the wanton sisters (vss. 1–21), then addresses sentences of doom to Oholibah (vss. 22–34). In detail, A's structure is this:

A1 (vss. 1–4): the setting. After the revelation formula (vs. 1), the sisters are introduced; their sexual arousal in Egypt, their identification, their marriage to God, and their bearing him children are related.

A2 (vss. 5–10): the adulterous career of Oholah-Samaria and her punishment. Although she was irresistibly attracted to Assyria's officers and cavaliers, Oholah did not give up her first lovers, the Egyptians (vss. 5–8); consequently (*laken*) the Assyrians, at God's bidding, inflicted exemplary punishment on her and took her children captive (vss. 9–10). These few verses are background and foil for the much longer story of Oholibah's surpassing outrages (A3) and the twofold recital of punishments in store for her (A4a, A4b).

A3 (vss. 11–21): the adulterous career of Oholibah-Jerusalem. After the generality that Oholibah outstripped her sister in lewdness (vs. 11), the particulars of her misdeeds are given in strict sequence. First she equaled her sister in defiling herself with Assyrians (vss. 12–13); then she outdid her, sending for Babylonian lovers and debauching herself with them till she loathed herself (vss. 14–17), and God loathed her (vs. 18), for it. She capped her excesses by reverting to the Egyptians, her first lovers, for an orgy (vss. 19–21).

A4a (vss. 22–27): Oholibah's punishment, first statement. Consequently (*laken*) God addresses a pronouncement of doom to Oholibah ("Thus said Lord YHWH"): he will stir up all of her Mesopotamian lovers to attack her, strip her of her finery, and kill her; that will put an end to her harloting and her yearnings for Egypt.

A4b (vss. 28–34): Oholibah's punishment, second statement. In another pronouncement of doom addressed to Oholibah ("Indeed, thus said Lord YHWH"), God stresses the hatred between her and her destroyers; they will strip and expose her naked, because of her harloting and her idolatrous defilement (vss. 28–30). This additional surge of passion expands on the mutual revulsion felt by Oholibah and her former lovers (cf. vss. 17b, 22a) and applies to her Oholah's humiliation (exposure of nakedness, vs. 10a$^{\alpha}$) and Oholah's sin of idolatry (vs. 7b) — with which Oholibah had not been previously charged. Oholibah's imitation of

Oholah is then expressly stated in vs. 31 ("You followed the course of your sister, so I will put her cup in your hand"), a counterpart of vs. 13 and a bridge to the climactic "poem of the cup" in vss. 32–34.

The ambiguous status of this poem, in which Oholibah "drinks" her sister's "cup" and goes berserk, consists in its relative independence — formally established by a fresh message formula ("Thus said Lord YHWH," vs. 32) and its own closure ("declares Lord YHWH," vs. 34). It develops a new figure — "the cup" — and has its own plot; yet it carries forward and fuses splendidly the dual trend of vss. 28–30 to focus on Oholibah's feelings and assimilate her to her sister. The poem portrays her disgrace, her appallment, her derangement, culminating in self-mutilation (vs. 25 taken to an extreme) as her hatred and loathing finally turn upon herself.

Vs. 35 opens with a formula of consequence ("*laken* thus said Lord YHWH") that immediately peters out in a truncated, general threat. It is unconnected with what immediately precedes, but its motive clause ("Because you forgot me, etc.") is antithetic to the theme of remembering Egypt and turning to it, sounded in vss. 19–21 and vs. 27. Forlorn here, vs. 35 could serve nicely as an opening to the sentencing of Oholibah instead of vs. 22a$^{\alpha}$ or 28a$^{\alpha}$. It is perhaps a variant to one of these verse segments, recorded as a footnote at the end of the oracle. (As only partial parallels to the present postposition of vs. 35 one may compare vs. 49a, at the end of oracle B, and 16:43 and 16:58 — all of which are unembarrassed by a *laken* clause, which marks an opening, not a closing.)

Oracle B (vss. 36–49) opens with an irregular revelation formula (see comment to vs. 36). It consists of a bill of indictment (vss. 36–45: terms of judgment [*špṭ*], adultery, and "bloody hands" mark the beginning [vs. 37] and the end [vs. 45] of the indictment) and a sentencing (vss. 46–49), demarcated by a message formula at its start and a recognition formula at its end. Its dependence on A is manifest from its assumption that Oholah and Oholibah need not be identified. The whole is pervaded by the language of previous oracles (see comment), yet exhibits its own peculiar emphases: the collection of cultic offenses (vss. 37–39), the preparations for the love feast (vss. 40–42), the radicalization of punishment (47) — effects, it would seem, of brooding over the theme of oracle A. B is remarkable for its incoherence, its linguistic oddities, and the disconcerting changes in number and person. The versions read more smoothly, but the confusion in MT is probably original. In the opinion of most critics it is due to successive accretions and glosses by late and later hands, but an alternative explanation is worth considering: what we have is a "preliminary expectoration" (to use Kirkegaard's term) of a supplement to oracle A, its rough, preliminary form as yet not submitted to the stylization and regularization that the rest of the book has undergone. Viewed from that angle, this passage is, in its rough-hewn state, a unique glimpse into the earliest form of Ezekiel's oracles, before the process of polishing at the hands of their editor (the prophet himself?) gave them their remarkable uniformity. Perhaps the blatant unreality of contemporizing the two sisters, in direct contradiction to the immediately preceding correct representation of their sequential careers, was too flagrant an excess even for the Ezekielian editor; and so the passage survived as a sacred fragment, but one too flawed for editorial attention.

Ironic touches and reversals characterize the oracles: promiscuous, excessive lovemaking eventuates in alienation, deadly hostility, and self-revulsion. The threefold itemization in A of the articles of power, pomp, and wealth by which the Mesopotamian paramours ravish the sisters' hearts is followed by a fourth listing of the paramours — now with the equipage of an army of executioners. And punctuating the whole of A is the repeated evocation of the women's breasts — organs of seduction and in the end objects of self-mutilation. In B the crowd of paramours at the love feasts is soon replaced by a crowd of lynchers. And it is bitter irony when the gentile executioners are termed "righteous" in comparison with the sisters.

The allegorization of Israel's relation to God as morbid marital infidelity has already occurred in ch. 16 in the figure of the faithless foundling wife, alongside which appeared the (three) wicked sisters, not identified as wives. Here sisters and wives are fused in a manner original with Jeremiah: "apostate Israel" and "faithless Judah" were sisters, wives of YHWH. Apostate Israel was destroyed for her rampant infidelity, yet faithless Judah did not take fright but followed in the path of her sister, until she made her sister look good by comparison (Jer 3:6–11).

Ezekiel shapes the allegory in accord with his concerns. Since theodicy required an enormous accumulation of guilt to account for the fall of Samaria and Jerusalem, the sisters are given a history of guilt that reaches back to their youth in Egypt (cf. I, 299, and ch. 20). Their marriage to God obligated the women to religious and political loyalty — exclusive worship of YHWH and exclusive dependence on him for national security (cf. I, 299). In Jeremiah's metaphor the sisters' infidelity is cultic only; here it is on both counts that the sisters failed — our oracle emphasizing the political infidelities, whereas ch. 16 gives prominence to the cultic. The allegory enabled Jeremiah to illustrate Judah's vice from a fresh angle: beside her stupidity in exchanging "a fount of living water" for "cracked cisterns" (Jer 2:11–13), Judah learned nothing from sister Samaria's disastrous career. Ezekiel's comparison of Ohola and Oholibah served an identical function: whereas the faithless wife of ch. 16 exemplified Jerusalem's obtuse ingratitude toward her savior, Oholibah embodied Jerusalem's ingrained inaptitude to take warning from the calamitous end of a sister city whose sins she replicated and augmented. Jeremiah breaks off without describing the parallel fate that awaits faithless Judah, but for Ezekiel that is the whole point of the comparison. Oholibah's addiction to infidelity, in which she outstripped her sister, will bring down upon her devastation more terrible than her sister's. The allegory serves Ezekiel's repeated argument during the years before the fall of Jerusalem that the crimes committed in the city against God and man made its destruction an unavoidable necessity. (Elsewhere Jeremiah uses a similar rhetoric when he invokes Shiloh's fate in order to undermine popular trust in Jerusalem's impunity, Jer 7:12–15.)

Comparison of the careers and ends of the sisters is extended and transformed in B into virtual identification: the life courses of the sisters are not merely analogous, they are joint and contemporary, and both will expire in the same judgment. (Since the same paramours and executioners must serve both women, to avoid historical difficulties they are left anonymous here, in contrast to A.) B's rhetorical heightening has not only defied history, it has nullified the force of the allegory, which resided precisely in the climactic sequence of the sisters' careers. Oholibah's extraordinary obtuseness, leading her into unheard-of promiscuity, resulting in unprecedented punishment all goes by the board if the sisters are coeval; this may be another reason for B's neglected state.

The sisters' pursuit of connections with powerful males was initiated by their youthful relations with the Egyptians, to whom they periodically reverted, thus incensing later paramours. The difference between the paramours is important: the Assyrians attract by the éclat of their military-political organization; the rich costume of Babylonian officialdom captivates eye and heart; both Mesopotamian lovers radiate power. The Egyptian appeal is neither power nor wealth, but purely erotic. Egypt can seduce Samaria and Jerusalem into abandoning their Mesopotamian lovers but cannot defend them against the evil consequences of such fickleness. This foreshadows the denunciation of Egyptian impotence in 29:6f.; 30:20ff., and points to the alliance with Egypt as a major issue at the time of this oracle (see ahead).

The "cup" of destiny, found only here in Ezekiel, is a familiar figure in Hebrew poetry. At bottom, it is a neutral metaphor, based apparently on the custom of the host to pour wine into the cup of each of his banquet guests (U. Cassuto, *Biblical and Oriental Studies*, II [Jerusalem: Magnes Press, 1975], p. 131), as in Ps 16:5, "YHWH is my allotted share and 'cup.'" More often it serves in the sinister sense of a toxic or intoxicating drink—a figure for divine punishment, as in Ps 75:9:

> There is a cup in YHWH's hand
> With foaming wine fully mixed;
> From this he pours;
> All the wicked of the earth drink,
> Draining it to the dregs.

The figure is common in the Judahite prophetic literature of the seventh and sixth centuries; e.g.:

> Take from my hand this cup of wine, of wrath, and make all the nations to which I send you drink of it; let them drink and vomit and act crazy, because of the sword I am sending among them. (Jer 25:15–16)

> Babylon was a golden cup in YHWH's hand;
> It made the whole earth drunk;
> The nations drank of her wine,
> That is why the nations are mad. (Jer 51:7)

A reminiscence of the drunkenness of Noah may be heard in Lam 4:21:

Rejoice and exult Dame Edom,
Who dwells in the land of Uz;
To you too the cup shall pass;
You shall get drunk and expose yourself.

This theme is elaborated at length in Hab 2:15–16.

The origin of the sinister figure is obscure. A connection with the ordeal-potion of Num 5 has been suggested, but the association with wine and frenzy points rather to "a banquet of death . . . the anti-banquet theme, the gruesome reversal of the benevolent host and wholesome hospitality" (W. McKane, "Poison, Trial by Ordeal, and the Cup of Wrath," *VT* 30 [1980], 487–92). Since the thought is always present that those to whom God gives the cup are powerless to refuse it (C. North, *The Second Isaiah* [Oxford: Clarendon Press, 1964], p. 216), a connection with the banquet-host metaphor seems most likely.

Of the circumstances and the time of these oracles this may be said: B has a relation to A recalling the halving pattern of many of Ezekiel's compositions. It skews the main theme of A, while at the same time resuming, not merely at the end, as is the usual case, but throughout, various elements of A in heightened or developed form. B thus seems a later return to certain themes of A, at a sufficient remove from it to allow for the divergent representation of the women as contemporaries. In both A and B the reminiscences of previous doom oracles are so extensive as to justify fully their location toward the end of Ezekiel's collection of doom prophecies. But inasmuch as both A and B regard the destruction of Jerusalem as still to come, their composition must antecede that event. Moreover, since A is especially contemptuous of Egypt and censorious of Jerusalem's reliance on it, a time of strong Egyptian influence on Jerusalem's policy may be assumed—viz., during the preparation of the revolt against Nebuchadnezzar and its first phase (I, 13; cf. ch. 17). This tallies with the allusion in the heading of the next oracle to the start of Nebuchadnezzar's siege of Jerusalem.

Note on the Feminist Critique of Ch. 23

One of the chief aims of a feminist reading of Scripture is to lay bare what feminists hold to be Scripture's specifically male construction of experience/reality—an instrument (as they see it) of male domination. Feminist critics consider the prophets' metaphor of Israel as the adulterous wife of God a particularly blatant instance of a male viewpoint, since it takes for granted the subjugation of the female to the total control of males (humans and God) and views women as the source of pollution and evil.

The allegorical/metaphorical survey of Israelite history in Ezek 23, like its mate in ch. 16, has accordingly been repeatedly subjected to a feminist critique. Two examples will serve to represent the genre.

Both chapters are studied in depth in Julie Galambush's monograph *Jerusalem in the Book of Ezekiel: The City as Yahweh's Wife*, SBL Dissertation Series 130 (Atlanta: Scholars Press, 1992). Some lines from the final paragraph convey the substance and style of the whole:

The metaphor of the city as Yahweh's wife fulfills, among various roles, the role of mediating between prophet as visionary and prophet as voyeur. The woman Jerusalem functions as a metaphor of the chaos and castration that threaten Yahweh in light of both the desecration of his temple, and ultimately, its destruction. Yahweh's struggle for control emerges over the course of Ezekiel as a struggle between male and female depicted in chaps 16 and 23 through a form of pornography, a whore's biography with the woman's sexual subordination as its goal.

Ch. 23 is criticized by Fokkelien Van Dijk-Hemmes in "The Metaphorization of Woman in Prophetic Speech: An Analysis of Ezekiel xxiii," *VT* 43 (1993), 162–70. After a brief statement of theory the author finds male "misnaming of female experience" throughout the chapter, beginning with vs. 3, which she rephrases from a female perspective: "They were sexually abused in Egypt, in their youth they were sexually abused." Oholah's later doting upon Egypt "is explained [in vs. 8] by her having enjoyed the violence, done to her in her youth" (*škbw* is said to mean "rape")—a male perspective on rape. It might be questioned (the author anticipates) whether androcentrism is really served by a metaphor that identifies male Israelites with a "pornographic" female figure. She answers by pointing to the "escape" available to males of identifying themselves with the "male" God-husband of the allegory, or with the righteous judges of vs. 45 who execute the wantons, while no authentic representative of feminine experience is at all available to women.

There can be no doubt that such readings are authentic expressions of the pain and outrage experienced by feminists searching Scripture for reflections of their constructions of reality and meeting with Oholah and Oholibah. The feminist project, promoting a new female reality, necessarily clashes with Scripture—one of the fashioners of the reality to be superseded. At bottom, what feminists criticize is not what the texts meant to those who composed and received them in their historical context, but what the text means in today's context. Van Dijk-Hemmes would presumably not be consoled by evidence that the women in Ezekiel's audience were persuaded by his rhetoric and identified with his pillorying of the wanton sisters. She demands a text that reflects her identity; for that purpose Ezekiel is but a negative countertext, whose male-centered agenda must be exposed and disarmed in terms of today's values, psychology, and anthropology.

Whether aiming to savage Scripture or to salvage it, feminists are judgmental. They applaud or decry, approve or disapprove. They write to promote a new gender reality.

Their project differs fundamentally from the (quixotic?) historical-philological search for the primary, context-bound sense of Scripture that is the project of this commentary. Hence reference to feminist criticism will be as rare in the following pages as it has been in the preceding ones.

XXIII. The Filthy Pot
(24:1–14)

24 [1]The word of YHWH came to me in the ninth year, in the tenth month, on
the tenth of the month: [2]Man, write down the name of the day, this very day: the
king of Babylon laid siege to Jerusalem on this very day. [3]And frame a parable for
the rebellious house, and say to them: Thus said Lord YHWH:

Put the pot on, put it on,
And then pour water into it,
[4]Gather her cuts into her,
Every good cut, thigh and shoulder,
Fill [her] with the best limbs.
[5]Take the best of the flock!
Then pile the bones around under her.
Get her boiling,
So that her limbs are cooked within her.

[6]Now then, thus said Lord YHWH:

Woe to the bloody city,
Pot whose filth is in her,
Whose filth will not be gone from her.
Take her cuts out one by one;
No lot has fallen on her.
[7]For the blood she has shed festers in her,
She set it on a glaring rock;
She did not pour it on the ground, to cover it with earth.
[8]To kindle fury, to take vengeance I put that blood on
a glaring rock, not to be covered.

[9]Now then, thus said Lord YHWH:

Woe to the bloody city!
I for my part will make a great pyre,
[10]Heap the wood,
Light the fire,
Cause the flesh to be consumed,
And mix the aromatic compound,
Till the bones be charred.
[11]Then I will let her stand empty on her embers

For her copper to heat up and be scorched,
So that her impurity melts away within her,
Her filth is consumed.
12[a]She has frustrated all effort,[a]
And her great filth is not gone from her;
In fire her filth [will go].

13For your depraved impurity, because I tried to purge you but you would not be purged, you will never more be purged of your impurity until I assuage my fury against you. 14I YHWH have spoken; it is coming and I will do it; I will not annul and I will not spare and I will not relent. According to your ways and according to your misdeeds they[b] shall punish you, declares Lord YHWH.

COMMENT

24:1. Parker-Dubberstein reckon the date as January 15, 588. The date formula, whose wording and location in the sentence are alien to Ezekiel's style (I, 10 n. 8), is almost identical with that of II Kings 25:1 (Jer 52:4). It is likely that originally no date appeared in the revelation formula (as, e.g., in 23:1 and mostly), and that the present one was subsequently copied from Kings into the margin and later into the text. Had a date originally appeared—presumably a different (wrong) one—we should have expected it at the beginning of the sentence (as, e.g., 29:1) or after *wyhy* (as, e.g., 26:1), and in either case followed by *hyh dbr YHWH*. Its replacement by the present, correct date would then not have resulted in the anomalous shape of the current text. The date appears in all ancient versions and so entered the text early on, endowing the prophet with exact supersensory knowledge that medievals interpreted in the only possible way:

> He was commanded to write down the date and show it to the exiles, because on that day the king of Babylon laid siege; and when they would later receive the report that it really happened on the very day the prophet had written down they would know that a prophet was among them and what he said in God's name was true, and they would no longer pay heed to the false prophets. (Kimḥi)

Such confirmatory purpose and procedure are not even hinted at in the following oracle, hence we may doubt that originally its opening lines contained an exact date that would lead one to suppose them (as Kimḥi and others did).

2. *the name of the day, this very day.* This is usually taken to mean the date formula of vs. 1. But *ʿṣm hywm*, lit. "the day's self," serves here uniquely as direct object; elsewhere it is in a temporal adverbial phrase, as at the end of this verse. Moderns delete it, noting its omission in S; but that is probably a simplification,

[a–a]Not in G; S "like sick figs," as from *tᵉʾenim ḥolot*; T "you were full of false accusations," as from *toʿᵃnot malet*.
[b]Versions and some mss. "I."

since G, though unclear, represents the "day" of this phrase. If, as was argued in the preceding comment, no date originally appeared in vs. 1, then "the name of the day" and "this very day" will belong to the following sentence, designating the day by what happened on it. See *NEB*, cited in the following comment.

laid siege to (samak 'el). Lit. "leaned, pressed heavily, on"; as intransitive, the verb recurs only in Ps 88:8 (with *'al*), but is common in Syriac and in the Hebrew and Aramaic of the Talmud.

This sentence ("the king . . .") is usually taken as the ground of the preceding command: "He was commanded to write down the date . . . because (*ki*) on that date the king . . . laid siege" (Kimḥi). But if so, the lack of a connective (such as *ki*) between the two is remarkable. Further, the occurrence of a verb in the perfect (*samak*) before the adverbial temporal phrase ("on this very") is unique; elsewhere the temporal phrase always precedes a verb in the perfect (cf. 40:1 and Gen 7:13; 17:26; Exod 12:17, 41, 51). The combined effect of these anomalies is to make this sentence appositional to the "name of the day" in the preceding clause. In other words, "the king of Babylon laid siege . . ." is the title of day, which the prophet is commanded to write down (so *NEB*: "Man, write down a name for this day, this very day: This is the day the king of Babylon invested Jerusalem"). The unusual placement of *samak* before the temporal phrase stresses the fateful fact that hostile contact had actually been made. It was the beginning of the end that the prophet had been predicting for years to an unbelieving community.

3. *frame a parable.* God's meaning will be conveyed under the likeness (*mašal;* see comment to 17:2 [I, 309]) of a cooking scene, whose components signify a political reality. The discourse is oral ("say to them: Thus said Lord YHWH"); there is no reason to suppose it was accompanied by action of any kind.

for ('el) *the rebellious house. 'el* is ambiguous; it can mean "directed to" or "about." In 17:2 I translated *um^ešol . . . 'el* "tell a fable to." Here the sequel "and say to them" makes attractive the alternative interpretation of *'el* as "about": "frame a parable about" (as in 16:44; so *BHS*), thus avoiding a tautology ("tell a parable to . . . and say to them"). In 17:2 ("tell a fable to") the indirect object pronoun does not reappear in the sequential clause (*w'mrt* "and say"—correct my translation accordingly!). Either way, whether those addressed as "the rebellious house" are the exiles (the usual case, e.g., 2:5, 6; 12:2, 3, 9; 17:12) or homelanders (Jerusalemites; cf. 12:22, 25) cannot be determined; see discussion in I, 16–17.

Put the pot on, put it on. So one gave orders to a cook, as in II Kings 4:38: "Put the large pot on and cook a stew . . ." Here the cook is imaginary and the cooking process is particularized in order to call vividly to mind the care that went into it so as to heighten the shock of the sequel. Repetition of the verb expresses exhortation and is characteristic of Ezekiel; e.g., "Will you arraign" in 20:4; 22:2; "Prophesy" in 37:9. The address to the cook (vss. 3b–5) is couched in short lines typical of poetry.

4. *her cuts.* The cuts of meat readied for cooking in the pot, now construed as feminine (as in II Kings 4:38; in Jer 1:13 masculine), perhaps anticipating its

resolution, in vss. 6, 9, as a city (*ʿir*, feminine). Other appurtenances of the pot are termed "hers"—"her limbs" (vs. 5) and "her embers" (vs. 11); G S, lacking the pronoun, do not reflect this Hebrew usage.

limbs. When *ʿeṣem* "bone" is pluralized with masculine afformatives (e.g., *-ym*), it sometimes means "limbs," as in Judg 19:29, "he cut her up (*ntḥ*) limb by limb (*lʿṣmyh*)"; Eccl 11:5, "the limbs (*ʿṣmym* = fetus) in the belly of pregnant woman." In this prophecy the distinction between this form and *ʿṣmwt* "bones" (vs. 10) is clear; it is not always so (see KB³, s.v. "*ʿeṣem*"). Cf. Kimḥi: "Since limbs are divided into cuts according to bones, limbs are called bones."

5. *Take the best of the flock!* Climactic: not only the best cuts, but the best animal(s). G saves the narrative sequence by translating "taken (as though *laquaḥ*) from choice (as though *mmbḥr*) beasts"; *BHS* wonders whether the line is merely a variant of the foregoing line. Such expedients are prosaic pedantry, denying the poet the right to subordinate narrative order to climactic order. *laqoaḥ* is an infinitive absolute serving as an imperative—a variation on the preceding imperatives (GKC, § 113 bb; for a similar variation in series, cf. Isa 14:31). DNF (by letter) compares Amos 4:45, where there are seven consecutive imperatives—the fifth, as here, an infinitive absolute.

pile the bones. The verb *dur* (imperative) and its related noun *mᵉdura* "pyre" (vs. 9; Isa 30:33) may ultimately derive from the root *dwr* "circle," having reference to the circular arrangement of logs in a pyre (so KB³). G S render *dur* "kindle"; T "arrange"; the medievals are divided between these two meanings.

"Bones" (*ʿṣmym*) as fuel is strange, both because of their unfitness and because in vss. 4b and 5b *ʿṣmym* refers to the limbs cooking inside the pot. "It is as if to say that the bones of the slain victims (of Jerusalem's rulers, 11:6) fueled the fire, i.e., brought on punishment"; so Kimḥi ingeniously but unconvincingly, since this intrudes an alien figure into an otherwise realistic and straightforward cooking scene. Menaḥem bar Shimʿon rejects a suggestion that *ʿṣmym* here means *ʿeṣim* "pieces of wood," but all critics agree that only *ʿeṣim* can be read here; cf. the sequence "pyre" (*mᵉdura*)–"wood" (*ʿeṣim*) in vss. 9b–10a. It was miswritten under the influence of *ʿṣmym/h* preceding and following it. Zimmerli notes that in the Vulgate of vs. 10 an error in the opposite direction occurred: Heb. *haʿeṣim* is translated *ossa* "bones." In Kara's commentary the copyist wrote the wrong member of the pair in both vss. 5 and 10.

Get her boiling. Lit. "boil her boiling (*rtḥyh*)"; but *ʿṣmyh* in the next line recalls the pair *ntḥyh* "her cuts"–*ʿṣmym* "limbs" in vs. 4, and speaks for Luzzatto's interpretation of *rtḥyh* as equivalent to *ntḥyh* "(boil) her cuts," with the initial *n* replaced by *r* (both are liquids) in order to alliterate with the verb *rtḥ* "boil." Some medieval mss. do read *ntḥyh* here.

So that her limbs are cooked. Taking *gm bšlw* as equivalent to *wbšlw* (perfect consecutive; so Menaḥem bar Shimʿon). *Minḥat Shay* cautions to vocalize *bšlw* with qameṣ (i.e., as a qal perfect), not with pataḥ (as a piʿel imperative plural), attesting to an early tendency to assimilate this verb to the other imperative-form verbs in the passage. Emending to *baššel* "cook!" with most critics yields a smoother clause, but how did the present text arise from that? Ehrlich assumes that the *w* of *bšlw* was detached erroneously from the following word, which originally began the circumstantial clause *wʿṣmyh btwkh*. Accordingly he would render the last lines of vs. 5: "Let her cuts boil and cook, while her bones are within her." This is clever, but what purpose does the encumbering circumstantial clause serve?

MT's reading of this last clause of the ditty signals a closure by a syntactic shift: heretofore the sequence was: transitive verb–object, but here it is: intransitive verb–subject.

6. *Now then*. As always, *laken* introduces the consequential part of an oracle—here, as in 15:6 and 17:19, the decoding of a parable.

Woe to the bloody city. Not an apostrophe; see comment to 12:3 (I, 235). On "bloody city," see comment to 22:2.

whose filth (ḥlʾth) *is in her*. The meaning of *ḥelʾa* is disputed. Our phrase reverberates in vs. 7, lit. "her blood is in her," and again in vs. 11, "her impurity melts away within her." Hence *ḥelʾa* is a defiling substance inside the pot—the copper pot (vs. 11)—that will yield only to overheating. G translates by *ios*, which means "rust" on iron, "verdigris (patina)" on copper; T by *zhmʾ* "filth" (followed by some medievals, B-Y); Rashi, NJPS "scum"; BDB and most moderns "rust." Since one wouldn't need to overheat the pot in order to get rid of scum in it, nor would scum, itself liquid, "melt" in the heating; and since long-exposed copper doesn't rust but gets a patina, we must choose between "verdigris" (*NEB* "green corrosion") and "filth." In the present context, the representation of *ḥelʾa* as a solid substance melted down by overheating inclines one to Ehrlich's view that it is the encrusted residue of cooked matter stuck to the inside of the pot that fouls it disgustingly; hence "filth." On the other hand, a verb, *yḥlyʾ*, occurs in the Hebrew Ben Sira 12:10: "for like copper [the enemy's] evil *yḥlyʾ* i.e., produces *ḥelʾa*" (G: "For as copper is be-verdigrised so is his evil"); hence *ḥelʾa* serves for verdigris, though in our context elimination by overheating goes against that identification. The difficulty may be resolved by assuming that *ḥelʾa* denotes any distasteful soiling and foulness; Ibn Janaḥ (*Haschoraschim*, p. 32) suggests an apt derivation from *ʾlḥ*, by metathesis; cf. *neʾelaḥ* "(morally) tainted, befouled" (Job 15:16; Ps 14:3; 53:4).

For the quiescence of the suffix *h* in *ḥlʾth* before the stop *b* (in *bh*), see GKC, § 91 e.

will not be gone from her. All attempts to dislodge the filth have failed; see vss. 12–13.

Take her cuts out . . . Lit. "By her cuts by her cuts take her out." The translation is somewhat conjectural, but the contrast in the text between "her filth will not be gone (*yṣʾh*) from her" and "take her cuts out" (*hwṣyʾh*) is salient, and suggests that the presence of the filth entails the expulsion of the cuts. A suggestively similar contrast occurred in 11:7, 9, where the Jerusalemite aristocrats say, "She (the city) is the pot and we are the flesh (in her)," and they are rebuffed by the prophet, who declares that their slain victims are the flesh in the pot, while the aristocrats shall be taken out (*hwṣyʾ*) of her and punished. As there explicitly, so here implicitly, there seems to be a causal relation between removal of choice flesh from the pot and the presence in it of impurity. T reads here, "Through exile after exile will the people be brought out"—which may well approximate the referent of this line. The question is whether it is part of the parabolic story or, though couched in terms of the parable, merely masks the referent without any story function. This question applies even more aptly to the next line.

No lot has fallen on her. That is, apparently, on her contents ("her cuts")—an obscure line. Casting lots was a form of divination by which something was discovered, allocated, determined (Num 33:54, landholdings; Obad 11 and Ps 22:19, booty; I Chron 25:8, order of work in shifts; Jonah 1:7, guilty person). Taken with the previous line, this has been understood to say that contact with the filth in the pot so spoiled the flesh that no one was interested in claiming a share in it, but it would be all thrown out piece by piece (Menaḥem bar Shim'on). This interpretation is noteworthy for its appreciation of the connection of the parts of the verse and for its remaining within the story of the parable. More common (especially among moderns) are interpretations that are meaningful only in terms of the supposed referent: there will be no order in the removal of the cuts (the inhabitants of the city), but their expulsion will be haphazard; moreover, the Jerusalemites will not be consigned to one common fate ("lot" = fate, destiny, Isa 17:14), but "those destined for captivity—to captivity, those destined for the plague—to the plague; those destined for the sword—to the sword" (Kimḥi; cf. Jer 15:2). Cooke supposes a contrast between the threatened indiscriminate future deportation and the past one (597), when lots may have been drawn to determine who would go. For Ehrlich the point emerges from connecting this line with the following one: it was unnecessary to cast lots over the city to discover the guilt and the guilty, for she flaunts her bloodguilt for all to see. Ewald (cited by Smend) and Malbim recall the divination scene of 21:27 and render *lo* "not" interrogatively (as, e.g., in II Kings 5:26; Jer 49:9): "Has not the (enemy's) lot fallen on her?" L. C. Allen, "Ezekiel 24:3–14: A Rhetorical Perspective," *CBQ* 49 (1987), 409 n. 16, proposes that "lot" has here a secondary sense "retribution" (so, according to BDB, in, e.g., Isa 47:11), the whole clause meaning: till now retribution matching Jerusalem's bloodguilt has not fallen on it. But "lot" never means retribution; in, e.g., Isa 47:11 it means "fate, assigned destiny," and only the context tells us that the fate alluded to is punishment. Moreover, with "fall" as its verb, only the instrument of divination is denoted.

7. *For the blood she has shed.* Lit. "her blood."

festers in her. Lit. "is in her"; for "fester," see 7:4 and comment thereto, I, 147. A midrash tells of the blood of the murdered priest Zechariah (II Chron 24:20f.) "boiling" until avenged by the Babylonian conqueror, citing our verse as prooftext (*Lamentations Rabba* to 2:2).

She set it on a glaring rock. Human and animal blood that was shed was customarily covered with earth in order to put the evidence of killing out of sight and mind (Gen 37:26; Lev 17:13). Poets implore the earth to uncover, or not to cover, the blood of innocents so as to ensure vengeance (Isa 26:21; Job 16:18). Jerusalem's rulers, careless of divine punishment, shed blood and left it on bare rock where it could not be absorbed, to attest enduringly to their guilt.

8. Jerusalem's flaunting her guilt is really God's doing: he wills that her crimes remain manifest so that his fury against her be inflamed. For the idea that God deepens the guilt of sinners, see I, 369. Ehrlich interprets God's action as with-

holding rain from the rock, recalling (though he doesn't mention it) 22:24; there may indeed be a vague connection between these verses.

kindle. That is what *heʿela* ("cause to rise") means in Exod 27:20; Num 8:2–3 "to kindle an eternal light"; cf. Judg 6:21, where fire "rises," i.e., is ignited. Fury, like fire, "burns" (Ps 89:47), "leaps forth" (Jer 4:4), and "is kindled" (*nṣth*, II Kings 22:13, 17) or "rises" (II Chron 36:16). The fire imagery of the context is continued.

to take vengeance (lnqm nqm). To exact just retribution. H. G. L. Peels, "The Vengeance of God," has established that with God as subject, *nqm* signifies punishing in order to restore right and justice for victims of injustice, by doing which God defends his honor.

9. *Now then*. The consequentiality of vs. 9 upon the preceding is articulated by Menaḥem bar Shimʿon: "Since there is so much blood and so much filth inside her, I for my part will make a great pyre under her to cause her filth to be consumed."

pyre. See comment to *pile the bones*, vs. 5.

10. *Heap* (harbe), *light* (hadleq), *cause to be consumed* (hatem), *mix* (harqaḥ). These alliterating words are all infinitive absolutes, continuing the initial finite verb "I will make great" (*ʾagdil*); GKC, § 113 z.

Cause the flesh to be consumed (hatem). That is, boil it away and burn it up, as in vs. 11b, *ttm ḥlʾth* "her filth is consumed," i.e., melted away. It cannot mean "make it ready," i.e., finish cooking it (Zimmerli). This representation of the destruction of the contents of the pot by overcooking is inconsistent with vs. 6's call to remove the cuts from the pot. See Structure and Themes.

mix the aromatic compound (harqaḥ hammerqaḥa). G "and the broth (*zomos*, in Judg 6:19, 20 = Heb. *mrq*) be diminished." G's evocation of *mrq* "broth" is preferred by most critics to MT *mrqḥh* "aromatic compound"; various emendations of MT are based on it, such as *whrq hmrq* "empty out the broth" and *whrḥq hmrq* "remove the broth" (*BHS*). But the proponents of these emendations mistake the process described in vss. 10–11, which is the consumption of the contents of the pot by overcooking and overheating (hence the "great pyre" of vs. 9b). Kara: "Keep it boiling until the flesh inside it is overcooked and vanishes in its broth (*mrq*); then *mix the aromatic compound*, that is, stir it in the caldron with a ladle until it all melts away, even the bones, and disappears." Kara's mention of "broth" (*mrq*) and his understanding of the gradual diminution of the mixture in the pot shows that MT may be interpreted as it stands in a manner approximating G, thus raising a doubt as to whether G's *Vorlage* was really different from MT. As for the choice of *mrqḥh* "mixture of spices" to describe the pottage, Rashi explains: "When the flesh falls off the bone, shrinking then blending into its gravy, and he stirs it with a ladle, it resembles the mixing of a spice compound, which requires much blending."

Till the bones be charred. As the cooking of the limbs (ʿ*ṣmym*) closes the normal procedure described in vss. 3–5, so the charring of the bones (ʿ*ṣmwt*) closes the overcooking procedure of vss. 9–10. The limbs are the main feature of the stew, hence their gradual consumption is particularized: the flesh dissolves into a broth (an "aromatic compound") and that burns away till even the bones are charred.

The placement of the subject (*wh'ṣmwt*) before the intransitive verb (*yḥrw*) in this closing line of the section is a closural change from the pattern of the foregoing clauses (transitive verb–object). It parallels the syntactical change from the foregoing in the last, closural clause of vs. 5 ("so that cooked are her limbs"—intransitive verb–subject in contrast to the preceding pattern of transitive verb–object). Both call attention to what happens to the limbs—innocent cooking (vs. $5b^{\gamma}$) ends in ruthless cremation (vs. $10b^{\beta}$). G lacks our clause; in preferring it to MT, critics (e.g., Zimmerli, *BHS*) miss the point and the artful design of the Hebrew.

11. *Then I will let her stand* (wh'mydh). Infinitive construct with direct object suffix (only the infinitive construct can take suffixes), picking up the string of absolute infinitives–objects in vs. 10 (which continue the initial finite verb in vs. 9b, "I will make great").

So that her impurity melts away within her. The language evokes the smelting image of 22:20–22 and the related use of "impurity" there in vss. 3–5, especially vs. 15, where it is a general term for Jerusalem's sin and wickedness, equivalent to "filth" here in the next clause (note the similarity between *whtmty ṭm'tk* "I will purge your impurity," 22:15, and *ttm ḥl'th* "her filth will be consumed," both phrases using the verb *tmm*). On the scope of *ṭm'h* "impurity," see Structure and Themes to ch. 22.

12. *She has frustrated all effort.* So, essentially, NJPS, which aptly characterizes the rendering of the entire verse as uncertain. The noun *t'nym* may derive from *'wn* "strength," the plural form as in *'wnym,* Isa 40:26, 29, but its noun pattern (plural of **t'wn?*) is otherwise unexampled. The verb (lit. "she has exhausted, worn out") shows the original feminine ending *-at* as in *hirṣat* "she paid back" (Lev 26:34; GKC, § 75 m). The conjectured translation is in accord with the next verse; Smend compares the figure in Jer 6:29–30 of the futile efforts of the smith to refine base ore; see also Ezek 22:18–22. The versions indicate divergent *Vorlagen*—see text note (G's omission may reflect bafflement). The graphic resemblance of *t'nym hl't* to the immediately preceding *ttm ḥl'th* (end of vs. 11) arouses suspicion that the former is a corrupt dittograph of the latter.

her great filth. Lit. "the abundance of (*rabbat*) her filth"; *rabbat* on the pattern of *dallat ha'areṣ* "the poor element of the land" (II Kings 25:12), and occurring absolutely in the sense of "many people" in II Chron 30:17, 18. (The masculine *rab* serves identically in *rab ṭub^{e}ka* "your great goodness," Ps 145:7.)

In fire her filth [*will go*]. NJPS: "into the fire with its scum!"—a happy rendering that hides the suspicious abruptness of the verbless Hebrew, which all interpreters must somehow supplement. Kimḥi fuses this clipped expression and the short closure of the preceding verse: "Since her filth is so great there's no remedy but that it be consumed in fire." And indeed such a sentence as "her filth will be consumed in fire" (*b'š ttm ḥl'th*) would be a fit ending of vs. 12.

G "her verdigris will be ashamed" associates *b'š* "in fire" with *bwš* "be ashamed." Luzzatto surmised an original *b^{e}'oš* "the stink of (her filth)"—an echo phrase of "her great filth" in the preceding clause. Though Malbim and Ehrlich also propose this revocalization (apparently independently), the intrusion of such an isolated allusion to smell is more ingenious than convincing (but note the resultant contrast with "aromatic mixture" of vs. 10).

13. *For your depraved impurity*. Lit. "For your impurity of depravity"; the placement of the suffix on the first word of a pair is discussed in the comment to 16:27 "your depraved way" (I, 283). The sentence breaks off and a new start is made ("because, etc."). S simplifies by formulating both motive clauses identically (*ʿl d-* "because"). On *zimma* "depravity," see again comment to 16:27.

I tried to purge you. Lit. "I purged you"—i.e., I applied cleansers to you to no avail. This may be a metaphor for the graduated futile chastisements inflicted on the people in the manner described in Lev 26, on which see I, 124–25 (Eliezer of Beaugency thinks of the disasters of the siege). Another possibility is the succession of prophets sent to warn against God's wrath; so Jer 25:3–4; 26:5, and more particularly II Chron 36:15–17, with possible echoes of this oracle.

14. *it is coming*. This phrase is inserted into the standard formula "I have spoken and I will do it," on which see the comment at 22:14. It expresses the imminence of the threatened disaster—unlike the contexts of the other occurrences of the standard formula, which refer to distant events. Cf. 33:33 *hinne baʾa* "it is on its way!" (lit. "behold it is coming").

I will not annul. For *prʿ* in the sense of "set at naught, spurn," see Prov 1:25; 13:18.

they shall punish. The foreigners to be brought by God against Judah, as in 23:45. The reading "I will punish" in the versions and a few medieval Hebrew mss. probably reflects an early variant. The interchange of God and his earthly agents as executioners occurs repeatedly; see, e.g., 23:25–27; 16:38 versus 23:45. *BHS* favors "I" (as in 7:3, 8; 16:38), which is doubtless better suited to the context, but that very fact may speak for the preferability of "they" as the more difficult reading. The verb is in the "prophetic perfect," representing a future event as already accomplished (Joüon-Muraoka, § 112 h).

STRUCTURE AND THEMES

The dreadful message of this oracle is disposed climactically, from the homely scene of a cook putting up a fine stew to the ghastly image of God in a transport of fury reducing his city to a burned-out shell. Vss. 1–2 state the occasion of the oracle, the day on which the king of Babylon started to besiege Jerusalem. On that day, the doom of the city finally began to work itself out; the prophet was to depict the process in parable and metaphor. The oracle shows the by-now-familiar intrusion of referent into figure typical of Ezekiel's parables; it is complicated by inner tensions that indicate stages of composition.

It may be divided into three main parts: vss. 3–5; 6–8; 9–14.

A (vss. 3–5): the parable. An imaginary cook is addressed in a ditty calling on him to prepare a stew. The ditty ends with the cuts cooked and ready for serving; there is no hint of the sinister sequel.

B (vss. 6–8): the first clarification, formally marked by *laken* and the messenger formula. God, as speaker, metaphorizes the "bloody city" as a cooking pot whose interior filth cannot be dislodged, and whose contents will, in consequence, be thrown away (conjectured sense of vs. 6). The figure of interior filth is then explained as the blood of murdered innocents that cries to heaven for vengeance — the motive of the divine punishment that will be spoken of in the next section. The style of B passes from the short, enigmatic, poetry-like lines of vs. 6, through transitional verse 7, of mixed style, into the long prose line of vs. 8.

C (vss. 9–14): the second clarification and complement of the parable, formally marked by *laken*, the messenger formula, and the closing "declares Lord YHWH." The repeated "Woe to the bloody city" evokes vs. 6a and the figure of the city as a filthy pot. God declares he will pick up where the cook left off (end of vs. 5), but, in a travesty of a cook's work, he will burn up the contents of the pot in order to cleanse it of its filth (vss. 9–11). Vs. 12 (so far as we can tell) reflects on the intractability of the filth, leading to the apostrophe that follows. To this point, C's style is that of A.

In a nonmetaphoric prose summary (vss. 13–14) God apostrophizes the city: all efforts at cleansing you having failed, nothing is left but to vent my fury upon you ruthlessly.

The complex oracle is unified by pervasive thematic and linguistic features — first of all by its figures: the pot standing for the city, the cuts of meat for the inhabitants, the burning pyre for its punishment, and filth for its guilt. It is mostly in poetic style, with prose exposition coming in rarely; short imperative and infinitive clauses predominate. Recurrent words and usages lend it coherence: *ʿeṣem* in its various meanings ("self," "bone," "limb") in vss. 2, 4, 5, 10; "in it/her/you(r midst)" in vss. 3, 5, 6, 11, 13; "fury" in vss. 8 and 13; the association of other objects with the pot through use of the possessive suffix "her" ("her cuts," vss. 4, 6; "her boilings," vs. 5; "her limbs," vs. 5; "her embers," vs. 11).

In this oracle, one of the last before the fall of Jerusalem, several themes of Ezekiel's pre-fall repertoire are inventively merged.

The start of the siege must have been decisive for the prophet's vindication. Previously his threats of doom had been effectively discounted; he could retort only by insisting that what God had spoken would come to pass sooner than later (12:21–28). Now finally anyone could see that "it is coming" (24:14); the fat was in the fire and the end was unavoidable. The command to record the day by the event that happened on it (whenever the command came) reflects the critical turn marked by the investment of the city. The prophet was to represent in a parable how henceforth events would march in uninterrupted escalation to disaster.

The gist of the oracle is the final apostrophe (vss. 13–14): having tried in vain to purge Jerusalem, God has now irrevocably committed himself to its destruction. Seeking a vivid figure with which to clothe itself, this message finds a point of departure in a saying coined by the Jerusalemite aristocracy, "She (= the city) is the pot and we are the flesh (in it)"; i.e., we are the valuable content for which the pot exists and which the pot protects (11:3; see Herrmann ad loc.). This static figure is activated by the prophet in a parabolic cooking scene. Rather than protecting its valuable contents, the pot now serves to prepare them for consumption. In the light of the subsequent clarifications (vss. 6–12), medievals (following

T) strove to identify every item of the ditty-parable with components of the siege event. Thus, for example, they identified the cook with Nebuchadnezzar; putting the pot on refers to the start of the siege; pouring in water refers to laying in stocks of provision; "her cuts," to the outlying population that fled into Jerusalem; "every good cut," to Judah's aristocracy; choice limbs, to the best fighters; and so forth. (Cf. T's particularized decoding of the allegory in 16:3–13, cited in I, 302.) Now, while it is true that there must be some correspondence between the cooking figure and the siege event, else it could not serve as a parable, not every element of a parable need have an external referent. Some elements may belong to the story and have no correspondence in reality (pouring in water would seem to be a story element, for example). A graver stricture on the rush to decode is its obscuring the purely retrospective nature of such decoding; no hearer of vss. 3–5 could suspect that anything sinister lurked in the ditty. Indeed some critics have conjectured, plausibly, that a culinary work song underlies it; if so, not even the general similarity between preparing meat and setting up a population for destruction (cf., e.g., Num 14:9, "they are our food!"), or between being cooked and being afflicted, would have immediately occurred to the audience. Hence the clarifications that follow.

Extraordinarily, two clarifications appear, each introducing elements that go beyond the ditty, thus establishing that it merely set the stage for events outside its scope.

The first clarification (section B) identifies the pot with "the bloody city" (cf. 22:2) and introduces the new concept of interior filth in the pot—immediately interpreted as bloodguilt (cf. 22:3–13). These appear to have attracted another component of the earlier pot figure of ch. 11—the prophet's rebuff of the Jerusalemites' boast in his asserting that the flesh in the pot are their slain victims, while they themselves will be flung out of it (11:9, 11). In our present passage the contrasted elements are transmuted: not flesh versus flesh but unyielding interior filth (bloodguilt) versus outcast cuts (Jerusalemites). In this first clarification, little use has been made of the cooking figure, nothing more than the pot and the cuts. Into the innocuous figure the disgusting element of the pot's filth has been injected, resuming and transforming older themes. By the end of this first clarification the referent of the parabolic pot has been established, as well as the motive for the punishment to be described in the next section. But the division between what is in the pot (filth) and what is ejected from it (cuts) disappears in the following account of the fate of the pot and its contents.

The second clarification (section C) repeats the identification of the pot with the bloody city, thus connecting directly with the cooking ditty (like section B). In wholly metaphoric terms it represents God as stepping into the cook's role and carrying through his work to a terrible conclusion. The metaphor needs no interpretation, since its pervasive imagery of burning and overheating is readily translated on the basis of everyday experience into destruction and purgation. In the course of the oracle this imagery grows in intensity. In the cooking ditty only the realistic and innocuous terms "boiling" and "cooking" occur. In the first clarification the phrase "to kindle fury," itself metaphoric, supplies the divine referent to the parabolic cooking scene. In the second clarification the cooking metaphor is resumed with a vengeance as God builds up the pyre, kindles, and cremates. The absence of reference to the firing of the pyre in the ditty underlines the emphasis laid on it in section C.

Vss. 11–12 in C take up the theme of the filth, so suddenly introduced in B. Capping the destruction of the stew is the melting down of the filth inside the pot—now resembling a crucible. For the image of vs. 11 recalls that of 22:17–22: Jerusalem a smelting pot into which base ore will be gathered and smelted away (expressed in both passages by *nittak* b^{e}*tok*- "[s]melt [away] inside of"). Vs. 11, with its reversion to the infinitive clause at its beginning, adroitly integrates the filth motif into the C section as a super-climax to vs. 10. But an indication that vs. 11 begins an addendum is the closure signaled in the preceding verse by the altered syntax of its final clause ($10b^{\beta}$—see comment to "till the bones be charred," vs. 10). That a similar syntactic change occurs in the final clause of the ditty ($5b^{\beta}$) speaks for an original connection of vss. 3–5 and 9–10; both share common terms and equally lack any allusion to filth. A more telling sign of the unoriginality of the filth motif is the difference in disposition of the flesh between vs. 6 and vs. 10: in vs. 6—the "home" section of the filth motif—the cuts are ejected from the pot on account of its internal filth, while in vs. 10—the continuation of the ditty—the flesh is boiled away.

A desire to concentrate previously scattered themes, and at the same time to produce something like the A, B, C (= AB) pattern lies behind the present shape of our oracle. The basic elements appear to have been the parabolic cooking song, ending with cooked limbs (vss. 3–5), and the metaphoric complement to it, ending with charred bones (vss. 9–10). A component explaining the motive for the destruction of the stew was lacking. For that, the pot image of ch. 11 in its context of bloodguilt was adapted, with bloodguilt transmuted into interior filth—which in turn suggested the ejection of the stew as a parallel to the expulsion of Jerusalem's aristocracy. Supplying the motivation for God's fury against the "pot," this section, B, now appears between the ditty and C.

The combination of interior filth and cooking evoked the crucible image of ch. 22 and served to enrich the oracle by a second climax (vs. 11) in which the pot's filthy residuum would go the way of the base ores in the crucible. C now included the themes of A and B. The apostrophe adds yet another count against the city, "depravity"—taken from chs. 16 and 23—and sums up prosaically the meaning of the figures: since all efforts at purging failed to rid the city of its impurity, only God's ruthless, unrelenting fury lay ahead. That was what the start of the siege portended.

Who was the author of the secondary elements of this oracle? The date in vs. 1 is plausibly ascribed to a glossator or an editor familiar with its source in the Book of Kings (see comment). The complex interweave and transformation of past themes, overlooking the resultant inconsistency of vss. 6 and 10, may be more readily assigned to a sovereign prophet-author than to a hypothetical disciple or traditionist who (we surmise) should have been too subservient to his master to have fabricated such a synthesis.

XXIV. Disaster That Constrains and Releases (24:15–27)

24 [15]The word of YHWH came to me: [16]Man, I am going to take away from you
your eyes' desire by a stroke, and you shall not lament, and not weep, nor shall
your tears come. [17]Groan a moaning for the dead, but into mourning you shall
not go: bind your turban on you, and put your sandals on your feet; you shall not
cover your mustache, and not eat the food of [other] men.
[18]I spoke to the people in the morning; my wife died in the evening, and in
the morning I did as I was commanded. [19]When the people said to me, "Do tell
us what these things mean for us, that you should be doing them," [20]I said to
them: The word of YHWH came to me: [21]Say to the house of Israel: thus said
Lord YHWH: I am going to desecrate my sanctuary, your pride of strength, your
eyes' desire and your soul's care, and your sons and daughters whom you left
behind shall fall by the sword. [22]Then you shall do as I have done: your mustache
you shall not cover, and you shall not eat the food of [other] men; [23]and with
your turbans on your heads and your sandals on your feet you shall not lament
and not weep, but you shall pine away in your iniquities and roar at one another.
[24]Ezekiel shall be your sign: just as he did so will you do; when it comes you
shall know that I am Lord YHWH.
[25]And you, man, see, at the time I take away from them their stronghold, their
joyful glory; their eyes' desire and their soul's yearning—their sons and their
daughters—[26]at that time a survivor will come to you to let hear of it. [27]At that
time your mouth will be opened, with the survivor, and you shall speak and be
dumb no longer. You shall be a sign for them, and they shall know that I am
YHWH.

COMMENT

24:16. *take away . . . your eyes' desire by a stroke.* "Eyes' desire" means what you love to gaze on—"the apple of your eye." As a general term it includes objects and persons (I Kings 20:6; cf. vss. 3, 5); in Lam 2:4 it means beloved humans, apparently youths. The prophet would know from the immediate sequel—the ban on mourning rites—that a beloved person was meant, but unless he was childless he could not know that it was his wife. "A stroke" renders *maggepa*, an ambiguous word derived from *ngp* "strike." It often means "plague"—an epidemic causing rapid death (e.g., in Pharaoh's Egypt, Exod 9:14; in the towns of

Philistia, I Sam 6:4); less often, the slaughter inflicted on a defeated army (I Sam 4:17; II Sam 17:9). Here, where only one person is to be carried off, a rapid death not preceded by sickness is intended (Kimḥi). Cf. Num 14:37, where the ten who maligned the land of Israel die *bammaggepa*, which S renders (as it does here) "by a sudden plague."

The language of vs. 16a recalls the threat of pillage sent by a victorious Aramean to the king of Israel: "All your eyes' desire [my men] will seize and take away" (I Kings 20:6), in whose light our passage serves to foreshadow the national reality to which the private misfortune of the prophet points.

lament . . . weep . . . tears. In this and the following verse the prophet is forbidden to perform the ceremonies by which a mourner expressed his misery and implicitly solicited the condolences of his community. Before burial one recited laments ("Ah, brother," "Ah, sister," and for a king, "Ah, lord," "Ah, his majesty," are mentioned in Jer 22:18) and (ritually, but no less feelingly for that) wept (Gen 23:2; II Sam 1:12). The pair of two-stress bans on lamenting and weeping (*lo tispod / w^{e}lo tibke*) are capped by a third ban of three stresses on even shedding a tear (*w^{e}lo tabo dim'ateka*)—a climax in which form and content meet. The third phrase is unique; its absence in G may be due to a *Vorlage* in which a scribe's eye jumped from *tbkh* to the end of the verse (*tb . . . k*), omitting the phrase altogether (DNF's suggestion).

17. *Groan a moaning for the dead* (dom metim). A problematic clause, as indicated by the accents, which disjoin *metim* "the dead" from what precedes and what follows it—a syntactic straddle. It has been traditionally construed with the following *'ebel* "mourning" as though it were possible to reverse the normal construct sequence **'ebel metim* "mourning for the dead" in this way (it is not). In the sequence *he'aneq dom* (disjunctive accent on *dom*), *dom* has traditionally been taken as an imperative (or infinitive) of *dmm* "be still," and the pair rendered "Groan silently" or the like—an oxymoron. Nahmanides (Spain, thirteenth century), in a treatise on death and its rites, connects *dom* to *metim* and assumes an ellipsis of a cognate accusative: *dom dim^{e}mat metim* "keep silent the silence customary for the dead" (Ch. Chavel, ed., *Kitve Rabbenu Moshe ben Naḥman* II [Jerusalem: Mosad Harav Kook, 1964], p. 176). Sh. Abramsky, in *Beth Mikra* 88 (1981), 15 (in Hebrew), renders the clause "Groan in deathly silence" (*bdmmt mwt*). The oxymoron remains.

Taking *dom* with *metim*, it is best to derive it from *dmm*^{2} "moan, murmur" (in Isa 23:2 || "wail" in vs. 1), in form a verbal noun (infinitive) related to *d^{e}mama* "murmur" (Job 4:16; I Kings 19:12) as **ron* "joyous shout" (plural *ronne-* in Ps 32:7) is to *r^{e}nana* (same meaning). Ugaritic *dmm* occurs in parallel to *bky* "weep (over the dead)" and Akkadian *damāmu* "moan, sigh, mourn," and related nouns occur in identical contexts (*CAD* D 60, 143, 144). A more usual Hebrew construction would have employed the cognate accusative **he'aneq 'enqat metim*, but *dom metim* "moaning for the dead" may have been a fixed expression that resisted adaptation.

By construing the first three words of vs. 17 thus, the semantic and grammatical difficulties disappear, the balance of the clauses in the verse is regularized (stress pattern: 3:3/3:3/3:4—a longer closing clause, as in vs. 16), and a parallel in the prophet's behavior to the "roaring" predicted of the people in vs. 25 is gained. The sense is: no mourning rites implying social solidarity and sympathy are to be performed (see Structure and Themes), only private, isolated groaning and moaning.

A discussion of our expression appears in B. Levine, "Silence, Sound, and the Phenomenology of Mourning in Biblical Israel," *JANES* 22 (1993), 89–106; see esp. 99–100. Levine's renderings ("Groan! But lament over the dead [and] mourning do not perform," or "Groan! Moan! But do not perform mourning over the dead") do not provide the rhythmic advantage or the syntactic normality of my proposal.

but into mourning you shall not go. The adversative nuance ("but") is conveyed by the initial position of the object (*'ebel*), lending it emphasis. "Mourning" means the conventional actions whose contraries are immediately to be described.

bind your turban on. "Turban" renders *pᵉ'er*, ornamental headgear worn by priests (Exod 39:28; Ezek 44:18), wealthy women (Isa 3:20), and bridegrooms (Isa 61:10, emending *ykhn* to **ykbn* "bind on" [Aramaic, Mishnaic Heb.], according to H. L. Ginsberg, orally), not worn during mourning.

sandals. A luxury those in grief denied themselves (II Sam 15:30).

cover your mustache. A sign of disgrace and self-abasement (Lev 13:45 [the leper]; Mic 3:7). Medievals combine this with David's covering his head in disgrace (II Sam 15:30; cf. Jer 14:3) as follows: one removes his headgear and wraps his head with cloth whose edges drop along his cheeks; he then fastens the edges above his upper lip (covering his mustache and beard — male "ornaments"). This custom may be alluded to in II Sam 19:5 as "veiling the face" (in mourning).

food of [*other*] *men.* "Other," with Menaḥem bar Shim'on, who takes this unique phrase, with T ("food of mourners") and other medievals, to allude to the custom that those who comfort mourners provide them with the first meal after burial (Rashi, Kimḥi). Jer 16:7 may reflect this custom: "They shall not break bread (read *lḥm* with some mss. and G) for a mourner (read *'abel*) to comfort him for the dead." Such, too, was the meal "all the people" came to feed David after Abner's funeral (II Sam 3:35). Moderns prefer to emend *'nšym* "men" to *'wnym* as in the unique phrase *leḥem 'onim* (Hos 9:4) "food of mourners" (most probably), "but if that were the original reading, why did the scribes turn it into the difficult *bread of men* [twice, here and in vs. 22]?" (Cooke).

These instructions, special to Ezekiel on this occasion, imply that in normal circumstances on the death of his wife he would have lamented and wept, and gone into mourning — by removing his turban and shoes, covering his mustache, and eating food prepared by others. These mourning customs were considered legitimate in Israel, as opposed to, e.g., self-wounding (Lev 19:27–28; Deut 14:1–2), "and from [our passage] it is inferable that ordinarily priests did not refrain from performing them . . . To be sure, after the death of his wife the priest Ezekiel did not behave in accord with these rules, but his behavior is interpreted as a symbolic act that puzzled the people, not as a normal priestly stricture" (M. Haran, *EM* 4.30b). E. Feldman, *Biblical and Post-Biblical Defilement and Mourning: Law as Theology* (New York: Yeshiva University Press, 1977), p. 103, wrongly regards the restrictions imposed on Ezekiel as applicable to any priest "because he is a priest" and must therefore be separated from all that involves death. If this were so, the puzzlement of the people at Ezekiel's behavior would be inexplicable. However, the question may be posed to both Haran and Feldman: is the behavioral norm of priests in active temple service (which is what both are defining) inferable from the behavior of the exiled Ezekiel? Perhaps an inactive—but only an inactive—priest, such as Ezekiel, could follow the ordinary lay customs of mourning (which is why Ezekiel's refraining from them was astonishing), but a priest in active service might have been forbidden to show any sign of mourning (as were the father and brothers of the slain Aaronides Nadab and Abihu, Lev 10:6).

18. *I spoke to the people in the morning.* Presumably, reporting to them the substance of vss. 16–17 (see Structure and Themes). That evening, the person called his "eyes' desire" proved to be his wife. The next morning (so S) he broke with conventions of mourning as he had been ordered to do.

19. *Do tell us.* Exemplifying the emphatic-affirmative sense of *hl(w)*ʾ, on which see H. A. Brongers, "Some Remarks on the Biblical Particle *hᵃlo*ʾ," *OTS* 21 (1981), 177–89 (on p. 187 he renders our instance and its mate in 37:18 as "please"); Michael L. Brown, "'Is It Not?' or 'Indeed!': *HL* in Northwest Semitic," *Maarav* 4 (1987), 201–19, with a valuable survey of earlier lexicographic recognition of this sense.

that you should be doing them. This *ki* clause does not qualify "these things" (as G S T render it: "these things that you are doing"), for such a clause would have been introduced by *ʾᵃšer.* For *ki* "that" expressing "consecution especially after a question," see BDB, p. 472, def. f., in which this verse is cited. On omission of the object ("them"), see GKC, §§ 117 f, and cf. 36:32 *ʾᵃni ʿośe* "I am doing this."

The people's question reflects their habituation to Ezekiel's histrionics: "these unconventional things you are doing must convey something of importance to us, otherwise you would not be doing them." Their expectation of being addressed is pointed to by MT *lanu* "for us," just before this clause; G and S, which misconstrue the clause, also omit "for us."

20. Here the prophet tells how he delivered the divinely authorized interpretation of his actions to the people, in contrast to his custom of relating only how he received the interpretation, as in 12:9 (see Structure and Themes). From this verse we learn that the revelation formula "the word of YHWH came to me" that regularly appears in the written record of Ezekiel's oracles occurred also in their (prior) oral delivery.

21. *desecrate my sanctuary.* By giving it into the hands of foreigners; see 7:24 and comment, I, 155.

your pride of strength. In Lev 26:19 the phrase is general—pride in power, vainglory; and so it is in Ezek 30:6, 18; 33:28. Here the reference is to the Temple, the source of vainglory, in whose impregnability, as the seat of YHWH, the people trusted. "They lean on YHWH, saying, 'Isn't YHWH in our midst? No misfortune will come upon us'" (Mic 3:11). A similar notion is ascribed to gentiles in Lam 4:12: "Kings of the earth and all the inhabitants of the world did not believe that foe and enemy would enter the gates of Jerusalem." In Ps 78:61 "strength" and "glory" refer specifically to the Ark, enshrined in the inner sanctum of the Temple, and called in Ps 132:8 "your mighty Ark."

your eyes' desire. In Isa 64:10 the people call the Temple "all our desirable things" (*mḥmdynw*).

your soul's care (mḥml npškm). *npš* "soul" here denotes the feeling, passionate faculty; *mḥml* denotes the object of care (*ḥml*). The verb *ḥml* "feel pity, concern for, care about, spare" often expresses the feeling God will banish when he punishes (5:11; 7:4, 9; 8:18, etc.); in 36:21 it denotes God's positive concern (for his reputation). The people's care for the Temple may be illustrated by the laments over its destruction, e.g., Lam 1:10; 2:1, 6–7; esp. 4:1, where the spilled "sacred stones" ambiguously refer to the demolished Temple or to precious youth (vs. 2). Since *ḥml* expresses also tender feelings toward children (Mal 3:17; Exod 2:6), this epithet—"your soul's care"—prepares the way for the following topic, "your sons and daughters."

Some have noted that in vs. 25 "soul's *maśśa*" stands in the position of "soul's *maḥmal*" in our verse; accordingly they invoke Arabic *ḥml* "carry," equivalent to Hebrew *nś*ʾ "carry" (from which *maśśa* is derived) to infer that *maḥmal* = *maśśa* and therefore both phrases are identical, "soul's yearning" (see comment at vs. 25). This is ingenious but unnecessary.

your sons . . . whom you left behind. From this it may be inferred that among the exiles were many elders and clan heads (Ehrlich).

22. *as I have done.* The prophet slips momentarily into the first person, as in 12:11, but without the signal of a change given there: see comment to "Say" (12:11), I, 212. By vs. 24 he has reverted to speaking in God's name.

23. *you shall pine away in your iniquities.* In its previous occurrence, 4:17, the expression refers to physical wasting under siege of a population steeped in sin; here to spiritual desolation as each languishes in his private sorrow.

roar at one another. In unrestrained, unmitigated grief. The verb *nhm* and its derivatives denote the roaring of lions (Prov 19:12; Isa 5:29, ‖ *š*ʾ*g*), of the ocean (Isa 5:30), of an attacking army (Isa 5:29–30), and the cries of grieving and remorseful persons (Ps 38:9; Prov 5:11). This inarticulate, unritualized expression of sorrow was foreshadowed by the prophet's groans and moans (vs. 17a). G (S) "you shall (be) console(d)," as though reading a form of *nḥm*, egregiously subverts the sense; see Structure and Themes.

24. *when it comes.* The predicted calamity, as in vs. 14.

25. *see.* For this sense of *h*ᵃ*lo*, see comment to 12:8 (error for 9 [I, 211]) and Brongers (cited above in comment to vs. 19), pp. 180f., 183f.

at the time. Lit. "on the day," in a future undefined as to its onset or extension, as in Deut 31:17–18 (Kimḥi; BDB, p. 400, def. h). This is required by the resumptive "on that day" in the next verse, on which see comment.

their stronghold. The form *ma*ʿ*uzzam* fuses features of the root ʿ*wz* "take refuge" (long *u*) and the root ʿ*zz* "be strong" (doubled *z*), which semantically are hard to distinguish (KB³). In Dan 11:31 the Temple is explicitly called "the stronghold"—perhaps in dependence on this passage. The word echoes "pride of strength (ʿ*uzz*-)" of vs. 21.

their joyful glory (mśwś tp'rtm). The glory they rejoice in—an epitome of the intense popular affection and reverence for the Temple. One may compare such expressions as, "In his temple are strength and glory" (*'z wtp'rt,* Ps 96:6); when the Temple was destroyed, God hurled to the ground "the glory of Israel" (Lam 2:1).

and their soul's yearning. Lit. "the lifting up (*maśśa,* from *nś'* 'lift up') of their soul" (objective genitive), based on the idiom *nś' npš 'l* "lift the soul to(ward)" = set one's heart on, crave. In Deut 24:15 the idiom expresses the hireling's urgent need of his wages; in Jer 22:27, the exiles' yearning to return home.

The objects of "I take away from them" glide from the Temple epithets—"their stronghold, their joyful glory"—through ambiguous epithets—"their eyes' desire and their soul's yearning" (see ahead)—to the specific "their sons and daughters." The ambiguity of the second pair is abetted by syntax. As indicated by the *atnaḥ,* the caesura falls after "their joyful glory" (Temple epithet). The list of objects of "I take away" is then resumed with the direct object sign *'t.* Lacking the copula, *'t* seems to introduce the pair, "their eyes' desire [in vs. 21 an epithet of the Temple] and their soul's yearning," as appositional to the foregoing Temple epithets. At the same time, however, the selfsame pair is drawn forward by "their sons and daughters" that follows it appositionally. "Eyes' desire," referring to a person in vs. 14 and to the Temple in vs. 21, thus serves in our verse in a double capacity, expressing the equivalence of the two.

S resolves the syntactic ambiguity of the verse—and impoverishes its meaning—by separating "their sons and daughters" from the preceding by attaching a copula to it ("and their sons, etc."). *NEB* falls in with S and fills it out: "I am taking their sons and daughters." As far as these translations are concerned, the artful deployment of epithets in this verse and throughout the oracle was in vain.

26. *at that time* (lit. "on that day") *a survivor* (hplyṭ) *will come to you.* As in Gen 14:13 *hplyṭ* is literally "one who escaped"; the article indicates "a certain one" there for the purpose (*BHSyn,* pp. 243f.). This cannot mean that coincident with the fall of the Temple and city a survivor would arrive in Tel Abib with news of it; in fact he arrived only months later (33:21). Rather "day" expresses a time of indefinite extension, as noted in the second comment to vs. 25.

to let hear of it. Lit. "to make hear (*lhšm'wt*) ears"; the infinitive with *wt* ending is aramaizing; GKC, § 54 k. Ancient and modern translators make the prophet the addressee of the survivor's message (e.g., NJPS: "to let you hear it with your own ears"), and some critics propose to emend the text accordingly (**lhšmy' 't 'znyk*); after all, the survivor is said to come to the prophet. Nevertheless, MT makes a point by its indeterminateness: the news the survivor bears is for the whole exilic community to hear. While the change in the prophet's career is the subject of these verses, the news—which the survivor will convey personally to the prophet—will effect the change precisely because word of it will be brought to the entire community; see comment to the next verse.

27. *with the survivor.* Best taken with T temporally: "with the coming of the survivor."

and be dumb no longer. You shall be a sign. "This terrible concurrence of events with [Ezekiel's] reiterated prophecies of doom vindicated him, gave him at once the credit he had lacked for seven years — gave him 'a claim to be heard,' 'an opening of the mouth.' And the restoration of the prophet to normal intercourse with his neighbors reflected and expressed[— was a "sign" of —]the great turn of God toward his people, now that they were broken by the punishment; for concurrent with Ezekiel's release from 'dumbness' is the second period of his prophecy — the predictions of Israel's restoration" (I, 121; see the argument there on pp. 120–21).

STRUCTURE AND THEMES

The oracle has two main parts:

A (vss. 15–24): the symbolic act of the prophet and what it portends for the people, beginning with a revelation formula (vs. 15) and the address "Man" (vs. 16a), and ending with the recognition formula ("you shall know . . . ," vs. 24).

B (vss. 25–27): the prediction of the prophet's release from dumbness, beginning with "And you, man," and ending with another recognition formula.

A, in turn, consists of two addresses:

A1 (vss. 16–17): God to the prophet, foretelling the death of his "eyes' desire" and forbidding him to go into mourning.

A2 (vss. 21–24): the prophet to the people, interpreting his actions as prefiguring what would take place among the exiles at the catastrophe.

The two addresses are linked by a narration of the external events between them (vss. 18–20), resulting in a structure similar to the account given in 12:3–16 of the symbolic act of exile. But here the time sequence is more complex.

The address to the prophet (A1) seems to have come at night, for it was in the — presumably following — morning that he relayed it to the people (vs. $18a^{\alpha}$). Our impression that the speech alluded to in vs. $18a^{\alpha}$ consisted of A1 derives from the presence in A2 of the key epithet "eyes' desire" repeated from A1 but with a new referent — Temple instead of wife. The point of using this vague epithet in A1 (instead of "your wife") was that it might serve as a link between A1 and A2, indicating that the Temple was as dear to the people as the wife of the prophet was to him. But if A1 were not spoken to the people, this point would have been lost. In the evening of the same day, the prophet's wife died (vs. $18a^{\beta}$); the next morning, when the prophet abstained, on divine orders, from ritual mourning, he was asked to explain his strange — hence portentous — behavior.

Quite unusual for Ezekiel is the framing of the people's query (vs. 19) as an external event, not, like 12:9 or 21:12, as a component of God's speech to the prophet. Of a piece is the framing of vs. 20, not as an account of the prophet's initial reception of God's message, but as an account of how the prophet delivered it. One is reminded of the speeches of Moses in the last triad of plagues in Exod 10:3–6; 11:4–8, in which he delivers messages of God that have not previously been mentioned in the text (in contrast with the previous pattern, as, e.g., 7:14–18, 26–29, in which messages are given to Moses whose delivery is not reported — the regular pattern in Ezekiel as well). As in the case of Moses in the story of the Ten Plagues, this externalization of the prophetic message — relating how it was delivered rather than its interior reception — is both a closural change of pace and a heightening. It lends a vividness to the confrontation of prophet and audience suitable to the climax of a series, in this case the series of Ezekiel's pre-fall prophecies.

A1 and A2 are parallel in construction:

verse		*verse*	
16a	I am going to take away from you your eyes' desire by a stroke	21	I am going to desecrate my sanctuary, your pride of strength, your eyes' desire, and your soul's care, and your sons and daughters . . . shall fall by the sword
16b–17	no lament, weeping, tears but groan, moan turban, sandals no cover of mustache no bread of men	22–24	no cover of mustache no bread of men turban, sandals no lament, weeping pine away, roaring

In the case of vss. 16a ‖ 21 the parallel is arranged in the same sequence in both verses in order to facilitate equating the different beloved things to be lost. In vss. 16b–17 ‖ 22–24, where the phraseology of the two series is nearly identical, their arrangement is roughly chiastic in order to avoid monotony.

B (vss. 25–27), unlike A, is a word to the prophet, not to the people. It harks back to A1 by its use of "take away from" (cf. vs. 16), and back to A2 by its string of epithets, so far an echo of vs. 21 as to cap the epithets with an express mention of "sons and daughters." Through B, the oracle as a whole exhibits something of the familiar pattern of A + B + AB (here A1 + A2 + A1, A2). B's salient structural feature is the threefold "at the/that time" marking the coincidence of three events: the fall of Jerusalem, the arrival of the news in the hearing of Ezekiel and the exiles, and the end of Ezekiel's dumbness. The interval between the event of the fall and its report among the exiles is overlooked in order to emphasize the inner connection of the three: when events would publicly corroborate Ezekiel's doom prophecy, the prophet's alienation from his environment would end. This, too, would be portentous.

Unique to the oracle are the prominence of epithets and their accumulation. "Eyes' desire" occurs in each of the three sections: what Ezekiel himself loves to gaze at in A1 proves to be his wife; in A2 the desire of the people's eyes is the Temple, but that bears two more epithets—the first, "pride of strength," is suitable to it alone, the last "soul's care" fits "sons and daughters" as well, though in A2 these are clearly distinguished from the Temple. In B four epithets appear: the first pair clearly alludes to the Temple (stronghold, joyful glory), while the second (eyes' desire, soul's yearning) is applicable at once to Temple and children. By the end of the oracle, then, Temple and children are represented as equal in the affections and concern of the exiles, and the pain of loss of both as comparable to the desolation entailed by the death of a beloved wife. Such expressive equivalences are the effect of the skillful employment of epithets, particularly the inclusive "eyes' desire," throughout the oracle. They were not lost on later readers:

> R. Yohanan (Palestine, mid 3rd c. C.E.) said: When a man's wife dies on him, it is as though he experienced the destruction of the Temple. The text says, "Man, I am going to take away your eyes' desire by a stroke"; it goes on to say, ". . . my wife died in the evening," and then, "I am going to desecrate my Temple . . . your eyes' desire." (*b. Sanhedrin* 22a)

Themes from Hosea and Jeremiah are combined here in a manner characteristic of Ezekiel. Hosea's metaphorization of his blighted marriage is the model for Ezekiel's making over a domestic calamity into a prophetic sign. Everything that happens to the prophet may be put to the service of his mission. Ezekiel experienced the death of his beloved wife, so close to the fall of Jerusalem, as a portent of the exiles' loss of their two funds of hope: the Temple and their children. In his response to his bereavement a Jeremianic motif came into play: Ezekiel the repressed widower is like Jeremiah, who at God's command may not marry or live in society (Jer 16:1–9). Both anticipate in their private desolation the disintegration of Judahite society.

Jeremiah portrayed the breakdown of solidarity, the disuse of rituals of consolation, that would occur in the face of the mass death in the siege and collapse of Jerusalem:

> Great and small alike shall die in this land. They shall not be buried; people shall not lament them . . . They shall not break bread (read: *leḥem*) for a mourner (read: *'abel*) to comfort him for a bereavement, nor offer one a cup of consolation for the loss of his father or mother. (Jer 16:6–7)

Like Jeremiah, Ezekiel is ordered to act out beforehand the inability to observe social norms that will result from universal bereavement. Rashi (at Ezek 24:22) paraphrases Ezekiel's message thus: "You shall not go into mourning for you shall have no comforters, inasmuch as not one of you but shall be a mourner; and when there are no comforters, there are no mourning rites." Those who survive in the exile will be able only to roar to each other in self-absorbed, in-turned grief.

The breakdown of mourning rites in the face of universal grief, mentioned only in Jeremiah and Ezekiel in the Hebrew Scriptures, is vividly portrayed in a passage from the ancient Egyptian "Prophecy of Neferti" describing the collapse of the social order of the Old Kingdom:

> There is no one who weeps because of death; there is no one who spends the night fasting because of death; (but) a man's heart pursues himself alone. (Dishevelled) mourning is no (longer) carried out today, for the heart is completely *separated from* it. (*ANET*[3], p. 445b)

The extreme introversion of the grief-stricken is explicitly noted, throwing a direct light on the biblical passages.

The imminent disaster would validate Ezekiel's doom prophecy in the face of the enmity, or at best the skepticism, of his audience. Hence the ambivalence toward the disaster that suffuses vss. 25–27, the concluding word to the prophet. The temporal clause of vs. 25 seems almost to savor the losses to be suffered by the exiles, else why particularize them at such length? The function of the survivor to broadcast the news of Jerusalem's fall is underlined by the unusual phrase "to make ears hear"—without a specific object. Then, with the survivor's awful verification of all of his doom oracles, the prophet would be dramatically released from his "dumbness." The moment of Ezekiel's deepest alienation from his community (due to their contrasting estimations of the disaster) would mark the turn toward his identification with them. Inhibitions upon his intercourse with them entailed by their hostility would be removed at a stroke. Their calamity would be the start of his fortune—his and God's—as the people would eventually realize the redemptive significance of Jerusalem's fall.

This oracle complements the preceding one (24:1–14). As the previous oracle focused on the inexorable process of Jerusalem's destruction—the analogy of cooking a stew to the point of its evaporation—this one focuses on its immediate, momentary aftermath. If the start of the siege stimulated an anticipatory parabolic survey of its disastrous course, this preview of its aftermath must belong to a more advanced stage in the reduction of the city. Its occasion was the presentiment of sudden personal loss, made luminous and prophetic by application to the great issue agitating the exiles at Tel Abib. It is Ezekiel's final word of doom.

XXV. AGAINST FOUR BAD NEIGHBORS (25:1–17)

25 [1]The word of YHWH came to me: [2]Man, set your face toward the Ammonites
and prophesy against them, [3]and say to the Ammonites: Hear the word of Lord
YHWH! Thus said Lord YHWH:

Because you said "Aha!"
over my sanctuary, for it was desecrated,
and over the soil of Israel, for it has been desolated,
and over the house of Judah, for they have gone into exile,
[4]therefore I am giving you to the People of the East as a possession.
They shall place their encampments in you,
and set in you their dwellings;
It is they who shall eat your produce,
and they who shall drink your milk.
[5]I will turn Rabbah into a pasture for camels,
[the city of] the Ammonites into a resting-place for flocks;
and you shall know that I am YHWH.

[6]Indeed, thus said Lord YHWH: Because you clapped your hands and
stamped your feet and rejoiced with wholehearted contempt over the soil of Israel, [7]therefore, see, I am stretching my hand out against you and giving you up
to the nations for plunder.[a] I will cut you off from among the peoples and make
you perish from among the lands. I will destroy you, and you shall know that I
am YHWH.

[8]Thus said Lord YHWH: Because Moab [b]and Seir[b] said: "See, the house of
Judah is like any other nation," [9]therefore I am laying open Moab's flank, the
cities, [c]its cities,[c] at its extremity, desirable land—Beth Hayeshimoth, Baal-meon
and Kiryataim. [10]To the People of the East—together with the Ammonites—I
will give it as a possession, so that the Ammonites shall not be mentioned among
the nations. [11]And on Moab I will inflict punishment, and they shall know that I
am YHWH.

[12]Thus said Lord YHWH: Because Edom acted vindictively against the house
of Judah, and incurred guilt when they avenged themselves on them, [13]therefore

[a] So Q; K *lbg*; see comment.
[b–b] Not in G.
[c–c] Not in G.

thus said Lord YHWH: I will stretch my hand out against Edom and cut off man and beast in it. I will turn it into a ruin from Teman, and to Dedan they shall fall by the sword. [14]I will take my vengeance against Edom by means of my people Israel; they shall deal with Edom according to my anger and my fury. So they shall know my vengeance, declares Lord YHWH.

[15]Thus said Lord YHWH: Because the Philistines acted vengefully, and avenged themselves with wholehearted contempt, ruining, with hatred immemorial, [16]therefore thus said Lord YHWH: See, I am stretching my hand against the Philistines, and I will cut off the Cherethites and make the remnant by the seacoast perish. [17]I will work in them great acts of vengeance, with chastisements of fury, and they shall know that I am YHWH, when I take my vengeance on them.

COMMENT

2. *set your face.* See comment to 6:2 (I, 130).

3. *Because you* (second person feminine singular) *said.* In this first address to the Ammonites (vss. 2–5), beginning and end are in the masculine plural ("Hear," vs. 3; "you shall know," vs. 5), agreeing with *bny ʿmwn,* lit. "sons of Ammon." In vss. 3b–4 the feminine singular appears—a common way of referring to cities and nations (see, e.g., 32:19–29). The second address to the Ammonites (vss. 6–7) is couched entirely in the masculine singular (as, e.g., Egypt in Jer 46:14–15), perhaps agreeing with the nouns "people, nation" or with reference to the king as representing the nation.

"*Aha!*" Expressing malicious glee; G "capital!," T "joy!" See 6:11 and comment (I, 135).

over (ʾl = ʿl) *my sanctuary, for* (ky) *it was desecrated* (niḥal—perfect, like the two following verbs, with lengthened *a* in pause). Or: "over my sanctuary that (*ky* = *š*) was desecrated" (so S and some moderns); for the ambiguity of this construction here and in the following two clauses, see comment at 21:12 on "because of news that is coming." Here I prefer the alternative to my preference there because the *ky* clause here appears to be causal ("for/because . . .") rather than qualifying ("that/which . . .").

4. *People of the East* (bny qdm). Tent-dwelling nomads of the Syro-Arabian desert (as in Isa 11:14; Jer 49:28) whose incursions were a constant threat to the settled population on which they bordered (see, e.g., Judg 6:3). On the range of the term, see I. Ephʿal, *The Ancient Arabs* (Jerusalem: Magnes Press, 1982), pp. 9–10.

place. For this sense of the hapax, see *j. Shabbat* 13c: "A mason who emplaced (*yiššeb*) a stone at the head of a row"; its appropriateness is confirmed by the object of the verb; see next note.

encampments. The singular *ṭira* (alternating with *ṭur*) appears in 46:23 as "row of masonry"; since nomadic encampments are marked off by rows of stones, the word comes to refer to the encampment as well. "'Dîra,' the Beduin circuit, is heard also in some cases for their town settlement" (Ch. Doughty, *Travels in Arabia Deserta*, I [New York: Boni and Liveright, n.d.], p. 261). In Gen 25:16

ṭira stands in series with "unwalled villages" (*ḥaṣerim*); in Ps 69:26, in parallelism with "tents" (*ʾohalim*).

your produce (pryk). Cf. the curse of Deut 28:33: "The produce (*pry*) of your soil and all you toiled for shall be eaten by a people you knew not."

your milk. A regular food of nomadic herdsmen; cf. in the Egyptian "Tale of Sinuhe": the nomads supplied the hero with "milk in every (kind of) cooking" (*ANET*[3], p. 20).

5. [*the city of*] *the Ammonites.* The elements of the city name *rabbat b*ᵉ*ne ʿAmmon* (21:25) are divided between the two parallel versets, innovatively extending a device commonly used with appositional noun phrases to a construct noun phrase ("Rabbah of the Ammonites"). For the normal usage (as when "Balak, son of Zippor" is divided into, "Up Balak and listen; / Give ear to me, son of Zippor," Num 23:18), see E. Z. Melamed, "Break-Up of Stereotype Phrases . . . ," Scripta Hierosolymitana 8 (Jerusalem: Magnes Press, 1961), 115–53, esp. 122; our example is cited in the Hebrew version, *Sefer Segal* (Jerusalem: Israel Society of Biblical Research, 1965), p. 193.

6. *clapped your hands and stamped your feet.* Cf. 6:11, where the first verb is *hikka*, whereas here it is the aramaizing *maḥa* (so in Isa 55:12; Ps 98:8)—used perhaps to lend a foreign color to the address to the Ammonites. Elsewhere the object of "clap" is *kap* "(palm of) hand" (6:11; 21:19, 22; 22:13; II Kings 11:12); here only it is *yad* "hand," providing a counterpart to God's punishing "hand" in vs. 7.

The anomalous *a* as the first vowel of the infinitive *raqʿ*- (for normal *roqʿ*- or *riqʿ*-) arises from assimilation to the preceding *maḥʾ*-, where *a* is regular before a laryngeal.

wholehearted contempt. Lit. "all your contempt in soul." *š*ᵉ*ʾaṭ* "contempt" (36:5) is vocalized with long *a* on an Aramaic pattern (like *k*ᵉ*tab* "document"). With a pronominal suffix **š*ᵉ*ʾaṭ*- becomes *šaṭ*- as in an analogous case **m*ᵉ*ʾatayim* "two hundred" becomes *matayim* (GKC, § 23 c). The triconsonantal root *šʾṭ* is a by-form of the hollow root *šwṭ*, from which the vocalization of the participle *šaṭim*/-*ṭot* (16:57; 28:24, 26) derives. For a similar triconsonantalization of a hollow root, see *lʾṭ* "cover" from *lwṭ* (II Sam 19:5).

7. *see, I am stretching my hand out.* The double indication of the subject *hnNY ntyTY* (instead of the normal, unemphatic *hnny* or *hnh ʾny nwṭh*, or *hnh nṭyty*, 16:27; cf. 3:8) contrasts "I" to "you" with respect to "my hand" countering "your hand" (vs. 6). For this double indication of subject, see also Jer 44:26 (I swear, countering your vows) and Jer 23:39 (punning on *nśʾ*; cf. previous verse). Related to this is Ezek 34:11—a triple stress on "my" tending the sheep in contrast to "your" neglect of them.

giving you up to the nations for plunder. Adopting the Q *bz* with all the ancient versions and most moderns. The medieval attempt to justify K *bg* by a folk-etymological analysis of *patbag* (Dan 1:15, etc.) as though from *pat* "morsel" and *bg* "food" breaks down in the face of its true derivation from Old Persian *patibaga* "allocation." Perles's invocation of a Persian word with these consonants (*bg*) meaning "fief, domain" is far-fetched (cited by G. R. Driver, *Aramaic Documents of the Fifth Century* B.C., abr. and rev. ed. [Oxford: Clarendon Press, 1965],

p. 40 n. 1). Another g miswritten for *z* is *gh* in 47:13 (see comment there); both here and there g recurs in the following word. Variants of this expression recur: *natan labaz* "give up for plunder" in 7:21; 23:46; *hayᵉta labaz laggoyim* "be for plunder for the nations" in 26:5. On the pair *baz/la'ag* in 36:4, see comment there.

I will destroy you. An abrupt, unintegrated (one-word) clause, uncharacteristic of closures. S V lamely prefix a copula "and," which does little to improve the anomaly. One may conjecture that our text is conflate, a result of combining alternative sequels to "I will cut you off from among the peoples," namely,

(a) *wh'bdtyk mn h'rṣwt* "and I will make you perish from [among] the lands"
(b) *wmn h'rṣwt 'šmydk* "and from among the lands I will destroy you"

For the pattern of (a), see vs. 16; for that of (b), cf. the perfect consecutive–imperfect sequence in 23:49 (and Amos 2:3), and the pair *hšmyd/hkryt* in Isa 10:7.

8. *and Seir.* This runs against the pattern of the chapter, in which each nation is addressed separately; moreover, Seir and Edom are synonymous (Gen 32:4; 36:8–9; Ezek 35:15), and Edom is addressed in the following section (vss. 12–14). In G "and Seir" does not appear; how it came into being is a mystery.

like any other nation. On the implicit blasphemy, see Structure and Themes.

9. *I am laying open Moab's flank* (ketep-). An obscure expression. Eliezer of Beaugency notes that in 40:40–44 *katep* (lit. "shoulder") appears in *ketep haš-ša'ar* "the shoulder of the gate," denoting the wall flanking a gate on either side. With this he combines the metaphoric "The gates of your land have opened themselves to your enemy" (Nahum 3:13), according to which our passage will mean: I am opening an indirect approach to the heartland of Moab (presumably from the west; see next notes) by which the proper "gate" of Moab (presumably the more fortified eastern approaches) would be outflanked. Moderns (e.g., Smend, Herrmann, B-Y, KB³, NJPS) suppose that *ptḥ* (normally, "open") has here the sense of "lay bare, denude" (as in 21:33 "unsheathed [sword]"—suggestion of Ilana Goldberg), and, taking *ketep-* to refer to the high ridge of Moab as seen from Jerusalem (Cooke), interpret: I am making the highland of Moab open country. For *ktp* = the slope or sub-summit stages of a mountainside (Josh 15:10) and by extension "side," see E. Dhorme, *L'emploi métaphorique des noms de parties du corps en hébreu et en akkadien* (Paris: P. Geuthner, 1963), pp. 94f.

the cities, its cities, at its extremity. Taking initial *m-* prefixed to each noun as merely indicating position (GB, p. 433, def. lc), and defining the "flank" of Moab. G does not represent "its cities," which may well be a variant of "the cities" and hence the result of conflation. According to the view that *ptḥ* means "lay bare, denude," *m-* prefixed to "cities" is taken privatively: I will make the highland of Moab open country, without (= deprived of) cities.

According to the first view, *mqṣhw* "at its extremity" will refer to the generally western location of Moab's "flank"; according to the second view, it might mean "in its entire extent," as in Isa 56:11; Jer 51:31.

Ilana Goldberg observes that in Akkadian *naglabu pattua* "bare (lit. 'open') shoulder" is disgraceful in a woman courtier (*CAD* N/1 119), which raises the possibility that the following consonantal sequence *mhʿrym mʿryw* contains the roots *ʿrm*/*ʿry* "strip naked."

desirable land. Cf. the inverted order of the words in Dan 11:16, 41 *ʾereṣ haṣṣᵉbi* "land of desire" (= land of Israel; see Ezek 20:6 and comment, I, 364). Is the eulogistic epithet used owing to the Israelite claim on the territory delimited by the three towns that follow in apposition to it? (in Josh 13:17, 19, the three are accounted to the tribe of Reuben); or is it owing to the excellence of the location? On the richness of Transjordan and its periodic devastation by nomads, see G. A. Smith, *Historical Geography*, pp. 519ff. All three towns lie north of the Arnon River, recognized by Israel as Moab's northern boundary (Num 21:13; Judg 11:18), and in the west, near the Jordan Valley and the Dead Sea (their order is northwest to southeast). King Mesha asserted control of Kiryataim and Baal-meon (Mesha Inscription, lines 9–10, *ANET*³, p. 320), and by Ezekiel's time all three may be assumed to have been long since in Moab's possession.

10. *To the People of the East—together with the Ammonites.* Moab together with the Ammonites will be devastated by the nomads. "He reverted to the Ammonites in the oracle against Moab because the Ammonites afflicted Israel excessively . . . cf. Amos 1:13, 'because they split open the pregnant women of Gilead in order to enlarge their territory,' and Zeph 2:8, 'I hear the taunt (singular) of Moab, the revilings (plural) of the Ammonites' . . . Here too [the charge against the Ammonites consists of two counts]: 'Because you said, "Aha!"' and 'Because you clapped your hands.' Hence he doubled her doom [in the oracle devoted to her—vss. 5–6; 6–7], and repeated it in the Moab oracle, since Moab and Ammon were kindred (Gen 19:36–38) and their lands were adjacent to one another" (Kimḥi).

I will give. The prefixed *waw* is semantically redundant, marking off the verb clause, as in *wslḥt* of Ps 25:11 and *wnṣth* in II Kings 22:17; see S. R. Driver, *Tenses*, § 123 (γ). Alternatively, *wnttyh* may be construed as starting a new clause, understanding the preceding "to the People of the East, together with the Ammonites" as distant complements to "I am laying open Moab's flank." Thus: "I am laying open Moab's flank . . . (exposing it) to the People of the East, (it) together with the Ammonites; and I will give it (viz., Moab) as a possession (to them)." The alternative construction is somewhat strained, but its construal of *wnttyh* is more natural.

shall not be mentioned. The verb is feminine, as in vss. 3–5; perhaps the implied subject is Rabbah (of the Ammonites), explicitly supplied by S; cf. comment to vs. 5 above. Oblivion ("shall not be mentioned") frequently complements the punishment of "being cut off" (vs. 7), as in Jer 11:19; Zech 13:2; Ps 83:5. This is another connection of the Moab oracle with the oracle against the Ammonites.

Critics regard the complicating references to Ammonites in this verse as accretions that mar its original simplicity; see notes in *BHS*. This is a plausible conjecture, and for the motive of the accretions we need look no further than Kimḥi's comment cited three paragraphs above.

12. *acted vindictively.* The combination *ʿaśa b* + noun = "act" + adverb re-

curs in vs. 15 (*ʿaśa binᵉqama* "act vengefully"), and in 22:7; 23:25, 29. Here the noun phrase is replaced by an infinitive with cognate accusative (*binqom naqam*), for emphasis (Cooke). The infinitive phrase (with prefixed *l*) occurs in 24:8. S omits the virtually untranslatable infinitive.

when they avenged themselves. Lit. "and avenged themselves," specifying the foregoing "incurred guilt" (Zimmerli). The perfect appears instead of an imperfect consecutive, an indication that the avenging was not the consequence of incurring guilt, but its specification.

13. *from Teman, and to Dedan* (dᵉdane[h]). These two Edomite locations have not been certainly located; they are mentioned together again in Jer 49:7–8 (on Dedan, see further at 27:15, 20). The expression seems telescoped from: ". . . a ruin from Teman [to Dedan], and [from Teman] to Dedan they shall fall." Note the alliteration: *WNTTyh ḤRBh . . . WDDNh BḤRB*. The *-e(h)* locative ending, normally *a(h)*, recurs in *ʾane(h)*, I Kings 2:36, 42, and in *nobe(h)*, I Sam 21:2; 22:9.

15. *hatred immemorial.* Adverbial, without prefixed *b*; cf. *ṣdq*, Deut 1:16 = *bṣdq*, Ps 96:13, "justly"; *myšrym*, Ps 58:2 = *bmyšrym*, Ps 96:10, "equitably."

16. *cut off the Cherethites.* Probably the Cretans. The Philistines came from the Aegean; here and in Zeph 2:5 Philistines, Cherethites, and seacoast dwellers are synonymous. Cf. I Sam 30:14 where the "Cherethite south" is equivalent to "Philistine land" in vs. 16. The alliteration of *whKRTY ʾT KRTYm* is exploited by T: "I will annihilate those liable to be annihilated."

the remnant by the seacoast. "Remnant" (*šʾryt*) commonly refers to those surviving a calamity; so, of Judahites, in 5:10; 9:8; 11:13. In 36:3–5 the sense seems to be: nations outliving Judah, remaining after its collapse. Here a clue to the sense is Amos 1:8 (also a verdict against the Philistines): "I will cut off inhabitants from Ashdod . . . from Ashkelon . . . Ekron . . . and those left of (*šʾryt*) the Philistines shall perish"; the last clause refers to those surviving the visitations mentioned in the preceding clauses. Here "the remnant by the seacoast" should accordingly be understood as in sequence to "Cherethites," not as a synonym of it.

STRUCTURE AND THEMES

Four nations surrounding Judah are condemned for having exploited Judah's fall. The order in which they are treated (from the vantage point of Judah) is: east, the Ammonites (vss. 2–7); southeast, Moab (vss. 8–11); south, Edom (vss. 12–14); and west, Philistia (vss. 15–17) — that is, orienting, then turning to the right. After the revelation-event formula and a command to address the Ammonites, four oracles, each introduced by the message formula, appear. We miss a specific command to address the remaining three nations, a token of the relative perfunctoriness with which they are treated. The oracles follow the pattern: because (*yaʿan*) the nation in question committed a certain offense, therefore (*laken*) God will punish it in such and such a way. Characteristically, variations are introduced in the pattern at each repetition: The Ammonites are addressed directly, the three others are spoken of, not to (in line with the absence of an order to address them). The Ammonites and Moab are indicted for insulting speech and gesture, while the other two are indicted for vengeful acts. God's punishment of the Transjordanian nations, Ammon and Moab, will be mediated through invasion by the nomads of the east; his punishment of Edom, through the agency of Israel; that of Philistia is unmediated. Cutting athwart the pairing of Ammonites and Moab, Edom and Philistia (the halving pattern), is the resumption of vs. 7's formula "I will stretch my hand out . . . and cut off . . . and make perish" partly in vs. 13 and wholly in vs. 16—but altered with each repetition. The impression is of a highly structured, well-knit piece.

Specificity and color diminish as the oracle unfolds. The Ammonites are condemned on two counts: insulting speech and gesture (the combination, whose performance by Ezekiel against the sinful house of Israel is commanded by God in 6:11, is here broken down in order to heighten the Ammonites' offense; see ahead). To each count a subsection introduced by the message formula is devoted (vss. 3–5; 6–7). Each contains a distinct verdict: for the first count, devastation by nomads, for the second, delivery into the power of "the nations" for spoliation (the two verdicts are not essentially in conflict). The first subsection (vss. 3–5) is colorful and poetic; the second (vss. 6–7), prosaic and formulaic.

Moab is indicted on the single count of insulting speech, but its punishment is particularized by reference to the towns that will be taken over by nomadic marauders. (Listing of Moabite towns occurs even more elaborately in the oracles against Moab in Isa 15–16 and Jer 48.) Neither the offense nor the punishment of Edom is particularized; we hear only of its vague "vengeance"—which God will requite with his vengeance (measure for measure), through the agency of Israel (a unique delegation). The case of the Philistines is again vengeance for vengeance with no identifying features, and expressed in general formulas. It is as though after an initial burst, the prophet's creativity waned.

These four nations had at some time or other either lost territory to Israel or borne its yoke. Although these issues are veiled here, they alone can account for the animosity toward Israel denounced in this oracle.

Ammon and Moab bordered on the Transjordanian holdings of Israel on the east and on the south respectively. According to the Deuteronomist (Deut 2:9, 19), the Israelites on their way to Canaan scrupulously respected the inviolability of the lands of these "sons of Lot" (cf. Gen 19:36–38); but the very emphasis put on this betrays a live issue. For Israel, Moab's northern border was the Arnon River (Deut 2:24); north of the river (all Gilead to Mount Hermon) lay the former kingdoms of Sihon and Og, Amorites whose land Israel took in a just war. To be sure, Moab formerly possessed (part of) Sihon's territory north of the Arnon (Num 21:26), but Sihon's subsequent capture of it "laundered" it of Moab's claim; in Israel's view, its conquest of Sihon's land gave it clear title. Towns north of the Arnon are listed in Josh 13:15–20 as the tribal domain of Reuben.

Regarding the Ammonites, the biblical record is inconsistent: while the Deuteronomist insists (2:19) that Israel did not encroach on Ammonite land, according to Josh 13:25, "half the land of the Ammonites" was allotted to the tribe of Gad.

These "sons of Lot" maintained their claims on the tribal allotment of Reuben and Gad through the centuries. In the time of the Judges, Jephthah the Gileadite fought the Ammonite king (who appears to have represented his Moabite "brother" as well) over the disputed ground (Judg 11). King Mesha of Moab boasts of retaking towns north of the Arnon and evicting Gadites (ninth century B.C.E.; *ANET*[3], p. 320). Amos (1:13) denounces Ammonite atrocities in Gilead, committed in the course of "expanding their territory"; evidently the Lotides exploited Israel's weakness during its century of warfare with the Arameans. Most of the identifiable towns of Moab mentioned in the prophecy of its fall in Isa 15:1–16:9 are north of the Arnon. Zephaniah (seventh century) condemns Moab and Ammon for "reviling my people" and "gloating" over their territory (2:8)—the historical reference is obscure, but the witness to continuing conflict is clear. Jer 49:1 speaks of Ammonite occupation of Gad—likewise an unclear reference, but another clear attestation of conflict.

After defeating Egypt at Carchemish (605; see I, 12), Nebuchadnezzar took possession of Syria-Palestine, and we may suppose that the Transjordanian kingdoms submitted to him, too. But their policy vacillated: they sent troops, as loyal vassals, to quell Jehoiakim's rebellion against the Babylonian (II Kings 24:2), but took part in the anti-Babylonian conclave in Jerusalem called by Zedekiah (see I, 10, 13). Only Ammon actually rebelled alongside Judah (to judge from Ezek 21:25), though it gave no help to Jerusalem, if we can credit Lam 1:2: "All her companions played false to her, / They became her enemies." After the fall, Judahite refugees were accepted by Moab, Ammon, and Edom (Jer 40:11), and, on the principle that "My enemy's enemy is my friend," King Baalis of Ammon supported the assassination of the Babylonian-appointed Jewish governor of Judah (Jer 41). Whatever hopes the two nations had of establishing their independence in their former wide borders now that Judah was gone must have been dashed in 582/1 when Nebuchadnezzar campaigned against Coele-Syria and Moab and Ammon (I, 13). From this blow the two countries never recovered, as we know from archaeological indications (I. Eph'al, *The Ancient Arabs*, pp. 176ff.).

With Edom, to the south of Judah, the Israelites were in conflict from the beginning of the monarchy. Conquered and massacred by David, the Edomites broke free during the reign of Solomon (I Kings 11:14–22). From Ahaz's time onward the Edomites prevailed in the seesaw struggle whose prize was access to the Red Sea port of Elath and control of caravan routes from Arabia (II Kings 16:6). Although Edom conspired with Zedekiah to overthrow the Babylonian rule, when the revolt came, at first it held aloof, but, if the biblical evidence may be trusted, it took part in the spoliation of the defeated (Obad 1:12–15). Several biblical passages express outrage at this treachery—as it appeared to the Judahites (Ps 137:7; Lam 4:21).

J. R. Bartlett has argued that the portrait of Edomite treachery drawn by prophetic and poetic texts is much exaggerated; see, e.g., his *Edom and the Edomites*, JSOTSup 77 (1989), 150ff. His detailed assessment of the biblical diatribes, largely discounting them, appears in his "Edom and the Fall of Jerusalem, 587 B.C.," *PEQ* 114 (1982), 13–24. On the other hand, Bert Dicou, *Edom, Israel's Brother and Antagonist: The Role of Edom in Biblical Prophecy and Story*, JSOTSup 169 (1994), 174ff., 182ff., admits some historical basis to the biblical accusations of Edomite hostility and land-grabbing at the time of the collapse of Judah. The end of the Edomite kingdom may have resulted from the campaign of Nabonidus in the west in the mid-sixth century (see Bartlett; article "Edom" in *ABD* II, p. 293).

On the centuries-long conflict between the Philistines and the Israelites, see comment at 16:26–29 (I, 282). After the battle of Carchemish, Nebuchadnezzar deported the rulers and people of Gaza, Ashdod, and Ashkelon, who presumably had been allies of the defeated Egyptians. The Philistines did not participate in the anti-Babylonian conclave of Zedekiah. What unsettled accounts existed between Philistia and Judah in Ezekiel's time are not known.

Remarkably, no reference to the standing territorial disputes between Israel and these neighbors appears here (although in the oracle against Mount Seir [= Edom] in 35:1–15 it does—in line with the context of territorial restitution). Instead the nations' mocking and victimizing Israel is presented as in some way an injury to God. The punishment to be inflicted on Edom and Philistia is expressly called "my (= God's) vengeance"—a more direct involvement of God than the graded language of Num 31:2–3, in which the campaign against Midian is motivated in God's speech by "the Israelites' vengeance" and only in Moses' transmittal of that speech is it called "YHWH's vengeance against Midian." The offenses committed are all against Israel, but their implications are blasphemous. The Ammonites gloat over the profanation of "my Temple" and the disaster that befell God's special possessions—the land and the people of Israel. Now, gloating over a fallen enemy is condemned in ancient literature as an offense to, or in the sight of, the deity:

> When your enemy falls, do not rejoice;
> When he stumbles, let your heart not exult;
> Lest, when YHWH sees it, it will displease him,
> And he withdraw his anger from him. (Prov 24:17–18)

The implication is: he will withdraw his anger from your enemy and direct it at you.

> Who mocks a pauper reviles his Maker;
> Who rejoices at [another's] misfortune will not be held innocent. (Prov 17:5)

> Do not disdain one embittered [by misfortune];
> Remember, there is One who lifts up and brings low. (Ben Sira 7:12)

> Do not tease a man who is in the hand of the god [i.e., mad or ill] . . .
> For man is clay and straw,
> And the god is his builder.
> He is tearing down and building up every day. (Wisdom of Amenemopet, ch. 25; *ANET*^{3}, p. 424)

The teaching is: misfortune is a divine decree and ought to put the fear of God into one who witnesses it. As an occasion for derision it is an insult to God's grave and serious (if not always transparent) purpose, of which it is a manifestation. Rightly perceived, misfortune enhances God's authority. He alone is entitled to gloat—or to order his prophet to gloat—over Israel's fall, 6:11 (cf. Deut 28:63).

Moab's offense is to deny Israel's incomparability. The gist of the offense, as we gather from Deuteronomist(ic) writings, is to negate God's special grace and providence evident in Israel's fate, which is the ground of its incomparability. "What nation," asks the Deuteronomist, "[be it ever so] great, has gods so near to it as YHWH our God [is to us] whenever we call upon him" (4:7). Or again: "Did ever a people hear the voice of God . . . as you heard it . . . Did any god ever attempt to come and take for himself one nation from the midst of another nation . . ." (4:33–34). Or again: "Who is like your people, like Israel, unique on earth, whom God went and redeemed as a people for himself" (II Sam 7:23; I Chron 17:21). Moab infers from Israel's fall that Israel's destiny is no different from any other—by implication, that to be YHWH's people confers no special status. The saying ascribed here to Moab corresponds to the blasphemous saying of the emissary of the Assyrian king at the siege of Jerusalem:

> Did any of the gods of other nations save his land from the king of Assyria? Where were the gods of Hamath and Arpad? Where the gods of Sepharvaim, Hena and Ivvah? Did they save Samaria from me? Which of all the gods of those countries saved their countries from me, that YHWH should save Jerusalem from me? (II Kings 18:33–35)

By deflating Israel, Moab discredits Israel's God; that is the view of the prophet, in accord with a general biblical doctrine that the gentiles judge of the (im)potency of YHWH by the (mis)fortunes of Israel; see above, 20:8–9, 14, 22, and comments. God will punish both the Ammonites and Moab for insulting his authority, "that they may know that I am Lord YHWH."

Highlighting the motive of divine self-interest is the nature of the punishment: no material advantage to Israel results from it. Moab and the Ammonites will be devastated and pillaged by the eastern nomads; their lands will become the possession of the nomads. The territorial dispute with Israel is no open claim that will be ultimately satisfied in Israel's favor.

Edom and Philistia are charged with a display of hate-filled vengeance (for wrongs presumably held against Israel); God will take his vengeance on them for it. The five occurrences of the root *nqm* in the three-verse oracle against Edom and the four occurrences (once in a noun-plural form; is that equivalent to twice?) in the three-verse oracle against Philistia make it clear that the basic motif here is "*nqm* for *nqm*." A concession to national feeling is the delegation of Israel to execute God's vengeance against Edom, reflecting the intensity of Israel's rage against its "brother" for having exploited its collapse to settle old scores. It is not clear whether the offense of these two nations consists in the very act of taking revenge—as though *nqm* were a prerogative of God alone (see G. E. Mendenhall, *The Tenth Generation* [Baltimore: Johns Hopkins University Press, 1973], pp. 69–104)—or in the exploitation of Jerusalem's fall, striking it when it was down. Cf. the characterization of Amalek's cowardly attack in the wilderness:

"how he surprised you on the way when you were famished and weary, and cut down all who straggled in your rear, not fearing God" (Deut 25:18). Again, the punishment of Edom and Philistia does not satisfy territorial aspirations or grievances Israel may have had regarding their lands.

These brief prophecies against the nations may profitably be compared to their analogues in Amos 1:1–2:3, consisting of denunciation of six foreign nations. In both series the oracles are brief and formulaic, but the order of the two series diverges widely. In Amos the offense of each nation is a specific violent breach of elemental humanity toward its neighbor (Moab's victim is not Israel), while, as we have observed, Ezekiel regards their offenses against Israel in the light of insults to God. In each book, then, the oracles against the nations embody a characteristic concern of the prophet: in Amos the primacy of morality; in Ezekiel the injured majesty of God. (On the contrast between the denunciation of the nations here and in the next five chapters, see J. B. Geyer, "Mythology and Culture in the Oracles against the Nations," *VT* 36 [1986], 129–45.)

Since the oracles of this series refer to the nations' reaction to the fall of Judah and the exile, they cannot precede that event (summer 586). A clue to the latest date by which they must have been composed is the prophecy that the Transjordanian kingdoms would be destroyed by the People of the East. In the event, it was Nebuchadnezzar's campaign of 582 that appears to have finished Moab and Ammon off; hence the prophecy must antedate 582.

Geography may have determined the location in the book of this series of oracles: starting from the east (of Jerusalem) and circling clockwise, the next nation after Philistia is Tyre — the subject of the immediately following prophecies.

XXVI. Tyre Wiped Out
(26:1–21)

26 [1]In the [a]eleventh year on the first of the month[a] the word of YHWH came to me: [2]O man, because Tyre said of Jerusalem,

Aha! "The doors of peoples" has been broken!
It has passed to me!
[b]I shall be filled;[b]
She has been ruined!

[3]Therefore thus said Lord YHWH: I am coming at you, Tyre! I will heave many nations against you as the sea heaves[c] its waves. [4]They shall destroy the walls of Tyre and tear down her towers. I will scour her rubble off her and leave her a glaring rock. [5]She shall be a spreading-place for nets amidst the sea, for I have spoken, declares Lord YHWH. She shall be spoil for the nations, [6]while her daughters that are in the country shall be slain by the sword; and they shall know that I am YHWH.

[7]Indeed thus said Lord YHWH: I am bringing against Tyre Nebuchadrezzar king of Babylon from the north, king of kings, with horse and chariot and horsemen, and an assemblage of a great army. [8]Your daughters in the country he will slay by the sword. He will set a siege-wall against you and throw a ramp up against you and erect shields against you. [9]The storm of his battle he will direct at your walls, and your towers he will tear down with his swords.

[10]From the multitude of his horses their dust will cover you; from the sounds of [d]horseman and wheel and chariot[d] your walls will quake, when he enters through your gates, the entering of a breached city. [11]With the hoofs of his horses he will trample all your streets; your people he will slay with the sword and your mighty stelae [e]will descend[e] to the ground. [12]They[f] will plunder your wealth and make spoil of your merchandise and tear down your walls and demolish your lovely houses. Your stones, timber and rubble they will throw into the water.[g] [13]I[h]

[a–a] G Alexandrinus "twelfth year, [day] one of the first month."
[b–b] G T "the full one" (as from *hmlʾh* instead of MT *ʾmlʾh*).
[c] G S T "rises" (as from *kʿlwt* for MT *khʿlwt*) + G "to," S "in," T "in the agitation of."
[d–d] G S "his horsemen and the wheels of his chariots" (*BHS* retroverts: *pršyw wglgly rkbw*).
[e–e] G S T "he will bring down" (as from *ywr(y)d*).
[f] G renders all verbs in this verse in the singular.
[g] G S and some T texts "sea" (as from *hym*).
[h] G "He."

will put an end to the noise of your songs, and the sound of your lyres shall be heard no more. [14]I will leave you a glaring rock; a spreading-place for nets she shall be, never to be rebuilt, for I YHWH have spoken, declares Lord YHWH.

[15]Thus said Lord YHWH to Tyre: Surely at the sound of your downfall, when the mortally wounded groan, when the slain are slain in your midst, the coastlands will quake. [16]All the sea chiefs will descend from their thrones. They will remove their robes and take off their variegated garments. They will clothe themselves in tatters, sit on the ground and tremble every minute, appalled at you.

[17]They will utter a lament over you, and say to you:
How have you [i]perished,
  who were inhabited[i] from [j]the seas,[j]
  city that was celebrated;
that was strongest in the sea,
  she with her inhabitants;
who inspired dread of them,
  every one of her inhabitants.
[18]Now the coastlands tremble
  [on] the day of your downfall.
Horrified are the coastlands that are on the sea
  by your departure.

[19]Indeed thus said Lord YHWH: When I make you a ruined city, like cities without inhabitants, heaving Tehom against you so that the deep sea covers you, [20]I will make you descend, [to be] with those descended into the Pit, to an ancient people; and make you inhabit the nether regions, like ancient ruins, [to be] with those descended into the Pit, so that you not be inhabited. [k]I will make "glory[k] in the land of the living"—[21]a horror will I make of you, and you shall vanish; you shall be sought and never found again, declares Lord YHWH.

COMMENT

26:1 *In the eleventh year.* Of Jehoiachin's exile, spring 587 to spring 586; MT lacks a month. G Alexandrinus reads "the twelfth year, [day] one of the first month"—i.e., 1 Nisan (March/April) 586—a variant independent of MT. Some critics prefer "twelfth," among other reasons because *ʿšth ʿśrh* is not the term for "eleven" in 30:20 and 31:1 (where *ʾḥt ʿśrh* appears); but note that both terms occur in close sequence in II Kings 24:18 and 25:2 (= Jer 52:1, 5). Since Jerusalem fell only in the summer of 586, both the defective MT and G Alexandrinus date this response to Tyre's gloating over Jerusalem's misfortune (vs. 2) before that city's fall. Wevers applies the date formula to the prediction of the fall in vss. 7–14, to which (he avers) vss. 2–6 were later added. Other critics leave the sequence of the text intact, and, taking into account the fact that (according to 33:21) news of Jerusalem's fall did not reach the prophet until the tenth month

[i–i]G "been banished" (as from *nišbat(t)*; *ʾbdt* is not represented).
[j–j]Rashi adduces a variant, "of old" (*mymym* as plural of *yom*); G "the sea" (singular).
[k–k]G "nor stand."

(winter) of the twelfth year (January 585), they emend the date formula to "twelfth year twelfth month." However, by early spring of 586, after more than two years of siege, Jerusalem's fall and ruin might well have seemed a foregone conclusion to any but its most fanatical defenders.

2. *Aha!* See comment to 25:3.

"The doors of peoples" has been broken! While the feminine singular verb may occur with a plural subject (GKC, § 145 k; see vs. 11 below [*trd*] and Isa 34:13; Jer 4:14; 12:4; 51:29), here the subject, a noun phrase, looks like an epithet of Jerusalem, as "trader for peoples to many islands" (27:3) is of Tyre. As such it is the feminine singular subject of the verb. Kimḥi took the epithet to signify an emporium, "where traders from all peoples came and went with their merchandise." In recounting the exports of Judah to Tyre in 27:17 Ezekiel mentions "wheat from Minnith," east of the Jordan, showing that Jerusalem imported wheat not only for her own use but to sell it again to the Phoenicians, thus indicating that it was a center of exchange (G. A. Smith, *Jerusalem*, I [1907; reprint, Jerusalem: Ariel, n.d.], p. 316). In the reigns of the Judahite kings of the mid-eighth to the seventh centuries an upsurge in the population of Jerusalem and its economic vitality occurred that might account for the prophet's conception of the city as a trade center (see M. Broshi, "The Expansion of Jerusalem in the Reigns of Hezekiah and Manasseh," *IEJ* 24 (1974), 21–26; N. Avigad, *Discovering Jerusalem* [Nashville: Th. Nelson, 1983], pp. 45–60). M. Elat collects the data on commerce during the monarchy in A. Malamat and I. Eph'al, eds., *The World History of the Jewish People*, V, *The Age of the Monarchies: Culture and Society* (Jerusalem: Massada, 1979), pp. 173–86. He cites Zeph 1:8–11 as an indication of the economic growth of Jerusalem in Manasseh's time (cf. his *Economic Relations in the Lands of the Bible* [in Hebrew] [Jerusalem: Bialik Institute, 1977], p. 224). "The people of Canaan" in Zeph 1:11 may well be Phoenician merchants who had markets in the city, as they did later in the time of Nehemiah (Neh 13:16). These attestations of commercial ties between Jerusalem and Tyre lend some color to the otherwise surprising representation of the cities as commercial rivals. But then Tyre may have regarded the elimination of any market in its vicinity as a gain for itself. (In the last analysis, we do not know whether the citation is authentic or a rhetorical invention to ground the prophecy of doom.)

T brings out the rivalry through its identical translation of the epithets of the two cities; it renders "doors of peoples" here and "trader for peoples" in 27:3 by "the supplier of merchandise to peoples."

The above interprets "doors" as entranceway (as, e.g., in Prov 8:34; Song 8:9); however, it may also mean a barrier, as in Isa 45:2. Jerusalem intercepted traders that otherwise would have reached Tyre (Eliezer of Beaugency, Davidson).

It has passed (fem.) *to me!* "The same expression as 'their houses shall pass to others' in Jer 6:12, only there the houses themselves passed [= changed hands], whereas here what passed was [Jerusalem's] importance. Render, 'I will take over her position'" (Ehrlich [Hebrew]). Rashi and Kimḥi supply "merchandise" (*s*ᵉ*ḥora*) as the subject of the feminine verb. The expression is indeterminate and admits any notion of advantage accruing to Tyre from Jerusalem's fall.

I shall be filled; / She has been ruined! Like the foregoing, this pair of clauses (in Hebrew each consisting of a verb) contrasts the two cities in disjoined verbs that ring like whoops of joy. Rashi comments: "I shall be filled from the ruined city of Jerusalem"—a bold ellipsis, since what will fill Tyre is not the ruins of Jerusalem but the material consequences of her ruin. Apparently Rashi read the second word not as a hofʿal verb (*hoḥ°raba*) but as an adjective (*haḥareba*; cf. *BHS*). This reading at least maintains the contrast between the two cities, as the version of G and T does not ("The full one has been ruined"), sounding limp alongside MT.

On the anticipatory character of "She has been ruined," Kimḥi remarks: "Since [Jerusalem] was besieged, by the eleventh year of Zedekiah [properly, of Jehoiachin's exile] they knew she could not escape destruction, so they regarded her as ruined even before the fall." The first half of the eleventh year of Zedekiah coincided with the last half of the eleventh year of Jehoiachin's exile: Tishri (fall) to Adar (spring) 587/6.

3. *as the sea heaves its waves* (lglyw). As the sign of the direct object, *l* is common in Aramaic and not rare in later Biblical Hebrew (BDB, p. 511, def. 3; R. Polzin, *Late Biblical Hebrew: Toward an Historical Typology of Biblical Hebrew Prose*, Harvard Semitic Monographs 12 [Missoula: Scholars Press, 1976], 64–66; M. F. Rooker, *Biblical Hebrew in Transition*, pp. 97–99). The enemy is figured as a rampant sea oversweeping a country in Jer 51:42: "The sea has risen (*ʿala*) over Babylon; she has been covered by the mass of its waves." In Jer 46:7f. the advance of Egypt's army is likened to the surge (*ʿala*) of the Nile in flood. The presence of *ʿala* in these parallels favors the versional reading here of *kʿlwt* (qal for MT hifʿil); indeed Isa 8:7 shows precisely the sequence reflected here in the versions: *mʿlh–wʿlh* (Ilana Goldberg). In that case, *l* serves to divide the whole into its parts, as in 24:6 *lntḥyh* "cut by cut" (KB³, p. 484, def. 20), here: "(as the sea heaves [intransitive]) wave on wave." On the other hand, MT *khʿlwt* accords with the parallel hifʿil verb in the foregoing clause (*whʿlyty* "I will heave" [transitive]). These are irreducible variants, each of which has its rationale.

4. *walls, towers.* Tyre's city wall, like most in the iron age, had towers at set intervals; see the ninth-century depiction of Tyre in *ANEP*², #356, upper register, upper left corner.

I will scour her rubble. From the root *sḥh* "scour" is derived the noun *s^eḥi* "offscourings" in Lam 3:45. That *ʿapar* here means the rubble of demolished buildings comes out clearly in vs. 12.

glaring rock. A phrase characteristic of Ezekiel, only in 24:7f. and here (repeated in vs. 14).

5. *a spreading-place for nets.* G "a drying-place for seine-nets." In the vision of 47:10 the coast of the Dead Sea, destined to be desalinated, is called "a spreading-place (*mišṭoaḥ*) for nets" of fishermen "from Ein Gedi to Ein Eglaim." The picture is of an uninhabited coast, used only by fishermen to spread out their nets to dry (*šaṭaḥ*, to spread out in order to dry, in Num 11:32 [of meat]; II Sam 17:19 [of fresh grain]; "to cast a net" for hunting is *paraś*). After its destruction the site of Tyre will be so devastated only fishermen will use it (Wevers); not a trace of its former bustling commerce will be left.

6. *her daughters that are in the country.* Tyre's dependencies (see comment to 16:46) on the mainland (erroneously called "Old Tyre" by the Greeks). Luzzatto aptly compares the Venetians' speaking of Padua and its neighbors on the mainland as *in campagna* "in the country." "Slaying the daughters" is an ambiguous metaphor for destroying the dependent settlements and their inhabitants; T demetaphorizes: "he will slay the inhabitants of your villages," thus losing the allusion to the destruction of the sites as well. H. J. Van Dijk (*Ezekiel's Prophecy on Tyre*, Biblica et Orientalia 20 [Rome: Pontifical Biblical Institute, 1968], 12–14) proposes to take "daughters" as a nonfigurative reference to women, comparing the Ugaritic Keret epic, lines 111–14, which tell of women menials swept(?), or running in, from the open country before the attack of an enemy.

7. *Nebuchadrezzar.* Closer to the Babylonian original *Nabūkudur(ri)-uṣur* (note the spelling *nbwkdr'ṣr* in 29:18–19 and Jer 49:28) "Nabu, protect the eldest son!" than the commoner Nebuchadnezzar (*n* dissimilated from *r*). Only the form with *r* is used in Ezekiel. A Babylonian tablet does in fact attest to Nebuchadnezzar's presence at Tyre sometime during its siege (J. Katzenstein, *The History of Tyre* [Jerusalem: Schocken Institute, 1973], p. 332).

from the north. The direction from which the last stage of approach to Tyre would start: departing from Babylonia in the east, the route of march would skirt the Syro-Arabian desert in a northwesterly curve toward the Mediterranean, thence south to Tyre. To the Israelites, the north was the traditional origin of enemy invaders (see *IDB*, s.v. "North Country").

king of kings. An epithet of Assyrian kings (e.g., Assurbanipal, *ANET*^{3}, p. 297b) and Persian (e.g., Xerxes, *ANET*^{3}, p. 316b), but unattested outside the Bible for Neo-Babylonian. Nebuchadnezzar is so titled in Dan 2:37, from which Cooke surmises that here the epithet—somewhat awkwardly placed—is a late annotation. See S. M. Paul, "Hosea 8:8 *ms' mlk srym* and Ancient Near Eastern Royal Epithets," in J. Blau and Y. Avishur, eds., *Studies in the Bible and the Ancient Near East* (in honor of S. Loewenstamm) (Hebrew volume) (Jerusalem: Rubinstein, 1978), p. 312 n. 31.

The second half of the verse gathers phrases denoting a formidable army: "horse and chariot" (e.g., Deut 20:1; I Kings 20:1), "chariot and horsemen" (e.g., Exod 14:28; I Kings 10:26), "a great assemblage" (Ezek 38:4). That *parašim* here means "horsemen" and not "span-horses," as S. Mowinckel contends in *VT* 12 (1962), 290–94, appears from 23:6, 12, where the word is explained as "riders of horses."

an assemblage of a great army. Taking *(w)qhl w'm*, lit. "(and) an assemblage and an army," as equivalent to the construct pair *qhl 'mym* "an assemblage of armies (or: peoples)" in 23:24. S repeats the *b* preposition of the preceding items with these last two ("with an assemblage and with a numerous people"), and this may be the sense, since prepositions may be dropped in a series (König III, § 319 l). Alternatively, this last phrase may be a direct object of "bringing against Tyre," coordinate with Nebuchadnezzar, etc.

8. The conquest of the mainland dependencies precedes the siege of the mother city, a realistic touch (in contrast to the position of vs. 6). For the siege terminology, see 4:2 and comment. The description of the stages of the siege and

conquest of the city is the most detailed in the Bible and is based on the repeated experience of victims of Assyrian and Babylonian attack. Tyre never underwent the experience (for which reason the prophet had to amend his prophecy in 29:17ff.). "We must assume that the siege . . . was actually a blockade of the island from the mainland opposite . . . But the island was surrounded by strong and high walls . . . Thus Tyre defied the Babylonian army . . . the destruction of the city . . . prophesied by Ezekiel did not come to pass" (Katzenstein, *Tyre*, p. 331). The most a Mesopotamian attacker could do to Tyre is described thus in an inscription of Assurbanipal:

> I threw up [earthworks] against him. [To prevent the escape] of his people, I kept a strong guard (on the watch). On sea and the dry land I seized his roads, I prevented him from going (anywhere). I let little water and food, which would keep them alive, reach their mouths . . . I threw a mighty, unescapable cordon around them. (Luckenbill, *ARAB* II, § 847)

erect shields. See comment to "shield and buckler" at 23:24, and the Assyrian illustrations referred to there. Nothing like the Roman *testudo* (a cover of overlapping shields) is known in the Assyro-Babylonian military art (as supposed by Luzzatto; Smend; G. R. Driver, 1954 [= *NEB* "screen of shields"]), while body-length shields with backward-curved tops are prominently figured in all Assyrian siege scenes.

9. *The storm of his battle.* A guess based on Akkadian *meḫu* "storm" and *qablu* "battle" (though these do not occur together). The versions diverge widely, indicating no firm tradition of the sense: G "his spears before you" (taking *qbl-* as from a root meaning "be opposite, confront"); S "his spear points" (both G and S supply a parallel to "his swords" in the sequel); V "his rams" (cf. Kara: "what strikes [from Aramaic *mḥh* "strike"] that which confronts it"); T "the stroke of his projectiles" (whence other medievals: catapults).

with his swords. Daggers and swords were used in the attempt to breach walls alongside, and at times apart from, battering rams; see Yadin, *Warfare*, p. 316, and illustrations on pp. 420–21, 448, 462, of soldiers dislodging brickwork. There is no need to give *ḥereb* here the unattested sense of "axe" (Van Dijk, *NEB*, etc.).

10. *the multitude. šip'a*, derived from *šp'* "be abundant," combines also with "camels" (Isa 60:6) and "water" (Job 22:11), and stands alone as "troop" in II Kings 9:17—where G renders "dustcloud," as does Rashi, whence NJPS "from the cloud raised by his horses" (and in Isa 60:6, "dustcloud").

horseman and wheel and chariot. "Wheel" and "chariot" separated, as in 23:24. The second, short *a* of *paraš* (a construct form) is anomalous. G S smooth the text; it is not clear that they had a different *Vorlage* (e.g., *pršyw wglgly rkbw*, as *BHS*).

the entering of a breached city. "When he captures you he will enter through your gates as though there were no gates, doors or bars, only breaches and gaps [in the wall]" (Eliezer of Beaugency). For the form of *mᵉbo'e*, cf. *moṣa'e* "a setting-out" in 12:4 and comment. The prefixed *k* is *kaf veritatis* ("in the manner of"; Joüon-Muraoka, § 133 g).

11. *your mighty stelae* (mṣbwt ʿzk). The Baal temple built in Samaria for the Phoenician Jezebel had in it stelae, including a "Baal stela" (II Kings 10:26f.). Hence Tyre's "mighty stelae" may have been temple fixtures, symbols of the divine presence in which the Tyrians trusted for protection, as did the Israelites in their Ark (cf. "your mighty Ark," *ʾrwn ʿzk,* Ps 132:8) and Temple (cf. "your pride of strength," *gʾwn ʿzkm,* Ezek 24:21, an epithet of the Jerusalem sanctuary). Cf. the stelae in the inner sanctum of a thirteenth-century Canaanite temple at Hazor, *ANEP*², #871. On the interpretation of such stelae, see C. F. Graesser, "Standing Stones in Ancient Palestine," *BA* 35 (1972), 34–63, esp. 44ff.

Fohrer and Zimmerli see a connection with "two pillars, one of pure gold, the other emerald" that Herodotus (2.44) counts among the offerings adorning the Tyrian temple of Heracles (= Melkart); these in turn being related to the external pillars (*ʿammudim*) of the Solomonic temple (I Kings 7:21)—presumably modeled on a Tyrian prototype (cf. the two external pillars of the Tyre temple depicted on an Assyrian relief, Harden, *Phoenicians,* plate 50, and see R. D. Barnett, "Ezekiel and Tyre," *EI* 9 [1969] [*W. F. Albright Volume*], 6–7 [English section]). But this is doubtful in view of the difference in terms and location. On the possibility that *mṣbwt* is not a true plural, see next comment.

will descend to the ground. Singular verb with plural subject; see comment to "The doors of peoples," in vs. 2. Curiously, the stelae of the Tyrian Baal temple of Samaria are also treated as singular in II Kings 10:26: "They brought out the stelae (*mṣbwt*) of the Baal temple and burned it (*wyśrpwh*)" (noticed by Ilana Goldberg). The Phoenician context of both occurrences inclines one to view the *-wt* ending as reflecting the Phoenician feminine singular afformative, *-ot* (< **at*; see J. Friedrich and W. Röllig, *Phönizisch-Punische Grammatik,* Analecta Orientalia 46 [Rome: Pontifical Biblical Institute, 1970], § 228), the native pronunciation of the word having clung to the object it signified.

G S T reflect a variant reading, *ywr(y)d* "he will bring down," continuing the subject of the previous verb; probably an ancient leveling (cf. the versional leveling in the next verse).

12. *They.* Nebuchadnezzar's soldiers; the shifts in subject portray the action from different viewpoints. In G all the verbs of this verse are singular, continuing the person of the previous verb.

stones, timber and rubble (ʿapar). The debris of the demolition (*nataṣ*), the verb and the three objects as in the priestly regulation of Lev 14:45: "[the priest] shall demolish it [the "leprous" house], its stones, its timber, and all the earth-plaster (*ʿapar*) of the house." In our verse *ʿapar* is the crumbled earth plaster mingled with the stone and timber debris. With this picture cf. (1) Ben Hadad's boast that "the rubble (*ʿapar*) of Samaria [= its pulverized remains] will not suffice for handfuls [for my soldiers]" (I Kings 20:10), and (2) Hushai's fantasy: "And if he [David] withdraws into a city, all Israel will bring ropes to that city and drag it (T: + and its stones) to the wadi until not a pebble is left there" (II Sam 17:13). Ezekiel imagines the Babylonian army sweeping the debris of Tyre into water ("to render them unfit for reuse in building," Eliezer of Beaugency; but the expected word is not "water" *mym* but "the sea" *hym* as in some versions), till nothing is left but the bare "glaring rock" (vs. 4). "Throw" properly renders *śym* here (so G S), as it does in Gen 40:15, "they threw (*śmw*) me into the pit" (so G)—where it is equivalent to *wyšl[y]kw* "threw" of Gen 37:24.

The predicted destruction of Tyre resembles the account of Sidon's destruction in 677 by Esarhaddon: "Abdimilkutte, king of Sidon . . . threw off the yoke of the god Ashur, trusting the heaving sea (to protect him). As to Sidon, his fortress town, which lies in the midst of the sea, I leveled it as (if) an *abubu* -storm (had passed over it), its walls and foundations I tore out and threw (them) into the sea destroying (thus) its emplacement completely" (*ANET*³, p. 291). Did the prophet have a model to work with, or was there a common store of idioms to describe the fall of port cities?

13. Cooke rightly hears in the wording of this verse an echo of Amos 5:23 ("Take away from me the noise of your songs; / The music of your lutes I will not hear"). Tyre's gaiety is alluded to again in the epithet "Jubilant" (*ʿalliza*) in Isa 23:7.

In G the subject of the first verb continues to be "he" (see the preceding verses), but all versions agree with MT that in the next verse (14) God is the subject; they diverge from it only as to the location of the shift in subject. However, if the versional "he" from the end of vs. 11 through vs. 12 is secondary leveling (see comments to vss. 11, 12), then so must be G's "he" at the beginning of this verse.

14. See comments to vss. 4–5.

she shall be . . . never . . . rebuilt. An echo of and supplement to vs. 5a; hence I have translated *thyh* (and by implication *tbnh*) as third person (according to its context in vs. 5a), though the present context calls for second person verbs—as G S render them. Indeed these verbs might be construed as second person in the light of the occurrences in 22:4; 23:32 (see comments there), were it not for the interference of vs. 5a.

15. The prophet imagines the sounds of Tyre's fall and the groans of her dying carried far and wide to the "sea chiefs"—the rulers of coasts and islands with whom Tyre traded—and terrifying them. Similar expressions occur in other prophecies against foreign nations (27:28; 31:16; Jer 49:21) and evidently belong to the vocabulary of this genre.

when the slain are slain. The noun *hereg* is normally abstract (e.g., Est 9:5 ‖ *ʾobdan* "destruction"); here as the subject of the passive infinitive *behareg* (contracted from *bᵉhehareg*, GKC, § 51 l) it is used concretely, "slain ones." Cf. the concrete use of *ṭebaḥ* "slaughter" in Gen 43:16, "slaughter an animal (*ṭebaḥ*)," and in Prov 9:2, "she has slaughtered her animal (*ṭibḥah*)."

16. *descend from their thrones.* In the ancient Near East thrones were either high chairs with footstools (*ANEP*², ##332, 458, 463) or chairs set on platforms (##306, 518, 525); Solomon's throne had six steps leading to it (I Kings 10:19). Van Dijk adduces a parallel to our verse from a Ugaritic description of the god El's lament over Baal's death (uncertain words italicized):

Straightway Kindly El Benign
Descends from the throne,
Sits on the footstool;

From the footstool,
  And sits on the ground;
Pours dust of mourning on his head,
  Earth of mortification on his pate;
  And puts on *sackcloth and loincloth* (*ANET*^{3}, 139a)

variegated garments. See comment at 27:7.

clothe themselves in tatters. Normally, *ḥ^{a}radot* would be taken for the plural of *ḥ^{a}rada* "trembling" and has been so taken here, on the analogy of "clothe himself in appallment" (7:27); cf. BDB, p. 528, def. b for other abstractions figured as clothes. The plural is unusual in this figure, but may be taken to signify intensification (GKC, § 124 e), like *ballahot* "horror" in vs. 21. However, the appearance in the sequel of the verb *w^{e}ḥar^{e}du* "they shall tremble," with the same meaning, is infelicitous and spurs the search for an alternative meaning for the noun. The context suggests that it is a concrete contrast to "variegated garments," hence Malbim's explanation, "garments of trembling, namely, of sackcloth and ashes to show they are trembling (with anxiety)," and N. Lohfink's "mourning-clothes" ("Enthielten die im AT bezeugten Klageriten eine Phase des Schweigens," *VT* 12 [1962], 271 n. 3). B-Y defines our word "rags," combining it with *ḥarod* "ragged clothes" (*Semaḥot,* 9 end), a hapax in Rabbinic Hebrew whose conjectured cognate is Arabic *harada* "tear clothing." The sequence in our verse of *ḥ^{a}radot–ḥar^{e}du* would then be a wordplay with homonymous roots. Others simply emend the word to *qadrut* "darkness" (of mood, cf. Isa 50:3), for which Ezekiel's use of the verb *hiqdir* "darken" in a mourning context offers some support (31:15; 32:7f.).

every minute (lrg'ym). Repeatedly, at short intervals, as in Job 7:18, "every morning (*lbqrym*) ‖ every minute" and Isa 27:3, "every minute I water it [my vineyard]." G "(they shall tremble) at their (own) destruction" and T "because of their (own) calamity" derive our word from a questionable **rg'* "afflict, break, strike"—as do Rashi and Kara—evidently influenced by 32:10: "they shall tremble *lrg'ym* each for his own life" (G: "awaiting their own fall"). M. D. Goldman, cited approvingly by Van Dijk, renders our word "with tremor" (agreeably with S at 32:10, which translates *lrg'ym* freely "and they shall be agitated"); but this sense is inappropriate to the two other occurrences of our word, in Job 7:18 and Isa 27:3.

17. *who were inhabited from the seas* (nošebet miyyammim). I.e., Tyre became peopled and prosperous owing to (thanks to, on account of) the seas, which carried trade to her from their shores (Kimḥi); *m(n)* "of the remoter cause, the ultimate ground . . . ," BDB, p. 580, def. f; e.g., "On account of (*m-*) winter the sluggard does not plow" (Prov 20:4). By way of ironic contrast, "the ship Tyre" of the next oracle is *nišberet miyyammim* "broken by the seas" (note the assonance with our phrase)—she who was built up by the sea will be destroyed by the sea. "Seas" (*yammim*) is a real plural (the singular appears in 27:3), and while its use is mostly in poetry (as here), where its sense is not always distinctive, the few high prose occurrences (e.g., in accounts of creation, Gen 1:10; Neh 9:6) indicate that

plurality evokes the vastness and the variety of the world ocean. A quaint expression of this is the following Tannaitic comment on the plural "seas" in Gen 1:10: "But it is one sea, isn't it? Why, then 'seas'? For a fish caught at Acco tastes different from a fish caught at Tyre; and the one at Tyre from the one caught at *Aspamia* (Apamea? Spain?)" (*Genesis Rabbah* 5.8).

Rashi mentions a variant vocalization of the graph *mymym*, with the first *y* vocalized with qames and the *m* simple, i.e., the plural of *yom* "day." The expression is interpreted in the light of a more explicit phrase in Isaiah's Tyre prophecy: "Is this your jubilant one, since days of old, of yore" (*mime qedem qadmatah*) (Isa 23:7); accordingly here: "who was inhabited from olden times" (Luzzatto). There is no other support for this reading.

G does not represent "perished" and translates the graph that in MT appears as *nošebet* "were inhabited" as though it read *nišbat(t)* (passive of *hšbyt* "bring to an end"): "(How) have you been banished (from the seas)"—both words easily derived from a consonantal *Vorlage nšbt*. The acceptability of this reading is vouched for by, e.g., Isa 17:3: "Fortress(es) shall be banished from, *nišbat* . . . *me*-Ephraim)." The construction is the passive of the active expression in vs. 13 (*whšbty*), or more fully, e.g., in 30:13, "I will banish (put an end to) idols from Nof" (*whšbty* . . . *m*-). The relation of G's *Vorlage* to MT may be conjectured thus: Early on, two versions of the first clause of the lament were extant:

(a) *ʾyk nšbt mymym* "How have you been banished from the seas"
(b) *ʾyk ʾbdt mymym* "How have you perished from the seas"

Version (a) was in G's *Vorlage*. The antecedent of MT was a text that read as (b) in which *nšbt* was copied after *ʾbdt* as a conflate synonymous reading (see 3:15 and 6:8 and comments thereto; for an illuminating explication of the phenomenon, see S. Talmon, "Double Readings in the Massoretic Text," *Textus* 1 [1960], 144–84). Later, when the origin of the reading *ʾbdt nšbt* was no longer known, the second word was read *nošebet* for intelligibility—thus setting up reverberations between our verse and the following section (*nošabu*, vs. 19; *wᵉhošabtik*, *tešebi*, vs. 20) and the ironic contrast in 27:34a. If this conjectured text history is correct, we have here a prime example of literary value generated by misunderstanding.

that was celebrated. The verbal form with penultimate stress is perfect; the prefixed *ha* serves as a relative with the perfect as occasionally in late Biblical Hebrew (e.g., *hhšyb* "who brought home," Ezra 10:14). The versions translate as if it were a passive participle without preformative *m*-.

that was strongest in the sea. On the superlative pattern of *qṭn bgwym* "smallest of the nations" (Jer 49:15); *gbwr bbhmh* "bravest of animals" (Prov 30:30). The more splendid Tyre's past, the greater the impact made by her fall.

The next line ascribes to Tyre terrorization of her surroundings in the manner of all the nations consigned to the Pit in ch. 32; they all "inspired fear of them in (*b*-) the land of the living" (32:24–26, 32?). Tyre and her inhabitants inspire fear of themselves *lkl ywšbyh*—a difficult phrase. Abarbanel explained it "in all her (i.e., the sea's) inhabitants"; but *ym* is never feminine, nor is the preposition *l*- suited for this idiom, but rather *b*- (as above) or *'l*; cf. Gen 35:5; Deut 2:25; 11:25. The only available antecedent for "her" is Tyre, hence—with diffidence—I follow Zimmerli and construe *l* of *lkl* as introducing an explication of the preceding subject: "namely, each and every one of her (i.e., Tyre's) inhabitants" inspired fear of themselves. *lkl* functions similarly in 44:9, "(no foreigner) . . . namely, any (foreigner)"; Ezra 1:5, "namely, all those" (*BHSyn* 11.2.10h takes this *l*- as marking an apposition).

The stereotypical ascription of terrorization to Tyre must not be pressed; unlike the imperial dead of ch. 32, Tyre did not in fact wield political-military control over her trading partners. It was her primacy in commerce that "inspired terror"—which is a hyperbole for acknowledgment of that primacy.

18. *coastlands*. The first occurrence of this word in the verse shows an Aramaic plural ending *-in*, perhaps to avoid the succession of three *m* sounds (*'*yM ywM Mpltk*).

[*on*] *the day*. As expressly in 32:10 *bywm*; for the elision of the preposition *b*-, cf. Ps 56:4 *ywm 'yr'* "[on] the day (= when) I am afraid."

by your departure. Taking *ṣ't* as the infinitive of *yṣ'* and in the sense it has in *bṣ't hšnh* "at the end (lit. 'departing, exit') of the year" in Exod 23:16. Eliezer of Beaugency filled out the meaning as departure "from being a city." Van Dijk derives the infinitive from *nṣ'* "fall into ruins" (as in Jer 48:9), as *ś't* "carrying" is the infinitive of *nś'*. The balance is even between an unusual meaning of a common verb (*yṣ'*) and the regular meaning of an uncommon verb (*nṣ'*).

19. *cities without inhabitants*. And fallen into ruins.

heaving Tehom against you. Absence of a subject suffix on the infinitive (*bh'lwt*) is common; e.g., *bldt* "when she gave birth" (Gen 25:26); *bhpk* "when he overturned" (Gen 19:29); *kpgš* "at his encountering" (Jer 41:6). Tehom is the primeval sea, in allusions to creation said to have originally covered the earth (Gen 1:2; Ps 104:6). Here it is allowed (as it were) to reclaim a spot of land it was forced to relinquish (that, rather than the Flood, is evoked by Ezekiel's image here). Treated as a proper noun (Tehom never takes the article, and when direct object, as here, is nonetheless preceded by *'t*), and cognate with the name of the ancient Mesopotamian primordial ocean goddess Tiamat, Tehom is a biblical relic of ancient myth, like "the deep sea" (lit. "the many waters") with which it is synonymous; in Ezekiel both are reduced to geographical terms (see comment to "the deep sea" at 1:24).

The simile of vs. 3 has been transformed into a metaphor; the primeval sea is a figure of Nebuchadnezzar and his armies, not (as literal-minded medievals thought) to a subsequent tidal wave.

20. [*to be*] *with those descended into the Pit*. Like *npl*, *yrd* can be a stative as well as an active verb—respectively "be fallen, prostrate" as well as "fall"; "be low" as well as "descend." E.g., "cedars *napal*, are fallen . . . the forest *yarad*, is laid low" (Zech 11:2). Thus *yorᵉde bor* are not "those who descend" but "those who have (already) descended into the Pit" (the grave, the netherworld, see *IDB*, s.v. "Dead, Abode of the"), who have already died. The preceding *'t* is not a miswritten *'l* "to" or equivalent to it, but means "[to be] with" and is distin-

guished in similar contexts from *'l*; e.g., "to (*'l*) the netherworld, with (*'t*) those descended into the Pit," 32:18; and note well *yarᵉdu 'itto* "lie low with him" (Egypt's company with Pharaoh, in Sheol), 31:17. The emphasis on Tyre's joining the dead in the netherworld, achieved through repetition in this verse, resulted in inelegance.

an ancient people. The masses of dead from of old; called *mty 'wlm* "the immemorial dead" in Lam 3:6; Ps 143:3.

the nether regions ('rṣ tḥtywt [plural]). Lit. "the land of lowest places" (BDB); so again in 32:18, 24); in 31:14, 16, 18 *'rṣ tḥtyt* (singular) "the lowest land" (BDB). As the location of Egypt in the netherworld the terms interchange (31:18; 32:18), which speaks against distinguishing between them (as N. J. Tromp tries to do in *Primitive Conceptions of Death and the Nether World in the OT*, Biblica et Orientalia 21 [Rome: Pontifical Biblical Institute, 1969], 180–83). However, there do appear to be levels in the netherworld; see below, comments to 32:19, 23.

like (k-) *ancient ruins.* "Exact manuscripts have *k-*" (*Minhat Shay*), and this is reflected in G (*hos* "as"). Other witnesses have *b-* "in (ancient ruins)." Both readings seem to depict the netherworld as a scene of ruins, which the dead haunt—an otherwise unknown notion (cf. E. Jenni, "Das Wort *'ōlām* im AT," ZAW 64 [1952], 225; Tromp, *Primitive Conceptions*, pp. 72f.).

you not be inhabited. The qal of *yšb* has this meaning, e.g., in 29:11; Joel 4:20. Kimḥi adds "again" to his paraphrase of the verb, as in the next verse, a felt lack that Ehrlich's emendation, to be noted below, fills.

I will make "glory in the land of the living"—. A *casus pendens* picked up at the start of the next verse ("a horror will I make you"). "Glory (or: beauty; or: desire; see 7:20 and comment to 20:6 [I, 364]) in the land of the living" is interpreted by Moshe ben Sheshet as an epithet of Tyre (cf. her "beauty" and "splendor" in 27:3, 10), an ingenious effort to make sense of MT. G renders the graphs *wntty ṣby* ("I will make glory") as "nor stand up," with the Greek verb that translates *htyṣb* "stand" in Num 22:22. Evidently G's *Vorlage* read here *wttyṣby*, from which MT appears to have been corrupted. Based on this, Ehrlich goes on to revocalize the foregoing verb as *tašubi*, adverbial to the following verb, "so that you shall not stand / take your place, again in the land of the living." The impulse that misdirected a scribe into corrupting such a clear text may be analyzed in two parts: (a) the effect of repeated derivatives of the verb *yšb* in preceding verses on the perception of the graph *tšby*, and (b) the prevalence of the pattern *ntn* X *b'rṣ ḥyym* in 32:24, 25, 32, under whose influence an original *wttyṣby* was perceived as *wtty ṣby* and "corrected" to *wntty ṣby* (cf. *tth* in II Sam 22:41 = *ntth* in Ps 18:41).

21. *a horror.* Plural in Hebrew, of intensification or amplification (GKC, § 124 e); the root is *bhl* (vs. 18b) metathesized to *blh*.

STRUCTURE AND THEMES

The island fortress-port of Tyre, chief city of Phoenicia at this time, had no political ambitions on the mainland opposite it (where lay its "daughter" towns, such as Ushu, wrongly called by Greeks "Old Tyre"). It did aspire, though, to concentrate "world" trade in its hands (H. J. Katzenstein, *The History of Tyre* [Jerusalem: Schocken Institute, 1973], p. 329). Tyre sought to be on good terms with the Egyptian Pharaoh Hophra, who commanded a large navy, and at the same time to maintain correct relations with the great Asiatic land power, Babylon. But to strike a peaceful balance between the rivals was impossible. Tyre took part in the anti-Babylonian conclave in Jerusalem in 594 (I, 10, 13) but did not come to Jerusalem's aid when she revolted. Egypt's continuing concern to control the coastal land bridge to Asia may be seen in Hophra's repeated sallies against it by land and sea. Jer 37:5 recounts his campaign to Judah during the siege of Jerusalem, and Greek writers record a naval battle with the Tyrians and an attack on Sidon, about whose time and purpose scholars disagree (Katzenstein, pp. 318–19, 332; Freedy-Redford, p. 483; the Greek sources are Herodotus 2.161; Diodorus Siculus 1.68.1).

Nebuchadnezzar sought to secure his hold on Syria-Palestine by subjugating Egypt. To do this, he needed to control the coastal approach to Egypt, and perhaps even to possess a fleet and a base for it. Such considerations may be supposed to explain his starting a campaign in Phoenicia soon after Jerusalem's fall. First the mainland, including Sidon, must have fallen to him, to be followed by a thirteen-year siege of the island of Tyre (see Table of Dates, I, 10 n. 10). Nebuchadnezzar personally took part in the campaign at some point, as is attested by a cuneiform tablet consisting of a receipt for provisions "for the king and the soldiers who went with him against the land of Tyre" (Unger, *Babylon*, pp. 36–37; cited by Katzenstein, p. 332).

Nebuchadnezzar must have blockaded the city from the mainland (as Assyrian kings had done), and Tyre's trade must have been severely curtailed. In the end the two sides must have come to an agreement of sorts. King Ethbaal III was deposed, and in all probability is "the king of Tyre" who appears among other royal captives deported to Babylon in the "Court List of Nebuchadnezzar" (*ANET*[3], p. 308a). A Babylonian royal high commissioner was appointed over the town. But Tyre remained intact; it evidently was not even subjected to pillage (see Ezek 29:17ff.). "The war was, therefore, hard for both sides, and Tyre was the actual loser, but the destruction of the city itself, prophesied by Ezekiel, did not come to pass" (Katzenstein, p. 331).

Ezekiel's Tyre prophecies present the doom of the city from four perspectives: a pair of oracles about the city itself, the first realistic and the second allegorical; then a pair about her ruler, the first realistic, the second allegorical. Ch. 26 contains a realistic description of the destruction of the city by the Babylonians, and grounds it on Tyre's intention of supplanting Jerusalem, "being filled" from her ruin. Ch. 27 is an allegory of Tyre as a gorgeous ship filled with the world's merchandise that is (for that very reason) wrecked on the high seas. Ch. 28 comprises two oracles addressed to the ruler of Tyre, whose pride in his wealth has given him delusions of divinity.

The motives given for the other dooms indicate that the present condemnation of Tyre's boast of supplanting Jerusalem is not an outburst of patriotic petulance on Ezekiel's part, but an indictment of Tyre's soaring ambition to win hegemony over world trade. Her boundless self-exaltation, epitomized in her ruler's apotheosis, has trenched on God's prerogative and sealed her doom. Thus Ezekiel's concern over God's injured majesty, the central issue in his denunciations of Israel, retains its centrality in his oracles against Tyre.

The two dates given at the extremes of the Tyre prophecies—year eleven (26:1) and year twenty-seven (29:17) after the first oracle against Egypt—precede the start of the siege and extend some years after its unsuccessful end. Except for 29:17ff. the oracles either predict the attack of the Babylonians (26:11–14, 19–21; 28:7–10) or anticipatorily lament the destruction of Tyre or its ruler (26:15–18; 27; 28:11–19). Since Tyre was not in fact destroyed or pillaged, the latest oracle promises a consolation prize to Nebuchadnezzar for his futile effort—viz., the conquest of Egypt. But that prophecy, too, was destined for failure, though Ezekiel did not live to see it. The failure of all Ezekiel's prophecies against Tyre is the surest warrant for their authenticity: they have not been revised to harmonize with events. A summary of exploded conjectures denying the authenticity of these oracles is given in Guy Bunnens, *L'expansion phénicienne en Méditerranée* (Rome and Brussels: Institut Historique Belge de Rome, 1979), pp. 79–83.

There is no explicit handhold for dating any of the oracles during the siege. Y. Hoffman (*The Prophecies Against Foreign Nations in the Bible* [in Hebrew] [Tel Aviv: Tel Aviv University, 1977], pp. 137–43) surmises that the shift in the motive of God's rage at Tyre from her taking advantage of Jerusalem's ruin (26:2) to her inordinate pride (27–28) reflects the march of events from the agony of Jerusalem to the unbroken resistance of Tyre for many long years. Hoffman supposes that Ezekiel repeatedly took up the theme of Tyre out of anxiety lest the disparity between her fate and that of Jerusalem give rise to doubts about the sovereignty of YHWH. This reasonable hypothesis is undercut by the fact that the *hubris* motive first appears in an oracle that represents the attack on Tyre as still to come (28:7–10). Hence we are constrained to conclude that from the beginning the prophet associated Tyre's gloating over Jerusalem's ruin with her boundless self-exaltation.

The first oracle against Tyre extends from the revelation-event formula in 26:1 to the next one in 27:1, and has four clearly marked sections in which three themes are developed: A, the fall of the city; B, the shock of the sea chiefs and their lament; C, Tyre's descent into the netherworld. A is divided into a shorter and longer presentation, thus:

A1 (vss. 2–6): the cause and brief account of Tyre's fall. Beginning with the address, "Man," the section exhibits the indictment-punishment sequence familiar from the brief oracles of ch. 25 ("Because . . . therefore thus said Lord YHWH . . . I will make . . . and they shall know that I am YHWH"). Remarkably, there is no initial form of address to Tyre; indeed, apart from the fleeting second person speech in vs. 3, God speaks about Tyre in the third person, as in the continuation oracles of 25:8ff., 12ff., 15ff. The composition of A1 thus seems to bear the impress of the immediately preceding material of ch. 25 (for the chronological complication, see ahead).

A2 (vss. 7–14): Tyre attacked and destroyed. The section opens with the supplemental *ki* "Indeed" (see at 23:28) and ends with the closure, "for I YHWH have spoken, declares Lord YHWH." It describes all the stages of the attack on Tyre, from the mustering out of the army to the reduction of the city to "glaring rock," resuming the skeleton narrative of A1 and filling it out in sequential order:

(a) Nebuchadnezzar arrives with a huge army.
(b) The mainland dependencies are annihilated.
(c) Siegeworks are emplaced, walls and towers attacked.
(d) The enemy pours through the breaches into the city.
(e) The population and defenders are slaughtered.
(f) The city's wealth is pillaged.
(g) Its walls and homes are demolished.
(h) Its debris is swept into the sea.

As G. Jahn observed: "The entire description of the siege [especially item (c)] despite its beauty, does not suit the island of Tyre, and seems to have been drawn according to the customary scheme of siege without regard for the situation of Tyre" (*Das Buch Ezechiel* [Leipzig: E. Pfeiffer, 1905], p. 186). See the extracts from the Assyrian inscriptions cited in the comments to vs. 8 and vs. 12, above.

If in A1 Tyre was now spoken of, now spoken to, in A2 Tyre is consistently spoken to (by God), but the agents of her destruction vary: now Nebuchadnezzar (vss. 8–11), now his soldiers (vs. 12), now God (vss. 13–14). The shifts vivify the description, while affirming the merely agential status of the Babylonians in these events.

B (vss. 15–18): the stunning effect of Tyre's fall on the rulers of the coastlands with whom Tyre traded. Their mourning rituals are described in stately prose, their lament, in poetry, with the variety of metrical variations that appears in the Book of Lamentations:

1. How have-you-perished / who-were-inhabited from-the-seas / city that-was-celebrated	2:2:2 (Lam 3:56; 4:20a)
(G: How have-you-been-banished from-the-sea / city celebrated)	3:2 (the dominant measure in Lam)
2. That was strongest in-the-sea / she with-her-inhabitants	4:2 (Lam 2:3b; 3:1, 64)
3. who inspired fear-of-them / every-one-of her-inhabitants	3:2
4. now the-coastlands tremble / [on]-the-day-of your-downfall	3:2
5. terrified-are the-coastlands that-are on-the-sea / by-your-end	4:1 (Lam 3:27)

Lines 2 and 3 begin and end with the same word (*'šr . . . ywšbyh*); lines 4 and 5 are bound by identical subject ("coastlands") and synonymous verbs ("tremble / be terrified") and assonant endings:

YoM MappalTEK "[on] the day of your downfall"
bayYaM Miṣṣ̣eTEK "on the sea by your end"

C (vss. 19–21): Tyre descends into the netherworld, in temporal sequence to A.

The narrative sequence of the oracle, its main integrating factor, is reinforced by verbal links among all its parts. A2 is most closely linked to A1, as it elaborates Tyre's fall, incorporating A1's terms. B, telling of the impact of Tyre's fall, repeatedly recalls the language of A: "the sound of your downfall" (vs. 15) recalls "the sound of your lyres" (vs. 13); "the slain" of vs. 15 picks up "the slain" daughter towns of vs. 6, and the slain population of Tyre in vs. 11. The "quaking" coastlands (vs. 15) echo the "quaking" walls of Tyre (vs. 10). The "descent" of her mighty pillars "to the ground" (vs. 11) is paralleled by the "descent" of the sea chiefs from their thrones to sit "on the ground" (vs. 16). Within B, the prose and poetry share many terms: "downfall," "sit/inhabit (*yšb*)," "coastlands," "tremble."

C, collecting language from A and B, as is the custom of Ezekiel's codas, carries the oracle to an imaginative climax. Tyre, who gloated over Jerusalem's ruin (vs. 2), shall herself be made a ruin (vs. 19). A's Tyre is an island built high, whose aspect is governed by walls and towers which are fated to be brought to the ground; likewise B depicts a sympathetic descent of the sea chiefs to the ground. C carries Tyre's descent below the earth's surface, to its nether limit, the Pit.

A corresponding intensification occurs in the imagery. The terms of A and B are almost entirely realistic—this-worldly—and nonfigurative. The lone simile for the enemy assault, "as the sea heaves its waves" (vs. 3) stands out against its prosaic background. C uses two similes for Tyre—likening her to "cities without inhabitants" and "ancient ruins"—and a bold metaphor: Tyre will be made "a horror" (*blhwt*), a concretization of the "terror" (*bhl*, vs. 18b) her fate inspired in the sealands. Most striking is the conversion of the sea simile for the enemy (vs. 3) into the heightened metaphor, with mythic overtones, of Tehom being raised up, of the deep sea covering the doomed city (vs. 19). The ambience of unworldliness is confirmed by the following scene (vs. 20) of Tyre's descent to join the eternal inhabitants of the underworld of death. Thus she will share the fate of the ancient ruins, condemned to eternal oblivion. The augmenting of imagination in C, as it gathers and transmutes ideas of A and B, brings the prophet to the initial stage of the next oracle, where the metaphor of submergence of the island generates a full-blown allegory.

According to the date at the head of A1, Tyre's gloating over Jerusalem's ruin preceded that city's fall. The formal resemblance of A1 to the immediately preceding brief oracles against Judah's neighbors has been noted, but those oracles assume the fall of Jerusalem. If A1 is to be dated as MT dates it (prior to the fall), then the brief oracle against the nations (consisting of indictment and punishment), like those of Amos 1–2, is a form Ezekiel inherited from earlier prophecy, adapted to his own style, and used before Jerusalem's fall. This oracle against Tyre is its first attested use, but as ch. 25 shows, Ezekiel continued to use the form after the fall in inveighing against the small states to the east and south of Judah. With the exception of Edom, who received further attention in ch. 35, the prophet exhausted his rage against those paltry objects in brief oracles. Tyre, a vortex of world trade and fabled for its wealth, stirred the imagination and gave it scope. Ezekiel warmed to his theme as he uttered it, and returned to it again and again. To the brief oracle of A1 he added a narrative of siege and eradication (A2); to that, a scene of mourning and a lament (B). That in turn stimulated a glimpse into the netherworld (in C)—here fleeting, but in subsequent oracles fully developed. That these augments are integrated and in good sequence does not mean that they originated at the same time. They may have been generated in series by sustained brooding over the scandal of Tyre's *hubris*, and at close enough intervals for the terms of each section to influence its successor.

The placement of the Tyre oracles after the brief dooms of ch. 25—out of chronological order as it seems—was explained above on geographical grounds; a formal reason can now be proposed in addition: in order to juxtapose the brief oracle of A1 to its like in ch. 25.

XXVII. The Shipwreck of Tyre
(27:1–36)

27 1The word of YHWH came to me: 2And you, man, recite a dirge over Tyre,
3and say to Tyre, who dwells at the entrances to the sea, dealer for peoples to
many coastlands: Thus said Lord YHWH:

Tyre! You said, "I am a perfect beauty."
4In the midst of the seas were your borders;
    your builders perfected your beauty.
5Of junipers from Senir they built
    all your ribs;
A fir from Lebanon they took
    to make a mast on you;
6Of oaks from Bashan
    they made your oars;
Your planking they made of ivory-inlaid cypresses[a]
    from the Kittean islands;
7Of variegated linen from Egypt
    was your sail,
    serving as your ensign;
Of blue and purple cloths from the islands of Elishah
    was your awning.
8Inhabitants of Sidon and Arvad
    were your oarsmen;
Your wise men, Tyre, were in you;
    they were your sailors;
9Gebal's elders and her wise men were in you,
    [serving as] your breach-repairers.
All seagoing ships and their seamen were in you,
    bringing you imports.
10Persians, Lydians and Putians were in your force,
    [serving as] your fighting men.
Shield and helmet they hung on you;
    they lent you splendor.

[a] Reading *bt ʾšrym* as one word (*bit*^{e}*ʾaššurim*), with T.

[11]Men of Arvad and Helek were on your walls all around,
and Gammadians on your towers;
Their quivers they hung on your walls all around;
they perfected your beauty.

[12]Tarshish was your trader—because of [your] abundant wealth of every kind—in silver, iron, tin and lead [that] they gave you for exports.

[13]Javan, Tubal and Meshech—they were your dealers in human beings and bronze vessels [that] they gave you as imports.

[14]From Beth-togarmah, horses and steeds and mules were given to you for exports.

[15]Men of Dedan[b] were your dealers, many islands were agents of your trade: ivory tusks and ebony they delivered to you by contract.

[16]Aram[c] were your traders—because of the abundance of your enterprises—in turquoise, purple and variegated cloths, and linen, and coral and rubies [that] they gave you for exports.

[17]Judah and the land of Israel, they were your dealers in wheat of Minnith and meal and honey and oil and balm [that] they gave you for import.

[18]Damascus was your trader—due to the abundance of your enterprises, because of the abundance of [your] wealth of every kind—in wine of Helbon and wool of Sahar.

[19][d]And Dan and Javan—yarn[d] as exports they gave you; iron ingots, cassia and calamus were among your imports.

[20]Dedan was your dealer in woolen cloths for riding.

[21]Arabia and all the chiefs of Kedar, they traded as your agents in lambs, rams and goats: in them they traded for you.

[22]Dealers of Sheba and Raamah, they were your dealers in all choice perfumes and in all precious stones and gold [that] they gave you for exports.

[23]Haran and Kanneh and [e]Eden, the dealers of Sheba,[e] Ashur Kilmad /were your dealers/ [24]They were your dealers in gorgeous clothes, in cloaks of blue and variegated cloth, and in coverlets of multicolored trim, tied with ropes and preserved in cedar [f]in your market.[f]

[25]Tarshish ships traveled for you [with] your imports.
So you were full and very heavy
in the midst of the seas.
[26]To the great deep brought you
those who rowed you;
The east wind wrecked you
in the midst of the seas.

[b] G "Rhodes" (as reading *rdn*).
[c] G "men"—perhaps reflecting *'dm*, i.e., Edom, as Aquila and S.
[d–d] Heb. *wdn wywn m'wzl;* conjectural emendation *wdny yyn m'yzl (wᵉdanny yayin me'izal*[*a*]) "and casks of wine from Izalla"; these and the following words up to the *atnaḥ* (in translation, the semicolon) to be attached to the preceding verse.
[e–e] G "they (were) your merchants" (as from *hmh rklyk*).
[f–f] Not in G S.

[27]Your wealth and your exports; your imports; your seamen and your sailors; your breach-repairers and those who bring you imports; all your fighting men that are in you—all your company that is within you will fall into the midst of the seas at the time of your downfall.

[28]At the sound of the cries of your sailors
the waves will toss.
[29]All who wield oars
will come down from their ships;
Seamen, all sailors of the sea,
will stand ashore.
[30]They will raise their voices over you
and cry out bitterly;
They will throw earth on their heads,
dust themselves with ashes.
[31]They will pluck their hair out over you
and gird sackcloth;
They will weep over you, embittered,
a bitter lament,
[32]And in their wailing they will recite over you a lament, [g]lamenting you [thus]:
"Who was like Tyre, like a tower
in the midst of the sea?[g]
[33]When your exports, [collected] from the seas, went forth
you satisfied many peoples;
Through your abundant wealth and imports
you made kings of the earth rich.
[34]Now wrecked by the seas,
in the watery depths
your imports and all your company within you fallen,
[35]All the inhabitants of the coastlands
are appalled over you;
Their kings are in turmoil,
their faces lower.
[36]Traders with the peoples
whistle over you;
A horror you have become,
and are gone forever."

COMMENT

27:3. *who dwells at the entrances to the sea.* This and the next clause (to "coastlands") are best taken as appositional to "Tyre" rather than as vocatives ("O you who dwell . . . ," NJPS), since there is a clear vocative ("Tyre") in the second part of this verse following the message formula. Two similar participial expressions

[g-g]G "and Tyre's lament."

in Jer 10:17 and 22:23 that are vocatives are embedded in second person addresses and lack the article. The K *hyšbty* shows the ornamental, poetic suffix *-y* (GKC, § 90 m–n).

"Entrances to the sea," i.e., seaports (portals), in plural, refers perhaps to Tyre's two ports—a natural harbor to the north and an artificial harbor to the south (D. Harden, *The Phoenicians* [Harmondsworth: Penguin, 1971], p. 30).

dealer for peoples to many coastlands. With *rklt h'mym,* lit. "the peoples' dealer," cf. *sḥry hmlk* "the king's traders" in I Kings 10:28: the first term of the pair does the business of the second. Tyre serves as middleman for the world, transferring products to and from the most distant ports. From vs. 12 on it is the various trading partners of Tyre who are called her dealers and traders—as it were, her commercial agents—who kept up the flow of merchandise into her stores. Note especially the double function of "dealers of Sheba" (vs. 22) who are subsequently called "your (Tyre's) dealers": i.e., Sheba's trading agents were Tyre's trading agents; serving their homeland they serve Tyre.

"Coastlands" renders *'iyyim,* which G translates "islands," but which serves to designate the coastal region of mainlands as well; e.g., Isa 20:6, where Philistia is called "this *'y.*" Here the notion of distant lands across the sea is conveyed, as when *'iyyim* is explicitly paired in parallelism with "the ends of the earth" (Isa 41:5; 42:10).

You said, "I am a perfect beauty." The dirge opens with Tyre's boast introducing the description of her past glory. "You said" (or a variant thereof) as the preface of a blameworthy utterance is frequent in Ezekiel's prophecies against the nations; see 25:3, 8; 26:2; 28:2; 29:3. In describing herself as a perfect beauty (*k^elilat yopi*) Tyre appropriates Jerusalem's epithet: "Heretofore all people praised Jerusalem as 'a perfect beauty (*k^elilat yopi*), the joy of the whole earth' (Lam 2:15) now you vaunt yourself saying 'I [= it is I who] am a perfect beauty'!" (Rashi). That this epithet was regarded as proper to Jerusalem is likely in view of its additional (variant) occurrence in Ps 50:2, "From Zion, perfection of (*miklal*) beauty . . ." and the even closer occurrence in Ezek 16:14, where allegorized Jerusalem's beauty is "perfect" (*kalil*) through the "splendor" God bestowed on her (cf. Tyre's splendor, below, vs. 10). "Beauty" and "splendor" are synonyms in this oracle and refer to the imposing magnificence and opulence that Tyre manifested to the beholder; note the parallel "they lent you splendor (vs. 10) . . . they perfected your beauty" (vs. 11). S aptly uses the same term for beauty here and for splendor in vs. 10 (*šwbḥ'*).

Some critics, troubled by the unannounced shift to metaphor between vss. 4 and 5, rewrite vs. 3b so as to announce it. Wellhausen (cited by Smend) inserts after "you said": "a ship, *'^{o}niyya* I am," etc., yielding a text in which the lamented one metaphorizes herself—a device unprecedented (yet in Hellenistic inscriptions Tyre did call herself a ship; see Structure and Themes). Allen reads: "you are called (*'ummart*[!]) a ship, etc.," while Zimmerli shortens the text to "you are a ship of perfect beauty" (see *BHS*). The two latter emendations in the interest of a pedestrian clarity (as though the poet must specify his metaphor before employing it) do away with Tyre's boastful appropriation of Jerusalem's epithet, present only in MT.

4. *In the midst of the seas were your borders.* Being an island, Tyre's borders were the sea. It is unclear whether the terms of this verse are already metaphoric; viz., whether "borders" is a geographic term, referring to the city of Tyre, or an architectural term referring to the rim or circumference of the ship (in 40:12 the word *gbwl* means a "barrier" in a building; in 43:13, 17, 20, the "rim" of an altar). Similarly, "builders" can have its ordinary sense, or (what seems here more likely) the sense of "shipwrights." The latter sense certainly imposes itself after reading the verb "build" in the next verse, in which the metaphor is fully operative.

In the midst of the seas. Lit. "in the heart of the seas"—here meaning no more than "in the water" (close by the mainland), referring either to the island of Tyre or to the metaphoric ship being built (or loaded, vs. 25) by the shore. But in vss. 26–27 the same phrase means "on the high seas." Akkadian *(ina) qabal tamtim* "in the midst (cognate with Arabic *qalbu* 'heart') of the sea" is similarly used both for the location of Tyre (e.g., *ANET*³, p. 295b) and for "on the high seas" (*ANET*³, p. 287b "overseas").

5. *junipers from Senir.* The names of the woods/trees used in constructing the ship are all uncertain. For recent discussion, see Eva S. Krantz, *Des Schiffes Weg mitten im Meer* (Lund: CWK Gleerup, 1982); Jehuda Feliks, *Plant World of the Bible* (in Hebrew) (Tel Aviv: Massada, 1957). Mount Senir is, according to Deut 3:9, the Amorite name for Mount Hermon, the southern spur of the Anti-Lebanon range lying to the east of the Baka Valley; in Assyrian inscriptions it is called Saniru (Luckenbill, *ARAB* I, §§ 663, 672). However, Song 4:8 and I Chron 5:23 place Senir and Hermon side by side as though distinct.

all your ribs. Heb. *luḥot* serves for the wooden boards of which the desert altar was made (Exod 27:8). Here with dual ending it has been supposed to denote "the two [sets of] ribs of the ship, corresponding to one another" (Davidson, Cooke). *kl* defines the noun, which is therefore preceded by *'t* (the marker of the definite direct object); cf. Gen 1:29; 8:21; 9:3. The pronoun *lk* "for you" serves for the possessive suffix (built for you all the ribs = built all your ribs).

A fir from Lebanon. Preferred by Krantz (pp. 156–58) to cedar in this context on the basis of Egyptian evidence for the use of fir for masts; in Greco-Roman antiquity "pine and fir were the woods preferred for masts and yards" (Lionel Casson, *Ships and Seamanship in the Ancient World* [Princeton: Princeton University Press, 1971], p. 233). Evidently the ancients did not classify trees with precision. Note the following item taken from Nathan ben Yeḥiel's twelfth-century Talmudic lexicon, *He'aruk*, s.v. *'šwḥy* (*'ašuḥe*) (ed. A. Kohut, I, p. 309a); "A kind of tree called in Arabic *šuḥ* [fir], from which masts of good quality ships are made. It is a species of cedar (*kᵉmin 'erez*) only it is taller than the cedar and stronger than it."

6. *oars.* In vs. 29 "oar" is *mašoṭ* (stress-long *a*, simple *š*); the present *miššoṭ-* arose, presumably, from the variant **maššoṭ-*, short *a*, doubled *š* (unstressed short *a* in a closed syllable becomes *i*).

planking. Heb *qereš* is a collective; in Exod 26:15 "planks" of the Tabernacle are mentioned. Is this planking for the deck or for the passenger cabin?

ivory-inlaid cypresses. "Ivory" translates *šen* "tooth," short for *šenhab* (*hab* represents the Egyptian word for elephant). The full form appears in I Kings 10:22, but the short form is more common; e.g., Amos 3:15 *bty šn* "houses of ivory [decorations]." T renders *bt 'šrym* with *'škr'yn* "boxwood," by which it renders *t'šwr* in Isa 41:19, and medievals (Rashi, Moshe ben Sheshet) follow it, reading the two Heb. words as one—the only reasonable reading. The best surmise identifies *t'šwr* with cypress (Feliks). *šen bitᵉ'aššurim* is formally like *šeš bᵉriqma* in the next verse; but the latter is "linen in variegation" (see ahead), while our phrase is "ivory (lit. '[elephant's] tooth') in cypress wood," which has been understood as cypress with ivory inlays. Some critics find this a strange concept (but Luzzatto compares *Aeneid* 10.137: "a medallion of ivory [inlaid] in terebinth or boxwood") and prefer to cancel the graph *šn* "ivory" as a dittograph of the last two consonants of *'św*; in that case one would have to cancel *b-* of the following word as well (see *BHS*).

from the Kittean islands. The Kitteans are presumably the inhabitants of Kition, an important Phoenician colony in southeast Cyprus; whence the name was extended to the entire area of the Greek islands (so apparently Jer 2:10; cf. Josephus, *Antiquities* 1.6.1). Cypress trees still abound in the forests of Cyprus.

7. *variegated linen from Egypt.* "Egyptian linen was celebrated in antiquity . . . Ordinarily garments were of bleached linen, though those of the wealthy were often interspersed with colored threads as bands or otherwise decorated" (J. M. Myers, "Linen," *IDB* III, p. 134). Krantz argues persuasively that the usual translation of *riqma* and its cognate *roqem* as "embroidery, -er" (based on G and medievals) is inapt at Ps 139:15, where *ruqqam* "woven, knit" is said of the formation of the embryo, and proposes "linen woven in designs/patterns" (such as has been found in ancient Egyptian sites). See further, Dalman, *AuS* V, pp. 125, 173, in support of the position advocated by Krantz. Nonnos describes a ship whose sail was made of linen (see Structure and Themes).

serving as your ensign. Heb. *nes* is a military standard or flag (T *'at* "[en]sign"), raised high, set on an eminence as a rallying point (Isa 13:2; Jer 51:27); here the sense appears to be that the design on the sail served to identify the ship. Depictions of ancient Phoenician ships do not show flags (Harden, plates 47–50).

blue and purple cloths from the islands of Elishah. In Akkadian *takiltu* (Heb. cognate *tᵉkelet*) denotes a dark shade of blue-purple, while *argamannu* (Heb. cognate *'argaman*) denotes a red shade (A. L. Oppenheim in *ANET*³, p. 282 n. 6). The dyes stand for cloths (usually woolen) colored by them. It is strange that Phoenicia, so famous for its dyes that the name given it by the Greeks derived from *phoinix* "purple" (M. C. Astour, "The Origin of the Terms 'Canaan,' 'Phoenician,' and 'Purple,'" *JNES* 24 [1965], 348f.), should have imported dyed cloths. Perhaps Elishah (in Gen 10:4 a "son" of Javan [Ionia]) was a Tyrian colony whose dyes were richer or more costly, possibly Alashia in the El-Amarna tablets (= Cyprus?), or Carthage, named here after Elissa/Dido, a Tyrian princess who was its legendary founder ("islands" = coastlands).

awning. Lit. "covering," a pi'el participle, the same in Isa 14:11: "Under you will be spread maggots / and your covering will be worms." There is no cause for revocalizing to *mikse* (as in Gen 8:13, of Noah's Ark). Krantz guesses that the costly fabric covered the captain's quarters or those of the passengers, as depicted in Egyptian ship models.

8–9. All three towns lay on the coast north of Tyre: Arvad, at about 110 miles, Byblos at about 60, Sidon about 25; all appear here as subservient to Tyre, their leading citizens ("elders" and "wise men") in the service of ship "Tyre." No significant order of location or tasks is evident, except that the navigating of the ship is entrusted to Tyre's own "wise men" (i.e., experts). "You did not have to import wise men from elsewhere . . . to navigate skillfully, for such were in you . . ." (Kimḥi).

they were your sailors (ḥoblayik). Lit. "rope-men"; "*ḥobel* denotes one who is expert in handling the ropes of (*ḥable-*) the sail; they must be handled wisely (= expertly) in order to catch the wind properly. The master is called *rab* [*haḥobel*, Jonah 1:6], since he directs the other sailors to handle [the ropes] as he sees fit. Moreover, he is the helmsman . . . and steers the ship . . . all of which involves wisdom (= expertise)" (Kimḥi).

While all the other crewmen are from subject towns (for which reason many critics alter the first words of the line to "the wise men of Zemer" — a Phoenician town; cf. "the Zemarites" of Gen 10:18), the key navigational role of "rope-men" is reserved for Tyre's own "wise men." This foreshadows the association of wisdom with Tyre in the following oracles (28:5, 7, 17; F. L. Moriarty, "The Lament over Tyre," *Gregorianum* 46 [1965], 86).

your breach-repairers. I.e., ship's carpenters. Virtually the same phrase appears in II Kings 12:6, 8, etc., in the sense of repairing damage (to a building).

All seagoing ships and their seamen were in you. This refers apparently to the city of Tyre rather than to the metaphoric ship. Yet vs. 27, speaking of the wreck of the ship, mentions "your seamen" and "those who bring you imports" (see end of this verse) as sinking with it — and hence aboard. Evidently the ship and the city are not clearly distinguished. "The representation is that the great ship was attended by all the ships of the sea with their sailors, who . . . delivered her wares to her, or were busied with them" (Davidson).

bringing you imports. The verb *ʿarab* "offer, bring in" is attested in Phoenician and South Arabic (it may appear in Hos 9:4, where "They shall not pour wine-libations to YHWH" is paralleled by "nor shall *yeʿerbu* to him their sacrifices"; the verb is usually rendered "be pleasing," but "they offer" is a better fit). The noun *maʿarab*, in this sense only in this oracle, will accordingly mean "import(s)" (N. Avigad and J. C. Greenfield, "A Bronze *phiale* with a Phoenician Dedicatory Inscription," *IEJ* 32 [1982], 124–25). G vacillates wildly: here "west," in the following verses mostly "mixture" (of goods?), once (contextually) "merchandise." The other versions are no better; clearly there was no tradition of the meaning of these words. Medievals generally associated them with *ʿrb* "pledge, guarantee," which yields an apt sense (such as "commerce, business") only with a strain. The first to ascertain the correct sense was D. H. Müller, "Ägyptisch-Minäischer Sarkophag in Museum von Gizeh," *Wiener Zeitschrift für die Kunde des Morgenlandes* 8 (1894), 4.

10. By "Persia(ns), Lyd(ians) and Put(eans)" Ezekiel designates peoples lying at the outermost limits of the known world: these have contributed their mercenaries to the greater glory of Tyre. Persia came into the purview of Assyria as early as the ninth century B.C.E. (e.g., Adad-Nirari III's annals, *ANET*^{3}, p. 281b), long

before its imperial rise. Lydian auxiliaries served Egypt in the seventh century (see M. J. Mellink in *IDB*, s.v. "Lud, Ludim," and Jer 46:9) and together with Puteans (probably Libyans; so G, usually, see T. O. Lambdin in *IDB*, s.v. "Put") appear in Ezek 30:5 as Egypt's helpers. On soldiers aboard ship (unless the city is intended), see the following comment.

Shield and helmet. The Tyrian custom of decking both warship's railings and city walls with shields is nicely illustrated in Hardin, plate 50, a scene depicting the flight of King Luli of Tyre (a beshielded turret appears on an Assyrian relief picturing the siege of Lachish, *ANEP*², #373). That here a cargo vessel is so equipped (unless, as in vs. 9b, the city is meant) may well be realistic: the freighter and warship cannot have differed much; since any ship coasting along the Mediterranean had to be ready to fight, it was economical to have vessels built for double purpose (S. Smith, "The Ship Tyre," *PEQ* 85 [1953], 97–110; cf. Krantz, pp. 147–51). This consideration allows for the image of the ship to be sustained; part of the crew were soldiers—as is explicitly stated in the account of the shipwreck in vs. 27.

That helmets, too, were hung on ships (or walls) is unattested from the Near East; possibly the pair "shield and helmet," repeated in 23:24 and 38:5, was simply a stereotype. Krantz (pp. 149–50) cites a picture from Minoan times showing helmets hung on a cabin amidship.

they lent you splendor. Often the pronominal suffix on a noun indicates a dative idea ("to/for you"): here lit. "they gave *hdrk*, your splendor" = you splendor. An example recognized as early as G occurs in Exod 2:9: "I will give *śkrk*, your wage" = G "I will give you the wage." Other examples: "I will give your rains" (Lev 26:4) = I will give you rains; "they made their asherahs" (I Kings 14:15) = made (for) themselves asherahs; "hidden in the ground is his rope(trap)" (Job 18:10) = hidden for (catching) him . . . is the rope(trap). See Joüon-Muraoka, § 129 h.

11. *and Helek* (wḥylk). The form of this noun is identical with that translated "your force" in vs. 10, and is so understood by the ancient versions and the medievals; Smend: "with your army." But in 1874 J. Halévy connected our *ḥylk* with Akkadian *Ḫilakku* "Cilicia" = Aramaic and Phoenician *ḥlk* (*klk*); his proposal was later strengthened by the occurrence of an Aramaic gentilic *ḥylky*ʾ "Cilicians," whose base *ḥylk-* is spelled identically with our word (see G. R. Driver, *Aramaic Documents*, p. 61, note to *lgbrn ḥlkyn*). The parallelism with Arvad, calling for another place-name, also favors this proposal. For the unusual double government of *bny*, cf. *bny nf wtḥpnḥs*, Jer 2:16, "Men of Nof and Tahpanes."

Gammadians. Evidently another gentilic, though vocalized as a common noun. Explanations vary: G S "watchmen," seemingly a guess from context; V *Pygmaei* "pygmies" (from Greek *pygme*, the span from elbow to knuckles), a Jewish interpretation based on *gomed* (Judg 3:16), a measure of length conventionally rendered "a short cubit" (see Rashi citing Menaḥem ben Saruq). Revised Version (1885) margin "valorous men" derives from Syriac *gmd* "be bold." T "Cappadocians" takes the word as a gentilic; others relate it to *Gomer* (Menaḥem bar Shimʿon, citing R. Ḥananel; cf. 38:6)—by which Cimmerians are usually understood—or to a Syrian town, Kumedi (referred to in the Amarna letters; GB). Note the alliteration with the following word (*GMDym bMGDlwtyk*).

on your walls . . . on your towers. The metaphor—the ship—gives way to the underlying referent—the city—a shift characteristic of Ezekiel's extended metaphors (e.g., 17:9; 23:46).

quivers. For this meaning (as G here, and medievals) Jer 51:11 is decisive: "Polish arrows, fill quivers"; the cognate Syriac word has this meaning, too. See further, H. Tadmor and M. Cogan, *II Kings*, AB, p. 128 (to II Kings 11:11).

12. Tarshish appears in the Bible as the farthermost location reachable by the Mediterranean Sea. Jonah flees from the land of Israel on a ship bound for Tarshish (Jonah 1:3); the two extremes of the world in Ps 72:10 are Sheba to the south and Tarshish to the west. A similar span, but confined to the sea, is Esarhaddon's phrase, "from Iadnana (Cyprus) to Tarsisi" (*ANET*³, p. 290), i.e., Sardinia, or more likely Spain (possibly Tartessus, on the Guadalquivir River; see M. Elat, "Tarshish and the Problem of Phoenician Colonisation in the Western Mediterranean," *Orientalia Lovanensia Periodica* 13 [1982], 55–61). Classical writers refer to deposits of silver, iron, tin, and lead in the region of Tartessus (Cooke). Jer 10:9 mentions "beaten silver imported from Tarshish."

Starting with this verse and continuing through vs. 24 is a list of Tyre's trade and trading partners, whose pattern is described below in Structure and Themes. Vs. 20 shows the basic sentence structure of the list: "Dedan was your dealer in (*b*-) woolen cloths for riding." From this we learn that *b*- is prefixed to an item of trade originating in the named country and supplied by it to Tyre. *soḥer b*-X is lit. "one who goes about with X (wares, etc., BDB, p. 695)" = trader in X; *rokel b*-X is synonymous. This basic sentence is enlarged by adding to it *ntnw m'rbk*, lit. "they gave (as/for) your import," alternating with *ntnw 'zbwnyk*, lit. "they gave (as/for) your *'*zbwnym* (in vs. 16 explicitly *b*- "as/for"; the dispensability of *b*- in such constructions is shown by the free alternation of *latet 'et ha'areṣ bᵉnaḥᵃla* [Num 36:2] with *latet . . . 'et 'arṣam naḥᵃla* [Deut 4:38] "to give the land for/as a patrimony"). The added clause is syntactically problematic; I construe it, with due diffidence, as an asyndetic relative clause (lacking the marker *'šr*; Joüon-Muraoka, § 158 a–d), qualifying the preceding trade items: "[that] they gave . . ."; cf. II Chron 28:9: *bz'p 'd hsmym hgy'* "in a rage [that] reached heaven."

'izzabon, the counterpart to *m'rb* "import," was explained by Moshe ben Sheshet as "the merchandise that one who trades in a land leaves (*'azab*) [there]"—in our context, exports (see Avigad and Greenfield, cited above). To be more precise, the articles so called are imported by Tyre for re-exportation (as Diakonoff rubrics them correctly, p. 193 of his article cited in Structures and Themes; thereby he abandons the definition proposed elsewhere in the article: "space for storing goods"). Why it should be in plural while its mate *m'rb* is in singular is not clear. The suffix is to be treated as a dative ("gave as your exports" = "gave to you as/for exports"; cf. "lent you splendor" in vs. 10, and comment).

your trader (sḥrtk). Feminine, as referring to city or country, both grammatically feminine (so, too, in vss. 16, 18, and *rkltk* "your dealer" in vss. 20, 23). In the plural the form is always masculine as referring to the traders (vss. 13, 15, 17, 22, 23, 24). The variation in terminology and morphology is typical of Ezekiel's style.

because of [*your*] *abundant wealth of every kind.* Because of Tyre's abundant stock of commodities, Tarshish traded with her, furnishing, in exchange for Tyre's goods, its own mineral resources, which Tyre in turn exported to others (whether in raw state or as finished products).

13. *Javan, Tubal and Meshech.* The first mentioned are the Ionians, the Greeks of western Asia Minor (cuneiform *Iamani*, *ANET*^{3}, p. 286a n. 12); the latter two are peoples of central and southeastern Asia Minor; cuneiform *Tabali* and *Muški* (Phrygia, *ANET*^{3}, p. 284a). They are mentioned in the same order in Gen 10:2, the Table of Nations. Joel 4:6 mentions Phoenician sale to Javan of Jewish captives. Cuneiform texts and archaeological finds confirm the metallurgical fame of the latter two peoples.

14. *Beth-togarmah.* Togarmah appears adjacent to the aforementioned peoples in Gen 10:3; it corresponds to Hittite *Tegarama* (*ANET*^{3}, p. 318a), Assyrian *Til-garimmu*, a city in the region of the Tabali. The area supplied horses as tribute to the Assyrians (Luckenbill, *ARAB* II, §§ 781, 848, 911) and, earlier, as items in Solomon's commerce (from Kue, southern Cilicia, I Kings 10:28). The element *beth* in place-names is common Semitic (see ahead, on Eden in vs. 23), but in this name it is not found elsewhere (the region is not Semitic). Diakonoff (article cited in Structure and Themes) explains the place-name as lit. "The house (= dynasty) of Tugdamme (the Cimmerian who founded it)," the land and people—located in Cappadocia or western Armenia—being named after the dynasty (he compares Elishah [vs. 7], which he takes to be Carthage, named after Elissa, its legendary founder).

steeds. Heb. *parašim* would normally be translated "horsemen" (so G and NJPS here), but such passages as Joel 2:4 ("they have the appearance of horses (*susim*); / Like steeds (*parašim*) they run") show that, like Arabic *faras*, Heb. *paraš* can also mean "steed." Properly, the plurals of "steed" and "horseman" ought to have differed: "horsemen" *parašim* (from **parrašim*), "steeds" **p^{e}rašim* (like *d^{e}barim* from *dabar*); but the distinction was lost on the vocalizers; see the discriminating entry in KB^{3}, s.v. *paraš*. Kimḥi offers both possibilities and, on the analogy of the human trade items of vs. 13, decides in favor of "horsemen" here. Cooke and others prefer the "steeds," although what the difference between "horses" and "steeds" was cannot be said.

15. *Men of Dedan.* G "of Rhodes" (confusion of *d* and *r*, as occurred in *ddnym* [Gen 10:4] = *rdnym* [I Chron 1:7], on which Kimḥi comments astutely). Cooke argues for the MT on the ground that the tropical products mentioned in this verse would have reached Tyre by way of north Arabian Dedan (recurring in vs. 20) rather than by way of Rhodes (Diakonoff, however, finds it acceptable that Rhodians got the items from Egypt and Ethiopia and delivered them to Tyre). I. Eph'al (*The Ancient Arabs*, p. 62) concurs with most critics in preferring G "Rhodes" for its association with the aforementioned "Japhethites" (see Gen 10:2–4), and the recurrence of Dedan in vs. 20, in its proper context. One may

add that the following appositional phrase, "many islands (coastlands)," fits Rhodes, but hardly an oasis such as Dedan.

agents of your trade. An obscure phrase, lit. "the merchandise of your hand (*sᵉḥorat yadek*)," which appears to be an abstraction of *soḥᵃre yadek*, lit. "traders of your hand," of vs. 21 (said of Arab tribes; does this favor Dedan here?). See comment there. For use of abstracts for concrete terms, consult Dahood's list in *Psalms III*, AB, p. 411; a good example is Ps 36:12, where *ga'ᵃwa* "pride" (= the proud) is parallel with *rᵉša'im* ("the wicked").

ivory tusks and ebony. Lit. "horns (so called from their shape) of tooth" from African or Asian elephants. *hwbnym* from Egyptian *hbny* is a black wood conventionally rendered "ebony" (derived, through Greek, from the Egyptian word), but the exact sense is uncertain. The wood originated in regions south of Egypt (see M. Zohary, *EM*, s.v. *hwbnym*). The Phoenicians were famed for their ivory work.

delivered to you by contract (hšybw 'škrk). According to the parallelism of Ps 72:10—"tribute (*mnḥh*) they deliver (*yšybw*) / '*škr* they offer"—our phrase has been translated "rendered you tribute" (NJPS). But the trading partners of Tyre were not her tributaries. Hence I ascribe to the loanword '*eškar* (from Akk. *iškaru*) the sense "product to be delivered"—i.e., under agency contract—an attested meaning of the Akkadian word (*CAD* I–J 246ff., def. 3).

16. *Aram.* Other witnesses (see text note) attest to *Edom,* which is preferable, since in vs. 18 Damascus, the chief Aramaic kingdom, will appear. Moreover, a better south-to-north sequence is obtained by reading Edom (south) here, followed by Israel (center) in vs. 17, then Damascus (north) in vs. 18. The wares that follow do not help to identify the locality, since it is doubtful that they are native to either Aram or Edom.

enterprises. Your many commercial undertakings. For *ma'ᵃśe* "business enterprise," see II Chron 20:37. Tyre's great enterprise made trade with her advantageous.

turquoise. Heb. *nofek* is commonly derived from Egyptian *mfk(t)* "turquoise, malachite" (T. O. Lambdin, "Egyptian Loanwords," p. 152; KB[3]); it was mined in Sinai.

variegated cloths. See comment to *riqma* in vs. 7.

linen. Heb. *buṣ* "byssus" (the English word from Greek, where it is evidently a loanword from Semitic) occurs in late Biblical Hebrew (e.g., II Chron 3:14) where Pentateuchal Hebrew (P) uses *šeš*. Whereas *šeš* has an Egyptian etymology—vs. 7 has it coming to Tyre from Egypt—*buṣ* has an Aramaic and Akkadian distribution, more suitable to its being an item of Aramaic or Edomite trade. The occurrence of both words for linen in the same oracle accords with Ezekiel's straddling early and late Hebrew; see A. Hurvitz, "The Usage of *šš* and *bwṣ* in the Bible and Its Implications for the Date of P," *HTR* 60 (1967), 117–21; also *Revue Biblique* 81 (1974), 33–35, 47 n. 40; M. F. Rooker, *Biblical Hebrew in Transition,* pp. 159–61).

coral. Heb. *ramot* occurs once again in Job 28:18 paired with *gabiš* "rock crystal(?)"; see M. Pope, *Job,* AB, ad loc. Interpretations vary widely; e.g., V "silk" (connecting with the foregoing cloth), T "precious stones" (connecting with the following word, on which see ahead). Wellhausen adduced Arabic *ra'matun* "seashell," coming nearer the conventional "coral," whose earliest attestation is in Ibn Janaḥ, followed by Kimḥi (each of whom records this sense as conjectural). The word *r'imt* denoting an ornament on a female's breast occurs in the Ugaritic "Palace of Baal" epic (Gibson, *Canaanite Myths and Legends,* p. 48, C1), "coral," according to Gibson, evidently following the Hebrew convention.

rubies. Heb. *kadkod* recurs only in Isa 54:12 (|| "burning stones" [carbuncles?]), apparently a gem of some kind; Semitic cognates have red as a common feature, hence the conjecture that rubies (red stones) are meant.

17. *Judah and the land of Israel.* The narrow sense of "the land of Israel," excluding Judah, belongs to the terminology of the dual kingdoms (e.g., II Kings 5:2, 4; 6:23; contrast the usage in Ezek 40:2, where it includes the city of Jerusalem, and in 47:18, where it refers to all Cisjordan). In later times it could still refer to the territory of the former northern kingdom, as in II Chron 30:25 (resident aliens from "the land of Israel" and Judah in the time of Hezekiah) and, probably, II Chron 34:7 (the cultic installations of vss. 6–7 belong to "the land of Israel" while those of vss. 4–5 belong to "Judah and Jerusalem"—this in the time of Josiah). Here it is so used, but, as the usage in Chronicles shows, this does not signify that this list dates back to the dual monarchy (against B. Mazar, *The Early Biblical Period* [Jerusalem: Israel Exploration Society, 1986], p. 82 n. 37). Here "Judah and the land of Israel" may refer to trade relations of Tyre with the still extant kingdom of Judah and the inhabitants of the territory of the former kingdom of Israel, under foreign domination to be sure, but no less "the land of Israel" for that (Zimmerli).

wheat of Minnith. Eusebius (*Onomasticon* 132.1) identified Minnith (mentioned as an Ammonite city in Judg 11:33) with a town Maanith "4 miles out of Heshbon on the [northeasterly] road to Rabbah." The Ammonite kingdom was rich in wheat as evidenced by the large grain (wheat and barley) tribute they paid King Jotham of Judah (II Chron 27:5). Israelite traders mediated Transjordanian products to Tyre.

meal. Taking the hapax *pannag* as equivalent to Akkadian *pa/ennigu* "a type of meal" (borrowed from Hittite; von Soden, *AHw,* p. 818). In an Esarhaddon text listing food commodities the Akkadian word appears associated with *dišpu* "honey" as here (H. R. Cohen, *Biblical Hapaxlegomena* [Missoula: Scholars Press, 1978], p. 118).

Honey and oil are typical products of the land of Israel (Deut 8:8); balm is characteristic of Transjordanian Gilead (Jer 8:22; 46:11). For the export value of these products of Cis- and Transjordan, cf. their role in the Joseph story: Gen 37:25; 43:11.

18. Helbon is modern Syrian Ḥelbūn, a town north of Damascus, of which Baedeker's *Guide to Palestine and Syria,* 5th ed. (1912), pp. 323f., after noting our passage, has this to say:

> Its wine is also mentioned in Assyrian (= Akkadian) chronicles of the time of Nebuchadnezzar [S. Langdon, *Die Neubabylonischen Königsinschriften* (Leip-

zig: J. C. Hinrich, 1912), p. 90, lines 22–23], and this appears to agree with the statement of Strabo [15.735] . . . that the kings of Persia imported their wine from *Chalybon*. The country is admirably adapted for the culture of the vine, the valley being bound by vast slopes of fine chalky rubble. Some of these are still covered with vines, but the grapes are now all dried to form raisins.

wool of Sahar. Perhaps identical with the wilderness *eṣ-ṣaḥrā'* (Arabic "desert") northwest of Damascus (Rüger at Zimmerli); S "white" (so Kimḥi and NJPS: "white wool"), cf. Arabic *ṣaḥira* "be tawny, sand-colored."

19. The translation divides the verse according to the accents; the result is quite anomalous and obscure. The pairing of Dan—otherwise a north Israelite tribe—and Javan—otherwise the Ionian Greeks—is inexplicable. "Yarn" is Rashi's guess based on Talmudic Aramaic *'zl* = *'zl* "spin," the MT form taken as pu'al passive participle, "spun stuff." The second clause of the verse has no place from which the imports come. No construction of MT is satisfactory, and emendation is called for. By vocalizing the first consonant of *m'wzl* (whose *waw* is anomalous in a passive participle) as *me-* "from," the rest of the graph becomes a place-name, "from Uzal" (so Eliezer of Beaugency, who compares South Arabian Uzal in Gen 10:27; G "from Asel"). Since vs. 18 lacks the standard conclusion, it seems that vs. 19 belongs with it; its doubling of final phrases ("exports . . . imports") agrees with the duplication of "abundance" phrases (in MT; G lacks the first). The consonants of the first three words of vs. 19 were brilliantly, and minimally, emended to read "and wine casks from Izalla" by A. R. Millard ("Ezekiel xxvii 19: The Wine Trade of Damascus," *JSS* 7 [1962], 201–3), who recognized in them a cognate of Akkadian *dannu* (= Aramaic *dan[na]*) "vat, cask," then the word *yyn* "wine," followed by the place-name Izalla, a town joined with Ḫilbuni (Helbon) in the Neo-Babylonian records of wine trade. For a brave but unpersuasive attempt to make do with MT, see M. Elat, "The Iron Export from Uzal (Ezekiel xxvii 19)," *VT* 33 (1983), 323–26.

they gave you. The pausal form, normally *natanu* (second *a* stress-lengthened), appears here as *natannu* with a euphonic doubling of the second *n*; cf. the *l* of *ḥadellu* in Judg 5:7 (GKC, § 20 i).

iron ingots. Lit. "thick (? *'ašot*) iron," relating the adjective to the verb *'štw* "became gross(?)" paralleling *šmnw* "became fat" in Jer 5:28, and the noun *'ešet* "bar(?)" in Song 5:14; all uncertain. G S V translate "worked (wrought) iron"—as though from *'śh* "do, work"; Kimḥi and other medievals: "purified, whitened iron," i.e., steel (cf. a quotation in Samuel Johnson's dictionary, s.v. "steel": "Steel is a kind of iron refined and purified by the fire with other ingredients, which render it white, and its grain closer and finer than common iron"); NJPS: "polished."

cassia and calamus. If correctly identified, these spice plants are native to China and Persia/north India respectively. If the source of Tyre's import of iron and spices is still Damascus (vs. 18), then Damascus will herself have imported the iron, perhaps from north Syria and Asia Minor (a ninth-century Assyrian king received five thousand talents of iron as tribute from Damascus, *ANET*^{3}, p. 282a), and the spices, probably from south Arabia (see comment to vs. 22).

were. Disaccord between postpositional *hyh* (sing.) and plural subject occurs in 16:49; 40:21; cf. 36:2.

20. The verse exhibits the basic sentence, without the alternating end-clauses that serve as a refrain. Dedan is mentioned again in 38:13 together with Sheba (see ahead, vs. 22) as international traders. Listed in Gen 25:3 among the north Arabian "sons of Keturah," Dedan was located at the northwest Arabian oasis of al-ʿUla. Local inscriptions from the sixth century B.C.E. have been found, and the town (Dadanu) is mentioned in inscriptions of Nabonidus (sixth century); see F. V. Winnett and W. L. Reed, *Ancient Records from North Arabia* (Toronto: University of Toronto Press, 1970), pp. 38, 113ff.; I. Ephʿal, *Ancient Arabs*, index, s.v. "Dedan." Ephʿal (pp. 233, 237–38) contrasts the luxury items in the trade of the kingdoms of Dedan and Sheba (ahead, vs. 22) with the herd items of the nomad Arabs in the next verse. Dedan was a major station in the overland trade route from south Arabia northward (Ephʿal, p. 14; G. Van Beek, "Frankincense and Myrrh," *Biblical Archeologist Reader*, II [Garden City: Doubleday, 1965], p. 107).

woolen cloths. For *beged* "cloth" (usually clothes), see Num 4:6 (the semantic range is similar to English cloth-clothes); *ḥopeš* usually "freedom" is taken here, with Zimmerli, as cognate with Akk. *ḫibšu*, a kind of wool (*CAD* Ḫ 181; NJPS "saddlecloths" interprets the phrase according to the sequel "for riding"). T and Kimḥi, "costly garments," understand *ḥopeš* as "nobility" (status of a freeman; for the semantics, cf. *ḥorim* [I Kings 21:8] "nobility," cognate with post-biblical *ḥerut* "freedom").

for riding. The Hebrew form *(lᵉ)rikb*a is an infinitive (verbal noun) on the pattern of *(lᵉ)yirʾa* "to fear" (Deut 10:12); *(lᵉ)ribʿa* "to couch" (Lev 20:16).

21. *Arabia*. The dwelling place of the *ʿᵃrabi* "Arab," viz., the north Arabian desert; the lands of the bedouin (cf. Jer 3:2, "like an Arab in the wilderness"). Kedar, a "son of Ishmael" (Gen 25:13), was a bedouin tribe; the phrase "chiefs of Kedar" suggests a federation of nomad tribes; for details, see I. Ephʿal, *Ancient Arabs*, pp. 223–27. Being nomads, their trade was in their livestock.

traded as your agents. Lit. "(were) traders of your hand"; cf. Ugaritic Akkadian *tamkaru ša qatiya* "merchants of my hand" (= under my jurisdiction, serving as my agents); A. F. Rainey, *A Social Structure of Ugarit* (in Hebrew) (Jerusalem: Bialik Institute, 1967), p. 61. The demoting of Tyre's trading partners into her agents (see also vs. 15) is rhetorical rather than factual (M. Liverani, p. 76 of article cited in Structure and Themes).

in lambs (bkrym), *rams and goats*. G read the first word as "camels" (plural of *beker* [Isa 60:6])—fitting indeed for Arabia. The *b*, however, is prepositional, in accord with the pattern of initial items in this trade list. The series repeats itself, without the preposition, in 39:18 (rams, lambs, and goats). These commodities resemble the booty Ashurbanipal (seventh century) seized in his campaign against the Kedarites: "donkeys, camels, large and small cattle" (*ANET*³, p. 299b).

22. *Dealers of Sheba*. See comment at catchword "dealer for peoples" in vs. 3. According to the Tyro-centric view of our passage, Sheba's merchants are Tyre's (i.e., act on Tyre's behalf).

Sheba, paired with Dedan in 38:13, is its "brother" according to the list of north Arabian "Keturites" in Gen 25:3 (in Gen 10:7 Sheba is among peoples of uncertain location; Eph'al, p. 227). But in Gen 10:28 Sheba appears among South Arabian peoples (ibid.). Extra-biblical evidence supports both locations, and scholars differ regarding their relation (e.g., is the northern Sheba the original home of the later, well-documented southern kingdom, or is it a commercial colony of the latter?). Similar uncertainty surrounds the provenance of the queen of Sheba who visited Solomon (I Kings 10); see A. K. Irvine in D. J. Wiseman, ed., *Peoples of Old Testament Times* (Oxford: Clarendon Press, 1973), pp. 298f., and Eph'al, pp. 63f., 227–29.

Raamah is an unknown place or people, "father" of Sheba and Dedan in the list of Gen 10:7. Transcribed *ragma* in G, it has been identified with a South Arabian town *RGMT*, though the representation of South Arabian g by Hebrew ' is unexampled. "The tradition preserved by the Hebrews is usually taken merely as evidence of . . . close cultural and commercial ties between the Dedanites and Sabaeans, but it may well be that the two peoples had a common origin. One group may have moved from the original homeland, Ra'amah (wherever that was), and established itself at Dedan, the other may have moved in a different direction and founded the kingdom of Sheba . . ." (Winnett and Reed, p. 113).

The gifts brought by the queen of Sheba to Solomon are identical with the items mentioned here: gold, very many spices and precious stones (I Kings 10:10). Partially congruous are the ingredients of the sacred anointing oil in Exod 30:22–24: choice spices (*bᵉśamim roš*) listed there include myrrh, cinnamon, aromatic calamus (*qane*), and cassia (*qidda*). Myrrh was produced in South Arabia, cinnamon originated in Ceylon and South India, calamus (if that is the correct identification) in Persia and India; cassia (if that is correct) in China. Presumably these commodities reflect South Arabian/Indian trade documented only for classical times but judged to be much older (Van Beek, pp. 109–10). The overland trade route from South Arabia to Tyre ran through Dedan, Transjordan, branching off in Gilead to Tyre (Eph'al, p. 15, map, p. 241).

The commodities imported from Arabia accord well with a list of tribute offered to Tiglath-Pileser III by defeated Arabians (*ANET*³, p. 283b): gold, silver, camels, and "all kinds of spices."

23. The text of this verse appears to be in disorder. Haran—a city famed for its connection with the Patriarchs (Gen 11:31; 12:4f.; 28:10ff., etc.)—is located in northwest Mesopotamia on the upper Balikh River. Eden, shortened from Beth Eden (Amos 1:5), is the name of an extensive Aramaean state on the upper Euphrates, west of Haran, since the ninth century B.C.E. an Assyrian province. Kanne is otherwise unknown but perhaps is the town Kannu, of uncertain location but whose population was related to the Harranians (GB; cf. A. T. Olmstead, *History of Assyria* [New York: Scribner's, 1923], p. 514). A main east-west trade artery passed through this territory, with Aleppo, Carchemish, and Haran in its western part, and Nineveh (a capital of Assyria) at its eastern part.

Ashur Kilmad. Suspiciously asyndetic, these look like interpolations. Kilmad is otherwise unknown; T "(and the provinces of Ashur) and Media" appears to be analyzing *klmd* as "all (*kl*) Med[ia]" (so Kara). "Dealers of Sheba" is represented in G only by the stock refrain "they [were] your merchants"; indeed Sheba seems out of place, having been mentioned in the previous verse; is it a scribal error?

/were your dealers/. The singular form (*rkltk*) is out of concord with the previous items; it repeats the form at the head of vs. 20. G T translate a plural, but so do they in vss. 12, 16 (in vs. 18 T is plural, G singular), and 20. S renders all these cases with the identical paraphrase "marketplace." "They were your dealers" (*hmh rwklyk*) in the immediate sequel at the head of vs. 24 suggests conflation, indicated by slashes in the translation.

24. *gorgeous clothes. maklul* evokes Akkadian *maklalulu* a type of garment and Hebrew *miklol* "perfection" (23:12; see comment thereto), the combination yielding this conjectural translation, following BDB, KB³.

cloaks. Conjectural translation based on Aramaic *glym'* "cloak" and Hebrew *galam* "wrap up" as in II Kings 2:8.

coverlets of multicolored trim. Hebrew *bᵉromim* is cognate with Akkadian *birmu* "multicolored trim"; *ginze* is obscure, its attested sense of "treasury" (derived from Persian; e.g., Est 3:9) being inappropriate (unless the phrase means "goods worthy of being kept in a treasury"; cf. Kara, "worthy of being stored away in a chest"). "Coverlets" is based on the Aramaic Targum to Est 1:3: "(diners) reclining on *gnzy* (so in Lagarde; in Sperber [IV A, p. 181] *zege*) of wool." KB³ renders our word "carpet"—so, too, NJPS—with reference to the Esther Targum; but there the reference seems to be to the coverings of couches, hence "coverlets."

tied with ropes and preserved in cedar. So NJPS, understanding *'ᵃruzim* as derived from *'erez* "cedar"; cf. G "bound in ropes and cypress-wood"; T "bound in ropes of linen and . . . laid in myrtle-wood," explained by Rashi: "bound with ropes . . . and placed in chests (lit. towers) of myrtle-wood, that is, a kind of cedar" (taking *'aruz* as "boxed in cedar"). NJPS follows A. Shalit's attractive suggestion that *'aruz* means "smeared with cedar-oil (for preservation)," comparing Assumption of Moses 1:16, in which the scrolls of Torah are said to be "cedar(-oil)ed" so that they might last. Here it is the baled cloth(e)s aforementioned that are "cedar(-oil)ed" to preserve them from mold and moth ("ḥbšym 'rzym bmrkltk,") *Lešonenu* 7 [1935–36], 131–35; cf I. Löw, *Die Flora der Juden*, III, p. 28, citing classical references to items preserved in cedar oil (*cedratos*). Arabic *'araza* "be drawn into oneself, be firm" underlies alternative renderings; e.g., *RSV* "bound with cords and made firm"; *NEB* "rolled up and tied with cords." Zimmerli separates the phrase as an additional item of trade: "(your dealers) in firm, twisted ropes" (reversing the order of the Hebrew adjectives). This is a more natural construction of the sequence, whereby *bḥblym* is taken as an item of trade with preposed *b*, and the two following passive participles as qualifying it; but *ḥabuš* nowhere means "twisted," and one expects the last item in the series (*ḥblym*) to bear the copula *waw* "and."

in your market (bmrkltk). A word difficult to construe; not in G S. T translates it like *bm sḥryk* at the end of vs. 21, as though it construed the consonants as *bm rkltk*, picking up *rkltk/hmh rklyh* at the end of vs. 23 (as *bm sḥryk* reprises *hmh sḥry ydk* in vs. 21) "in them (i.e., the aforementioned items) they were your dealers."

25. *traveled for you.* Lit. "your travelers," understanding *šarot-* as feminine plural participle of root *šw/yr,* a Hebrew cognate of Arabic *sara* (medial *y*) "travel," perhaps recurring in Song 4:8 "travel (*tašuri*) from the top of Amana." "Tarshish ships," originally ships built for trade with far-off Tarshish (see vs. 12), came to designate larger seagoing merchant vessels regardless of origin or port of call (C. Gordon in *IDB*, s.v. "Tarshish").

[*with*] *your imports.* An awkward expression, lacking the expected preposition *b-* (supplied by G, medievals). The clause recalls vs. 9b, in which "all seafaring ships" are said to have been "in" the ship Tyre bringing her imports (which she subsequently exported). The sense of vs. 25a is: "The famous Tarshish-ships of Tyre's merchant fleet were the middlemen for the 'display-ship' Tyre—as traveling merchants in her service" (Herrmann).

and very heavy. Hebrew *kbd* suggests at once being heavy, rich, and honored (cf. English "weighty"), as in Job 14:21 "be heavy (= honored)" is opposed to "be diminished (= dishonored)"; cf. Gen 13:2: Abraham was "heavy" in herds, silver, and gold. The primary sense here is that the ship lay low in the water because of its weight; paired with "full," it connotes "rich(ly stocked)" as well.

in the midst of the seas. I.e., offshore; the ship has not yet put to sea.

26. The wreck of "Tarshish-ships" by the east wind is mentioned in Ps 48:8—perhaps a reference to the historical wreck of I Kings 22:49. "In places where the mountains come close to the coast, as at Haifa and farther north [where Tyre is], a strong sirocco [east wind] will pour down the steep slopes like a river in spate and may at times reach sixty miles an hour and over. The harbors, of course, provide little protection from a descending storm of this nature and farther out to sea it can become exceedingly rough, sufficiently so to be very dangerous to the small ships of ancient times" (D. Baly, *The Geography of the Bible* [London: Lutterworth, 1957], pp. 68f.). On the metaphorical meaning of this passage, see Structure and Themes.

27. "Wealth," "exports," and "imports" are terms drawn from vss. 12f., the beginning of the trade list. The first, asyndetic "imports" looks like an addition, perhaps a misplaced variant of "your wealth." The terms denoting members of the merchantry and crew are drawn from vss. 8b–10.

all (wbkl) *your company.* The *w-* is explicative ("namely"); see comment to 3:13 (I, 71). The *b-* does not appear in some Heb. mss. and is not translated in G S T. Likely it arose from an erroneous repetition of the sequence *bk* in the preceding word.

28. *waves will toss.* Ibn Janaḥ (*Schoraschim,* root *grš*) connects *mgršwt* with "like the agitated (*ngrš*) sea" (Isa 57:20), "whose waters toss up (*wygršw*) muck and mud" (ibid.); "it will be agitated (*wngršh*) and subside like Egypt's Nile" (Amos 8:8): the sound of the cries of the drowning sailors will set the sea churning (cf. G. R. Driver [1954], who all unknowingly follows suit). That is preferable to the meaning "outlying (pasture-)lands" = *mgršh* (as in Num 35:3; so, e.g., T), in whose favor only the distantly similar "the islands will quake" of Ezek 26:15 can be invoked.

29. Sailors will abandon their ships and come ashore for fear of suffering a like shipwreck ("If that ship, so much stronger than ours, was wrecked . . ." [MenbSh, Smend]); or in order to gather to honor the memory of the ship by their mourning and dirges. Cf. 26:16 "all the sea chiefs will descend from their thrones."

30. Throwing earth on one's head (Josh 7:6; Job 2:12) and dusting oneself with ash (Jer 6:26) were conventions of grief. The tradition vacillates regarding the sense of *htplš*: G "spread under"; S V "sprinkle themselves" (so G in Jer); T "rub themselves." Medievals and many moderns have fixed on "wallow," and interpret Ugaritic *ʿpr pltt* "dust of wallowing" (so Gibson, *Canaanite Myths and Legends*, p. 73, line 15: though since it is poured on the crown it is hard to imagine the crown wallowing). Ginsberg, in *ANET*[3], p. 139a, renders the Ugaritic phrase "earth of mortification," whence *htplš* should mean "mortify oneself."

31. *pluck their hair out.* Lit. "make themselves a bald spot"; for this and sackcloth, see 7:18. With the entire verse cf. Isa 22:12: "On that day YHWH of Hosts will call for weeping, for lamenting, and for baldness and for girding sackcloth." Also similar to our passage is Jer 6:26: "Dame My people! Gird sackcloth / Take up mourning as for an only child / Bitter lamenting." Comparison with the Ugaritic passage cited above (and in comment to 26:16) shows the currency of these practices in the Syro-Palestinian area in antiquity.

32. *in their wailing* (bnyhm). T translates this word and the following *qynh* with *bʿnwyhn ʾlyʾ* "in their lamenting a dirge"; in Jer 9:19 the pair *nhy/qynh* is translated by a reverse sequence *ʾlyʾ/ʿnwyʾ*. The two Aramaic words are semantic equivalents. Hebrew *nhy* "wailing" when not associated with a synonym is regularly translated in T by *ʾlyʾ* (which also serves as the regular translation of *qynh* "dirge"). Clearly T analyzed our base word *ny* as = *nhy* "wailing." Medievals and some moderns agree—e.g., König II, pp. 63 f, who compares the elision of the *h* in the name element *yo(yakin)* contracted from *yᵉho(yakin)*. G S "their sons" attests to the same consonantal text; yet some critics (Cornill, *BHS*, Zimmerli) regard it as a "gloss" and a metric overload (though it is not explanatory, and the metrics of Ezekiel are anything but determined). G. R. Driver (1938) regularizes the form by metathesis **bᵉniyham*. A notable conjecture is Tur-Sinai's *bᵉnaham* "in roaring" (*Pešuṭo šel Miqra*, III/2, p. 337); cf. the verb *nhm* in 24:23 in a context of lamentation.

like a tower (kdmh). In this opening line of the dirge (absent in old G, perhaps because of its difficulty) we expect reference to past glory. This is most simply gained by taking *duma* (simple *m* in Aleppo, Leningrad [*BHS*], Cairo, and other mss.; in printings, doubled *m*—reflecting differing views on derivation, see ahead) to be cognate with Akkadian *dimtu* "tower, siege tower, fortified area, pillar"; first suggested by B-Y, again by Dahood (*Biblica* 45 [1945], 83f.). Cf. Josh 19:29 "the fortress city (*ʿyr mbṣr*) of Tyre"; Zech 9:3 "Tyre has built herself a fortress (*mṣwr*). The verticality of Tyre was striking: "The city was closely built. Some of its buildings were many stories high. The natural slope of the ground showed the buildings tier on tier . . ." (W. B. Fleming, *The History of Tyre* [New York: Columbia University Press, 1915], p. 5, citing classical authors).

T "there is none that resembled (*dmy*) her" is followed by some medievals, and, since the MT cannot be so construed, has inspired the emendation *ndmh* (*nidma*) "be like" (resulting in awkward word order). Others, disregarding the dirge pattern, have taken the word as denoting Tyre's misfortune. G Alexandrinus and some hexaplaric versions render "stilled, silenced" as from *dmh/dmm;* this view, too, has its medieval proponents (e.g., Kimḥi, who defines the sense as "cut off") and has inspired moderns to read *nidma* "annihilated" or *nadamma* "stilled." J. Reider ("Etymological Studies in Biblical Hebrew," *VT* 4 [1954], 276–95; citation, 279) posits a Hebrew root, *kdm* "bind," on the basis of Arabic, of which *k*ᵉ*duma* is a passive participle "captive (or enslaved)"; but Tyre is not described in the sequel as captured but as annihilated.

33. The story of Tyre's past glory is continued in poetic parallelism; for the shift from speech about Tyre (vs. 32b) to address to Tyre, cf., e.g., the shifts in David's dirge, II Sam 1:22–26.

The first verset of vs. 33 is difficult; lit. "When your exports went forth from the seas." Some interpret, "were landed/unloaded from the seas" (Smend, NJPS), but passage from sea to shore is indicated by *ʿlh* "go up" not *yṣʾ* "go forth" (Dan 7:3 Aramaic *slq;* Isa 63:11 [hifʿil]). On the other hand, derivatives of *yṣʾ* are specific terms for export: *moṣa* "source," *yaṣa* "be exported" (I Kings 10:28f.), a sense appropriate here where the subject is "exports" (Van Dijk). "From the seas" appears to have the sense we attribute to 26:17 *(nošebet) miyyammim* (see comment thereto), *mi-* having an originative sense, as the seas brought Tyre her exports.

wealth and imports. The Hebrew nouns are, exceptionally, plural (*-yk*) assimilating to the form of "exports."

34. *Now.* So G T render Hebrew *ʿt,* here adverbial = *bʿt* "at/in the time of, when," as in *ʿt hdrykh* "when it is trodden" (Jer 51:33), *ʿt rṣwn* "at an acceptable time" (Ps 69:14)—just as *ywm* in 26:18 = *bywm* "on the day"; see comment there. On the nuance "now," cf. 16:57 *kmw ʿt* and comment (I, 290). The absence of a subject pronoun with the participle *nišberet* is unusual, though it has an analogue in Jer 2:17 *bʿt mwlykk* "when he was guiding you"; in both cases the context provides a subject. But critics prefer to emend the text in accord with G T to: *ʿtta nišbart* "Now you have been wrecked" (*BHS;* cf. König III, §§ 239 h, 331 b; S. R. Driver, *Tenses,* § 135 [6] obs. 2), which is more regular.

Kimḥi notes the significance of the repeated *miyyammim* in this verse (here *mi-* causal as in Gen 9:11 "by the water [*mimme*] of the flood"): "From the seas came your wealth and riches (vs. 33) and the seas swept all away (vs. 34)."

in the watery depths. This phrase looks in two directions: on the one hand, it locates where the aforementioned wreck occurred (cf. vs. 26b: "wrecked . . . in the midst of the seas"); on the other, it locates the place of the following clause, where it was that all fell (= drowned)—as in vs. 27b: "will fall into the midst of the seas."

In this verse (34) the contents of the ship are summarized as "imports" (*mʿrbk*) (alternating, as in the list, with "exports" [*ʿzbwnyk,* vs. 33]; both meaning merchandise in general) and company—covering all the offices in vs. 27.

35. *appalled* (šmmw) . . . *are in turmoil* (śʿrw śʿr). The same sequence of verbs appears in Jer 2:12, where G renders the second verb as related to *śeʿar* "hair," viz., *ephrixen* "feel the hair bristle (from fear), shudder"; Eliezer of Beaugency compares Job 4:15, usually taken as "making the hair of my flesh bristle" (*tśmr*

ś'rt bśry; G *ephrixan*), and so BDB, GB. Alternatively, Ibn Janaḥ, Rashi, Kimḥi, and some moderns regard *ś'r* as equivalent to *s'r* "storm, be in turmoil" (e.g., II Kings 6:11 "the King of Aram's heart was agitated [*wys'r*]"). G renders here "were astonished," and when derivatives of **šmm* and **ś'r* appear in Job 18:20, it renders the second (a nominal form) "astonishment." The association with "thunder" (see the next word) tips the scale in favor of "storm" (so B-Y).

their faces lower (r'mw pnym). The verb is from a root *r'm* whose derivatives in Hebrew and Syriac denote thunder, rage, and complaint (Mishnaic Heb. *htr'm* = Syr. *'tr'm* "be angry, complain"). Our passage is literally "they 'thunder' as to their faces"; for the construction, cf. Lam 4:7b "their limbs were ruddy," lit. "they were ruddy as to limb (*'dmw 'ṣm*)" (König III, § 328 f). Since the verbal idea is here associated with the face, a look rather than a sound, conveying anger or complaint is suggested, whence the rendering "lower" (look sullen; be dark, gloomy, and threatening). The verb is associated with the face again in I Sam 1:6, 18: Hannah's cowife vexed her in order to exasperate her (*hr'ymh*); but after Eli gave Hannah a sympathetic hearing she no longer "had her (sullen) face" (*pnyh l' hyw lh*).

36. *whistle over you.* Connected with appallment over ruins in I Kings 9:8 and, in identical circumstances, with clapping of hands and shaking of head in Lam 2:15 and elsewhere. These expressions of consternation have been widely explained as originally intended to ward off demonic harm "especially at ruins or unpopulated wastes"—so Fohrer here, referring (as does Holladay, *Jeremiah*, Hermeneia, p. 525) to R. Lasch, "Das Pfeifen und seine Beziehung zu Dämonenglauben und Zauberei," *Archiv für Religionswissenschaft* 18 (1915), 589–92. But Lasch's evidence is all to the effect that whistling stirs up the demons and must be strictly avoided, except in the special case of raising a wind in a becalmed sea.

A *horror.* These are the prophet's words, as in 26:21; only he can say "are gone forever."

STRUCTURE AND THEMES

The lament of 26:15–18 is elaborated here into an imposing, complex oracle, answering to a divine charge to recite a dirge over Tyre. In accord with the scheme of dirges the oracle has two parts, a description of past (in reality, present) glory, vss. 3b–25, and an account of its sudden end and the repercussion thereof, vss. 26–36. The introduction, summoning the prophet to his task, opens with the usual revelation-event formula (vs. 1), but the charge ("And you, man," vs. 2) enlarges on the bare summons to lament (seen in 19:1f, and the more or less similar 28:2 and 32:2 [32:18 falls outside the pattern]). Tyre's special character as a port city-state, the agent of commerce to a far-flung clientele, is stated, sounding the main theme of the oracle.

A (vss. 3b–25a): Tyre in its glory. Tyre is described metaphorically as a splendidly outfitted merchantman, laden with all the wares of the world. The ship and the list of wares constitute distinct literary units.

A1 (vss. 3b–11): the ship. This section opens with the message formula ("Thus said Lord YHWH") and Tyre's praise of herself as a "perfect beauty." The prophet concurs ("your builders perfected your beauty," vss. 3b–4) and goes on to particularize. The resumptive phrase in vs. 11, "they perfected your beauty," marks the close of the unit. (A subunit, vss. 9–11a, in which *hyw b-* is iterated, is closed by the reversal of these elements in vs. 11a$^{\beta}$, *b- hyw* [Ilana Goldberg].)

A1 works out in detail the metaphor of the ship Tyre: her parts are made of choice materials imported from many lands (vss. 5–7); her company of seamen and warriors is drawn from far and near (vss. 8–11). Vessel and crew together are a magnificent sight. In vs. 11 and probably in vs. 9b the referent intrudes into the metaphor, but the main line of imagery is preserved. The mention in vs. 9b of ships and sailors "bringing you imports" anticipates the subject and terminology of the next portion of text, vss. 12–25a, the itemization of Tyre's trade. This anticipation indicates that the register of trade items no less than the human cargo—the crew, seamen, and soldiers—belongs to the tale of the ship's splendor.

A2 (vss. 12–25a): the list of Tyre's trade. The list is naturally understood to comprise the cargo with which ship Tyre is loaded. Hence we include the list in the first part of the lament that describes Tyre's glory. The final words of this section, "in the midst of the seas" (vs. 25), resume the first words of vs. 4, "in the midst of the seas was your boundary."

The list begins and ends with "Tarshish" (vss. 12, 25a) and exhibits an alternating pattern with typical variations, which dissolves toward the end. In its fullest form the pattern (a) names the trading partner, (b) qualifies it by a noun (phrase) derived from **sḥr* or **rkl*, (c) grounds its connection with Tyre in Tyre's wealth, (d) enumerates the wares traded and (e) how they functioned (e.g., as imports or exports). The alternations of terms, and the variations for their own sake, are salient literary features of the passage.

In the following table, + denotes presence of an item, − its absence.

	a	*b*	*c*	*d*	*e*
Verse	Trading partner	Qualification	Tyre's wealth	Wares traded	Function
12	+	*sḥrt*	*hwn*	+	exports
13	+	*rkly*	−	+	import
14	+	−	−	+	exports
15	++	*rkly* / *sḥrt yd*	−	+	delivery by contract
16	+	*sḥrt*	*mʿśy*	+	exports
17	+	*rkly*	−	+	import
18–19a	+	*sḥrt*	*mʿśy*/*hwn*	+	exports
19b	−?	−	−	+	import
20	+	*rklt*	−	+	for riding
21	+	*sḥry yd* / *sḥry*	−	+	−
22	+	*rkly*	−	+	exports
23–24	+	*rklt*/*rkly*	−	+	in markets?

Columns *a* and *d* are virtually perfect; columns *b* and *e* show a dominant tendency to alternate the terms of qualification and function, realizing a general intent to vary the recurrent terms so as to avoid monotony. The major divergences from pattern in vss. 19, 23–24, seem to be textually corrupt. But enough remains in which deliberate variation is manifest to preclude classifying the passage as simply prosaic, a dry (Fohrer) commercial inventory. Our list is a poetic adaptation of such an inventory. That there is no inherent opposition between list and poetry is shown, in ancient literature, by Homer's catalogue of Greek ships (*Iliad* 2.484–785) and his catalogue of Trojan forces (ibid., 786–877). Moreover, embedded in a Sumerian myth about the divine couple Enki and Ninhursag is a list, strikingly comparable to ours, of the trade of the paradisiacal port city of Dilmun. Couched as a blessing, it reads thus in the translation of Thorkild Jacobsen, *The Harps That Once* . . . [New Haven and London: Yale University Press, 1987], pp. 188 f.):

May Dilmun become (an emporium,)
  a (store)house on the quay
  for the country's produce!
May the land Tukrish
  [offer you for exchange]
  gold of the river-bends,
may it exchange lapis-lazuli
  and clear [lapis lazuli!]
May the land Meluhha
  load precious desirable sard,
mesu wood of the plains
  the best *abba* wood
  up into large ships!
May the land Marhashi me[et] you
  with precious stones,
  topa[zes],
May the land Magan
  offer you [for exchange]
  strong copper gongs, . . .
May the Sealands
  offer you [for exchange]
  ebony wood
  fit for a king's chest!
May the "Tent" lands
  offer you [for exchange]
  fine multicolored wools!
May the land Elam
  offer you for exchange
  choice wools, its produce!
May the manor Ur,
  the royal throne dais,
  city of hea[rt's delight,]
[load up into] large ships for you
  sesame, august raiment,
  and fine cloth!

May the wide sea
  [yield you] its wealth!

Jacobsen observes that the countries mentioned are on the periphery of the world as known to the Sumerians. To stress how far-flung was the trade involved, their names are presented in diametrically opposed pairs: Tukrish-Meluhha for north and south, Marhashi-Magan for east and west (p. 188, n. 16). As we shall see directly, Ezekiel's list is constructed on similar principles. Though we cannot identify links between the Sumerian poem from the end of the third millennium B.C.E. and our mid-first millennium prophecy, as a structural forerunner, the former supports the authenticity of the latter. One cannot leave this subject without paying respects to the exquisite effects of the commodity lists in John Masefield's gem "Cargoes"—a definitive confutation of the notion that trade lists and poetry are incompatible (brought to my notice by my lamented student, Nehamah Leiter).

A certain order is discernible. Tarshish, Javan, Tubal, Meshech, Beth-togarmah, and Rhodians all are Japhethites according to the list of nations of Gen 10:2–4, the outermost, uttermost zone of the inhabited world known to ancient Israelite authors, to the west and north of Tyre. This is followed by the innermost strip of locations most adjacent to Tyre, including Aram (or Edom) Judah and "the land of Israel," Damascus (and if correct, Izalla) nearby the east and northeast of Tyre. Then Arabian Dedan, Kedar, Raama, and Sheba to the southeast of Tyre; and finally far east, north Mesopotamian Haran, Eden, Assur. The extremes of west and east thus bound the list, and express vividly Tyre's worldwide connections. To the merchant ship Tyre stream goods—raw and manufactured—from everywhere.

B (vss. 25b–36): the shipwreck and worldwide laments.

B1 (vss. 25b–27): a sirocco strikes the ship on the high seas and wrecks it; the brief account of its loss particularizes the main heads of the vessel's contents, thus bringing home the extent of the disaster.

B2 (vss. 28–36a): the effect on the commercial world of Tyre's destruction: a paralysis of seafaring (vss. 28–29), general mourning and lament (vss. 30–32a). The text of the seamen's lament follows (vss. 32b–36a)—a miniature of the prophet's. First, a recall of Tyre's past success, which benefited all her trade partners (vss. 32b–33); then the tale of the shipwreck and the ensuing universal consternation (vss. 34–36a).

The oracle ends with a briefer version of the "horror and disappearance" formula with which ch. 26 ends (again in 28:19).

The initial appellation of Tyre as "dealer (*rklt*) for peoples" (vs. 3) is echoed in the second member of the recurrent pair "trader-dealer" that alternates ten times in the trade list, and crescendoes in a manifold occurrence of the root *rkl* at the close of the list (vss. 22–29). The "dealer for peoples" is echoed again by "traders with the peoples" who mourn Tyre in the final verse of the lament (vs. 36). The concentration of derivatives of the synonymous roots *sḥr* and *rkl*, together with repetition of the (Phoenician?) terms *m'rb* and *'zbwn*, lends a pervasive mercantile ambience to the oracle.

As befits a depiction of wealth and splendor, the governing form of discourse throughout is inventory: counting off item by item so as to make an impression of great quantity. The description of the ship's construction is as much inventory as the trade list, the regular order of items being: material, origin, verb, product (variation in vs. 6b: product, verb, material, origin). The ship's company (vss. 8–12) lists origin and task of each functionary — with constant variation in length of statement.

The sections of the oracle are interconnected verbally. In vs. 9b "bringing you imports" foreshadows the list of imports and exports that is to come, and the construction "they lent you splendor" heralds the identically constructed refrain in the trading list, "they gave you [as/for] import/exports." The trade list fleshes out the commercial terms "import, export, wealth" by which the wealth of Tyre will be alluded to in vss. 27, 33–34, of the lament section (B). The functionaries referred to in the second part of the oracle have all been introduced in the description of Tyre's past glory. Thus the present text integrates the diverse parts of the oracle through terminological anticipation and resumption.

Most critics deny the originality of the trade list, and consequently of all the passages in which its characteristic terms "import," "export," and "wealth" appear, scattered though they be throughout the oracle. This position misconceives the notion of originality. It is highly probable that the ultimate origin of the data of the trade list is Tyrian; that says nothing about the present form of the list. Its artificiality (noted above, and on which see more ahead) speaks for adaptation to its present purpose; the working of its terms into the fabric of the oracle is part of that adaptation. Perhaps the most important argument in favor of the integrality of the list is that something like it is needed and would have been missed if it didn't appear where it does. In A1 the ship is built and manned; at the beginning of B1 the ship lies low in the water, heavily laden. Without the list of wares (A2), the summary "so you were full and very heavy" (vs. 25b), which is admitted by those critics to belong to the original oracle, would lack reference, and one would have to posit an alternative, "lost" list of cargo which the present trade list "replaced."

Efforts to evaluate the list and determine its historic setting have been baffled by its obscurities (see comments) and the insufficiency of extraneous data. No consensus has been reached. I. M. Diakonoff concluded from a detailed study that it is what it purports to be: a knowledgeable and exact survey of the navy and trade of Tyre as it was at the beginning of the sixth century B.C.E. To account for Ezekiel's amazing familiarity with the subject, Diakonoff raises the possibility that the prophet made a stay in Tyre before its siege, or that in Babylonia the data were leaked to him by Babylonian intelligence ("The Naval Power and Trade of Tyre," *IEJ* 42 [1992], 168–93). M. Liverani, too, considers the picture of Tyrian trade as basically reliable (though "deformed by ideology") and seeks to work out the rationale of its literary presentation in terms of geographic "belts" ("The Trade Network of Tyre according to Ezek. 27," in M. Cogan and I. Ephʿal, eds., *Ah, Assyria* . . . [Festschrift Ḥayim Tadmor], Scripta Hierosolymitana 33 [Jerusalem: Magnes Press, 1991], 65–79). Earlier, B. Mazar supposed its "poetic" character to antedate its adoption by the prophet (an unlikely idea). "We may assume that . . . Ezekiel learned this poem from the inhabitants of Bīt Ṣurraia, a colony of Tyrian exiles [mentioned in Neo-Babylonian inscriptions] in the neighborhood of Nippur on the Chebar [canal]" (*The Early Biblical Period* [Jerusalem, Israel Exploration Society, 1986], p. 81). Fohrer supposes an Egyptian origin, since otherwise Egypt would not have been omitted as a major trading partner of Tyre; but would Tyre be omitted from a list of Egypt's trade? Zimmerli notes that the list of trade and the earlier list of items describing the ship's material and crew are mutually exclusive — so Egypt (vs. 7) is mentioned after all. On his part, Zimmerli speculates that at first the list was "a matter-of-fact enumeration stemming from a great commercial house or from a government agency."

G. Garbini considers the first half of the eighth century to be the best fit for the ethnic entities listed as active in trade (e.g., Israel was no longer extant in Ezekiel's time [but that may be the force of "the land of Israel" — its territory rather than its kingdom]). G. Bunnens regards the very abundance of geographic-ethnic terms as suspicious and ascribes the trade list to a post-Ezekiel redactor, of the school that composed the Table of Nations of Genesis 10 (whose post-exilic origin is itself debatable); for these opinions, see G. Bunnens, *L'expansion phénicienne en Méditerranée* (Rome and Brussels: Institut Historique Belge de Rome, 1979), pp. 88–90. H. J. Katzenstein, following B. Mazar, dates the entire chapter to the ninth century, as reflecting the flourishing of Tyre under Ethbaal I (*History*, pp. 154 ff.). We must admit that we have not the means for checking the details of Ezekiel's picture, or for determining its precise date, let alone separating the rhetorical from the factual components. Nor can we say how the prophet came by his information, though as he was a priest we may assume he had access (before his deportation) to the full range of information stores of temple and palace. The closest biblical analogue to the trade list is the Table of Nations in Gen 10, whose greater part is derived from the Priestly source. The table is generally dated to the seventh century, and it is pertinent to our inquiry that a recent study concludes that the source of its data on lands distant from Judah was the Phoenicians (Y. B. Tsirkin, "Japheth's Progeny and the Phoenicians," in E. Lipinski, ed., *Phoenicia and the Bible* [Leuven: Peeters, 1991], pp. 117–31). The mention of "Judah and the land of Israel" in the trade list (vs. 17) attests to a commercial relation between Jerusalem and Tyre from which knowledge of the latter's far-flung trade network may have sprung.

We turn to the themes of the oracle.

The island situation of Tyre generated the image of the merchant city as a splendidly outfitted and fortified merchant ship. While this image might have come unaided to the prophet's mind, related data from later times deserve mention for the possibility that they reflect earlier notions that may have influenced Ezekiel.

On coins and inscriptions of Hellenistic-age port cities the honorific Greek epithet *nauarchis* "admiral's flagship, command ship" appears. Liddell and Scott, *Greek-English Lexicon*, s.v., list the cities of Tyre, (Phoenician) Tripoli, and Laodicea by the Sea (in Syria), and interpret the epithet to mean "mistress of a fleet." A. Fitzgerald adduces Sidon, and compares our "ship Tyre," remarking that in both cases "an older typically Phoenician point of view may well be reflected"

("The Mythological Background for the Representation of Jerusalem as a Queen and False Worship as Adultery in the O.T.," *CBQ* 34 [1972], 403–16; citation, p. 406 n. 16).

A curious literary kinship exists between elements of Ezekiel's oracle and reports about Tyre found in classical authors. According to the fabulous account given of the founding of Tyre by the fifth-century-C.E. Greek epic poet Nonnos in his *Dionysiaca* 40.428ff., Tyre originally consisted of two floating rocks (*ṣor* "rock")—a rough analogy to a floating ship. The god Herakles instructed men to build the first-ever ship in order to get to the islands, and to make a sacrifice by which a juncture of the two would be effected and they should become anchored to the ground (Pliny records a tradition that the cargo ship was an invention of one Hippus of Tyre, *Natural History* 7.46.208). Nonnos's detailed account of the building of the ship (lines 443ff.) and Ezekiel's of the building of the ship Tyre are mutually illuminating. In the following extracts from Nonnos, terms that have equivalents in Ezekiel are emphasized:

Clear me this [mountain-]ridge of *pinewoods* . . .
And make me a *clever* [*sophon* "wise"] work . . .
Set a long row of . . . *ribs* and rivet *planks* to them . . .
Let there be a *tall spar* [= a mast] upright in the middle . . .
Fasten a wide *linen cloth* to the middle of the pole . . .
Keep the *sail* extended . . .

In subsequent lines Nonnos refers to plugging gaps between the timbers (cf. Ezekiel's "breach-repairers," vs. 9a) and to the tiller that guides, steers, and drives the craft (cf. Ezekiel's "oarsmen" and "sailors" [lit. "rope-men"] vs. 8). Although these authors were centuries apart, the basic elements of Phoenician ships, fit for a narrative of construction, remained constant.

For her fall to produce the desired effect, Tyre had to be magnified, and it was not difficult to do this, in view of the actual wealth of the enterprising city. The list of trade items serves this purpose: it gives substance to Tyre's title "dealer for peoples to many coastlands" by enumerating the many coastlands (and islands) from which Tyre imported and to which she exported. The artificial alternation of the terms "exports" and "imports" expresses vividly the middlemanship of Tyre: what she imported she exported, so that to trade with her was effectively to trade with the whole world. Whatever was available anywhere for exchange was available from Tyre's ships; she was everyone's commercial agent and all were enriched by her service as a vortex of goods to be exchanged.

How varied and rich the cargo of a single ancient Mediterranean (fourteenth century B.C.E.) merchantman could be is shown in the contents of the shipwreck recovered off the southwest Turkish town of Ulu Burun (reported by George F. Bass, "Oldest Known Shipwreck Reveals Splendors of the Bronze Age," *National Geographic* 172/6 [December 1987], 692–733): copper ingots, mined from Cyprus, shaped in forms known from Ugarit; tin ingots (from Afghanistan? Turkey?), weighing six tons (pp. 719–20); Canaanite jars, ebony-like wood (from Africa), Baltic amber; ivory tusks (elephant? hippopotamus?); Canaanite jewelry, blue glass ingots (Mycenean? Egyptian?); silver and gold ornaments; sailor's sword. The multifarious cargo of the ship Tyre is not utterly fantastic. (A summary of information on Mediterranean trade drawn from cargoes of ancient shipwrecks is included in S. Wachsmann, "On the Syro-Canaanite Sea Trade in the Late Bronze Age," in B. Kedar, et al., eds., *Commerce in Palestine Throughout the Ages* [in Hebrew] [Jerusalem: Yad Izhak ben Zvi and Israel Exploration Society, 1990], pp. 42–66 [cargoes itemized on pp. 43ff.]; I thank Israel Eph'al for directing me to this work.)

The very abundance of Tyre's merchandise proves to be her undoing. In the terms of the metaphor, the heavily loaded ship lies low in the water, and once taken out to sea is an easy victim of an east wind (a reference to divine agency, now no longer figured as a rising sea [26:3, 19] but, as in 17:10, the deadly east wind). "Had your oarsmen taken notice of your overload, they would not have moved you from the port without lightening your load . . . The sailors are the cause of your settling in the sea" (Kara). Kara goes on to draw the implication of our passage that pride of wealth and success led to Tyre's fall—the theme of the following oracles (ch. 28). But in fact it is the distinctive feature of this oracle that no ground for Tyre's destruction is contained in it. The focus is entirely on the contrast between the past (in reality present) glory of Tyre and its lamented (in reality future) downfall. True, the sinking of the ship (vs. 26) is ominously juxtaposed (vs. 25) to its being weighted down with merchandise. But as opposed to the preceding and following oracles, no explicit justification of Tyre's fate is given here; the dirge is nonjudgmental, virtually sympathetic.

As a consequence of Tyre's extensive commercial relations the scope of those lamenting her fall is vast, "all the inhabitants of the coastlands, all their kings, traders with the peoples" (vss. 35–36)—generalities particularized in the list of trading partners. Once again (as in 26:16) the details of mourning rites are described (but different from and complementing those of 26:16). The prophet's lament is then reinforced by an echoing sub-lament in the mouth of the affected parties—an artful device to heighten the effect. Like the rulers' lament in 26:17–18, the seamen's lament summarizes what precedes it, highlighting one point: the benefit and enrichment Tyre bestowed on all who dealt with her.

This oracle is fitly placed between chs. 26 and 28. In ch. 26 Tyre culpably gloats over Jerusalem's fall: "The 'doors of the peoples' has been broken; I will be filled." We are not told there what the nature of that fullness might be; here it is minutely described. In ch. 26 all the sea chiefs go into mourning and lament Tyre's fall, but the dimensions of the calamity are not revealed. Here the background for the universal extent of mourning is vividly set forth. In ch. 28 Tyre's offense, the justification of her fall, is spelled out at length: it is *hubris* arising from her commercial skill and success. After reading ch. 27 the justification of Tyre's *hubris* is manifest.

Tyre's unique island situation and appearance generated two striking figures of her destruction: in ch. 26 a tidal wave oversweeps her, reducing her built-up splendor to bare rock; here a gale causes her, a magnificent merchantman, to founder in the open sea. One cannot but admire the imaginative power of the prophet, in truth a master of figures.

XXVIII. THE FALL OF TYRE'S HUBRISTIC LEADER (28:1–10)

28 [1]The word of YHWH came to me: [2]Man, say to the leader of Tyre: Thus said Lord YHWH:

Because your heart has grown haughty and you say, "I am a god; the dwelling of a god I dwell in the heart of the seas"—
But you are a human and not a god, yet you hold your heart to be like the heart of a god—
[3]Surely you are wiser than Daniel; no mystery baffles you.
[4]Through your wisdom and understanding you have got
wealth; you have got gold and silver in your treasuries.
[5]Through your great wisdom in your dealing you made your
wealth great;
And your heart has grown haughty because of your wealth—

[6]Therefore thus said Lord YHWH: Because you hold your heart to be like the heart of a god, [7]therefore I am bringing upon you strangers, the most terrible of nations. They shall unsheath their swords against the beauty of your wisdom and desecrate your radiance. [8]They shall bring you down into the Pit, and you shall die the death of one slain, in the heart of the seas.

[9]Will you still say "I am a god" in the face of your killer,[a] when you prove to be a human and not a god [b]in the hands of your desecrators[c]? [10]You shall die the death of the uncircumcised[b] at the hands of strangers, for I have spoken it, declares Lord YHWH.

COMMENT

28:2. *the leader of Tyre.* The term *nagid* is used here as a synonym of *melek* "king" in the following oracle, 28:12, as it is in Psalms 76:13 (*ngydym* ‖ *mlky ʾrṣ*). T. N. D. Mettinger argues that in early texts (as I Sam 9:16) it means "king designate, crown prince" (*King and Messiah,* Coniectanea Biblica OT 8 [Lund: Gleerup, 1976], 151–84); but here and in post-exilic literature it has the general

[a] Hebrew witnesses and G S V "killers."
[b–b] G "among the multitude of uncircumcised you shall die."
[c] Hebrew witnesses "your desecrator."

sense of "leader." The king of Tyre at this time was Ethbaal III (Katzenstein, pp. 325ff.), but nothing in this oracle is known to be specific to him.

your heart. Hebrew *leb(ab)* "heart" occurs eight times in this brief oracle, in various senses: the seat of pride (vss. 2, 5, with *gbh* "be high, haughty"; see I, 358), the seat of wisdom, "mind" (vss. 2, 6), and the inner part—as opposed to the shore—of the sea (vss. 2, 8; as in 27:4, 26).

I am a god (ʾel). When the Tyrian's boast is repeated in vs. 9, *ʾel* is replaced by *ʾelohim*, indicating that the former, like the latter, is a common noun and not an allusion to the Canaanite god El, known from Ugaritic myths as "father of the gods" (see the range of opinion summarized in S. Rummel, ed., *Ras Shamra Parallels*, III [Rome: Pontificium Institutum Biblicum, 1981], p. 340). The less common shorter term here is probably conditioned by the following rebuttal *ʾdm wlʾ ʾl* "a human and not a god," in which it is preferred as befitting the epigrammatic terseness of the phrase (again in Isa 31:3, and cf. *lo ʾiš ʾel* "not man is God," Num 23:19).

On the theme of self-deification, see Structure and Themes.

the dwelling of a god I dwell. Construing *mošab* as a cognate accusative, as in Exod 12:40: "the Israelites' dwelling (*mošab*) that they dwelt (*yašebu*) in Egypt." Variants of this construction appear in vs. 8 *wmth mmwty ḥll* "you shall die the death of one slain," and vs. 10 *mwty ʿrlym tmwt* "you shall die the death of the uncircumcised." From his inaccessibility in his island fastness, and the wealth that he has amassed (vss. 4f.), Tyre's leader infers his divinity.

Another possibility is to take *mošab* concretely "seat, abode" (as in 8:3, the seat [= site] of the image): "in a god's seat I sit." Is there then some allusion to a sea-girt divine abode? The Ugaritic gods dwell each in his or her *mtb* "abode" (*ANET*³, p. 131b). El is located "at the sources of the floods, in the midst of the Headwaters of the Two Oceans" (e.g., *ANET*³, p. 129b); cf. the allusions in Xenophon's *Anabasis* (1.4.7, 10) to royal palaces built on river sources. But these are symbols connecting deity and royalty with fertility (cf. the fecundating stream that issues from the Temple in 47:1ff.), remote from the image of the island fortress of Tyre. The added phrase "in the heart of the seas" lends support to the straightforward interpretation of godlikeness as remoteness from human reach.

But you are a human and not a god. Cf.: "But Egypt is human and not a god, and its horses are flesh and not spirit" (Isa 31:3), possibly the inspiration of our phrase.

you hold your heart to be like the heart of a god. The leader's haughtiness springs from his success and prosperity, which puff him up to thinking he is equal to a god in his wisdom. The heart is the seat of wisdom (= mind), as in Exod 31:6; Prov 23:15. Divine wisdom is mentioned in Isa 31:2 (outstrips human devices), Jer 10:7 (outstrips all sages), and Dan 2:20; 5:11 (a divine possession); II Sam 14:20 speaks of the wisdom of God's angels.

3. *Surely you are wiser than Daniel.* Sarcastic? The biblical Daniel is recognized by the pagan Nebuchadnezzar as having "the spirit of the holy gods in him, and exceeding illumination and understanding and wisdom is found in him" (Dan 4:6). This trait, dominant in the biblical character, is not prominent in the Ugaritic Danʾel (renowned for his justice), the probable ancestor of this

Dan(i)el—who, however, by Ezekiel's time had acquired the virtue of wisdom as well; see I, 257.

no mystery baffles you. Of the biblical Daniel it is said, *kol raz la ʾanes lak* "no mystery baffles you" (Dan 4:6), perhaps an Aramaic version of our expression (Ilana Goldberg); cf. T here: *kol raz la ʾitkassa minak* "no mystery is concealed from you." *satum* "mystery, secret" is a passive participle of *satam* "stop up, block"; in Dan 8:26; 12:4, 9, the verb means "keep secret"—the sense applicable here. "Baffles" renders *ʿmmw-* from *ʿmm* "darken" (related to Aram *ʿmʾ* "be dark, troubled" and Arab *ġamma* "grieve, trouble"). In 31:8 the verb appears in its primary sense: "cedars . . . did not darken—i.e., overshadow—it"; here the sense will be "cast a (metaphoric) shadow over, trouble" (Eliezer of Beaugency; so, too, H-P. Müller, "Mantische Weisheit und Apokalyptik," SVT 22 [1972], 268–93; citation, 278). Cf. Lam 4:1, "How has gold become dim (*yuʿam*)." Akkadian *ešû* "become dark, confused, troubled" (*CAD* E 412) offers a semantic parallel (I. Goldberg).

An alternative interpretation invokes a hypothetical **ʿmm*, the root of *ʿim* "with," having the sense "be equal to, be a match for"; but such a verb is unexampled in Semitic.

The subject *kl stwm*, lit. "every mystery," is treated as a collective and hence takes a verb in plural (*ʿmmw-*); cf. Gen 7:22, "every [living thing] that had breath of life in its nostrils . . . [they] died."

4. *wisdom and understanding.* With these God endowed the skilled craftsmen who built the desert tabernacle (Exod 36:1; to these gifts is added "knowledge" [*daʾat*] in 31:3; 35:31). Here a genius for commerce is meant, and for making money; see the next verse and the like depiction of the Phoenicians in Zech 9:2–3 as "wise" in amassing wealth.

got, lit. "make" in the sense of "acquire, amass, gather" (BDB aptly compares English "make money"), is idiomatic, as in "make riches (*ʿošer*)," Jer 17:11; "property, wealth (*kabod*)," Gen 31:1. S T actually translate the second *got* by "gather" as a better fit for the following preposition "in (your treasuries)"—Hebrew being more flexible.

5. *in your dealing.* G S separate this word from the preceding: "wisdom and trading," as in vs. 4a "wisdom and understanding," are separate. MT varies the pattern, preferably. Vs. 5a augments vs. 4a, adding "greatness" (*rb*[*h*]) and specifying "dealing" (*rklh,* here with a more general meaning than in 26:12, where it is "merchandise") as the realm in which the Tyrian's wisdom (= skill) was displayed.

7. *strangers, the most terrible of nations.* The Babylonians, according to 26:7ff. Hab 1:6–10 describes them as "dreadful and awesome." For similar expressions, cf. Ezek 7:21–22. "Strangers ‖ terrible ones" recurs in Isa 29:5; Ps 54:5. With the hostile connotation of *zar,* Luzzatto (at Isa 29:5) compares Latin "hostis," which originally meant "stranger" but afterward "enemy," a (public) foe "because in antiquity most peoples were hostile to one another." Cf. Akkadian *nakru* (cognate with Hebrew *nokri* "foreign[er]"), meaning "alien, strange, hostile," and as a substantive "enemy" (I. Goldberg).

the beauty of your wisdom. The splendor (see comment to 27:3 "I am a perfect beauty") in which your wisdom is embodied (after Davidson); cf. the synonymy of beauty and wisdom in vs. 12 below.

desecrate. G T "injure," S "sully" are both inexact; see next note.

your radiance. Hebrew *yipʿa*, only here and in vs. 17, is derived from the same base (*ypʿ*) as the verb *hopiaʿ* "shine forth" (usually of God's revelation). G does not distinguish it from *ypy* "beauty"; however, S "glory, splendor" and T "dread radiance" (*zw ʾymt-*) point to a conception well documented in ancient Mesopotamia. "The sanctity of the royal person is often said to be revealed by a supernatural and awe-inspiring radiance or aura . . . characteristic of deities and of all things divine . . . [Akkadian] *melammu*, something like 'awe-inspiring luminosity,' is [the] most frequent [term for this phenomenon]" (A. L. Oppenheim, *Ancient Mesopotamia*, rev. ed., completed by E. Reiner [Chicago: University of Chicago Press, 1977], p. 98). Hence *ḥllw* "desecrate" is aptly used for the demotion of the king to his mortal status.

8. *the Pit.* Hebrew *šaḥat* is a frequent equivalent of *bor* "Pit," in the sense of the abode of the dead (26:20). In Ps 30:10 *šaḥat* takes the place of *bor* of vs. 4. For the nonfigurative sense, see above 19:4, 8.

the death of one slain. Not a natural death. The abstract *memote* "death, dying" has the form of *mebo'e* "entering" 26:10, on which see comment. For another unnatural death, see Jer 16:4 "die a death of/by diseases" (*memote taḥaluʾim*).

in the heart of the seas. An ironic twist to vs. 2a: to the Tyrian, dwelling in "the heart of the seas" bestows on him godlike invulnerability and splendor. But the long arm of God's agent will reach him in his island fastness, where he will die as one slain, a mortal, not a god.

The student Noah Hayyot notes the affinity of the language of this verse (8) to that of the description of calamity in Jonah's psalm: "You cast me in the deep in the heart of the seas (*blbb ymym*) . . . you brought up my life from (vs. 8: they shall bring you down into) the pit (*šḥt*)" (Jonah 2:4, 7). If the terms of vs. 8 were indeed borrowed from psalm language, the conversion of "the heart of the seas" from a general figure of troubles to the location of Tyre (throughout the Tyre prophecies of Ezekiel) is noteworthy.

9. *Your killer . . . desecrators.* The shift from singular to plural may be a scribal compromise between a reading in which both nouns were singular and another in which both were plural. The versions and mss. show leveling in one or another direction. Or the actual slayer is thought of as one, while the desecrators are many.

"Your desecrators" renders *mḥllyk* according to the usual sense of the piʿel of *ḥll*—as *wḥllw* "they shall desecrate" in vs. 7. But the proximity to "one slain (*ḥalal*; vs. 8)" invites construing the word as a denominative, "those who make you a *ḥalal*," i.e., "your slayers" (|| "your killer"); the passive denominative occurs in 32:26: *meḥulele ḥereb*, lit. "those rendered *ḥllym* by the sword."

10. *the death* (mwty) *of the uncircumcised.* The unique *mwty* is a shortened variant of *mmwty* of vs. 8. Uncircumcision is a disgrace (*ḥrph*) to the circumcised Israelites (Gen 34:14), and "uncircumcised" a term of contempt among them;

see how it is used with "Philistines" in, e.g., Judges 14:3; 15:18; I Sam 14:6; 17:26. Hence the expression "die the death of the uncircumcised" is presumably the Israelite equivalent of our "die like a dog" (or: "a dog's death") — i.e., a disgraceful or miserable death. A concomitant of such contempt is the abuse of the corpses of uncircumcised enemies: David produced the foreskins of two hundred slain Philistines as a bride price for his first wife (I Sam 18:25–27). The Egyptians, who likewise practiced circumcision, tallied the corpses of uncircumcised enemies by their severed penises (J. Breasted, *Ancient Records of Egypt*, III, p. 588; E. Meyer, *Geschichte des Altertums*, II/1, p. 558: "To be uncircumcised was a disgrace, and thus one showed even toward corpses the abhorrence of the unclean"). That the Phoenicians practiced circumcision is attested by Herodotus, who records their assertion that they adopted it from the Egyptians (2.104); the expression would therefore be as insulting to the Tyrian as to an Israelite.

To "die the death of X" describes the circumstances of death; see comment above to vs. 8 "the death of one slain," and add "die the death of the righteous" (Num 23:10) — i.e., not premature or violent but peaceful and in a good old age (Gray, *Numbers*, ICC); "die the death of a base man" (II Sam 3:33) — be cut down unceremoniously. This militates against the common opinion that our phrase refers to the humiliation of the ghost of the uncircumcised, who, it is alleged, is consigned to the lowest level of the underworld. See comments to 31:18; 32:19ff.

STRUCTURE AND THEMES

Ch. 28 contains two oracles against Tyre's ruler, the first nonfigurative, the second figurative (similar to the sequence of chs. 26 [nonfigurative] and 27 [figurative]). In both there is a movement from prideful height to abased lowliness, from sanctity to profanation.

Vss. 1–10 are a doom oracle and show its usual pattern of indictment — punitive consequence. The revelation-event formula (vs. 1) is followed by an address to the prophet commanding him to deliver God's message to Tyre's leader (vs. $2a^{\alpha}$). This consists of:

A (vss. $2a^{\beta}$–5), the Tyrian's sin, opening with *ya'an* "because," followed by B (vss. 6–10), his punishment — opening with *laken* "consequently" and ending with a closing formula ("for I have spoken it, declares Lord YHWH").

A is a beautifully wrought complex. Vs. 2 sets the themes of "haughty heart" and self-deification, repeating the keywords "heart" and "god" (*'l/'lhym*) and ending with a combination of the two: "heart of a god." Vss. 3–5 give particulars of the indictment, introducing them with the particle *hnh* (here "surely"), as in 16:49 and 22:6. The cause of the Tyrian's offense is specified through keywords — derivatives of the root **ḥkm* "wise," referring to commercial genius, and thrice-occurring *ḥyl* "wealth," the fruit of wisdom. This leads us back, at the end of vs. 5, to the leader's "haughty heart."

B negates A, echoing its language. Vs. 6 resumes the accusation of vs. $2b^{\beta}$, "you hold your heart to be like the heart of a god" (for such restatements of the ground of punishment introducing the punishment, producing a sequence of *laken–ya'an–laken*, see 22:19 and the delaying tactic of 5:7ff.). Vss. 7–10 depict the leader's punishment at the hands of "strangers"—a term encasing the passage at its beginning and its end. The Tyrian's violated "radiance" (vs. 7) counters his "unshadowed" wisdom (vs. 3). "High of heart," he will be brought low into the Pit, from his fastness in "the heart of the seas"—vss. 8–9, repeating the leader's boast of his divinity (vs. 2) in grim contradiction of it.

Phonetic and syntactic elements connect B to A. Both employ assonance: threefold *ḥll* "desecrate; slain" in vss. 7–9 counterpoints threefold *ḥyl* in vss. 4–5. Within A, *bḥkmtk wbtbwntk* (vs. 4) resonates in (the syntactically different) *bḥkmtk brkltk* (vs. 5). The long form of "heart" in vs. 6 (*lbbk*) links up with *lbbk* at the end of vs. 5, thus bridging the passage from A to B. Within B *ypy* resonates in *yp't-* (vs. 6). A and B share the peculiar cognate noun construction of *mwšb* X *yšb* (vs. 2) "dwell the dwelling of X," *mt mmwty* Y (vs. 8), and (vs. 9) *mwty* Z *tmwt* "die the death of Y/Z" (with chiastic alternation of parts [I. Goldberg]). The structural and formal bonds within and between the components of this oracle speak for its integrity.

Several themes are interwoven in this oracle. The universal principle against which the leader of Tyre has offended is stated succinctly where we should expect it—in the wisdom literature: "Every haughty person (lit. 'high of heart') is an abomination to YHWH" (Prov 16:5; see the additional citations in I, 358). As in Deut 8:12–18 pride (*rwm lbb* "heart be high") results from acquisition of wealth (*'śh ḥyl*). As in the Garden of Eden story (Gen 2) a hankering after godlikeness and divine wisdom eventuates in the fall of the overweening humans. Whether in fact the ruler of Tyre in Ezekiel's time claimed divinity is moot. A recent theory gives him a role in the ritual of "Awakening (revival) of Melkart"—the chief god of Tyre (*milk qart* "king of the city")—in which the king was a hypostasis of the god (C. Bonnet-Tzavellas, "Le dieu Melqart," in F. Gubel et al., eds., *Studia Phoenicia*, I–II [Leuven, 1983], p. 196), and Aelian (second century C.E., Rome) reports that the Phoenician royal family claimed descent from the gods (*Varia Historia* 14.30). Israel's prophets ascribed self-deification to pagan kings as an expression of their supreme arrogance and self-reliance. Mesopotamian kings contemporary with the prophets have left us plenty of examples of self-vaunting, but they attribute their triumphs to their gods. No Mesopotamian king contemporary with Isaiah can be cited in support of Isaiah's alleged quotation: "I will climb to the sky; higher than the stars of God I will set my throne. I will sit in the mount of [the divine] assembly . . . I will match the Most High" (Isa 14:13–14). But in the prophets' view the pagan world was truly godless, its worship of idols effectively solipsistic, the worship by humans of human handiwork. Thus the functional god in the prophetic view of paganism was the human repository of power, wisdom, and wealth that made things happen. The intimate knowledge Ezekiel had of Tyre's commercial success was displayed in the previous oracle. Here he depicts the commander of that success as afflicted with typical pagan blindness (as the prophets understood it), conceiving success as evidence for his divinity.

Thus this chapter links up with the preceding description of Tyre as a glorious, prosperous emporium by providing the justification of its fall. The king's role as the emblem of his state (I, 219) makes possible the representation of the city's fall by a story of the downfall of its hubristic ruler. His claim to divinity enables the prophet to term his humiliating death a "desecration," thus preparing the way for the mythologized recasting of the story in the following oracle.

XXIX. The Fall of Tyre's King: A Mythical Version (28:11–19)

28 [11]The word of YHWH came to me: [12]Man, recite a dirge over the king of Tyre
and say to him: Thus said Lord YHWH:

You were the [a]sealer of proportion,[a]
full of wisdom and perfect in beauty!
[13]In Eden, the garden of God, you were,
every precious stone your hedge:
carnelian, peridot, and diamond,
beryl, onyx, and jasper,
sapphire, turquoise, and emerald;
And of gold was the work of your tambours and settings,
fixed in you on the day you were created.

[14] [b]You were a great shielding cherub!
And I set you
in the holy mountain of God[b] you were;
amidst fire-stones you walked about.
[15]Unblemished were you in your ways
from the day you were created,
until wrongdoing was found in you.

[16]Because of your many dealings
your midst was filled with lawless gain, and you sinned.
So I desacralized [and barred] you from the mountain of God,
and [c]I banished you, shielding cherub,[c] from
amidst fire-stones.
[17]Your heart grew haughty on account of your beauty,
You corrupted your wisdom together with your radiance.
To the ground I hurled you, before kings I set you,
for [them] to gaze on you.

[a] G S V and some Hebrew witnesses "seal of likeness," as from *ḥotam tabnit.*
[b–b] G "with the cherub I set you in [the] holy mountain of God"; S "and you were with the anointed and shading cherub, and I set you in the holy mountain of God" (S attaches "you walked" to the beginning of the next verse: "and you walked unblemished," etc.).
[c–c] G "the cherub led you"; S "the shading cherub banished you."

[18]By your many iniquities, because of your wrongful dealings
You desecrated your holy precincts.[d]
So I caused fire to break out from your midst;
it consumed you.
I turned you into ashes on the ground
before the eyes of all who gazed on you.

[19]All among the peoples who knew you are appalled over you;
You have become a horror and are gone forever.

COMMENT

28:12. *the king.* The same as the "leader" of 28:2; here called "king" in anticipation of his disgrace in the sight of his royal peers (vs. 17). Note the similar variation of terms between 26:16 "chiefs of (*nśy'y*) the sea" and 27:35 "their (i.e., the coastlands') kings."

You were the sealer (ḥotem) *of proportion* (toknit). An obscure expression, meaning, perhaps, "you consummated, perfected measurement" (*toknit* "measurement, proportion" [BDB] again only in 43:10, where it is the object of *wmddw* "they shall measure"; related to *token* "measure"); i.e., you were perfectly proportioned. The figurative meaning of *ḥtm* posited in this conjecture is not attested in Hebrew but is in Syriac and Arabic. Accordingly Ibn Janaḥ utilizes it in his gloss (*Schoraschim*, s.v. *ḥtm*): "you seal perfection (Arabic *'itqān*) and (= i.e.) consummate it—that is, in you beauty is consummated" (see the end of the verse). Ibn Janaḥ regarded *tknyt* (<**tkn*) as cognate with Arabic *'atqana* "make perfect" (<**tqn*), a view held by moderns (see, e.g., KB³, s.v. *toknit*), who compare as well Akkadian, Hebrew, and Aramaic derivatives of **tqn* "be in good order, be right." This yields a translation: "You set the seal on perfection" (e.g., *NEB*), or, with the reading *ḥotam* (see below), "you were the seal of perfection" (e.g., NJPS). According to the following narrative, the figure addressed was an inhabitant of the Garden of Eden, later expelled—a figure somehow related, therefore, to the first human in the Paradise story of Gen 2–3. Hence "set the seal on / were a seal of perfection" will mean either you were a perfect creature or you capped a perfect design (i.e., the design of creation; so, e.g., Ibn Janaḥ in *Schoraschim*, s.v. *tkn*).

Aquila and Theodotion translate "seal (reading *ḥotam*) of preparation," deriving *toknit* from *kwn*, in hif'il *hekin* "prepare, make ready, make." Kara's comment illumines this rendition: "What are you like? Like a seal by which one prepares other seals in imitation of it. That is, you are fashioned like a beautiful implement, serving to fashion a beautiful implement in imitation of it; for I stamped you with my stamp-seal, as it is said, 'in the likeness of God he made him' (Gen 5:1)."

G S V translate as though they read *ḥotam tabnit* "seal[-impression] of likeness"; T *mn' dṣwrt'* "implement of (= with?) a figure" also seems to have read *tbnyt*, since it renders *tbnyt* by *ṣwrt'* in I Chron 28:12, 18, 19 (though elsewhere

[d]*mqdšyk*; some Hebrew witnesses show *mqdšk* (the noun in the singular).

it is usually by *dmwt'* "likeness"). As descriptive of the Adam-like figure in the sequel *ḥotam* refers to Adam, who both received as a stamp-seal the likeness of God (Herrmann: he was "an exact copy of God"), and in turn served as a stamp-seal to impress the divine (= his own) likeness on succeeding generations. Both the passive and the active aspects of Adam as a seal are expressed in Gen 5:1 and 3 respectively: "[1]When God created man, in the likeness (*dmwt*) of God he made him . . . [3]Adam . . . begot a son in his likeness (*bdmwtw*) after his image (*kṣlmw*)."

Allusion to our phrase in the form *ḥotam tabnit* (S *ṭbʿ' ddmwt'*) with reference to Adam appears in Tannaitic sources: in *m. Sanhedrin* 4.5, God is said to "stamp (*ṭbʿ*) all humans with the stamp-seal (*ḥwtm*) of the first human (*adam*), yet none resembles (*dmh*) his fellow." Moreover, the Tannaitic wedding benediction (on its date, see D. Flusser and Sh. Safrai, "bṣlm dmwt tbnytw," in A. Rofé and Y. Zakovitch, eds., *Sefer Yiṣḥaq 'Arye Seeligmann* [Jerusalem: E. Rubinstein, 1983], pp. 453–61 [Hebrew section]) speaks of God's fashioning of man *bṣlm dmwt tbnytw*, a construct chain of synonyms (Y. Avishur, "bṣlm dmwt tbnytw," *Lešonenu* 51 [5647 (1987)], 231–34). The first two words derive from the biblical story; the third has a biblical association with man's creation only in the para-Masoretic form of our phrase. I say para-Masoretic (rather than non-Masoretic) because, as noted by *Minḥat Shay*, a Masoretic authority records *ḥotam*, though the best mss. read *ḥotem*. Abarbanel writes: "[the king of Tyre] is compared to the likeness on a seal (*tabnit haḥotam*)," thus attesting the currency of this alternate reading in the sixteenth century.

For a structural argument in favor of the noun form *ḥotam*, see Structure and Themes.

full of wisdom. An echo of vss. 3–5, recalling also the "wise (= expert) seamen" of Tyre in 27:8.

perfect in beauty. An echo of 27:3—Tyre's boast, here as in 27:11 concurred in by the prophet.

13. *In Eden, the garden of God*. In Gen 2:8, 10, Eden (first *e* long [*ṣere*] to distinguish it from the Aramaic kingdom Eden [first *e* short (*segol*)] of 27:23) is a (mythical) eastern region in which God plants his garden, *gan ʿeden* "the garden of (= which is in) Eden." But here and in 31:9, 16, 18 (and Isa 51:3), Eden is elliptically the garden itself (hence 36:35 is probably "the garden of [= which is] Eden"; as in English "the city of Philadelphia"). Elsewhere called "the garden of YHWH" (Gen 13:10; Isa 51:3), the invocation of the intimate name of Israel's God would have been inappropriate for the present pagan referent.

New light has been shed on *ʿeden* from the Tell Fekheriye bilingual inscription, in which the Aramaic participle *mʿdn* (line 4)—the root hitherto unattested in old Aramaic—has as its Assyrian counterpart (line 6) *mutaḫ[ḫ]idu* "make abounding, luxuriant, prosperous." Hence the attractive conjecture that the name of the mythical biblical garden/region means "abundance, luxuriance" (A. R. Millard, "The Etymology of Eden," *VT* 34 [1984], 103–6; Jonas C. Greenfield, "A Touch of Eden," in *Orientalia J. Duchesne-Guillemin emerito oblata*, Acta Iranica 23 [Leiden: E. J. Brill, 1984], 219–24).

every precious stone your hedge. "Hedge" renders *ms/ś(w)kh/t-* in Mic 7:4, Isa 5:5, and Prov 15:19, and there is no reason to take it otherwise here (some medievals "canopy," as from *skk* "cover, provide shade," some moderns following G S and T "girdle, cover, clothes"). In Isa 5:5 the hedge protects a vineyard; here, the splendid inhabitant of the garden (and incidentally the garden itself). That the hedge should be of precious stones recalls the picture in Isa 54:11–12 of the future Jerusalem, built of jewels, whose boundary stones are all precious (*'bny hpṣ*). Jeweled vegetation grows in an otherworldly grove "of stones" met with by Gilgamesh in his search for eternal youth:

> The carnelian bears its fruits;
> It is hung with vines good to look at.
> The lapis bears foliage;
> It too bears fruit lush to behold. (*ANET*[3], p. 89b)

The final clause of the verse complicates judgment, however, since it speaks of appointments on the person of the inhabitant. That favors taking *mswkh* as that which bound or girt the creature (G S), or clothed him (T), a sense otherwise unevidenced. Beset by uncertainties, we prefer to stay with the attested meaning of *mswkh* and hesitate adjusting it to the obscurity of the final clause (see ahead).

The list of precious stones, arranged in three sets of three, contains—in differing order—nine of the twelve stones of the high priest's breastplate in Exod 28:17–20, omitting the third set of the breastplate. G, listing twelve stones, reproduces its Exodus version, inserting here, inaptly, "silver and gold" between the sixth and seventh stones. But the stones of the breastplate are twelve because they stand for the twelve tribes of Israel, a symbolism irrelevant to this context. G's reading its Exodus version here appears to be a secondary adjustment of the Ezekiel text to that of Exodus; so Y. Zakovitch, *"For Three . . . and for Four": The Pattern of the Numerical Sequence Three-Four in the Bible* (in Hebrew), II (Jerusalem: Makor, 1979), pp. 475–77. It is hard to say what the relation of the two lists is. Was there a version of the Paradise story that told of these stones, which our passage reflects directly, and from which ultimately derived the stones of the priest's breastpiece (increased to twelve—one for each Israelite tribe)? Or was the reference to a hedge (or garment) of precious stones particularized by borrowing from Exodus' list, reducing it by a set of three and changing its order so as to forestall associating the Tyrian king's regalia with that of the Israelite priest (an association made by, e.g., K. Yaron, "The Dirge over the King of Tyre," *Annual of the Swedish Theological Institute* 3 [1964], 28–57; citation, 39f.)?

[DNF: Ezekiel is indicating that these stones go back to the beginning of things—the Creation story and the high priest's breastplate. So he would have every reason to keep the lists the same. A mechanical explanation of the divergences is to be preferred to an ideological one. Thus Ezekiel may not have had the same list that is now found in Exodus. The layout of four registers with three items in each—as in Exodus—is shown by G to have existed in Ezekiel as well, although G's present list is secondary, having been conformed to Exodus. Changes in the order of items are not vital. But MT here is also not original, having suffered loss of a line in the course of transmission—in all likelihood by a scribal error.]

Whatever the origin of the list, the genre was not foreign to the priest-prophet; the priestly writings of the Pentateuch are famous for their lists. The hand that spelled out Tyre's trade (ch. 27) would have delighted in fleshing out the allusion to "every precious stone." There is no compelling reason to deny that it was the prophet's own.

The identification of the stones is uncertain; for detailed treatment, see Zimmerli and *IDB*, s.v. "Jewels."

And of gold, etc. The accents connect this word with the stones (cf. T's paraphrase: "in gold settings"), but gold ought to be separated from them (G outdoes MT, listing "silver and gold" among the stones). Exod 28:20b concludes the enumeration of the stones with the sentence: "They shall be framed in gold in their settings," thus clearly distinguishing the gold work from the precious stones. What gold objects are intended here is obscure. "Tambour" (*tp*) recurs in Jer 31:4(3) as an ornament with which dancers adorn (*'dh*) themselves, perhaps one shaped like a tambourine, with *nqbym* "holes," i.e., settings or housings for jewels (Cooke). Note Ugaritic gold *nqbn* "trappings" (J. C. L. Gibson, *Canaanite Myths and Legends* [Edinburgh: T. & T. Clark, 1978], p. 115) or "housings" (Ginsberg, *ANET*^{3}, p. 153b). The decoration of the person of the creature from its creation appears to be referred to. For this part of the verse comparison with the gold-girt divine being in Dan 10:5f. is apt; for extensive Mesopotamian evidence, see A. Leo Oppenheim, "The Golden Garments of the Gods," *JNES* 8 (1949), 172–93.

T's explanatory paraphrase links vs. 13b with the theme of pride in vs. 17:

> All these (namely, the preceding precious items) were the work of your adornment (*tqwnk*, the word by which T translates *tpyk* in Jer 31:4). And so your heart grew haughty; but you didn't consider that your body is made with cavities and orifices (*nqbyn*) needful for you—since you cannot live without them—fixed in you from the day you were created.

Contemplation of his body's alimentary canal would have checked the Tyrian's pride.

14. *You. 'att* is normally feminine, but here and twice again (Num 11:15; Deut 5:24) masculine; accordingly the creature in the garden is a cherub. G S translate "with (as reading *'et*) the cherub"; accordingly there were two beings in the garden, a resplendent inhabitant and a cherub.

"Great" guesses at *mimšaḥ*—a hapax—connecting it with Aramaic *mšḥ* "measure" (S "anointed" is based on the Hebrew homonym), and inferring the meaning of *krwb mmšḥ* from its Hebrew analogue *'iš midda* (I Chron 11:23) "a large man," lit. "a man of measure" (T *'nš dmšht'*). NJPS "with outstretched shielding wings" is based on an extrapolated sense of the Aramaic verb; cf. Hebrew *hitmoded* "stretched himself" (I Kings 17:21), lit. "measured himself." "Wings" is imported from the description of the cherubs on the desert Ark and in Solomon's temple:

> The cherubs shall have their wings spread out above, shielding (*skkym*) the cover with their wings (Exod 25:20).

> For the cherubs had their wings spread out over the place of the Ark, so that the cherubs shielded the Ark and its poles from above (I Kings 8:7).

It is not clear what shielding function this cherub had, but the image of the Ark cherubs appears to have attracted this descriptive term. G omits the two words MT has after "cherub," perhaps on account of their difficulty.

And I set you. Isolated by the accents, the verb clause (*wnttyk*) appears incomplete—like *wntty* of 17:22 and *wnttym* of 37:26; T (followed by medievals) supplies a complement, translating: "I gave you greatness." G omits the *w-* and connects the verb with the foregoing, on which basis critics have conjectured a rhythmic sequence of three clauses ending in a verb:

> with (= G) the cherub I set you (*nttyk*);
> in the holy mountain of God you were (*hyyt*);
> amidst fire-stones you walked about (*hthlkt*)

NJPS translates *'t krwb . . . wnttyk* "I created you as a cherub" (noting that the meaning is uncertain). It thus joins *wnttyk* to the foregoing, evidently taking *w-* as pleonastic (Williams, *Syntax*, § 435; e.g., *wyṣrtyk* in Isa 37:26—where IQIsa[a] actually omits *w-*); but *ntn* is never "create" but rather "turn into / make (into)"; e.g., Ezek 26:19 "when I make you a ruined city" or vs. 21, "I will make you a horror."

in the holy mountain of God you were. For the noun phrase, see Dan 9:20 ("the holy mountain of my God")—a reference to the Temple mount ("the holy mountain," Isa 27:13; Jer 31:23[22] and frequently). "God" stands in the place of the pronominal possessive suffix attached to *qdš* as in the phrase *hr qdšw* "his holy mountain"; an analogous construction occurs in I Chron 22:19 *kly qdš h'lhym* "the sacred vessels of God." For the relation of this mountain to Eden, see Structure and Themes.

Disregarding the accents, the MT of vs. $14b^{\alpha\beta}$ may be resegmented thus: *wnttyk bhr qdš / 'lhym hyyt*, etc. "and I set you in the holy mountain; a divinity you were." Separating *qdš* from *'lhym* does not fundamentally change the sense. "Holy mountain" is a valid construction by itself, and *'lhym* will mean "divinity," a generic term for transhumans; e.g., angels—Gen 32:3, 29, 31. According to the MT, then, the inhabitant of God's garden/mountain was a divine being, a cherub. The Hebrew is unexceptionable, but the clash with the preceding oracle, which mocks the claim of Tyre's ruler that he is divine, is too much for most commentators. Yet as noted above in connection with Tyre's boast of being a perfect beauty, the prophet may concur in Tyre's self-conceits.

Finally, the possibility must be admitted that the MT of vs. $14b^{\alpha}$ is a conflation of two versions, resulting in an anacoluthon:

wnttyk bhr qdš 'lhym	(cf. vss. $17b^{\beta}$, $18b^{\beta}$)
bhr qdš 'lhym hyyt	(‖ vs. $13a^{\alpha}$)

amidst fire-stones. Perhaps a reference to (or a transformation of) the hedge of sparkling gemstones (vs. 13 [MenbSh]); otherwise unknown. Some support for this view is offered by Akkadian *aban išati* "fire-stone," glossed in lexical texts by *pe/indu*, a stone that appears in magic and ornamental contexts (*AHw*, s.v. *pe/indu*, p. 854). For inconclusive speculations about Ugaritic *'abn brq* (Ginsberg: "thunderbolts[?]," *ANET*³, p. 136b; contrast Gibson, *Canaanite*, p. 49, line 23: "I understand [**byn*] lightning"), see the bibliographic summary in L. R. Fisher, ed., *Ras Shamra Parallels* I, pp. 387f.

15. *wrongdoing was found.* A masculine verb (*nimṣa*) preceding a feminine subject is not a rarity; see, e.g., 47:9b (*whyh hdgh*); GKC, § 145 o; König III, § 345 b. The locative-like *'wlth* "wrongdoing" (with final unstressed *a*) occurs elsewhere in elevated speech or poetry, e.g., Hos 10:13; Ps 125:3. Here, as in Ps 92:16, the form may have been chosen to avoid the contact of two stressed syllables (Joüon-Muraoka, § 93 j). Other feminine nouns appear in this form, all in poetic texts; e.g., *'mth* "terror," Exod 15:16; *swpth* "stormwind," Hos 8:7.

16. As happens repeatedly, the referent breaks through Ezekiel's figures. Here "your many dealings" necessarily alludes to (the king of) Tyre's commercial success, which—we hear for the first time—entailed corruption. "Lawless gain" is a meaning of *ḥamas* found first in Amos 3:10: "They treasure up lawless gain and rapine in their palaces" (in our passage G and T paraphrase "your midst" with "your treasuries"). Homer describes the Phoenicians as "mariners renowned, greedy merchant men" whose piratical behavior is related in the sequel (*Odyssey* 15.415). For Hosea (12:8) the typical trader (called "Canaan," whose "firstborn" was Phoenician Sidon [Gen 10:15]) is a cheat:

> The merchant (*kn'n*)—false scales are in his hands
> He loves to overreach.

Israel's merchants are condemned wholesale as a crooked and predatory lot (Amos 8:4–6). Pursuit of commerce by Jew and Tyrian alike overrode the sabbath rest in post-exilic Jerusalem (Neh 13:15–16). The very epitome of filthy gain is Tyre in Isa 23:15–17, whose wide network of trading partners is metaphorized as the clientele of an international whore, and whose wealth is figured as harlot's hire.

malu (for *malᵉ'u*) "they filled" (like *naśu* for *naśᵉ'u*, 39:26) shows assimilation of final-alef verbs to the final-he paradigm, a process much further advanced in Mishnaic Hebrew (Joüon-Muraoka, § 78 e–g). The verb is transitive (as is the qal form in 8:17; 30:11) and impersonal = passive ("they filled" = "was filled"). The motif of being filled with lawlessness (*male ḥamas*) is a commonplace in Ezekiel's speeches of reproof (7:23; 8:17; 12:19). Is the sequence *tokka ḥamas* a skewed echo of *mittok* (<**tkk*) *umeḥamas* "from fraud and from lawlessness," Ps 72:14? Cf. *tok umirma* "fraud and deceit," Ps 55:12.

Alternatively, might not the *ḥms* "lawlessness" and "sin" of this verse be restated in vs. 17 as haughtiness and corruption, recalling vss. 2–5 above, in which the king's commercial success and wealth are said to have led him to think himself divine?

So I desacralized [and barred] you from. Lit. "I held you desecrated"—a declarative-estimative pi'el (Joüon-Muraoka, § 52 d)—"from the mountain of God."

This is a pregnant construction, one in which a verb—here *ḥll*—is construed with a preposition not proper to it—here *mn*—that implies an unsaid verbal element to which the preposition is proper—here an expression of exclusion or expulsion. Spelling it out: I held you desecrated by your wrongdoing and as such barred you from my holy mountain. For an identical construction, see Ezra 2:62: *wayᵉgoʾᵃlu min hakkᵉhunna* "they were held defiled (= desacralized) [and expelled] from the priesthood."

G "you were wounded, S "I killed you" treat the verb as from *ḥll* "slay" (see comment to "your desecrators," vs. 9 above), thus avoiding the ascription of sanctity to the Tyrian. But there is no ambiguity in the usage of the verb here; it is based on the acceptance, for the sake of the figure, of the king's hubristic self-apotheosis.

and I banished you. The form *waʾabbedka* is contracted from piʿel first person *waʾᵃʾabbedka* of the base **ʾbd* (GKC, § 23 d). Qal has the sense "perish, vanish, be lost" (19:5; 26:17; 34:4); piʿel is causative, "destroy, banish" (6:3; 22:27; Jer 23:1).

G and S render a text in which the cherub expels the inhabitant of paradise; see Structure and Themes.

17. *Your heart grew haughty on account of your beauty.* Cf. the theme of the adulteress whose beauty was her undoing (16:15).

together with. *ʿal* has this meaning in 16:37. In the previous oracle wisdom, beauty, and radiance are attributes of Tyre's leader that the foreign enemy will destroy. Here they are royal qualities that the king himself has corrupted, for which he suffers debasement in front of his royal peers.

To the ground I hurled you. This language recalls 19:12: the soaring vine from which scepters branched that was hurled to the ground—an image of the fall of Judah's royalty. Similar language appears in the roughly contemporaneous Lam 2:1: "he hurled from heaven to the ground the glory of Israel."

to gaze on you. Misfortune is more painful when its victim is exposed to the curious, if not scornful, stares of unscathed erstwhile peers; the crowning disgrace of exposure to the public at large is reserved for the conclusion of the figure in vs. 18. *rʾh b-* has the connotation of looking with satisfaction on another's calamity; e.g., Mic 7:10; Ps 54:9. The noun form *rʾwh* is patterned on feminine infinitives (verbal nouns) such as *(l)ʾhbh* "to love" and *(l)yrʾh* "to fear."

18. *iniquities.* The base of *ʿwnyk* onto which the suffix is attached is plural *ʿwny-*, less common than *ʿwnwt-*, but yet common enough (as in Jer 14:7; Isa 64:5; Ezra 9:13). *rb* "many" combines regularly with plural nouns (e.g., 27:16; Prov 16:8), hence there is no reason to prefer (as does *BHS*) the singular form *ʿwnk*, which to be sure is well attested in Hebrew mss., but is suspect of assimilation to the following *rkltk*.

You desecrated your holy precincts. The holy garden/mountain of God, in the figure of this oracle; the godlike seat in the heart of the seas in the previous one. The plural denotes extension or complexity (see comment to 21:7), and the attestation of a singular reading (see text note) shows that the plural form was equated with a singular. Noteworthy is the interpretation of *mqdš* (singular) as "sanctity" by Symmachus, V, Rashi, and Eliezer ("wherewith I sanctified you so that you might dwell on the holy mountain of God").

Tyre's commercial crookedness desecrates in the same way as Israel's moral faults pollute (see ch. 21, Structure and Themes). In both instances a cultic concept is extended to the realm of morality.

fire from your midst. The picture of evil causing its own destruction is repeated here from 19:14. Burning is the punishment for desecration; e.g., for unchastity the daughter of a priest is condemned to be burned, "because she desecrates her father" (Lev 21:9).

STRUCTURE AND THEMES

The singular structure of this lament was set forth in Ilana Goldberg's study "The Poetic Structure of the Dirge over the King of Tyre" (in Hebrew), *Tarbiz* 58/2 (1989), 277–81; the following remarks are based on her findings. Like all laments, this one is divided into two parts: a description of past glory (A, vss. $12b^{\beta}$–15) followed by an account of disaster, here justified as punishment (B, vss. 16–19). Vs. 15b ("until wrongdoing was found in you") marks the transition from the first to the second part. Each part consists of a pair of stanzas (A1, A2, B1, B2) in an unusual parallelistic interrelation: the second stanza of each pair repeats expressions of the first with variations but in roughly corresponding positions. Repetition is the agent of seconding rather than synonymous equivalents. Each stanza except the third has three lines (*a*, *b*, *c*); the third has four. The last verse of the lament (vs. 19) falls outside the pattern, but its first line is linked to the preceding line by a paralleling phrase: "all who knew (**yd*ʻ) you" / "all who gazed (**r*ʼ*h*) on you."

The structure and correspondence of parts (according to the MT) appears from the following scheme:

	A1, vss. 12b–13		A2, vss. 14–15
a)	you . . . sealer . . . full of wisdom . . . beauty	*a*)	you . . . shielding cherub I set (**ntn*) you
b)	in Eden the garden of God you were every precious stone	*b*)	in the holy mountain of God you were amidst fire-stones you walked about
c)	. . . in you (*bk*) on the day you were created	*c*)	from the day you were created . . . in you (*bk*)

	B1, vss. 16–17		B2, vs. 18
a)	because of your many dealings (*brb rkltk*) . . . was filled	*a*)	by your many . . . dealings (*mrb . . . rkltk*)
b)	I desacralized you . . . from the mountain of God from amidst fire-stones	*b*)	you desecrated your holy precincts fire from your midst

B1, vss. 16–17 (cont'd)	B2, vs. 18 (cont'd)
c) beauty . . . wisdom	*c*) I turned (**ntn*) you . . .
d) to the ground . . .	on the ground
before kings I set (**ntn*) you	before the eyes of all
to gaze on you (*bk*)	who gazed on you
	Closure: vs. 19
	all who knew you

These correspondences constitute the skeleton of overlapping scenes of past glory and present calamity climactically arranged and intricately interwoven.

The subject of A is the blissful existence of the exquisite creature in God's domain. A1 and A2 are constructed alike: in both, line *a* addresses and qualifies the creature (this favors MT's *'att* "you" in vs. 16a against G's "with" [= *'et*]); line *b* describes its setting; line *c* qualifies it again with reference to "the day you were created." The end of every internal stanza (A1, A2, B1) is marked by the occurrence of *bk*. B2, being the last stanza, needs no marker. To signal formally the end of part A, the elements "in you / day . . . created" of the last line of its first stanza (A1*c*) are reversed in the last line of its second stanza ("day . . . created / in you"; A2*c*).

Just as in poetic line-parallelism the second verset (the restatement) heightens (some part of) the first verset (the statement), so it is in the peculiar stanza-parallelism of this oracle:

The perfect creature in God's garden of A1 becomes in A2 a cherub—a celestial—on "God's holy mountain" (his location through the rest of the oracle—but note the subsequent graded distribution of the components of the epithet in vs. 16 [B1*b*], "the mountain of God," and in vs. 18 [B2*a*], "holy precincts"). A1's "precious stones"—from the real world—are replaced in A2 by otherworldly "fire-stones," from which the cherub is ultimately banished (vs. 16; B1).

While A1 gives a static picture of the creature (a point in favor of the reading *ḥotam*—a noun—rather than the active participle *ḥotem*), A2 introduces dynamism and change: the cherub "shielding," God setting him in place, he walking about, his "ways" (conduct) at first unblemished, then found iniquitous. The static "on the day" of A1*c* contrasts with the dynamic line *c* of A2: "from the day . . . until."

B describes the sin and the punishment of the divine creature. B1 alternates them in two paired statements: line *a*, you sinned in commerce; *b*, I desacralized you from God's mountain; *c*, you grew haughty (high) by reason of your excellences; *d*, I hurled you to the ground in the sight of kings.

B2 aggravates each component. "Your many dealings" (B1*a*) is expanded into "your many iniquities, your wrongful dealings." In place of God "desacralizing and barring you from his mountain" (B1*b*), you committed the ultimate sin of desecrating your holy place (line B2*a*—corresponding to B1's *a* + *b*). So I burned you (*b*), and I turned you into ashes before all who knew you (*c*). The series of punishments in B is carefully graded: being expelled from God's mountain (1*b*), hurled to the ground (1*d*), consumed by fire (2*b*), reduced to ashes (2*c*). The first degradation was before royal peers (B1*d*); the second "before the eyes of all" (B2*c*).

Thematic words connect the parts: The pristine creature was "full of wisdom" and beautiful (A1*a*); corrupted by commerce, his insides were "filled with lawlessness" (B1*a*), and his beauty and wisdom abused (B1*c*). External stones evolve into internal fire: "precious stones" hedge the creature in A1*b*; he walks about amidst fire-stones in A2*b*; in B1*b* he is banished from amidst fire-stones; in B2*b* fire breaks out "from your midst." Even the troubling *wnttyk* (A2*a*) gains in credibility from the repetition of the verb in the following two stanzas (B1*d*, B2*c*).

In the light of this intricate, integrative construction, the various critical dismemberings of this text appear to be misguided. It has been trimmed to fit the so-called lament-meter ("which can only be restored by radical interferences with the words in their present form, for which it is difficult to find reasons," Eichrodt, p. 392), and to eliminate its repetitiveness and its ever-shifting imagery (see, e.g., Zimmerli; Wevers; O. Loretz, "Der Sturz des Fürsten von Tyrus (Ez 28:1–19)," *Ugarit-Forschungen* 8 [1976], 455–58; R. R. Wilson, "The Death of the King of Tyre: The Editorial History of Ezekiel 28," in J. H. Marks and R. M. Good, eds., *Love and Death in the Ancient Near East* [Festschrift M. H. Pope] [Guilford, Conn.: Four Quarters Publishing Co., 1987], pp. 211–18). Aside from the list of precious stones in vs. 13, scarcely a word can be removed without damaging the correspondence of its parts. We do not understand every term—in part because the text is not always sound—but the formal integrity of the MT seems demonstrated.

Doubtless the most difficult aspect of the oracle is its polymorphism: persons and settings keep changing from stanza to stanza. A1's creature perfect in form, wisdom, and beauty—but not called divine—is transformed in A2 into a cherub. The creature is set in the Garden of Eden, the cherub on the holy mountain of God; the creature is adorned or hedged by precious stones, the cherub walks among "fire-stones" and is eventually banished from them. The cherub's offense in B1 is commercial malfeasance and pride; in B2 it is desecration of a holy place. Its punishments are multiple: banishment, casting down to the ground, fire, being turned to ashes. Such polymorphism is disconcerting and one sympathizes with critics' efforts to eliminate it. (But we are cautioned against rash foreclosing of poetical possibilities by Ps 23, in which God as a shepherd and the psalmist as a sheep are abruptly replaced by God as a host and the psalmist his guest at a banquet. For the difficulties some critics have had in allowing the unity of this psalm, see H.-J. Kraus, *Psalmen*, BKAT, pp. 187f.; for a unifying interpretation, see D. N. Freedman, *Pottery, Poetry, and Prophecy* [Winona Lake: Eisenbrauns, 1980], pp. 275–302.)

If form means anything, then the repetitive overlap of the second stanzas suggests that somehow their nonrepeated elements are identical with or equivalent to their correspondents in the first stanzas. The consummate creature in A1 is the cherub in the rest of the oracle. The garden of God (A1) is the holy mountain of God (A2, B1), is the holy precinct (B2), and so forth. What we seem to have is a concentration of figures in a single oracle instead of their isolation in discrete ones. The latter is the rule and the literary norm: Jerusalem is a nymphomaniacal adulteress in ch. 16, inutile vine-wood in ch. 15; the Davidic king is the top of a cedar in ch. 17, a lioness's cub in 19:2–9; a soaring vine-branch in 19:10–14.

However, in one and the same oracle we find "illogical" polymorphism in multiple incompatible punishments; see the remarks on "overkill" in I, 355. Why this peculiar mixture with the king of Tyre?

The answer seems to lie in the combination of Tyrian pretensions displayed in the previous oracles. The king of Tyre boasts he is a god, living in an inaccessible, invulnerable place in the heart of the seas — a fastness we can visualize as a mountain rising out of the flat surface of the sea. The city is a perfect beauty and has wise helmsmen who have brought her great wealth. Tyre's king epitomizes its beauty, wisdom, and wealth, all of which have generated in him a self-image of superhuman endowments (so the prophet alleges; on the verifiability of the allegation, see section XXVIII, Structure and Themes). Ezekiel addresses the royal self-image here as in ch. 27 he addressed the city's (alleged) self-image of a splendid, richly laden merchantman: he does not deny it, he rather exploits it in order to turn it into a figure of disaster. It is as though he says to the king: "Granted that you are a divine being, that does not put you beyond the reach of God's just retribution. Your story is one we have heard the likes of before, and it ends with your destruction." The prophet then fabricates a poetical allegory of the fall of Tyre's king out of motifs familiar to us from biblical materials, presented as a series of transformations, and so altered as to make it impossible to decide what was innovated by the prophet and what was traditional but divergent from our texts.

References in vss. 12–13 to the Garden of Eden, and to creation, relate to the combined J and P narrative of Gen 1–3. The perfect creature of vs. 12 evokes the first human, Adam. That is how the ancients took these verses — viz., as belonging to the Paradise story and supplementing it with new details.

> We know [from Gen 2:8–9] that the Holy One (blessed be he) planted for the first human (*adam*) every sort of tree and all sorts of choice plants; but we did not gather [from the Genesis account] that [he also] created for him wedding canopies of gold and precious stones and pearls. Whence do we learn that? From the address [of Ezekiel] to Hiram [= the king of Tyre]: "In Eden, the garden of God were you, of every precious stone was your canopy etc." God said to Hiram: "[Do you think] you are the first human to whom I did all this honor?" (*Midrash "Thirty-two Rules,"* § 17; *b. Baba Batra* 75a)

In this first comparison, the perfect and beautiful city (of 27:1–11), the inaccessible city of the splendid king (of the previous oracle), is metaphorized as God's garden hedged in precious stones in which a perfectly formed, consummately wise and beautiful creature lived.

The cherub of the second stanza is, in the G version ("with the cherub I set you"), a companion (perhaps more accurately: a monitor) of the perfect creature in God's garden (see comment to vs. 14a), and the executor of punishment upon the creature (vs. 16b; see comment). This brings him closer to the cherubs of the Paradise story, whose duty it is to prevent the expelled sinners from returning to the garden (Gen 3:24). But G's approximation of Ezekiel to Genesis may well be the first step to the later midrashic harmony of the two; preference is to be given to the more difficult MT.

The cherub, the holy mountain of God, and the fire-stones evoke the Temple mount of Jerusalem (the only "holy mountain of God" in Scripture) and its furniture: "shielding" cherub statues, I Kings 6:23ff.; cherub decorations, ibid., vss. 32, 35; 7:29, 36; and Ezekiel's own vision of cherubs at the Temple site, among whom moved coals of fire (Ezek 10:2).

In the second comparison the king of Tyre, insulated on his island fastness jutting up from the sea, is metaphorized as a member of the divine entourage, who lives on God's holy mountain. As bounded and inviolate divine territory, the Garden of Eden is fused with the holy mountain of God, Mount Zion—whose epithet *yrkty ṣpwn* "the far distant north" (Ps 48:3) retained an allusion to the Canaanite Mount Saphon, sacred to the god Baal (L. R. Fisher, ed., *Ras Shamra Parallels*, II, Analecta Orientalia 50 [Rome: Pontifical Biblical Institute, 1975], 318–23). "The superimposition of Eden, the holy mountain, and the Temple mount is a commonplace of religious language," M. Bogaert, "Montaigne Sainte, Jardin d'Eden et Sanctuaire (Hiérosolymitain) dans un Oracle d'Ezéchiel contre le Prince de Tyr [Ez 28:11–19]," in H. Limet, ed., *Le mythe, son langage et son message* (Louvain-la-Neuve, 1983), p. 139; see further J. D. Levenson, *Theology of the Program of Restoration of Ezekiel 40–48*, Harvard Semitic Monograph Series 10 (Missoula, Mont.: Scholars Press, 1976), 25ff. The sacred site that the divine being occupied is given the highest degree of sanctity in the final stanza, where it is called "holy precincts" (*mqdšy-*), so aggravating the guilt of its desecration.

If the Paradise story serves as the model of the fatal results of human *hubris*, Ps 82's account of God's demotion of his divine courtiers from divinity to mortality because of their corruption may serve as a hint of the concept underlying the cherub's fall in Ezekiel:

I thought: You are divinities (*'lhym*),
  you are all sons of the Most High;
But indeed as Adam (or: humans) you shall die;
  you shall fall as any prince.

The opening line of a sarcastic dirge over a Mesopotamian conqueror in Isa 14:12 seems comparable to our dirge:

How have you fallen from heaven,
  O Shining One, son of Dawn!
How cut down to the ground,
  O conqueror of nations!

In both dirges the real mortal is metaphorized in a superhuman figure who was demoted from divinity to mortality. But if we can detect in Ezekiel's dirge plot and motifs that appear elsewhere in biblical literature, that literature fails us entirely in the case of the "son of Dawn" (for efforts at identification, see bibliography at O. Loretz, *Ugarit und die Bibel* [Darmstadt: Wissenschaftliche Buchgesellschaft, 1990], p. 160).

There has been much inconclusive speculation about the mythical background of Ezekiel's dirge (surveys in A. J. Williams's "The Mythological Background of Ezekiel 28:12–19?" *Biblical Theology Bulletin* 6 [1976], 49–61; and in Wilson's article mentioned above). No Phoenician myths have turned up by which to illumine our passage, so resort is made to partial handholds; e.g., J. Dus identified the cherub with the Phoenician god Melkart (< **mlk qrt* "king of the city"), with whom the king of Tyre (*mlk ṣr*) is compared ("Melek Ṣor — Melqart?" *Archiv Orientální* 26 [1958], 179–85). The conjectured Ugaritic myth of El's fall, supposedly underlying this and the preceding oracle (M. Pope, *'El in the Ugaritic Texts,* SVT 2 [Leiden: E. J. Brill, 1955], 98 ff.), has not survived criticism; see, e.g., the magisterial counterportrait of El by H. Gese in *Die Religionen Altsyriens, Altarabiens und der Mandäer* (Stuttgart: Kohlhammer, 1970), pp. 94–118, esp. n. 22 and pp. 112, 117f.; also the brief but trenchant remarks of W. J. Fulco in the Macmillan *Encyclopedia of Religions* (1987) 5.73f., s.v. "El." J. Van Seters looks to a Neo-Babylonian text on the creation of the king as the foreign element in Ezek 28 (which Ezekiel transformed, and which transform was further transformed in the Paradise story of Genesis); see his *Prologue to History: The Yahwist as Historian in Genesis* (Louisville: Westminster/John Knox Press, 1992), pp. 60ff., 119ff. The biblical parallels in terminology and plot lines offer material with which to construct variations on extant stories. That Ezekiel was using Israelite mythical motifs familiar to his audience is the most plausible assumption. Here is an example of a scholarly guess as to the myth that Ezekiel adapted, and its relation to the Genesis story:

> There was a tradition about a cherub that resided in the Garden of Eden, located on the Mountain of God, which was as high as heaven. At first the cherub was blameless in his conduct but later he sinned, whereupon he was hurled from the Garden of Eden to the ground, was burnt and became ashes. The Torah, which sought to purge mythological traditions — such as those about angels that sinned and were cast out of heaven — tells that the sinner in the Garden was not a cherub or an angel but a human. The task of caring for the garden, entrusted to the "shielding" cherub in the primitive tradition . . . was, according to the Torah, assigned at first to the human, and only after he sinned was it transferred to the cherubs. (M. D. Cassuto and R. D. Barnett, *EM* 4.242, s.v. *krwb*)

Cooke, too, reconstructs a similar "popular story" which "belonged, no doubt, to the common stock of Semitic myths . . . [I]n Ez[ekiel] the purifying process has not gone so far [as in Genesis]."

Such reconstructions tailored ad hoc are not more convincing than the ad hoc dismemberment of the poem to suit extraneous canons of coherence and consistency. Once the general integrity of the passage is recognized, its character as a figurative version of the preceding oracles against Tyre, especially the oracle against its king in vss. 1–10 of this chapter, stands out. Taking his departure from the self-apotheosis of Tyre's king—the quintessence of pride induced by invincibility and prosperity—Ezekiel metaphorizes him in allusions to traditional superhuman figures located in traditional sites of splendid isolation and sanctity. Utilizing whatever components of tradition would add color, he tells a simple story of pride or sin going before a fall. As obvious as are the allusions to tradition, no less obvious are the features specific to Tyre's king: the extensive trade and the sin of lawless gain (incongruous with a cherub living in God's mountain); haughtiness, wisdom, beauty, and radiance (characterizing the king in the previous oracle); the disgrace before kings. We recall the artificial features of the parable of the two eagles (ch. 17), where birds and plants act out of character in order to simulate the political conduct of humans. Such artifice is typical of Ezekiel's figures, and its presence here is a signature of our prophet. It also, finally, undermines the search for a unified subtext for our oracle, because Ezekiel, "a master of figures," drew on the full range of tradition material and tailored whatever he took of it to suit the rhetorical needs of the moment (cf., e.g., his revision in ch. 20 of the Pentateuchal depiction of Israel's relation to its God during the Egyptian bondage). Even one who posits that Ezekiel used a "less purified" Paradise myth must admit that such use "did not carry with it any force to compel Ezekiel to follow slavishly the lines of the myth" (Eichrodt, p. 394). Why then invoke an unknown myth when known mythical motifs freshly combined in a unique structure are enough to explain the origin and impact of this poem?

The anger of the prophet (speaking for God) toward Tyre's ruler in both oracles directed against him in ch. 28 is not motivated by any explicit offense committed against Israel. The two stated grounds are self-deification born of wealth and splendor (vss. 2, 5, 17), and corruption incident to commerce—offenses against a universal morality. In the absence of any relation to Israel, Tyre's judgment recalls Jeremiah's warning to the nations, as he introduces his oracles against them: "If the city that bears my name is the first against which I am bringing calamity, do you [nations] expect to go unpunished? You will not go unpunished, for I am summoning the sword against all the inhabitants of the earth" (Jer 25:29). God has not singled out Jerusalem for punishment when all the nations stand guilty before him. The fate of Jerusalem is a signal to all that the time of punishment for their various sins has arrived.

XXX. Sidon's Doom; God's Vindication (28:20–26)

28 [20]The word of YHWH came to me: [21]Man, set your face toward Sidon and prophesy against her, [22]and say; Thus said Lord YHWH: I am coming at you, Sidon, and I will gain glory in your midst, and they[a] shall know that I am YHWH, when I work judgments in her[a] and assert my holiness through her.[a] [23] [b]I will let loose against her plague and bloody death in her streets, and the slain shall fall in her midst, when the sword comes against her from all around [her],[b] and they shall know that I am YHWH. [24]Then the house of Israel shall no longer suffer the malignant thorns and the wounding briers of all who are around them who despise them; and they shall know that I am Lord YHWH.

[25]Thus said Lord YHWH: When I gather the house of Israel from the peoples among whom they have been scattered, and assert my holiness through them in the sight of the nations, and they dwell on their soil, which I granted to my servant, to Jacob— [26]dwell on it in security, building houses and planting vineyards and dwelling in security, when I work judgments against all who despise them who are around them, then they shall know that I am YHWH their God.

COMMENT

28:21. *set your face.* As in 25:2.

22. *I am coming at you, Sidon.* Cf. 26:3, but unlike the case of Tyre, no motive appears here.

and I will gain glory in your midst. "When the nations see that I have the power to inflict punishment on you they shall give glory to my Godhead, as it is said, 'The Egyptians shall know that I am YHWH when I gain glory through Pharaoh through his chariots and through his horsemen' (Exod. 14:18)" (Kara). "In your midst" = "through what I do in your midst"; *btwk* and *b-* interchange freely in Ezekiel, as in 22:6–9.

"Gain glory" is said of God in 39:13 in connection with the defeat of Gog; in 39:21 it is paraphrased "I will set (= manifest) my glory (*wntty kbwdy*) amidst the nations."

[a]G "you."

[b–b]G "blood and death in your streets and wounded shall fall by the sword in you around you."

and assert my holiness through her. This concept appears in 20:41 in connection with the future restoration of Israel; it will recur in 38:16 (the defeat of Gog) and is developed in the context of 39:27. In Num 20:13 God's holiness is asserted through provision of food in the wilderness. Both signal benefits and signal punishments vindicate God's holiness.

For the pairing of glory and holiness, cf. God's statement after the calamitous death of Nadab and Abihu: "Through those near me I shall assert my holiness and gain glory before all the people" (Lev 10:3). The order of the two verbs has no apparent significance.

G maintains second person for MT's third through this verse, changing only with the last verb in vs. 23; this appears to be a secondary adjustment. The second person address to a fictive audience (Sidon) changes into speech about Sidon to a real audience (the exiles). For an identical change in person see, e.g., 5:12–17: address to Jerusalem changes into speech about her.

23. *plague and bloody death.* So 5:17 (against Jerusalem) and 38:22 (against Gog).

and the slain shall fall. So 6:7. The duplication of the final radical (*npll* for the normal *npl*) seems to be an erroneous assimilation to the following *ḥll.*

when the sword comes against her. The temporal force of the verbless phrase *bḥrb ʿlyh* is similar to that of the familiar *bṣr ly* "when I am in distress" (e.g., Ps 18:7).

24. *suffer.* Lit. "have" (*yhyh l-*); the verb is in the singular, as it is usually uninflected in this sense (Joüon-Muraoka, § 150 j–l). With the destruction of the last of its malign neighbors Israel will no longer suffer their insult and injury. *slwn mmʾyr* "malignant thorn" combines Ezekiel's term (plural *slwnym*, 2:6) with a priestly one qualifying morbid eruptions (Lev 13:53f.; 14:44; cf. Arabic *mʾr* "reopen"—intransitive, said of wounds). It and "wounding briers"—both unique expressions—recall Num 33:55: "stings in your eyes and thorns in your sides," said of gentiles remaining in the land of Israel. For "wounding" (alternatively, "painful"), see Job 5:18: "he wounds (*ykʾyb*) and binds up."

25–26. Retribution will be dealt out to Israel's contemptuous neighbors at the time of the ingathering of its exiles; the concurrence of events will make manifest their connection and demonstrate the power of YHWH and his protection of Israel. The subject of the last clause, "they shall know, etc." is ambiguous: it could be the nations (as in vs. 24b) or, more likely, Israel in view of the added "their God"; cf. 34:29; 39:22, 28, where the expanded clause has Israel as its unambiguous subject. In either case the point is that through his restoration of his people YHWH's holiness and glory will be established among men.

The grant of the land "to my servant, to Jacob" (again in 37:25) names the last patriarch, all of whose sons shared in the promised land—unlike Abraham and Isaac, who each had a son excluded from the promise; cf. "the heritage of Jacob" in Isa 58:14. In the Talmud (*b. Shabbat* 118a) the association of Jacob with the eschatological restoration of the land to the people is explained by the "heritage without limits" promised to Jacob, and to him only of all the patriarchs, in Gen 28:14: "you shall burst forth westward and eastward, and northward and southward."

Building houses and planting vineyards are typical acts of permanent settlement (as in Deut 20:5–6; Isa 65:21). They are precluded in contexts of doom or threat such as Deut 28:30, Amos 5:11, and Zeph 1:13, and in the nomadic rule of the Rechabite order, Jer 35:7. Vineyards are replaced by gardens in Jeremiah's exhortation to the exiles to reconcile themselves to a long stay in Babylonia, 29:5f. (an allusion to Deut 20:5–6; see A. Berlin, "Jeremiah 29:5–7: A Deuteronomic Allusion," *Hebrew Annual Review* 8 [1984], 3–11). "Dwell in security" is a priestly expression of reward for observance of God's laws (Lev 25:18f.; 26:5); it recurs regularly in Ezekiel's prophecies of restoration (e.g., 34:25, 28).

STRUCTURE AND THEMES

Some twenty-five miles north of Tyre on the coast of Lebanon, Sidon rivaled Tyre as the chief city of southern Phoenicia. Even when Tyre predominated, its king was titled "King of Sidonians" (e.g., Ethbaal, I Kings 16:31). In 677 B.C.E. King Esarhaddon of Assyria destroyed Sidon (*ANET*³, p. 291a), but the city recovered after the fall of Assyria (612). Its history during the struggle between Egypt and Babylonia over control of Syria-Palestine is obscure. This much is clear: Sidon is the last named of the small western monarchies convened by Zedekiah in 594 in Jerusalem to plan a revolt against Babylonia (Jer 27:3), and "the king of Sidon" appears in a list of Nebuchadnezzar's captive kings (*ANET*³, p. 308). Eventually, then, Sidon (like Tyre) came under Babylonian rule; whether that entailed the devastation presaged by Ezekiel we cannot say. Under Persian rule the city regained its premier rank.

The revelation event introduced by the conventional formula (vs. 20) comprises two distinct but related utterances, each introduced by the message formula: A (vss. 21–24), Sidon's doom, removing the last thorn in Israel's side; and B (vss. 25–26), the restoration and prosperity of Israel, contemporaneous with the punishment of the contemptuous neighbors. The frequency of the recognition formula ("they shall know that I am YHWH [their God]"), four times in five verses, highlights the chief concern of the oracle.

Ezekiel's counting Sidon among Tyre's "crew" (27:8) may explain his perfunctory treatment of it. That he noticed it at all may be due to Sidon's entering the orbit of Judah's fate through participation in Zedekiah's conclave (the other participants have already been dealt with in chs. 25–28:19). Yet, though the doom of vs. 23 is stereotypical, the opening of the oracle (vs. 22) strikes a fresh note. In place of an indictment of Sidon appears a statement of the motive of its punishment: God's resolve to defend his glory and holiness that have been impugned by the contempt shown toward Israel by its neighbors. The downfall of Israel's enemies will put an end to the stinging reproaches Israel suffers from them. The themes of the gentiles' contempt and of God's vindicating punishment link the short oracle against Sidon (A) to the opening set of brief dooms against Israel's neighbors (see 25:6, 15). Echoing that opening, A serves to close the series of oracles against the small nations who were Judah's closest neighbors.

B is related to A through the concepts of punishment of the contemptuous neighbors and God's assertion of his holiness. But now God's attributes are demonstrated by his ingathering of Israel's dispersion and their resettlement in their land in perfect security. Whereas section A makes punishment of the gentiles the means of vindicating God's honor, B achieves that vindication by the wonderful restoration of Israel. Punishment of contemptuous neighbors is still there, as an adjunct of Israel's restoration, but the instrumentality of God's glorification is now the blessedness of his people. While A sums up what has preceded, B foreshadows the consolatory visions of chs. 34ff.—Israel's return to its land and its reconciliation with its God; the destruction of prideful gentiles; the divine stake in both. Taken together, A and B form a transition from the dooms against the nations to the prophecies of restoration. Chs. 34ff. would follow very naturally, but the arranger of Ezekiel's prophecies placed the oracles about Egypt in between; the reason for that will be discussed in the next section.

Note on Criteria of authenticity: The Sidon oracle as an example

The criteria employed by leading critics for determining primary and secondary elements in Ezekiel's oracles can be nicely exhibited by sampling their judgments on the brief Sidon oracle.

Fohrer: No part derives from Ezekiel. Not vss. 20–22 because vs. $22a^{\beta}$–b depends on "glosses" (= accretions) to Ezekiel's words in 5:15 ("work judgments"), 38:16 ("be sanctified"), 39:13 ("get glory"), and on editorial additions to Exod 14:4, 17f., and on Hag 1:8 ("I will get glory"). Vs. 23 is entirely a "supplementary gloss" to vss. 20–22. Vs. 24 is a later interpretation of the oracles against foreign nations, and 25 is a still later extension of it.

Remarks: One has to believe in Fohrer's "gloss" phenomenon; in his assertions of literary pedigree (what preceded what); and in his disallowance of a development of a thought within a unit.

On glosses, see G. Fohrer, "Die Glossen im Buche Ezechiel," *ZAW* 63 (1951), 33–53; K. S. Freedy, "The Glosses in Ezekiel I–XXIV," *VT* 20 (1970), 129–52; M. Dijkstra, "The Glosses in Ezekiel Reconsidered: Aspects of Textual Transmission in Ezekiel 10," in J. Lust, *Ezekiel and His Book*, pp. 55–77. E. Tov protests against the indiscriminate use of the term "gloss." Properly speaking, glosses are "marginal or interlinear interpretations of difficult or obsolete words," and for such, hardly any evidence exists in the ms. tradition of the Hebrew Bible. See his study "Glosses, Interpolations, and Other Types of Scribal Additions in the Text of the Hebrew Bible," in S. E. Balentine and J. Barton, eds., *Language, Theology, and the Bible* (Festschrift J. Barr) (Oxford: Clarendon Press, 1994), pp. 40–66.

Wevers: "The recurrence of the recognition formula at verses 22, 23, 24, and 26 shows the composite nature of this section." This in line with what is postulated *a priori* in Wevers's Introduction: "If the text of an oracle has more than one introduction and/or conclusion formulae, only one of each can normally be original" (§ 4 a). The kernel of the passage is vs. 22a—the part of vs. 22 that is in direct address; accretions through vs. 23 "can easily be identified since they are in the 3rd fem. singular." (G's continuation of direct address in vs. 23 is overborne by the *a priori* postulate. Contrariwise, *Biblia Hebraica*[3] [1937] adopted Cornill's adjusting MT to G, and was followed in this by Eichrodt [1965]. Cooke kept MT [third masc.] in 22b—as a sign of "later enlargement"—but in vs. 23a$^{\alpha}$, the second line of the original oracle, Cooke changed MT's "her" to "thee, thy" to agree with the first line [22a].) Wevers calls vs. 24 an "expansion" concerning all the oracles in chs. 25–28. Vss. 25–26 are "late" "excerpts from chapters 34–39" with "build houses, plant vineyard" taken from Trito-Isaiah.

Remarks: A *priori* expectations of how prophets express themselves cannot serve in place of descriptions of the stylistic habits of given prophetic collections. In Ezekiel there are at least seven instances of double (or more) recognition-formula closures: 6:13f.; 11:10–12; 12:15f.; 28:22–26; 30:25f.; 34:27f.; 37:13f. Only a prejudgment can declare this phenomenon beyond the stylistic reaches of the original author. This is even more the case with changes of person, etc., in the prophecies. As for the assertion that a given instance of an idiom is earlier or later than its repetition—how can we possibly know, when (as is the present instance) the idioms are common to several works preceding and contemporary with Ezekiel (on the alleged borrowing from "Trito-Isaiah," see Berlin's article cited above in the comment to vs. 25).

Eichrodt: This cliché-ridden oracle is an "unnecessary piece of padding" likely to have been "inserted" here to bring the number of condemned neighbors of Israel to seven. Holiness, glory, and punishment are joined here and in the priestly narrative of Exod 14:17f. and Lev 10:3, and in vs. 24 a priestly lexical term appears. This points to "a priestly recension of the text," and a "reviser" who interpreted the previous oracles "in a way agreeing closely with Ezekiel's conception of how God judges the world." On the same grounds as Wevers, Eichrodt dates vss. 25f. "at least half a century" after the prophet's time.

Remarks: The motivation alleged for composing the oracle borders on the flippant (Allen: "has little to commend it"); citation of a precedent or an analogy might have lent it some weight. As to the insipidity of the oracle: *de gustibus* . . . Moreover, whence arises the expectation that in an extensive corpus like this all original pieces shall be equally scintillating? The signs of a priestly reviser fit Ezekiel himself: was he not a priest and as such conversant with the literature and vocabulary of his profession?

Zimmerli: Vss. 20–23, in spite of the change in person and the double recognition formula, are a unity ("one must simply accept the change in style"). The double recognition formula in vss. 23–24 is "redactional" (Introduction, p. 59* [E.t. p. 39]); i.e., vs. 24 is an expansion of the previous verses "by the same hand," which by its language is "the hand of the prophet" Ezekiel, reviewing the whole block of previous prophecies. Vss. 25f. are very late, no longer from Ezekiel: they include matter (such as living in safety) based on more fully developed formulations in chs. 33–39, and "building houses and planting vineyards"—from Jeremiah (again, see Berlin).

Remarks: Here is a measure of recognition that the prophet cannot be held to rigid stylistic rules, and an equally important allowance of the possibility that additions and annotations may be Ezekiel's own additions to extant matter. It is an *a priori* (even paradoxical) assumption that the more fully developed a thought is the earlier it is. As to the evidence of lateness of vss. 25f., see end of remarks to Wevers.

Conclusion: The identification of the original elements, or the elements attributable to the shaping hand of the prophet, rests on too limited a range of explanations; there seems to be a premium on discovering multiple layers and many hands. A passage in which nothing is un-Ezekielian in thought or style, and nothing literary alien to his times, is to a greater or lesser extent excluded from his corpus by critical operations characterized by misplaced confidence in the conjectural dating of other passages (in the book and elsewhere; of such Jacob Licht wisely said, "Our conjectures are too frail to sustain a second storey"); on *a priori* expectations and assumptions concerning literary creativity, the relation of quality to originality, and the limits of Ezekiel's familiarity with contemporary writings. The product of such operations can be persuasive only to partisans of the operators. Others may be moved to embrace a literary-historical version of Occam's razor: not to multiply authorial or editorial hands unnecessarily.

XXXI. Egypt's Fall and Restoration (29:1–16)

29 [1]In the tenth year, in the tenth month, on the twelfth of the month the word of YHWH came to me: [2]Man, set your face toward Pharaoh king of Egypt, and prophesy against him and against all Egypt. [3]Speak and say: Thus said Lord YHWH:

I am coming at you, Pharaoh king of Egypt, the great monster couching in his Nile-streams, who says, [a]"Mine is my Nile, and it is I who made [it] for me."[a]

[4]I will put hooks in your jaws,
and stick the fish of your Nile-streams[b] to your scales.
I will haul you up from your Nile-streams,[b]
and all the fish of your Nile-streams[b] [c]shall stick to your scales.[c]
[5]I will cast you out into the desert,
you and all the fish of your Nile-streams;
you shall lie fallen on the ground,
not collected and not gathered.[d]
To the beasts of the earth and the fowl of the sky
I consign you as food.

[6]Then all the inhabitants of Egypt shall know that I am YHWH.
Because they[e] were a staff of reed to the house of Israel—
[7]when they grasped you in hand[f] you would splinter,
and split [g]every shoulder;[g]
And when they leaned on you you would break,
and collapse all loins—

[8]therefore, thus said Lord YHWH: I am going to bring a sword upon you, and cut off man and beast from you. [9]The land of Egypt shall be a desolate ruin, and they shall know that I am YHWH.

[a–a] G "Mine are the rivers and I made them"; S "Mine is the river and I made it."
[b] G S "your river."
[c–c] Not in G.
[d] T "buried" (as from *tqbr*).
[e] G S "you."
[f] G S "their hand."
[g–g] S "their hands"; G renders the verset: "and when every hand prevailed against them."

Because [h]he said:[h] [i]"A Nile is mine, and it is I who made [it],"[i] [10]therefore I am coming at you and at your Nile-streams; I will turn the land of Egypt into ruins of parched desolation from Migdol to Syene, to the border of Cush. [11]There shall not pass through her the foot of a human, nor shall the foot of any beast pass through her; and she shall not be inhabited for forty years. [12]I will make the land of Egypt a desolation among desolated lands, and her cities among ruined cities shall be [j]a desolation[j] for forty years. I will scatter Egypt among the nations and disperse them among the lands.

[13]However thus said Lord YHWH: When forty years are over I will gather Egypt from the peoples where they were scattered, [14]and restore the fortunes of Egypt, and return them to the land of Pathros, the land of their origin, and they shall be there a lowly kingdom. [15]Of kingdoms she shall be most lowly, and not exalt herself over nations; I will reduce them so as not to dominate nations. [16]It[k] shall not serve again as a source of Israel's trust, bringing iniquity to mind in their having turned to them; and they shall know that I am Lord YHWH.

COMMENT

29.1 *the tenth year,* etc. The date is 7 January 587 (Parker-Dubberstein, p. 28; see now the chronological table in A. Malamat, *Israel in Biblical Times* [in Hebrew] [Jerusalem: Bialik Institute, 1983], between pp. 288 and 289), a year after the start of the siege of Jerusalem ("in the ninth year," 24:1). This first oracle against Egypt is earlier than the first Tyre oracle ("in the eleventh year," 26:1); on the disorder, see Structure and Themes.

2. *set your face toward.* See comment to 6:2 (I, 130).

against him and against all Egypt. Accordingly the gender-specific morphemes in the sequel vacillate freely between masculine singular, referring to Pharaoh; feminine singular, referring to the land (*'ereṣ,* fem.) of Egypt; and masculine plural, referring to the Egyptians.

3. *Speak and say.* Shortened form of the solemn parallelism of 14:4 and 20:3.

the great monster. Hebrew *tannin* (here and in 32:2 *-m,* perhaps resulting from a misconstrual of *-n* as an Aramaic plural ending and its "correction" to Hebrew *-m*) is a mythical primeval sea monster (G "dragon") defeated by God (Isa 51:9; Job 7:12), symbolizing one of the forces of chaos ultimately to be vanquished (Isa 27:1). It is cognate with Ugaritic *tnn* "dragon," among the mythic powers struck down by the goddess Anath (e.g., *ANET*[3], p. 137a). But it also denotes a mundane creature found in Egypt (Exod 7:8–12), who functions in the priestly Plague narrative as the equivalent of the "serpent" in the nonpriestly narrative (Exod 4:2–5), and is usually identified as the reptilian crocodile. Here, too, as a denizen of the Nile, *tnym* is generally taken to refer to the crocodile—especially in the light of the strong coloration of this oracle by Egyptian concepts; see Struc-

[h–h] G "your saying" (as from *'mrk*); S "you said" (as from *'mrk* or *'mrt*).
[i–i] G "The rivers are mine and I made them"; S = S in note a–a.
[j–j] Not in G.
[k] G S T "they."

ture and Themes. (J. Day's discussion of Ezekiel's *tnym*, in his *God's Conflict with the Dragon and the Sea* [Cambridge: Cambridge University Press, 1985], pp. 93ff., ignores the mundane *tnyn* of priestly literature; to be sure, in ch. 32 Ezekiel does draw on a richer mythical vocabulary, including terms associated with the mythical *tnyn*.) Luzzatto aptly notes that in Arabic *far'un* "Pharaoh" denotes "crocodile."

his Nile-streams. Plural of *y'wr*, the Hebrew form of Egyptian *'rw* "great river, Nile," the plural apparently denoting the many branches and canals of the Delta (so, too, e.g., in Exod 7:19; Isa 7:18; Ps 78:44). The Egyptians called each of the major Delta branches "a Nile" (Freedy-Redford, p. 471 n. 37). In this oracle *y'wr* is treated as a common noun and hence has a plural and can bear pronominal suffixes. In the west-central part of the Delta lay Sais, the capital of the twenty-sixth (Saitic) dynasty contemporary with Ezekiel where Pharaoh "couched." MT has the singular in Pharaoh's speech (here and in vs. 9), the plural in the addresses to Pharaoh; G, the plural in vss. 3 and 9, the singular in between (cutting across the speakers in each instance); S has the plural only once, in vs. 3a. The variation in MT seems most regular, though its significance is unclear.

"Mine is my Nile, and it is I who made [*it*] *for me."* The structure of this sentence—dative pronoun at the head of clause *a*, emphatic subject pronoun at the head of clause *b*—recalls that of attribution to God of his creations: "His is the sea and it is he who made it" (Ps 95:5); "Yours is the day; yours the night too; it is you who established luminary (= moon) and sun" (74:16); cf. also Ps 89:12. What stands out in Pharaoh's boast is the self-reference in every word, peaking in *'śytny*—a unique form with the first person object suffix attached to a first person verb. One's first inclination to render the word "I made me" is checked by the consideration that such a colossal boast should have headed the sentence, not come as a seconding of the claim on the Nile. Moreover, the reformulation in vs. 9 of Pharaoh's boast, though differing in nuance (see comment there), must be substantially similar, and it lacks the object suffix and so cannot be construed as a claim of self-making. I therefore follow the proposal (of Moshe Kimḥi [cited in MenbSh], David Kimḥi, NJPS) that the direct object of the verb is unexpressed—as in the case of *'śyty* ("I made [it]") of vs. 9 (and often; GKC, § 117 f; Joüon-Muraoka, § 146 i), and the object suffix is dative (paralleling *ly* in clause *a*), like the suffix of *nttny* "you gave to me" in Josh 15:19 (see König III, § 21; Joüon-Muraoka, § 125 *ba*; Dahood, *Psalms III*, AB, pp. 377f.). Accordingly the sense of clause *b* is: it is I who made the Nile for my benefit or glory.

G reads Pharaoh's boast here and in vs. 9 as virtually identical (as does S, but in a different way), and their readings are smoother than that of MT (see text notes); such levelings are not preferable to MT.

4. *hooks.* For this meaning, see comment to 19:4 "shackles." Herodotus (2.70) describes the procedure: "The hunter baits a hook with a chine of pork, and lets it float into the middle of the river; he himself stays on the bank with a young live pig, which he beats. Hearing the cries of the pig, the crocodile goes after the sound, and meets the chine, which it swallows; then the hunters pull the line" (trans. A. D. Godley, in the Loeb Classical Library).

stick the fish . . . scales. A fantastic image; God the hunter prepares to haul up the crocodile with its adherents: he hooks its jaw and attaches the fish to its scales. The referent of fish has been understood as either the army of Pharaoh or, more likely, the teeming Egyptian population; cf. the verb *dgh* "to teem" (lit. "be like fish").

I will haul . . . After setting up the victims in the water, he hauls the monster out of the river with all its fish stuck to it. Each stage of the operation is deliberately spelled out for vividness.

and all the fish of your Nile-streams shall stick. The subject "all the fish" of the intransitive verb "shall stick" (vs. $4b^{\beta}$) is preceded by the object marker *'t* under the influence of the preceding transitive construction ($4b^{\alpha}$) as though it were absorbed into it: "I will haul you up . . . [you] and all the fish" (= G, which lacks the predicate of the second clause—"shall stick to your scales"—possibly because of its awkwardness). Such syntactic contamination, resulting in anacoluthon, was furthered here by the foregoing construction of the same components in vs. $4a^{\beta}$, where "the fish of your Nile-streams" is the object of the transitive verb "stick." This type of anacoluthon occurred in 17:21 and 20:16; see J. Blau, "Zum angeblichen Gebrauch von *'t* vor dem Nominativ," *VT* 4 (1954), 7–19, esp. 8; T. Muraoka, *Emphatic Words and Structures in Biblical Hebrew* (Jerusalem and Leiden: Magnes Press and E. J. Brill, 1985), pp. 146–57, esp. p. 153.

5. *cast . . . into the desert.* There to die, separated from your natural habitat. Though crocodiles are amphibious and can make long overland journeys, they cannot presumably survive long in the desert any more than other unadapted land animals. But cf. 32:4, where "the land" replaces the desert; Ezekiel may not have been familiar with the amphibious nature of the crocodile.

not collected. But left strewn in the open (the crocodile and the fish are addressed as a single entity).

not gathered (tqbṣ). A synonym of the preceding verb (*t'sp*); the two are paired in 11:17 (and Mic 4:6) referring to the ingathering of exiles. Here, in the figure, it replaces the expected "buried" (*tqbr*)—paired with "collected" in Jer 8:2; 25:33—and thus foreshadows the nonfigurative statement in vss. 12–13 on the eventual ingathering of Egypt's exiles. In the figure the scattered, exposed corpses suffer the ultimate disgrace: they are eaten by animals—a common curse or threat in ancient writings (Deut 28:26; Jer 34:20; Ezek 39:17–20; and elsewhere; see D. R. Hillers, *Treaty-Curses and the Old Testament Prophets* [Rome: Pontifical Biblical Institute, 1964], pp. 68–69). The entire verse is a figure forecasting Pharaoh's going into exile together with his people, where all of them would perish (MenbSh).

T *ttqbr* is taken to reflect a reading *tqbr* "be buried," which according to *BHS* appears in some medieval mss. and is preferred by it to MT, although this reading is not supported by other versions. V supports MT. G *peristales* "enwrapped, laid out" and S *ttḥml* "enshrouded" do not render *qbr* elsewhere, and had their *Vorlage* read it here, no reason can be shown for their having reached for so uncommon a rendering. Could their *Vorlage* have read *tqbṣ*?—nowhere else is *qbṣ* so translated! Yet it could have, for *'sp*—a synonym of *qbṣ*—serves in Ben Sira for burying (38:16; 44:14), evidently abbreviated from "gathered (= laid in)to a grave" (II Kings 22:20). The Greek of Ben Sira 38:16 renders *'swp* by *peristeilon* "lay out" just as it renders *qbṣ* in our Ezekiel passage. J. C. Greenfield kindly calls my attention to a Phoenician inscription from Persian times in which the dead man speaks of himself *'sp bmr wbbdl[ḥ](?)* "laid out (i.e., embalmed) in myrrh and bdellium"; see F. M. Cross, *IEJ* 29 (1979), 40–44. So G (and S) could have arrived at their peculiar rendition of *tqbṣ* through a transfer of the burial sense of post-biblical *'sp* to our *tqbṣ* in order to conform the sense of the pair *'sp/qbṣ* to that of *'sp/qbr* which was expected in this context. T *ttqbr* is thus either the product of a similar semantic transfer or a reflection of a variant Hebrew reading *tqbr*. The versional evidence favors *tqbṣ*, and the echo of it in vs. 13 indicates that it is employed here in its usual sense.

6. The mention of "all the inhabitants of Egypt" in the *a* clause explains the vacillation in what follows between "they" of MT (i.e., the inhabitants) and "you" of G (i.e., Pharaoh).

staff of reed. Nile-reeds (cf. Isa 19:6) afford another image of Pharaoh: he is as treacherous as a staff made of a hollow reed, which may suddenly fracture and give way under the weight of a body. Ezekiel's belittlement of Egypt (vss. 6b–7) recalls that ascribed to the Assyrian Rab-shakeh in II Kings 18:21 (Isa 36:6): "This staff of splintered reed, which when one leans on it enters his palm and punctures it." (A few years earlier Sargon II of Assyria characterized his Egyptian contemporary as "a king who cannot save"; see M. Cogan and H. Tadmor, *II Kings*, AB, p. 231; *ANET*^{3}, p. 287a.) Ezekiel enlarges upon the apparently traditional image by poetically doubling its elements with typical parallelistic heightening. At first, in this verse, Pharaoh (Egypt) is called merely a "staff (made) of reed," without the anticipatory qualifier "splintered" which appears in Kings/Isaiah; that belongs to the dynamic of the image as it is developed in the next verse.

7. The little drama of the treacherous reed staff is spun out in two climactic poetic lines (7a, 7b). The first verset of each line ($7a^\alpha$, $7b^\alpha$) tells how the house of Israel relied on the reed staff; the second verset ($7a^\beta$, $7b^\beta$) tells the injury the staff inflicted.

α	β
7a: grasped you . . . you would splinter	split every shoulder
7b: leaned on you, you would break	collapse all loins

In each category the second line surpasses the first: grasping with the hand results in damage to the shoulder (7a); leaning with the whole body results in total collapse (7b).

you would splinter, and split . . . you would break, and collapse. The verbs are durative — imperfect (*trwṣ, tšbr*) followed by perfect consecutive (*wbq't, wh'mdt* — note the final stress), indicating habitualness: Egypt was ever an unreliable ally.

in hand (Q: bkp). Without possessive suffix as in 21:16; in both cases G supplies an appropriate suffix presumably to suit Greek idiom. The K *bkpk* is apparently a scribal error, the suffix inadvertently copied from preceding *bk*.

split every shoulder. An upgrading of the injury in relation to the Kings/Isaiah formula, though not entirely clear: the splintered end of the staff "breaks open" (*bq'*)—shatters? dislocates?—the shoulder, a body part that carries the brunt of labor (e.g., 12:6ff.; 29:18; Isa 46:7) and expresses rebellion, Neh 9:29. G. R. Driver (1954, p. 299) tries to depict the mishap: "[I]f a man falls heavily on a breaking staff, it may wound his hand and even, if he slips over it [?], pierce his arm-pit. Here therefore *ktp* means the shoulder viewed from underneath, i.e., the arm-pit."

S reads "their hands" for "every shoulder," and G's puzzling reading of the verset includes "every hand"; this appeals to critics (e.g., Zimmerli, Wevers) who require Ezekiel to conform to the wording of Kings/Isaiah ("punctures his palm"). But it also obliterates the radicalization of traditional elements that is the hallmark of Ezekiel's creativity. The splintered staff "splits," not merely "punctures"; it damages the shoulder, not merely the hand.

collapse all loins. This rendering takes *h'md* as a metathesis of *hm'd*, as in the phrase "make their loins collapse (*hm'd*) always" (Ps 69:24). For a suggestive list of metatheses in Biblical Hebrew, see Ibn Janaḥ, *Riqma*, ch. 32 (31) (this example is not found there). On the loins as the seat of the body's strength, see comment to 21:11.

8. *upon you . . . from you.* Feminine singular, addressing "the land (feminine) of Egypt," as in the next verse. Cf. 14:17 and 25:13 for the stereotypical doom phraseology.

9. *a desolate ruin* (lšmmh wḥrbh). Absence of preposed *l-* before the second noun suggests a hendiadys, whose meaning is expressed in 36:4 by noun+qualifier: *lḥrbwt hšmmwt* "to the desolate ruins" (for a nonhendiadyl sequence, with repeated preposition, cf. 5:14 *lḥrbh wlḥrph* "a ruin and a reproach").

Because he said. This resumes vs. 3b, hence the third person (as in 3b) where we expect (from the sequel)—and G S actually have—second person forms (see text note).

"A *Nile is mine, and it is I who made* [*it*]." The components of the first clause of Pharaoh's boast in vs. 3b are here reversed, indicating reference; see comment to 9:9 (I, 178) and fuller discussion at I, 198. The initial position of "Nile" and the absence of a first person suffix on it bring the river into prominence over against Pharaoh's ego (note also the absence, to the same effect, of the first person object suffix on the verb *'śyty*).

The first clause *y'r ly* exhibits the nominal sentence pattern: noun—dative as in *'z l'lhym* "might is God's (= belongs to God)" (Ps 62:12); *dwdy ly w'ny lw* "my beloved is mine and I am his" (Song 2:16). The difference between this formulation and that of vs. 3b is thus minimal. But this pattern also appears in, e.g., *śmlh lkh* (Isa 3:6) "you have a garment"; *ph lhm* "they have a mouth" (Ps 114:5 and the series there); *'ḥwt lnw* "we have a sister" (Song 8:8). Accordingly this reformulation of Pharaoh's boast is translatable: "I have a Nile" with the nuance: I am secure in possession of my life source. To this corresponds the doom of drought announced in the following verse.

MT's divergent formulations of Pharaoh's boast take precedence over the versions of G and S, in which the first and second citations are virtually identical.

10. *ruins* (ḥrbwt) *of parched* (ḥrb) *desolation.* This generality is made specific

in 30:12: "I will turn Nile-streams into dry land (*ḥrbh*)." For another wordplay on *ḥoreb*, see Jer 50:35–38, where a series of imprecations against Babylon beginning "A sword (*ḥereb*) against . . ." (as vs. 8 here above) ends with "A drought (*ḥoreb*, lit. 'parching') against its waters, so that they dry up."

from Migdol to Syene, to the border of Cush. Migdol ("tower," a Semitic borrowing in Egyptian place-names) is the name of several military stations on Egypt's northeastern frontier (cf. *ANET*³, p. 259b). A Migdol figures in the Exodus story (Exod 14:2); it reappears in Jeremiah (44:1; 46:14) as the location of a Jewish colony (of garrison troops?). Here Migdol marks the north(eastern) border of Egypt. Syene (Heb. *sᵉwene*; in Egyptian, "market, trading post") is modern Aswan, just north of the first cataract of the Nile—anciently the southern limit of Egypt. Beyond it lay Cush—the prevailing Egyptian designation of all known territory south of Egypt. Jews were also to be found at Syene in the sixth century B.C.E. (Isa 49:12: "the land of the Syenians"), and the Jewish garrison in the island of Elephantine opposite it is well documented from the fifth century (B. Porten, *Archives from Elephantine* [Berkeley: University of California Press, 1968]. See E. Oren, "Migdol: A New Fortress on the Edge of the Eastern Nile Delta," *BASOR* 256 [1984], 7–44, esp. 30ff.).

In the Aramaic papyri from Elephantine, Syene is written *swn;* MT's consonantal form, *swnh,* should have been vocalized *sᵉwena(h),* with unstressed directional suffix *a(h).* The *waw* of the following *wʿd* is then explicative: "that is, to the border of Cush." The MT vocalization *(sᵉwene[h])* and the translations of G ("and Syene") and S ("of S.") betray ignorance of the historical geographic reality.

11. *forty years.* The period in which one generation flourishes and then dies off (the full term of "judges" [e.g., Judg 3:11; 8:28] and kings [e.g., II Sam 5:4; I Kings 11:42]); hence a period of temporary national punishment: the Israelite generation of the Wandering (Num 14:33; 32:13) and the predicted exile of Judah (Ezek 3:6; see comment in I, 105–6). King Mesha of Moab gives forty years as the length of Israelite occupation of part of his land during the time of his god's anger (*ANET*³, p. 320b; on the chronology, see F. M. Cross and D. N. Freedman, *Early Hebrew Orthography* [New Haven: American Oriental Society, 1952], p. 39 n. 13).

12. *a desolation among desolated lands.* Usually taken as a superlative: most desolate; Joüon-Muraoka, § 141 j n. 1. But see below.

among ruined cities shall be a desolation (šmmh). We expect "shall be a ruin" (*ḥrbh,* which complements *šmmh* "desolation" in vs. 9). This second *šmmh* is not in G and appears to be a secondary assimilation of the second clause of the verse to the first. But 30:7 shows that the second clause in such a sequence need not be constructed like the first, for it reads:

They shall be desolate among desolate lands,
  and his cities among ruined cities shall be.

This was probably the original reading of vs. 12a$^{\beta}$ here as well, with "ruined" expressed here by hofʿal participle *mḥrbwt,* varied in 30:7b to nifʿal *nḥrbwt*—a typical Ezekielian touch.

Modern translations (e.g., NJPS, *REB*, *NAB*) do not recognize the difference of 30:7b, and translate all four of the clauses in 29:12a and 30:7 as superlatives (*REB* renders both passages identically: "the most desolate of desolate lands . . . the most derelict of derelict cities" — a beautiful example of versional leveling). But if leveling is at all in order, it should start from 30:7b, which is clearly nonsuperlative: "its cities shall be [reckoned] among ruined cities." Agreeably the clauses concerning the land may be understood: Egypt shall be a desolation, (reckoned) among other desolate lands. Membership in a class is the point, not superlative exemplification of it.

13. *However.* For the contrastive sense of *ki* introducing a new stage of an oracle, see comment to 23:28, "Indeed thus said Lord YHWH."

14. *restore the fortunes.* See comment to 16:53–55 (I, 290).

the land of Pathros. An Egyptian name, "the southern land," designating all Egypt above (= south of) Memphis. King Esarhaddon of Assyria (681–669 B.C.E.) called himself king of Musur (= north Egypt; Hebrew *miṣrayim*), Paturisi (south [= upper] Egypt) and Kusu (= Cush, the country south of Egypt) (*ANET*[3], p. 290) — a north-to-south sequence found as well in Isa 11:11. An ancient Egyptian tradition is reflected in Ezekiel's assertion that the Egyptians originated in the southland; see Structure and Themes.

16. *It shall not serve again as a source of Israel's trust.* "It" is glossed by MenbSh "the Egyptian people" in order to supply a masculine singular subject (*ʿam*); the versions adjust to plural ("they") according to the context (note the subsequent "[turned to] them"). In fact, the sentence appears to be an anacoluthon: it starts with "(source of) trust" as the implicit subject, "There shall no longer be for the house of Israel a (source of) trust" (*mbṭḥ* with no preposed *l*-). Under the influence of *lbyt (yśrʾl)* the next word received *l*- (*lmbṭḥ*) and the construction changed, leaving *yhyh* "shall be" without a proper subject.

The thought is somewhat tangled, too. The verse seems to say two things: (1) reduced Egypt will no longer tempt Israel to look to it for help; (2) it will no longer serve to remind God of the offense Israel gave in so doing. As in vss. 6b–7 Israel's crediting the unfounded pretensions of Egypt to be a world power has dire consequences. On "bring iniquity to mind," see comment to 21:28.

turned to them. The construction of *pnh* "turn" with *ʾḥry*, properly "after," is an Aramaism for regular Hebrew *pnh ʾl* "turn to" (see, e.g., Ps 40:5); cf. Targumic Aramaic *ʾtpnh btr* for Hebrew *pnh ʾl* as in Lev 19:4. J. C. Greenfield calls my attention to the expression in the Aramaic Sefire Inscription (mid-eighth century B.C.E.) III, 7: *wʾl tpnw bʾšrh* "pay no attention to him" (*ANET*[3], p. 660b; *bʾšr* = *b*[*ʾ*]*tr* "after").

Vs. 16 recalls Ps 40:5: "Happy is the man who makes YHWH his (source of) trust (*mbṭḥw*) / Who turns not to (*pnh ʾl*) *rhbym* 'rahabs' (conventionally: the arrogant)." Since Rahab is a mythical monster associated with *tannin* in Isa 51:9 (cf. our vs. 3), and a symbol of Egypt in Ps 87:4, our Ezekiel verse may be a specific application of Ps 40:5.

STRUCTURE AND THEMES

Since the Assyrian domination of Palestine-Syria in the eighth century, Egypt pursued its interests by stirring up the small states of the area to rise against their overlord. The calamitous revolt of Hoshea of Israel against Shalmaneser V involved a mission to Egypt (II Kings 17:4; see Alberto R. W. Green, "The Identity of King So of Egypt—an Alternative Interpretation," *JNES* 52 [1993], 99–108). Its continuation, in alliance with other western states, was abetted by an Egyptian army—which alliance was defeated by Sargon II in 720, at Raphia (*ANET*[3], p. 284a). A few years later Sargon had to put down another rebellion that began in the Philistine city of Ashdod, but implicated Judah as well as other statelets. The Egyptian Pharaoh was "bribed" (so the Assyrian put it) to help, but proved to be "a king who could not save" them (see comment to vs. 6). In this situation Isaiah predicted the downfall of the Egypto-Ethiopian helpers, their exile by the Assyrians, and the disappointment of those who looked to them for aid (ch. 20; in vss. 4–5 he calls Egypt *mbṭm* "the object of their gaze").

In an oracle also apparently dating from this period (H. L. Ginsberg, *EJ* 6.56) Isaiah predicts the destruction of Egypt with especial attention to the failure of its life source—the Nile: "The Nile-streams of (*y'wry*) Egypt will dry up (*wḥrbw*)," and all industries dependent on them will cease (19:1–15).

After Sargon's death, Hezekiah king of Judah organized a revolt against his successor, Sennacherib. Once again missions went to Egypt and got promises of aid. Isaiah bitterly attacked this reliance on human power (30:2–7; 31:1ff.):

"Ho! Those who go down to Egypt for help
And lean (= rely) upon horses
And trust in chariots so many . . .
And do not turn to the Holy One of Israel . . .
But the Egyptians are humans, not God
And their horses flesh, not spirit . . ."

The Egyptian army that was sent against Sennacherib's force was defeated at Eltekeh (near Ekron) in 701. A century later as the Assyrian empire collapsed, Pharaoh Necho made an effort to acquire the Assyrian holdings in Syria-Palestine. He was decisively defeated by the Babylonian army at Carchemish on the Euphrates in 605. Jer 46 reflects this defeat and foretells that the victor (Nebuchadnezzar) would conquer Egypt's home territory and exile its inhabitants. But an afterword declares that Egypt's former state would be regained after a while (vs. 26).

The kingdom of Judah, subject to Nebuchadnezzar, continued to look to Egypt for aid. King Jehoiakim, raised to the throne by Necho (II Kings 23:34), rebelled against his new Babylonian overlord, hoping for Egyptian support that never materialized (judging from the laconic reference to Egypt's inaction in II Kings 24:7). The final item in Egypt's record of fruitless interventions and disappointments was Pharaoh Hophra's dispatch of an army to relieve besieged Jerusalem that provided a flicker of hope before it retreated (Jer 37:5, 11; see Lam 1:2, 7, for a post-fall view of Egypt's impotence). For the integration of biblical and extra-biblical data on these events, see the relevant chapters in M. Cogan and H. Tadmor, *II Kings*, AB (1988).

The main themes of the Egyptian oracles of the Judahite prophets were thus established by the time of Ezekiel: the prideful kingdom's illusion of power, based on the Nile-plenty; the disastrous consequences of misplaced reliance upon it; God's dooming it to defeat and exile (entailing the drying-up of the Nile) in order to humble it; and its eventual restoration.

Ezekiel's first oracle against Egypt opens with the dated revelation formula of 29:1, and its three main sections all close with the recognition formula (vss. 6a, 9a, 16). It contains the fullest justification of Egypt's coming doom, together with the only statement concerning its future restoration; subsequent oracles develop only aspects of the doom. The structure of the oracle is somewhat obscured by the verse division in vss. 6 and 9 that conjoins in one verse the end of one section and the beginning of another. The clue to the correct division is Ezekiel's usage: *ya'an* "because" precedes *laken* "consequently," and the closing recognition formula is never followed by *ya'an* (though it may be enlarged by other formal elements). Thus the oracle's structure is as follows:

A (vss. 2–6a): first figure — Pharaoh the river monster and his adherents. Both will be hauled out of the Nile and cast into the desert, there to die and be prey for wild creatures.

B (vss. 6b–9a): second figure — Pharaoh/Egypt the unreliable reed staff. For having induced Israel to rely on them, then collapsing in the event, Egypt will be devastated.

C (vss. 9b–16): a nonfigurative elaboration of the foregoing.

C1 (vss. 9b–12): the devastation and desiccation of the Nile country and exile of its population for forty years (related to A).

C2 (vss. 13–16): the ultimate restoration of Egypt as a lowly kingdom. This is a supplement to C1 ("when forty years are over") and is related to B in that Egypt will then be unable to tempt Israel into relying on them for help.

The structure recalls the tripartition ("halving" plus "coda") of Ezekiel's earlier oracles, in that it sounds two themes (A, B) and then fuses the two (C) — although in view of its size C cannot be called a mere coda.

A feature of this oracle is the constantly shifting object of address and reference, the condition for which was set at its start (vs. 2) by the double target of God's anger: Pharaoh and all Egypt (the land, its inhabitants). In A the two are explicitly figured by the monster and the fish respectively. The shift from second person ("you" = Pharaoh) in vss. 3–5 to "all the inhabitants of Egypt shall know" (vs. 6a) is abrupt but not exceptionable. A more complicated movement occurs in B: influenced by vs. 6a, 6b retains "they," followed in vs. 7 by "you" (singular masculine = Pharaoh). Vss. 8–9 run the gamut of possibilities of reference to "Egypt": in vs. 8 "you" (feminine singular, as reflecting *'rṣ* "land"), in vs. 9a "she," and in vs. 9b "they" (the inhabitants). C1 shifts from Pharaoh, spoken of in third person (vs. 9b, perhaps a textual error in MT; see comment), then spoken to in second (vs. 10a), to the land, in third person singular (vss. 10b–12a), and finally to the inhabitants, in third plural (vs. 12b). C2 continues in third plural (vss. 13–14); vs. 15a enlarges on "lowly kingdom" of vs. 14b (third feminine singular), returning to third plural in 15b. In vs. 16 an anacoluthon (see comment) initially breaks the third plural sequence, which is immediately resumed.

The MT of this passage exhibits a maximum of shifts over against any version. This absence of adjustment and leveling is a warrant of originality and illustrates splendidly the stylistic "untidiness" of the prophet, from which some of his critics labor to redeem him, invoking for support the more harmonious readings of the versions.

The main issue of the oracle is Egypt's pride as epitomized in the boastful self-sufficiency of Pharaoh. The government's management of the assured annual Nile inundation gave the Egyptians a sense of security unknown to the inhabitants of the land of Israel. Herodotus reports the complacency of Egyptian priests who contrasted their safety with the insecurity of a country like Greece, which was dependent on rainfall (2.13–14; the negative reflection of such complacency appears in the reversal of values evident in Deut 11:10–17; see Martin Buber, *Israel and Palestine: The History of an Idea* [London: East and West Library, 1952], pp. 24–26). Our oracle assails Pharaoh's self-assurance.

Section A figures Pharaoh as the Nile-monster couching in his life sphere, which he "has made for himself"—tailored to his needs. Fittingly, then, the doom takes the form of the fatal separation of the monster and his dependents from their natural environment (this is spelled out as exile in the nonfigurative C1). In section B, Pharaoh's boast is reformulated, with a stress on his possession of "a Nile"—a permanent resource—of which he is master. Fittingly, then, the doom is portrayed as a failure of the resource—a drying-up of the Nile and the consequent desolation of the countryside.

As with the first oracle against Tyre (and all the small oracles against nations in ch. 25), the first oracle against Egypt, and that alone, mentions a specific wrong done to Israel: the false trust Egypt inspired in her of support in her revolt against Babylonia. Ezekiel elaborates a traditional Israelite gibe about Egypt's dangerous impotence, but in doing so he poses a question for the interpreter: can the prophet who denounced the Judahite alliance with Egypt (ch. 17) and who consistently condemned Judah to destruction, now turn and blame Egypt for not helping Judah in her death throes? Is this a display of sympathy for the desperate homelanders, for whom the prophet has never had a good word? The thematic connection of the gibe with the future reduction of restored Egypt (vss. 14–16) suggests that we need not go so far.

The pretension, never fulfilled, to be a bulwark against and a counterforce to the Mesopotamian power (Assyria or Babylonia) involved Egypt in two offenses, one ethical, the other religious. The ethical offense is embodied epigrammatically in Prov 25:19, "Like a broken tooth, or an unsteady leg is trust in a faithless person on a day of trouble." The terminology of this epigram recalls Ezekiel's language about Egypt:

Prov 25:19	*Ezek 29:7, 16*
rʿh "broken"; Aramaism from *rʿʿ* = Hebrew *rṣṣ*	*trwṣ* (from *rṣṣ*) "you would splinter"
mwʿdt "unsteady"	*hʿmdt* = *hmʿdt* "collapsed"
mbṭḥ "trust"	*mbṭḥ* "source of trust"

Menaḥem Ha-Meiri's comment to the Proverbs passage explicitly compares the Kings/Isaiah characterization of Egypt as "a splintered reed staff" (though as we have just seen Ezekiel offers a closer comparison). The universality of this condemnation and its elevation to a theological issue appears in an Akkadian proverb: "To create trust and then to abandon / To [promise] and not give / Is an abomination to Marduk" (W. W. Hallo, "Biblical Abominations and Sumerian Taboos," *JQR* 76 [1985], 30). Pharaoh's fickleness toward Israel was thus a generally recognized ethical offense—one engendered by overweening. Condemnation of it signifies no particular favor toward the victimized Judahites (whom, indeed, God had long since abandoned). God will punish Egypt not as the avenger of a wrong done to Israel but as the guardian of a universal morality.

The religious offense resulting from Egypt's pretensions was to deflect Israel from reliance on God. The future reduction of Egypt to a lowly kingdom will prevent any future Israelite state from faithlessly turning to Egypt for help. We have here a detail of the grand program of Israel's restoration, described in chs. 34ff. At that time, God will purge Israel of its past sins and hard-heartedness (cf. esp. 36:25–29), but that will not be all. As when God punishes he puts a stumbling block before sinners (3:20; see comment), so when he restores he will remove all cause of iniquity from their view. However, like the acts of purgation as interpreted in 36:16–32, the elimination of Egypt as a source of temptation is ultimately rather for the glorification of God than out of concern for his people.

The terminology of Egypt's restoration in vss. 13f. is identical with that of Israel's—see, e.g., 11:17; 20:41. While it may be a misnomer to call this and the rest of C2 universalistic (W. Vogels, "Restauration de l'Égypte et universalisme en Ez 29:13–16, "*Biblica* 53 [1972], 473–94), Ezekiel's excepting Egypt from the doom of all the other gentiles is remarkable. It is doubtless because Egypt did not exploit or rejoice over Israel's defeat as they did; the harm it caused was not out of malice. However, the promise of restoration is never repeated, and when 30:23, 26, repeat 29:12b ("I will disperse Egypt among the nations and scatter them among the lands"), it is without the limit of forty years that appears at the end of 29:12a. This raises suspicions that C2, and the "forty years" of vs. 12a, are a mitigating afterthought. The appending of a prophecy of restoration to the first oracle (which we may suppose was originally of unmitigated doom like the rest) indicates that it applies to all the subsequent oracles concerning Egypt. It could have been composed and emplaced at any time, but not likely before the formulation of the last Egypt oracle. It expresses a deliberate judgment that takes Egypt's lesser guilt into consideration and, after a purgative devastation of the land and exile of its people, allows it a place in God's new world order—on humbling terms.

Several elements of the oracle correspond strikingly with Egyptological data. The conjunction of Pharaoh, the Nile, and a river monster has strong local coloration. The Egyptian god Sobek "was manifest in the crocodile and represented the power of the Nile to rise and fertilize the land" (H. Frankfort, *Ancient Egyptian Religion* [New York: Harper Brothers, 1961], p. 26). Pharaoh was compared or identified with the crocodile, as in the declaration of the god Amon-Re to the victorious Thutmose III: "I cause them [the enemy] to see thy majesty as a crocodile, / the lord of fear in the water, who cannot be approached" (*ANET*[3], p. 374b). A Pyramid text describes the appearance of the dead king Unas as the crocodile-god, Sobek (M. Lichtheim, *Ancient Egyptian Literature* I [Berkeley: University of California Press, 1973], p. 40).

Ezekiel's description of Pharaoh's boast corresponds to attested Egyptian notions. The ancient Egyptian king did in fact ascribe to himself the benefits of the Nile. "He controlled the water which made Egypt and made her fertile. 'The Nile is at his service, and he opens its cavern to give life to Egypt' [from a scarab of Thutmosis III]. As his courtiers told him: 'If thou thyself shouldst say to thy father, the Nile, the father of the gods: "Let water flow forth upon the mountains!" he will act according to all that thou hast said'" (J. A. Wilson, in H. and H. A. Frankfort, et al., *The Intellectual Adventure of Ancient Man* [Chicago: University of Chicago Press, 1948], p. 80; cf. at length, H. Frankfort, *Kingship and the Gods* [Chicago: University of Chicago Press, 1948], pp. 57–59, 194–95).

That Ezekiel was familiar with the topography of Egypt (vs. 10 and the additional data in 30:13–18) is less remarkable (though it is that) than his knowledge of the curious antiquarian concept that the land of the Egyptians' origin was southern Egypt (vs. 14). Herodotus, who lived a century after Ezekiel, reports this as an Egyptian priestly tradition (2.4): before Min (the first king and unifier of Egypt) the name Egypt referred to the district of Thebes alone; north of that, the land was under water. With time, the silting of the Nile raised the land farther and farther north, and "as the land grew in extent many of [the people] spread down [from the higher south] into the new country, and many stayed behind" (2.15). It is a historical fact that the unification of the country did begin, and was several times renewed, by southern rulers gaining control of the north. We can only guess at the source of Ezekiel's Egyptology: perhaps it entered into the education of the young priest, along with other Egyptian scribal and sapiential lore that flowed into Judah from the eighth century onward (on the impact of Egypt on Israel, see R. J. Williams's contribution to J. R. Harris, *The Legacy of Egypt*, 2d ed. [Oxford: Clarendon Press, 1971], pp. 257–90, esp. pp. 276ff.).

The message of the oracle fits the situation in Judah in January 587, in which beleaguered Jerusalem vainly hoped for help from Egypt. The precise relation of this oracle to the expeditionary force of Pharaoh Hophra is unclear; see I, 10 n. 11. We have noted above indications that C2 and "forty years" of vs. 12 are later additions. However, nothing in the text as we have it points to a hand other than Ezekiel's; his may be the original oracle and his the reflective afterthought.

The dating of this oracle to the tenth year places it earlier than the previously dated (Tyre) oracle, "in the eleventh year" (26:1). Likewise, the last-dated Egypt oracle (32:17; see I, 10–11 nn. 12, 13) postdates the next dated oracle on exilic matters. In other words, the Egypt oracles are a unit, self-contained chronologically and topically, that has been inserted en bloc with disregard for the slight chronological disturbance at either end. The treatment of Egypt separately from the nations mentioned in chs. 25–28 accords with its differing political-military stance toward Israel. Israel's smaller neighbors are blamed for rejoicing over its fall or exploiting the event for their own advantage. In Tyre's case a crass theological offense is added: the king of Tyre's claim to divinity. Egypt, however, differed on both counts: it was a failed ally, but an ally, of Judah; and its king's *hubris*, as Ezekiel describes it, stopped short of claiming divinity. Hence, its chastisement is lesser: it will be humbled but not annihilated.

Since the first-dated Egypt oracle precedes in time the only dated oracle in the unit of chs. 25–28, why was the Egypt-block postpositioned? Perhaps because of the link in the next unit (29:17–21) between the Egyptian and the Tyrian oracles. And since the next unit is (aside from the enigmatic date in 1:1) the latest-dated item in the book, it seems that its placement and that of the two blocks both belong to the same editorial operation. See further, Structure and Themes of the next section.

XXXII. An Amendment to the Tyre Oracles (29:17–21)

29 [17]In the twenty-seventh year, the first month, on the first of the month, the word of YHWH came to me: [18]Man, Nebuchadrezzar king of Babylonia made his army labor mightily against Tyre—every head rubbed bald, every shoulder abraded—yet neither he nor his army got wages out of Tyre for the labor which he performed against her.

[19]So thus said Lord YHWH:

I am going to give the land of Egypt to the king of Babylonia. He shall carry off her horde and plunder her and despoil her, and that shall be wages for his army. [20]As his pay, which he labored for, I am giving him the land of Egypt, [a]which they did for me,[a] declares Lord YHWH.

[21]At that time I will make a horn sprout for the house of Israel, and I will enable you to open your mouth among them; and they shall know that I am YHWH.

COMMENT

29:17. The date is 26 April 571 (Parker-Dubberstein), a year or two after the end of the siege of Tyre (573/2, see I, 10 n. 10).

18. *rubbed bald . . . abraded.* From protracted carrying of burdens on the head and shoulders, as would be entailed, e.g., by throwing up earthworks. Such were used in blockading the land approaches to Tyre; see the Assyrian citation in the comment to 26:8.

wages. Booty in the form of persons, animals, and possessions; on the ancient view of booty as soldier's wages, see my article "Is there a Mari Parallel to the Israelite Enemy-*ḥerem*?" (in Hebrew), *EI* 24, *Avraham Malamat Volume* (Jerusalem: Israel Exploration Society, 1993), 49–53. Although in the end Tyre surrendered to the Babylonians, it evidently was able to obtain exemption from ravaging and despoiling in exchange for yielding. Ezekiel's prophecy to the contrary (e.g., 26:3–14) was not fulfilled.

19. *her horde* (hmwnh). On the basis of the parallelism of *hmwn* and *ḥyl* "riches" in Isa 60:5, and that of *ḥyl* and *šll* "spoil" in Isa 8:4, a case can be made here for S "her possessions." However, throughout the Egypt oracles *hmwn* occurs (sixteen times in MT) in the sense of horde (cf. 7:12 "masses," and com-

[a–a]Not in G S.

ment, I, 150), as in 30:10, 15; 31:2, 18; etc.; see L. Boadt, *Ezekiel's Oracles against Egypt*, Biblica et Orientalia 37 (Rome: Pontifical Biblical Institute, 1980), 51, 64. T renders it so: "he shall take her throng captive," which is supported by 30:17–18: Egyptian villagers shall go into captivity (*bšby tlknh*).

Booty is represented as a gift of God in Deut 20:14 ("the spoil of your enemy, which YHWH your God gives you") and I Sam 30:23. I. Eph'al and J. Naveh, "Hazael's Booty Inscriptions," *IEJ* 39 (1989) 192–200, esp. pp. 194f., cite these verses and adduce extra-biblical examples as well; e.g., "the enemy's booty, of all sorts, which Aššur, king of the gods, granted me as the share due to me as king"—from an inscription of Esarhaddon.

20. *As his pay, which he labored for* (bh, lit. "for her"). G S construed the suffix of *bh* not as a reference to nearby *p'ltw* "his pay" but as a reference to distant Tyre (in vs. 18): "in return for the service that he served at Tyre (= her)." This results in a parallel to vs. $18b^{\beta}$: "the labor which he performed against her (= Tyre)," but the distance put by this construction between the suffix of *bh* and its antecedent seems too great.

which they did for me. Which labor they (i.e., Nebuchadnezzar and his army) performed on my behalf. This relative clause (so it is perceived, on the analogy of the relative clauses of vss. 18b and 20a) is awkwardly placed, has no explicit noun that it modifies, and is absent in G and S. Cornill and Allen hesitantly suggest it is a variant or an explanatory note to one or the other of the relative clauses. I concur in regarding it as a secondary annotation that did not get into all copies of the oracle, but I take it to apply, loosely and summarily, to both relative clauses. It declares (climactically) that Nebuchadnezzar was working for God in pursuing the siege; the event, despite its disaccord with prophecy, was thus under God's aegis and his agent would therefore be rewarded, even if not as originally foretold.

A neater translation ignores the contextual pressure to take this as a relative clause, and renders it "because they worked for me" (*RSV, NRSV*). That *'šr* can mean "because" is recognized by BDB, 83, def. c; cf. I Kings 8:33 (*'šr*) = II Chron 6:24 (*ky*): "because they have sinned against you."

T construes the clause as relative and attaches it to the immediately preceding "land of Egypt," which necessitates a periphrastic continuation: ". . . I have given him the land of Egypt, who sinned (plural) before me, to punish them." The medievals, not surprisingly, and the *REB*, surprisingly, follow suit; *REB*: "I have given him Egypt . . . because they have spurned my authority" (no textual basis other than MT is claimed for this "translation").

21. *At that time.* Lit. "On that day"; coincident with Egypt's conquest by Nebuchadnezzar in the indefinite, but near, future. Near, so as to reward the soldiers who participated in the campaign against Tyre.

I will make a horn sprout for the house of Israel. NJPS gives the sense: "I will endow the House of Israel with strength." An animal's horns are tokens of its power, hence a figure of strength (Deut 33:17; Ps 92:11). Mesopotamian gods are regularly portrayed with horns; e.g., *ANEP*², ##514–16, 525–26. As God "hewed off" Judah's horn when he caused its fall (Lam 2:3), so he will ultimately restore it to power by "making a horn sprout" for it. The exact phrase recurs in vs. 17 of the royal Ps 132: "There [in Jerusalem] I will make a horn sprout for David / I will tend a lamp for my anointed one." But it is not at all evident that here the allusion is to a restored kingdom. Indeed the expression is so vague as to preclude any definition beyond the inauguration of an era of new vigor for the people. Is it that the Babylonian conquest of Egypt, predicted here, will herald Israel's restoration? Our perplexity matches that of the medievals who confessed it, then proceeded each in his own way to try and anchor this passage in the framework of biblical history. Their many solutions are a sure sign of no solution.

and I will enable you to open your mouth. Lit.: "and to you I will give an opening of the mouth," i.e., a claim to be heard, a vindication of your credibility. *piṯḥon pe* (also in 16:63) is discussed in I, 121. Evidently the prophet expected to live to see the turn in Israel's fortunes (Ehrlich [Hebrew]).

STRUCTURE AND THEMES

Following the dated revelation-event formula (vs. 1), the fact is noted that Nebuchadnezzar's Tyrian campaign was bootless (vs. 18). This serves as the ground (equivalent to a *yaʿan* clause) for the prediction in vss. 19–20 (the *laken* clause) that the king and army would be compensated out of Egypt's loot. To this are appended two sentences of consolation; coincidentally with Egypt's fall, Israel would be reinvigorated and the prophet vindicated.

This brief passage — the latest-dated in the book, aside from the enigmatic 1:1 — amends the unfulfilled oracles on Tyre and Egypt. By the twenty-seventh year of the exile (571) the thirteen-year siege of Tyre by Nebuchadnezzar had ended with the city subjected but intact — contrary to Ezekiel's predictions. Moreover, when seventeen years earlier, around the time of Jerusalem's agony, Ezekiel had proclaimed Egypt's fall and devastation, he had expected it to occur imminently (see esp. 30:3–4: YHWH's doomsday against Egypt and its helpers is near). But after Pharaoh Hophra's futile intervention in Jerusalem's behalf there had been no hostilities between Egypt and Babylonia down to this twenty-seventh year of exile.

Hophra's last years were marred by a war against Greek colonists in Libya in which his army was overwhelmingly defeated. Discredited, he would soon be deposed by his general Amasis, who usurped his throne (570). It may have been some inkling of these internal troubles that aroused Ezekiel's expectation (a year earlier) that at long last the Babylonian conquest of Egypt would occur.

However that may be, in the extended siege and final capitulation of Tyre Ezekiel saw a partial fulfillment of his Tyre dooms. Nebuchadnezzar had done God's work (according to the best rendering of the explanatory addition in vs. 20b) and had thus earned a reward that he failed to get from Tyre. The unfulfilled dooms against Egypt now came to be understood as God's manner of compensating the Babylonians for their service to him. The promise of remuneration was relevant only for those — king and soldiers — who participated in the siege of Tyre. That means that the conquest and plundering of Egypt must be close at hand. Vs. 21 goes on to connect the fall of Egypt with the reinvigoration of Israel, and both with the vindication of the prophet. We sense a crisis of faith in prophecy, similar to that reflected in 12:21–28.

By year twenty-seven of the exile, in twenty-two years of prophesying Ezekiel had only one realized prophecy to his credit: the fall of Jerusalem back in the seventh year of his career. That event had vindicated Ezekiel in the sight of his fellow exiles (see 33:21f., 30ff.), but only for a while. His doom prophecies on Tyre, Sidon, and Egypt date from just before and after the fall (see Table of Dates, I, [8]–11), and their fulfillment was somehow linked to Israel's restoration (28:25f.; 29:16). As the years went by and none of his predictions materialized we may plausibly suppose the rise of new doubts about his calling. At the start of his career his fears were answered by supportive personal oracles (see I, 121, 123); now again his God responded to his need for support by revealing an amendment to the unfulfilled Tyre prophecies. Since it affected the interpretation of all the oracles about Egypt, it was appended by the editor to the first Egypt oracle. This may well have determined the placement of the Egypt oracles after those of Tyre (despite the earlier onset of the former), since it made Egypt's doom consequent on the fruitlessness of Nebuchadnezzar's Tyrian campaign.

The prediction made in the amendment that Nebuchadnezzar would (soon) conquer and plunder Egypt also failed to materialize. A damaged cuneiform tablet dated to the thirty-seventh year of Nebuchadnezzar (568/7) refers to some sort of Babylonian military action against Hophra's successor, Amasis (*ANET*[3], p. 308b). This datum has been integrated with an Egyptian description of a defeat Amasis inflicted, in that year, on an invading force of Asiatics, presumably Babylonians (E. Edel, "Amasis und Nebukadrezar II," *Göttinger Miscellenen* 29 [1978], 13–20). In 562 Nebuchadnezzar died, never having conquered Egypt (A. Gardiner, *Egypt of the Pharaohs* [Oxford: Clarendon Press, 1961], pp. 360–63; see esp. D. J. Wiseman, *Nebuchadrezzar and Babylon* [Oxford: British Academy, 1985], pp. 39–40, who cannot find evidence for Nebuchadnezzar's interventions in Egypt alleged by Josephus, *Antiquities* 10.9.7, or in the prophecy of Jer 43:8–13; Jeremiah's expectations were no more realized than Ezekiel's).

Perhaps the most momentous aspect of this amendment is its testimony to the prophet's procedure in the case of invalidated (not merely unfulfilled) prophecies. He did not suppress them, but let them stand in their contradiction to events. He awaited a new message from God to interpret the discrepancy, and when it came, he set it alongside the failed prophecy. DNF: "I think it is clear that Ezekiel didn't agree with the assessment of the Deuteronomist about how to tell the difference between true prophets and false prophets [Deut 18:21f.: if his prediction failed to come true, he is a false prophet]. Ezekiel knew from personal experience that he was a true prophet, and hence if some of his predictions didn't come out, there had to be a different explanation from the one that would make him a false prophet. His God could change his mind, or some factor might require a shift in strategy, but that was all in the mystery of the Godhead, whereas a prophet . . . could only report what he had seen and heard in the heavenly assembly."

It is remarkable that the transmitters of these materials also shrank from altering the texts so as to do away with the embarrassing evidence of failure. No less remarkable is the survival of the amendment though itself contradicted by later events. The prophet himself added the amendment on the basis of a new oracle, but by the time Nebuchadnezzar died — foreclosing forever the validation of the amendment — Ezekiel was no longer alive, or at least no longer prophesying, so as to amend the amendment. The fact that no subsequent addition was made to bring the amendment up to date suggests that the transmitters of the material did not venture to invent oracles for such purposes. Such evidence strongly advises caution in the ascription of material in the Book of Ezekiel to updating by later hands.

(Calling this amendment an "adaptation" through "hindsight" of the original oracle [when it is rather an avowal, evincing no hindsight, that events have invalidated the original oracle], and regarding it as an example of *vaticinium ex eventu* "'prediction' based on the event" — on a level with I Kings 13:2 [when the only event predicted here never came to pass] — R. P. Carroll misses its true significance in his *When Prophecy Failed* [London: SCM Press, 1979], pp. 174ff., 227 n. 46.)

XXXIII. Egypt's Doomsday (30:1–19)

30 [1]The word of YHWH came to me: [2]Man, prophesy and say: Thus said Lord YHWH:

Wail, "Alas for the day!"
[3]For near is [a]a day;
yes, near is[a] YHWH's day—
a day of clouds, a time of nations it shall be.
[4]A sword shall enter Egypt,
and convulsions shall be in Cush,
When slain fall in Egypt,
and they take away her horde,
and her foundations are demolished.
[5][b]Cush and Put and Lud, and all the mixed units and Kub, and men of the land of the covenant[b] with them, shall fall by the sword.

[6][c]Thus said YHWH[c]:
The supporters of Egypt shall fall,
and its pride of strength shall sink;
From Migdol to Syene by the sword they shall fall in her, declares Lord YHWH.
[7]They[d] shall be desolate among desolate lands,
and his[e] cities among ruined cities shall be.
[8]And they shall know that I am YHWH, when I set fire to Egypt, and all her helpers are broken.
[9]On that day messengers shall go forth [a]at my bidding[a] [f]in boats to make confident Cush tremble.[f] Convulsions shall be in them on[g] the day of Egypt. Indeed it is coming!

[a–a]Not in G.
[b–b]G "Persians and Cretans and Lydians and Libyans and all the mixed ones and the sons of my covenant."
[c–c]G "in her" (conjoined to the preceding).
[d]G singular (viz., the land).
[e]G "their."
[f–f]G S "hastening (as from *'aṣim?*) to destroy (as from *lᵉhaḥᵃrib*) Ethiopia (S: Cush)."
[g]*b(ywm)* as Cairo, Aleppo, Leningrad mss., G S; other witnesses *k(ywm)* "as (the day of)."

10Thus said Lord YHWH: I will put an end to Egypt's horde by the hand of Nebuchadrezzar, king of Babylon— 11he and his army with him, the most terrible of nations, brought to destroy the land. They shall unsheath their swords against Egypt, and fill the land with slain. 12I will turn Nile-streams into dry ground, [a]and deliver the land into the hands of fierce men;[a] I will desolate the land and all that is in it by the hands of strangers. I YHWH have spoken.

13Thus said Lord YHWH: [h]I will destroy idols and put an end to images[h] in Noph; a native chief of Egypt shall be no more; and I will put fear in the land of Egypt.

14I will desolate Pathros,
and set fire to Zoan,
and work judgments in No.
15I will pour out my fury on Sin, Egypt's fortress,
and cut off the horde of No[i]
16I will set fire to Egypt;
Sin[j] shall be convulsed,
And No readily breached,
[k]and Noph—enemies by day.[k]
17The youths of Aven and Pi-beseth shall fall by the sword,
and they shall go into captivity.
18In Tehaphnehes the day withholds,[l]
when I break the bars[m] of Egypt there,
and her pride of strength is ended in her.
She shall be covered with clouds,
and her daughters shall go into captivity.
19I will work judgments in Egypt, and they shall know that I am YHWH.

COMMENT

30:2. *Wail, "Alas for the day!"* The addressees (a plural audience as in Isa 13:6) are whoever may be affected by "the day"—e.g., the Egyptians themselves—after the pattern of Jer 25:34, where the "shepherds" are called on to wail over their own doom (see also Jer 47:2); or sympathetic onlookers (cf. 32:16: gentile women lament [*qnn*] over Egypt's destruction, as do the world's seafarers over Tyre's, 27:32). The words to be wailed (cf. S T: "Wail and say"), "Alas (*hh*) for the day," recur in Joel 1:15 with the regular full form of the interjection *'ahah;* it is clipped here for the sake of alliteration with the preceding verb *hylylw: HYLyLw HH LYwm.* G "O, o, the day" may be a haplographic reduction of MT.

3. *For near is a day; yes, near is YHWH's day.* These two phrases climactically

[h–h] G "I will destroy great men" (as from *gdwlym;* cf. G at Jonah 3:7; Nahum 3:10).
[i] G "Memphis" (Hebrew *np*).
[j] G "Syene."
[k–k] G "and waters will be dispersed" (as from *wnpwṣw mym?*).
[l] *ḥśk* as Cairo, Aleppo, Leningrad mss.; other mss. *ḥšk* = G V S T "darkens." Cf. *Minḥat Shay.*
[m] G "the scepters" (as from *maṭṭot*); S singular.

augment the preceding "the day": *qrwb ywm* "near is a day" preposes an adjective and removes the article from "day," as it were preparing it for the following periphrastic genitive construction *ywm lyhwh* "YHWH's day" (elsewhere *ywm yhwh;* cf. *ḥrb lyhwh* "YHWH's sword," Jer 12:12). The periphrastic expression alliterates more fully with the opening cry *hylylw lywm.* The breakup of the expression *qrwb ywm YHWH* into two stages, connected by *w-* "yea, yes," recalls the augmenting parallelism of numbers "for three, yes (*w-*) for four" (Amos 1:3, 6, etc.). The short text of G (see text note) — and similarly of T in some mss. — may reflect a simplification in the *Vorlage* or by the translators, erroneous or intentional. *BHS*'s evaluation of the MT as dittographic misses its art.

The proclamation that the day of YHWH is near is a commonplace of prophecy; see Isa 13:6 (with "Howl!"); Joel 2:1; 4:14; Zeph 1:7, 14ff. Ezek 7:7, 12, refers to this doomsday, though not explicitly naming it YHWH's day.

a day of clouds. Similarly in vs. 18; shortened from "a day of clouds and gloom" as in 34:12, Zeph 1:15, and Joel 2:2, all describing a calamitous time. The darkness figure is developed in 32:7–8.

a time of nations. "Time" is doom time, as in 7:7 ("time"–"day" paired as here); 22:3 (Isa 13:22); so T: "time of disaster for nations." The "nations" have been understood to be all heathens ("a final reckoning with evil everywhere," Skinner), but they need be no more than those listed as Egypt's allies in vs. 5.

4. *shall enter.* The irregular ultimate stress is noted by *Minḥat Shay*, and is to be compared with similar anomalies in Lev 22:13 (*wšbh*) and Isa 23:17 (*wšbh*). All these forms are converted perfects and normally have penultimate stress.

convulsions (ḥlḥlh) . . . *in Cush.* "Trembling" or "anguish" does not do justice to this powerful derivative (by reduplication) of *ḥwl* "writhe, be convulsed," associated with the throes of childbirth (Isa 21:3); see further on *ḥwl* at vs. 16 below. Note the alliteration of *ḤLḤLh* with preceding *ḤRb* "sword" and following *ḤLL* "slain." On Cush, see comment to 29:10.

take away her horde. T "they take her throngs captive"; see comment at 29:19.

her foundations are demolished. A more thorough destruction than that described in 13:14 (foundations exposed). Perhaps, though, the expression is metaphoric (cf. "the righteous man is an everlasting foundation [*yswd ʿwlm*]," Prov 10:25) for the supporters of (*smky*) Egypt enumerated in the following verse. For the synonymy of **ysd* and **smk*, cf. Tannaitic Hebrew *smwkwt* "supports" (of the sky) in *Genesis Rabba* 38:1 = Biblical *mwsdwt* "foundations" (of heaven), II Sam 22:8.

5. *Cush and Put and Lud.* On the latter two peoples, see at 27:10. Jer 46:9 lists these three in the same order, as components of Pharaoh Necho's army at Carchemish. From various extra-biblical sources it is known that the army of the Saite rulers comprised, beside Egyptians, also Greeks, Ionians, Rhodians, Carians, Libyans, Phoenicians, and Jews (E. Drioton and J. Vandier, *L'Égypte*, 4th ed. [Paris: Presses Universitaires de France, 1962], pp. 582, 594).

and all the mixed units. The word *haʿereb*, a common noun, occurs in Jer 25:20 denoting a nonnative element of Egypt's population (see McKane, *Jeremiah*, ICC, p. 637) and in Jer 50:37, a nonnative element in the population of Babylon. It is distinct from *ʿᵃrab* (no article), a proper noun (Ezek 27:21 and elsewhere) "Arabia," though S so renders here. (In I Kings 10:15 *haʿereb* is to be corrected to *ʿarab*, as in the parallel II Chron 9:14.) Here the reference must be to mercenary units, as T "all the auxiliaries (or: supports)."

and Kub. Unknown; on the basis of G it has been emended to *Lub*, from which Lubians (= Libyans), coupled with Put in Nahum 3:9 may be derived.

and men of the land of the covenant. Presumably a reference to soldiers of an unnamed allied country. Jerome supposed them to be Judahites (Cooke) and indeed in the Letter of Aristeas 13 reference is made to Jewish auxiliaries in the army of a Psammetichus. Taken in connection with Ezek 17:13ff., a case can be made for the allied country being Judah, the "covenant" being a pact of mutual assistance concluded between it and Saite Egypt during the reign of Zedekiah (see, e.g., M. Hadas, *Aristeas to Philocrates* [New York: Harper & Brothers, 1951], p. 100 note). G "men of my covenant" will signify the same, though the covenant is here between God and Israel. The coded epithet for Judah will be designed to avoid direct implication of Judahites in Egypt's disaster.

with them. Though absent in G (as is "with him" in vs. 11), it is a list closure characteristic of priestly style (Cooke, citing S. R. Driver, *Introduction to the Literature of the Old Testament*, 9th ed. [Edinburgh: T. & T. Clark, 1913], p. 132 #10; see, e.g., in the priestly components in the Flood story, Gen 6:18; 7:7, 13; 8:16, 18; 9:8).

6. *Thus said YHWH.* This introductory formula ending with the tetragram alone (for Ezekiel's regular form see vs. 2) occurs in Ezekiel only twice again, in 11:5 and 21:8, where its location is unimpeachable. Here, however, it breaks into a continuous passage, vss. 4–8, that describes the collapse of Egypt and its helpers. G reads "in her" instead, forming, with the end of vs. 5, an expression identical with vs. 6b: "shall fall by the sword in her." Perhaps the original was as in G *bh* "in her"; it was first miswritten *kh* "thus" and then filled out (irregularly for Ezekiel) with the prophetic messenger formula. Cooke regards the formula as original and as opening a new section.

The supporters of Egypt shall fall. Irony; cf. Ps 145:14: "YHWH supports all who fall."

its pride of strength shall sink. On the noun phrase, see comment at 24:21. The verb (*yrd*) "descend" replaces the commoner *nšbt* "be ended" (vs. 18; 33:28; cf. 7:24) as a better parallel to *npl* "fall."

From Migdol to Syene. As 29:10; see comment thereto.

7. This verse rephrases 29:12; see comment there. The pronominal elements of the two clauses of the verse are inconsistent in both MT and G. The shift in number in MT ("they, his") is reversed in G (singular feminine verb ["she"], "their"). In the first clause MT is attracted to the previous verse's verb (*yplw* "they shall fall"), while G carries on the preceding preposition phrase (*bh* "in her"). In the second clause MT's "his (cities)" has no referent (Smend: Pharaoh — but he is not mentioned in the foregoing). G's "their cities" is inconsistent with its singular verb in the preceding clause but agrees with MT's "they (shall be desolate)." S T also read "their cities" (agreeing with their preceding plural subject. Some moderns (e.g., NJPS) prefer "her cities" in accord with 29:12 (and to be consistent some adopt G's singular ["she"] in the first clause [*RSV*]). The state of both

MT and G indicates early textual variations that were represented by inconsistency in the choice of number for each of the two clauses (but MT's "his [cities]" is likely an error for "her").

8. *helpers.* I.e., allies; cf. I Kings 20:16—thirty-two kings, "helpers" of Ben Hadad (*'wzr 'tw*); Isa 31:3 "the helper (Egypt) will stumble and the helped will fall."

9. *messengers . . . at my bidding in boats.* MT depicts God spreading panic in Cush through the report of the fall of its northern neighbor. "Rivers of Cush" separate the country from the rest of the world (Zeph 3:10; Isa 18:1–2; cf. vs 2: "[whose land] is cut off by streams" [NJPS; *RSV*: rivers divide]), so communication with it is by "swift messengers" on boats (Isa 18:2 "papyrus vessels"). Remote Cush's confidence in its inaccessibility will be shaken.

The Hebrew for "at my bidding" is "from before me," i.e., "proceeding from me" (BDB, 818); e.g., Est 1:19 "let the king's edict go forth by his order" (*mlpnyw*). This usage occurs only in late Biblical Hebrew and is probably an Aramaism; cf. Ezra 7:14 "commissioned by order of (*mqdm*, lit. 'from before') the king."

"Boats" (*ṣym*) is a rare word derived, so it is commonly held, from Egyptian (T. O. Lambdin, "Egyptian Loanwords in the Old Testament," *JAOS* 73 [1953], 153f.; KB³). It occurs in Isa 33:21 in an expression of inaccessibility that evokes our passage:

> [YHWH] will be for us [like] a region of rivers
> of broad streams (*y'rym*);
> Rowing ships cannot go there,
> and no mighty boat (*ṣy*) can traverse it.

The pair *hḥryd/bṭḥ* "trouble, agitate" / "confidence, security" regularly occurs in the combination "dwell in security with none to trouble" (*yšb lbṭḥ w'yn mḥryd*) Lev 26:6–7; Ezek 34:28; 39:26. Ehrlich observes that *hḥryd* connotes to take by surprise, comparing II Sam 17:2. In our passage *bṭḥ* has no verb that it qualifies, but is attached directly to Cush, just as in Gen 34:25 it appears to refer to the state of the Shechemites: "[Jacob's sons] came against the unsuspecting city" (*h'yr bṭḥ*; cf. Targ. *dytb' lrwḥṣn* "that was dwelling in confidence"; here, too, S and T both insert "dwelling" before their rendering of *bṭḥ*).

The integrity of the MT of vs. 9 is established by the context field of its terms.

G S reflect a different reading of keywords (see text note): Cush will not merely be convulsed, it will be destroyed by "hastening messengers" (cf. "swift messengers" of Isa 18:2)—God's commissioned executioners. Medievals understood MT in this way. For Rashi the messengers are "troops of soldiers going on my mission" (cf. T: "messengers . . . with legions"). Kimḥi expands on this: "After the destruction of Egypt I will bring upon Cush an army of nations, in ships . . . Cush, that dwelt in security will be agitated by the army that will come upon them unexpectedly." The medievals go well beyond what is said in MT, but their interpretation raises the possibility that the *Vorlage* of G S evolved out of it.

on the day of Egypt. T "the day of Egypt's punishment"; cf. "the day of Midian," Isa 9:3, when Midian was defeated; "the day of Jerusalem('s fall: *NRSV*)," Ps

137:7. The other (inferiorly attested) reading "as the day of Egypt" coheres with the understanding (of G and medievals) that vs. 9 predicts the destruction of Cush: "As they were convulsed at the destruction of Egypt [vs. 4] so they shall be convulsed concerning themselves" (Kimḥi).

Indeed it is coming. Doomsday: see comment at 24:14, 24.

11. *the most terrible of nations, brought.* The passive participle is a typical (active-passive) variation on 28:7 "I am bringing (active participle) . . . strangers, the most terrible of nations." (Another variation: "I will bring [perfect consecutive] the fiercest [so! see comment to vs. 12 *rʿym*] of nations," 7:24—note, too, the varied terms for the enemy.) After "by the hand of Nebuchadrezzar" in vs. 10, the passive participle here emphasizes that the Babylonian is but an agent, an executor of God's purposes. This is lost in S and T's "coming."

unsheath their swords. As in 28:7; lit. "they shall empty [their scabbards of] their swords," forming a contrast with the sequel "and fill the land with slain" (Ehrlich). The transitive use of *male* recurs in 10:3 and characterizes priestly writing; e.g., Gen 1:22, 28; 9:1; Exod 40:34.

12. *deliver the land into the hands of fierce men.* Lit. "sell (the land)," a usage of *mkr* frequent in the frame passages of the book of Judges (e.g., Judg 2:14; 3:8; 4:2), found also in the stories (Judg 4:9) and in Moses' song (Deut 32:30) but nowhere else in Ezekiel. *byd* "into the hand(s) of" differs in meaning from *byd* "by the hand(s) (= agency) of" in vss. 10 and 12b, thereby adding another touch of otherness to the clause. With "fierce men" (*rʿym*) cf. "a band of fierce messengers" (executors of God's wrath), Ps 78:49, and "the fiercest [rather than "worst"] of (*rʿy*) nations" in Ezek 7:24, an earlier doomsday oracle; see BDB, s.v. *rʿ*, p. 948, def. 1–2. The whole clause is absent in G; is it a variant of the following clause?

desolate . . . by the hands of strangers. Expressing again the instrumental role of humans; for "strangers," see comment at 28:7.

13. *I will destroy idols.* Punishment of a people includes its gods, as stated explicitly in the Plague narrative of Exodus (12:12): "I will work judgment on all the gods of Egypt as well." The future judgment of Egypt described in Isa 19 repeats the idea: the idols of Egypt shall reel before God (vs. 1). Jer 43:12f. predicts the destruction of Egypt's places of worship ("the houses of Egypt's gods"). The closest parallel to our passage is Jer 46:25, where Egypt's doom involves both Amon, chief god of Thebes, and Pharaoh (in the sequel, Egypt's "gods and kings").

The model of YHWH's judgment of an idol-god is the story of the dismemberment of the Philistines' Dagon (I Sam 5; see the discussion in Y. Kaufmann, *The Religion of Israel* [Chicago: University of Chicago Press, 1963], pp. 11f.).

images (ʾlylym). A term for heathen god-images favored by Isaiah, it appears in the Holiness Code as well (Lev 19:4; 26:1), but only here in Ezekiel. Instead of the two parallel clauses G shows only, "I will destroy great men (*megistanas*) from Memphis." The Greek word translates *gd(w)lyw/h* "his/her great men" in Jonah 3:7 and Nahum 3:10; G's *Vorlage* here evidently had *gdwlym* (a term otherwise not used by Ezekiel). The logic of the reading is clear: it makes vs. 13 speak only of the human leaders. But the forerunner of MT read Ezekiel's choice term *glwlym,* and in order to defend that reading against its rival, the second clause ("and [explicative *waw*] I will put an end to images") was added by way of explanation, using the un-Ezekielian synonym of idols—*'lylym.* Presumably, then, the original reading of vs. 13a$^{\beta}$ was simply, "I will destroy idols in Memphis."

Most critics follow Cornill in equating *megistanas* with *'lylym,* although it occupies the latter's position only in those Greek versions (such as A) that have been adjusted to the expanded MT (see Ziegler or Rahlfs); in the primary, short versions (such as B) it corresponds to *glwlym.* This dubious equation entails emending the Hebrew to *'ylym* "leaders"—which is never translated by *megistanes*—and ignoring *gdwlym,* which is so translated. Ehrlich criticized this procedure (in 1912), but only Herrmann has taken account of his argument (in 1924). One need not agree with Ehrlich's conclusions (I do not) to appreciate the cogency of his critique.

Noph. In Hos 9:6, Moph; both derived from late Egyptian *mnf,* grecized as Memphis: a chief city and religious center of northern (lower) Egypt, at the apex of the Delta, just south of modern Cairo. It was a refuge of Judahites after the fall of Jerusalem (Jer 44:1).

a native chief. Lit. "a chief from the land of Egypt"; cf. "a man from the highlands of Ephraim" (Judg 17:1), i.e., a native of the highlands (Ehrlich). Ezekiel uses *naśi* (G *archon*) "chief" for king in 26:16; 27:21; 38:2 (all foreign kings)—see 7:27 and comment thereto, I, 156f. The meaning seems to be: after Egypt is conquered it will never have a native ruler again.

The verse describes the extinction of the twin repositories of highest authority, deity and king—the maintainers of order in ancient society. Cf. the gravest rejection of authority pairing the two in the capital offense of "cursing (reviling) God and king," I Kings 21:13, an act of ultimate despair, Isa 8:21; in the prohibition of Exod 22:27 king is replaced by "a chief" (*naśi*), as in Ezekiel.

I will put fear in . . . Egypt. With "put fear in" cf. 32:32: "I have put dread of me in the land of the living"; and Jer 32:40: "I will put fear of me in their heart." The term *yr'h* "fear" occurs again in Ezekiel in 1:18 in the sense of fearsomeness. In the oracle on Egypt in Isa 19:16f. fear of God is meant: "In that day, the Egyptians shall be like women, trembling and terrified because YHWH Sebaot will raise his hand against them . . ." But in the present context it is rather terror of anarchic chaos, resulting from the absence of authority (see previous comment). *yr'h* as existential (not "fear of God") appears in Ps 55:6, Jonah 1:10 (as opposed to vs. 16, where it is "God-fearing"); equally nonreligious is "fear of thorns and briers" in Isa 7:25.

14. *Pathros.* Southern (upper) Egypt. See at 29:14.

Zoan. Grecized as Tanis, a town in the eastern Delta, an important administrative center in the eighth and seventh centuries (cf. the "officers" of Zoan in Isa 19:13; 30:4).

No. Full name No-Amon (Nahum 3:8) "City of (the god) Amon." Grecized as Thebes, the chief city of southern (upper) Egypt; surrounded by a great aggregate of sacred precincts.

15. *Sin.* "Fortress" in Egyptian; a fortress town in the extreme northeast fron-

tier, commonly identified with Pelusium; a key position in Egypt's defensive system in our period.

the horde of No (h^{a}mon no). A wordplay on No Amon? (Nahum 3:8; I. Goldberg). G "Memphis."

16. *Sin shall be convulsed.* G Syene. The Q *ḥul taḥul* vocalizes the imperfect as from middle-*w* (as in Ps 114:7 imperative *ḥuli*), and the infinitive absolute, instead of the regular *ḥol*, is assimilated to it. K implies a vocalization of *ḥol taḥil*, following the pattern of middle-*y* verbs (cf. *ḥilu*, Ps 96:9), as *śom taśim*, Deut 17:15. The verbal construction is a variation on the consonantal duplication of the root in the noun *ḥlḥlh* of vss. 4 and 9.

readily breached. I.e., her walls (T); cf. II Kings 25:4: "the city was breached"—meaning her walls. "Readily" renders *hyh l-* as expressing destination; e.g., Deut 31:17: *whyh l'kl* "shall be ready prey" (NJPS; lit. "for eating"). See S. R. Driver, *Tenses*, § 203.

And Noph—enemies by day. A noun (*ṣare*) in construction with an adverb (*ywmm*) is unusual but attested (e.g., *qllt ḥnm* "gratuitous curse" Prov 26:2; *pḥd pt'm* "sudden terror" Prov 3:25; König III, § 318 c); but some kind of ellipsis must be assumed, and the sense is far from clear. T paraphrases: "Memphis, enemies shall surround her every day." Abarbanel fills in: "Though Noph's fortifications be high, the enemies . . . will assault it by day, not by night like thieves; in broad daylight they will attack Noph to capture it." The text is likely to be corrupt. G (see text note) puts us on a trail that leads to the description of No (= Thebes) in Nahum 3:8: ". . . which sat by the Nile, surrounded by water—its rampart a sea, its wall water" (read *mayim*). The consonantal sequence conjectured from G (see text note) may be corrupted from **wnfrṣw mymyh* "her water shall be burst through"—her (i.e., No's) protecting wall of water. The questionable accuracy of this picture of Thebes (*Nahum*, ICC, pp. 341f.) is not a relevant objection to this suggestion; Ezekiel and Nahum can have had the same misconception of the relation of the Nile to Thebes.

17. *Aven* and *Pi-beset* represent Egyptian names of towns grecized as Heliopolis (so G here: "city of the sun[-god]"; again at Jer 43:13, for Hebrew *Beth Shemesh* "house of Sun[-god]") and Bubastis. The first is vocalized disparagingly like the Hebrew word for "evil"; elsewhere (e.g., Gen 41:45, 50) it appears as *On*. Its location is at the apex of the Delta, just north of modern Cairo. Bubastis lies in the Delta.

and they (whnh). To whom does this feminine plural pronoun refer? G "the women," counterbalancing "the youths"; cf. Kimḥi in the name of his father: "the wives of the slain young men." Simpler (but less balanced): "the (rest of the inhabitants of the) two cities," since Hebrew "city" (*'ir*) is feminine.

18. *Tehaphnehes.* Vocalized as Tahpanhes in Jer 43:7f. G renders the name as *Taphnas*, which has generally been identified with Daphnae, a fortress town on the eastern frontier of Egypt. According to Jeremiah, it was a refuge of Judahites and a royal residence city (vss. 7–9). Though mentioned in a sixth-century Phoenician inscription found in Egypt (*KAI* 50.3), a corresponding Egyptian placename has not yet been found, but Lambdin (following Albright) reconstructs one with the meaning "Fortress of Penhase" (*IDB*, s.v. "Tahpanhes").

withholds. The translation follows the reading *ḥśk* in the best mss. and all copies seen by *Minḥat Shay;* an object must then be supplied — say, "light." A similar ellipsis occurs in Job 16:5: "the movement of my lips (= my utterance) would check" (*yḥśk*), viz., pain (cf. the next verse). Other witnesses (see text note) read or translate *ḥšk* "darkens," which is so fitting one wonders at the obstinate evidence for the unusual reading. Could it be assimilation to the last syllable of *tḥpnḤS* — an entirely local phenomenon?

The darkening of the heavenly lights on YHWH's day is detailed in Isa 13:9, and further developed in Ezek 32:7–8. Gloom is an accompaniment to disaster.

break the bars of Egypt. T's "strength" seems to get the correct sense of "bars" (*moṭot*) here, though the expression is problematic. Usually it is yoke bars (*mṭwt ʿl*) that are broken — the two parallel beams above and below the head of the animals pulling the plow (Y. Feliks, *Ha-ḥaqlaʾut beʾereṣ yisraʾel* . . . [Tel Aviv: Dvir, 1963], pp. 66–68), and the image is of liberation from servitude (e.g., Lev 26:13 and Ezek 34:27; *mṭ-* without *ʿl* in Nahum 1:13). Accordingly our expression has been referred to Egypt's vassals, whose subjugation would end with her fall (Kimḥi). Moderns, guided by the context, prefer G "scepters" (Hebrew *maṭṭot;* on the plural, cf. 19:11 and comment; S in singular: Hebrew *maṭṭe*), i.e., the royal power. But if *maṭṭe* is brought into play, the commonplace "break the staff of bread" (*maṭṭe leḥem;* Ezek 4:16; 5:16; 14:13) reminds us of its basic sense of "staff, support," whence *bšbry mṭwt mṣrym* here would mean "when I break the supports of Egypt" — a figurative active transform of the nonfigurative passive *wnšbrw kl ʿzryh* "and all her helpers are broken" (vs. 7). (The connection is strengthened by the equivalence of "her helpers" to "the supporters of Egypt" in vs. 6.) God will break Egypt's supports (*maṭṭot*) as Egypt broke under Israel as a "staff (*mšʿnt*) of reed" (for the equivalence of *maṭṭe* to *mšʿnt,* cf. Judg 6:21 with II Sam 14:27).

her pride of strength. As 24:21; see comment thereto. "Her" = Egypt's.

is ended in her. In Tehaphnehes; "in her" parallels "there" in the previous verset.

She . . . her daughters. The antecedent of these pronominal elements is unclear: the women of the town? of all Egypt? or, alternatively, the outlying villages (so T *kprnhʾ*) dependent on the town (see at 16:46)?

STRUCTURE AND THEMES

The unit opens with the revelation formula (vs. 1), of all seven prophecies about Egypt the only one without a date (see below on the consequence). The oracle proper falls topically into three parts:

A (vss. 2–9): Egypt's doomsday announced. After the standard address to the prophet and the message formula (vs. 2a), the day is heralded when Egypt and her supporters will fall (vss. 2b–6; closing formula). Devastated, Egypt will recognize YHWH (vss. 7–8; closing formula). Epilogue: far-off Cush, receiving the report, will be convulsed with fear (vs. 9). The subjects of this section are mostly Egypt and her allies, the verbs mostly intransitive or passive; the causes and agents of doom are scarcely mentioned.

B (vss. 10–12): God's commissioning of Nebuchadnezzar to carry out Egypt's doom. The section is defined by the opening message formula and the closure, "I YHWH have spoken." The relation of B to A is similar to that of 26:7–14 to 26:3–6; see there Structure and Themes). The double causality of execution, God working both directly and through human agents, is stressed.

C (vss. 13–19): the destruction of authority and of centers of population. The section opens with the message formula and closes with the recognition formula. In contrast to B (and A) it is God who carries out the judgment.

The unity of the oracle is pronounced. Within A, the key term "day" occurs at the beginning and the end—seven times in all—five times in vss. 2–3, twice in vs. 9. Vs. 3 announces the day of YHWH, the general theme, whose components are set out in vs. 4: the devastation of Egypt and the convulsion of Cush. These are enlarged upon in the sequel. At the very end (vs. 10b) elements of the beginning are resumed: "day of Egypt" defines "day of YHWH"; "it is coming (*b'h*)" echoes "will enter (*wb'h*)"; "there will be convulsion in them" echoes "there will be convulsion in Cush." Vs. 7—a variation on 29:12—introduces two terms, "land" and "cities," that will dominate sections B and C.

The theme of Babylon's agency in B is expressed through the twofold occurrence of "by the hand of" (vss. 10, 12b) and the passive "brought" (vs. 11). Connection with A is established through "horde," vs. 10 (cf. vs. 4), but especially through the fourfold repetition of "land," the object of baneful divine activity in vss. 11–12 (cf. vs. 7a).

Section C starts with the destruction of Egypt's order, divine and governmental (vs. 13)—another aspect of the collapse of Egypt's "foundations" (vs. 4), "supporters" (vs. 6), and "helpers" (vs. 8). It continues with a list of her destroyed cities (cf. vss. 6b, 7b), remarkable for its repertoire of expressions of destruction, many of which are repeated from A and B:

Verse		
13	destroy	
13	put an end to	B (10)
13	be no more	
14	desolate	B (12) A (7)
14, 16	set fire to	A (8)
14, 19	work judgments	
15	pour out fury	
15	cut off	
16	be convulsed	A (4, 9)
16	readily breached	
17	fall by the sword	A (5, 6)
18	break	A (8)

The "day" of gloom and the cover of "clouds" with which C ends (vs. 18) break up "the day of clouds" of the beginning of the oracle (vs. 3) "thus ending with what he began" (Eliezer)—a grand *inclusio*.

The list of Egyptian cities in C follows no discernible order, the few variants in G being of no help. First comes Memphis (Noph) in the north (vs. 13); next the southern region of Pathros, then the Delta city of Tanis (Zoan), and back south to Thebes (No) (vs. 14). There follow: Pelusium (Sin) in the extreme northeast, Thebes (G Memphis) again (vs. 15), Pelusium (G Syene), Thebes, and Memphis again (vs. 16). Finally come three northern town: Heliopolis (On), Bubastis (Pi-beseth; vs. 17), and Daphnae (Tehaphnehes; vs. 18).

The need to repeat and the lack of order suggest a superficial and limited acquaintance with Egypt's topography. Moreover, the literary quality of this passage hardly rises above mediocrity. Critics do not allow Ezekiel to produce anything less than the best quality (that he is capable of, in their estimate), nor are they willing to ascribe to him error or limited knowledge. Hence they agree in relieving him of responsibility for authoring these verses, and foist them on his "school" or his "editors." Since we have no warrant to identify authenticity with accuracy and aesthetic excellence, or to expect consistent quality in a literary record of this scope, we must ask rather whether the passage departs saliently from the style of the prophet or contains matter reflecting a situation other than his. Put in these terms, the comments to the entire oracle show that (saving an explanatory phrase here and there) the language throughout, and the repetitive style, are unmistakably Ezekiel's. Nothing in the oracle betrays historical circumstances later than what may be surmised were his.

The oracle blends motifs of "the day of YHWH" oracles with other motifs specific to Egypt. Among the first are the announcement of the imminence of doomsday (see above, 7:7; and, presumably earlier than Ezekiel, Obad 15 and Zeph 1:7; presumably later, Isa 13:6 and, undated, Joel 2:1; 4:14; see I, 160–61) and its characterization as a day of preternatural gloom and universal fatality (see esp. Zeph 1:15, 18). Specific to Egypt is the enumeration of allies and of native towns. With this Jer 46:13–26 (roughly contemporaneous with Ezekiel) is comparable:

> 14Tell it in Egypt, proclaim in Migdol,
> Proclaim in Noph and Tahpanhes!
> Say: Take your posts and be ready,
> For the sword has devoured all around you.
>
> 19Make yourself an exile-pack,
> Fair Egypt, you who dwell [secure]!
> For Noph shall become a desolation,
> It shall be a ruin without inhabitants.
>
> 21Her mercenaries, too, in her midst . . .
> They too shall turn about,
> Flee as one, and make no stand.
> Their day of disaster has come upon them,
> The time of their doom.
>
> 25. . . I will punish Amon of No and Pharaoh—Egypt, her gods, and her kings—Pharaoh and all who rely on him. 26I will deliver them into the hands of . . . King Nebuchadrezzar of Babylon . . .

The ancient Egyptian "Prophecy of Neferti" (composed in the twentieth century B.C.E. and preserved in a fifteenth-century copy) when describing the chaotic period between the Old and Middle Kingdoms employs phrases strikingly similar to some in our oracle: "The sun disc is covered over. It will not shine (so that) people may see. No one can live when clouds cover over (the sun)." "The rivers of Egypt are empty (so that) the water is crossed on foot. Men seek for water for the ships to sail on it. Its course is become a sandbank." Earlier there is a suggestive allusion to the necessity for the god Re to "begin the foundations (of the earth over again)"; the line is italicized by Wilson in *ANET*³, p. 445a, but W. K. Simpson ed., *The Literature of Ancient Egypt* (New Haven: Yale, 1972), p. 236, gives an equivalent without indicating doubt: "Re must begin by refounding the land." The similarities point to parallel concepts rather than to direct borrowing.

The fall of the great is made the more impressive by depicting its effect on onlookers. In the Tyre prophecies, the sea chiefs and all sailors play the onlooker's part, and their grief and terror (over what Tyre's fall bodes for them) is given much space. In our oracle, Cush, Egypt's southern neighbor, plays a similar role. During the time of the late Judahite monarchy (from mid-eighth to early sixth centuries B.C.E.) Cush and Egypt alternated as the dominant member of a dual realm. The twenty-fifth dynasty (760–656) was Cushite; the twenty-sixth, the Saitic (ruling from Sais, a city in the western delta, 664–525), was Egyptian. Ezekiel's contemporary King Psammetichus II (594–588) conducted a victorious campaign to secure his control of Cush. Both Isa 20:4 (Assyria will conduct "the captives of Egypt and the exiles of Cush") and our oracle bind Egypt and Cush to a single destiny, with the northern member, historically the dominant one, given priority. It is to be observed, however, that contrary to Isaiah, Ezekiel (in MT) does not contemplate here the fall of Cush to Nebuchadnezzar; Cush serves, through its terror, to enhance the enormity of Egypt's collapse.

The absence of a date formula from this oracle leaves open its relation to the foregoing matter. There is no way to tell whether this oracle continued the late addition in 29:17–21 — in which case such verbal links as "the day," "on that day," "the horde of Egypt," "Nebuchadrezzar king of Babylon," would be temporally close as well — or whether it rather goes back to 29:8–12, carrying on such themes of that passage as "sword," desolated lands, ruined cities, and exiled population. It is at any rate from before Nebuchadnezzar's foray against Egypt in 568, and editorially its fitness as a continuation of the generalities of ch. 29 is clear.

XXXIV. Egypt Disarmed, Babylon Armed (30:20–26)

30 [20]In the eleventh year, in the first month, on the seventh of the month, the word of YHWH came to me:

[21]Man, I have broken the arm[a] of Pharaoh, king of Egypt, and see! it has not been dressed—[no] remedies applied [nor] bandage put on, to dress it so that it might heal and grasp a sword. [22]So now, thus said Lord YHWH: I am coming at Pharaoh, king of Egypt, and I will break [both] his arms, [b]the sound one with the broken one,[b] and I will make the sword fall from his hand. [23]I will scatter Egypt among the nations and disperse them through the lands.

[24]I will strengthen the arms of the king of Babylon, and put my sword in his hand, but I will break the arms of Pharaoh, and he shall utter before him groans of the mortally wounded. [25]I will hold up the arms of the king of Babylon, while the arms of Pharaoh shall fall. And they shall know that I am YHWH, when I put my sword into the hand of the king of Babylon and he stretches it against the land of Egypt. [26]I will scatter Egypt among the nations and disperse them through the lands; and they shall know that I am YHWH.

COMMENT

30:20. The date is 29 April 587 (Parker-Dubberstein); see Table of Dates, I, [8] and 10 n. 11.

21. The arm is the symbol of aggressive power (see, e.g., 4:7; 17:9 [= "force" in vs. 17]; 22:6); breaking the arm signifies rendering impotent: Ps 10:15; 37:17. On G's plural, see Structure and Themes.

and see! I.e., take note that from the time that I broke it till now it has not mended. The suggestion is that enough time has passed for Egypt to have taken remedial measures, and since it hasn't, the injury is irreparable; cf. Jer 46:11: "Go up to Gilead and get balm, maiden daughter of Egypt. In vain do you seek many remedies; there is no healing for you."

dressed. Lit. "bound" (24:17, of a turban), probably passive qal, since all occurrences of the verb but one are in the qal pattern (in Ps 147:3 pi'el, as having many objects). Here *ḥbš* "dress" is a general term, followed by two specifying

[a]G "arms."
[b–b]Not in G.

infinitives, *ltt* "apply" and *lśwm* "put" (on such infinitives, see comment at 16:31 *lqls* "in that you scorned"; I, 284). *ḥittul* "bandage" is cognate with "swaddled" in 16:4. *lḥbšh* "to dress it" resumes "not . . . dressed" and is followed by two infinitives of purpose: (1) *lḥzqh* "so that it might heal," an intransitive construction, like *l'mdh* "that it might endure" in 17:14. For the sense "heal," see, e.g., Isa 39:1 *ḥlh wyḥzq* "he fell sick and recovered." (2) *ltpś* "[so that it might] grasp" a sword. Properly one is said to grasp with the hand (*bkp* 21:16); here, to maintain focus, the arm includes the hand.

22. *So now* (laken). Supply a ground mentally: because of Pharaoh's impenitence in spite of his disabling, by which he should have been warned that he offended.

I will break [*both*] *his arms.* Since only the other arm is meant, logic has given way to rhetoric: I will now see to it that he has two broken arms, the already broken one and the hitherto "sound one"—*hḥzqh*, lit. "the strong one," but here "sound" as contrasted with "the broken one."

On G's text, see Structure and Themes.

make the sword fall. Since the other arm will be as incapacitated as the already broken one.

23. Repeats 29:12b.

24. *I will strengthen the arms.* Both arms, giving him maximum power, contrasting with "break the arms of Pharaoh" (= render him maximally impotent) in the sequel.

my sword. Whose ruthless work in Israel is described vividly in 21:8–16. Nebuchadnezzar's sword is really God's; he is God's agent to execute judgment on Egypt as on Israel, and he will succeed, being thus armed.

groans. The phrase repeats 26:15, with transposition of the radicals: *n'q* for *'nq*. Pharaoh has heretofore been a collective figure for Egypt's military might; now he is individualized in his death groans in the presence (= at the feet) of Nebuchadnezzar. The shift from collective to individual is absent in G, which renders vs. 24b: "and he [= Nebuchadnezzar] shall bring it [viz., the sword] to Egypt and plunder its plunder and loot its loot"—a prosaic transfer of the core of 29:19. G (or its *Vorlage*) resisted the sudden shift.

25. *I will hold up* (whḥzqty). This verb with direct object *yad* "hand" here as in 16:49 signifies "sustain, keep from falling" as shown by the contrast with the fall of Pharaoh's arms in the sequel.

stretches it against the land of Egypt. A menacing gesture indicating intention to attack; see I Chron 21:16: the plague angel appeared to David "with drawn sword in hand, stretched against Jerusalem." Cf. also Josh 8:18: by outstretching his lance against Ai Joshua signals an attack.

STRUCTURE AND THEMES

The oracle has a structure similar to 29:17–21. The dated revelation-event formula is followed by A (vs. 21), the description of a situation, and B (vss. 22–26), its consequence, introduced by *laken* and the message formula. B is divided into B1 (vss. 22–23), God's declaration that he will incapacitate Egypt and exile it, and B2 (vss. 24–26), an elaboration thereof, in which the agency of Nebuchadnezzar is repeatedly affirmed. Closure is effected by an expanded recognition formula and an iteration of the coming exile of Egypt, ending with a second recognition formula (vss. 25b–26b). (For such double closures, see above, § XXX, Note on Criteria . . . , under *Wevers*.)

The oracle is extremely focused and consists of variations on the theme of enabling and disabling; keywords are *zrwʿ* "arm" (five times singular and plural) and—each four times—*(n)šbr* "break (broken)," *(h)ḥzq* in a range of meanings, and *ḥrb* "sword." Part A tells of the partial disabling of Pharaoh, from which, by apparently preternatural hindrance, he has not recovered. B1 describes God's intention to complete the job by totally disabling the king; he acts directly against Pharaoh and his people. B2 nuances the foregoing, introducing the Babylonian king as God's agent. But in both parts of B God directly effects the exile of Egypt.

Displaying a concept from different angles is characteristic of Ezekiel—here, his exploitation of nuances of the root *ḥzq*, and the sudden conversion of Pharaoh from a figurative broken-armed man (i.e., a king whose army was defeated) to a real individual, dying at the feet of Nebuchadnezzar. Similarly the Babylonian king is figuratively armed with God's sword (i.e., the Babylonian army, which serves a divine purpose), but then he stretches that sword against Egypt—a realistic attack signal.

The initial defeat of Pharaoh's forces from which he had not recovered fully has been variously interpreted. The Bible records the defeat of Pharaoh Necho at Carchemish (Jer 46:2) and, in II Kings 24:7, Egypt's subsequent inability to undertake a campaign beyond its borders (to support Jehoiakim's rebellion?). Hence the medievals take the Carchemish defeat as the referent of Pharaoh's already broken arm (vs. 21), from which Egypt never fully recovered. All modern commentators, however, refer the broken arm to the much more recent failure of Pharaoh Hophra's effort to relieve more than momentarily the siege of Jerusalem (Jer 37:5–11), a failure of immediate concern to Ezekiel's audience. Opinions differ about the exact relation of the date in vs. 20 to the failure. Both Freedy-Redford and Malamat (see I, 10 n. 11) regard this and the following passage, dated three months later (31:1), as reflecting two stages in the Babylonian defeat of Hophra's expeditionary force (one arm broken, then two). This is doubtful, since the predicted second stage is the defeat of Egypt on its native soil (Nebuchadnezzar's sword signals an attack on "the land of Egypt") and the death of Pharaoh. This goes well beyond a repulse of Hophra's expeditionary force, looking rather to Egypt's ultimate total collapse—which the prophet mistakenly believed to be imminent.

To take the breaking of Pharaoh's arm (vs. 21a) as an allusion to Hophra's aborted campaign seems in itself reasonable. The tenor of vs. 21b, suggesting that a considerable time has passed without its being healed, can be suited to this view if Hophra's campaign be dated well before April 587 (the date of our oracle). The image of a broken arm is best accounted for by crediting Josephus, *Antiquities* 10.108–10, who writes specifically of a battle in which Hophra's army was defeated and put to flight. But the fact is that otherwise nothing is known of any battle; Jer 37:7 predicts only that the force that has marched out of Egypt will march back again. Wiseman can even surmise that the Egyptians "retreated before contact was a possibility, leaving Jerusalem to be sacked" (*Nebuchadrezzar*, p. 30).

In the face of such uncertainties there is just room for one more surmise: that the broken arm of Pharaoh alludes to the drawn battle between Babylonian and Egyptian forces somewhere near the borders of Egypt back in 601, of which the Babylonian chronicler admits that each side inflicted heavy losses on the other (*ANET*³, p. 564a). That battle "effectively ended any Saite control in Asia by land" (Wiseman, pp. 29–30)—i.e., figuratively, Egypt's fractures were never healed though fourteen years passed. Now—our oracle declares—by God's decree the two arms of Babylon, fully recovered, will be brought to peak strength and invincibly armed in order to dispatch Egypt finally. Whether this prediction was stimulated by a report of Hophra's intent to help Jerusalem, or by his retreat from his purpose—defeated in battle or not—it anticipates a disaster much greater than a thwarted sally to help the Judahites: viz., the complete collapse of Egypt, soon to come under attack by the Babylonians on its own soil.

The lesson of this oracle is: nothing can be hoped for from Egypt; Jerusalem's doom is not to be averted through its help. (If we combine the message of 29:16, the teaching is: the very hope that the Judahites put in Egypt was a ground for its defeat!)

It is probably a mere coincidence, but a noteworthy one, that the figure of the broken arm of Pharaoh is an ironic echo of Saitic Pharaoh's royal epithets. "Under the Saites the 'monarch with biceps' was a popular concept, and the very king in question here, Apries, took as the second formal name of his titulary . . . the title . . . 'possessed of a muscular arm, strong-armed man'" (Freedy-Redford, pp. 482f.). Although Ezekiel might have learned this from Egyptian prisoners in Babylon (ibid.), since his own store of images included the arm as a metaphor of power, such a derivation is unnecessary.

One cannot leave this oracle without an uneasy feeling. The contrast "one arm" / "two (both) arms" which seems essential is not linguistically explicit, but inferred from the singular noun in vs. 21 over against the plural in vs. 22, which plural is somewhat lamely glossed by "the sound one and the broken one"—a gloss missing in G. Moreover, G fails to distinguish "arm" from "arms" but pluralizes them both. The suspicion is aroused that the present text overlays an oracle that did not distinguish two stages in Pharaoh's fall, and that it has been imperfectly adapted to convey that idea. If that is so, then a new field of speculation is opened about the circumstances and meaning of the underlying oracle, with twice the number of variables; let chess lovers rejoice.

The juxtaposition of this to the previous oracle may have been determined by the resemblance of the theme *šbr zrwʿ(wt)* "break the arm(s) of" of this oracle to the sound and substance of *wnšbrw kl ʿzryh* "all her helpers shall be broken" (29:8), and to the figure *šbr mṭwt* "break bars/staffs" (29:18). Cf. U. Cassuto, "The Arrangement of the Book of Ezekiel," in his *Biblical and Oriental Studies*, trans. I. Abrahams, I, *Bible* (Jerusalem: Magnes Press, 1973), pp. 227–40, esp. p. 237.

XXXV. Assyria a Lesson to Egypt (31:1–18)

31 [1]In the eleventh year, in the third month, on the first of the month, the word
of YHWH came to me: [2]Man, say to Pharaoh king of Egypt and to his horde:

To whom are you comparable in your greatness?
[3]Here was Assyria, a cedar in Lebanon,
of beautiful branches, [a]a shading wood,[a] and of lofty stature;
whose crown was among the clouds.
[4]Water made him grow, Tehom made him tall:
her rivers she made flow around her[b] planting,
but her canals she sent forth to all the [other] trees of the field.
[5]Therefore his stature was loftier than that of all the other trees of the field,
and his limbs were numerous and his branches long,
because of the abundant water in his channel.
[6]On his limbs nested all the birds of the sky,
and under his boughs all the wild beasts gave birth,
and in his shadow all the many nations dwelt.
[7]He was beautiful in his great size,
in the length of his branches,
for his roots were in abundant water.
[8]Cedars in God's garden could not overshadow him;
junipers could not compare with his limbs,
nor plane-trees match his boughs;
No tree in the garden of God could compare with him in beauty.
[9]I made him beautiful by his many branches,
and all the trees of Eden envied him,
that were in the garden of God.
[10]Therefore thus said Lord YHWH:
Because you[c] grew lofty in stature,
and he[d] set his[d] crown in among the clouds,
and his heart grew haughty on account of his height,

[a–a]Not in G.
[b]G S "his" (i.e., the cedar's).
[c]S "he."
[d]G "you/your."

11I [e]will deliver[e] him into the hand of the leader of nations;
he [f]shall deal with him.
According to his wickedness[f] [a]I banished him,[a] 12and strangers, most terrible of nations, cut him down and cast him away.
On the mountains and[a] in all valleys his branches fell,
and his boughs lay broken in all the gullies of the land.
All the peoples of the earth left his shadow and forsook him.
13On his fallen trunk all the birds of the sky live;
and on his boughs are all wild beasts.
14So that none of the well-watered trees should grow lofty in stature,
and set their crown in among the clouds;
and none of [g]their leaders[g] should stand high,
all drinkers of water;
for all of them are consigned to death,
to the netherworld, amongst mortal men,
to those gone down into the Pit.

15Thus said Lord YHWH: On the day he went down to Sheol I caused to mourn; [a]I covered[a] Tehom on his account. I restrained her rivers so that the abundant water was held in check; I made Lebanon gloomy on his account, and on
his account all the trees of the field languished. 16At the sound of his downfall I
made nations quake, when I brought him down to Sheol, with those gone down into the Pit. In the netherworld all the trees of Eden, [h]the choicest and best[h] of Lebanon, all drinkers of water, consoled themselves. 17They too like him went
down to Sheol, to those slain by the sword, [i]and his arm [who] dwelt in his shadow amidst the nations.[i]

18To whom are you so fitly comparable in glory and in greatness among the trees of Eden? You shall be brought, with the trees of Eden, to the netherworld. Amidst the uncircumcised you shall lie, with those slain by the sword.
That is Pharaoh and all his horde, declares Lord YHWH.

COMMENT

31:1. The date, 21 June 587 (Parker-Dubberstein), is a bit under two months later than that of 30:20.

2. *To whom are you comparable in your greatness.* Complete the thought: that a parallel might be drawn between his fate and yours, so as to make plausible the prediction of your fall. Indeed there was one of comparable greatness, yes of greatness even exceeding yours — the king of Assyria.

The question is not, as G and medievals interpret it, "To whom do you [think

[e–e] G "delivered."
[f–f] G "worked his destruction."
[g–g] So according to MT vocalization, *ʾelehem;* some mss. vocalize *ʾ[a]lehem* "to/against them" — a reading reflected in G T.
[h–h] G "and the choicest."
[i–i] G "and his seed [as reading *zarʿo*], those dwelling [as reading *yšby*] in his shadow, in the midst of their life, perished."

to] compare yourself?" since boastful Pharaoh presumably would not think himself comparable to any mortal (cf. the pagan king's boast in Isa 14:14 "I liken myself to the Most High"), and hence the following argument from the fate of Assyria would carry no weight. Such a question would have been phrased, as we learn from the Isaiah passage, *lᵉmi hiddameta / dimmita napšᵉka*. Ezekiel's question is not about Pharaoh's self-image, but about fact: to whom (of your class) can you fitly be compared (see vs. 18a) by an objective beholder? Answer: to another great king greater than you, who nonetheless fell.

3. *Assyria.* S T "the Assyrian," i.e., the king of Assyria, recognizing, as did all the medievals, personification of the people in its king. The same usage is found in Isa 10:5–11: "Assyria" in vs. 5 is carried on in the rest of the passage as "he," whose identity is assured by the equivalence of "his heart" (vs. 7) with "the . . . heart of the king of Assyria" in vs. 12. Thus "Assyria" here is of the class of Pharaoh, a monarch embodying a people.

a cedar in Lebanon. Moderns suggest that the tree figure applies to Pharaoh and that, accordingly, not *ʾšwr* (Assyria) but *tʾšwr* "cypress" (see comment to 27:6) should be read here (see Boadt's indecisive discussion, pp. 96–97). But it is awkward to have two kinds of tree at the outset of the figure, the main one being the obscure *tʾšwr* "cypress" — never elsewhere used as a figure — glossed, or explicated, by *ʾerez* "cedar," and thereafter supplied with all the attributes of a cedar familiar from other parables of Ezekiel. See further, Structure and Themes.

of beautiful branches. Their beauty consisted in their length (vs. 7) and their abundance (vs. 9); hence the great tree amounted in itself to:

a shading wood. A unique phrase, differing from its neighbors in being a participial rather than a binominal construction, and unlike them, a functional rather than a descriptive expression. Absent in G, it may be an afterthought anticipating "in his shade" of vs. 6, and attached to the first mention of the tree's branches — the origin of the shade.

among the clouds. As 19:11; see comment thereto (I, 353). Here G recognizes this sense of *ʿbtym;* cf. the great tree of Dan 4 (a reincarnation of Ezekiel's cedar) "whose height reached the sky" (Dan 4:8).

4. *Water* may refer to rainwater (Judg 5:4; II Sam 21:10; Job 5:10) as opposed to Tehom (see 26:19), the subterranean ocean (= *yam;* Isa 51:10) that irrigates vegetation from beneath; cf. "blessings of the sky above, blessings of Tehom, that couches below" (Gen 49:25). However, *mym* can also refer to subterranean water, as in Jonah 2:6 (|| Tehom); cf. Gen 1:2; Ps 136:6. Since the sequel mentions only the latter, *mym* and *thwm* are most likely separated components of a construct pair *my thwm* "water of Tehom" (cf. Isa 51:10; for such separation, see comment to 25:5). In Jonah 2:6 *mym* is in parallelism to *thwm* in a clearly subterranean context.

made him grow . . . tall. The pair *gdl* and *rwmm* recur only in Isa 1:2; 23:4, in the borrowed sense of rearing and raising children; here the reference is to Tehom's nurture of the great cedar.

her rivers. On (Tehom's) subterranean rivers (or "currents" [Dahood, *Psalms,* AB, p. 151]), see Ps 24:2. Tehom showed partiality toward the cedar — "her planting" (G S "his" obscures the point) — by directing her main currents to irrigate it, while feeding the rest of the trees by her canals, i.e., smaller watercourses (Ehrlich). The contrast between rivers and canals is emphasized by the initial position of each in its clause. Kimḥi, paraphrasing MT *hlk* in the first verset by *holika* "she made flow" (cf. 32:14), identified it as hifʿil, thus agreeing with G "(she) led." Critics emend MT to Kimhi's reading; but MT may be read as an infinitive absolute, which regularly continues discourse after a finite verb (GKC, § 113 y). Its post-initial position (like that of *šlḥh* in the next verset), anomalous with an infinitive, may be due to the desire to give prominence to the object "her rivers," contrasting with "her canals" in the sequel.

but her canals she sent forth. Hebrew *tʿlh* is a ditch (I Kings 18:32) or a conduit (II Kings 18:17) for water. Here the context indicates an irrigation ditch, in contrast to a river. The verb *šillaḥ* (piʿel) serves for releasing water, or making it gush forth (Ps 104:10; Job 12:15); on the absence of dagesh in *l* of *šlḥh*, see GKC, § 20 m.

all the [*other*] *trees of the field.* "Field" = open country. "Other" is implied by the exclusion from the totality of trees of the cedar, which is watered by the rivers. Cf. Gen 3:2: "We may eat of the fruit of all the [other] trees of the garden"—"other" implied by the exclusion of the "tree in the middle of the garden" in the sequel (Ehrlich). The reference is to king(dom)s lesser than Assyria (cf. vs. 5a); in vs. 6b this is made explicit in a mixed image: "in his (the cedar's = Assyria's) shade all the many nations dwelt."

5. *Therefore.* Anticipates "because" (*m*[*mym*]) at the verse-end, hence is, strictly speaking, redundant; similarly Est 9:26a: "Therefore . . . by reason of." Cf. Mishnaic Hebrew *lpykk . . . l-/š-* "Therefore . . . in order to / because" (*m. Sanhedrin* 4.5; *b. Qiddushin* 30a). This is a feature of later Hebrew.

was loftier. The irregularly spelled *gbh*ʾ shows the Aramaic preference for ʾ as the feminine marker; the normal Hebrew spelling *gbhh* appears in many medieval mss.

limbs. Heb. **sarʿappa* is derived from **sᵉʿappa* (vs. 6) by insertion of *r* between the first two radicals; cf. *šarbiṭ* "scepter" (Est 4:11) from *šebeṭ* "staff"; this is another late Biblical Hebrew (Aramaic-like) feature. See GKC, § 85 w.

abundant water. Lit. "many waters," on which see comment at 1:24 (I, 48). The phrase simultaneously evokes commonplace water and the primeval great deep (Tehom).

in his channel. Taking *šlḥw* as from *šelaḥ* "water conduit" (Neh 3:15), cf. Mishnaic *bet šᵉlaḥin* "irrigated field" (lit. "place of irrigation ditches"). The dagesh in the *l* will then be *dirimens* ("separating [the syllables]") like that of *ḥallᵉqe* Isa 57:6 (GKC, § 20 h; so approximately Ehrlich). The word is semantically related to *šillaḥ* "release (water)" in vs. 4. The figure has changed: now the great cedar is fed by an irrigation channel full of water—all for itself.

6. The items of this verse (excepting the cedar) are all real, not symbolic; on the reality of the birds, beasts, and nations, see comment to 17:3 (I, 316f.).

With the hyperbolic totality of birds that nested in the great tree, compare *j. Taʿanit* 69a (cited by J. Feliks, *Plant World of the Bible* [in Hebrew] [Tel Aviv: Massada, 1957], p. 78), which tells of a fabulous cedar on the Mount of Olives, from which were extracted, monthly, forty *seahs* (over five hundred liters) of sacrificial birds. The low-lying branches of Ezekiel's cedar also offered shade and shelter for animals giving birth.

In Near Eastern literature shade commonly expresses the protection afforded by the king to his subjects—here the vassals of Assyria (see further on vs. 17 below). On the widespread figure of the king's shadow, see D. Hillers, *Lamentations*, AB, p. 92, to Lam 4:20.

all the many nations. An awkward phrase, due to *kol* "all," which has been repeated here under the influence of the previous two versets; for the normal phrase ("many nations"), see, e.g., 38:23. S does not translate *kol,* probably a simplification. The translation "all great nations" (e.g., NJPS) saves the text by invoking an uncommon sense of *rb* (mostly in poetry and titles—e.g., *mlk rb* "great king," Ps 48:3), out of place in such a banal expression.

dwelt. Vocalization as an imperfect, alternating with prior perfects, is not abnormal in poetry (so again in vs. 13); A. Berlin calls it grammatical parallelism (*The Dynamics of Biblical Parallelism* [Bloomington: Indiana University Press], 1985, p. 36). For many examples in Psalms, see Dahood, *Psalms III*, AB, 420ff. (discounting emendations).

8. *overshadow.* As in 28:3; see comment thereto. Here, too, interpreters divide between "be the like of" (G, NJPS; see Boadt, who connects with *ʿm* = *k* "like" [cf. *hyw k-* in the third verset of our verse] as in Job 9:26) and "darken, eclipse" (BDB, etc.).

"No cedar was more splendid than it, even among those in the garden of God, where they are more excellent and beautiful and tall than any of the cedars of Lebanon" (Eliezer of Beaugency). It is not implied that the great cedar was among those of the garden, only that the cedars of the garden were fabled for their size and beauty. The juniper is a lofty tree whose height may reach twenty meters; the plane tree, too, stands out for its height, its broad and dense boughs, and its beautiful foliage (Feliks, *Plant Life* [citation in comment to vs. 6], pp. 80, 120). For the characterization of the trees, cf. Gen 2:9: God caused to grow in Eden every tree delightful to behold.

9. *I made him beautiful.* The splendor of the tree is God's doing, "not as [Assyria] was in the habit of asserting, 'By the strength of my hand I did it'" (Isa 10:13; Kimḥi). But the attribution to God is not emphasized here; the clause is not in G.

envied him. The direct object construction with *qinne* is unusual in this sense; elsewhere only in Gen 26:14; Isa 11:13.

10–12. Person and tense vacillate disconcertingly in these verses. In vs. 10 the prophet tells Pharaoh what God declared (years ago!) to the king of Assyria—"Because you (Assyria) grew lofty"—but he continues in third person ("he set his crown") (Rashi, Kimḥi, MenbSh; cf. J. Levi, *Inkongruenz*, pp. 149f., citing among others Isa 14:30; Ps 81:17). Vs. 11 begins with *waw* of apodosis with the imperfect, as in Hos 4:6: "because you have rejected knowledge, *wᵉʾemʾasᵉka* I will reject you" (‖ *ʾeškaḥ* "I will forget" in the next line); see S. R. Driver, *Tenses*, § 125. "I will deliver . . . he shall deal" are construable as continuing in third person God's dooming of Assyria (so MenbSh²). The end of vs. 11 ("I banished him"), and the sequel, then narrate the fulfillment of the doom.

G takes the whole of vs. 11 as the narrative, reading *w'tnhw* as preterite (so, too, e.g., Kimḥi) "I delivered him." While G largely reproduces MT's inconsistency, S renders a consistent viewpoint: "Because his stature was lofty . . . I will deliver him . . . and he shall do"; S even includes vss. 12–13 in the doom proclamation. But S leaves it unclear whether Assyria or Egypt is the referent of these verses.

10. *and he set his crown.* A subtle shift from vs. 3, where the height of the cedar is a neutral given, not an act of self-exaltation.

grew haughty. Hebrew *rm* only here in Ezekiel—otherwise *gbh* (28:2, 5, 17)—but found in Deut 17:20 and Jer 48:29, and in theological context in Deut 8:12–14 and Hos 13:6 of the pride of the affluent, who forget God.

11. *leader.* Lit. "ram"; as in *'yly h'rṣ* "leading men of the land" 17:13; see comment thereto, I, 314. The leader is the Babylonian destroyer of Assyria, Nabopolassar, though it is likely that the prophet confused him with his son Nebuchadnezzar, especially since the finality of Assyria's defeat was established only when its Egyptian ally was expelled from western Asia by the then crown prince Nebuchadnezzar in 605 (battle of Carchemish).

shall deal with him. MenbSh (like G) takes the sense to be past, comparing *y'św* "they made" (Ps 106:19).

According to his wickedness. Mss. vacillate between *b/k(rš'w)* "for, because of" / "according to (his wickedness)," the best ones reading the latter (*Minḥat Shay*). The translation follows the accents, which disjoin *krš'w* from the preceding *lw* "with him"; but (as Kimḥi observed) the word can be connected with both what precedes it and what follows.

I banished him. From his privileged plot (cf. MenbSh). The expression is odd, evoking the expulsion from Eden and the banishment of Cain (Gen 3:24; 4:14); Ehrlich [Hebrew] suggests the sense: I ended my gracious care of him (= Malbim). The referent—the king of Assyria—momentarily replaces the cedar figure. The word is not in G; it has been judged a dittograph of the preceding *krš'w* (*BHS*).

12. *strangers, most terrible of nations.* As in 28:7; 30:11–12, a code word for Babylonians.

cast him away. The verb *nṭš* appears in this verse with two meanings, nicely discriminated in S, which renders the first by *rm'* "cast (down, away, out)" (so, too, at 29:5) and the second by *šbq* "leave, forsake." The full sense of the verb is a combination of the two: "left him prostrate" (MenbSh).

On the mountains and in all valleys. So MT according to the accents; but G, lacking "and," starts a new clause with "in," thus: "and cast him down on the mountains. In all the valleys, etc." The structure of 29:5a$^{\alpha}$ supports G insofar as *nṭš* has an adverbial complement; but MT at the verse-end shows that *nṭš* can do without it.

branches . . . boughs. In the nonfigurative depiction of Mount Seir's doomsday in 35:8 what fills mountains and valleys are corpses; whence we infer that the severed limbs of the fallen tree strewn across the landscape represent the Assyrian dead (MenbSh).

All the peoples . . . left (yrdw) *his shadow.* Undoing vs. 6b. For this sense of *yrd,* cf. I Sam 15:6 ". . . depart (*rdw;* T *'tprš* "separate yourself") from among the Amalekites." Note, too, I Sam 29:4, 9, where *yrd* and its antonym *'lh* both serve for "march out" into battle. How these idiomatic usages relate to the basic sense "descend" is not clear. In the present case the idea might be that the protection of the shadow put the clients above the reach of enemies; departing from the shadow is in this respect a descent.

13. *all the birds . . . wild beasts.* Undoing vs. 6a (note the chiastic order of undoing). The birds and animals that enjoyed the shelter afforded in and under the cedar now rudely exploit its scattered parts. In 32:4 they reappear as feeding on the cadaver of the Pharaoh-monster (as in 29:5). The figure of the fallen cedar is not amenable to this role for them.

14. *So that.* The fate of the towering cedar must be a lesson to all favored ("well-watered") trees. The Assyrian king's fate is a warning to all mighty kings not to strive for preeminence and grandeur.

Vs. $14a^{\alpha-\beta}$ ("So that . . . clouds") speaks figuratively of trees; vs. 14b ("for all . . . Pit") speaks nonfiguratively of humans (for trees don't go down to the netherworld; but vs. 16b shows that the human inhabitants of Sheol can still be figured as trees!). Vs. $14a^{\gamma}$ is ambiguous and obscure.

and none of their leaders ('lyhm) *should stand high.* MT's vocalization *'elehem* recalls *'yl* (*'el*) of vs. 11—there a human "leader of nations," here possibly the leader of "well-watered trees." Or does the possessive suffix *-hm* refer to the following "all drinkers of water"—a broader circle than "well-watered trees" for it includes humans. If the latter, then "their leaders" faces both backward to the tree figure and forward to the human referents of the second part of the verse. (Kimḥi interprets *'lyhm* as "their trees," comparing *'el(a)* in Isa 1:29; 6:13; 61:3; but this word never means "tree" in general.)

"Stand high" is the conjectured sense of a unique expression, lit. "stand in their height." With the idea that the very act of standing high trenches on God's domain, cf. the judgment of God bringing low whatever is high, Isa 2:12–14 (cf. Zech 14:10). A talmudic dictum based on Isa 6:3 is apposite: "If one walks even four cubits with erect stature it is as though he pushed aside the divine presence, for it is said, 'His glory fills the earth'" (*b. Berachot* 43b).

The alternative reading *'ᵃlehem* (see text note g–g), from *'el* = *'al,* yields an entirely different sense: *'md 'l* (Judg 6:31) = *qwm 'l* (Gen 4:8) "rise against, attack." Taking account of the distinction between "well-watered trees" and "drinkers of water" (humans), we may render: "and that none of the drinkers of water should attack them on account of their height." Towering prideful trees call down on themselves an attack by human drinkers of water.

Awareness of the common fate of all mortals, sovereigns included, to go down to the grave punctures delusions of grandeur.

15. *I caused to mourn* (h'blty). The same verb in Lam 2:8: "He caused rampart and wall to mourn (*wy'bl*). *NEB:* "I closed (the deep over him) as a gate" reflects a highly speculative derivation from Akkadian *abullu* "gate" (H. Zimmern, *Akkadische Fremdwörter* [Leipzig: Hinrichs, 1917], p. 14 ["perhaps"]), whose chief

virtue for soberer translations that adopt it (e.g, NJPS, *NRSV*) would seem to be that it offers a kind of synonym to the following "I covered" (which *NEB* omits, following G).

I covered Tehom on his account. The asyndetic pair of verbs (*h'blty ksty*) is problematic. The Masoretic accents separate them, perhaps intending the first to be taken as a generality—"I caused many to mourn over him" (Rashi, Kara)—followed by particulars. This is artificial but probably the best that can be done with MT. Boadt (crediting Dahood) takes the two verbs as a hendiadys: "I covered with mourning garments the Tehom"—a resourceful try for which no support can be mustered. G lacks "I covered," yielding a smooth Hebrew reading "I made Tehom mourn" (G: "the abyss mourned him"). But the presence of "I covered" (awkward though it be) is supported by 32:7f., in which there is a two-fold occurrence of the sequence "cover–make gloomy" that appears in the MT of our verse. The two verbs appear to be alternative beginnings of their clause:

h'blty		I caused Tehom to mourn over him
	'lyw 't thwm	
ksty		I covered Tehom on his account

"On his account (*'lyw*)," i.e., "over/for him," like the repetitions of the word in the second part of the verse; cf. the same usage in 31:8, 10. Moderns incline to take 26:19 (Tehom will cover Tyre) as the clue to interpreting our clause, thus: "I (closed the deep over it and) covered it" (NJPS, *NRSV*) = "I covered him over (*'lyw*) with [= drowned/buried him under] Tehom." But if this were the meaning here, the following clauses about the cessation of Tehom's nurture would not have much point.

The difference between the two verbs *h'blty* and *ksty* affects the understanding of the rest of the verse. The first verb stamps all that follows with the mark of mourning: Tehom benumbed by the death of her protégé ceases her watering functions. The other trees are gloomy and languish on his account, because their paragon and patron has gone. The frame of reference is clearly the story of the fallen majestic cedar.

The second verb brings to mind God's extinguishing of the heavenly lights associated with judgment day (32:7f.), which is its frame of reference. Tehom is incapacitated, the trees are devitalized; the two are linked in a causal chain. The beginning of the chain is: "I covered . . . Tehom," where "cover" means "put a cover on," as in Exod 21:33: "If a man digs a pit or opens a pit and does not cover it . . ." What follows in our verse has the appearance of the physical consequence of that covering (e.g., drought). Such a reading dominates medieval exegesis.

As the medievals saw clearly, vs. 15 answers in detail to vss. 2–5, undoing what was done there. The following is an amalgam of comments exhibiting their close reading (italics are lemmas from vs. 15, quotation marks enclose echoes of vss. 2–5).

> *I covered Tehom,* who constantly watered him and made him grow—as was said above: "Tehom made him tall"—so that she should not well up and water him.

I restrained her rivers, that "flowed around her planting."
The abundant water was held in check, which "made his limbs long."
The rest of the trees of *Lebanon* blackened and shriveled because of the drought,
and all the trees of the field to whom "her canals were sent forth"
languished from thirst; cf. ". . . maidens and young men shall languish from thirst" (Amos 8:13). (Extracted from Rashi, Kara, Eliezer)

These medievals miss the subtle difference in meaning of the terms common to our verse and 32:7f. In 32:7f. the covering (of the sky by smoke) and the gloom (caused by extinguishing the luminaries) are physical phenomena, and are directly caused by God. But here the governing idea is expressed by the initial "I caused to mourn": Tehom's inactivity, expressive of her deep mourning, and the despondency of the cedar's tree clients are both psychic effects of the death of the cedar and are only indirectly caused by God. Judgment-day terminology ("I will cover, I will make gloomy") here is once removed from its primary meaning. The direct attribution to God "serves to make known," explains Kimḥi, "that the calamity was brought about by God."

I made . . . gloomy. As *qdr* in qal serves for "be/grow dark" (Mic 3:6, || "sun set") and metaphoric "be gloomy, dejected" (Jer 8:21, || "seized with desolation"), so in hif'il *hqdyr* serves for "darken" (transitive; Ezek 32:8, || "bring darkness [*ḥšk*]) and metaphoric "make gloomy"—which is the sense here, as required by the context, the object of the verb being the personified forest of Lebanon.

languished (ʿulpe). The versions translate as a third person plural verb (as I do perforce!), but the form is nominal, like *topte* (Isa 30:33) an extremely rare form of the *qotel* pattern with final *-e(h),* from the root *ʿlp* "be enwrapped, be faint." It is the predicate of a nominal sentence: lit. "all the trees of the field (were) languishment," where the predicate noun functions as a qualifier; e.g., "his hands (were) firmness (= firm)" Exod 17:12; "you were nakedness and nudity (= stark naked)" Ezek 16:22.

16. *At the sound . . . I made nations quake.* This interprets the fainting of "all the trees of the field" of the preceding verse as a figure for the universal consternation caused by Assyria's fall. The language echoes 26:15, save that what is there depicted as a terrestrial act (*yrʿšw hʾyym*) is in our passage ascribed to God's doing (*hrʿšty gwym*); cf. 32:9a, 10a.

The second part of the verse takes place in Sheol, where the other choice trees of Eden and Lebanon (the two are now combined) who are in Sheol are comforted—after the Eden trees' previous envy (vs. 9)—by the sight of cedar-Assyria's fall.

the choicest and best of Lebanon. "Other great powers who have already waned" (Allen). Two governing nouns (*mbḥr, ṭwb*) are in construct with the same governed one (*lbnwn*); see König III, § 275 b, who compares Isa 11:2b *dʿt wyrʾt yhwh* "knowledge and fear of YHWH" (so, too, Kimḥi, ad loc.); Dan 1:4 *spr wlšwn kśdym* "the writings and the language of the Chaldeans." G read only one noun; perhaps MT is conflate.

"All drinkers of water" now expressly fuses the figure and its reference (trees = humans), both sharing a common neediness and mortality.

17. *They too like him* (*'itto*) *went down to Sheol.* An explanation for the presence in Sheol of "the choicest and best of Lebanon." For the comparative sense of *'itt-*, cf. Lev 10:9: intoxicants are banned to all priests, "you (Aaron) and your sons alike" (*wbnyk 'tk;* lit. "and your sons with you"). Cf. the use of *'im* (a synonym of *'itt-*) as "like" in Eccl 2:16 "the wise man and the fool alike" (lit. "with the fool"); Jer 6:11 "Men and women alike (lit. 'with women') shall be captured."

to those slain by the sword. The soldierly dead, fitting company for royalty cut down in battle—an anticipation of the vivid imagery of the oracle in 32:17ff.

and his arm [*who*] *dwelt in his shadow.* Apparently an allusion to the vassal king(dom)s whose forces were incorporated into the Assyrian army; cf., e.g., the list of twenty-two kings who accompanied Assurbanipal with their troops (*ANET*[3], p. 294). "Arm" as a figure for military force resumes 30:21ff. The connection of this clause is unclear. Those who "dwelt in his shadow" alludes to the clients of vs. 6b; here they are called Assyria's "arm." The whole clause appears to add this "arm" to those in Sheol. But those dwelling in the shadow have already been disposed of in vs. 12b ("they left his shadow"). To this difficulty must be added the evidence of G for a very different reading (see text note). Altogether this clause looks like a stray or mutilated passage whose placement here is secondary.

18. The verse expands the rhetorical question with which the oracle opened (vs. 2b). The sense is: to no tree in Eden are you, Pharaoh, so comparable, with respect to glory and greatness, as to the cedar Assyria. Yet you saw that he was brought down to Sheol. So also you shall share the fate of all trees of Eden—to be thrust into Sheol.

amidst the uncircumcised you shall lie. Another foreshadowing of the netherworld panorama of 32:17ff.

That is Pharaoh . . . Identifying the person addressed in this verse, who has not been referred to since vs. 2a. This is an indication that the main body of the oracle has been dealing with another than Pharaoh—viz., the king of Assyria.

STRUCTURE AND THEMES

This fourth oracle against Egypt, dated (vs. 1) two months later than the previous one (30:20), reiterates, by way of a comparison, the ineluctable doom of Pharaoh and his army. The long comparison, which comprises the body of the oracle (vss. 3–17), is encased in an introduction and a closure that form an *a b / b' a'* pattern:

vs. 2a: "Pharaoh . . . and his horde"
 2b: "To whom are you comparable"
vs. 18a: "To whom are you . . . comparable"
 18b: "Pharaoh and all his horde"

The body of the oracle has three main parts:
A (vss. 3–9): an extended metaphor of the king of Assyria as a splendid cedar

of Lebanon to whom all creatures are drawn (vss. 3–7), envied by all the trees of the Garden of Eden (vss. 8–9).

B (vss. 10–14): the disastrous consequence (*laken*) of the cedar's pride: cut down by cruel strangers, its broken members scattered over hill and vale, it is abandoned by all its former adherents. The fate of the cedar warns all trees to shun prideful towering, since all are destined to die.

C (vss. 15–17): an after-scene in Sheol: the felled cedar joins in death other mortals (arboreal and human), who are comforted by its fate.

The theme of the oracle is the downfall of the proud. Human grandeur is in itself an offense to God, before whom only a lowly spirit is appropriate (see further, I, 358). Pride is symbolized by a great cedar (for the cedar as a royal image, see comment to Lebanon at 17:3 [I, 310]). Ezekiel's cedar has attributes praised in the inscription of his contemporary Nebuchadnezzar II: "mighty cedar, high and strong, of precious beauty and of excellent dark quality, the abundant yield of the Lebanon" (*ANET*[3], p. 307). Centuries earlier a Hittite ritual for a new palace described, in lines that might have inspired Ezekiel, the king's prayer for "the timber which the rains have made strong and tall" (in what follows, italics mark doubtful renderings):

> Under the heavens ye [trees] grew. The lion would rest beneath you, the panther would rest beneath you, the *snake* would *coil up* in you . . . Cattle pastured beneath you, sheep pastured beneath you. (*ANET*[3], p. 357)

In typical fashion, the prophet combines disparate features to complexify his figure. As foils for his towering cedar he presents first the common "trees of the field"—in 17:24 also representing lesser king(dom)s. Then in a second, climactic round of imagery it is the trees in God's garden of Eden whose envy of the cedar underlines its glory. Here the prophet elaborates on the Eden scene of Gen 2:8–9, specifying three species of trees (not mentioned in Genesis) that could not rival the cedar. In the Sheol finale, Lebanon, trees of the field, and Eden's trees all join in taking comfort in the cedar's downfall.

The hurtling down of the haughty from their heights to the ground has already appeared in 19:12 (the Judahite vine-bough) and 28:17 (the king of Tyre).

Though in a sense the message of the oracle is complete at the end of B (vs. 14), where its lesson is drawn, the prophet is not content to leave the cedar broken on the ground. As in his first Tyre prophecy (26:19ff.), he follows the condemned down into Sheol. This Sheol scene, however, has distinctive features that relate it to Isaiah 14:9–10—especially the comfort that the underworld peers of the new arrival take in his downfall (in Isaiah, the downfall of "the king of Babylon"):

> Sheol below was agitated to greet your coming;
> The ghosts of all the chiefs of the land were roused for you.
> All the kings of nations were upraised from their thrones;
> All of them speak up and say to you:
> You too have been stricken as we were;
> You have become like us.

This is not the only contact of our oracle with Isaiah. Isaiah speaks repeatedly of hewing down cedars: in 2:13 God's ultimate exaltation will bring low "all the cedars of Lebanon, the high and uplifted"; in 14:8 junipers and cedars of Lebanon will rejoice at the downfall of the Mesopotamian king, for that will end their fear of his axe—an image related to 37:24, Sennacherib's boast that he has climbed Lebanon and cut down its lofty cedars, its choice junipers.

The most striking parallel, however, is Isa 10:33–34:

> See, the Lord, YHWH of hosts will prune the boughs with an axe;
> The lofty of stature will be hewn down,
> The high ones brought low,
> The thickets of the forest shall be hacked away with iron,
> And Lebanon['s trees] shall fall by the Majestic one.

It appears likely that the Isaiah passage inspired the imagery of our oracle. Though there is uncertainty about the referent of the felled "Lebanon" in Isa 10:33–34 (see the sensitive treatment by K. Nielsen, *There Is Hope for a Tree*, JSOTSup 65 [1989]), to judge from our oracle Ezekiel saw in it an allusion to the fall of Assyria. The presence of so many motifs belonging to Isaiah's Assyrian imagery, fused in Ezekiel's fashion into a new alloy, supports the view that the great cedar represents Assyria.

However, many critics (Smend, p. 246; see the brief survey in Allen, p. 122 n. 3.a) take the direct address in vs. 10 to indicate that a present addressee is represented by the cedar—viz., Pharaoh—and that the verbs in the future in vs. 11 point to a future punishment, not a past one (the fall of Assyria). Vs. 18 is taken as identifying the cedar with Pharaoh. The cedar is a mythological, cosmic tree. The predominantly past tenses of the narrative of the cedar's fall are explained as the style of a parable (e.g., Jotham's, Judg 9:8–15) or a prophetic lament. This view of the whole as comparing Pharaoh to a (mythological cosmic) tree entails emending *ʾaššur* in vs. 3 to *tᵉʾaššur* and regarding the consequent awkwardness of a double name for the tree ("Here is a cypress, a cedar in Lebanon") as the result of a clumsy gloss (see Zimmerli for this and other speculative emendations). The grounds for taking the text as it stands are as follows:

1. To emend "Assyria" away in vs. 3 goes against the confirming witness of all versions.

2. The past-tense narrative of our oracle is most naturally accounted for by reference to the past fall of Assyria, rather than to a future fall of Egypt. To be sure, parables are couched in the past tense; but in our oracle the time frame of the judgment (parts B and C) is also past (except for vs. 11, on which see comment to vss. 10–12). Punishment of the cedar has been accomplished, and its descent to Sheol has occurred. Contrast this with ch. 26 in which Tyre's expected punishment and descent into Sheol are in the future. The "lament" over Egypt (ch. 32), whose terms resemble those used here to describe the fall of the cedar, is also couched in future verbs. The past time-frame of the true prophetic laments of ch. 19 and 28:11ff. over events that in reality had not yet occurred is a

convention: laments are normally over past calamities. But the allegory (or extended metaphor) of the cedar is not a lament, and there is no compelling reason to consider false or artificial its representation of events as past.

3. The pronoun *mi* "(To) whom (are you comparable)" (vss. 2, 18) invites comparison with a human, not a tree.

4. The rhetorical situation is better met by comparison of Egypt to fallen Assyria than to a mythical-metaphoric cedar, as will be seen immediately.

Bar Hebraeus epitomizes this oracle thus: "If the Assyrian, who was so lofty, could not get the better of the Babylonian Nebuchadnezzar, how will you, Pharaoh, get the better of him?" He makes the oracle an argument *a fortiori*, but its tenor recalls rather arguments of straight comparison such as II Kings 19:10–13: the Assyrian Rab-Shakeh compares Jerusalem to a string of city-states that fell to the Assyrians in order to blast its hope of surviving their assault. More apt is the comparison in Nahum 3:8–10, of Nineveh, the Assyrian capital, with the great Egyptian capital of Thebes: "Are you [Nineveh] better than No-Amon [= Thebes], located by the Nile . . . ?" Strong as it was, Thebes was vanquished; an identical fate awaits Nineveh. Such comparison made an otherwise implausible prediction credible. And that is precisely the purpose of this one. Egypt was a giant power (in the estimate of Judahites), the gift of a great river system; it controlled many vassal kings (cf. Jer 46:9, 25). It was natural for Judah to turn to it for help, and for the exiled Judahites to pin on it their hopes of withstanding Babylonian pressure. What could the prophet conjure up to undermine his countrymen's confidence? What better than comparison with the other giant power on the ancient Near Eastern scene, to whose might Egypt herself had been subject, and that now lay in ruins. If Assyria could fall, so could Egypt—and it would.

As in all of Ezekiel's extended metaphors, strains, inconsistencies, and intrusion of referents creep in. The heroic cedar is contrasted first with all the other trees of the field (vss. 4–5), then climactically with the trees of God's garden of Eden (vss. 8–9). Felled, the cedar's limbs are strewn over the land like cadavers and the creatures that once enjoyed its protection now haunt the ruins—waiting, it would seem, for their transformation into preying creatures on a corpse (their role in 29:5 and 32:4b ff.). Unmetaphorically, "all nations, all peoples of the earth" dwell in the protection of the cedar; when the ruthless destroyer hews it down, they abandon it. The stern lesson of the allegory is couched in terms moving in stages from "trees of water" to "drinkers of water"—inclusive of plants and humans—to "human beings," in a single verse (14).

The final scene in Sheol combines all the aforementioned *personae*: vs. 15 recaps Tehom, rivers, abundant waters, Lebanon, and trees of the field from the first stage of the story. Vs. 16 mentions "nations," and Eden-trees who are now categorized by the inclusive expression "drinkers of water" to enable them to live in Sheol (whose population is human!). Confusion peaks in vss. 10–11; to argue from them that the cedar represents Egypt is to build on sand.

Extended metaphors have to some extent narrative exigencies that generate elements for which no correspondent exists in the referent; the figure has a life of its own. That such elements appear in the present case is demonstrated by the signal failure of Targum consistently to decode its details. Here is a sampling, with the Hebrew correspondent italicized and in parentheses:

> [3]Here [was] the Assyrian [king], like a cedar in Lebanon whose crown was beautiful, etc. . . . [4]Through [conquered] nations (*water*) he grew great, through auxiliary troops (*Tehom*) he grew mighty (*tall*). Kings (*rivers*) he subjugated (*made flow*) under his kingship (*planting*), and his governors (*canals*) he appointed over all the provinces of the earth (*trees of the field*). [5]Therefore he was loftier than all kings of the nations (*trees of the field*) and his armies (*limbs*) grew great (*numerous*), and his auxiliaries (*branches*) were superior (*were long*) to many nations (*abundant water*) through his superiority (*channels*). [6]By his armies (*limbs*) he conquered all mighty cities (*birds of the sky*) and under his governors (*boughs*) he subjugated all provinces of the earth (*wild beasts*), and in the shadow of his kingdom dwelt all the many nations. [7]He was superior (*was beautiful*) through his auxiliaries (*greatness*) through the abundance of his brave men *(the length of his branches)*, for dread of him (*his roots*) was over many nations (*abundant water*). (Cf. S. H. Levey, *The Targum of Ezekiel*, The Aramaic Bible, XIII [Wilmington: M. Glazier, 1987], pp. 89f.)

As with other figures of Ezekiel, scholars have speculated as to whether some lost myth underlies the story of the cedar. A detailed study by Fritz Stolz ("Die Bäume des Gottesgartens auf dem Libanon," ZAW 84 [1972], 141–56) tries to distill a core myth from all the references in Scripture to cedars, Lebanon, and God's garden. There is not much of a story: Someone sought to conquer the seat of a Lebanon god—Lebanon being the god's garden—in order to share the divine nature. The venture failed and the sinner was condemned to Sheol. Ezekiel was the first to conjoin the Eden myth to this other one and to compose a story out of the negative elements of both. The cedar and garden trees became symbols of anti-godly arrogance, and they suffer the fate of the sinful someone in the original Lebanon myth. Such speculation answers to a powerful critical impulse to suppose that there is always something behind a text, that every text must be derivative (a reflection of the critics' contingent creativity?). It does not add anything to the understanding of our figure and is not more convincing than the supposition (not current among scholars, but why not?) that the presumptuous, towering vine of ch. 19 is a reflex of another myth, similar to Stolz's.

XXXVI. A Dirge Over Pharaoh (32:1–16)

32 [1]It was in the twelfth[a] year, in the twelfth month, on the first of the month
that the word of YHWH came to me: [2]Man, recite a dirge over Pharaoh king of
Egypt and say to him:

You seemed to be a lion of the nations,
While you were [really] like the monster in the seas:
you lunged in your rivers;
you muddied the waters with your feet,
and made their rivers turbid.
[3]Thus said Lord YHWH:
I will spread over you [b]my net, with an assemblage of many armies,
and they[b] shall haul you up in my meshes.
[4]I will cast you away on land,
leave you fallen on the ground.
I will cause all the birds of the sky to settle on you,
and the beasts of all the earth to feed on you to their fill.
[5]I will set your flesh on the mountains,
and fill the valleys with your bulk.
[6] [c]I will irrigate your flood-land with your blood[c] up to the mountains,
and gullies will run full of you.
[7]I will cover heaven when you are snuffed out,
and make its stars gloomy.
The sun—I will cover it with cloud;
the moon shall not give out its light.
[8]All light-giving bodies in the sky
I will make gloomy over you.
I will set darkness over your land,
declares Lord YHWH.

[a]G S "eleventh."
[b–b]G "nets of many peoples and I," as from *ršty ʿmym rbym whʿlytyk*.
[c–c]G "the land shall be drenched with your fluxes from your multitude" (as from *mhm[w]nk/mrbk?*—corrupted from *mdmk*).

[9]I will vex the hearts of many peoples when I bring [d][word of] your calamity[d] among the nations, to lands you never knew. [10]I will cause many peoples to be appalled over you. Their kings shall be agitated over you when I brandish my sword in their faces. They shall tremble every moment, each for his life, on the day of your downfall.

[11]For thus said Lord YHWH: The king of Babylon's sword shall overtake you.

[12]I will fell your horde by the swords of warriors,
the most terrible of nations all of them.
They shall devastate the pride of Egypt,
and all her horde will be destroyed.
[13]I will cause all her beasts to vanish from beside abundant waters;
Muddy them no more shall the foot of man,
nor shall hooves of beast muddy them.
[14]Then will I make their waters limpid,
and their rivers run like oil,
declares Lord YHWH,
[15]When I turn the land of Egypt into a desolation,
and the land is emptied of all that fills her;
When I smite[e] all her inhabitants,
and they know that I am YHWH.
[16]This is a dirge, and they shall keen it—
women of the nations shall keen it—
over Egypt and all her horde shall they keen it,
declares Lord YHWH.

COMMENT

32:1. The date in MT is 3 March 585 (Parker-Dubberstein), which is later than the date in 33:21 and for that very reason is preferable to G's harmonizing reading; see Table of Dates, I, 10–11 n. 12. It is three months after the report of Jerusalem's fall reached the prophet.

2. *You seemed to be a lion of the nations.* Taking the verb as passive of pi'el *dimma* "imagine" (Num 33:56), "compare" (Song 1:9), close in meaning to and echoing the qal form used in Ezek 31:2: "To whom are you comparable." It might also be taken in a reflexive sense: "You imagined yourself." For such a relation of nif'al to qal and pi'el, see B-L, pp. 289–90 (note especially the semantics of the triad *ḥala* "be ill," *ḥilla* "inflict illness," *neḥ*[e]*la* "be ill"; Bergsträsser II/1, 90–91). For the absence of a preposition ([']*l-/k-*) before *kpyr,* see the analogous construction in Prov 17:28 (*ḥkm yḥšb* "is thought to be wise"). While *ndmh* in this sense does not appear elsewhere in Biblical Hebrew, it is commonplace in Talmudic (e.g., "To the righteous the evil impulse seems [*nidme*] like a mountain" [*b. Sukkah* 52a]). Most moderns, however, prefer to derive the verb from *dmh* "be cut off, annihilated"—the attested nif'al sense in Biblical Hebrew (e.g., Isa 6:5)—

[d–d]G "your captives," as from *šbyk.*
[e]G "scatter," as from *bhpyṣy* (so G at 30:23a, 26a).

and translate, e.g., "Young lion of the nations, you are undone" (*NEB*). But this obscures the explicit contrast with the next figure and makes the change of figure inane.

The lion served as a symbol of despotic kingship in the parable of ch. 19; here, in the unique epithet "lion of the nations" (cf. *'el goyim*, lit. "ram [= leader] of the nations" [31:11]—the Babylonian king), it alludes to the reputation of a great power that Egypt had unjustifiably enjoyed among the statelets of Syria-Palestine. For the lion "goes forth from his lair" (Jer 25:38) nightly, spreading terror with his roaring as he roams the wild in search of prey (Ps 103:20–22). How differently Pharaoh behaved, the verse proceeds to say.

while you were [really] like the monster in the seas. For the adversative force of *w'th* in nonverbal clauses, cf. 28:9: "Will you say I am a god . . . *when you [prove to] be* a mortal . . ."; I Sam 28:12: "Why did you lie to me, *when you are [really]* Saul!" On the form *tnym* (for *tnyn*), see comment at 29:3.

The monster is located not in the Nile (as is that of 29:3) but in "seas" and (at the end of the third verset) "rivers." These cosmogonic terms (Ps 24:2) evoke the primeval water monsters whose uprising God crushed (e.g., Isa 51:9–10; Ps 74:13) but whose menace will not be finally removed until the eschaton (Isa 27:1). However, the reference is clearly to the same Nile-creature as in 29:3—probably the crocodile (see comment there), and in view of the minor local disturbance ascribed to it in the sequel, the evocation appears ironical. Cf. *Meṣ. David*: "You are like the sea-monster whose might is confined to the water but if ever he comes onto land he dies; so your power is limited to your country."

you lunged in your rivers. When this verb—qal or hif'il of **gwḥ* "gush/rush forth"—occurs elsewhere with a preposition, it is with *m-* "from" (ambush, Judg 20:33; womb, Job 38:8); here alone it occurs with *b-* "in," pointedly indicating motion that, vigorous as it may be, is confined to bounds. As such it neither menaces nor benefits land-livers (e.g., mankind). "Your rivers" recalls Pharaoh's boast "Mine is my Nile" (29:3), the plural referring to the Nile's branches (29:4).

you muddied the waters. Rendering them obnoxious to man and beast for drinking (cf. 34:18). The actions of the Pharaoh-monster effected no more than could any human or animal, as vs. 13 below indicates.

and made their rivers turbid. The root **rps/ś* (34:18) appears to be a variant of **rms* "tread, trample" (ibid.) with the specific sense of fouling water by trampling it. The antecedent of "their" is "waters" of the previous verset. G has "your rivers," as two versets before; this makes for easier reading, but it is characteristic of Ezekiel to make a change in repetition.

3. A mixture of figurative language ("my net . . . my meshes") and nonfigurative ("with an assemblage of many armies"—Nebuchadnezzar's multinational army, 23:24). While such mixture is common in Ezekiel (e.g., 31:6), this picture of God as a commander amidst, or accompanied by, the enemy's forces (that is what is conveyed by the *b-* of *bqhl*, as in 17:17; 23:24; cf. *b'm* in Num 20:20) goes further than the divine commissioning of the enemy expressed by *byd* "by the hand (= agency) of," as in 30:10. From G (see text note) one may infer an original reading with God as the sole subject—as in all the following verses: *"I will spread over you my net (*rišti*), / and I will haul you up in my meshes." *'mym*

rbym "many peoples/armies," already present in G's *Vorlage,* entered the text as a gloss to "my net," but the translators misconstrued the *y* of *ršty* as the sign of a plural construct state, whence their "nets of many peoples." In MT we have the gloss expanded by a preposed *bqhl,* after the idiom of 23:24 + 38:6, 22, and construed as the subject of the following verb, which was adjusted to third person plural.

my meshes (ḥrmy). Lit. "my fish net," *ḥerem* being specific (26:5, 14; 47:10; Hab 1:15–18) as against the generic *rešet.* The common hunting figure—on which see comment to 12:13 (I, 214)—is here adapted to a water creature. In 29:4 the monster is more fitly captured by hooks.

4. With the language of vs. 4, cf. 29:5 and comment thereto. For *hṭyl* "leave fallen," see Ps 37:24: "If he falls he will not remain fallen (*ywṭl*)."

5. *your bulk* (ramutka). Meaning uncertain; lit. "your height" (from *rwm* "be high"), apparently, the high mass of your carcass (with the form cf. **lazut* "perversity" from *lwz*). The choice of this unique word may be due to its overtone of haughtiness—as in 31:10 ("your heart grew haughty [*rm*]")—fitly punished by being cast down into valleys (*g'ywt,* assonant with *g'wn* "pride" [see vs. 12 below], as though like shall be cast into like/unlike).

S translates "your worms"—either reading or associating with *rimma* (so, too, Rashi[2] and Moshe ben Sheshet). The pairing of (rotting) flesh (in the previous verset) and worms recurs in Job 7:5 ("my flesh is clothed with worms") and, if this reading is followed, we have here another example of the division of a construct phrase (**b^eśar rimma* "flesh of [= infested with] worms") between parallel versets, as in 25:5 (see comment thereto). The pair appears in the Mishnaic epigram: "The more flesh [on one's body] the more worms [in the grave]" (*m. 'Abot* 2.7).

G's reading of the verset is, "and I will fill from your blood all the land." This indicates a *Vorlage* made up of elements of MT's vss. 5b and 6a, inferior to MT (so *BHS*) and shedding no light on *rmwtk.*

6. *your flood-land* ('rṣ ṣptk). The Masoretic accents join the two words, making them the compound object of the verb "irrigate." The word *ṣapa,* a hapax, may be derived from *ṣwp* "float, flow (over)"—as in "water flowed over (= submerged) my head" (Lam 3:54)—to which "flood (i.e., a flow-over)" is related as *qama* "a stand [of grain]" is to *qwm* "stand up." The reference will be to the vast areas annually inundated by the Nile in flood (cf. T "fat land").

But G separates *'rṣ* from *ṣptk,* making the latter serve as the means to irrigate the former: "And the land will be irrigated by your excreta (lit. "issue," interpreting *ṣptk* by, or reading it as *ṣ'tk* [cf. 4:12] or *ṣp'k* [cf. 4:15]). Symmachus renders *ṣptk* "by your *ichor*"—which may mean "foul discharge" (= G), but also—and more fittingly here—"serum, watery animal fluid" (the primary sense of Greek *ichor* is the fluid that serves the gods for blood). Adopting this syntactical construction and the basic sense "flow" for *ṣapa* as proposed in the previous paragraph, we translate: "I will irrigate the land with your ichor"—the uncommon expression having been chosen to denote the life fluid of the river-monster. The following "with your blood (*mdmk*)" arose as a simplifying alternative reading to the hapax *ṣapa,* and was so early incorporated into the text as to appear in all ancient versions (corruptly in G; see text note c–c).

up to (ʾel) *the mountains.* To the cliffs bounding the Nile valley on each side (after Kimḥi); or, since in Ezekiel's idiom the phrase is equivalent to "on (*ʿal*) the mountains" (vs. 5; see the interchange in 18:11, 15, and the usage of 7:16; 31:12), we may so render here (with, e.g., T): the fluid flowing down out of the flesh on the mountains (vs. 5a) will irrigate the land. That the blood of the slain can be both on the mountains and in the valleys (as in the next verset) is no anomaly, as the Assyrian parallels adduced in Structure and Themes show; but the phrase is awkward, and may have been added in order to pair with "gullies" in the next verset, on the model of vs. 5.

will run full of you. Lit. "will be filled of you." Governed by the irrigating image of the preceding verset, the allusion is to the outpoured life-fluid of the monster that will fill the gullies, not to its carcass, as in vs. 5b.

7. *when you are snuffed out.* The active infinitive here serves a passive function; lit. "in the snuffing out of you." Compare Num 9:15: "And on the day the tabernacle was erected" (lit. "the day of erecting the t."); I Sam 18:19: "At the time Michal was given" (lit. "the time of giving M.").

The poet enriches the traditional image of doomsday as dark (30:18 and Structure and Themes thereto) by metaphorizing the judgment on Pharaoh as the extinguishing of a flame. Medievals developed the figure: "As though in his greatness he were a shining lamp and when he was snuffed out a cloud of smoke rose that covered heaven" (Kimḥi). Giving Pharaoh the attribute of a flame raises a doubt about the luminaries in the sequel: are they real or are they metaphoric fellow kings of Pharaoh? The issue comes to a head in vs. 8a.

8. *over you.* The echoing of 31:15b and the ambiguity of *ʿlyk* in vs. 8a permit two interpretations of vss. 7–8a. On the analogy of 31:15b ("I made Lebanon['s trees = fellow kings] gloomy on his account [*ʿlyw*]") vs. 8a should mean, I will make the aforesaid sun, moon, and stars gloomy on account of you[r extinction] (cf. vss. 9–10, esp. *ʿlyk* in 10); the luminaries are metaphors for other kings. Such an understanding can be sustained through vs. 8a. But vs. 8b's darkness over Pharaoh's land must result from the extinction of real luminaries, not metaphoric kings; the verbal similarity of vs. 8a to 31:15b proves to be misleading. Accordingly, vs. 8a will mean literally, I will darken sun, moon, and stars on/for you (as in Mic 3:6: "the day shall be gloomy for them" [*ʿlyhm*]). On this reading vss. 7–8 are a consistent nonmetaphoric picture of the darkness of doomsday that will envelop Egypt. Our translation "over you" seeks to reflect the ambiguity, which is removed only in vs. 8b.

Both the image and language of vs. 8b recall the darkness with which Egypt was afflicted as the penultimate of the Ten Plagues (Exod 10:21–22).

9. *when I bring* [*word of*] *your calamity.* Hebrew *šeber* may be used in a pregnant sense: "news of calamity," as in Jer 4:20 (see McKane's comment in *Jeremiah,* ICC, p. 105), in Zeph 1:10 "sound of great anguish" (NJPS), and in Jer 50:22 "sound" of the *a* verset lent to the *b* verset "of a great calamity." The expression is equivalent to "the sound of your/his downfall" in 26:15; 31:16, which will

shake the nations. G's "your captives" expands to all Egypt the local doom of 30:17–18 (several Egyptian towns "will go into captivity" [*šby*]), in accord with its reading "when I scatter all its inhabitants" in vs. 15 below. Resuming the prediction of Egypt's exile in 29:12; 30:23, 26, G appears to reflect a significant variant Hebrew *Vorlage*. T "your battle-broken ones" (*tbyry qrbk*) approximates the MT to the sense of G (cf. NJPS's expedient, "your shattered remnants"). For *hby*' ʿ*l* in the sense of causing a sound to reach one, see Job 34:28.

10. The wide reverberations of Egypt's fall recall the similar effect predicted of Tyre's collapse in 26:15–16 and 27:35; see comments there.

when I brandish (bʿwppy) *my sword*. The definition of English "brandish" (wave about by way of threat, etc.) and its etymology—related to "(fire)brand"—neatly parallel the two traditions of the sense of *b*ʿ*wppy* (polel of ʿ*w*/*yp*):

(1) "when I wave, flourish"—lit. "make fly" <*ʿ*wp* "fly"—Rashi, Kimḥi[2], and most moderns; cf. G, intransitive (as in Gen 1:20; Isa 6:2), "when my sword flies";

(2) "when I flash" <*ʿ*yp* "gleam, glance," as in Prov 23:5: "Your eye but glances (*t*ʿ*yp*) at it"; Job 3:9: "glimmerings of (ʿ*p*ʿ*py*) dawn"—S, Ibn Janaḥ, Kimḥi[1]. Favoring (2) is the attribution of lightning flashes to the sword in 21:15, 20, 33; cf. *lahab* "flame" (Judg 13:20) and "sword-blade" (Judg 3:22).

"'My sword' refers to Nebuchadnezzar, previously called [bearer of] God's sword (30:24) . . . 'and they shall tremble . . . each' thinking: he will fall upon me as he fell upon Egypt" (Abarbanel).

12. *the most terrible of nations*. An epithet of the Babylonians in 28:7; 30:11; 31:12.

13. *abundant waters*. Like "seas" and "rivers" of vs. 2, this cosmic term (see comment at vs. 2 and at 1:24 [I, 48]) enhances the Nile, which, without being named, is meant.

hooves (plural) . . . *muddy* (singular). Such grammatical disagreement is not uncommon (e.g., 11:5 "Your thoughts [*-wt;* plural]—I know it" [*-h;* singular]; Joel 1:20); it probably results from viewing the noun as a collective expression (J. Levi, *Die Inkongruenz im biblischen Hebräisch* [Wiesbaden: Harrassowitz, 1987], pp. 185–99). More examples are listed in comment to 26:2.

G renders the verb of the last verset (MT *tdlḥm*) as it renders *wtrps* "made turbid" at the end of vs. 2, indicating its *Vorlage* read *trpsm* here. While MT's use of the same verb in both versets is perfectly regular (e.g., II Sam 22:7; cf. A. Berlin, *The Dynamics of Biblical Parallelism* [Bloomington: Indiana University Press, 1985], pp. 69–70), the variation and resultant wordplay (*prswt* . . . *trpsm*) reflected in G are surely preferable to our taste. That is not to say that G's *Vorlage* is more original; see Berlin.

Vs. 13b in both its chiastic form and its content echoes 29:11a, at the same time elaborating on it and adapting it to its riverine context—Ezekiel's style of varying repetition.

14. *make their waters limpid*. Lit. "make [the mud in] their waters settle"; cf. the noun phrase for limpid water in 34:18: *mšq*ʿ *mym*, lit. "settling of [mud in] water."

run like oil. Which flows with surface undisturbed—a heightening of the previous verset: not only will subsurface water be limpid but also the surface will be perfectly calm.

15. *is emptied of all that fills her.* Taking *(w)nšmh* (nif'al feminine participle from **šmm*) with what follows, as do the versions (G T S; so, too, Kimḥi) and vocalizing it *našamma* (perfect, stress on penult.). For the sense, see comment to 12:19 (I, 224). The Masoretic accents strangely connect the word with what precedes, on the pattern of the pair *šmmh wmšmh* (33:28–29), laming the rest of the clause.

When I smite. On G "scatter," see above, comment to vs. 9.

16. This colophon expands its brief precursor in 19:14b (see comment at I, 354) into a poetic three-line incremental form — another example of varying repetition. On the gap between the title "dirge" and the content — a doom prophecy — see Structure and Themes.

women of the nations. Keening was a woman's work; so Jer 9:16: "Summon the keening women and let them come!" See the mourning women depicted on the sarcophagus of King Ahiram of Byblos (tenth century B.C.E.), *ANEP*², #459.

STRUCTURE AND THEMES

The literary unit is delimited by the dated revelation formula at its beginning (vs. 1) and the oracular colophon ("This is a dirge . . . declares Lord YHWH," vs. 16). The oracle proper (vss. 2–15) has a standard opening, "Man" (vs. 2), and closing recognition formula, "and they shall know that I am YHWH" (vs. 15). It is articulated by the message formulas ("Thus said Lord YHWH") in vss. 3 and 11 into three closely related parts:

A, an aborted pseudo-dirge over Pharaoh (vs. 2). Just as the dooms of Tyre are followed by dirges (26:17f.; 27; 28:11–19), so it seems will be the case with Egypt. But the dirge dictated to the prophet starts with a dubious allusion to Pharaoh's past glory ("you seemed to be a lion"), and goes on to reduce him to a farcical Nile-muddying "monster," thus violating the dirge pattern (cf. I, 357) — which in fact is abandoned in the sequel.

B, a doom prophecy against Pharaoh (vss. 3–11). A message formula opens God's address to the water monster, depicting his capture and gory dissolution (B1, vss. 3–6), and the ensuing eclipse of heavenly lights (B2, vss. 7–8). The formula "declares Lord YHWH" at the end of vs. 8 closes these densely symbolic passages. The terrifying effect of these events on the world's monarchs is then realistically described (B3, vss. 9–10), God's brandished sword remaining as a figurative element.

C, a doom prophecy against Egypt — its populace and fauna (vss. 11–15). In vss. 11b–12 the shift from address to Pharaoh to speech about Egypt is effected. God's sword (end of B) is transmuted realistically into that of the Babylonians, and their devastation of Egypt, its populace and fauna, is portrayed. The opening allusions to muddied waters (A) are resumed in the closing picture of Egypt's rivers, undisturbed by man or beast, running limpid through a desolated land.

The oracle collects themes and motifs of previous pieces, augmenting them or giving them a new, more biting twist.

In the first Egypt oracle the monster's carcass, cast away in the desert, is prey for birds and animals (29:5). Here in addition its parts are dispersed over hill, vale, and gully (32:5–6)—a motif related to the scattered limbs of the felled cedar in the preceding oracle (on whose trunk birds and beasts ominously but as yet innocuously settle; 31:12–13). In this motif, an Ezekielian topographical formula appears to have been influenced by an Assyrian commonplace.

D. H. Müller argued in his *Ezechiel-Studien* (1894), pp. 56–58, that the division of the monster's remains into flesh/body (vs. 5) and blood (vs. 6), and their distribution between highlands and lowlands, reflect Assyrian usage. From the inscriptions of Tiglath-Pileser I he cited:

> "Like a storm demon I piled up the corpses of their warriors on mountain ledges (and) made their blood flow into the hollows and plains of the mountains" (A. K. Grayson, *Assyrian Royal Inscriptions*, II [Wiesbaden: Harrassowitz, 1976], p. 9 [1.iii.23–27]). ". . . corpses . . . on mountain ledges . . . blood . . . into the hollows and plains . . ." (ibid., p. 14 [v.92–96]).

From the inscriptions of Ashurnaṣirpal II:

> "With their blood I dyed the mountain red like red wool, (and) the rest of them the ravines (and) torrents of the mountains swallowed" (ibid., p. 122 [1.i.53]). ". . . dyed the mountain red with their blood, (and) filled the ravines (and) torrents of the mountains with their corpses" (ibid., p. 135 [ii.114–15]).

Müller's observation can be strengthened. The Assyrian formula divides the scene of carnage in two: a single reference to "mountain (ledges)," then a pair referring to lowlands (e.g., "ravines and torrents"); corpses and blood can appear with either. Now, Ezekiel's topographic series normally consists of four terms (two pairs): mountains and hills, gullies and valleys (6:3; 35:8; 36:4, 6). Only in our vss. 5–6 and the related 31:12, where the victim's remains are, in the Assyrian manner, dichotomized, do three terms (again in the Assyrian manner) appear—"mountains" (in vss. 5–6 twice! to compensate for no "hills") + "valleys" and "gullies." And, as in the Assyrian formulas body and blood may be either in highland or in lowland, in vss. 5–6 body and blood are located both high and low. Significantly, the first reflection of this Assyrian formula appears, in a more diluted form, in 31:12, amidst the allegory of Assyria as a cedar.

(In 35:8 Edom's dead are strewn over all four locations—but whole corpses are spoken of there, in what would seem to be an expansion of a native Israelite battlefield image of corpses on highlands; cf. the refrain of David's lament over Saul and Jonathan, "slain on your heights" [II Sam 1:19, 25].)

The Assyria allegory mentions gloom over the tree's fall (31:15b); here gloom grows into actual extinguishing of heavenly lights (more drastic than the local blackouts of 30:18)—a reminiscence of the Plague of darkness (Exod 10:21ff.). The shock experienced by rulers around the world at hearing of the downfall of the great is a regular motif of Ezekiel's oracles against foreign nations: 26:15–18; 27:35; here it is expressly described as apprehension lest God's sword (= Nebuchadnezzar) should strike them. The annihilation of both man and beast in Egypt has already been predicted (29:8); here it is connected with the peace of the Nile, disturbed, as it were, by those who lived off of and in it. This leads us to the most mordant reuse of an established motif: Pharaoh as a water monster (*tnym*).

We noted above (Structure and Themes to § XXXI) that the Egyptian kings compare themselves to the crocodile (Hebrew *tnyn*), "the lord of fear in the water, who cannot be approached" (Thutmose III, *ANET*[3], p. 374b). Another favorite comparison was with the lion, especially as victor over foreign enemies: "His majesty prevailed over them like a fierce lion" (Seti I, *ANET*[3], p. 254b); in battle "his majesty is like an enraged lion" (ibid., p. 263b). A bit further in the Thutmose III inscription cited above we read: "I cause them to see thy majesty as a fierce lion, / as thou makest them corpses throughout their valleys" (ibid., p. 374b). The Psalmist, too, coupled the lion (*kpyr*) and the *tnyn* (a dread reptile) as terrors that the devotee of YHWH can trample (91:16). In our oracle, Ezekiel exploits the differences between them and the weak point of the *tnym*-monster (already disclosed in 29:4–5) in a brilliant subversion of the native comparisons.

Pharaoh is figured as a Nile monster in the first Egypt oracle (29:3–6); the image there is local — the Nile is specifically named as the creature's natural habitat, in which it couches as master of all the fish. But the figure has its dark side: in its element the monster may be invincible, but haul it out of the water onto dry land and it dies. In the present oracle Pharaoh's appearance as a lion — eminent among land powers (a lion of nations) — is declared imaginary. The contrast between *kpyr* and *tnym* is between a power who operates freely all over the land, and a local power, confined to water. In this light vs. 2 will mean: You, Pharaoh, were regarded (by the Asiatic statelets like Judah who sought your protection) as a lion — a power that could make its presence felt far and wide. But you proved to be a water monster — helpless outside your element. Whenever you sallied out of your country, you were defeated (see the summary of Israelite frustration with Egypt in Structure and Themes of § XXXI).

In vs. 2b the prophet's gibing reaches its peak. Even within its element, he goes on to say, this monster's effect was piddling. The "great monster" of ch. 29, though couching at rest in its Nile, radiates a *hubris* worthy of being crushed by God. The monster of the present oracle, whose watery element is described in cosmic terms, stirs up the mud with his lunging and thrashing about. We wonder about that "muddying" — is it a figure of cosmic convulsions? When we reach vss. 13f., it becomes clear that such disturbances are decidedly mundane and require no supernal potency to effect. The collocation of the cosmic and the trivial in the description of the monster turns out to be ironic. Not only is the monster effectual only in his limited element, all that he effects there is "muddying" — a disturbance of the peace.

But as the monster has shrunk in reuse, the Nile has gained stature: in ch. 29 it is merely the bed of the great monster who falsely claims to have made it. Here, from the beginning to the end of the oracle, it is, without being named, identified with cosmic waters controlled by God. Over against the monster's sullying them, God will clarify them; it is as though the proper state of the Nile were limpidity. Egypt's inhabitants/Pharaoh abused the gift of the river — they muddied it — and with their destruction the river will regain its pristine peace. This singular concept and its formulation are adapted from the threats of Lev 26:34–35, where the future desolation of the land of Israel is related to unkept sabbatical years:

> Then shall the land pay back its sabbaticals—during the time of its desolation while you are in the land of your enemies; then shall the land rest and pay back its sabbaticals. During the time of its desolation it shall keep the rest it did not keep in your sabbatical years, while you were living on it.

With the desolation of the land of Israel God's dominion is affirmed through enforced sabbaticals; with the desolation of Egypt it is affirmed through enforced limpidity of the Nile.

XXXVII. Pharaoh in the Netherworld (32:17–32)

32 [17]It was in the twelfth year,[a] on the fifteenth of the month, that the word of YHWH came to me:

[18]Man, lament for Egypt's horde and send it down—her and glorious nations—to the nether regions, with those [already] descended into the Pit. [19] [b]"Better than whom are you? Descend and be laid to rest with the uncircumcised!"

[20]Amidst those slain by the sword they shall fall.
[c]She has been consigned to the sword; draw her and all her hordes![c]
[21]Leaders of the mighty will speak about him from the midst of Sheol, [d]with his helpers.[d]
They descended, lay down, the uncircumcised, slain by the sword.

[22]There is Assyria and all her assemblage, around him its graves;
All of them slain who had fallen by the sword,
[23]Whose graves were set at the bottom of the Pit.
Her assemblage was around her grave,
All of them slain, fallen by the sword,
Who inspired dread in the land of the living.

[24]There is Elam and all her horde around her grave;
All of them slain, who had fallen by the sword,
Who descended uncircumcised to the nether regions,
Who inspired dread of them in the land of the living,
And bore their disgrace with those descended into the Pit.
[25] [e]Amidst the slain they set a resting-place for her,
With all her horde—around him its graves,
All of them uncircumcised, slain by the sword,
For dread of them was inspired in the land of the living,

[a] G adds "the first month."
[b] G reads this verse after "Sheol" in vs. 21.
[c–c] G "and all his force shall lie down."
[d–d] Not in G S.
[e–e] Not in G; probably omitted through haplography. With our text before him, the eye of the copyist of G or its *Vorlage* skipped from *bwr* "Pit" at the end of vs. 24 to *bwr* at the end of vs. 25. G renders the verb at the end of vs. 25 as plural (reading *ntnw*?) and connects it with what follows; see next note.

And they bore their disgrace with those descended into the Pit;[e]
Amidst the slain [f]it was[f] set.

26 There is Meshech-Tubal and all her horde, around him its graves,
All of them uncircumcised, pierced by the sword,
For they inspired dread of them in the land of the living.

27 They do not lie with the mighty, those fallen
[g]of the uncircumcised,[g]
Who descended into Sheol with their weapons,
And had their swords set under their heads;
Whose iniquities were on their bones,
For dread of the mighty was in the land of the living.
28 But you amidst the uncircumcised [h]shall be broken and shall
lie[h], with those slain by the sword.

29 There is Edom, her kings and all her chiefs,
Who were set, for all their might, with those slain by the sword;
With the uncircumcised they lie, with those descended into the Pit.

30 There are the princes of the north all of them,
And every Sidonian, who descended with the slain,
In dismay at their might, despairing;
They lay uncircumcised with those slain by the sword,
And bore their disgrace with those descended into the Pit.

31 Them shall Pharaoh see and be consoled for all his horde,
slain by the sword, Pharaoh and all his army—
declares Lord YHWH.
32 For [i]I will inspire dread of me[i] in the land of the living,
And he shall be laid down amidst the uncircumcised,
With those slain by the sword, Pharaoh and all his horde,
declares Lord YHWH.

COMMENT

32:17. The missing month is usually taken to be the twelfth, as in vs. 1; this oracle will then be dated two weeks later than the preceding one. For the preferability of MT to G, see I, 11 n. 13.

18. *send it* (or: him) *down—her and glorious nations.* "Send down" = consign to the netherworld in your lament; proclaim their posthumous existence there. Cf. Jeremiah's commission "to uproot and tear down, to destroy and overthrow, to build and plant" (Jer 1:10) = proclaim destruction and restoration. To what extent a prophet's utterance was considered effective must have varied with the audience (see I, 122, on the effectivity of symbolic acts).

[f–f] Versions plural; G connects with next verse ("There were set").
[g–g] G "of old," as from *m'wlm*.
[h–h] G "you shall lie"; S "you shall lie and sleep."
[i–i] So Q; K G S "I (in the Lucianic G: he) inspired dread of him."

The bewildering shifts in the gender of the pronominal elements here and throughout the oracle are perhaps due to confusion of the varying antecedents (cf. the similar gender confusion in the description of the divine vehicle in 1:5ff., on which see comment, I, 43–44). Thus "horde" is properly masculine, but it may be treated as an equivalent of "Egypt" (or another land/people-name), which may be feminine (e.g., Exod 10:7). On the other hand, the land-name may stand for its king (as does "Assyria" in 31:3; see comment thereto) and hence be referred to by masculine pronouns. Some such explanation that seeks to account for the persistent irregularities in the present text is preferable to the methodic "corrections" made by critics in order to adjust the text to grammatical propriety.

Here the juxtaposition of pronouns of differing gender (*-hw, 'wth*) is still more jarring. The second may be feminine (referring to Egypt) by attraction to the following epithet for "nations," with which it is paired as the object of the verb "send down." But see next comment.

nations (bnwt gwym). Lit. "daughters/women of nations," as in vs. 16, only here—conjoined to *'wth* "her," a reference to Egypt—in another sense, based on the personification of a nation as a female styled *bat* X "daughter/woman X"; e.g., *bat babel* "Fair Babylon" (Jer 50:42, NJPS). The nations called "glorious" (in 17:8, 23, said of royalty) are Assyria, Elam, etc., whose rulers and slain armies are depicted in the sequel inhabiting the netherworld. But this conjectured sense of *bnwt gwym* together with the explanation of *'wth* given above is dubious. Hence the attractiveness of the proposal to read *'atta* "you (and the women of the nations)," making the keening gentile women (as in vs. 16) and the prophet co-lamenters.

with those [already] descended into the Pit. See comment to 26:20.

19. "*Better than whom are you?* . . . " Great king that you may be, you are no better (**n'm* ‖ ** ṭwb*, Gen 49:15; Ps 133:1; 135:3; Job 36:11) than anyone else and must die; cf. Elijah's request for a speedy death "for I am no better (*ṭwb*) than my forebears" (I Kings 19:4).

be laid to rest (hškbh) *with the uncircumcised.* The verb is passive (hof'al), and like the preceding *rdh* a lengthened imperative; for the active *hškyb* in this funereal sense, see II Chron 16:14: "They laid him [King Asa] to rest in a resting-place that was filled with spices . . ."

There is good evidence that Egypt's priests and kings were circumcised (H. Bonnet, *Reallexikon der Ägyptischen Religionsgeschichte* [Berlin: de Gruyter, 1971], p. 110; J. Sasson, "Circumcision in the Ancient Near East," *JBL* 85 [1966], 473–76). The disdain the Israelites felt for the uncircumcised being well attested (e.g., the reproach of marrying into a family of uncircumcision, Gen 34:14; Judg 14:3), one may presume (or Ezekiel may have presumed) that Egypt's rulers felt the same. (Indeed some interpret "the reproach of Egypt" in Josh 5:9—referring to uncircumcision—in this very sense: that which Egyptians regard as a reproach.) Contempt of uncircumcision appears in the Egyptian and Israelite practice of cutting off uncircumcised penises of slain enemies. For the Egyptian custom—a way of verifying body counts (with circumcised slain, hands were cut off)—see J. H. Breasted, *Ancient Records of Egypt*, III (1906; reprint, New York: Russell and Russell, 1962), pp. 248–49; for an Israelite instance, see I Sam

18:25–27. For the slain Pharaoh to be placed in the netherworld together with uncircumcised dead, then, adds insult to injury. A. Lods conjectured that Israelite custom excluded the uncircumcised from family graves and funeral rites, and that Israelite belief consigned them to the bottommost level of the netherworld (see ahead, vs. 23). Ezekiel, Lods argued, applied such conceptions to the uncircumcised nations ("La 'mort des incirconcis,'" *Comptes rendues . . . de l'Academie des Inscriptions et Belles-Lettres* [1943], pp. 271–83). While there is no evidence for the alleged custom — on the alleged belief, see comment to vs. 23, below — some sort of separation, in the grave and the netherworld, between those who died circumcised and those who died not so seems implicit in Ezekiel's emphasis on Pharaoh's evidently degrading placement amidst the latter. See the sober evaluation of Lods by W. H. Propp, "The Origins of Infant Circumcision in Israel," *Hebrew Annual Review* 11 (1987), 363–65.

According to MT, this verse is the prophet's address to Pharaoh, "sending him down." But in G it appears in place of vs. 21b as the speech of the netherworld mighty to the new arrival; see further, comment to vs. 21b.

20. *Amidst those slain by the sword they shall fall.* Pharaoh and his horde will die slain on the battlefield and subject to ignominy. Battle-fallen corpses were stripped by the victors (I Sam 31:8–9; II Sam 23:10; see the naked and headless Elamite bodies depicted in *Assyrian Palace Reliefs* [London: Batchworth Press, n.d.], plate 128; similar naked corpses in Y. Yadin, *The Art of Warfare in the Lands of the Bible* [Jerusalem and Ramat Gan: International Publishing Co., 1963], pp. 420–21; E. Porada, "The Iconography of Death in Mesopotamia in the Early Second Millennium B.C.," in B. Alster, ed., *Death in Mesopotamia* [Copenhagen: Akademisk Forlag, 1980], pp. 259–60 and plate ix b), and their remains were buried in mass graves (Ezek 39:11–16). Contrast the honorable posthumous treatment of the "mighty" in vs. 27. If the expression "[those] slain by the sword" evoked a picture of corpses of the defeated stripped naked, the constant reference to their uncircumcision becomes intelligible: the eye of the circumcised is drawn to the despised member. (*'rlym* does not mean "naked," as A. Geiger asserted in *Urschrift und Übersetzungen der Bibel*, 2d ed. [Frankfurt am Main: Madda, 1928], p. 412 note.)

Vs. 20b is difficult, breaks with the terms of this oracle, and is hardly reflected in G; attempts at interpretation only enforce the suspicion that it is corrupt and out of place. Yet we must attempt.

She (= Egypt) *has been consigned to the sword.* So T, which supposes an anomalous ellipsis of the preposition *l-* "to" before *ḥrb* "sword" (cf. the usage of *ntn l-* in 15:4, 6). An alternative is: "A/The sword has been appointed [supply: against them — MenbSh]" as in 21:16; this is only less elliptical, and it fails to cohere with the following clause where "her" = Egypt; see next comment.

draw her (= Egypt) to the netherworld; dubious. The imperative (so the Masorah, see *Minḥat Shay*) is addressed to undefined agents (cf. 7:23). The short *o* of the first syllable (*mo-*) is a rare variant of normal *i* in qal imperatives (cf. *molki* "reign!" Judg 9:10; *ḥorbu* "be amazed!" Jer 2:12).

and all her hordes. The plural, alone in this oracle, may refer to the forces of Egypt's allies (30:5, 6, 7).

21. The following is an attempt to construe MT, whose soundness is in doubt.

Leaders. Lit. "rams" (written without the middle *y*) as in 17:13 (I, 314); 31:11. "The mighty" are the honorable dead of vs. 27; their leaders remark the new arrivals. Cf. the netherworld parties who mockingly usher the slain Mesopotamian king into Sheol in Isa 14:9–10.

will speak about him. About Pharaoh; according to this intepretation, *lw*, which with *dibber* "speak" means normally "to him," here has the anomalous sense "about him," and vs. 21b tells what they said (Rashi, Kara, Eliezer). Staying with "to him" leads one to expect an address to Pharaoh, which the sequel in MT lacks (as Kimḥi admits), rendering our clause somewhat inane. G reads: "will say to you" and follows with vs. 19a.

with his helpers. Egypt's helpers are mentioned in 30:8; here they seem to be spoken about along with Pharaoh. The phrase, tacked on awkwardly, looks like an afterthought — perhaps to identify "the uncircumcised" of the next clause. G lacks it.

They descended . . . How this sentence serves the context is unclear. Understood as what the mighty say about Pharaoh and his horde, equivalent to "Here come the uncircumcised!" (Smend), the point may be that Pharaoh is denigratingly assimilated to his barbarous hordes. Others (e.g., Kara, Kimḥi, Cooke) take their cue from vss. 19, 27, 29, in which *škb* "lie down" is followed by *ʾt* "with," and render: "They (i.e., Pharaoh and his hordes) descended, lay down with the uncircumcised," Pharaoh and his hordes being separate from the latter.

22. *There is Assyria.* Whose people did not practice circumcision (E. A. Speiser, *Genesis*, AB, p. 127).

and all her assemblage. Of armed forces, perhaps alluding to accompanying vassal armies; see discussion of *qahal* at 16:40 (I, 287). The land/people-name — Allen calls it a "figurehead" — is feminine; so again Elam (vs. 24), Meshech-Tubal (vs. 26a$^{\alpha}$), and Edom (vs. 29a$^{\alpha}$). It is not clear why Assyria's company are an "assemblage" while those of Elam and Meshech-Tubal are a "horde" (like Pharaoh's). Is the former more organized?

around him (the Assyrian king) *its* (the assemblage's) *graves.* This juggling of antecedents seeks to adjust the phrase to the clear statement of vss. 23a$^{\beta}$ and 24a that the company of the figurehead are deployed around her grave. In the repetitions of this phrase (vss. 25a$^{\beta}$; 26a$^{\beta}$) the suffixes referring to the figurehead are again masculine (*sbybwtyw* "around him"), those referring to the "horde" are now feminine (*qbr*[*w*]*tyh* "her graves"). This first occurrence of the phrase is not in G; taken with the reversal of genders in its repetitions, there is cause for seeing in it the touch of a later hand.

23. *Whose graves.* The many graves of the figurehead and her company.

at the bottom (lit. "*utmost part*") *of the Pit.* In Isa 14:15 — its only other occurrence — *yrkty bwr* is in apposition to Sheol, the diametric opposite of *yrkty ṣpwn* "the summit of Zaphon" (the abode of the gods), the equivalent of "heaven," to which the Mesopotamian king (under the mythical emblem of Helel son of Shaḥar) boasted he'd ascend (vss. 13f.; the apparently related *ʾbny bwr* "stones of the pit(?)" in vs. 19 is obscure, like much of that verse). Here, too — an echo of the Isaiah passage? — the term conveys the extreme humiliation of Assyria, which plunged in forty years from regional hegemony (conquest of Egypt in mid-seventh century) to utter ruin (destruction of its capital cities between 615 and 612). A fixed gradation of Sheol's inhabitants, with the worst at the bottom, is not implied by the contexts. The point is rather: the higher they rise, the lower they sink. Another contrast, between harmless, impotent afterlife in the netherworld and dreadfulness in this life, is also the point of the final qualifying clause, *who inspired dread in the land of the living.*

24. Elam was a state occupying the southwestern part of the Iranian plateau (modern Khuzistan); its chief city was Susa. Constantly at war with Mesopotamian kings, Elam was devastated by Ashurbanipal during a two-year campaign (647–646), in which its main cities and temples were systematically pillaged and demolished (Luckenbill, *ARAB* II, pp. 305–13: ". . . I ravaged Elam to its farthest border. The noise of people, the tread of cattle and sheep, the glad shouts of rejoicing, I banished from its fields. Wild asses, gazelles and all kinds of beasts of the plain, I caused to lie down among them, as if at home" [§ 811]). Elam is mentioned as an independent monarchy in subsequent Babylonian records, and was eventually (mid-sixth century) absorbed in the empire of the Medes and Persians (see H. Tadmor's article *'Elam* in *EM* 6.189–99). We may suppose that Ezekiel's picture of Elam as inhabiting Sheol reflects its catastrophic defeat at the hands of Assyria, from which it never fully recovered.

And bore their disgrace. The disgrace of defeat, battlefield death, and subsequent ignominy; see above, comment to vs. 20.

25. *a resting-place* (mškb). This term for the final resting-place of the dead—elsewhere simply "couch, bed"—recurs in II Chron 16:14 (see above, comment to vs. 19), and on a Hebrew tomb inscription from Second Temple times (M. Avi-Yonah, ed., *Sepher Yerushalayim* [Jerusalem, 1956], p. 354), and is attested in Phoenician (e.g., a curse on whoever disturbs the tomb of Tabnit of Sidon: "May he have no resting-place among the shades!" [*KAI* 13.8; *ANET*^{3}, p. 662a]; in Eshmunʿazar of Sidon's similar admonition, the term interchanges with "grave" and "sarcophagus," *KAI* 14.4–11; *ANET*^{3}, ibid.).

Vs. 25a$^\beta$ "With all her horde . . ." to the end of the verse appears to be a shorter, variant version of vs. 24 from "and all her horde" (*wkl hmwnh*) through vs. 25a$^\alpha$. Thus (the short version is italicized):

24–25a$^\alpha$: . . . and all her horde around her grave,
25a$^\beta$–end: *with all her horde, around him her graves,*
all of them slain, who had fallen by the sword,
all of them uncircumcised, slain by the sword,
who descended uncircumcised to the nether regions,
who inspired dread of them in the land of the living,
for dread of them was inspired in the land of the living,
and bore their disgrace with those descended into the Pit.
and they bore their disgrace with those descended into the Pit.
Amidst the slain they set (*ntnw*) a resting-place for her
Amidst the slain it was set (ntn).

The last word in vs. 25 (*ntn*) will then be all that remains of the full text represented at the beginning of the verse (*btwk ḥllym ntnw mškb lh*).

The variant (italicized), presumably at first written in the margin, was copied into the text, thereby producing the present conflated version. G lacks most of the variant, but its omission of the novel "resting-place" clause—surely original—indicates that its omission is an error rather than a better text (see text note e–e).

26. *Meshech-Tubal.* This Anatolian pair appears elsewhere as two separate peoples: in the Table of Nations, Gen 10:2, in Ezek 27:13, and as the combined domain of Gog in 38:2, 3; 39:1. (Here, too, G and S translate "and Tubal," but all immediately following pronominal elements are in the singular, supporting the MT.) In the eighth and seventh centuries they were among the independent kingdoms of Asia Minor that were ravaged by internecine war, conquest by Assyria, and invasion by barbarian hordes of Cimmerians from south Russia. As ethnic entities they survived, to be incorporated into the Persian empire (the Moschoi and Tibarenoi of Herodotus, 3.94; 7.78). In Ezekiel's purview they are among Tyre's trading partners (27:13), but principally they are warrior hordes—here of the past; in chs. 38–39, future barbarian invaders of Israel's restored land (Gog's horde). See R. D. Barnett, "Phrygia and the Peoples of Anatolia in the Iron Age," in *The Cambridge Ancient History*, 3rd ed. (1975), II, ch. 30; *EM* 5, s.v. *mešek* (A. Kempinski), and 8, s.v. *tubal* (H. Tadmor).

around him. Around the king.

pierced (mᵉḥulᵉle) *by the sword.* Taking the pu'al form as a passive denominative of *ḥalal* ("slain," lit. "pierced through"): lit., made into ones pierced through by the sword. In view of Ezekiel's habit of varying repetition there is no need to suppose (as does *BHS*) a textual error (for *ḥlly*). For the active denominative, cf. the double sense of *mḥllyk* in 28:9 (your desecrators / those who make you a *ḥalal*).

27. The mighty of vs. 21 are now portrayed lying in Sheol; they are the elite of the dead warriors and are mentioned only to stress Pharaoh's ignominy: he will not lie with them (vs. 28). The mighty lie not only apart from, but evidently on a higher level than, the uncircumcised hordes, for in vs. 21 Pharaoh and his horde, descending to Sheol, meet them first. Moreover, they retain their arms in death, signifying, it seems, that they were not among the defeated whose corpses were stripped on the battlefield. They died a heroic death in victorious battle and were buried with honor.

those fallen of the uncircumcised. This could qualify the mighty, or the "they" of "they do not lie"—viz., the above-mentioned figureheads and their companies. But the construction is odd (the normal way would have been *nplym ʿrlym*), and the mention of this feature in connection with the mighty raises the issue of their status—are they circumcised or not?—which is an unwanted diversion.

G translates *gbwrym . . . mʿrlym* as "giants fallen of old," an evocation of the myth of the divine-human marriages of Gen 6:1–4, whose issue were *hgbwrym ʾšr mʿwlm* = G "the giants who were of old." The implied *Vorlage* of G here—*gbwrym nplym mʿwlm* "the mighty fallen of old"—is smoother, the mythic evocation suits Ezekiel, and the MT reading is explicable as a miswriting due to the prevalence of *ʿrlym* throughout the oracle.

Who descended into Sheol with their weapons. "In the burial ground of Tell es-Saʿidiyeh in the valley of the Jabbok a grave of a warrior [of the early Iron Age] was discovered; the deceased was wrapped in a linen shroud on which his sword was laid" (E. Stern in *EM* 7.16). The use of a sword as a headrest for the dead is otherwise unattested.

Whose iniquities were on their bones. An obscure expression. Since it is the result of their terrorizing (see the next clause), it may refer to some visible stigma set on their limbs as punishment. Cornill felicitously emended *ʿwntm* "their iniquities" to *ṣntm* (*ṣinnatam*) "their shields" (cf. 23:24). Shields on bodies—now mere bones—complement swords beneath heads as the essential weapons of soldiers.

28. Since "amidst the uncircumcised" cannot be taken with "you [Pharaoh] shall be broken" (not his defeat but his afterlife will be amidst them), MT must be construed thus: *But you,* Pharaoh, *shall be broken* (tšbr) in battle (said of Egypt's allies in 30:8), then *you shall lie* (tškb) *amidst the uncircumcised.* The awkwardness of MT's "broken" is highlighted by its absence in G, while S invents a synonymous pair ("lie down and sleep") in order to get rid of it. The original text probably had only "you shall lie (*tškb*)" = G. In some manuscript this was miswritten as *tšbr* (under the influence of 30:8?)—the two graphs are very similar—which was later copied into the ancestor of MT as a variant reading.

29. *There.* Here and in the next verse *šmh* (properly "thither") serves as *šm* "there" in vss. 22, 24, 26. Such semantic erosion of *šmh* occurs in 23:3 (followed by *šm*); 48:35.

Edom. Unlike the aforementioned great kingdoms, the statelets noticed in this and the next verse—neighbors of Judah—have no hordes surrounding their rulers in Sheol. Instead, the rulers (plural) of each are depicted, lying among the dishonored dead. Kings of Edom are mentioned, e.g., in Gen 36:31ff.; Jer 27:3; chiefs (*nśyʾym*) are not; Kara equates them with the Edomite *ʾlwpym* "clans" or "chiefs" of Exod 15:15. The pair king/chief occurs in 7:27 and was commented on there (I, 156).

for all their might. For *b-* "despite," cf. Isa 47:9: "[Calamity shall overtake you] despite your many (*brb*) enchantments"; and the common *bkl zʾt* "for all that" (e.g., Isa 5:25).

With the uncircumcised they lie. To their disgrace, for they were circumcised, according to Jer 9:24–25a (on the problems in these verses, see W. McKane, *Jeremiah,* ICC, pp. 213–15).

30. *princes of the north.* Josh 13:21 speaks of "[tribal] chiefs of (*nśyʾy*) Midian" who were "princes of (*nsyky*) [king] Sihon"; from this it may be inferred that *nsyk* denotes a high authority just under a king (cf. the equation of *nsyk* and *śr* "royal officer" implied by juxtaposition of Ps 83:12 and Judg 7:25). In Neo-Assyrian and Neo-Babylonian texts *nasiku*—a foreign word—is used of Aramaean chieftains (cf. D.R. Hillers's emendation *nsyky *ʾrm* "Aramaean chiefs" in Mic 5:4 [*Micah,* Hermeneia (Philadelphia: Fortress Press, 1984), p. 68]), giving some support to the conjecture (Smend, Cooke) that our phrase refers to rulers of Aramaean (Syrian) statelets north of the land of Israel. On the other hand, since the context appears to consist of near neighbors of Judah who were hostile to it, these

"princes" may be rulers of the more northerly Phoenician towns, such as Gebal and Arwad, considered as subordinate to kings of Tyre and Sidon (cf. 27:8, 9); see the next phrase.

And every Sidonian. In the light of the foregoing the sense is probably every king of (Tyre and) Sidon; see 28:21–26, Structure and Themes, first paragraph.

In dismay at (bḥtytm m-) *their might, despairing* (bwšym). This carries further the allusion of the previous verse to the ultimate nullity of human might, and does so by a striking pun on *ḥtyt.* Heretofore *ḥtytm* has meant "dread of them" (vss. 24–26), the sense in which it first appeared in 26:17, in a lament over Tyre. Reappearing here in a Phoenician context, its association with *bwš* "be put to shame, frustrated" and the preposition *m-* "by, on account of [a failed source of hope]" gives it the sense, "their dismay at [the nullity of] their might." The keys to this passage are Isa 20:5: "They shall be dismayed at and despair of (*wḥtw wbwšw m-*) Nubia, their hope"; Mic 7:16: "The nations shall see [God's wonders] and despair of all their might (*wybwšw mkl gbwrtm*)."

The text of this three-word sequence is, however, suspicious. Ironic wordplay dictated the choice of the nominal form *bḥtytm* rather than the expected participle *ḥtym* || *bwšym.* But the late position of *bwšym,* the lack of the copula, and the absence of the word in G indicate some irregularity in its transmission. Perhaps the simplest explanation is that *bwšym* originated as a gloss or an alternative to *bḥtytm,* needed because of the semantic shift in the latter word in this verse (which none of the interpreters of this passage have caught). Or perhaps MT conflates two readings:

bḥtytm mgbwrtm
mgbwrtm bwšym

The gloss, alternative, or second reading (unknown to G) arose from the correct understanding that here, and here only, the noun derivative of *ḥtt* is used in the sense its verb has when paired with *bwš,* viz., "dismay [at failed expectation]."

They lay uncircumcised. This description conflicts with Herodotus (2.104), who expressly counts the Phoenicians and "the Syrians of Palestine" (along with "Syrians" of Asia Minor) among those who "learned the custom [of circumcision] from the Egyptians." Hence Cooke's attractive suggestion to read here, as in vss. 19, 29: "with the uncircumcised"—themselves being circumcised—and hence disgraced in death.

31. *Them,* i.e., the spectacle of death and dishonor of great kingdoms and small, *shall Pharaoh see and be consoled* in that he is not alone in disaster (cf. 31:6); for the idea that another's calamity mitigates one's own, see Lam 2:13: "What can I witness on your behalf, what can I liken to you, O Fair Jerusalem? / To what can I compare you so as to console you, O Fair Maiden Zion?"

Pharaoh and all his army. The phrase is drawn from the story of the Exodus, Exod 14:4, 17, 28.

32. "This verse states the purpose of all that has gone before: 'It is my will to inspire dread of me in the land of the living, that I may be feared; therefore I work all this retribution' " (MenbSh). The Q of the first part of the verse thus

transforms climactically the "dread (of them)" refrain (in vss. 23b, 24b, [25b], 26b, 27b), the ground for which had been prepared in vss. 29–30.

The innovative reading had to contend with the conventional one: G^L ("for he [Pharaoh] inspired dread of him") assimilates this occurrence to all the others (it gives the ground for Pharaoh's punishment; Kara arrives at the same sense by making Q Pharaoh's confession!); K (= G S: "I inspired dread of him"), which cannot be reasonably construed, seems to be a hybrid of Q and G^L.

STRUCTURE AND THEMES

The oracle opens with a dated revelation-event formula (vs. 17) and an address ("Man, lament . . . ," vs. 18), and runs without a formal break to a double closure (twofold "declares Lord YHWH") in vss. 31–32. Its main part is a panorama of Sheol's inhabitants, which falls into three sections marked by variations on a refrain-like sequence in which Pharaoh and his horde are said to "lie down with/amidst the uncircumcised, with/among those slain by the sword." At the beginning and the end of the oracle the sequence (vss. 19b–20a, 32) has the verb "lie" in the hofʿal (passive causative) "be laid to rest," thus creating an envelope structure. Within it the sections are:

A (vss. 19–21): Pharaoh is consigned to Sheol and is greeted by the mighty ones. The command, "Descend and be laid to rest with the uncircumcised," and the following "Amidst those slain by the sword . . ." is answered by the (problematic) "They descended . . . slain by the sword" (see comment). MT shows an envelope structure for this section.

B (vss. 22–28): a panorama of masses of gentile dead in Sheol—a litany-like section in which each nationality is introduced by "There is," followed by stock phrases repeated with changes. A subsection, distinguishing "the mighty ones" from the gentile masses, begins and ends with that term—another envelope (vs. 27). Each group of dead is reproached with having spread dread of themselves "in the land of the living," for which their present shame is the punishment. Vs. 28 closes the section with a renewed address to Pharaoh, echoing vs. 19: "And you amidst the uncircumcised . . . shall lie . . ."

C (vss. 29–32): lying "there" in disgrace are also rulers of Edom and the Phoenicians, despite their "might"—a verbal link with the immediately preceding section on "the mighty ones." Pharaoh will console himself at the sight of others' defeated hordes and others' disgraceful placement among the uncircumcised. With the fall of Pharaoh and his horde dread of God will be established in the land of the living.

Ezekiel's repetitive style is well illustrated here: on the one hand, he works with a stock of fixed phrases; on the other, he constantly changes their sequence and their components. It is no wonder that variations, omissions, and additions occurred in the transmission of such a text—as displayed in the textual notes and comments. In the circumstances, any attempt to reconstitute the "original" form of the oracle is vain.

This oracle elaborates on the motif of descent into the underworld as the finale of God's judgments, hitherto mentioned only briefly in a Tyre oracle, 26:20, and an Egypt oracle, 31:15–18 (both using the key verb *yrd/hwryd,* as throughout this oracle). As befits a conclusion to the oracles against the nations, it surveys a vast spectacle of erstwhile dreaded gentile kings and their armies now laid low. Reference in vss. 29–30 to Edom (singled out from the statelets of ch. 25) and the Phoenicians (= Tyre and Sidon of chs. 26–28) indicates an intention to sum up the topic as a whole, not only with regard to Egypt, in this vision of the graveyard of nations. Together with the absence of "hordes," the change of *šm* to *šmh* in these verses sets them off from the foregoing, but not so much as to warrant the assumption of another or later hand.

The passage as a whole is one of the most detailed descriptions in Scripture of the condition of the dead (see its citations in N. J. Tromp, *Primitive Conceptions of Death and the Nether World in the Old Testament,* Biblica et Orientalia 21 [Rome: Pontifical Biblical Institute, 1969]). They lie in their graves in Sheol ("Sheol is the entirety into which all graves are merged," J. Pedersen, *Israel, Its Life and Culture,* 2 vols. [London and Copenhagen, 1926], p. 462; see the fine statement, pp. 461ff., of the fusion yet separateness of the two concepts). Some continuation of their social circumstances obtains: kings are distinguished from their subjects; the dead of the victors from those of the defeated, presumably reflecting their different burials; perhaps the uncircumcised from the circumcised, again perhaps reflecting Israelite burial practices. Though no longer active, the dead are conscious, speak, and have feelings (shame, consolation). In the picture of the dead in Sheol in Job 3:17–19, prisoners, the great and the small, the servant and his master, are recognizable as such, but they no longer actualize their status. O. Eissfeldt, building on the argument of Lods [see above, comment to vs. 19], supposed that the interchange here in Ezekiel of "the uncircumcised" with "those slain by the sword" indicates that those who died before their time—such as the murdered and the executed—were buried apart and without honor, and by analogy were believed to lie apart in Sheol ("Schwerterschlagene bei Hesekiel," in H. H. Rowley, ed., *Studies in Old Testament Prophecy* [Festschrift T. H. Robinson] [New York: Charles Scribner's Sons, 1950], pp. 73–81). Passages describing the burial of such persons do not bear out his supposition. The murdered were buried in family graves—II Sam 2:32 (Asael); 4:12 (Ishboshet); II Kings 12:22 (Joash); II Kings 21:26 (Amon, cf. vs. 18); so, too, were the executed—II Sam 21:14 (add "and the bones of the impaled" as reflected in G); I Kings 2:34 (Joab); likewise suicides—II Sam 17:23 (Ahitophel). There are indications that to be buried with the wicked was an ignominy: Isa 14:20–21: "You shall not be joined with them [= the kings of the nations (vs. 18)] in burial, for you destroyed your land . . ."; 53:9: "His [God's servant's] grave was set with the wicked"; and cf. the Chronicler's statement that two wicked kings were denied burial in the royal graveyard—Jehoram (II Chron 21:20) and Joash (II Chron 24:25).

Biblical notions of the realm of the dead differed materially from those of other ancient peoples. Given monotheism, there are no distinctive divinities charged with managing that realm (for Mesopotamia, see W. G. Lambert, "The Theology of Death," in B. Alster, ed., *Death in Mesopotamia* [Copenhagen: Akademisk Forlag, 1980], pp. 53–66); indeed the godlessness of Sheol is quite astonishing (presumably a reaction to pagan conceptions, Y. Kaufmann, *The Religion of Israel* [Chicago: University of Chicago Press, 1963], pp. 311–16). Even the unburied go down to Sheol: Jacob believes his son, killed by wild beasts and unburied, is in Sheol (Gen 37:35); Helel son of Shaḥar (a mythical symbol of a Mesopotamian king) goes down to Sheol, although denied burial (Isa 14:19; S. Lowenstamm in *EM* 4.757), as do those who die untimely (e.g., infants: inferable from David's assertion that he is going to his dead baby, II Sam 12:23; Korah's company: Num 16:33). Contrast the Mesopotamian view that the unburied find no rest in the netherworld (Gilgamesh 12.153f.; A. Heidel, *The Gilgamesh Epic and Old Testament Parallels*, 2d ed. [Chicago: University of Chicago Press, 1949], pp. 155–57), or the Greco-Roman fear of the vagabond spirits of the unburied and those who died before their time—e.g., by violence, suicide, or shipwreck (F. Cumont, *Afterlife in Roman Paganism* [New Haven: Yale, 1923], pp. 64–69, 128–47).

In the visionary mixture of already fallen kingdoms (Assyria, perhaps Elam) and as yet existing ones (all the rest) lying in Sheol, this oracle carries to its extreme conclusion Ezekiel's view that the gentile kingdoms are essentially insolent encroachers on God's dominion. Dread of them eclipsed dread of God. For his kingship to be established, the earthly kings and their forces must be annihilated. "For I will inspire dread of me in the land of the living" (32:32).

XXXVIII. Doom Prophecy Is A Call to Repent (33:1–20)

33 [1]The word of YHWH came to me: [2]Man, speak to your fellow countrymen and say to them:

If I brought a sword upon a land, and the people of the land took one man of their number and appointed him as a lookout for them, [3]and he saw the sword coming upon the land and blew the horn and warned the people, [4]and someone heard the sound of the horn but did not take warning, and a[a] sword came and took him off—his blood is on his own head. [5]He heard the sound of the horn but did not take warning; his blood is on him. Had he taken warning he could have saved himself.

[6]But if the lookout saw the sword coming and did not blow the horn, so that the people did not take warning, and the sword came and took off one of them—that one was taken off because of his iniquity, but I will hold the lookout responsible for his death.

[7]Now you, man—I have appointed you as a lookout for the house of Israel. When you hear a word from my mouth you must warn them against me. [8]When I say to a wicked man, "Wicked man, you shall die!" and you do not speak up to warn the wicked man against his way, he, being wicked, shall die because of his iniquity, but I will hold you responsible for his death. [9]But if you warn a wicked man to turn from his way, and he does not turn from his way, he shall die because of his iniquity, but you will have saved yourself.

[10]Now you, man, say to the house of Israel: This is what you are saying, "Our transgressions and our sins are upon us, and because of them we are pining away; how then can we live?" [11]Say to them: By my life!—declares Lord YHWH—I do not desire the death of the wicked man, but rather that the wicked man turn from his way and live. Turn, O turn from your evil ways, for why should you die, O house of Israel!

[12]Now you, man, say to your fellow countrymen: The righteousness of the righteous man will not save him on the day of his trangression, nor will the wicked man fall because of his wickedness on the day of his turning from his wickedness; /nor will a righteous man be able to live [b]because of it on the day of his sinning[b]/. [13]When I say of the righteous man, "He shall live," then, relying on

[a]G "the," and so in the sequel where an expected article is absent in MT; see comment.
[b–b]Not in G; S T omit "because of it."

his righteousness, he does wrong, all his righteous acts shall be disregarded, and because of the wrong that he did he shall die. [14]And when I say to the wicked man, "You shall die," and he turns from his sin and does what is just and right—[15]the wicked man returns a debt-pledge, makes good what he has taken by force, follows the laws of life, not doing wrong; he shall live, not die. [16]All the sins he committed shall not be held against him; he does what is just and right, he shall live.

[17]Your fellow countrymen say, "The way of the Lord does not conform to rule," when it is their way that does not conform to rule. [18]When a righteous man turns from his righteousness and does wrong, he shall die because of that; [19]and when a wicked man turns from his wickedness and does what is just and right, on account of that he shall live. [20]And you say, "The way of the Lord does not conform to rule!" I will judge each one of you according to his ways, O house of Israel.

COMMENT

33:2. *your fellow countrymen.* Lit. "the sons (= members) of your people"; cf. "the daughters (= women) of your people" in 13:17. In 3:11 the phrase qualifies "the exiles," and in the oracles of this chapter, where all the remaining occurrences appear (vss. 2, 12, 17, 30), it likewise denotes the exiles as fellow Judahites of the prophet. "Fellow ethnics" would be closer to the Hebrew, setting them off from their gentile surroundings. This message is specifically for the exiles, despite its pan-Israel terms (vss. 7, 10, 20).

If I brought . . . upon a land. Lit. "A land if I brought upon it." In the priestly casuistic style, the normal, nonemphatic word order of the protasis places the person or thing affected in initial position; e.g., Lev 1:2, lit. "A person if he makes an offering of you" = if one of you makes an offering; 13:40, lit. "A man if his head is balded" = if the head of a man is balded; 13:47, lit. "And a cloth if there should be on it the blight of 'leprosy'" = if the blight of "leprosy" should be on a cloth. Ezek 14:13 shows the same pattern: lit. "A land if it sinned against me" = if a land, etc.

took one man of their number (mqṣyhm). The sense of *qaṣe* "limit, end" is extended to mean "entirety, sum total"—i.e., what is bounded by the limit; cf. the semantic range of *gbwl* "boundary" and "territory (enclosed by a boundary)." The word in this context connotes scanning the entire populace to pick the best man. The supposed sense "outstanding persons" (Malbim, Ehrlich, and Speiser at Gen 47:2 [AB]) is forced. The form of *mqṣyhm* is singular, the *y* being radical; cf. the alternation of *mḥn/y/k* "your camp" (singular, from **ḥny*) in Deut 23:15.

4. *did not take warning.* The verb *nizhar* is in the perfect, coordinate with the preceding perfect *šamaʿ* "heard" (so again in vs. 5; in vs. 6, it is coordinate with *taqaʿ* "blew"). The long *a* of *nizhar* in all its occurrences, instead of short *a* as is normal in the perfect, is a pausal form, somewhat uncommon with the minor disjunctive accent *zaqef* (as Kimḥi notes); cf. the long *a* of (perfect) *nilqaḥ* in vs. 6.

a (G: the) *sword came.* Absence of the article in MT where it is expected occurs too often in this oracle to be taken as a scribal error (vss. 6, 8, 9, 11, 15). See

BHSyn, p. 250: "The article is not consistently used even according to the best established patterns . . ." In what follows, English usage will be respected in the translation.

took him off. This figurative, euphemistic use of "take (*lqḥ*)" with the victim as direct object (again in vs. 6) is unique.

his blood is on his own head. I.e., blame for his death falls on him alone; see Josh 2:19: "Whoever steps out of your house [and is killed], his blood is on his own head, and we are blameless. But whoever is with you in your house—his blood is on our heads if a hand is laid on him." The priestly version of this formula is simply "his blood is on him" (e.g., Lev 20:9ff.), which variant appears in the next verse, derived from 18:13 (see comment, I, 331).

5. *Had he . . . he could have.* So S and Rashi. A condition contrary to fact is expressed by asyndetic sequence of two clauses with verbs in the perfect: "Had you let them live (*lw hḥytm 'wtm*) I should not have killed you (*l' hrgty 'tkm*)," Judg 8:19. Absence of a conditional particle (e.g., *lw*, *'m*) is unusual, but it occurs with real conditions (verbs in the imperfect): "If you trespass, I will scatter you (*'tm tm'lw 'ny 'pyṣ 'tkm*), Neh 1:8. G and Eliezer render: "but he [that] took warning saved his life"; this abrupt change of subject is harsh, but it at least keeps to the topic enlarged upon in vss. 4f., viz., the responsibility of the warned for their fate, where death was avoidable. The proposed emendation of *nzhr* to *hzhyr* (*BHS*; = "but he [the lookout] had warned, he saved his life") on the ground of symmetry with vs. 6b is equally harsh, changes the topic, and goes against the unanimous attestation of MT in all ancient versions.

6. *because of his iniquity.* For which he would have died in any case; so Zelophehad's daughters ascribe their father's death in the wilderness to some private sin of his (Num 27:3). The view is that no one dies but for some sin, and "there is no one who does not sin" (I Kings 8:46), so every death is justified.

7–9 = 3:17–19 with minor variations; see comments, I, 84–85.

10. *This is what you are saying* (kn 'mrtm). As in 11:5, this introduces a notion held by the people that the prophet contests. In the sequel, the particle *ky* merely introduces the direct speech of the people and is untranslatable (BDB, pp. 471–72); e.g., "You said to him *ky* 'A king you must appoint over us'" (I Sam 10:19).

The people say that they are languishing under the burden of their sin (and its punishment), and they despair of survival; they depict themselves in terms of Ezekiel's predictions (4:17; 24:23). The prophet cannot but agree with this self-depiction—indeed Kimḥi interprets *kn 'mrtm* "Rightly have you thought" (like *kn . . . dbrt* "rightly have . . . [they] spoken," Num 27:7): you do well to confess that your troubles result from your sins. But the example of 11:5 shows that this clause is disputational, and the rest of the oracle in fact contests the despair that the people infer from the (correct) premise of their sinfulness.

you are saying ('mrtm l'mr). The infinitive would seem to authenticate the quotation; "(This is what you are saying) and I quote: . . ." See its effect in vs. 24; 35:12 and Gen 42:22; II Sam 3:18; Jer 27:14.

11. ‖ 18:23, 30b–32, except that here God confirms with an oath—fittingly, by his life—his desire that the wicked should repent and live.

12. *on the day.* The sense, "when" (as, e.g., *RSV*, NJPS, render this phrase),

could have been conveyed by the simple infinitive construction as in vss. 18–19. "On the day" expresses the rapidity of the change: e.g., the wicked man turns from wrongdoing and on that very day is delivered from its destructive effect ("he will not fall"; *nkšl* = stumble-and-fall [cf. 3:20 "a stumbling block" and comment, I, 85]). Such temporal compression dramatizes the conversion and underlines its decisiveness. Vss. 13–16 represent it more as a process.

Vs. 12b ("nor will a righteous man . . .") is barely coherent, and what coherence it has is redundant; G renders only a fragment (see text note). Likely it is a variant of the "righteous man" clause in vs. 12a$^{\alpha}$, originally beginning with the words *ṣdqt ḥsdyq*: "The righteousness of the righteous man—he will not be able to live because of it, etc."

13. *When I say of the righteous man, "He shall live."* In the third person, dependent on the "verdicts" of 18:9, 17, 19. The G versions that assimilate this to vs. 14's direct address (see *BHS*) are secondary, and obscure the literary connections of our piece. The rest of the vs. = 18:24, 26; but only here is the backslider's faulty reasoning given: in his reliance on his virtuous past he fatally overlooks the annulling effect of his backsliding.

14–16. *to the wicked man, "You shall die."* Direct address in the second person, dependent on the "lookout" passages, vs. 8 above = 3:18. The rest of the passage is dependent on parallels in ch. 18 (e.g., 18:7, 19, 21–22, 27). Like them, it does not give the reasoning of the penitent sinner; instead it instructs the hearer in practical penitence by items drawn from the descriptions of righteous conduct in 18:7, 16, adjusted to the new context; e.g., "he makes good what he took by force," instead of "he takes nothing by force."

follows the laws of life (bḥqwt ḥyym hlk). The new, unique term, "laws of (= that give) life," is based on the proximity in 18:9, 17, of "follow my laws" to the verdict "he shall live." Cf. also the refrain, "my laws . . . by observing which one shall live," 20:11, 13, etc.

17–20. Condensed from 18:25–30a. What "way of God" is being caviled at and by whom? The obvious "way" is the one enclosed by the cavils in vss. 18–19; viz., to judge each person according to his present state. But it is hard to see why the demoralized audience of vs. 10 (or any other) should cavil at that hope-inspiring way of judgment or consider it "not conforming to rule."

According to A. Graffy (*A Prophet Confronts His People*, Analecta Biblica 104 [Rome: Biblical Institute Press, 1984], 77), the people's cavil should be translated, "YHWH's way cannot be fathomed." This is an expression of surprise and difficulty in understanding how they can avoid wasting away in their sin, and hints at reluctance to change their ways. God throws it back in their face, declaring that their way—knowing the way to life (= repentance) and not following it—is incomprehensible. Cf. Davidson's view on 18:15 cited in comment there, I, 334. See Structure and Themes.

18–19. *because of that* (lit. "them") . . . *on account of that* (lit. "them"). In Hebrew the plural pronoun may be used to refer to a single act/thing that is expressed by two terms (R. Gordis in *Louis Ginzberg Jubilee Volume* [New York: Jewish Theological Seminary, 1945], pp. 184–86 [English section]; Gordis compares 18:26 and Job 13:20f.; 22:21). Here the two terms are the two clauses describing the single act of reversal ("... turns ... and does ...").

20. *according to his ways.* His present ways, if the sentence is to suit the context.

STRUCTURE AND THEMES

This oracle consists of two main parts: after the revelation formula (vs. 1), A, vss. 2–9, an address to the exiles on the role of the prophet as a lookout, and B, vss. 10–20, a threefold assertion of the principle that God judges a person according to his present moral state, hence there is hope for the penitent wicked. There are no closing formulas; the end is indicated by the next revelation formula in vs. 21. Introductory formulas further divide the oracle as follows:

A1 (vss. 2–6): "Man, speak to your countrymen," opens the description of a lookout's warning task and his limited liability for the death of his charges. Two cases are presented: in the first, the lookout has given warning (vss. 3–5); in the second he has not (vs. 6). In the first case the unheeding citizen is solely liable for his own death—a point that is lingered over (vss. 4b–5). In the second case the delinquent lookout shares responsibility.

A2 (vss. 7–9): "Now you, man," opens the application to Ezekiel of the role of a lookout; = 3:16–19. Only cases in which the wicked die because of refusal to repent are presented. The order of the cases of A1 is reversed: first, where the prophet fails to warn; secondly, where he warns.

The pattern of the cases in A1–2 is thus *a b b′ a′*; this chiastic pattern, bonding the two sections of A, is maintained in B (as will be shown), formally linking the two parts.

B1 (vss. 10–11): "Now you, man, say to the house of Israel," introduces the exiles' confession of sin and their despair of living, to which God replies in an impassioned declaration of his desire that the wicked repent and live (sequence: wicked becomes good, symbolized by $-$ [minus] $>$ [becomes] $+$ [plus]).

B2 (vss. 12–20): "Now you, man, say to your fellow countrymen," introduces a triple statement of the principle of God's judgment in terms drawn from ch. 18:

(a) Past conduct, when reversed, will not operate on behalf of a good man who goes bad (vss. $12a^{\alpha}$; $+ > -$) or against a bad man who turns good (vss. $12a^{\beta}$; $- > +$).

(b) God's verdicts of life and death are based on one's record to date; reversal of conduct ($+ > -$, vs. 13, or $- > +$, vss. 14–16) cancels the record and reverses the verdict. How the wicked reforms is illustrated in detail (vs. 15).

(c) The gist of (a) and (b): $+ > -$ earns death (vs. 18); $- > +$ earns life (vs. 19).

Throughout B the chiastic (or alternating) pattern prevails in the presentation of cases. But more than a formal device, it results from all closures in God's speeches being iterations of the principle: if the wicked turns good he will live—God's heartening retort to the people's cry, "How then can we live?" (vs. $10b^{\beta}$).

The critical issue of this oracle is its integrity, affirmed by some critics (e.g., Cooke), denied by most (e.g., Zimmerli, Wevers, Eichrodt, Carley). There can hardly be a doubt that the material in A and B originated separately and that their combination here is secondary. The prevalence of chiasm is a unifying feature, but is not enough in itself to support an argument for the integrity of the secondary composition. We turn to other criteria.

The style of the oracle is uniform throughout: casuistic, quasi-legal, as in all of Ezekiel's disquisitions on principles of divine government (I, 94–95). The rhetoric of B, like its substance, is that of 18:21–32: repetition with variation, disputational language, stating a principle "roundly" — i.e., is, going beyond the immediate issue (God's acceptance of the penitent wicked) to its — for now irrelevant — symmetrical opposite (God's rejection of the backsliding righteous); cf. I, 337f.

Terminologically, there is a staged progression; each section carries some of the previous vocabulary while introducing new terms that are, in turn, carried forward (for a more elaborate instance of this structure, see the table for ch. 21). In the following table, x marks terms carried over from previous sections:

A1 (vss. 2–6)	*A2 (7–9)*	*B1 (10–11)*	*B2 (2–20)*
appoint as a lookout	x		
warn	x		
blood	x		
because of his iniquity	x		
self (*npš-*)	x		
	wicked	x	x
	die	x	x
	way	x	x
	turn	x	x
		transgression	x
		sin	x
		live	x

The large terminological overlap of B1 and B2 sustains the impression that they belong together. The same may be said of the relation of A1 to A2. The overlap of A2 and B1 is more like a pivot, and invites further inquiry as to their relation.

(Slight terminological discrepancies between A1 and A2 raise a doubt whether they were originally composed together [as is generally held]. "Save" in vs. 5 [A1] is *mlṭ*, while in vs. 9 [A2] it is *hṣyl;* the verbal element in the phrase "hold responsible for death" in vs. 6 [A1] is *drš*, while in vs. 8 [A2] it is *bqš*. Since Ezekiel is fond of variation, this is not a strong argument; but it adds a featherweight to the suspicion of separate origins for A1 and A2 that arises from the independent existence of A2 in ch. 3, and the lack of emphasis in A2 on the responsibility of the warned that is so prominent in A1 [see I, 90–92, and below].)

The ultimate test of (secondary) integrity must be thematic-ideational coherence. That the elements of A cohere well, as do those of B, is evident; is there a train of thought that binds all the elements together? Their combination was not mechanical, but the extant material was modified, augmented, and pruned. Can a thread of argument be discerned running through the whole that will account for the changes in the original, and for the present order of the material? I think it can.

All the components of vss. 1–20 in their present shape and order serve as a complex response to the new situation revealed by the people's despairing saying (vs. 10): "Our transgressions and our sins are upon us. . . how then can we live?" Let us imagine the background and implications of this saying.

Calamitous events have occurred which the people interpret as punishment for their sin; moreover, the sin must be overwhelming to have deserved such punishment. It may be supposed that news has reached the exiles of the imminent collapse of besieged Jerusalem (the report of its fall comes in the next piece, vss. 21–22). In this saying the people reveal that in their extremity they have bowed to the prophet's insistence — expressed baldly in ch. 18 — that they are not suffering for ancestral sins but for their own.

At the same time, the exiles show no understanding of the remedial purpose of Ezekiel's prophecy of inexorable doom for Jerusalem. It was intended in the first place to pull the exiles away from their attachment to "the bloody city." The ultimate goal — to bring them to repentance (ch. 18) — was never explicitly connected with the doom prophecy. So the exiles inferred from the dooms and from the realized calamity that they — like the homelanders — had no future, that their sin was too great for reconciliation with God.

That the people's acceptance of Ezekiel's estimate of their sinfulness should lead to paralyzing hopelessness was unanticipated. It required a restatement of the prophet's role so as to justify his message. The metaphor of the lookout had served at the outset of his career to assuage his own fears of failure (3:17–21): as a lookout is responsible only for giving warning but not for its effectiveness, so Ezekiel must announce doom, but will not be answerable for the course taken by those warned. Now, in typical fashion, the figure is reused in a new situation for a fresh purpose: to justify the doom prophecy as a spur to repentance. To this end the "realistic" preface was composed in which the saving role of the lookout is brought out, when his warnings are acted on appropriately. This is part A of the oracle.

But could a people lying under such a burden of sin ever purge themselves before God? Incredulousness resonates in the people's saying. To counter it, Ezekiel forcefully reiterates the corollary of his doctrine of the moral autonomy of generations (18:4–20), viz., the doctrine of the expungeability of one's moral record by a change of course (18:21–32). This is part B.

The modifications in the original materials lend support to this surmised train of thought.

Only the citizen who is "taken off" || the unrepentant wicked is mentioned in the two parts of A. The wavering righteous of 3:20–21 who is saved from perdition by heeding the warning is omitted here. That case is irrelevant to the context of B, in which unrepentant wicked (the prophet's audience) are addressed.

Thus abbreviated, the reused lookout metaphor is prefaced by a description of a real lookout's task, and since the object was to assuage the despair of the people, the oracle is addressed to the people (vs. 2) rather than to the prophet alone (as 3:16 ff.). The ampler realistic description points up gaps in the corresponding restatement of the prophet's role. These gaps can readily be filled mentally, and we may suppose that the audience did so — that it interpreted the prophet's role in the light of the preface's lookout. In what follows, the bracketed matter in the right-hand column is extrapolated from the left-hand one.

Lookout	*Prophet*
[2]I bring a sword on a land	[8aα]I doom the wicked (Israel)
people appoint a lookout for themselves	[7]I appoint you as a lookout for the house of Israel
[3]lookout sees sword coming	you hear my (doom-)word
blows horn to warn people	must warn them of/against me
	([8aβ]–b delinquent prophet)
	[9]you warned the wicked to turn
[4]someone heard the horn	[he heard your warning]
didn't take warning	he didn't turn from his way
sword came and took him off	he'll die in his iniquity
his blood is on his own head	you saved yourself
[5]he heard the horn	[he heard your warning]
he didn't take warning	[he didn't turn from his way]
his blood is on him	[he's to blame]
had he taken warning	[had he turned from his way]
he could have saved himself	[he could have saved himself]
([6]delinquent lookout)	

In the prefaced lookout story, stress is laid on the responsibility of the heedless person (= the wicked in the application). The verdict at the end of vs. 4 — "his blood is on his own head" — is repeated and enlarged upon for another full verse (5). Such a stress is apt for the audience of B, which had to be roused from the lethargy of despair.

This stress is underlined by the absence of corresponding clauses in the application to the prophet — the bracketed gap-fillers in our right-hand column. Since the language of the application (A2) is virtually identical with its doublet in 3:19, the application of the figure to the prophet originated presumably in different circumstances from that of the preface, and was reused here without substantial change. Taking the evidence at face value, the metaphor of the lookout was first applied to the prophet in a private message at the start of his career. On repeating it here in a public message he kept to its original formulation, adding the emphasis on the responsibility of the warned only in the newly fashioned preface; see further, I, 91–92.

An encouraging theological paradox emerges from the opening lines of the figure and its application. The theatened people of the land who appoint a lookout for their protection have as their correspondent God, who appoints Ezekiel as Israel's lookout. But God is also the enemy against whom warning must be given. God who ordains doom is at once God who seeks to avert it by sending the prophet to warn Israel against his onslaught (on the desire of God to block his own wrath, see 13:5; 22:30). His doom-word is not final but is contingent on the failure of the people to repent. Its desired effect is to bring about its annulment. Reading the application to the prophet in the light of the realistic preface puts a new aspect on the prophecy of doom: it is a sign of God's care for Israel, of his desire that they live and not die.

Having reinterpreted for the people his mission as a doom prophet, Ezekiel now can answer their cry, "How then can we live?" God's sentence of death to the wicked (vs. 8) is not final; on the contrary, by informing the wicked of that sentence God demonstrates his true desire—that the wicked repent and live. By their collective repentance the house of Israel can annul the sentence of death which has been issued for them (vs. 11).

The prophet proceeds to set forth the rule of God's judgment in terms drawn from ch. 18. Omitting the primary argument of that oracle—that the moral status of a given generation cannot be accounted to its successor—the prophet recalls here its corollary: that a person's moral record will not determine God's judgment of him if he has broken with it. The three statements of the rule of God's judgment are emphatic variations on this theme, typical of Ezekiel's style (see above). In vs. 15 he draws on the list of attributes of the righteous man in the omitted section of ch. 18 to spell out the generalization of vs. 14b that the wicked man "does what is just and right." He exemplifies such deeds by social virtues rather than religious (in the cultic sense), and by calling them "laws of life" he offers a response to the people's despairing "How then can we live?" as though it were a genuine question: "What must we do in order to live?"

The cavil about God's way (of judgment) "not conforming to rule" (vss. 17, 20) has been taken over from 18:25, 29, where it properly refers to the primary issue of the moral autonomy of generations. There the cavil reflects the conviction of the prophet's generation that they suffer for ancestral sins. To be sure, even there it appears somewhat misleadingly amidst the presentation of the individualistic corollary (as though disapproving of God's judging each person according to his present status). But at least there it is at home in the overall context of ch. 18: questioning God's justice. In the present context, however, the cavil is beside the point, since the popular mood is not of questioning his justice, but of despair of ever recovering from afflictions perceived as wholly justified. The function of the "quoted" cavils here in vss. 17, 20, can hardly be more than to serve as a foil for the iterated reassertion of God's rule of judging persons according to what they presently are. Presumably the original sense of vs. 20b ("I will judge each of you according to his ways" = 18:30) also rebutted the popular complaint that God was judging this generation by the sinful conduct of their ancestors. Reused in this context, it must mean "according to his present moral state (not a former, contrary one)."

Critics are almost unanimous in seeing in this oracle the beginning of "a new [post-fall] phase of Ezekiel's activity," as "a pastor to individual exiles" (Carley, pp. 218, 220). The lookout comparison contradicts such an interpretation (as Eichrodt expressly admits, while holding to the pastor idea; p. 446). For as the lookout serves the entire land, and his warning is directed not to individuals but to the collective, so the prophet's warning is to the collective "house of Israel." The individual address is conventional in Ezekiel's quasi-legal style and does not signify that the prophet is to be a pastor of individuals (see I, 93–97, for detailed argument).

Far from being a new phase of the prophet's mission, this oracle is the epilogue of his pre-fall mission as a prophet of doom. Nowhere in it is there so much as a hint that the lookout-prophet proclaims anything but doom. What is new is the benign face put on doom prophecy by comparing it to the blast of the lookout's horn. The prophet, like the lookout, is charged with protecting the people from disaster. By combining the lookout metaphor with the doctrine of the annullability of divine death-decrees through repentance, the messenger of doom is seen as a token of God's concern that exiled Israel live and not die. This ingenious twist is the result of the oversuccess of the doom prophecy: reinforced by calamity, it convinced the people of their guilt to the point of demoralization and despair. Dismayed, the prophet reinterprets his harsh mission to them in heartening terms, for without hope there can be no repentance.

This is Ezekiel's last call to repentance. In the prophet's estimate he failed to move his people to self-purgation. His own despair is reflected in his vision of the future amending of Israel's heart—by an act of God (36:16ff.).

XXXIX. Release from Dumbness (33:21–22)

33 [21]It was in the twelfth year, in the tenth month, on the fifth of the month, of our exile, that a survivor from Jerusalem came to me, saying, "The city has fallen." [22]The hand of YHWH had come upon me the evening before the coming of the survivor, and he opened my mouth by the time he came to me in the morning. Thus my mouth was opened and I was no longer dumb.

COMMENT

33:21. *the twelfth year . . . of our exile.* Year twelve of Jehoiachin's exile began in spring (month one [Nisan]) 586. The fall of Jerusalem and the deportation of Judah's exiles occurred in the summer of that year (months four [Tammuz] and five [Ab]). The survivor may have been in the exile train, and will have arrived in Babylonia about five months later, in the wintry tenth month of Tebet (19 January 585, according to Parker-Dubberstein). With this five-month trek may be compared the four months Ezra's immigrant train took to travel the return route from Babylonia to Judea (Ezra 7:9). For details, see notes 1 and 14 to the Table of Dates, I, 9, 11.

Some versional evidence exists for a reading "the eleventh year," perhaps mistakenly influenced by the regnal year dating of the events of summer 586 in, e.g., II Kings 25:2, 8. On the Judahite regnal year, see I, 10 n. 5.

a survivor (hplyṭ) *from Jerusalem came to me.* As predicted in 24:26. This construction rather than "came to me from Jerusalem" seems to be suggested by the accents that connect the words this way. On the presence of the article in *hplyṭ*, see comment at 24:26. (To be sure, it could be argued that in this instance "the [specific] survivor" is meant—viz., the one predicted in 24:26.)

22. *The hand of YHWH had come upon me.* A trance state presaging this time not an oracle (see comment at 1:3 [I, 41–42]) but a release from the years-long constraint on normal intercourse with his society.

by the time. For this idiomatic use of *'d* with *bw'*, cf. Num 10:21; II Kings 16:11; the expected form of the verb is *bw'w* "his coming."

STRUCTURE AND THEMES

This rare autobiographical notice, the fulfillment of the prediction in 24:26, marks a turning point in the prophet's relation to his society. The disaster vindicated his prophecies concerning Jerusalem and established his credit. The crisis of creditability occasioned by the unfulfillment of his prophecies against Tyre and Egypt (§ XXXII) was years in the future. For the time being he was believed and embraced by his hearers. (An indication that they began to see things his way somewhat before the news of the fall reached them is their confession in vs. 10 above). Now he could speak freely with them—perhaps as a public censor, admonishing them on his own (see comment to 3:26 [I, 102]). We have no evidence, however, of this new freedom, for the prophet's speech in subsequent chapters of the book is not more spontaneous than in the foregoing ones; as before, all that Ezekiel speaks is "the word of YHWH."

See further, the comments to 24:26–27 and the related matter in Structure and Themes to that passage.

XL. Unregenerate Communities (33:23–33)

33 [23]The word of YHWH came to me: [24]Man, these inhabitants of ruins on the soil of Israel say, "Abraham was only one man but he got possession of the land; we are many; surely the land has been given to us as a possession." [25]So say to them: Thus said Lord YHWH:

You eat over blood; you look for help to your idols; you shed blood—and you would possess the land?

[26]You live by your swords; you commit abominations; each of you has defiled his fellow's wife—and you would possess the land?

[27]Thus shall you say to them: Thus said Lord YHWH: By my life! whoever are in the ruins shall fall by the sword, and whoever is in open country—[a]I have consigned him to the beasts to eat him,[a] and whoever are in fastnesses and caves shall die by the plague.

[28]I will turn the land into an utter desolation, and her pride of strength shall be ended, and the mountains of Israel shall be desolate with none passing through. [29]Then they shall know that I am YHWH, when I turn the land into an utter desolation because of all the abominations they have committed.

[30]Now you, man: Your fellow countrymen who converse about you by the walls and in the entrances to houses—one speaks with the other, each with his fellow, saying, "Come now and hear what word issues from YHWH!" [31]They come to you in throngs and sit before you, my people, and they hear your words—but they don't do them. For erotic talk with their mouths [b]they do;[b] their hearts pursue their advantage. [32]To them you are like a singer of erotic songs, whose voice is melodious and who makes sweet music; they hear your words but do them they don't. [33]But when it comes—and it is coming!—they shall know that a prophet had been in their midst.

[a–a] G "to the animals of the field they shall be given for food"; S "(as) food for the animals I shall give them."
[b–b] Not in G S.

COMMENT

33:24. *these inhabitants of ruins on the soil of Israel.* Taking *'lh* "these" to refer to the whole construct phrase, not to the immediately preceding "ruins" as, e.g., *'my ht'bwt h'lh* "these peoples of abominable practices," Ezra 9:14. The demonstrative expresses contempt, as when Joseph's brothers call him *b'l hḥlmwt hlzh* "this dreamer (lit. 'master of dreams')," Gen 37:19. There is a grotesque incongruity between the claim and the claimants.

"Inhabitants of ruins" evidently refers to the survivors who lived in the Judahite towns ravaged by the Babylonians. In the aftermath of the war, people who fled into the open country straggled back to resettle abandoned sites (cf. Jer 40:7–12: the governor appointed by the conqueror bids the squatters to "settle in your towns that you have seized," vs. 10). The situation in this oracle is that some have returned while others still lived scattered about the countryside (see B. Oded in J. H. Hayes and J. M. Miller, eds., *Israelite and Judaean History* [London: SCM Press, 1977], pp. 475–79).

As in 12:22 and 18:2 the prophet is aware of a saying current in the homeland. Two-way communication between it and the exiles is attested in Jer 29:1, 25, 30f.

Abraham was only one man. The saying is based on a tradition represented in Gen 15, in which Abraham, still childless, is promised innumerable progeny and possession of the land—a promise sealed by a covenant ceremony. The surviving homelanders propound an *a fortiori* argument in quasi-syllogistic form: if one man is enough to establish title to a land, and they are "many" (relatively, for even two is twice as much as one), how much more secure is their title! For a conjecture as to the issue, see Structure and Themes.

25. *You eat over blood* ('l hdm). Not "eat the blood," as is usually translated. Lev 19:26 associates "eating over blood" with banned forms of divination. By way of explanation, Maimonides, *Guide of the Perplexed*, III, p. 26, cited the practice of the Sabians—a North Mesopotamian sect perpetuating ancient pagan elements into the Islamic age—of a communion meal in which humans ate meat whose blood was poured on the ground to attract the jinns, who fraternized with them and gave them knowledge of the future. Homer, *Odyssey* 11.24ff., describes in detail the raising of the shades for divination by pouring sacrificial blood into a pit. Abundant evidence exists for similar practices all over the ancient Near East; cf. H. M. Hoffner, "Second Millennium Antecedents to the Hebrew *'ÔB*," *JBL* 86 (1967), 385–401; Y. M. Grintz, "Don't Eat on the Blood," *Annual of the Swedish Theological Institute* 8 (1970–71), 78–105.

The following expression, "looked for help to your idols," appears in 18:6, 15, where it is preceded by "eat on the mountains" (*'l hhrym*). Since the latter is peculiar to Ezekiel (it recurs in 18:11; 22:9), perhaps it stood originally here as well. The present reading ("eat over blood"), though attested in all ancient versions, will then be a secondary assimilation to the more familiar (and graphically similar) expression, which beside Lev 19:26 appears also in I Sam 14:32–34.

look for help to your idols. An offense that defines the wicked in 18:12b.

shed blood. For which Jerusalem is indicted in 22:3 and throughout that oracle.

26. *You live by your swords.* A conjectural rendering that takes *ʿmd* in the sense "exist, last, be sustained" (e.g., "so that they may last [*yʿmdw*] a long time," Jer 32:14), with *ʿl* "by, on (the basis of)"; cf. Mishnaic Hebrew "By (*ʿl*) three things is the world sustained (*ʿwmd*)," "*m. ʾAbot* 1.2. It is equivalent to *ḥyh ʿl* "live by/on" as in Gen 27:40, "and you shall live by your sword." Lev 19:16 will accordingly mean, "Do not live by/on (*tʿmd ʿl*) the blood of your fellow," i.e., do not profit from his misfortune (cf. NJPS, following Ehrlich, on Lev 19:16; Ehrlich on this passage is otherwise). The substance of this charge is the same as the previous one, shedding blood.

you commit abominations. Although in Ezekiel this epithet usually attaches to idolatry (e.g., 8:6, 9, etc.; see comment to 5:9 [I, 113]), in 22:11 it denotes sexual immorality (as in the Holiness Code, e.g., Lev 18:26–30). Since the terms of our clause are obviously related to those of 22:11, it is plausible to take them in a sexual sense (Rashi specifies sodomy, to which the epithet is applied in Lev 18:22; 20:13). The anomalous feminine afformative on the verb (*ʿśy-tn;* Kimḥi[2]: it implicates females) may be a scribal error induced by the Aramaic masculine ending *-twn.*

each of you has defiled . . . Cf. 22:11.

27. *in the ruins* (bḥrbwt) . . . *by the sword* (bḥrb). Assonance underlines the appropriateness of the instrument of punishment: where there is a human habitation there is a sword.

in open country (bśdh) . . . *beasts.* Jer 40:7 tells of a post-war dispersal of soldiery "in the open country"; such survivors will be dispatched by animals who roam the wilds—*ḥyt hśdh* "wild beasts" (lit. "beasts of the field"; e.g., 31:13; 34:5, 8)—as G actually reads here, underlining again the appropriateness of the agent.

This middle clause of the triad of punishments differs grammatically from its neighbors in two ways: (1) God is its subject, and (2) the condemned is the object in the singular, whereas in the adjacent clauses the condemned is a plural subject. The change is reinforced by the singular object suffix on the infinitive (*lʾklw* "to eat him"), instead of the unsuffixed, substantive form (*lʾklh* "for eating/food") usual in this idiom (e.g., 29:5; 35:12), and read here by a few Hebrew mss. G and S more or less assimilate this clause to its neighbors and to the usual idiom (see text note), thus obliterating a characteristic feature of Ezekiel's style: variety in repetition.

in fastnesses and caves . . . plague. Caves and fastnesses (*m*ᵉ*ṣadot*) are mentioned as refuges in Judg 6:2; Arabic *maṣ(a)d* "mountaintop" associates well with the Hebrew word, which connotes inaccessibility (|| cliffs [*slʿym;* Isa 33:16]; located in the wilderness [I Sam 23:14]); see KB[3], **mṣd.* What is proof against man and beast succumbs to plague.

28. The threat in this verse accords with the utter desolation of Judah depicted in Jer 33:10–13. On "utter desolation/waste," see comment at 6:4 (I, 136f.); on "pride of strength," at 24:21; 30:18.

30. *who converse about you.* Lit. "who speak with each other (root **dbr,* nifʿal in reciprocal sense) about you (*bk*)." The expression appears again only in Ps 119:23 in a hostile sense: "Nobles sit, they speak against me." From Ezek 36:3 it appears that to be the topic of conversation was as a rule undesirable (since most

talk about people is gossip?). Is there a hint here of the hollowness of their interest in the prophet's message?

by the walls and in the entrances to houses. When outside (*bḥwṣ* "in the outside"); we should say, "in the street," but the Hebrew word does not connote a clearly bound strip set aside for traffic. People might stop to chat out of traffic's way by the house walls that bounded the lanes between them—the middle of the lane was for traffic—or in the entrances.

one speaks with the other. Having stated in vs. 30a the elaborately qualified subject ("Your fellow countrymen who converse, etc.") as a *casus pendens,* the verse continues with a resumption, in reverse order, of verb and subject: lit. "speaks one with the other."

It is uncommon for the verb in such a reciprocal expression to be in the singular, but it occurs: Isa 6:3 (*wqr' zh 'l zh w'mr* "one called to the other and said"); Jer 46:15 (*npl 'yš 'l rʿhw* "each fell over his fellow"). *ḥd* "one" is a clipped form (so in Aramaic; cf. Heb. *nḥnw* "we," clipped from *'nḥnw*), and the following *'aḥad* "the other" is a construct form (instead of the expected context form *'eḥad*). The phrase does not appear in G, which represents only the following common phrase "each with his fellow." The unique phrase, with its anomalies, is likely to be original (a vernacular idiom?).

what word issues from YHWH! Is this spoken by the people sarcastically or with a pretended reverence that is belied by their subsequent conduct?

31. *in throngs.* Lit. "as the coming of a people" (for the abstract *mbw'*, cf. *mbw'y* 26:10 and comment thereto); meaning doubtful. I follow Eliezer, NJPS ("in crowds"), *NEB* ("crowding"); T "as disciples" is influenced by the following:

and sit before you. "At your feet," as we should say (Kara: "deferentially, like disciples before their master"); so it is said of the elders who came to the prophet seeking an oracle, 14:1; 20:1.

my people. Apparently ironical: acting as though they were devoted to me.

erotic talk. Allen's happy phrase. *ʿgbym* "lust" (plural of emotional state, like *'hbym, dwdym* "love"; *rḥmym* "compassion"; König III, § 262) is a cognate of the verb *ʿagab* "lust (after)" recurrent in the diatribe of ch. 23 (from vs. 5 on). Verbal expression of lust is indicated by the adverb *bpyhm* "in/with their mouths" (Allen with most moderns: "on their lips"). G S translate "a lie" (whence *NAB* "lies"), T "scoffing," *NRSV* "flattery" (Ehrlich)—all evidently guessing, since they all translate *ʿgbym* in the next verse differently. The precise meaning of the clause (vs. 31b$^{\alpha}$) is not clear. NJPS admitting uncertainty renders: "they produce nothing but lust with their mouths."

An alternative line of interpretation accuses the audience not only of ignoring the call to act but of using the prophet's very words for bawdy talk. The first stage of this interpretation appears in Symmachus, who rendered *ʿgbym bpyhm* "a song in their mouth," connecting *ʿgbym* with *ʿwgb* "flute," which G translates "song" in Job 21:12; 30:31. V incorporated this in its rendering of the clause: "they turn them [viz., your words] into a song of their mouth." *ʿgbym* is construed as the second object of *ʿśym* "they make," the first object being an implied "them" (carrying over *'wtm* of the previous clause). The same construction appears in Moshe ben Sheshet[2]: "in their mouths they make the words of God

(= the prophet's words) love [talk]"; i.e., the prophet's words are put to profane, lustful use (it is not difficult to imagine the bawdy nuggets that can be mined in chs. 16 or 23 of our book). If this interpretation is correct, the offense anticipates the later scandal of the profane use of the Song of Songs: "[Rabbi Akiba taught:] Whoever sings the Song of Songs in a tremulous voice at a wedding feast and turns it into a [love] ditty (*'wśh 'wtw kmyn zmr*) has no portion in the World to Come" (*t. Sanhedrin* 12.10).

their hearts pursue their advantage. The context suggests that *bṣ'*, "gain, profit" (often ill-gotten), has a wider sense here—material advantages inclusively (cf. Isa 56:11). G renders "pollutions," by a term used for both sexual (Judith 9:2) and ritual (I Macc 13:50) defilements.

Whatever the precise meaning of *'gbym* and *bṣ'm* may be, the general purport of vs. 31b is to explain why the audience is not moved to do what the prophet requires of them: because (*ky*) their mouths and minds ("hearts") are devoted to mundane values (sex and wealth/power?). Mouth and mind are the movers of obedience to God's word: "Let these words that I command you this day be on your hearts . . . speak of / recite them when you stay at home and when you are abroad, etc." (Deut 6:7). The key terms in our passage appear in Deut 30:14: "For the word is very close (= readily accessible) to you; it is in your mouth and in your heart (= you need only your mouth and heart) to do it." To bring this point out is the aim of the awkward "they do" in vs. 31b$^{\beta}$: they don't do your words because they do X with their mouths, and their hearts do Y. The phrase is not in G or S; it is probably a secondary annotation to underscore the contrast.

32. *like a singer of erotic songs.* Lit. "like an erotic song"; the song stands for the singer, as also in Ben Sira 50:18: "Then the song gave forth its voice." To them the prophet is like a popular entertainer: they flock to hear his piquant performances but do not take him seriously.

who makes sweet music. Accompanying himself on an instrument; cf. Isa 23:16: "Take a lyre, go about the town, / Forgotten harlot; / Make sweet music, sing many songs, / That you may be remembered." It is not clear in the Hebrew whether the appositional phrases (in translation, the relative clauses) refer to the prophet—who then delivered his oracles to music that he played—or to the bawdy singer to which he is compared.

But when it comes. The predicted doom, = 24:24; *and it is coming!* = 7:9, 10, etc.; *they shall know that a prophet had been in their midst* = 2:5.

STRUCTURE AND THEMES

The revelation-event formula (vs. 23) opens a unit containing two disparate addresses to the prophet (A, B): each has an opening formula ("[Now you,] man", vss. 24, 30), and each ends with a recognition formula ("they shall know . . ." vss. 29, 33). There is no obvious connection with the preceding dated autobiographical notice.

A (vss. 23–29): a refutation, pervaded by triads, of the surviving homelanders' claim to the land.

A1 (vs. 24): God cites their claim, then—

A2, indignantly rejects it on grounds of their wickedness ("So say to them . . . ," vss. 25–26, each consisting of a threefold indictment + rhetorical question), and concludes with—

A3, an oath to extirpate them ("Thus shall you say to them . . . ," vs. 27) and to lay the land waste (vs. 28), each object of wrath treated again in three clauses. The oath thus does away with the elements of the claim—the survivors and the land.

Each of these divisions has a design of its own. A1 is an argument in the form of a quasi-syllogism (see comment on vs. 24). A2 interweaves the two triadic indictments thus:

vs. 25, two pagan practices + bloodshed
vs. 26, sword (murder) + two sex crimes

A3 has a syntactic variation in its middle clause (contra-monotony) and a precise logic in its fit of location and punitive agent.

As in the previous oracle, the theme is set by a popular saying that touches a theological nerve. Word has reached Ezekiel of the homelanders' claim to possess the land. We have heard that claim before: in 11:14–15 the prophet retorted to their smug assertion that the exiles were alienated from God, hence had forfeited their stake in God's land, which now devolved upon those left in it (see I, 203f.). Here the homelanders' claim is not against the exiles, and, agreeably, the retort does not assert the rights of the exiles (as 11:16f. does). What then is the issue?

The saying seems to rebuff a claim by a third party that the territory of the former kingdom of Israel, now emptied of the bulk of Israelites, is no longer Israelite. A nation's title to a land is vacated, so the claimant contends, when the population of that nation has vacated the land. The interested parties to this argument were Judah's neighbors, who are pictured in 36:2f. as gathering around the stricken country and exulting: "Aha! the ancient highlands are ours as a possession!" Ezekiel explicitly denounces the Edomites for asserting that the mountains of Israel, now desolate, were given to them "to devour" (35:12), and for saying: "The two nations and the two lands will be mine and we shall possess them" (vs. 10).

We have very few data concerning the extent of the depopulation of Judah after the fall of Jerusalem. II Kings 25:11f. speaks generally of a mass deportation of the inhabitants of Jerusalem and of a poor remnant left to eke out a living in the land as farmers. "It is known that no new settlers were brought to replace the exiled, or the thousands who no doubt were killed or escaped to neighboring lands" (M. Cogan and H. Tadmor, *II Kings*, AB, p. 324; cf. p. 327). To these meager facts we may add the testimony of our oracle.

The saying of the homelanders justifies their continuing claim to title of their land. It could carry no weight outside their community, but offered a measure of moral support within it. If the single "Israelite," Abraham, could obtain possession of (title to) the land, nothing but the extirpation of every last Judahite homelander could uproot that title. This argument bespeaks a miserable few clinging desperately to their heritage in the face of encroachers on all sides.

The pathetic reasoning outraged the prophet: as if the essential point of the Abraham tradition was his singleness and not his virtue! Ezekiel mocks the pretenders by arraying their depravity against their claim. Repeating parts of the indictment of Jerusalem in ch. 22, he epitomizes the unrepentants' conduct in three cardinal sins: idolatry, bloodshed, and sexual crimes. (The later Talmudic sages adopted this triad as the cause of the destruction of the First Temple, *t. Menaḥot* 13.22). He ends by assuring them that even on their own terms they will lose their title. They have survived so far, but in store is a final reckoning which will pursue them from the ruined towns, to the open country and into the mountain refuges. Not even one will be left to traverse the mountains of Israel. This oracle, then, implicitly addresses the apprehension of the exiles—presumably the immediate audience of the prophet—that their stake in their land would be contested by bands of unrepentant squatters.

Ezekiel's suppression of the traditions on the patriarchal origins of Israel's relation to God (see I, 300), which he shares with pre-exilic prophets, can now be better understood.

> In the patriarchal tradition the prophets could find no object lesson for their purpose. That tradition recorded only an act of grace. No special responsibilities were placed upon the Patriarchs or their descendants. It was the sort of tradition which the populace could use for its own purposes to stress God's unfailing fidelity regardless of their own sinfulness. (Simon Greenberg, "The Relation between God and Israel in the Bible" [Ph.D diss., Dropsie College, Philadelphia, 1933], ch. 9, pp. 13–14)

On the distinction between the Abrahamic and other covenants, see G. E. Mendenhall, *IDB*, s.v. "Covenant," I, pp. 717–18.

The survivors' reliance on the solitariness of Abraham for solace, while negated by Ezekiel, had a remarkable positive echo in the prophecy of his exilic successor. The Second Isaiah, no more than a couple of decades afterward, encouraged his audience (in the name of God) precisely by holding up Abraham to them. Here is the passage with some bracketed glosses of Ibn Ezra:

> Listen to me, you pursuers of justice, seekers of YHWH:
> Look back to the rock you were hewn from [that is, Abraham],
> To the mine from which you were extracted [that is, Sarah].
> Look back to Abraham your father,
> And to Sarah, who gave birth to you.
> For he was only one when I called him
> But I blessed him and made him many.
> Surely God will comfort Zion;
> He will comfort all her ruins [through the many children who
> will inhabit her]. (Isa 51:1–3)

The exiles, disheartened by their fewness, are reassured by the case of Abraham: solitary when summoned by God, by God's blessing he became a numerous nation. So God is perfectly capable of turning the dwindled remnant of the Judahites into a multitude.

Skinner (p. 292) would see the saying of the survivors as a travesty on this argument, but the difference between the local and moral circumstances of the two does not favor a direct relation. Abraham appears to have exercised a fascination upon the battered remnants of the national collapse in the homeland and in Babylonia. The solitary progenitor of Israel and grantee of its land served the masses as a guarantor of continued divine favor. But where the masses typically ignored the moral aspect of Abraham, the prophets regarded it as the very basis on which the unconditional grant was made. (Theirs was the truer concept of the divine grant, modeled as it was on the royal grant to faithful servants; see M. Weinfeld, "The Covenant of Grant in the Old Testament and in the Ancient Near East," *JAOS* 90 [1970], 184–203.)

Ezekiel disdained the unrepentant homelanders who arrogated to themselves the title of Abraham's heirs. Second Isaiah encouraged "pursuers of justice, seekers of YHWH" among the exiles—true heirs of that Abraham who had been singled out by God to charge his household to follow the way of YHWH by doing what is right and just (Gen 18:19). Ezekiel denied the former the right to the land that they claimed as Abrahamites in the flesh; Second Isaiah assured the latter that as Abrahamites in character as well as in the flesh they would be sufficiently numerous to sustain the blessings of restoration.

Part B (vss. 30–33) contrasts the success of the prophet at drawing crowds with his failure to convert them. At the start of Ezekiel's mission God had steeled him against failure by giving him notice that "the house of Israel will not listen to you for they will not listen to me" (3:7). This had never been true of the leaders ("elders") of the exiles who repeatedly came and "sat before him" (8:1; 14:1; 20:1). By the time of this revelation—a private one not meant for the public—his audience comprised throngs of ordinary people, eager to hear the latest word from God. But now a new cause of frustration emerged: the prophet's failure to persuade his audience to do what God's word required of them.

Like A, the point of departure of B is a saying of the people (*'m* "people" occurs three times in vss. 30f.): "Come now and hear what word issues from YHWH!" The key terms are forms of *bw'*, *šm'*, and *dbr*, and they recur in the continuation telling how the people carry their resolve out to the letter: they come to Ezekiel, and they hear his words. Then comes the wry pivot: "but they don't do them." The organs of obedience, their mouths and hearts, are otherwise occupied; what draws them to hear the prophet is his entertainment value. The pivot sentence is repeated, with closural inversion of the last clause: "but do them they don't." The section closes with a play on the opening words of the people, *bw'w n'* "come now": "But when it comes (*wBB'h*)—and it is coming (*hNh B'h*)!—they shall know that a prophet (*NBy'*) had been in their midst." God assures Ezekiel that coming events will show the people how wrong they were to have treated him as street theater (for the expression, see B. Lang, "Street Theater, Raising the Dead, and the Zoroastrian Connection in Ezekiel's Prophecy," in J. Lust, ed., *Ezekiel and his Book,* Bibliotheca Ephemeridum Theologicarum Lovaniensium 74 [Leuven: Peeters, 1986], 298–307).

The situation of this passage is not immediately clear. That the audience addressed is the exiles is established by their being neighbors of the prophet who congregate at his residence. From the contrast between the eagerness of the audience to hear God's word and their refusal to act on it we must posit a prophetic message that was at once soothing and demanding. The people latched on to the soothing component—a promise of well-being—and ignored the demand, for which they would soon be punished. All this is fairly explicit in these verses. The specifics of the message and its circumstances are at issue.

Moderns who have addressed the issue (not all have) generally identify the soothing component with the prophecies of restoration that set in with the next chapter. After the fall of Jerusalem "the situation for the prophet seems to be much more open . . . Here the word about the new life which Yahweh plans to establish (e.g., 37:1–14) could be proclaimed much more directly" (Zimmerli). "The singular figure of the singer of love-songs is best explained if the weal-proclamation of the prophet is presupposed. Thus this small piece, set in this location of the book, looks ahead to the following chapters" (Herrmann). "Hitherto the crisis has brought judgment: now it leads to restoration"; what "is coming" is "the glorious prospect that is opening before [the exiles] in chs. 34ff." (Cooke). "It is not the messenger of God whose word confronts his audience with the choice between life and death whom they rush to hear, but the master of words, who has done with his grim preaching of judgment and now speaks of all sorts of attractive possibilities of a new life, and of a hitherto unimagined national future . . ." (Eichrodt).

What of the component of demand? "The weal-proclamation of the prophet has a terribly serious undertone . . . [namely] the announcement of the still outstanding purgative judgment" (Herrmann). Is that tantamount to a demand for action?

Since we have no guarantee that our record contains every oracle of Ezekiel, we cannot be certain that this view is in principle wrong. Perhaps the popularity of the prophet was generated by conditional prophecies of restoration (with "undertones of purgative judgments"). What we can say with certainty is that no such have been preserved in chs. 34ff. A prominent feature of Ezekiel's visions of the future is their unconditionality. In that, they resemble the dooms hurled against Jerusalem and the nations: as repentance is not held out as a means to avert the dooms, so it is not made a condition of Israel's restoration. No extant prophecy of restoration contains a component of demand, so that one might embrace the consolatory message and ignore the demand that something must be done for it to be realized.

The only prophecies containing both components are the disquisitions on retribution and repentance in 18:21–32 and 33:1–20. The latter formulation adds emphasis to the good news proclaimed in the former that God does not desire to punish the wicked but to see him repent and live. The soothing effect on the desperate community that felt itself wasting away under the weight of its sin can only be imagined. But after the fall of Jerusalem it would be no wonder if this message of God's merciful readiness to forgive repentant sinners was received enthusiastically and the messenger rewarded with popularity. Nor is there reason to suppose that he did not repeat the good message time and again to grateful ears. That there was a demand to be met in order to merit forgiveness, people then (as ever) chose to ignore.

Can we identify the threat expressed by "it is coming"? We can, and it appears in the very same disquisitions.

The impassioned oath of God that he desires not the death of the wicked but his reformed life (33:11; cf. 18:31f.) concludes with a sanction toned down as a rhetorical question: "Why should you die O house of Israel?" The execution of this sanction fits the veiled admonition at the end of our passage "it is coming!" In this connection we recall the depiction in 20:35ff. of a grand sifting of the exiles at the time of the redemption, to purge them of irredeemable transgressors. That singular concept (but see, too, 13:9) accords with the death sentence on the impenitent.

It emerges that the catastrophic judgment of Jerusalem did not immediately generate in Ezekiel a new vision of God's government of Israel. All the elements of ch. 33 show the same principles operating as before: in the exilic community, the possibility of repentance giving hope for a future, but joined to a threat of doom if not acted upon (vss. 1–20; the background of vss. 30–33); in the ravaged homeland, an additional purge of incorrigible survivors (vss. 23–29). The momentum of pre-fall doctrine is visible in the adherence to the principle of retribution, grounded on human responsibility. In the next oracle, however, the first of the prophecies of restoration, a new concern for the injured majesty of God has overridden that principle and its ground as governing the actions of God toward Israel. Ch. 33 is the last gasp of Ezekiel's pre-fall theology.

XLI. Shepherds Bad and Good
(34:1–31)

34 [1]The word of YHWH came to me: [2]Man, prophesy against the shepherds of
Israel, prophesy and say [a]to them: To the shepherds[a] — thus said Lord YHWH:
Woe to the shepherds of Israel, [b]who have been tending them[b]! Surely it is the
flock the shepherds should tend! [3]The fat[c] you ate, and the wool you wore; the
fat one you slaughtered. The flock you did not tend.
[4]The weak you did not strengthen, and the sick you did not heal, and the fractured you did not bandage, and the stray you did not recover, and the lost you
did not seek, and [d]with force you ruled over them and[d] with rigor.
[5]So they scattered, for lack of a shepherd, and became food for every wild
beast. So they scattered, [6]/[e]went astray, [e]/ my flock, in all the mountains and on
every high hill. Over the whole face of the earth my flock scattered, and no one
cared for them and no one searched for them.
[7]Now then, shepherds, hear the word of YHWH: [8]By my life! declares Lord
YHWH, surely because my flock became spoil — my flock became food for every
wild beast for want of a shepherd, and my shepherds did not care for my flock,
but the shepherds tended themselves, and my flock they did not tend — [9]Now
then, shepherds, hear the word of YHWH! [10]Thus said Lord YHWH: I am coming at the shepherds and I will hold them to account for my flock. I will put an
end to their flock-tending, and the shepherds shall no longer tend themselves; I
will rescue my sheep from their mouths, so they shall not become their food.
[11]Yes, thus said Lord YHWH: I am coming to care for my flock and take stock
of them. [12]As a shepherd takes stock of his herd on a day when he is among his
dispersed flock, so will I take stock of my flock and rescue them from all the
places to which they scattered on a day of cloud and gloom. [13]I will take them
out of the peoples and gather them from the lands and bring them to their soil.
And I will pasture them on the mountains of Israel, in the gullies and in all the
settlements of the land. [14]I will pasture them in good pasture, and their grazing
ground shall be on the high mountains of Israel. There they shall lie down in

[a–a] G "to the shepherds"; S "to them, 'Shepherds . . .'"
[b–b] G "do shepherds tend themselves?" (as from *hyr'w* for MT *'šr hyw*).
[c] G V "milk" (vocalizing *ḥalab* for MT *ḥeleb*).
[d–d] G "the strong (reading *baḥ[a]zaqa*) you subjugated."
[e–e] Not in G (S translates it, but lacks previous verb).

good grazing land; they shall feed on rich pasture, on the mountains of Israel. [15]It is I who shall pasture my flock and I who shall make them lie down, declares Lord YHWH. [16]The lost I will seek, and the stray I will recover, and the fractured I will bandage, and the sick I will strengthen; [f]and the stout[f] and the strong I will destroy.[g] I will pasture them justly.

[17]As for you, my flock, thus said Lord YHWH: I am going to judge between animal and animal.

To the rams and to the he-goats: [18]Is it not enough for you that you feed on the best pasture, but you must trample with your feet the rest of your pasture; or that you drink limpid water, but you must muddy the remainder with your feet, [19]so that my flock feed on what your feet have trampled, and drink what your feet have muddied?

[20]Now then, thus said Lord YHWH to them: I am coming to judge between fat animals and lean animals. [21]Because you pushed with flank and shoulder, and butted with your horns all the weak ones, until you scattered them abroad, [22]I will save my flock so that they become spoil no more; I will judge between animal and animal.

[23]Then I will set over them a single shepherd, who shall tend them — my servant David. He shall tend them and he shall be their shepherd, [24]and I, YHWH, will be their God, and my servant David, a chief in their midst; I YHWH have spoken.

[25]I will make a covenant of well-being for them,[h] and I will make an end of harmful animals in the land, so that they may dwell secure in the wilderness and sleep in the forests. [26][i]I will make them and the environs of my hill a blessing.[i] I will cause the rain to fall in its season — rains of blessing they shall be. [27]The tree of the field shall yield its fruit and the land shall yield its produce. Thus they shall be secure on their soil, and they shall know that I am YHWH, when I break the bars of their yoke and rescue them from the hands of those who enslave them. [28]They shall no more be spoil for the nations, and the beasts of the land shall not eat them, but they shall dwell in security, with none to disturb [them]. [29]I will establish for them [j]a planting of renown,[j] so that they shall no more be carried off by famine in the land, and no more bear the taunts of the nations. [30]They shall know that I, YHWH their God, am [k]with them,[k] and they are my people, the house of Israel, declares Lord YHWH. [31] [f]And you,[f] my flock, the flock of my pasturage, you are human[f] — I[l] am your God, declares Lord YHWH.

COMMENT

34:2. *the shepherds of Israel.* The political leaders responsible for the disaster that befell Israel. The captive kings Jehoiachin and Zedekiah, along with their advi-

[f–f]Not in G.
[g]G "guard" (as from *ʾšmr*).
[h]G "David."
[i–i]G "I will set them around my hill"; S "I will give them my blessing around my hill."
[j–j]G S "a plant of peace" (as from *šlm* for MT *lšm*).
[k–k]Not in G S.
[l]G S "and I."

sors and officials, all in disgrace, are the putative audience (see Structure and Themes). For the exiled community—the real audience—the message is that this discredited leadership will be replaced by God.

and say to [ʾl-] *them: To* [l-] *the shepherds.* T "to them, to the leaders" treats the second, prepositional noun phrase as in apposition to the foregoing preposition (*ʾlyhm*). While this construction occurs in Biblical Hebrew (it is common in Aramaic), the rule is that the two prepositions are identical; e.g., *lhm lbny yśrʾl* "to them, to the Israelites (Josh 1:2); *ʾlyhn ʾl dltwt hhykl* "on them, on the doors of the shrine" (Ezek 41:25; GKC, § 131 n; Joüon-Muraoka, § 140 e). The variation in prepositions here speaks against T.

At first sight these phrases seem to be variants: the first on the pattern of 37:4 ("[prophesy to XX] and say to [*ʾl-*] them"), the second on the pattern of 13:2 or 21:2b–3a ("[prophesy to Y] and say to [*l-*] Y′). The absence of the first phrase in G suggests that MT is conflate, incorporating both variants. However, Ehrlich connected *lrʿym* with the syntactically difficult *lʾylym wlʿtwdym* of vs. 17, vacillating between construing *l-* as "concerning" (in *Randglossen*) and as "to" [Hebrew]. In either case, the usage is after Jeremiah, who introduces or entitles prophecies with such rubrics (Jer 23:9; 46:2, etc.). NJPS follows Ehrlich and I follow NJPS, noting the many connections of this chapter with Jeremiah—on which see Structure and Themes.

S renders the noun phrase "[O] shepherds," which probably is a free rendering of our difficult text rather than a trace of a supposed vocative *lamed* in Biblical Hebrew (proposed here by G. R. Driver [1954]; implanted by Dahood throughout Psalms [*Psalms III*, AB, pp. 407–8], and throughout Ezekiel by Van Dyke, *Tyre*, p. 29 [following Penar]). Driver and Allen lean on S here, and find the same vocative *lamed* in vs. 17 (*lʾylym* . . .), but S renders it there "between." KB^3 and Joüon-Muraoka do not recognize "vocative *lamed*"; *BHSyn* allows its possibility (p. 211).

Woe to the shepherds. So, e.g., T, V, OJPS, *NAB*; for this rendering, see comment to 13:3 (I, 235). Others (e.g., G, S, *RSV*, NJPS) see a vocative here: "Ah, [you] shepherds," with the following relative clause couched in the third person ("who were [*hyw*] tending them[selves?]") as is the rule with vocatives—e.g., 21:30; Isa 54:1; and with *hwy*, Isa 5:8 (*BHSyn*, p. 77 [4.7d]; D. R. Hillers, "*Hôy* and *Hôy*-Oracles: A Neglected Syntactic Aspect," in C. L. Meyers et al., *The Word of the Lord Shall Go Forth* [Festschrift D. N. Freedman] [Winona Lake: Eisenbrauns, 1983], pp. 185–88).

who have been tending them. I.e., who have till now been leading them and are therefore responsible for their fate. Repetition with morphological alteration—here a nominal expression (shepherds of Israel) is transformed into a verbal one—challenges the interpreter to find the semantic increment; cf. vss. 10 and 23 below. Kara took the clause ironically: "who were to have tended them but did not." G "do shepherds tend themselves?" anticipates vs. 8b, where the reflexive use of the object pronoun *ʾwtm* (as in Exod 5:19; Lev 22:16) is manifest. Although G, T, and all moderns render the object pronoun reflexively ("who were tending themselves/yourselves"), that is not the natural first reading of the word, but a retrospective reading in the light of the sequel. The reflexive possibility comes into view only after the following clause.

Surely it is the flock the shepherds should tend! Supply: and not themselves (Rashi). "Flock" renders *ṣ'n,* a feminine collective noun denoting small cattle (German *Kleinvieh*)—sheep and goats. The object "flock" precedes the verb for emphasis, suggesting that it contrasts with the preceding object pronoun, which will then retrospectively be interpreted not as "(tending) them" (the flock) but "themselves" (the shepherds). For the affirmative force of *hlw'* —as in Jer 38:15 ("surely you will put me to death!")—see GKC, § 150 e; *BHSyn,* p. 684 n. 48. That *r'h* (= "graze" in its transitive and intransitive senses, as well as "tend") has the sense "tend" here is shown by the answering negative clause at the end of vs. 3: "the flock you did not tend."

The retrospectively reflexive "tending themselves" momentarily makes our clause appear ambiguous: the syntactic-semantic parallelism of "the flock they tend/graze" (*hṣ'n yr'w*) with the following clauses (vs. 3), "the fat you eat" (*'t hḥlb t'klw*), etc., reflects on our clause the sense: "it is on the flock that the shepherds graze (feed)!"—the sense of *r'h* in vss. 14b, 19a. The ambiguity is resolved at the end of vs. 3 but is awakened again in vs. 10.

Kara exploits the absence of the object-marker *'t* before "the flock" to construe it as the subject of the verb, rendering: "Surely the flock has tended (= fed) the shepherds"; vs. 3 will then particularize this reversal. Since Ezekiel treats "flock" (*ṣ'n*) as plural feminine (e.g., *tr'ynh,* vss. 14, 19), and he does not use the plural masculine (*yr'w*) for the plural feminine (Levi, *Inkongruenz,* pp. 155–60; but cf. *yšgw* in vs. 6), this interpretation requires us to assume that the male referent of the flock, "the Israelites," determined the masculine verbal form (as it determined the masculine plural pronoun suffixes referring to "flock" in vss. 11–15).

3. The verse states three things the shepherds have done and a fourth that they have not. They have taken all the perquisites attached to their job—and more—without doing their job. Since these perquisites are all products of the flock, they stand accused of exploiting it rather than caring for it. How far have they exceeded their rights? Clearly they had no right to slaughter (*zbḥ* for food, I Sam 28:24) the fat (T S: fattened) animals: cf. Gen 31:38: "the rams of your flock I did not eat." The status of wool is unclear; later Jewish law (*t. Baba Qama* 11.9; see Saul Lieberman, *Tosefta Ki-fshuṭah,* ad loc.) allowed shepherds only an obscure type of raw wool; shearings and pluckings were not theirs to sell (but were they theirs to use for themselves?). The fat (*ḥeleb*) was considered a delicacy, to judge from its occasional metaphoric sense "best, choice part," as in Gen 45:18: "the best (*ṭwb*) of the land of Egypt" is called "the fat (*ḥeleb*) of the land." In the sacrifice of well-being (*šlmym*), though the meat was eaten by the offerers, the fat (*ḥeleb*) was reserved for God; in consequence, all fat was banned for human consumption (Lev 3:17; 7:23). Are the shepherds blamed for transgressing this ban? T "the best" and S "the fat one" appear to avoid the plain sense so as to obviate the cultic offense (it is indeed irrelevant). But on any reading the difficulty is that this first item in effect duplicates the third: for to eat the fat or the best/fat animal is hardly other than to "slaughter the fat one." On this ground all moderns prefer G V "milk" (*ḥalab*), which I Cor 9:7 indicates was a perquisite

of a shepherd: "Who shepherds a flock and does not eat (*sic*) of the milk of the flock?" The pairing of milk and wool occurs in the Mishnah: these mustn't be bought from a shepherd because he may have misappropriated them (*m. Baba Qamma* 10.9). On the other hand, "milk and cheese" may be bought from a shepherd "in the wilderness (*mdbr*)," because when away from civilization he has the right to use these products of the flock, since the owner has no expectation that they will last unspoiled till the shepherd comes home with the flock (*t. Baba Qamma* 11.9; see G. Dalman, *Arbeit und Sitte in Palästina*, VI, pp. 236–37, 307).

The use of *'akal* "eat" with "milk" (in 25:4: "drink") is remarkable, and doubtless contributed to the vocalization of the graph *ḥlb* as "fat." "Eat milk" in the Greek of I Cor 9:7 and an Aramaic locution cited in the Talmud, *ta'i d'okliyk ḥalba* "come (fem.), that I may feed you milk" (*b. 'Erubin* 53b; see J. Levy, *Wörterbuch über die Talmudim*, I, p. 74a), supports the emendation here and suggests that the reference to milk includes its thick and solid products (e.g., buttermilk, cheese — cf. *ḥryṣy hḥlb* "cuts of milk" = slices of cheese, I Sam 17:18).

In sum: the list of the shepherds' acts in vs. 3a starts with what is a recognized perquisite, continues with a doubtful appropriation, and ends with a gross violation of a shepherd's duty to care for his charges. The referent is the selfish conduct of Israel's leaders; they have fleeced their subjects.

the flock you did not tend. A closure that opens a series of omissions (duties not performed).

4. *The weak* (nḥlwt) . . . *the sick* (ḥwlh). The range of the nif'al and the qal of *ḥlh* is identical; here the specific sense in each case is determined by the accompanying verb. The identity is indicated by the appearance in vs. 16 of *ḥwlh* alone, accompanied by the verb found here with *nḥlwt*. In vs. 21 *nḥlwt* alone stands for the class of infirm and disabled animals. It may function so in our verse, too — hence it is in the plural — naming the class of which the next two terms ("sick," "fractured") are members.

you did not strengthen. Restore to healthy robustness; cf. vs. 16, where the object of "I will strengthen" is "the sick," and "the strong" is paired with "the stout." For a similar assortment of derivatives of *ḥzq*, see 30:21–25.

the stray. Lit. "one driven away"; cf. Rashi: "Driven abroad out of the herd," detecting an allusion to the scattering "abroad" of the weak animals by the strong described in vs. 21.

and with force you ruled over them and with rigor. "With force" describes the harsh oppression of a foreign ruler (Judg 4:3); "ruling over" an Israelite bondsman "with rigor" is forbidden by law (Lev 25:43, 46, 53, evoking the Egyptian bondage, Exod 1:13f.). For the separation of two coordinate words ("with force, with rigor"), cf. Deut 7:14: ". . . among you a barren male or female, or among your beasts" (also Gen 28:14; Exod 34:27). *rdh* "rule, have dominion over," though once used of man's subjugation of other creatures (Gen 1:26, 28), otherwise has a human object. Hence while its figurative meaning as used here is to bring animals harshly to heel (NJPS: "you have driven them with harsh rigor"), it evokes the referential meaning — the rulers' harsh oppression of their subjects. Intrusion of the referent is a common feature of Ezekiel's extended metaphors; here it accounts for the masculine object pronoun *'tm* (incongruent with the feminine collective "flock"). The clause, a general condemnation, breaks with the foregoing series of particular items, as befits a closure.

G has a notable variant: "and the strong (animal) you subjugated with toil," reflecting a *Vorlage: wbḥzqh rdytm bprk* ("and over the strong you ruled with rigor"). This effects a closure of the list of derelictions toward the needy by an abuse of the sturdy (a figure for extorting the wealthy). In its favor is the parallel in vs. 16, in which a corresponding list of God's caring acts is closed with a mention of "the strong (animal)."

MT originated, perhaps, through a dittography of the last two letters of the penultimate word: **rdytmtm* > *rdytm 'tm;* the slight adjustments entailed thereby resulted in MT. (With the verb *rdh* the preposition *b-* may introduce either an adverb [*bḥzqh* (-*ḥoz*-), *bprk*] with object marked by object pronoun ['*tm*] as in MT [cf. Lev 25:53], or both an adverb [*bprk*] and the object [*baḥ^{a}zaqa*], as in G's *Vorlage* [cf. Lev 25:46].)

5–6. Cf. the identical figure of a routed army in Micaiah's oracle in I Kings 22:17: "I saw all Israel scattered over the mountains like a flock that has no shepherd." Here the ruin of the leaderless flock is described in cumulative detail: their vulnerability to predators, their straying far from home pasture, but still in native land (mountains and hills; cf. vs. 14: "the high mountains of Israel"), and their eventual dispersion over the "whole face of (*kl pny*) the earth" (the idiom appears in Gen 2:6; 19:28; 41:56). The figure is more or less transparent: subjection to conquest and pillage, alien worship on hilltop shrines (6:13; 18:6; 20:28), dispersion in exile.

For these misfortunes Ezekiel holds the leaders of Israel responsible (see further, I, 322). The new note struck here is the portrayal of the people as innocent victims of bad government—a compassionate, forgiving note heightened by the variant reading that opens vs. 6.

6. */went astray/.* Missing in G but present in S (which lacks the preceding verb "scattered"), *yšgw* appears to be a secondary variant of the preceding verb *wtpwṣynh.* It is not in the imperfect consecutive as are the other verbs in its context; it is in the masculine plural, whereas elsewhere verbs whose subject is "flock" are in the feminine (Ezekiel distinguishes throughout between these forms, unlike later Hebrew; see Levi, cited in comment to vs. 2); its juxtaposition to "So they scattered" is awkward (and hardly mitigated by the Masoretic verse division). The effect of *yšgw* is to ambiguate the univocal "they scattered." *šgh* means "go astray" in a moral as well as a physical sense (Ps 119:10, 118, speaks of those who "stray (= deviate) from your commandments/laws"). It expresses perfectly the figurative as well as the referential meaning of vs. 6a: for lack of a leader to constrain them the flock strayed / the people practiced an erroneous worship on the mountains. Since *šgh* also means "err unwittingly," especially in cultic contexts (e.g., Lev 4:13; Num 15:22; Ezek 45:20), the interpolation of this verb underlines the tendency of the oracle to portray the people as more sinned against than sinning. Affection for the people is expressed also by the possessive suffix of—

my flock. Identifying them as God's precious own, and so to the end of the oracle (once more in vs. 6, in 8 [thrice], 10 [twice], etc.).

7. *shepherds.* Vocative without the article, varied in the next verse by one with the article. "Quite often the article is lacking when it is a case of persons not present or more or less imaginary . . . Isaiah 23:16 'O harlot' [= Ezek 16:35] . . . Besides there is sometimes much freedom [examples include Joel 1:2, 5, 13, in which four vocatives occur, two with and two without articles]" (Joüon-Muraoka, § 137 g).

8. *surely* (ʾm lʾ). On this usage, see comment on 3:6 (I, 69).

became spoil. Since beasts (metaphor for hostile nations) do not take spoil, this intrusion of the referent is immediately "corrected" in the next clause by "became food." The *w-* of *wthyynh* has the force of *waw*-explicative, indicated by the long dash in the translation (so NJPS). In the nonmetaphoric vs. 28 the restored Israel will not be spoil for the nations or food for the wild beasts.

my shepherds. Now identified as properly God's agents, charged with the care of his flock; cf. 45:8: "my chiefs"; Isa 44:28: "who calls Cyrus, 'my shepherd'"; so, too, Zech 13:7. As such they are answerable to him, vs. 10.

In vs. 8b the chiastic pattern (*wyrʿw . . . ʾwtm / wʾt ṣʾny lʾ rʿw* [verb-object / object-verb]), with the contrasting direct objects juxtaposed ("themselves / and my flock"), guarantees the reflexive sense of *ʾwtm* (as in Exod 5:19; Lev 22:16) and expresses vividly the shepherds' perversity.

Vss. 7–8 are an incomplete sentence, delaying the consequence of the shepherds' misdeeds in order to restate them. The consequential *laken* clause must therefore be repeated in vs. 9 (cf. 5:7–8; 36:1–7; similarly 11:16–17). Before announcing God's action the grounds for it are hammered home.

10. *I . . . will hold them to account* (wdršty). A play on "did not care for" (*dršw*) in vs. 8.

I will put an end to their flock-tending. I.e., I will discharge the discredited leaders from their offices; this personal disqualification is not a repudiation of the monarchic principle (so A. Rofé, *Introduction to the Prophetic Literature* [in Hebrew] [Jerusalem: Academon, 5752 (1991)], p. 27), since the entire political leadership is included.

shall no longer tend themselves. *ʾwtm* in noncontrastive position is ambiguous: in the narrow context of vs. 10a it is naturally taken as "them" (the animals of the flock); so G and evidently S, too (abbreviating the last two clauses: "I will discharge them that they no longer tend my flock"). But in the wider context of vs. 8b and the sequel of this verse it may be perceived as a pun—"themselves" being intended (T and medievals and most moderns).

In vs. 10b the shepherds—for whom the flock became food (= the last clause of vs. 3a)—behave like the wild beasts of vss. 5, 8a. In this light the two preceding clauses may be reread: "I will put an end to their flock-grazing, and the shepherds shall no longer graze (= feed) on them (= the flock)."

11. *Yes, thus said Lord YHWH.* On this formula, see comment to 23:28, and I, 260 (on 14:21) and I, 294 (on 16:59).

take stock of them. The range of *biqqer* is from the strong sense of "examine, inspect, check (for presence/absence of something)"—so here and Lev 13:36 (check the skin for yellow hair)—to the weaker "visit" (Mishnaic *biqqur ḥolim* "visiting the sick," and perhaps Ps 27:4 "to visit his temple"). The pair *drš-bqš* "care for / search for" of vs. 6 has been varied to *drš-bqr*, the second member foreshadowing the figure expanded in vs. 12.

12. *when he is among his dispersed flock.* A difficult passage that has resisted repeated efforts at explication; Zimmerli judges it as "obviously corrupt." MT is lit. "on a day of his being (*hywtw*) among his flock [they being] dispersed ones (*npršwt*)" (G. R. Driver [1954], p. 302). The indefinite nif'al participle of *prš* (= *prś* nif'al "be dispersed," 17:21; cf. B-Y, p. 5243) qualifies "flock" as an accusative attributive of state (Joüon-Muraoka, § 126 a); cf. *dbtm r'h* "the report of them [it being] bad" (Gen 37:2) = the bad report of them; *hzrw' bšlh* "the [lamb's] shoulder [it being] cooked" (Num 6:19) = the cooked shoulder.

A less strained construction of MT (cf. Moshe ben Sheshet) regards the suffix of the infinitive *(hywt)w* as an error (induced by false connection with *'drw* "his herd" as though that were the subject of the infinitive), and takes *npršwt* ("separated," the sense of *prš* in Mishnaic Hebrew and in Aramaic) as the subject of the infinitive: "when there are among his flock some [animals that have got] separated [from the body of the flock]"; followed by NJPS. (T renders: "when he is amidst his flock and separates [the tithe from] them"; cf. T^O to Gen 28:22 and the process described in Lev 27:32–33, where the verb *bqr* recurs.)

G "when there be darkness and cloud amidst the sheep that are separated" confirms the sense "separated" and inserts the last phrase of the verse (which it repeats at the end), by way of explanation of the breakup of the flock—on account of darkened skies. (Menaḥem bar Shim'on records a similar opinion that the verse ending "on a day of cloud and gloom" explains the separation of the animals; cf. Rashi.) S "on a stormy day" merely satisfies the context.

on a day of cloud and gloom. Judgment day; see 30:3 and comment. "Cloud and gloom" surround God in the hymnal opening of Ps 97:2, celebrating God's kingship and judgments.

13–14. The threefold mention of the mountains of Israel as the future pasturage of the ingathered under the care of God contrasts with the former mention of them in vs. 6 as the site of the flock's leaderless dispersal. By the mountains—plural—the entire land is meant. It is otherwise in 20:40, where a single holy high mountain of Israel—the Jerusalem Temple mount—is contrasted with the many illicit high places (20:28), and in 17:22–23, where the (singular) high mountain of Israel refers to Jerusalem, the seat of the Davidic dynasty. The plural "high mountains" in the MT of vs. 14 appears in G and T in the singular—in T as "the holy mountain of Israel" (so, too, in 17:23; 20:40), a leveling reflecting the symbolization of the entire land by Jerusalem in post-exilic rhetoric; cf. Neh 1:9 with Deut 30:5.

in all the settlements of the land. An intrusion of the referent: the habitations of humans.

15. *shall make them lie down.* In the midday heat (Song 1:7).

16. For the reversal of vs. 4a in vs. 16a, see Structure and Themes.

MT closes the list with a double change: two objects (instead of one) of a destructive act (instead of a caring one). Vs. 16b foreshadows the next section, in which judgment is worked between oppressor and oppressed within the flock (vss. 17–22).

the stout (šmnh). Anticipating the antonymous pair "fat" (*bryh*) / "lean" (*rzh*) in vs. 20, *šmnh* is a synonym of the former, as in Hab 1:16 and an antonym of the latter, as in Num 13:20.

the strong. Anticipating its antonym "the weak ones" in vs. 21 (cf. the contrasting **ḥlh/*ḥzq* in vss. 4a, 16a).

I will destroy. The destruction of the oppressors goes well beyond the dismissal of the shepherds announced in vs. 10 or the rescue of the flock from bullies in vs. 22. Kimḥi mitigates: "As for the stout and the strong, I will destroy their strength." The plain sense is so unexpectedly excessive as to cast doubt on the authenticity of the reading *ʾšmyd*; see ahead on G's reading.

I will pasture them. Lit. "her," that is, each animal—

justly. Giving each its due care; cf. Ps 72:2: "that he may rule your people rightly, your lowly ones justly." Not like the shepherds who ruled with violence (vs. 4b).

G reads the first part of vs. 16b: "and the strong one I will guard (*ʾšmr*)": I will watch over the healthy, robust animals so that no harm befalls them. This corresponds to G's reading "the strong one" (whom the shepherds treated harshly) in vs. 4b, and has the ring of authenticity. MT *ʾšm(y)d* may have arisen through a scribal error, which was suggested (or was facilitated) by linking "justly" of the next clause with the "judgment" on the bullying animals described in the following section. This entrained the gloss "and the stout" (not in G), which by anticipating the "fat/lean" pair of the sequel (vs. 20), served better than "the strong" alone to establish the transitional character of the verse-end.

17. *animal*. Hebrew *śh* denotes an individual of the flock, whether a sheep or a goat; Gen 30:32; Exod 21:37.

To the rams and to the he-goats. A necessary marker of the shift in the sequel from addressing the whole flock to addressing its leaders. The similar rubric in vs. 2 ("To the shepherds") is followed by the formula, "thus said Lord YHWH," which must be understood here as well (Ehrlich [Hebrew]). For the metaphoric use of "rams," see 17:13 and I, 314; for the leadership of he-goats, Jer 50:8.

The verse division in MT (= the versions) connects the phrase to what precedes, in apposition to the second "animal": "between (weak) animal and (strong) animal [vs. 20b]—(the latter being) rams and he-goats" (so, e.g., Kimḥi, Smend). But the absence of the phrase in the two resumptions of vs. 17b in vss. 20 and 22 speaks against the Masoretic verse division.

18–19. The viciousness of the leaders: not content with exhibiting their power by cornering the best pasturage and clearest water and leaving the inferior pasturage and the partly settled water for the rest of the flock, they willfully foul what they do not consume themselves (cf. the identical conduct of the fourth beast of Daniel's vision, Dan 7:7).

20. *fat* (birya) *animals*. The form of the adjective (instead of the normal *bᵉriʾa*, vs. 3) is common in Mishnaic Hebrew (e.g., Kelim 24.17; for vocalization, see Mishnah Codex Kaufmann); it is discussed by Y. Kutscher in S. Lieberman et al., eds., *Henoch Yalon Jubilee Volume* [Jerusalem: Kiryat Sepher, 1963], pp. 272–76.

21. Such dispossession was denounced by Isaiah: "Woe to you who make one house touch another, / Join one field to another, / Till there is no more room /

And you alone are left settled in the land" (Isa 5:8). Ezekiel railed at royal expropriation: "Put a stop to your evictions of my people" (45:9), ". . . so that my people do not scatter, everyone from his ancestral holding" (46:18).

22. *become spoil.* For the powerful expropriators — an intrusion of the referent, as in vs. 8.

23. *a single* (*'ḥd*) *shepherd.* Not two, as in the time of the two monarchies of Israel and Judah; the idea is elaborated in 37:15–22, 24, and is out of context here. G *heteron* "an other, a different (shepherd)" (= Hebrew *'ḥr*) refers obliquely to vss. 1–16, in that it foresees a different kind of shepherd than those bad ones, or perhaps a shepherd other than God. Like S, in which "shepherd" is not qualified, G mitigates the unsuitability of MT's "single" and is therefore suspect. Did the prophet anticipate here the subsequent doctrine of a single future Davidide (as he anticipated the "new heart" doctrine of 36:26f. in 11:19), or is this a later retouching made on the basis of the developed doctrine of 37:21ff.? See Structure and Themes.

my servant David. A standing title of King David; e.g., I Kings 11:34, 36, 38; II Kings 8:19; Ps 36:1; 78:70. For the meaning here, see § XLV, Structure and Themes.

The double statement of vs. 23b, in which a simple verb (*yr'h*) is seconded by *hyh* + a substantival derivative of the same verbal root (*yhyh lr(w)'h*), is in priestly style; cf. Lev 11:44: *whtqdštm whyytm qdwšym* "sanctify yourselves and be holy." The second clause expresses accomplishment of the first one.

The alternation in gender of the pronominal suffixes in this verse — m-f-m-f — anticipates the transition from metaphor (flock, feminine) to plain speech (humans, masculine) from vs. 24 on.

24. *and I, YHWH, will be their God.* This half of the mutuality formula of the covenant (I, 254) attaches at once to the previous clause, "He shall be their shepherd," and to the following nonmetaphoric restatement of it.

and my servant David, a chief in their midst. This marks the end of metaphoric language (except for the closing vs. 31). The epithet "chief" is also used in Ezekiel 45.

25. *I will make a covenant of well-being for them.* As a rule the subject of *krt bryt l-* is a superior who obligates himself (grants terms) to another; thus Joshua commits himself to spare the Gibeonites (Josh 9:15), and the Jabeshites ask for terms on which they can surrender (I Sam 11:1). "Covenant of well-being (*bryt šlwm*)" is a promise of security and prosperity, or of friendship and harmony (cf. the context of the phrase in Isa 54:10). The content of the covenant is spelled out immediately in the sequel. (On the relation of our passage to Hosea 2:20, see H. W. Wolff, "Jahwe als Bundesvermittler," *VT* 6 [1956], 316–20.)

G "for David" reflects the idea of monarchic mediation of well-being; see Structure and Themes.

Anciently, settlements were endangered by wild animals (Jer 5:6; Prov 22:13); in the blessed future even their haunts (forests and deserts: Jer 5:6) will be safe, and even at night (when they prowl; Ps 104:20f.), because they will be gone. Earlier exegetes (medievals, Skinner, Davidson) metaphorized the beasts as hostile nations (as they are in vs. 5). Against this reading is the separate mention of hostile nations alongside wild beasts in vs. 28 and in the parallel visions of blessedness, Lev 26:6; Hos 2:20.

26. The first half of the verse is unclear; the versions do not help since they appear to have had a text similar to MT. The sense of *ntn* X *(l-)Y* here is "make/ constitute X (into) Y"; e.g., "I will make you a(n object of) reproach" (22:4); "this city I will make a curse" (an exemplar of accursedness, Jer 26:6). "My hill"—the Temple mount (Isa 10:32; 31:4)—contrasts with the illicit cult sites alluded to by "every high hill" in vs. 6. If the antecedent of "(I will make) them" is the aforementioned wilderness and forests, as places, coordinate with "the environs of my hill," the meaning of vs. 26a will be: I will turn the uninhabitable places—wilderness and forest—along with the now ruined environs of the Temple mount into a blessing, an exemplar of blessedness (cf. Zech 8:13: as Israel had exemplified curse, it would exemplify blessing). The sequel tells how this will come about through seasonable rains. Another melioration of nature appears in 47:1–12: a miraculous stream emerging from the future Temple will fertilize the Judean desert. For a similar idea, cf. Isa 32:15: "[Today's] wilderness shall become farmland (*krml*) / While [today's] farmland will [then] rate as forest (= uncultivated ground)."

rain . . . in its season. Particularized in Jer 5:24 as "early and late rain" (*ywrh wmlqwš*), the former in Marheshvan (September–October), the latter in Nisan (March–April), as Sifre to Deut 11:14 specifies. Hence, the following plural "rains of blessing" ("rains" also in the parallel Lev 26:4), i.e., rainfalls in season, and in the right quantity. In *m. Ta'anit* 3.8 our phrase occurs in the story of Ḥoni the rainmaker, expanded into "rains of goodwill, blessing, and gift" (*rṣwn brkh wndbh*), characterizing beneficial rainfall, as opposed to mere drizzle or ruinous downpour.

27. *break the bars of their yoke . . . enslave them.* The idiom of Jer 30:8, except that "break bars of yoke" appears only here and Lev 26:13. G and S reflect "break yoke," in MT an expression found only in Jeremiah (e.g., 2:20; 5:5; 28:4, 11). "Enslave them" is lit. "work by means of them" (*'bdym bhm*), a locution found in priestly passages such as Exod 1:14 and Lev 25:39, 46 (beside *rdh b-*; cf. above in vs. 4), but mostly in Jeremiah (e.g., 22:13; 25:14; 27:7). On the combination of priestly and Jeremianic language, see Structure and Themes.

28. *they shall dwell in security, with none to disturb* [*them*]. Combines elements of Lev 26:5b–6a; "none to disturb" occurs in visions of restoration in Mic 4:4; Zeph 3:13; Jer 30:10; and Job 11:19.

29. *I will establish for them a planting of renown.* "This I will establish (= set up on a permanent basis) for them: that they shall be a planting of renown and glory, as Isaiah (60:21) prophesied: 'A shoot of my planting / My handiwork by which I get glory'" (MenbSh); cf. also Isa 61:3: "They shall be called 'Terebinths of righteousness' / the planting of YHWH by which he gets glory." Such is most likely to be the sense of this clause in view of the common figure of God's planting of Israel in, or uprooting it from, its land (e.g., Exod 15:17; II Sam 7:10; Amos 9:15; see esp. Jer 24:6; 32:41; 42:10). For the force of *lšm* "of/for renown (lit.

"name")," cf. its synonyms in the series "for praise, for renown and for glory" (Deut 26:19; cf. Jer 13:11). In the future God will execute a planting for Israel that will be famous for its radical reversal of Israel's fortunes.

In view of the immunity from famine promised in the next clause, moderns have taken "planting" literally, preferring *šl(w)m* "well-being"—the presumed *Vorlage* of G and S—to MT's *lšm*; e.g., *RSV* "prosperous plantations," taken to mean "fertile, productive fields" (Wevers). But, as the passages cited above show, "plant(ing)" in restoration prophecies is a metaphor for permanency rather than fertility (in Micah 1:6 "plantings of vineyards" signify depopulated regions!). The *Vorlage* of G and S echoes the "covenant of well-being" of vs. 25. Whether the planting be "of renown" (MT) or "of well-being" (G S), it is best referred to the permanent restoration of Israel to, its implanting in, its land. Thereafter the land will be immune to famine, which caused emigration to neighboring lands (see next comment).

carried off. This sense *ʾsp* has in, e.g., Gen 30:23: "God has taken away my disgrace"; Ps 26:9: "Do not sweep me away with sinners." Kimḥi nicely interprets T "removed by famine" in connection with what precedes and what follows it: "For in the event of famine the Israelites had to remove themselves to Egypt [e.g., Gen 12:10] and other lands [e.g., Moab, Ruth 1:1–2], where they had to bear the taunts of the nations."

the taunts of the nations. Who say that the land devours its people and loses its inhabitants, 36:13–15.

30. The verse is a unique fusion of three elements: (1) the recognition formula (see comment to 6:7 [I, 133]) expanded by (2) the covenant formula of mutuality (I, 254), made more solemn by the naming of the parties (YHWH, the house of Israel), and (3) the formulaic oracular assurance of God's presence. The kernel of the assurance formula is *ʾtk ʾn(k)y* "I am with you"—whether addressed to an individual (Gen 26:24; Jer 1:8, 19; 15:20) or to the collective (Jer 30:11; Isa 43:2, 5). It is taken up by humans in Num 14:9 ("but YHWH is with us") and Amos 5:14 ("So be YHWH God of hosts with you, as you have said!"). Here its interfusion with the covenant formula alters the syntax: instead of the symmetrical "I am YHWH their God and they are my people . . . ," we have an unbalanced pair: "I, YHWH, their God, am with them, and they are my people . . ." It is no wonder that G, S, and a few Hebrew mss. show the normal, balanced phrasing. That Jer 30:11, whose context resembles ours, contains the assurance formula offers some support to MT.

31. The verse resumes, by way of closure, the direct address to the flock of vs. 17. Its inelegant MT form specifically (and to our taste needlessly) identifies the flock with the humans who have taken over the scene since vs. 24. "Human" (*ʾadam*) seems to be a gloss inspired by the phrase "flocks of humans" in 36:37–38; it is not represented in G, which reflects a simpler unencumbered *Vorlage*, a continuation of the preceding verse: "my flock and the flock of my pasturage you are, and I am YHWH your God . . ." Even in this form, however, the verse appears to be superfluous after the closure of vs. 30. It may be an alternative closure.

STRUCTURE AND THEMES

This oracle begins a series of visions of restoration, whose theme is reversal, "amending the failures of [Israelite] history" (the title of a brief, insightful essay on these prophecies by Moshe [Goshen-]Gottstein, in A. Biram, ed., *Sefer Auerbach* [in Hebrew] [Jerusalem: Kiryat Sepher, 1955], pp. 175–78). As the doom prophecies of chs. 1–24 drew on the curses of the covenant documents (particularly Lev 26), so the restoration visions turn the blessings promised for obedience to the covenant laws (especially those of Lev 26) into unconditional prophecies of future bliss.

This first, complex oracle develops the theme of the renovation of the leadership of Israel in a rather clear progression. Israel's present misrulers will be discharged, God will ingather the exiles to their land, will appoint a Davidide to reign over them, and will ensure their enduring bliss through a covenant of well-being.

The oracle begins with the revelation-event formula and a charge to prophesy to a specific audience (vss. 1–2a). It ends with multiple closures—an expanded recognition formula (vs. 30) and "declares Lord YHWH" (vss. 30, 31—perhaps a doublet). Within this frame the oracle falls into several parts according to content and formal markers. Except for vss. 25–30 the metaphor of shepherds and their flock prevails.

A (vss. 2–16): denunciation of the bad shepherds and their replacement by God.

A1 (vss. 2–10): the indictment and the penalty, framed by the punning "shepherds tending them/selves" and mention of their eating the flock (vss. 2b$^{\gamma,\delta}$–3 and 8b, 10). Speech is both directly to the shepherds (vss. 3–4, 7, 9) and about them (vss. 5–6, 8, 10). A climactic series of abusive acts (vs. 3) is followed by a climactic series of derelictions of duty toward needy animals (vs. 4, ending with closure). As a result the flock scattered far and wide (vss. 5–6). Equal space is given to narrating the shepherd's misdeeds and the dispersal of the flock; the indictment must detail the crimes and their effects. The penalty is couched in the iterative, retarding pattern, *laken . . . ya'n . . . laken* (vss. 7, 8, 9; similarly 5:7–8; 16:35–37; 22:19; 28:6–7; and most extensively, 36:1–7): the bad shepherds will be discharged from their job.

A2 (vss. 11–16): God's assumption of the shepherd's role and his reversal of the disastrous course of events, starting with the last and working backward. Far more space is given to the restoration of the flock to its pastures (vss. 12–15) than to caring for individual animals (vs. 16); the harder task overshadows the simpler (in the table below the proportions are not kept). The closing formula of vs. 15 ("declares Lord YHWH") separates God's treatment of the entire flock from his treatment of the needy individuals within it. At the corresponding position in A1 (end of vs. 4) occurs the closure of the list of derelictions toward individuals. The matching list in A2 ends in vs. 16b with another closure. In both closures MT and G diverge significantly. G's closures are related (treatment of strong animals), and stay within the frame of A; MT's closures are unrelated, and the second (vs. 16b) looks ahead to section B. MT here gives the impression of a secondary adaptation of the end of A to the new theme of B1, in the interest of a tighter bond between them.

Shepherd's Faults (A1) (*read up*)	*God's Remedies* (A2) (*read down*)
none cared or searched for flock	[11]will care for and take stock of flock
flock scattered over whole face of earth	[12–13a]gather scattered from all lands
[6]flock scattered in the mountains	[13b–14]pasture flock on mountains of Israel
[5]flock ruined, lacking shepherd MT: ruled over them by force and rigor G: ruled over the strong with rigor	[15]I will make them graze, lie down (declares Lord YHWH)
didn't search for the lost animal or recover the stray or bandage the fractured	[16]will search for lost recover the stray bandage the fractured
[4]didn't heal the sick or strengthen the weak	strengthen the weak
———	MT: destroy stout and strong G: watch over the strong

Part A has a uniform iterative texture; it focuses attention by breaking down situations into their components, and by use of synonyms and repetition (with variation). The point-by-point reversal of the items of A1 in A2 is the structural principle, and its careful execution attests to the integrity of the section.

B (vss. 17–31): restoration in Israel of a just social order, peace, and prosperity. The opening address to the flock is answered by the closure, which marks off the section.

B1 (vss. 17–24): indictment of bullying animals and appointment of a shepherd to tend the flock; opening address and message formula (vs. 17), closing formula ("I YHWH have spoken"). Within the leaderless flock, the powerful monopolize goods and leave the scraps to the rest of the flock (vss. 17–19). God will put a stop to this and appoint a Davidic king as shepherd (vss. 20 [*laken*]–24). Vs. $24a^{\alpha}$ is a pivot: attached to the preceding vs. 23b, it states the interrelation of people, shepherd, and God—necessitated by B's interpolation of a human shepherd into A's simpler two-party order: God the shepherd, and his human flock, Israel. Attached to the following (vs. $24a^{\beta}$), it translates the shepherd metaphor into plain language and marks the transition from figurative to nonfigurative discourse. The (covenant) formula of mutuality has been skewed for expressing a hierarchical relation of three parties: people, shepherd/chief, God.

B2 (vss. 25–31): the future immunity of the restored people from natural banes, and their material blessedness. The direct covenant relation of God and Israel is resumed here; the versions of the mutuality formula in the closing (vss. 30–31) echo the end of B1, but without the mediation of a human shepherd.

B starts as a second thought about the shepherd-flock metaphor, responding to two issues: (1) what will be the place of the Davidic king (announced in 37:15–24) in the restored polity? (2) what of the dispossessed within the flock (cf. 22:29)? Both issues are resolved together. God himself will gather the exiles and restore them to their homeland (so A2, and so in all allusions to ingathering of the diaspora it is God himself who works the wonder: 11:17; 20:34, 41; 36:24). At that time he will take up the cause of the dispossessed against their bullying oppressors. Afterward he will appoint a Davidic king to govern the people. The same sequence of divine act of restoration followed by appointment of human rulers occurs in Jer 23:3–4.

In line with the old covenant promises and threats (Lev 26; Deut 28), the welfare of the restored community will again be a direct providence of God, not mediated by the king. Contrast the royal ideology expressed, e.g., in Ps 72 (for the ancient Near Eastern concept of the king's mediation of prosperity, see R. Patai, *Man and Temple* [London: Nelson, 1947], pp. 175–80; H. Frankfort, *Kingship and the Gods* [Chicago: University of Chicago Press, 1948], pp. 307–12). The "covenant of well-being" fuses the covenant concept of Hos 2:20 — immunity from natural predators, cessation of warfare, and "lying down in security" — with the promises of well-being as reward for obedience in Lev 26:4–13. The terms are adapted to Ezekiel's thought and circumstances. Since the restored state would not have to protect itself, being under divine protection (see chs. 38–39), victory in war (Lev 26:8) goes unmentioned. Israel's present situation is reflected in the new promise that it would no more be subjected to despoliation. Several signs, therefore, point to B being a secondary reflection, including motifs more at home in subsequent oracles (see comment to "one shepherd," vs. 23).

Verbal connections with A indicate that B was composed as a supplement to A: the metaphor of shepherd and flock; the terms: "justice" (16) / "judge" (17, 20); "fat" (3 / 28); "weak" (4 / 21); "scattered" (21 / 5, 6, etc.); "become spoil" (22, 28 / 7); "food for beasts" (28 / 5, 7); "rescue" (27 / 12). A salient feature of B is its affinities with the eschatological prophecy of Jer 30:8–11. Common terms include: breaking yoke, enslave, appoint David over them, quiet and tranquil with none to disturb, God with you to deliver you, the nations among whom Israel was scattered, justly. This is to be considered along with the Jeremianic origin of the main theme of this oracle, the shepherd metaphor.

The metaphor of shepherd for ruler — human and divine — is a common Near Eastern usage. Sumerian and Assyro-Babylonian kings regularly used this epithet: "wise" and "humble shepherd" (Lipit Ishtar, *ANET*[3], p. 159b); "the shepherd called by Enlil," "shepherd of the people" (Hammurabi, ibid., pp. 164b, 165b). For a comprehensive listing, see M.-J. Seux, *Épithètes royales akkadiennes et sumériennes* (Paris: Letouzey et Ane, 1967), pp. 244–50. The Babylonian gods exalt Marduk, saying, "May he shepherd all the gods like a flock" (*ANET*[3], p. 72a; cf. the anonymous divine "shepherd" who "pastures [his flock] as a god should," ibid., p. 604b). Egyptian hymns call gods herdsmen (ibid., p. 368a), "tending [all creatures] forever" (ibid., p. 371b), as well as kings (who were divine) — "the good shepherd" (Amenhotep III; Breasted, *Ancient Records*, II, p. 900; so, too, Seti I, ibid., III, p. 195; Merneptah ["I am the ruler who shepherds you"], ibid., p. 580).

In the *Iliad* "shepherd of the people" is the standing epithet of Agamemnon, leader of the Greeks against Troy (*Iliad* 2.243, etc.). The meaning of the epithet vacillates between the owner of the flock (as in the case of a god) and the agent of the owner who is responsible to him (e.g., Lipit Ishtar). But in all cases the connotation is of one who cares for his charges and exerts himself to answer their needs.

(Another Mesopotamian royal epithet germane to prophetic imagery is "gatherer of the dispersed people" of a given locality; e.g., Esarhaddon, "who gathered together the scattered [people of Babylon] and caused them to inhabit an abode of peace" [Luckenbill, *ARAB* II, p. 258; cf. G. Widengren, "The Gathering of the Dispersed," *Svensk Exegetisk Aarsbok* 41/42 (1976–77), 224–34]. In Mesopotamia this epithet is not combined with the shepherd image, nor is it applied to a god.)

The biblical shepherd metaphor has distinctive features. In the singular, the figure may serve for God ("YHWH is my shepherd," Ps 23:1; "Shepherd of Israel," Ps 80:2), with Israel as his flock ("O shepherd your people with your staff, your very own flock," Mic 7:14). His gathering-in of Israel's dispersion is imaged accordingly: "I will collect the lame animals / and the strayed I will gather" (Mic 4:6), as is his tender care of them: "Like a shepherd he tends his herd / In his arm he gathers the young / Carries them in his bosom / He provides for the nursing ones" (Isa 40:11; cf. Jer 31:10). Or it may serve for the ruler God appoints over his people: Moses is alluded to in Isa 63:11 as "the shepherd (sing. wth mss. and versions) of his (God's) flock," as is David in Ps 78:70–72 ("He took him from the sheepfolds . . . to tend Jacob, his people"). God even calls the foreign king Cyrus, whom he has commissioned to deliver Israel "my shepherd" in Isa 44:28.

Hebrew usage parts from its neighbors in pluralizing the term and thus extending it to the entire ruling class. In contexts surveying the past the reference may be to kings (as in Jer 2:8); the same holds for its use in eschatological contexts: "I will give you shepherds after my own heart"—perhaps a line of kings (Jer 3:15). But where "shepherds" are mentioned alongside a king (Nahum 3:18; a distinctly un-Assyrian usage applied to Assyria) or as contemporaries (Isa 56:11), the referent must be to the entire political leadership (king, counselors, officials, magnates; see comment at 7:26–27 [I, 156]). The extension of a royal epithet to a class may reflect the extent of power-sharing in late monarchic Judah; cf. the extraordinary power of king-making ascribed to that vague entity called "the people of the land" (II Kings 21:23–24; 23:30; Cogan and Tadmor, *II Kings*, AB, p. 129: ". . . the wealthy who by dint of their influential position could direct public affairs . . ."). Since the shepherds in our oracle are to be punished by being stripped of their commission (vs. 10), they must still be present—in the ruins of Judah or among the exiles. The captive kings Jehoiachin and Zedekiah would satisfy the grammatical plural address, but it seems more likely that the plural refers to the whole leadership class.

The theme of predatory misrulers has appeared in 22:25 (see text note and comment there): Israel's have preyed, lion-like, on their own people, devoured and pillaged them (mixed figurative and nonfigurative language). That passage was inspired by Zeph 3:3 ("lions . . . wolves . . . leave no bone till morning"), whose antecedent is Micah 3:2–3: Israel's misrulers "have eaten my people's flesh / And stripped them of their skin / And broken open their bones . . ."

Jeremiah appears to have innovated the theme of the delinquent shepherds, announced in a nutshell in 2:8: "the shepherds rebelled against me." In 10:21 the result of their fecklessness appears: "all their flock has scattered." Two amplifications of the theme supply almost all of the components that entered into Ezekiel's complex treatment. One adds the scattering of the flock on the mountains and their vulnerability to predators (50:6–7). The other (23:1–4) surveys the whole tale of delinquency and God's remedial intervention, an ideal whole that might be the bare outline of our oracle (and that has been subjected to critical dissolution; see McKane, *Jeremiah*, ICC, ad loc.):

> Woe to the shepherds who let the flock of my pasture get lost and scatter, declares YHWH. Now then, thus said YHWH God of Israel to the shepherds who shepherd my people: It is you who scattered my flock and let them stray, and did not attend to them; see I am going to attend to all your evildoing, declares YHWH. I myself will gather the remnant of my flock from all the lands to which I have banished them, and I will bring them back to their grazing ground, and they shall be fertile and increase. And I will appoint shepherds over them who will tend them, and they shall no more be afraid nor dismayed, and none shall go missing, declares YHWH.

The adjacent piece (vss. 5–6) predicts the appointment of a righteous descendant of David during whose reign "Judah shall be delivered and Israel shall dwell in security."

It was left for Ezekiel to combine the two themes — predatory rulers and delinquent shepherds — into the image of predatory shepherds feeding on their own flock, an extravagance typical of him; cf., e.g., "children shall eat their parents" (5:10), or the nymphomaniacal adulteress of ch. 16.

The influence of Jeremiah, both in the image and in the terminology, on both components of this oracle is patent. It is plausibly accounted for by the assumption that Ezekiel had access to the words of his older Jerusalemite contemporary. Perhaps the tender note audible in this oracle owes something to the influence of Jeremiah, too. For a succinct discussion of Jeremiah's influence on Ezekiel, see W. L. Holladay, *Jeremiah* 2, Hermeneia (Minneapolis: Fortress Press, 1989), pp. 81–84.

Echoes of this oracle are heard in the prophecies of Zechariah (e.g., chs 10–11). An indication that the post-exilic visionary knew a version in which A and B were already joined is the mixed figure of Zech 10:3: "I am angry at the shepherds (= A) and I shall punish the he-goats" (= B).

XLII. Reclaiming and Renewing the Land (35:1–36:15)

35 [1]The word of YHWH came to me: [2]Man, set your face toward Mount Seir
and prophesy against it, [3]and say to it: Thus said Lord YHWH:

I am coming at you, Mount Seir:
  I will stretch out my hand against you,
  and make you an utter desolation.
[4]Your towns I will turn into ruins,
  and you shall be a desolation;
  then you shall know that I am YHWH.

[5]Because you harbored eternal hatred, and delivered the Israelites to the sword
at the time of their disaster, at the time of [their] terminal iniquity, [6]therefore, By
my life! declares Lord YHWH, [a]I will make you all bloody, and blood will pursue
you.[a] Assuredly, you [b]were an enemy of[b] blood, so blood shall pursue you. [7]I will
make Mount Seir an utter desolation, cutting off from it all who come and go. [8]I
will fill [a]its mountains[a] with its[c] slain; your[d] hills and your[d] valleys and all your[d]
gullies—those slain by the sword shall lie fallen in them.[e]

[9]Eternal desolations I will make you;
  and your towns shall not be restored.[f]
  And you shall know that I am YHWH.

[10]Because you said: "The two nations and the two lands shall be mine, and [g]we
shall possess it[g]"—but YHWH was[h] there!—[11]therefore, By my life! declares
Lord YHWH, I will deal [with you[i]] in accord with your anger and your passion
with which you dealt, because of your enmity, with them; and I will make myself
known [j]among them[j] when I punish you. [12]And you shall know that I am

[a–a] Not in G.
[b–b] G "sinned (with respect) to" (as reading *ldm ʾšmt*).
[c] G "your."
[d] T "its."
[e] G "you."
[f] So Q (*tašobna*); K *tyšbnh* = *tešabna* (see comment) = G S T "inhabited."
[g–g] G S T "I shall possess them."
[h] G "is."
[i] G S "to you."
[j–j] G "to you."

YHWH — who heard all your blasphemies that you uttered about the mountains of Israel, to the effect that "they are desolate, they have been given to us to devour." [13]You spoke vaunting over me [a]and surfeited me with your words;[a] indeed I heard it.

[14]Thus said Lord YHWH: As the whole earth rejoices, I will deal desolation to you. [15a]As you rejoiced over the heritage of the house of Israel because it was desolated, the same will I have done to you.[a] You shall be a desolation, Mount Seir, and the whole of Edom, all of it, and they[e] shall know that I am YHWH.

36 [1]And you, man, prophesy to the mountains of Israel, and say: Mountains of Israel, hear the word of YHWH! [2]Thus said Lord YHWH: Because the enemy said about you, "Aha!" [k]to say,[k] "The eternal highlands have become our possession!" [3]therefore prophesy and say: Thus said Lord YHWH:

For the very good reason that on all sides you were panted after as a possession for the remaining nations, and were the theme of slanderous speech and popular defamation, [4]therefore, mountains of Israel, hear the word of Lord YHWH! Thus said Lord YHWH to the mountains and the hills, the gullies and the valleys, and to the desolate ruins and to the deserted towns that have become the object of plunder[l] and mockery for the remaining nations that are on all sides —

[5]Therefore thus said Lord YHWH: Surely in my fiery passion I speak against the remaining nations and against all of Edom, who made over my land to themselves for a possession, with wholehearted rejoicing, with wholesouled contempt, so that her pastureland [be] spoil —

[6]Therefore prophesy to the soil of Israel, and say to the mountains and the hills, the gullies and the valleys: Thus said Lord YHWH: See, I speak in my passion and my fury: Because you have borne the taunts of the nations, [7]therefore, thus said Lord YHWH: I do solemnly swear that the nations that are around you shall themselves bear taunts.

[8]But you, mountains of Israel, shall put forth your branches and bear your fruit for my people Israel, for they are coming soon! [9]For I am coming to you, and I will turn my face to you, and you shall be tilled and sown. [10]And I will make you teem with humans, with the whole house of Israel, all of it, and towns shall be resettled and ruins rebuilt. [11]I will make you teem with humans and animals, [a]and they shall multiply and be fertile.[a] I will resettle you as you were in your former state, and prosper [you] more than your original state, and you shall know that I am YHWH. [12]I will cause humans to walk upon you — my people Israel — and they shall possess you, and you shall be their heritage. And you shall never again lose them.

[13]Thus said Lord YHWH: Because they say to you: "You are a devourer of humans; you kept losing your nations,[m]" [14]assuredly, humans you shall no more devour, and your nations you shall not again lose, declares Lord YHWH. [15]No

[k–k] Hebrew *w-*; not in G; S "that says, that."
[l] T "derision" (as from *lbwz*).
[m] So Q; K and versions "nation."

more will I let you hear the taunts of nations, and the reproaches of peoples you shall bear no more, /[a]and your nations you shall no more cause to stumble,[a]/ declares Lord YHWH.

COMMENT

35:2 *set your face toward.* As 6:2, etc.; see comment thereto, I, 130.

Mount Seir. Seir is an ancient name (found, e.g., in the fourteenth-century Amarna tablets) of the mountainous regions south of the Dead Sea on both sides of the Rift Valley running south to the Gulf of Aqaba. Occupied by the descendants of Esau = the Edomites (Gen 36:8), who displaced the Horites (Deut 2:12, 22), the name became synonymous with Edom (e.g., Gen 32:4: "the land of Seir, the country of Edom"). Mount Seir = the high land of Seir; cf. "the mountains (= mountainous land) of Israel" at 6:2, and the comment thereto (I, 130).

3–4. Typical Ezekielian doom language: used against the high places (6:14), foreign nations (25:7, 13, 16), the land of Israel (33:28–29); "turn your towns into ruins" echoes Lev 26:31. For the expression *šmmh wmšmh* "utter desolation/ waste," see comment to 6:14 (I, 136f.).

your towns I will turn into ruins, and you shall be (wʾth thyh) *a desolation.* The pronoun in the second clause sets up a rhetorical contrast between the juxtaposed "your towns" and "you," giving each a (semantically fictitious) separate weight. Cf. Ezra 8: "whoever does not come . . . all his property shall be proscribed, and he (*whwʾ*) shall be separated from the congregation of the exiles" (Muraoka, *Emphatic Words*, pp. 56ff.).

5. *eternal hatred.* Ascribed to the Philistines in 25:15. Long-held ethnic grudges are a feature of the biblical world; e.g., I Sam 15:2 (against Amalek), with reference to Exod 17:8–16; Deut 23:4–7 (against Ammon and Moab). (Counterbalancing these are long-held memories of ethnic favors: e.g., Deut 23:8 [Egypt!]; I Sam 15:6 [the Kenites].) The hatred of Seir/Edom/Esau originated, according to Israelite tradition doubtless known to Ezekiel, with Jacob/ Israel's usurpation of his twin brother's firstborn-blessing (Gen 27:41: "Esau hated Jacob on account of the blessing . . .").

delivered (wtgr) . . . *to* (ʿl ydy) *the sword.* So S, Kara; literally, "spilled . . . into the hands of the sword." *higgir* (hifʿil of **ngr* "flow") with nonliquid object recurs in Micah 1:6: "I will spill (*whgrty*) her stones into the valley." Here, as in Jer 18:21; Ps 63:11, masses of humans are pictured as tumbled "into the hands (= charge/power) of" the sword (for the ascription of "hands" to baneful objects, see Job 5:20 [sword]; Ps 141:9 [trap]). The Mishnaic Hebrew sense of *ʿl ydy* "by means of" would fit nicely here, but is unattested in Biblical Hebrew; for the sense here, see II Kings 12:12: "they delivered the money . . . into the charge of the foremen"). Human mortality is compared in II Sam 14:14 to "water poured (*ngrym*) on the ground," and Lam 4:1 calls the slain sons of Zion "jewels spilled (*tštpknh*) at every street corner."

time of their disaster. The occasion of Judah's collapse is thrice called its "day of disaster" in Obad 13 and everywhere (Deut 32:35; Jer 46:21, etc.) except here, where "time" replaces "day" by assimilation to the following Ezekielian coinage:

time of [their] terminal iniquity. "Iniquity that fills the measure [and thus triggers punishment]" (*Meṣudah*); cf. 21:30 and the comment thereto.

'yd "disaster" occurs only here in Ezekiel; in its present, inflected form, *'edam*, it is assonant with the repeated *dam* "blood" in the next verse, and evokes (or was it evoked by?) an alias of Seir: Edom (vs. 15). Thus disaster, blood, and Edom are linked by sound.

6. Following the oath formula ("By my life"), vss. 6a$^{\beta}$ and 6b are two different asseverations. That of 6a opens with *ky* "[I swear] that," instead of *'m (l')* as everywhere else in this position in the book (e.g., 34:8), but *ky* is common outside of Ezekiel; e.g., I Sam 29:6; II Sam 12:5; Jer 22:24; 46:18–19. The asseveration consists of two death threats, in requital of Seir's massacre of Israelites. The meaning assigned to the first clause is uncertain and leans on its similarity to 16:38. The second clause personifies the blood shed by Seir as hounding him to death (as its own avenger? cf. the blood-redeemer's "pursuit" of the killer in the asylum law of Deut 19:6; Josh 20:5; for such personification, cf. the cry for vengeance of Abel's shed blood, Gen 4:10). There is no causal connection between the two clauses.

Vs. 6b is a second sequel to the oath formula of 6a; it opens with the standard conditional particle (*'m* [*l'*]) and follows with what sounds like a measure-for-measure statement: "you were an enemy of blood (*dm śn't*—a peculiar expression) so blood will pursue you." All three terms of this asseveration—*dm* "blood," *śn'* "be an enemy," and *rdp* "pursue"—belong to the vocabulary of the asylum law (e.g., Deut 19:6; cf. Num 35:20–21, where both *śn'h* "enmity" and *'ybh* "hatred," as in our vss. 5 and 11, appear). That law defines one who kills out of enmity and hatred as a murderer; the redeemer of blood (kinsman of the slain) is obligated to pursue and kill him. Our passage seems to draw on those terms to say that Edom's killing of Israelites was not in self-defense (excusable) or even for booty (understandable) but out of sheer blood-enmity—hostility toward the very life ("blood is life," Deut 12:23) of Israel (T: "your hate was hate of blood"; Malbim). The blood shed by such a murderer will hound him and be satisfied only by his death.

A striking interpretation of *dm* (though hardly defensible philologically) is foreshadowed in Symmachus ("you hated your blood"), recorded by Rashi ("some take it to mean your brother [Israel] who is your blood and flesh"), and is ascribed by Bar Hebraeus to S: "'The blood that you hate, that blood will pursue you.' It means . . . 'you are of the same family, of one blood with the Israelites, and you hate it! it will pursue you.'" This interpretation carries on the theme of "eternal hatred" of the previous verse, understood as a reference to Jacob and Esau.

Vs. 6a$^{\beta}$ is not in G, which may indicate that it is a variant of vs. 6b, originally recorded in a margin and eventually copied into the text. In vs. 6b, most critics take G's first clause as reflecting a *Vorlage* "you have incurred guilt with respect to blood" (*ldm 'šmt*; cf. 22:4 *bdmk . . . 'šmt*, and *'šm* in the Edom oracle, 25:12), and prefer it to MT without considering the terminological connection of MT with the law of asylum, which favors its more difficult reading.

7. *utter desolation.* The first word of the pair *l^{e}šim^{e}ma uš^{e}mama*, otherwise unattested, is a dissimilated form of the second; cf. *'ane w^e'ana* "hither and yon"

(I Kings 2:36); *kazo wᵉkaze* "this one and that one alike" (II Sam 11:25). This is a variation of *šmmh wmšmh*, otherwise employed for emphasis (e.g., vs. 3), and may be an error for it. (For the absence of the preposition in the second word, cf. *lšmmh wḥrph*, 29:9.)

cutting off from it all who come and go. Lit. "and I will cut off from it one who passes through and one who returns." The sentence is a novel combination of commonplaces: (1) the sentence pattern and verbal element of "I will cut off from it man and beast" (14:14, 17; 25:13, etc.; G actually renders so here), and (2) the participial element of "a desolation with none passing through" (*'ober*, 14:15; 33:28), referring to a human being in motion. In order to create a hendiadys meaning "every moving human being" corresponding to the hendiadys "man and beast" (= every living creature) as the object of "I will cut off," the prophet called up the pair *'br wšwb* (Exod 32:27: "Go back and forth") and added the participle *šab* to the already present *'ober.* The resulting pair recurs only among Zechariah's borrowings from Ezekiel (Zech 7:14; 9:8).

In vs. 7 God speaks about Seir, not to it as in vs. 6. This betrays the double audience of the oracle: the ideal one—Mount Seir—addressed in the second person, and the real one—the exiles—to whom God speaks about Mount Seir. Such shifts of perspective are common in oracles addressed to an unseen audience: e.g., 5:14–16 (Jerusalem); 26:3–4 (Tyre); 29:8–10 (Egypt, Pharaoh); 31:10 (the cedar). See the final comment to the next verse.

8. Seir's highlands will be emptied of living people (vs. 7), but filled with their corpses.

In 6:3 and 36:4, 6, the topographical terms are a consecutive set of alternating masculine and feminine nouns: *hrym wgb'wt 'pyqym wg'ywt* "mountains and hills, gullies and valleys." Here (for a change) the set is broken: "(its) mountains" is in a clause by itself with the assonant "its slain" (*HRYW ḤLLYW*), the clause serving as a summary which the sequel particularizes. The separation of the "mountains" clause is emphasized by its third person suffixes, connecting it with what precedes, while the sequel has second person suffixes, connecting it with what follows.

(G's omission of "mountains" breaks the set, and is perhaps a haplography due to the similarity of *hry-* and *ḥlly-*. G's supposed *Vorlage* **wml'ty ḥllyk gb'wt(yk)* "I will fill with your slain (your) hills" is unidiomatic: with the verb *ml'* "fill" the container regularly precedes the contents.)

The abrupt change of person in the second part of the verse is uncongenial to translators. G levels all pronominal suffixes in the verse to second person, T to third. The remedy is only local, however, because in any event a shift in person occurs between vs. 7 and vs. 9. In placing the shift in the middle of vs. 8 MT reflects an insouciance that is altogether characteristic of Ezekiel's style.

9. *Eternal desolations.* Corresponding to "eternal hatred" of vs. 5. The plural *šmmwt-*, as in Jer 25:12; 51:26, 62, is regularly used in the construct state (like *ḥrbwt-* "ruins"); it is not, with some critics (e.g., Fohrer), to be singularized in order to conform with the ancient versions. The "emended" form **šimᵉmat-* never appears (nor does **ḥorbat-*).

shall not be restored. The Q is *tašobna*, from **šwb* "be restored," standing alone as in II Kings 5:10: "your flesh will be restored." The full expression is *tašobna lᵉqadmatan* "be restored to their former state" (16:55). K *tyšbnh,* with its anomalous vowel-letter *y* (for *e*) parading its derivation from **yšb,* is to be vocalized *tešabnah* "(not) be inhabited." It underlies G (+ "any more") S V T and is the more common usage (e.g., 26:20; 29:11; 36:35).

And you (plural) *shall know.* Addressing the Seirites. In the MT the recognition clause shifts from second person singular (Mount Seir, vs. 4) to second plural (here), back to singular (vs. 12), finally to third plural (speaking of the Seirites/ Edomites, vs. 15). G levels all to second singular.

10. *two nations . . . lands.* Judah and Israel, called in 37:22 "two nations and two kingdoms." Since the two once were, and are destined to become again, one nation (ibid.), Ezekiel regards an encroachment on the southern flank of the land an offense against both temporarily separated constituents. By nevertheless calling them two lands Ezekiel heightens Seir's greed. (The formulation of the claim is Ezekiel's: Seirites would presumably seize only Judahite territory.)

The preposed *ʾt* before the two subjects is explained by J. Blau (*VT* 4 [1954], 14–15) as the result of perceiving the grammatical subject of *ly thyynh* "to me they shall be" as objects (= I shall have them).

we shall possess it (fem. sing.). "We" = the Seirites, the "us" of the iterated claim in vs. 12; "it" is the implicit "land" (*ʾrṣ* fem.; see 36:5). The shift from singular to plural speakers within the quotation was intolerable to the ancient translators, who conformed the second to the first clause of the speech (see text note). When in vs. 12 a "you" (sing.) is addressed who then speaks about "us," they let it stand, as not necessarily solecistic.

but YHWH was there! And so, we are to infer, even when desolate and abandoned by him it retains a trace of its former sanctity. The Seirites' claim to the land is an affront to God (vs. 12), for the presently desolate land is still God's ("my land," 36:5). The land is called "YHWH's land" in Hos 9:3 (see Andersen and Freedman, *Hosea,* AB, 524–25), and in Lev 25:23 the laws of the sabbatical and jubilee years are grounded on God's assertion that "mine is the land [of Israel]" (for some further consequences of the idea, see W. D. Davies, *The Territorial Dimension of Judaism* [Berkley: University of California Press, 1982], pp. 15–21).

G's "but YHWH is there" is startling. It contradicts Ezekiel's depiction of God's abandonment of the land (chs. 8–11), and incongruously anticipates the climactic renaming of restored Jerusalem at the end of the book, "YHWH is there" (48:35). But it agrees with the reverence for the ruined Temple shown by the North Israelite pilgrims as described in Jer 41:5. With that reverence has been compared the ruling of a Roman jurist: "A place in which sacred buildings are located remains sacred even when the building is destroyed" (Papinian, cited by Rudolph, *Jeremia,* HAT, ad loc.). One suspects G's version reflects *wyhwh šm,* a comment in the spirit of Jer 41:5 added in order to aggravate Seir's offense; MT's added *hyh* puts God's presence in the past so as to mitigate the contradiction. T removes all tension by rendering, "but to God are exposed the thoughts of the heart." This is made more pointed by the medievals: "but God was there and heard it"; cf. the end of vs. 13.

11. *I will deal* [*with you*] *in accord with your anger and your passion with which you dealt* (ʿśyt), *because of your enmity, with them* (bm). Cf. the similar phraseology in 25:14: "they shall deal with (*wʿśw b-*) Edom in accord with my anger and my fury," from which it appears that *bm* in our passage goes with *ʿśw*, not as generally held, with *mśnʾtyk* (yielding "because of your enmity toward them"). Indeed no form of **śnʾ* takes the preposition *b*. Accordingly, the initial *wʿśyty* must be complemented (in thought) by *bk* "with you"; so Kara, against G S and commentators who supply *lk* "to you." The anomalous form of *mśnʾtyk*—a singular noun with suffix of plural—has a few mates, e.g., *thltyk* (Ps 9:15).

I will make myself known among them. Among the Israelites, as a God of retribution; cf. 39:7: by destroying Gog God makes his name known amidst Israel. But G "to you" (reading *lk*; 20:5) is more to the point (see vs. 12: "and you [Seir] shall know . . ."); MT may have arisen by inadvertent assimilation to the preceding *bm*.

12. *blasphemies.* Seir's appropriation of Israel's land (vs. 12b), which is God's land (vss. 10b; 36:5b), is in contempt of God, as stated in the next verse. Derivatives of **nʾṣ* "contemn" almost always have God as their object, hence the fitness of "blaspheme/y."

"they are desolate." I.e., emptied of people (vs. 7) and therefore easy prey for us ("given to us to devour").

13. *You spoke vaunting over me.* Cf. the similar expression in Obadiah's oracle against Edom (vs. 12): "Do not rejoice over the Judahites on the day of their ruin; do not speak vauntingly on the day of distress." On rejoicing, see next two verses.

and surfeited (hʿtrtm) *me with your words.* An uncertain expression; S T: "multiplied words on (T: "before") me," as deriving the verb from *ʿ*tr*, Aramaic "be rich, abundant" = Hebrew *ʿ*šr*. There is no difficulty in assuming such an Aramaism in Ezekiel (or derivatives of the same root in Jer 33:6 "abundance"; Prov 27:6 "excessive"), but its meaning here is unclear. I compare it to "he multiplies (*wyrb*) his sayings" (Job 34:37) = "amasses (*ykbr*) words" (Job 35:16); cf. Eliezer: "you have overburdened me with your words." Alternatively, it might be compared to the preceding phrase, yielding "you talked big (against me)." In favor of the first alternative is 36:3, which condemns the constant talk about the takeover of Israel's land. A combination of both senses appears in I Sam 2:3: *ʾl trbw tdbrw gbhh* (G reflects only one *gbhh*), lit. "do not do much high (= boastful) talking."

The absence of this clause in G may be due to its difficulty.

14–15. *As the whole earth rejoices, I will deal desolation to you.* "When I shall accede to my kingdom, all the earth will rejoice, as it is said, 'The Lord reigns; let the earth rejoice (Ps 96:1)' and then I will make a desolation of you" (Rashi). MT invites some such eschatological reference, but the concept breaks the context; moreover, *ʿśh šmmh l-X* "do/deal desolation to" someone is unidiomatic (the idiom is *ntn/śm* X *(l)šmmh* "make X a desolation"; see vss. 3, 7).

Vs. 15a is suspiciously similar to vs. 14b; in fact it reads like a paraphrase of it. The absence of vs. 15a in G strengthens the suspicion that it is an explanatory addition, and leads us to read vs. 14b in its light. Vs. $14b^{\alpha}$ (which appears in G as in MT) agrees with vs. 15a$^{\alpha}$ if the consonants of *kl* are distributed to each adjacent word, thus:

**kśmḥk lh'rṣ* "as you rejoiced over the land (of Israel)"

The homeland is regularly called simply "the land" (e.g., 33:24); for retention of the article after *l*-, cf., e.g., 47:22; I Sam 13:21; II Sam 21:20; Neh 12:38; II Chron 10:7; 25:10. The restored text of vs. 14b$^{\alpha}$ = vs. 15a$^{\alpha}$, "as you rejoiced over the heritage of the house of Israel."

The next words in vs. 15a, "because it was desolated," fill out the elliptical formulation of vs. 14b: *šmmh* "desolation." As a noun, or revocalized as a participle (*šomema*), it may be an accusative of state: "[it being] desolate / a desolation."

The last clause of vs. 14b is filled out by its correspondent in vs. 15a: "[the same] will I do [= have done] to you." I will make you desolated and a cause of joy to your enemies.

Mount Seir, and the whole of Edom, all of it. The devastation will embrace the whole territory of the Edomites, whether mountainous or not. Edom is the commoner name of the hostile "brother"-people, and is singled out of "the rest of the nations" for blame in 36:5. "Mount Seir" is used in this oracle as a foil for the "mountains of Israel" in the sequel; but the ethnic appellation of the encroacher on Israel's land was Edom. The formula "all X, all of it" occurs with "the house of Israel" in 11:15; 20:40; 36:10; "Edom, all of it" occurs in 36:5. Here and (as in 11:15) G mistakes *klh* ("all of it") for a form of the verb "perish," a verb that doesn't occur in Ezekiel's oracles against foreign nations.

and they (the Edomites) *shall know.* G "you (sing.) shall know" assimilates to the foregoing; see comment to the recognition formula at the end of vs. 9.

36:1. "After he proclaimed punishment for Mount Seir he proclaimed consolation for the mountains of Israel" (Kimḥi).

2. *"Aha!"* (h'ḥ). A cry of exultation (T *ḥdw'* "O joy!"—cf. 35:15, "As you rejoiced, etc."), as in 25:3 (see comment), 26:2.

to say. Explicative *waw*, introducing an explanation of what this "Aha!" connotes; cf. the *waw* in Zech 9:9b (". . . an ass, that is, a foal . . ."), Prov 3:12b ("and that, as a father . . ."). G, seemingly at a loss, omits the copula; S spells out its sense (see text note).

eternal highlands. In the poetic Deut 32:13 Israel's mountainous land is called "the highlands of the earth" ("your highlands" in II Sam 1:19), and in Deut 33:15 its central part, the Josephides' tribal allocation, is called "eternal hills." Ezekiel combines elements of the two poetic appellations. "Eternal" in reference to hills and mountains expresses at once their ancientness and their permanence—"mountains ancient . . . hills eternal" (Deut 33:15; cf. Hab 3:6). G's "eternal desolation" reflects 35:9, which doesn't make it a preferred reading.

have become. The singular verb (*hyth*) accords with *mwršh* "possession."

3. *For the very good reason.* Similarly 13:10 (lit., "because, for because").

you were panted (šmwt wš'p) *after.* The difficult pair of infinitives is guessed at variously by the ancient versions; e.g., G "your being dishonored and your being hated"; S "you were despised and you were devastated and you were reviled"; T "they exalted themselves . . . they planned to destroy and to devastate you." But "devastate" (taking *šmwt* as a rare infinitive form of **šmm* [cf. *ḥnwt* from **ḥnn*, Ps 77:10] in transitive sense; Kimḥi) is not what the context calls for, and the other renderings have no basis. The pair recalls *ʾšm wʾšʾp yḥd* (Isa 42:14) "I will pant" (lit., "breathe out [**nšm*] and breathe in [Jer 2:24] together"). The consonants of *šmt* (disregarding the vowel-letter *w*) may represent a qal infinitive **šemet*, on the pattern of *gešet* from **ngš* "come near," mistakenly vocalized as though from **šmm* (see Kimḥi).

the remaining nations. Judah's neighbors who outlived her; see 25:16 and comment.

you . . . were the theme. Lit. "you were taken up," *teʿalu* being a mixed form of nifʿal and qal, perhaps signifying a double tradition.

slanderous speech. For *lšwn* "tongue" in this sense, see Ps 140:12 *ʾyš lšwn* "slanderer" (lit., "man of tongue").

popular defamation. Lit. "calumny (*dbh*) of people," perhaps an allusion to the view that as abandoned property the land was up for grabs, and/or to the jibe that the land devoured its populace (vs. 13). The latter reproach was first spread by the Israelite scouts who "uttered calumny (*dbh*) about the land" (Num 13:32; cf. 14:36f.); now it is heard from all sides.

4. *plunder and mockery.* "Plunder" (*lbz*) accords with the enemy's declaration in 35:12 that the land is theirs "to devour" (*lʾklh*); cf. the equivalence of the two terms in 34:8. "Mockery," *lʿg*, otherwise absent in Ezekiel, belongs to the terminology of gloating and contempt in the immediately preceding verses. Since *lʿg* is paired elsewhere with *bwz* "derision" (Ps 123:4; their verbal forms are paired as well, e.g., II Kings 19:21), it is no wonder that T *lḥy/wk* "for derision" occurs here, reflecting a reading *lbwz* (as in Gen 38:23) instead of MT *lbz*. Notwithstanding Kara's endorsement of this interpretation/reading, the divergent terms of MT cover the two aspects of the outrage and are to be considered an innovative, punning combination of Ezekiel.

5. *fiery passion.* Elsewhere only in Zeph 1:18; 3:8. As formerly God's passion was kindled by Israel's affronts to him (see comment to 5:13 [I, 115]), so now it flares against the arrogant gentiles.

I speak. An instantaneous perfect (see comment to 22:13; *BHSyn* 30.5.1d), but the speech is deferred till the end of vs. 6 and vs. 7.

all of Edom. Postpositional *klʾ* is miswritten for *klh* (as with Egypt [29:2] and Edom [35:15]), which some mss. give as Q. It is an Aramaic form, regularly placed after a noun; Ezra 5:7: *šlmʾ klʾ* "all well-being."

my land. See comment to 35:10, "But YHWH was there."

wholehearted rejoicing, with wholesouled contempt. These are examples of Ezekiel's play on the wording of his sources. The expression "hearty rejoicing" (*śmḥt lbb*, Isa 30:29) is augmented with the typically Deuteronomic "whole heart" (*kl lbb*, in the phrase *bkl lbb-* "with all X's heart") resulting in *śmḥt kl lbb*, lit. "rejoicing of whole heart." The Deuteronomic mate "with all X's soul" (*npš-*) appears to be echoed here by the following "with soul's contempt" (*bšʾt npš*, translated "wholesouled contempt"; see comment to 25:6).

so that her pastureland [*be*] *spoil.* The clause is justly suspected of being corrupt, though the versions support MT. The supplied verb is anomalously absent, and the conjectured sense is inappropriate, since much more than pastureland has been said to be subject to spoliation.

6. *to the soil of Israel.* "Soil" is appropriate for a prophecy of renewal of the land's fertility; a farmer is called "a tiller (lit. 'worker') of the soil" (*'wbd 'dmh,* e.g., Gen 4:2; Prov 12:11). Cf. "you shall be tilled (*n'bdtm,* lit. 'worked')," vs. 9.

taunts of the nations. As 34:29; specifically here, the malicious glee over Judah's desolation.

7. *I do solemnly swear.* Lit. "I lift my hand" (see 20:5 and comment [I, 363]); instantaneous perfect (above, comment to vs. 5). According to Muraoka (*Emphatic Words,* p. 54), the "redundant" pronoun *'ny* reflects the heightened self-consciousness of the speaker at the moment he takes the oath. Here, however, a factor is the shifting subjects of the verb *nś'* "lift, bear" in consecutive contrasting sentences: "Because you have borne (*nś'tm*) taunts . . . therefore I on my part lift (*'ny nś'ty*) my hand that the nations . . . shall themselves bear (*hmh . . . yś'w* taunts. See comment to 35:4 ("Your towns," etc.).

shall themselves bear taunts. When divine judgment overtakes them, measure for measure.

8. The presently desolate hilly landscape ("mountains of Israel"), upon which only stumps of dead trees stand, is summoned to renewed life and productivity. Branches and fruit are ascribed directly to the soil that nourishes them, and the order of mention is the natural sequence of branches first sprouting then bearing fruit. What can be done without human effort—the growing of edible fruit—precedes the return of the exiles and prepares their sustenance. Two items of the Garden of Eden story come to mind: fruit-bearing trees, planted by God, were readied for Adam before he was placed in the garden; and arboriculture preceded agriculture (Gen 2:5–16; 3:17–19). This accords with the relative importance of each in the natural economy of the land. "The regions of the land of Israel suitable for cultivation are located mostly in the highlands; these are especially fit for trees and shrubs and are not good for grains and vegetables. Trees thrived even on steep slopes, which were terraced for catching rain and preventing soil erosion . . . This accounts for the importance ascribed to fruit trees in the Bible. They dominate descriptions of vegetation . . . [and] comprise five of the seven species with which (according to Deut 8:8) the land is blessed: vine, fig, pomegranate, olive and date (honey)" (J. Feliks, *Plant World of the Bible* [in Hebrew] [Tel Aviv: Massada, 1957], pp. 12–14).

they are coming soon. Lit. "they are near (= soon) to come"; *qerebu* is an intransitive pi'el, derived from *qarob;* cf. "my deliverance is near (*qeroba* = soon) to come," Isa 56:1. A semantic and morphological parallel is *qiddamti libroaḥ,* Jonah 4:2, "I was beforehand with fleeing" (cf. *qedem* "aforetimes").

This declaration of a near return from exile has been connected with various hope-inspiring events: King Jehoiachin's release from prison in 561 (II Kings 25:27–30; Wevers), or the rise of Cyrus the Persian (ca. 550), which inspired the Second Isaiah (Carley; Malbim, too, takes Cyrus's reign to be the occasion of the prophecy); cf. the forty years of Judah's "punishment" (4:6), which, if calculated from 597 ("our exile"), would end in 557. But the prophet may have believed the deliverance would come much sooner in view of the need for YHWH to vindicate his honor.

Later Jewish chiliasts who combed Scriptures for clues to the time of the coming of the Messiah were advised by R. Abba (fourth century C.E., Babylonia) that "no sign of the end-time is more explicit than this one" (Sanhedrin 98a; Rashi glosses: "When the land of Israel yields its produce in abundance then the time will be near"). By calling Ezekiel's vague statement the most explicit clue R. Abba doubtless meant to discourage such speculation. In the event, it has inspired theurgic fantasies down to the present.

9. *I am coming to you.* The phrase that has heretofore meant "I am coming at (= to punish) you" (see at 5:8 [I, 113]), most recently in 35:3, means here: I am coming to you to help you.

turn my face to you. With favorable regard; opposed to "hide my face from you" (39:29), i.e., disregard and abandon you to misfortune because of your evildoing (Isa 59:2). See R. E. Friedman, "The Biblical Expression *mastir panim*," *Hebrew Annual Review* 1 (1977), 139–47.

The terms of this and the following verses echo the covenant blessings of Lev 26:9, save that what is there contingent on obedience is here predicted absolutely.

10. *the whole house of Israel, all of it.* Including the North Israelite diaspora (see 11:15 and comment thereto, I, 189), whose vacated land is prey to encroachers (35:10).

11. Vs. 11 augments vs. 10. This occurs explicitly in vs. 11b: "towns shall be resettled" of vs. 10b is first resumed by "I will resettle you (meaning "your towns," vs. 33) . . ." and then is augmented by "and prosper you more than (versions: "as," blunting the point) your original state." Vs. 11a bears the same relation to 10a: on the restored land not only humans but also domestic animals (*bhmh*) will be numerous, and they will be very prolific to boot. That is the force of *wrbw wprw*, which G lacks (as though it were superfluous). Since the regular sequence of members in this common verb pair is *prh–rbh*, the present reversal exemplifies late Biblical Hebrew's penchant for reversing traditional pairs, described by A. Hurvitz, "'Diachronic Chiasm' in Biblical Hebrew," in B. Uffenheimer, ed., *Bible and Jewish History* (in Hebrew) (Tel Aviv: Tel Aviv University, 1971), pp. 248–55.

former state (qdmwt-) . . . *original state* (r'šwt-). Plural nouns often serve for abstracts as signifying the diverse concrete manifestations of a quality or state (*BHSyn* 7.4.2). The singular *qdmt-* occurs in 16:55. The *i* vowel of *rišot-* (like that of *rišon* "first") is dissimilated from *o* (**rošot-*; cf. *roša*, Zech 4:7).

prosper (w^{e}heṭiboti) [*you*]. The vocalization of the hifʿil verb mixes that of **yṭb* (*heṭabti*) and **ṭwb* (*h^{a}ṭiboti*); the object is supplied from the previous clause (GKC, § 117 f).

12. *I will cause humans to walk on you — my people Israel.* Reversing your utter desolation (6:14); cf. 35:7: in a desolate land no one comes and goes. But the full portent of *whwlkty* is suggested only in the sequel.

and they shall possess you, and you shall be their heritage. As the depopulation indicated dispossession (see Structure and Themes on 33:24), so population entailed possession. More: in the conjunction of walking and possession there resonates the popular legal conception that ownership of land may be established by walking through it. Thus in Gen 13:17 God says to Abraham: "Up, walk (*hthlk*) through the land in its length and breadth for I will give it to you." It is likely that this passage underlies Josh 24:3: "I took your father Abraham from beyond the River and caused him to walk (*w'wlk*) through the whole land of Canaan." Comparable, too, is I Kings 21:16: King Ahab "set out for Naboth's vineyard to take possession of it" (see A. Kahana, *Commentary to Genesis* [in Hebrew] [Zhitomir, 1903], at Gen 13:17; discussion of the concept as "popular legal thought" in D. Daube, *Studies in Biblical Law* [New York: Ktav, 1969], pp. 37f.). The designs on Israel's patrimony (vs. 2; 35:10) will be finally quashed when God enables Israel's masses to assert their possession of it by walking on it. G's bizarre "I will beget" arose from an erroneous *Vorlage* (*whwldty*).

In midverse the pronouns change from plural to singular, as though the mountains have congealed into one; indeed the whole land is called "this fair mountain" in Deut 3:25. G S retain the plural.

never again lose them. G "be bereaved of them"; S "be left destitute"; V "without your own people"—all suit the context better than "bereave them" (of their children, as in 5:17; 14:15). The point is not that parents shall no longer be bereft of their children, but that the country shall never again be depopulated and thus subject to seizure by its neighbors. Depopulation is metaphorized as a country's loss of her children (cf. Isa 47:8f.); Rashi and other medievals refer it to deportation, a needless specificity (see next verses). The pi'el of *škl* "lose one's children" occurs in a similar metaphor in II Kings 2:19: "The water is bad and the land *mšklt* keeps losing her children" (= inhabitants, who drink the water and die; cf. Rashi and Kimḥi). In God's plaint in Jer 15:7b *šikkalti 'ibbadty 'et 'ammi* the first term is explained by the second; not "I have bereaved (= done away with the children of) my people," but, paralleling "I have destroyed," rather "I have lost (= done away with) my people" (Kimḥi: "He says *šikkalti* because they are his [metaphoric] children"). The difference from qal (e.g., "Let me not lose ['*eškal*] you both," Gen 27:45) in these passages seems to be that pi'el signifies an active rather than a passive losing of one's children, nearer to doing away with them or killing them off; see V's renderings: "strangling" (vs. 13), "killing" (vs. 14).

13. *they say to you* (pl.). Unspecified sayers; for the indefinite sense of the plural participle, see the identical phrase in Exod 5:16 ("they say to us"). The versions show "you" in the singular to agree in number with the addressee.

"*You are a devourer of humans.*" Previously said of the ravaging lion-kings of Judah (19:3, 6). As the kings perversely killed those whom they should protect (cf. the wicked shepherds of 34:3, 10), so the land, which should sustain its population, is reproached for having made an end of them (for this sense of "devour," see also Lev 26:38; Ps 79:7). The spies sent by Moses to scout Canaan defame the land similarly: "it is a land that devours its inhabitants," Num 13:32. Whatever pre-Israelite feature of Canaan may be referred to in that statement (alleged infertility? an internecine or international battlefield? See J. Milgrom, *Numbers*,

The JPS Torah Commentary [Philadelphia: The Jewish Publication Society, 1990], pp. 106–7), its echo here has solid grounds. For medievals, "that country habitually destroys her inhabitants: the Amorites perished in her and the Jews perished in her" (Rashi)—an interpretation that ascribes to the taunters a view of local history rooted in Israelite tradition. Perhaps grounds enough for the taunt are the famines that periodically ravaged the country (see IDB, s.v. "Famine," for a listing), causing death and driving people to seek refuge abroad, thus broadcasting the failure of the land to sustain its population.

"you kept losing your nations." The construction with *hyh* + participle is taken as past progressive (*BHSyn* 37.7.1b). The reference is to the repeated deportations suffered first by Israel and then by Judah, or to repeated famines, both of which may well have been common knowledge among Israel's neighbors. The versions translate "your nation" (singular), with K (= the ideal unified people of Israel); Q, in the plural, accords with "the two nations" of 35:10.

14. *lose.* With Q and versions, reading *tškly;* K *tkšly* "cause to stumble" is a scribal error; see ahead, last comment.

15. *taunts . . . reproaches.* Cited in vs. 13.

and your nations you shall no more cause to stumble. "Through sinning" (Malbim)—an alien idea, blaming the land for its people's sin. Not in G, the clause is identical with K of vs. 14a$^{\beta}$, repeated to no clear purpose.

STRUCTURE AND THEMES

This loosely organized, repetitive oracle develops two topics: (1) the enormity of the (intended?) encroachment on Judah's territory by its neighbors—especially the Edomites, and (2) God's answering assurance that Israel would repossess its land, and that, in greater prosperity than before. The topics do not coincide with the literary division of the oracle. By their headings, 35:1–15 is an address to Mount Seir while 36:1–15 is an address to the mountains of Israel. Topic 1, however, crosses the literary boundary, dominating the latter half of the first address and the adjacent first half of the second—where it might well be dispensed with. This raises the possibility that in the present oracle two originally separate pieces have been conjoined. However that may be, the duplication serves to underline the importance of topic 1; it not only motivates, it necessitates the divine response of topic 2.

After the revelation-event formula (vs. 1), the oracle has, as aforesaid, two equal parts: A, a doom addressed to Mount Seir, and B, a promise of restoration addressed to the mountains of Israel. The epithet "Mount Seir" is used for Edom to contrast it to "the mountains of Israel."

A (35:1–15): doom of Mount Seir. This part opens with a command to prophesy (vss. 2–3a$^{\alpha}$) and ends with a recognition formula (vs. 15), followed by a new command to prophesy—the start of part B. It is articulated by internal pauses—recognition formulas (vss. 4, 9, 12), and *yaʿn–laken* sets as follows:

A1 (vss. 3a$^{\beta}$–4): unmotivated doom prophecy, echoed in the conclusions of two motivated dooms that follow.

A2 (vss. 5–9): first motivated (*ya'an–laken*) doom prophecy: Seir delivered Israelites to the sword, so Seir will be filled with sword-slain, measure for measure.

A3 (vss. 10–15): second motivated doom prophecy. For its designs on Israel's/God's desolated land, Seir will be desolated. This loosely organized section comprises a motivated doom prophecy, citing Seir's expectation to take over the land (*ya'an–laken*–recognition formula; vss. 10–12a$^{\alpha}$); an *inclusio* stressing God's hearing Seir's blasphemous vaunting (vss. 12a$^{\beta}$–13); a promise that Seir's joy over the land's desolation will be requited in kind (vss. 14–15).

A1 and A2 agree with the picture of a hate-driven, vengeful Edom given in 25:12–14. Edom's participation in the defeat of Judah is denounced, rather than its later expansionist designs. But while the key term in 25:12–14 is **nqm* "vengeance," in A1–A2 the key term is **šmm* "desolation," conforming to the theme of A3: Mount Seir's future desolation for asserting its title to the desolated highlands of Israel. The sequence A2–A3 is chronological: Seir's massacre of Israelites "at the time of their disaster" (vs. 5) is followed by its later offense against the devastated land.

The function of the first part of all of Ezekiel's restoration prophecies is to depict the flawed past or present that will be repaired by divine intervention. That is why there is a second prophecy against Edom, this time among the restoration oracles. Edom's vengeance at the fall of Judah, included in the list of neighborly outrages in ch. 25 was not a hindrance to Israel's restoration. But Edom's encroachment on Israelite territory was, and must be countered before restoration could take place. I Esdras 4:50 is acutely aware of this: it asserts that the Persian government's decree permitting the Jews to return to Judah included an express order that "the Edomites give up the villages that they took over from the Jews." A3 thus prepares the way for B. But what need was there for A2, which goes over the same ground as 25:12–14? Why not attach A3 directly to A1? In order to present a complete indictment; A2 is a new version of 25:12–14 adapted to the terms of the present context (Mount Seir, mountains, desolation).

The desolation of Mount Seir is the prelude and foil for the restoration and blessing of the mountains of Israel (B). But B also serves to undo the condemnation of the selfsame mountains in ch. 6. The relation of these three (literary) events is shown by their common terminology:

Israel's Mts. Doomed ch. 6	*Mt. Seir Doomed* ch. 35	*Israel's Mts. Blessed* ch. 36:1–15
set your face [vs. 2]	vs. 2	——
prophesy [2]	vs. 2	vss. 1, 6
mts. of Isr. hear the word of YHWH [3]	——	vss. 1, 4
mts., hills, gullies valleys [3]	vs. 8	vss. 4, 6
slain fall [4, 7]	vs. 8	population numerous [10f.]
towns ruined [6]	vs. 4	towns, ruins restored [10]
Aha! [11]	——	vs. 2
outstretched hand [14]	vs. 3	——

B (36:1–15) is an oracle of restoration addressed to the highlands of Israel. Its first half (vss. 1–7) grounds the restoration in God's rage at the designs and slurs of the nations on his land. There are repeated charges to prophesy (vss. 1, 3, 8), summonses to hear (vss. 1, 4), messenger formulas (vss. 2, 3, 4, 5, 6, 7), abortive *ya'an–laken* sequences (vss. 2–3, 3–4; *laken* alone: vss. 5, 6); only 6b[β]–7 comes to an issue. Critics routinely suppose that several hands have been at work here, and speculate variously about an "authentic kernel" of the oracle. What the present text (which is reflected in all the versions) points to is repeated formulations—whether by the prophet himself cannot be proved or disproved—of the divine motive for renewal of the land. Skinner calls it "divine patriotism" (p. 371), an identification of God with his land such that a rival claim of ownership, or an aspersion on its character—both made possible by its depopulation—infuriates him.

Provoked by the arrogance of the gentiles, God proclaims the imminent renewal of the land—its refructification, its repopulation, its recultivation, its resettlement, all better than before. This will reveal to the redeemed YHWH's glory (vss. 8–11). The large restored population will establish an unchallengeable ownership of their heritage, and the motherland shall never again lose her children (vs. 12). Thus the reproach of the land as a devourer of her inhabitants, justified by her past, will be silenced (vss. 13–15).

B is obviously related to A in subject as in language, but there is a reversal of key terms: A is dominated by derivatives of **šmm* (ten occurrences), with only one occurence of **yrš*. This accords with its main theme—the destruction of Mount Seir as a foil to the restoration of Israel. B on the other hand has but one occurrence of **šmm* with four **yrš*, in accord with its main theme—the thwarting of gentile designs on the land in favor of Israel. Furthermore, while A knows of only one encroacher on Israel's territory, B names as culprits "the remaining nations who are all around." These divergences suggest that A was not originally composed as a prelude to B, and that B at one time was a self-contained oracle. Hence the need to state the gentiles' offenses in the first half of B, which now appears redundant after the parallel account of Seir's offenses in A.

The burning issue of this oracle was an unanticipated challenge to God's sovereign control over the disposition of his land, and a slur on that land that resulted from its devastation and depopulation. This was not taken into account in the earlier doom prophecy (e.g., ch. 6) or in the threats of punishment for breach of covenant in the Torah. Indeed one indication of the pre-exilic outlook of the covenant-curses of Lev 26 (and Deut 28) is their ignorance of this issue. Lev 26, which inspired so much of Ezekiel's thought, depicts as the ultimate punishment such a desolation of the land as will appall the enemies that occupy it (vs. 32). Far from being "panted after" or "devoured," the desolate land will lie fallow ("pay back its sabbaths") until its exiled population, contrite, stirs God's memory of his ancient covenant (vss. 34–45). In the event, our oracle contends, the destruction of the land and the exile of its inhabitants produced gentile blasphemy and land grabbing. That required a revision of the conditions for restoration. Ezekiel portrays God, stung by the gloating land sharks, sentencing them to desolation on the one hand and shortening the term of exile on the other ("for they are coming soon," 36:8). Vindication of his honor necessitates a more than complete restoration of Israel on its land—a restoration and an enduring prosperity that have nothing to do with contrition, and cannot wait for it, but are demanded by the mockery of the gentiles.

This oracle, like many others, is formulated as a reaction to attributed statements, the threat of deeds rather than deeds themselves. More than ever it is difficult to assess the reality of these attributions. Did reports of intent to grab land reach the prophet and did he fashion the statements? Allusion to "the two nations and two lands," in Ezekiel's time no more than a historical memory, would not likely have been an Edomite manner of speech about Judah. The vilification of the land by gentiles can be accounted for by information foreigners might have had about the country. But the clear echoes of the story of the spies sent by Moses to reconnoiter the land ("defamation," "a land that devours its inhabitants") make one wonder whether the prophet has not externalized some bitter reflections of the exiles themselves on the inhospitability of the homeland, with its droughts and other natural disasters, its wars and deportations. Ezekiel would have regarded such reflections as comparable to the faithless report of the spies that caused the forty-year wandering (Num 13:17–14:35). Whether externalized or truly external, such reflections on God's land were an intolerable injury to the divine majesty. The following oracle is the boldest conceptualization of the redemption of Israel as a divine necessity, drawing from the concept its ultimate conclusion concerning the future of human nature.

XLIII. Restoration for the Sake of God (36:16–38)

36 [16]The word of YHWH came to me: [17]Man, while the house of Israel dwelt on their soil they defiled it by their ways and their deeds; to me their ways were like the impurity of a menstruous woman. [18]So I poured my fury on them on account of the blood they poured on the ground—and by their idols they defiled it—[19]and I scattered them among the nations so that they were dispersed among the lands. I punished them in accord with their ways and their deeds.

[20]When they[a] came to the nations to which they came they desecrated my holy name, in that it was said of them, "These are YHWH's people and from his land they have gone forth." [21]I was moved to save my holy name that the house of Israel desecrated among the nations to which they came.

[22]Now then, say to the house of Israel: Thus said Lord YHWH: It is not for your sake that I am about to act, O house of Israel, but for my holy name that you desecrated among the nations to which you came. [23]I will sanctify my great name that has been desecrated among the nations, which you desecrated amidst them; and the nations shall know that I am YHWH, declares Lord YHWH, when I assert my sanctity through you in their sight.

[24]I will take you from the nations,
and gather you from all the lands,
and bring you to your soil.
[25]I will throw purifying water on you and you will be purged;
of all your impurities and of all your idols I will purge you.
[26]Then I will give you a new heart,
and a new spirit will I put inside you.
I will remove the heart of stone from your flesh,
and give you a heart of flesh.
[27]I will put my spirit inside you,
and so bring to pass that you shall follow my laws,
and my rules you shall carefully observe.

[28]Then you shall dwell in the land that I gave to your fathers; you shall be my people while I will be your God. [29]I will deliver you from all your impurities, and summon the grain and make it abundant, and not put famine upon you. [30]I will

[a]MT singular, G S V T plural; see text note a to 14:1 (I, 247).

make the fruit of trees and the produce of fields abundant so that you shall no more take the reproach of famine among the nations. [31]Then you shall remember your evil ways and your doings that were not good, and you shall loathe yourselves on account of your iniquities and your abominations. [32]Not for your sake am I about to act, declares Lord YHWH; let it be known to you! Be ashamed and disgraced by your ways, O house of Israel!

[33]Thus said Lord YHWH: At the time that I purge you of all your iniquities, and resettle the towns, so that the ruins are rebuilt, [34]and the desolate land is tilled, instead of being a desolation in the sight of every passerby, [35]they shall say: "That [once] desolate land has become like the Garden of Eden, and its towns, [once] ruined, desolated and demolished, have been repopulated and fortified." [36]The nations that remain around you shall know that I YHWH have rebuilt what was demolished, have replanted what was desolate. I am YHWH; what I have spoken I will do.

[37]Thus said Lord YHWH: I will further respond to the house of Israel by doing this for them: I will make them teem with humans like flocks—

[38]like flocks of small cattle for sacred offerings,
like the flocks of Jerusalem on her holy days—

so shall the [once] ruined towns be filled with human flocks, and they shall know that I am YHWH.

COMMENT

36:17. *while the house of Israel dwelt on their soil.* A circumstantial clause, like I Kings 13:20: "While they were sitting at the table"; I Sam 9:11: "As they went up the ascent to the town." "The house of Israel" is the subject of the following clause, which is the predicate ("they defiled it . . ."). For *wa* + imperfect (consecutive) introducing a predicate, see, e.g., Gen 30:30: "for the little you had before I came, *wyprṣ* it has increased" (S. R. Driver, *Tenses,* §§ 165–66).

they defiled it. According to the laws, the land of Israel contracts impurity by certain gross offenses: unchastity (Lev 18:25–28; cf. Deut 24:4), unexpiated bloodshed (Num 35:34), and exposure overnight of an executed criminal (Deut 21:23). The impurity of idolatry is a widely attested notion (e.g., Ezek 5:11, see D. P. Wright, *The Disposal of Impurity* [SBLDS 101. Atlanta: Scholars Press, 1987], pp. 283–85); in Jer 2:7 and here it is said to defile the land. In Lev 18:25–28 the defiled land vomits out its defilers; cf. vs. 19 below.

by their ways and their deeds. A fixed pair in Ezekiel: 14:23; 20:43f. (idolatry); 24:14 (bloodshed).

like the impurity of a menstruous woman (kṭmʾt hndh). G S T and the medievals understand *hndh* to be the menstruous woman, as in 18:6 (and Mishnaic Hebrew; see comment there), rather than its usual sense "(menstrual) impurity." The article of *hndh* is generic, as in *hʿṣ* "trees" of vs. 30 below.

In the priestly law (Lev 15:19–24, on which see J. Milgrom, *Leviticus 1–16,* AB, pp. 952f.) the menstruant is in an untouchable state of separation from society. In nonlegal biblical texts menstrual impurity is "a metaphor for extreme pollution, ultimate revulsion" (Milgrom). Note the parallelism of Ezek 7:19: "fling into the streets || be as *ndh*" (see comment, I, 152), and the polar terms of II Chron 29:5 "Take the *ndh* out of the holy place (*qdš*)." Here the defiling inhabitants will be expelled from the holy land (vs. 19).

The *ndh*-state of a given population (incurred by their evildoing) is communicated to their land; e.g., Canaan prior to its takeover by Israel was "a *ndh*-land because of the *ndh* of the peoples of the lands" (Ezra 9:11).

18. *on account of the blood they poured on the ground.* This answers to and motivates the foregoing "I poured my fury on them," while interpreting (as an allusion to blood) the *ndh* element of the simile *kṭm't hndh* of vs. 17. Just so, the following clause, "and by their idols they defiled (*ṭm'w*) it" interprets *ṭm't-* of the simile. *ṭm't hndh* thus alludes to the bloodshed and idolatry so often denounced in Ezekiel's oracles (e.g., 22:3–13; 23:37f.).

and by their idols they defiled it. The shift in construction (a parallel to the preceding clause would have read "and on account of their idols with which they defiled it") is almost identical to that in Jer 30:14f.: "on account of your many iniquities—and your sins were numerous—I did these things to you." Similar is the shift in coordinate clauses from infinitive (*bhpyṣy*) to finite verb (*wzryty*) in 12:15.

The two clauses interpreting vs. 7's *ṭm't hndh* do not appear in G; they may be an elaboration that did not enter all early mss. of the book.

19. *I scattered . . . so that they were dispersed.* A typical sequence of action (active verb)–achieved state (passive); so, e.g., 6:3b–4a; (reversed sequence in 15:3); 30:18; 32:12; and in our oracle vs. 33b. G S obliterate the distinction by rendering both verbs as active, a leveling facilitated by the fact that in all other (previous) occurrences of this verb pair both verbs are indeed in the active (12:15; 20:23; 22:15; 29:12; 30:23, 26). In this last occurrence the prophet makes a change, as it were a closure of the series.

Medievals gave the comparison of dispersed Israel to a woman in menstrual impurity a silver lining: "Since the congregation of Israel is metaphorized as God's wife, she is compared in her sinful state to a menstruant whose husband puts her away all the days of her impurity, but draws her near once she becomes pure" (Kimḥi).

20. *they came to the nations to which they came.* A manner of speaking when there is no desire to be precise, called by S. R. Driver (*Deuteronomy*, ICC, at 1:46, p. 31) the *idem per idem* ("the same by the same") idiom; see Ezek 12:25 and comment (I, 229). Here the imprecision (repeated in vss. 21, 22) intimates a scattering of exiles and refugees among many countries, which gave the calamity a publicity that aggravated the insult to God.

they desecrated my holy name. NEB, NJPS: "they caused my holy name to be profaned"; *NRSV*: "they profaned my holy name." Moderns vacillate because of the new sense the expression has here. Heretofore "desecration" meant conduct deliberately flouting God's decrees, in disregard of his holiness (so in 13:19; 22:26). But here exiled Israel desecrates (profanes) God('s name) involuntarily, not by any act of defiance, but by the way her condition reflects on her God; see discussion in I, 384, and Sheldon H. Blank, "Isaiah 52.5 and the Profanation of the Name," *HUCA* 25 (1954), 1–8.

in that it was said of them, etc. "The nations of the world would say of them: 'Being YHWH's people, they are dear to him, and if he were able to help them they would not have gone forth from his land. He would have prevented it, but his strength has failed.' Thus although they have gone into exile for their iniquities the nations do not say that their iniquities are the cause, but rather that 'God's hand is inadequate to save' (after Isa 59:1)" (Kara). This interpretation is supported by the similar thought and terms of 20:8f., 13f., 21f.; there God is said not to have "poured his fury on" sinful Israel in olden times so that "his name not be desecrated in the sight of the nations"; i.e., he would be discredited by the misfortune that would befall the people associated with him; see I, 365f., 384. This is the generally held interpretation of the insult to YHWH alluded to here.

However, our passage contains terms connecting it with the depiction of the deportees of Jerusalem as exemplars of depravity. When the Judahites are "scattered among the nations and dispersed among the lands," their remnant will tell all their abominable acts "in the nations to which they have come" (12:15–16); the survivors will "go forth (from Jerusalem)" to the exiles who, when they see "their ways and their deeds" — how corrupt they are — will be convinced that the disaster was deserved (14:22–23). Combine this with Ezekiel's condemnation of Israel's conduct as worse than the heathens' (5:6–7), as shocking even by their standards (16:27), and an alternative interpretation suggests itself: God's name is dishonored by association with such miscreants.

In this alternative, the expression "from his land they have gone forth" refers not so much to exile as to origin, like "Caphtoreans who originated in (lit. 'went forth from') Caphtor" (Deut 2:23). The depraved exiles are YHWH's people and their origin is YHWH's land, and disgraced is the god whose land spawned then spewed out such a people.

It is difficult to choose between the alternatives; the sequel fits both. Perhaps the suggestion of both was intentional.

21. *I was moved to save my holy name.* From discredit. *ḥml ʿl* elsewhere takes a tangible object, and is rendered "take pity on" (16:5; Exod 2:6); here where the concern is to save reputation, the appropriate rendering is as above. G and Kara obviate the peculiar use of the verb by interpretively supplying a personal object: G "I spared them (Kara: Israel, taking them out of the exile) because of my holy name." But *ḥml* conveys a positive regard for its object, and that is inappropriate for Israel here, inasmuch as vs. 22 emphasizes that it is not out of concern for Israel but in order to save his reputation that God will act. Fohrer mistakes G's interpretive rendering — guaranteed to be such by Kara's concurrence — for a witness to a different *Vorlage* (and translates unacceptably "I was sorry for them because of my holy name").

23. *I will sanctify my great name.* Win for it the awe and dread due to the holy name of God, made great through his mighty acts (cf. Josh 7:9 "[If we are defeated] what will you do about your great name [hitherto associated with triumphs]?"). On the innovated term *qiddeš šᵉmo*, see I, 384.

when I assert my sanctity through you in their sight. As in 20:41; see comment there. The sequel spells out the wondrous reversals of Israel's condition that will manifest God's dread sanctity to all in whose sight it had been impugned.

24. Reversal of vs. 19.

25. Reversal of the personal impurity ("like the impurity of a menstruous woman [*hndh*]") incurred by the evils of vss. 17–18. The figure uses terms drawn from the ritual of the "water of lustration" (*my ndh,* lit. "water of/for impurity") which was "thrown" on persons or objects to cleanse them of corpse-impurity (Num 19:13, 20). T actually renders "purifying water" here by the same term used by T^{O} in Num 19 for "water of lustration."

purifying water. Lit. "pure water," a unique phrase. Ehrlich takes it to be a euphemism for the lustral "water of impurity" (see previous comment), but it is more likely a resultative adjective—water that effects purity—like *yg'ym* "weary" in Eccl 1:8 "All thing are wearisome" (make one weary); cf. Mishnaic *'nbym qhwt* "unripe (lit. 'blunt') grapes" (*m. 'Abot* 4.20; grapes that "blunt" the teeth; see comment to Ezek 18:2).

Absolution is described in terms drawn from the realm of purity/impurity, according to the priestly view underlying vss. 17–19 that the exile resulted from the accumulated impurity caused by bloodshed and idolatry.

of all your impurities . . . I will purge you. Terms taken from Lev 16, the ritual of the Day of Atonement; note especially the plural "impurities" that occurs only there (vss. 16, 19) and here (see also ahead, vs. 29). In vs. 35 below, what God purges is "all your iniquities (*'wnwt*)," whence it appears that the broader category of ethical wrongs defile. On the predominantly ethical character of *'wnwt,* see Milgrom, *Leviticus,* AB, p. 25.

26–27. Elaborates 11:19–20 and contrasts with 18:31: "Make yourselves a new heart and a new spirit"; see I, 341. Vs. 26a is explicated by vss. 26b–27a. At present Israel's heart (the seat of the mind, of inclinations and resolutions; BDB, pp. 524–25) is stony; Israel is "tough/hard-hearted"—obdurate and obstinate (2:4; 3:7; see comment). After its purification its heart will be "of flesh"—yielding, malleable, impressionable—of the same element as its body. Implicit is the idea that presently Israel's inner nature is at odds with its mortal, creaturely frame.

my spirit. God, who "fashions the spirit of man"—his animating impulse (1:12 "will")—"inside him" (Zech 12:1), will replace Israel's hopelessly corrupted spirit with his own impulsion to goodness and righteousness, his "good spirit" of Ps 143:10: "Teach me to do what pleases you . . . May your good spirit lead me on level ground."

and so bring to pass. With this use of *'śh* Cooke rightly compares Eccl 3:14: the sage climaxes his reflection on the immutable decrees of God with the deterministic assertion: "and God has brought to pass that men revere him" (NJPS; following H. L. Ginsberg, *Qohelet* [in Hebrew] [Tel Aviv: Newman, 1961], p. 73, who compares our Ezekiel passage).

that you shall follow my laws, etc. After the language of Lev 26:3: "If my laws you follow, and my commandments—you carefully observe them." Just as the sequel in Lev 26:4 states the result of obedience ("I will give you rains in their season"), so does the sequel here in the next verse.

28. *Then you shall dwell in the land.* "Since you shall follow my laws and my rules you shall dwell (= stay put) in the land, and she shall not lose you again

[as said above, 36:12], for it was your failure to observe them that was the cause of the exile" (MenbSh).

that I gave to your fathers. Only here in Ezekiel, repeatedly in Jeremiah (e.g., Jer 16:15; 24:10).

while I (w'nky). Only here in Ezekiel is this long form of the first person pronoun found; however, it is frequent in Jeremiah and in his covenant formula of mutuality (Jer 11:4; 30:22); see esp. Jer 24:6–7, like our passage a promise of future restoration. For the contrastive function of the pronoun, see Muraoka, *Emphatic Words,* pp. 54ff.

29. *I will deliver you from all your impurities.* "That bring upon you punishments of exile, sword, plague and famine" (Eliezer). "Impurities" = defiling evil deeds; for similar energizing of evil deeds, cf. Ps 39:9: "Rescue me from all my transgressions"; 38:5: "for my iniquities have submerged me / they are like a load too heavy for me to bear." That Ezekiel energizes impurities is characteristically priestly.

and summon the grain. Lit. "call to the grain" to come into being; similarly Isa 48:13 "when I summoned them (namely, heaven and earth), they sprang into being" (*NEB*).

30. *produce of fields.* A unique prosification of the poetic *tnwbwt śdy* of Deut 32:13; Lam 4:9.

take the reproach of famine among the nations. "Reproach of famine" specifies the "reproach of the peoples" of vs. 15; cf. 34:29: "they shall no longer be carried off by famine and no longer bear the taunts of the nations." Kimḥi explains "among the nations" as alluding to the emergency emigration of Israelites to other lands: "The land of Israel is more dependent on rain than other lands, hence it is liable to famine . . . and when a person has to depart his land for another country because of famine, that is a disgrace."

31. *you shall remember* (S: + "there") *your evil ways.* S assimilates our passage to 20:43 (where I erroneously omitted "there" in my translation) and thereby emphasizes the priority of restoration to contrition. Only after their spiritual recreation in their land will they be capable of remorse over their past evildoing. And when their obduracy will be removed, the memory of their past misconduct will remain, to arouse self-reproach.

evil ways . . . doings that were not good. "Way(s) and doings" (*m'lly-*) is characteristic of Jeremiah's idiom (e.g., Jer 4:18; 7:3, 5; 17:10) and occurs only here in Ezekiel (contrast "ways and deeds [*'lylwt*]" in vss. 17 and 19 above.

"That were not good" is a litotes (see comment to the same expression in 18:18 [I, 332]), an emphatic parallel to "evil" in the preceding clause. A good example of emphatic paralleling by a double litotes is Ps 36:5: "Lying abed he plots mischief; / he stands on a no-good path; / he does not reject evil." The repetition that was avoided by our author appears in Zech 1:4: "evil ways . . . evil doings."

32. *Not for your sake.* Repeated from vs. 22, hammering home the utter lack of merit — indeed the viciousness — of the audience, for which the prophet calls on them to —

Be ashamed and disgraced. Anticipating their post-restoration remorse; cf. the similar call to the wanton sister in 16:52. S reads: "Be ashamed and disgraced by your evil ways so that you do not die, O house of Israel," adapting the verse to the call for repentance of 33:11 ("Turn, O turn from your evil ways, for why should you [S: "so that you do not"] die O house of Israel!"). But assimilating the two passages obliterates the crucial difference between them: in 33:11 (and 18:31f.) repentance is enjoined as a precondition of Israel's restoration ("life"); but the shame and self-reproach that the prophet enjoins here cannot be a condition of their restoration, which is explicitly grounded on God's interest and not on the people's deserts. The course of this theme in Ezekiel's thought can be traced from 6:9—where it is the exiles who will feel shame over their past—through 16:61–63, 20:43, our passage, 39:26, 43:10f., and 44:13 (in all these, it is the restored Israelites who will be shamed by the memory of their past wickedness). See discussion in I, 141, 306.

33–34. Echoes vss. 25 ("purge"), 10b ("resettle towns, rebuild ruins"), 9b ("be tilled"); note the reverse order, intimating deliberate allusion. "Purge of iniquity" occurs only here and Jer 33:8, but here "iniquity" replaces "impurities" of vs. 25, evoking the identical exchange of terms in the two acts of the annual purgation ritual of Lev 16, vss. 16 and 21. See Structure and Themes.

instead of being. Lit. "instead of that it was," a sense of *tḥt ʾšr* found again only in Deut 28:62 (elsewhere it means "because, inasmuch as," e.g., I Sam 26:21; Jer 29:19).

in the sight of every passerby. As 5:14 indicates, the phrase goes with "desolation" rather than with "tilled" (as Ehrlich [Hebrew] proposes). The phrase is unique to Ezekiel; see comment to 5:14 (I, 115f).

35. The admiration of people at the land's renewal is conveyed by a quotation; cf. the more frequent use of quotation to express wonder at its ruin: Deut 29:21–23; I Kings 9:8. Some medievals (Kimḥi, MenbSh) read wonder here, too, taking the subject of "they shall say" to be the aforementioned passersby: "This desolate land was once like the Garden of Eden, and the ruined . . . cities once were populated and fortified." Possible, but with strain on *wʾmrw*, which is naturally read as perfect consecutive (= future) with impersonal subject: "and they (= people) shall say."

The natural reading—admiration—conflicts with 38:11, which depicts the future Israelite towns as unwalled and defenseless, a conflict avoided by the alternative reading. Zimmerli accounts for the conflict by assuming that "the particular theological statements of 38:11 were not yet available to the author of 36:35." Perhaps a simpler explanation is that the ancient model of a city built to perfection included, as a matter of course, defensive structures. The author of our verse was intent on imagining the model city in contrast with ruins; in 38:11 his point was to motivate distant hordes to attack Israel, for which unwalled cities supplied a good ground. Not working to a systematic theology, but for immediate rhetorical effect, he sometimes fell into inconsistencies. See above, § XX, Structure and Themes.

That (hlzw). A unique feminine form of a rare demonstrative, whose masculine form, *hlz(h)*, usually refers to objects at a distance from the speaker (e.g., Gen 24:65; Judg 6:20).

ruined. The anomalous vocalization of the first syllable ḥ° (instead of ḥ^a, as in the singular *ḥ^{a}reba,* Neh 2:3) shows the influence of the noun *ḥ°rabot* "ruins" (end of vs. 33).

36. *The nations that remain around you.* As in vs. 4, the neighbors that outlived Israel and gloated over its fall. From this it is inferable that they will be punished only after seeing Israel's restoration and the vindication of God.

"(Re)build, demolish, (re)plant" is a combination unique in Ezekiel, common in Jeremiah (e.g., Jer 1:10; 45:4).

37–38. Echoes vss. 10a, 11, and the flock metaphor of ch. 34.

I will further respond to the house of Israel. Beside making the land abundantly fertile and rebuilding and resettling the towns, God will more than make up for the decimation of the population. His responding (nif'al of *drš*) to Israel's concern here contrasts with his refusal to do so in 14:3; 20:30f.

like flocks of small cattle for sacred offerings. Proverbially numerous; on one occasion three thousand are said to have been offered (II Chron 29:33). The time and place at which they would have been most numerous was in Jerusalem, on pilgrimage festivals, when multitudes converged on the royal sanctuary, not "empty-handed, but each with his own gift" (Deut 16:16f.). II Chron 35:7–9 reports that at King Josiah's celebration of the paschal sacrifice 30,000 + 2,600 + 5,000 small cattle were supplied to the public.

human flocks (ṣ'n 'dm). Lit. "flocks of [the class of] humans"; cf. *pr' 'dm* "a wild ass of a man" (Gen 16:12).

STRUCTURE AND THEMES

This closely woven interpretation of the motive of Israel's destiny is presented in the form of an oracle depicting A, a bad present situation (vss. 16–21), leading to B, a remedial consequence (*laken,* vss. 22–32). To B are attached two appendixes, C1 (vss. 33–36) and C2 (vss. 37–38).

The bad present situation is simply and swiftly described in two stages:

A1: Israel's defiling conduct caused their expulsion from their land and their dispersion "among the nations" (vss. 17–19). A1 is framed by repetition of the phrase "their ways and their deeds."

A2: this caused a widespread "desecration of God's holy name" (vss. 20–21). A2 is framed by repetition of the phrase "among the nations to which they came" and is linked to A1 by "among the nations."

The remedial consequence of this calamity is set forth in stages in B, a section framed by repetition of the phrase "not for your sake am I about to act" (vss. 22, 32):

B1: an introductory generality, the motive of all that is to follow: God will act on Israel solely for his name's sake, to assert its sanctity (vss. 22–23). "I am about to act (*'śh*)" looks forward to the string of first person active verbs in the sequel, particularly the peculiar, climactic expression of vs. 27 "I will bring to pass (*w'śyty*)," alluding to Israel's enforced obedience to the law. The rest of the section, looking backward, states three times the terms of sanctity-sanctification (*qdš*) and of public desecration (*ḥll bgwym/btwkm*). These terms link B1 to A2. Vs. 23 closes the section with an expanded recognition formula.

B2: stages of God's re-creation of Israel (vss. 24–32):

(a) Gathering the exiles back to their land (vs. 24) — contra vs. 19 (scattering)
(b) Purgation from impurity (vs. 25) — contra vss. 17b–18 (N.B. "throw purifying water on" versus "pour fury on")
(c) Implantation of new heart and spirit, causing obedience to the law (vss. 26–27), the necessary condition for —
(d) Permanent dwelling in the land as God's people (vs. 28) — contra the interrupted dwelling there (vs. 17a), and the disgrace of having "gone forth from his land" (vs. 20)
(e) Fertilization of land and deliverance from disgrace of famine (vss. 29–30); adjunct to permanency of dwelling in the land (d) and to public disgrace (B1)
(f) Israel's self-reproach, after their restoration, on realizing that it was undeserved (vss. 31–32)

Closure of B2 is by repetition in vs. 32 of "not for your sake" of vs. 22 (vs. 32's "your ways" echoes A1), and a skewed recognition formula: "let it be known to you."

To the account of Israel's renovation in B are appended two supplements on themes of previous oracles. Each is introduced by a message formula.

C1: Appendix I: onlookers and gentiles marvel at the prodigy of the refertilized land and rebuilt towns (vs. 33–36). The initial temporal clause "At the time I purge you" connects with B2b (vs. 25), but the description of the restoration is based on the terms of the previous oracle: vss. 9 ("be tilled") and 10b ("towns resettled, ruins rebuilt"). "Saying" praises of the restored land (vs. 35) distantly counter-echoes the disparaging "saying" of vs. 20b ("in that it was said of them"). Appendix I ends with an extended formula of recognition by the nations of God's prodigy — an implicit fulfillment of God's design to assert his sanctity publicly through his acts in Israel (cf. vs. 23).

C2: Appendix II: God's response to Israelite concern over reduced population (vss. 37–38; cf. the issue of 33:23: "Abraham was but one"): he will make the inhabitants of the once ruined towns as numerous as sacrificial small cattle (vss. 37–38). The vivid figure resumes and innovatively combines the terms of the previous oracle (vss. 10a, 11) and the one before that (34:14: "you are the flock of my pasturage"). It ends in a recognition formula unrelated to the issue of saving God's reputation.

The two appendixes are linked by the expression *h'rym hḥrbwt* "the ruined towns," found only in vss. 35 and 38.

The argument of A–B is tightly organized, with *inclusios* (framing repetitions) effecting coherence within sections, and key terms linking them. Moreover, there is a close relation between A–B and ch. 20 (see ahead). C1 touches only obliquely on A–B's concern about saving God's reputation; C2 does not allude to it at all. By subject both belong to previous oracles; they appear here to reinforce the message of restoration, by which God will become "known" in Israel and the world.

The main oracle (A–B) carries on the grand theme of ch. 20: the indissoluble link between the fate and destiny of Israel and the general recognition of YHWH

God of Israel as true God. This link had in the past checked God's intention to "pour his fury" on faithless Israel lest their misfortune "desecrate his holy name" among the nations. This link cannot be unilaterally annulled by Israel. The oracle of ch. 20 was inspired by what the prophet perceived to be the intention of the exiles to assimilate to the idolatrous nations. His (God's) response was to proclaim the impossibility of Israel's ever escaping its subjection to God (20:33: "with a strong hand . . . I will be king over you!"), because Israel's extinction would desecrate God's name among the nations. The present exile would end in a severe culling out of rebels and a forced restoration of the remainder to the homeland, for the greater glory of God.

Our oracle was inspired by the gentiles' deriding of "the people of YHWH" who "have gone forth from his land." The oracle of ch. 20, issued before the fall of Jerusalem and the attendant deportations, had not dealt with the insult to God entailed by the mere fact that remnants of his people were scattered among the nations. Whether the exiles betokened YHWH's weakness or their depravity besmirched his name (see comment to vs. 20), the way must be found to restore the glory of his name. This could only happen by putting an end to the degradation of his worshipers, and afterward ensuring that the disastrous course of events would not be repeated.

That course had been determined by a strict consequentiality: in priestly terms the people's base conduct had polluted the land; the pollution set in motion the covenant curses, including crop failure and famine (Lev 26:19f.), climaxed by expulsion from the land (cf. Lev 26:33 "and you will I scatter among the nations"). But in the event, an unlooked-for consequence emerged: by the very condition of being exiles Israel desecrated God's name among the nations. The remedy would consist of reversing the sequence: first, the dispersed would be gathered and brought to their land, while still in their unregenerate state. The rehabilitation of God's reputation cannot depend on the chancy repentance of the stonyhearted people. There they would be purged of their pollution—absolved from their guilt—by a unilateral act of God. Then the root of their evildoing, their obdurate heart, would be altered to yield to God's will that would henceforth animate it. As a result of their enforced obedience they would never again be uprooted from their land, but would reside in it forever as God's covenant partners. Nor would famine ever again bring disgace on the reformed people. All this would come about not out of any regard for or merit of Israel but for the glorification of God's name.

Ezekiel's doctrine of a new heart combines a radical despair of Israel's repenting with a radical certainty that God's holiness (majesty, authority) would be vindicated and acknowledged by all nations, through the agency of Israel. The indissoluble link between God's reputation and Israel's fortunes guarantees that Israel shall be restored; but so that God's name never again suffer disgrace, Israel's restoration must be irreversible. Such it can be only if Israel be denied the ability ever again to disobey God's laws. God's uninterrupted glorification entails the curtailment of human freedom.

That national reconciliation with God was not achievable by human initiative alone is an iterated theme in the literature of the period of the fall. It transfers to the collective the sense of natural inadequacy expressed by the penitent psalmist of Ps 51. After lamenting his congenital tendency to sin (cf. Ezek 16's metaphor of the congenitally corrupt harlot Jerusalem), the psalmist prays, using priestly imagery:

> Purge me with a hyssop till I am pure;
> Wash me till I am whiter than snow . . .

After being ritually cleansed by God he prays for a change of nature:

> Fashion a pure heart for me, O God;
> Create in me a steadfast spirit.

Jeremiah's oracles vacillate between affirming, on the one hand, that repentance, initiated by humans, will precede and induce forgiveness (e.g., 36:3), and, on the other, that the cooperation of God is involved in the very process of repentance. Jer 24:7 is typical in its ambiguity; speaking of the exiles, he says:

> I will give them understanding (lit. "a heart") to know me, that I am YHWH; and they shall be my people and I will be their God, for/when they shall turn to me with all their hearts.

More clearly in 31:18f., he depicts Ephraim, already contrite, imploring God's help in repentance:

> You have disciplined me and I have been corrected
> Like an untamed calf.
> Bring me back that I may turn back,
> For you, YHWH, are my God.
> For, having turned back, I am remorseful;
> Having become aware, I strike my thigh.
> I am ashamed and humiliated,
> For I bear the reproach of my youth.

In Lamentations 5:21 the post-fall community prays for help in repentance in virtually identical terms: "Bring us back, O YHWH, to you that we may turn back."

But there are also passages in Jeremiah that announce the future bliss without the precondition of repentance. Such is 33:6–9, where the healing of the people and their rebuilding precede purgation and forgiveness. And in 32:37–41 the physical restoration to the homeland is sealed by the formula of mutuality and the change of heart:

> They shall be my people and I will be their God. And I will give them a single heart and a single way, to fear me all the days . . . and I will make for them an eternal covenant not to turn away from them, [but] to do good to them. And I

> will put fear of me in their heart so they not fall away from me. And I will rejoice over them to do good to them and I will plant them in this land . . .

This language is related to Deut 30:1–10, where the whole process of restoration is depicted: the exiles will turn back in obedience to God; God will gather them into their land and prosper them more than before. Then he will "circumcise your hearts and the hearts of your offspring, to love YHWH your God with all your hearts and souls, for the sake of (*lmʿn*) your lives" (vs. 6). He will "rejoice over you for good . . . when you shall turn back to YHWH your God with all your hearts and all your souls." In Deuteronomy the people's longing to be reconciled with God is answered by God's enabling them to be permanently obedient, so they might live.

The crowning expression of reconciliation is Jer 31:31–34 (30–33), the promise of a new covenant written on the hearts—i.e., imprinted on human nature:

> See, the days are coming, declares YHWH, when I will make a new covenant with the house of Israel and the house of Judah. Not like the covenant that I made with their fathers . . . which covenant of mine they violated . . . But this is the covenant that I will make with the house of Israel . . . : I will put my teaching inside of them and write it on their hearts; I will be their God and they shall be my people. So they shall no longer teach one another—each his fellow—"Know God!" For all of them shall know me, from the least to the greatest of them; when/for I will forgive their iniquity and not be mindful of their sin any longer.

The future change will consist of a total identification of the human will with the divine teaching; "knowledge of (= devotion to) God" will be internalized, so that a perfect harmony will exist between God and man. It is a scene of bliss unmarred by coercion or remorse.

Thus the motifs of post-restoration repentance and change of human nature belonged to the dialectic of pessimism and optimism of the end of the monarchy. The old order had failed, but God was faithful to his covenant and would restore Israel, and restore it permanently. It was not clear whether this would depend on Israel or be an act of total or partial divine grace.

Ezekiel sounds a new note in his appropriation of these motifs. He, too, vacillates between calling on the exiles to repent and despairing of their capacity for it. But there is no question that for him the change of human nature was not an act of grace. In 11:17–21 the change of nature is an element of rebuke (I, 204). The returned exiles will be given a new heart "so that (*lmʿn*)" they obey God's laws, in contrast to the idolatrous homelanders. In that passage the motif seems too big for its context; it has certainly not realized there its full implications.

The insult to God's majesty in the mockery of the gentiles gave the theme a setting that released its potential. The restoration would not be a gracious divine response to human yearning for reconciliation (as in Deuteronomy and Jeremiah). It would be an imposition on wayward Israel of a constraint necessary for saving God's reputation. The development of the motif is epitomized in the "for the sake of" (*lm'n*) clauses: in Deut 30:6 the change of nature is "for the sake of your lives (= that you may live)"; in Ezek 11:20, "for the sake" of obedience to God's laws, as yet not further motivated. In our oracle, obedience serves a higher cause: "for the sake of my holy name that has been desecrated among the nations." Ezekiel remains true to his ruthless focus on the majesty of God, the safeguarding of which is, in his view, the prime motive of Israel's history. That linkage to God guarantees that Israel, undeserving as it is, will be restored and prosper as never before. As a prophecy of consolation it is singularly harsh; but its logic is ironbound.

The external origin of the purification of the exiles, not from a turn of heart, is underlined by imagery drawn from purgation rituals. Vs. 25 recalls the "water of lustration" that purges corpse pollution (see comment to vs. 25), a pollution strictly "objective" whose removal requires no contrition. The other ritual evoked is the annual Day of Atonement (Milgrom: of Purgation) in which sacrificial blood purges the sanctuary of Israel's "impurities" while the scapegoat removes Israel's "iniquities" (Lev 16:16, 21–22). The distinction that the ritual text makes (J. Milgrom, *Leviticus*, AB, pp. 24f., 1033, 1043) is obliterated in the figurative usage of the prophet: the "impurities" of vs. 25 are the "iniquities" of vs. 33. For the prophet the terms are coextensive, embracing offenses against God and fellowman. Evocation of the rituals of Lev 16 suggests that just as they are effective in themselves (the people's role in the Day of Purgation is only to fast; repentance is not called for), so God's purification of impenitent Israel takes effect without Israel's volition.

Innovative conception correlates with a clustering of unique or rare expressions (see comments): "have pity on my holy name (vs. 21)," "sanctify my holy name (vs. 23)," "purifying water," "impurities (pl.)" (vs. 25), "bring to pass" (vs. 27), "deliver from impurities," "summon grain," "put famine upon you" (vs. 29), "produce of fields," "take the reproach of famine" (vs. 30), "instead of being" (vs. 34), *hlzw* "that" (vs. 35), "human flocks" (vs. 38). The unusual vocabulary injects freshness into what otherwise might have been only an anthology of Ezekielian speech and is now a vehicle for a new idea.

Once again, as in ch. 34, we note Jeremianic language: see comments to *'nky* "I," "the land I gave to your fathers" (vs. 28), "doings" (vs. 31), "purge of iniquity" (vs. 33). For the connection with Jeremiah, see Structure and Themes to § XLI.

The originality of vs. 23b$^{\beta}$ (from after the recognition formula) to vs. 38 has been challenged by Johan Lust ("Ezekiel 36–40 in the Oldest Greek Manuscript," *Catholic Biblical Quarterly* 43 [1981], 517–33). These verses do not appear in the earliest witness of the Old Greek (Septuagint) text of Ezekiel, Papyrus 967 (second to third centuries C.E.; the earliest form of the Old Latin text of Ezekiel, deriving from the Septuagint, also lacks these verses). Moreover, the present Greek text of these verses differs in style and terminology from its surroundings (this had been established by H. St. John Thackeray, in *The Septuagint and Jewish Worship* [London: Oxford University Press, 1921], pp. 124–29). Lust concludes from these two facts that the present Greek text is a later supplementation, and that the Hebrew *Vorlage* of the Old Greek lacked these verses. The unique and rare terms in the MT of these verses and their Jeremianic coloration point, in Lust's estimate, to their having been composed by a late redactor, familiar with Jeremiah's way of speaking (p. 523), but of pedestrian mind. Lust admits that the passage

> presents a culmination of the prophet's theological thinking. On the other hand, it looks like a mere summary, borrowing from the surrounding chapters. Its most famous thought, the gift of a new heart and a new spirit, is almost a literal repetition of Ezek 11:19. (p. 519)

That such "an anthology" should contain so many singular expressions signifies to Lust a later, "redactional" hand. Lust takes all the signs of interrelation of these verses with what precedes and what follows as the design of the late redactor.

How conclusive are Lust's arguments?

As for the Greek text, the long omission in Papyrus 967 was explained by F. V. Filson as due to haplography ("The Omission of Ezek. 12:26–28 and 36:23b–38 in Codex 967," *JBL* 62 [1943], 27–32), the eye of the Greek scribe having jumped from "that I am Lord (*kyrios*)" in vs. 23b to "I [am] Lord" at the end of vs. 38. While Fohrer and Wevers adopt this explanation (DNF, too, regards it as "entirely possible"), Lust doubts that such a large omission could be a mere haplography, and advances his theory of a shorter Hebrew *Vorlage* in its stead. M. V. Spottorno proposes a different mechanical explanation: a codex page of 1,512 letters in the past history of the papyrus was lost either by frequent use in the synagogue or through haplography ("La omision de Ez. 36.23b–38 y la transposicion de capitulos en el papiro 967," *Emerita* 50 [1981], 93–99 [cited from Allen]).

Precisely what was the origin of the short text of Papyrus 967, and whether it reflects an accident in the course of the transmission of the Greek or of its Hebew *Vorlage*, are questions that cannot at present be answered definitively. But even if we concur with Lust, that the omission of vss. $23b^{\beta}$–38 in the earliest witness to the Old Greek version (together with the divergent ordering of the sequel: ch. 37 after ch. 39) points to a Hebrew *Vorlage* that differed from MT, the superiority of that supposed *Vorlage* to MT is not decided thereby. Indeed Lust's strictures against the authenticity of MT argue against him.

The mixture of commonplaces and originality in both the thought and the terminology of the verses in question is of a piece with the texture of the preceding verses. The reuse with innovations of older material is a standing feature of Ezekiel's style: "anthology" along with unusual language, especially when some striking new thought is presented (as in ch. 16). Furthermore, Lust does not appreciate the advance our passage makes over 11:19 (see above). As for reminiscences of Jeremiah, these occur throughout the book, and especially in the oracles of restoration; they are explicable as direct borrowings.

If in line with the papyrus the *laken* passage, beginning with vs. 22, is cut off after the recognition formula in vs. $23b^{\alpha}$, it is incomplete (Zimmerli). Lust's comparison with 25:12–14 works against him: there the *laken* clause spells out fully the consequences of the foregoing indictment, while here the consequences are heralded but not even hinted at in vs. 23, making indispensable their specification in vss. 24ff.

The unpublished Masada Hebrew text of Ezekiel, which cannot be later than the first century C.E. and is thus earlier than all the extant versional witnesses, contains clear remains of vss. 24–34, all identical to MT (courtesy of Sh. Talmon, who has been entrusted with its publication). All in all, the long omission in Papyrus 967 would appear to "pose a problem for the history only of G, not of MT" (Zimmerli).

The placement of this oracle is appropriate: it carries forward the theme of gentile mockery of the land of Israel set at the end of the previous oracle (36:13–15). The land did lose its inhabitants, and in so doing gave an opening to further mockery, whose target now was Israel's God. In his comment to vs. 17 Kara links the two oracles by the common ground on which both are based: the secret virtue of the land of Israel:

> This passage is linked to the previous one: "Because they say to you: 'You are a devourer of humans, [you kept losing your nations]'" (36:13), meaning: you expel your nation. The gentiles regard this as a fault but it is really a virtue. For the land is pure and cannot tolerate inhabitants who defile it. When the [Canaanite] nations occupied it they defiled it and it expelled them, as it is said, "the land was defiled . . . and the land vomited its inhabitants" (Lev 18:25). It did the same to Israel, for "while the house of Israel dwelt on their soil they defiled it" (vs. 17). What resulted? "they were dispersed among the lands" (vs. 19).

Trust the medievals to find a transcendent value in expulsions.

XLIV. The Resurrectional Metaphor of National Restoration (37:1–14)

37 [1]The hand of YHWH came upon me, and he brought me out by the spirit of YHWH and let me down in the midst of the plain, and it was full of bones. [2]He made me pass all around them, and lo, they were very many on the surface of the plain, and lo, they were very dry. [3]He said to me: Man, will these bones come to life? And I said: Lord YHWH, you know.

[4]Then he said to me: Prophesy over these bones and say to them: O dry bones, hear the word of YHWH! [5]Thus said Lord YHWH to these bones: See, I am going to make [a]breath enter you and you shall come to life.[a] [6]I will put sinews on you and grow flesh on you and cover you with skin, and I will put breath[b] in you and you shall come to life; and you shall know that I am YHWH.

[7]So I prophesied as I was commanded. There was a noise, as I prophesied, and lo, a quaking, and the bones came together, bone to proper bone. [8]I saw and lo, sinews [were] on them, and flesh grew, and skin formed into a cover over them—but there was no breath in them.

[9]Then he said to me: Prophesy to the wind; prophesy, man, and say to the wind: Thus said Lord YHWH: From the four winds come, O wind, and breathe into these slain that they may come to life. [10]So I prophesied as he commanded me, and the wind entered them and they came to life and stood up on their feet—a very, very great army.

[11]He said to me: Man, these bones—they are the whole house of Israel. See, they are saying, "Our bones are dried up and our hope is lost; we have been clean cut off." [12]So prophesy and say to them: Thus said Lord YHWH: See, I am opening your graves and I will raise you from your graves, my people, and I will bring you to the soil of Israel, [13]and you shall know that I am YHWH—when I open your graves and raise you from your graves, my people. [14]I will put my spirit in you and you shall live, and I will settle you on your soil, and you shall know that I am YHWH: what I have spoken I will do, declares YHWH.

[a–a]G "breath of life (as reading *rwḥ ḥyym*) enter you."
[b]G "my spirit."

COMMENT

37:1. *The hand of YHWH came upon me.* For this expression of trance seizure, see comment to 1:3 (I, 41–42). In all prior occurrences the verb appears with *waw*-consecutive (*wthy*, 1:3; 3:22; cf. *wtpl*, 8:1); here it is in the perfect (cf. initial position perfects in vss. 2, 7, 8, 10). G keeps to the regular pattern, reflecting *wthy*.

and he brought me out of the Tel Abib settlement; cf. 3:15 + 22: "I came to the exiles at Tel Abib . . . he said to me: Get up and go out to the plain."

by the spirit of [brwḥ] *YHWH*. T "by a spirit of prophecy that rested on me from before (= at the instance of) the Lord"; i.e., the transportation was in prophetic vision, not in reality. Standing alone, *rwḥ* signifies "wind," an external force by which the prophet felt himself transported (see comment at 3:12 [I, 70]), 14. *rwḥ YHWH* / *'lhym* signifies spiritual enablement to receive prophetic messages or visions (see comment at 8:5 [I, 187]). The difference comes out in 11:24: "Then a wind (*rwḥ*) lifted me and brought me to Chaldea . . . in vision by the spirit of God (= in a vision for which I was capacitated by the spirit of God, *rwḥ 'lhym*)."

G and S construe the second clause of the verse thus: "The Lord brought me out by a wind"; but if this were meant, the placement of the subject (*YHWH*) after the adverb (*brwḥ*) is awkward. This forced reading may reflect an interpretation of the event as real rather than visionary (see Note following Structure and Themes).

"The spirit of YHWH" is a fixed phrase, hence the Tetragram is repeated instead of being replaced by a pronoun ("by his spirit").

and let me down (wayᵉniḥeni). The same vocalization of the verb as in 40:2; the perfect is *heniᵃḥ*, the imperfect appears in Exod 17:11: "When Moses would raise his hands . . . let down (*yaniᵃḥ*) his hands." It is to be distinguished from *hinniᵃḥ* "settle" in vs. 14 (*whnḥty*).

the plain. See comment to 3:22 (I, 101).

full of bones. Not skeletons, but a sea of disjoined bones each separated from its mates—an extreme of deterioration.

2. *He made me pass all around them.* To impress on me their vast quantity and extreme dryness, indicating that a long time had passed since life had left them. The verb in the perfect (*wh'byrny*) is not in the classical prose style, which calls for an imperfect consecutive here (*wy'byrny*); see end of comment to 20:22 (I, 368) and below, Structure and Themes.

The pronominal suffix *-hm* "them" is masculine, though the gender of the noun *'ṣmwt* "bones" is feminine, as is evident from its adjective *ybšwt* "dry." Most pronominal elements referring to bone(s) throughout the passage are masculine, such a preference for masculine forms being present throughout the book, and characteristic of late Biblical Hebrew (Joüon, § 149 b; many examples from Ezekiel are given by Levi, *Inkongruenz*, pp. 164ff.; see now M. F. Rooker, *Biblical Hebrew in Transition: The Language of the Book of Ezekiel*, JSOTSup 90 [1990], 78–81).

3. God's question about the reanimation of the bones highlights its improbabil-

ity. The prophet avoids encroaching on God's freedom in his deferentially evasive reply. Eliezer of Beaugency does not regard the reply as evasive; he glosses, "*you know* since you are their creator. The craftsman [who made it] has the expertise to tell whether a broken vessel can be mended or not."

5. *See . . . you shall come to life.* The astounding product of divine activity is declared at the outset; the declaration is followed in vs. 6 by the detail of its execution and is repeated in its proper final position. For this manner of storytelling, cf. Gen 27:23: "So he did not recognize him and he blessed him," followed by the details of Jacob's deception (vss. 24–27) and ending with repeated "and he blessed him."

G does not show this structure, since it reads the last two words of the verse as "breath of life" (see text note), reflecting a Hebrew text influenced by the language of Gen 6:17; 7:15.

6. The sequence of reconstitution evoked comparison "with one who goes to a bathhouse: whatever article of clothing he takes off last he puts on first when he dresses to leave the bathhouse" (*Genesis Rabba* 14.5) Kara rewords in terms of our verse: "The first to decompose and be stripped off [a corpse] is its skin, then the flesh, then the sinews, then the bones [fall apart]. And when he 'gets dressed' (= is recomposed), first he 'puts on' (= reconnects) the bones, then the sinews, then the flesh, and finally the skin."

I will put breath (rwḥ). The airy element identified in vs. 9 with the wind. G "my spirit" (as from *rwḥy*) imports the different conception of vs. 14 (see ahead) into our passage.

7. *There was a noise* (wyhy qwl) . . . *and lo, a quaking* (whnh rʿš). The combination *qwl rʿš* of 3:13f. (translated there "rumbling noise") is here separated into its components to heighten the effect as by slow motion. This results in parallelistic clauses.

and the bones came together (wtqrbw), *bone to proper bone.* It is unclear whether the quaking (of the ground) set the bones in motion ("*then* the bones came together") or whether the stir of the myriad bones, animated by the prophesying, made the ground of the plain quake ("*as* the bones came together"). "Came together" does not convey the range of movement implied in the compact Hebrew, which may be paraphrased but not translated: the inert mass resolved into bones headed for (*qrb* "nearing"), and finally arriving at (*ʾl*), their proper joins. The rare (poetic?) form of the verb ("with only one sign of the feminine" [Kimḥi], viz., the initial *t-*, but without the afformative *-nh* that marks the feminine plural) recurs in Jer 49:11 (*tbṭḥw*) and serves as the base for pronominal suffixes, e.g., *trʾw-ny* "you (fem. pl.) stare at me" (Song 1:6); *tḥšb(w)-ny* "they (fem. pl.) regard me" (Job 19:15). The absence of the article with "bones" accords with its sporadic absence in other passages of high prose; e.g., *ḥrb*/*hḥrb* in 33:3–6; *hydym*/*brkym* in 7:17. (The article is often omitted in poetry; *BHSyn*, 13.7.)

bone to proper (lit. "its") *bone.* I.e., to the bone(s) it was originally joined to; the disjoined bones thus recombined into skeletons.

8. *formed into a cover* (wayyiqram). As indicated by its *a* vowel, and in line with the preceding intransitive *ʿlh* "grew," *(way)yiqram* is qal intransitive with "skin"

as its subject. But in vs. 6 *wqrmty* "I will cover you" is transitive with "skin" as its direct object. That the qal of *qrm* should be both transitive and intransitive is unusual. The intransitive sense alone is evidenced in later Hebrew; e.g., "Bread may not be put into the oven when darkness is falling [on the eve of the sabbath] . . . unless there is time for its top surface to form into crust (*yiqrᵉmu paneha*)" (*m. Shabbat* 1.10). The transitiveness of Biblical Hebrew *qrm* qal is established by the function of *wᵉqaramti;* its intransitive counterpart would regularly be a nifʿal **niqram,* imperfect **yiqqarem,* whose vowelless biblical spelling would be *yqrm,* as here. Since only the intransitive sense of *qrm* qal existed in post-Biblical Hebrew, wherever the spelling permitted, an intransitive *yqrm* would naturally be read as qal. Hence the present qal intransitive vocalization (*yiqram*) may be late, having overridden an original nifʿal formation—**yiqqarem* "was formed into a cover," the passive of an active, transitive Biblical Hebrew *qrm* that did not survive in post-Biblical use.

9. *Prophesy . . . prophesy.* Repetition expresses urgency, tension.

the wind. Wind and life-breath are conceived of as the same element. Death and stoppage of breathing ("ex-spiring") are one and the same; therefore, revival entails "in-spiring." In the homey account of Gen 2:7 the artisan God himself breathes "breath of (*nšmt*) life" into his earth model of a single human creature. Here a vast army must be revived; hence God summons his titanic servant the wind ("he makes the winds his messengers," Ps 104:4; "storm wind that carries out his command," 148:8) to muster its forces from the four cardinal compass points to do the job.

The concept "four winds/directions" is found only in late books: e.g., Jer 49:36, "four winds, from the four extremes of heaven"; Zech 6:5, "the four winds of heaven." Ezek 42:16–20 names them in the course of measuring the four sides of the Temple area as east, north, south, and west. The concept seems to have originated in Mesopotamia, where Akkadian *šār erbetti* "four winds / cardinal points" is used identically.

and breathe into these slain. The verb, from the root *npḥ,* is the very one used with God as subject in the creation of man in Gen 2:7. An allusion to that story is unmistakable. The lifeless bodies lying on the plain appear to the prophet to be battle-slain. The same perception is shown in the next verse, where the revived are called "a very, very great army."

10. *So I prophesied as he commanded me.* A variation, typical of Ezekiel's style in repetition, of vs. 7a. The initial *wnbʾty* (nifʿal) of vs. 7a is replaced by the anomalous form *whnbʾty* (perhaps under the influence of the repeated imperatives *hnbʾ* in vs. 9), vocalized as hitpaʿel, with the preformative *t* (**hitnabbeti*) assimilated to the following radical (*hinnabbeti*). Cf. *wᵉhinneḥamti* (<**hitneḥamti*) in 5:13 (see *BHSyn,* p. 360, for a brief discussion).

army. The meaning of *ḥyl* in 17:17; 29:18f; 32:31; 38:4, 15. The prophet is not yet aware of the reference of his vision.

11. *these bones—they are the whole house of Israel.* The dry bones represent the people of both past kingdoms: Israel and Judah, now largely in exile. Together they comprise "a very, very great" population. The representation literalizes the metaphor used by the people to describe themselves, as in the immediate sequel.

The sentence parses thus: the subject, "these bones," stands in *casus pendens;* a nominal clause follows in which the predicate *kol bet yisra'el* "the whole house of Israel" precedes the resumptive subject pronoun *hemma* "(are) they"—a pattern that lends emphasis to the predicate. This pattern is common in interpretations of visions and dreams, where the predicate, as here, decodes the symbol; e.g., Gen 40:12, "The three tendrils—three days are they"; similarly vs. 18 and 41:26f. Other examples: Exod 3:5, "The place on which you are standing—holy ground is it"; Exod 32:16, "The tablets—the work of God were they" (not of man, yet Moses dared to break them). See Muraoka, *Emphatic Words*, pp. 17, 75f.; *BHSyn*, § 16.3.3d.

they are saying. Plural participles with no specified subject often denote an indefinite subject, "they": see 36:13 and comment; preceded, as here, by *hnh* in II Kings 6:25 "and they were besieging (*wᵉhinne ṣarim*) it." That the versions supply a subject here does not necessarily point to a different text (such as *BHS*'s "probably *whnm*"); in Josh 8:6 G provides *nasim* "(they) are fleeing" with a subject, "these," that is dispensable in Hebrew. See König III § 324 n.

Our bones are dried up. A metaphor meaning, we are utterly dispirited. High spirits and good cheer are figured as moist, oily, or sappy bones: "[God-fearing conduct] will be a cure for your body / a drink for your bones" (Prov 3:8); "Good news oils the bones" (Prov 15:30, referring to the marrow); ". . . your heart shall rejoice / your bones shall bloom like grass (Isa 66:14; "bloom" contrasts with "wither, dry up" as in Ezek 17:24). Despair and grief are figured as the opposite: "A stricken spirit dries up the bones" (Prov 17:22). In our passage, the following clause, "and our hope is lost," is a nonmetaphoric explanation of this one; the connecting *waw* is explicative (as in 3:13; see I, 71).

we have been clean cut off. The nifʿal of *gzr/grz* "cut off" serves to depict one who is dead and buried; e.g., "For he was cut off from the land of the living . . . And his grave was set among the wicked" (Isa 53:8–9). It recurs in psalms of complaint to express the anguish of being abandoned by God and man, figured as descent to the grave/Pit/Sheol: "Alarmed [by my stricken state, described before (vs. 13) as one "put out of mind like the dead"], I thought: I am cut off from before your eyes" (Ps 31:23). The images cluster in Ps 88:4–6:

For I am sated with misfortune;
I am at the brink of Sheol.
I am counted with those who have gone down into the Pit
I am a helpless man,
  abandoned among the dead,
  like bodies lying in the grave
  of whom you are no longer mindful
  and who are cut off from your care.

Or again in Lamentations 3:54f.:

Water rose over my head;
I thought: I am cut off!

I called your name, YHWH, from the depths of the Pit.

Deliverance from such distress is figured as resurrection and raising from the grave:

From the belly of Sheol I cried out . . .
I thought: I have been driven away (*ngršty*; or = *ngrzty* "I have been cut off") from before your eyes . . .
But you raised my life from the Pit. (Jonah 2:3–7)

Or again in Ps 71:20:

You who have made me see many troubles and misfortunes
shall revive me again,
and shall raise me from the depths of the earth.

The pronoun *lnw* "for us" added after the verb serves to focus on its effect on the subject of the verb (*BHSyn*, pp. 208f.). For its use with passives, see Job 7:3; Ps 122:3. How to express this in translation is problematic; "clean cut off" alliterates, as Hebrew *nigzarnu lanu* rhymes. The clause needs no emending, but F. Perles's inspired emendation involving a redistribution of the consonants deserves mention: *nigzar nolenu* "our web (Syriac *nwlʾ* "web [of fabric]") has been cut off (from the loom)" = we are finished—in an ominous sense ("*nwl* = 'Gewebe' im Alten Testament," *Orientalische Literaturzeitung* 12 [1909], 251f.). This ambiguates the preceding noun *tqwh* "hope," which has a homonym meaning "thread" (Josh 2:18). All this is quite needless and indeed ruins the consistency of the imagery.

The association of the expression "be cut off" with the grave generated the shift of the metaphor in the sequel.

12. *I am opening your graves and I will raise you. . . my people.* = "I will deliver you from the Slough of Despond into which you have sunk." This is the terse equivalent, in the new metaphor, of vss. 5–10 in the old one. At the words "my people," the people have been raised from their graves and are awaiting the next move by God—as was the "very, very great army" at the end of vs. 10. That move is described in the climactic last clause of our verse: "and I will bring you to the soil of Israel."

13. *and you shall know that I am YHWH.* This closes the prophecy of vs. 12, but to it is attached (vss. 13b–14) an afterwave that resumes lingeringly and emphatically the first two clauses of vs. 12 but augments its third clause with fresh matter.

13b–14. After the disinterment and raising of the buried they will be lifeless clay until God inspirits them—analogous to the two-stage resurrection of the dry bones (note the almost identical language of vss. $6a^{\delta}$ and $14a^{\alpha}$). But, unlike the case of the restored bones into whom it was the wind that breathed life, the disinterred are vivified by God with "my spirit." Now in 36:27 "my spirit" defines what was just called "a new spirit" (36:26) to be implanted in the people, that will bring about conformance to God's laws (36:27). God not only will "bring" the resurrected to their soil (37:12b), but by infusing them with his spirit he will "settle / let them stay" there (vs. 14a$^{\beta}$). For this sense of *hinniᵃḥ*, cf. Isa 14:1: "YHWH will have compassion for Jacob . . . and he will settle them (*wᵉhinniḥam*) on their soil"; Judg 2:23: "YHWH let those nations stay (*wayyannaḥ*), not hurrying to drive them out." This is the very idea expressed in 36:27f., that the ultimate effect of God's implanted spirit on the people will be to conform them to his commandments and thus assure their lasting settlement in the land.

I am YHWH: what I have spoken I will do. My hallmark; see comment at 22:14.

STRUCTURE AND THEMES

This passage, probably the best known of Ezekiel's prophecies, deserves its fame. It conveys a powerful, inspiring message of national restoration in a rhetorically perfect vehicle (see Michael V. Fox, "The Rhetoric of Ezekiel's Vision of the Valley of the Bones," *HUCA* 51 [1980], 1–15). First comes a dialogic vision, in whose action the prophet participates (vss. 1–10), in the same way he took part in the Temple vision of chs. 8–11. Lastly comes a prophecy, entirely a speech of God (vss. 12–14). In between, and linking the two, is the saying of the people expressing their hopelessness in two metaphors (vs. 11). The preceding vision (dry bones) responds to the first metaphor (our bones are dried up), and the following prophecy (disinterment) responds to the second (we are clean cut off).

The despondency of the exiles, betokened by their drastic death and burial metaphors, is met by the prophet's stunning counter-metaphors of resurrection and disinterment. The vividness of these metaphors was so great as to mislead later interpreters into taking them literally, as will be shown in the Note that concludes this section.

The vision is constructed in suspenseful steps. Vss. 1–3 set the ghastly scene of a plain filled with dry human bones, and end with tension created by God's question, "Will these bones come to life?" unrelieved. Vss. 4–10 contain the divine resolve to revive the bones, and the word-by-word fulfillment of that resolve. Unexpectedly the process halts before life is restored to the reconstituted bodies, delaying, and thus highlighting, the climax. The final state of the revived is "a very, very great army" standing on its feet, ready — for what?

Throughout, the prophet plays an ambiguous role: on the one hand, he is God's agent and witness — much as in the Temple vision of chs. 8–11. On the other hand, he is an outsider astonished by what he sees, as his audience are astonished by what they hear — an identification with them conducive to winning their hearts (Fox). A verbal sign of the repeated surprises experienced by the prophet is the number of "lo's" (*hnh*) he employs:

vs. 2: lo, they were very many
lo, they were very dry
vs. 5: lo, I will make breath enter you
vs 7: lo, a quaking
vs. 8: lo, sinews were on them

The repetitions and detail of the narrative make it impressively solemn; the audience has time to take in the amazing panorama. Keywords recur over and over: "spirit/wind/breath," nine times; "bone(s)," eight times; "prophesy," six times; "come to life," five times.

Tracing the last item leads to the double climax of the vision. All along we have been told that the final stage of the bones will be that they "come to life" (vss. 3, 5, 6, 9). In the event (vs. 10), there is one more stage: having come to life, the revived "stood up on their feet—a very, very great army." The vision ends at a new beginning; it asks for a continuation.

Instead, the oracle continues with the citation of the people's threefold saying, the first clause of which ("Our bones are dried up") inspired the vision. Note that it is introduced by *hnh* "lo, see" (vs. 11b), whereas the normal antecedent to *laken* (vs. 12) is *yaʿan*. Had *yaʿan* been employed, it would have made the saying the ground only of the subsequent prophecy (vss. 12ff.). But the saying contains both the key to the preceding vision—"These bones are . . ."—and, in its third clause, "we have been clean cut off," the ground of the new metaphor in the following prophecy (raising from the grave). Hence the choice of the neutral "See," which allows attaching the saying to what precedes and to what follows.

The continuation of the vision is the prophecy of vss. 12–14. In a new metaphor the multistaged resurrection of the vision is reduced to two stages—opening of graves and raising those in them. The unfinished business of the vision (what will the very great army do?) is then completed by the restoration of the people to their land (vss. 12–13a). Here again the momentum of inspiration generates an augment: the vivifying *rwḥ* of the vision is upgraded to the reforming divine *rwḥ* of 36:27, and the bringing to the land of vs. 12 is augmented by the promise of the people's lasting settlement therein (cf. 36:28).

The bizarre image of a plain filled with bones may be an adaptation by Ezekiel of a Mesopotamian motif occurring in battle accounts. Sennacherib boasts, "With the bodies of [the enemy's] warriors I filled the plain, like grass" (D. D. Luckenbill, *The Annals of Sennacherib* [Chicago: University of Chicago Press, 1924], p. 46, lines 9–10). One of the curses by which vassal kings of Esarhaddon were bound to loyalty reads: "[If you are disloyal] may Ninurta, leader of the gods . . . fill the plain with your corpses, give your flesh to eagles and vultures to feed upon" (*ANET*^{3}, p. 538b; for further examples, see *CAD* M/1 186). F. C. Fensham inferred from this curse that in his vision of dry bones the prophet alluded to the punishment (military defeat) Israel suffered for disloyalty to its God, which was now to be rescinded ("The Curse of the Dry Bones in Ezekiel 37:1–14 Changed to a Blessing of Resurrection," *Journal of Northwest Semitic Languages* 13 [1987], 59–60). It would seem, however, that the major stimulus of the vision was the despairing metaphor in the popular saying, whose literalization was imagined by the prophet—perhaps under the influence of the Mesopotamian motif. (As the disposition of the water monster's remains in ch. 32 also suggests a connection with a Mesopotamian motif; see § XXXVI in Structure and Themes.) This conjecture is more plausible than B. Lang's derivation of the dry bones imagery from the sight of a Zoroastrian graveyard ("Street Theater, Raising the Dead, and the Zoroastrian Connection in Ezekiel's Prophecy," in J. Lust, ed.,

Ezekiel and His Book, pp. 307–14). Literalization of figurative language is a feature of Ezekiel; see 3:1, 3, and I, 77; 5:1 and I, 126.

The use of perfects with *waw*-conjunctive where imperfect consecutives would be expected (verbs in initial position in vss. 1, 2, 7, 8, and 10) is a feature of later Biblical Hebrew that appears throughout the book of Ezekiel (e.g., 9:7; 13:6, 8; 19:12b; 20:22; 25:12; 40:24, 35; 41:3, 8, 13, 15; 42:15; see Rooker, *Biblical Hebrew*, pp. 100f.). Although the phenomenon occurs sporadically in early texts (e.g., notably in the Song of Deborah, Judg 5:26), it becomes more frequent in the books of II Kings, Jeremiah, Ezekiel, and Chronicles (S. R. Driver, *Tenses*, pp. 158–64). Since contemporary Aramaic has no *waw*-consecutive forms, nor does the later Mishnaic Hebrew, strongly influenced by Aramaic, it is plausible to assume that the occasional appearance of ordinary perfects instead of imperfect consecutives in those biblical books is due to the influence of Aramaic on the speakers and writers of late Biblical Hebrew. E. Y. Kutscher leaves open the possibility of an inner Hebrew development in his *A History of the Hebrew Language* (Jerusalem: Magnes Press, 1982), §§ 67, 104. In any case it is unnecessary to ascribe instances of this usage to later scribes (Joüon-Muraoka, § 119 z, za) or, in the case of our passage, to a "middle Hebrew / Aramaic reworking" (R. Bartelmus, "Ez 37:1–14, die Verbform *wᵉqatal* und die Anfänge der Auferstehungshoffnung," ZAW 97 [1985], 366–89). To be sure, the clustering of the phenomenon in this oracle is curious; might it betray an adjustment to later usage resulting from the incorporation of the passage in the liturgy (see the concluding Note)?

The connection of this oracle of re-creation to the preceding oracle of re-formation is patent. The various functions assigned to *rwḥ* in this passage enlarge on its single, yet crucial, role in the reformation of Israel described in 36:27.

Note on Early Jewish and Christian Interpretation of Ezek 37:1–14

In view of the vivid metaphors and powerful rhetoric of this passage it is no wonder that it was understood literally by interpreters living in an age when the doctrine of a future resurrection had (on other grounds) taken hold in the Jewish and Christian communities. (On the origin of this doctrine, see H. Birkeland, "The Belief in the Resurrection of the Dead in the Old Testament," *Studia Theologica* 3 [1949], 60–78.) In the New Testament, allusion to this passage has been seen in Matt 27:51–53: when Jesus expired, ". . . the earth shook [cf. our vs. 7] . . . the tombs were opened, and many bodies of the saints who had died were raised, and coming out of the tombs . . . they went in to the holy city . . ." [cf. our vs. 12]. Language taken from Ezek 37 depicts literal, individual resurrection, part of a messianic agenda (J. Grassi, "Ezekiel xxxvii 1–14 and the New Testament," *New Testament Studies* 11 [1964-65], 162–64). "Many church fathers found the final resurrection of the dead proclaimed here" (Zimmerli, with reference to W. Neuss, *Das Buch Ezechiel in Theologie und Kunst bis zum Ende des XII. Jahrhunderts* [Münster: Aschendorff, 1912]). The Peshitta entitles the passage, "On the resurrection of the dead"; agreeably it translates the beginning of vs. 11: "These bones are *of* the whole house of Israel" — belong to all their dead, rather than "are (a figure for) the whole mass of Israel's exiles." (We recall that the metaphoric status of the dry bones is assured by the exiles' use of the expression with reference to themselves; they cannot mean literally "we are dead." Ezekiel's vision concretizes the metaphor, but it remains a metaphor for all that.)

Early Jewish interpretation also understood the passage to represent a literal resurrection of the dead. Whether the event really occurred or it was just in vision was disputed. In *b. Sanhedrin* 92b, apropos of a discussion as to whether those who will be resurrected at the end-time would die, a dictum of R. Eliezer is adduced in favor of their dying: "The dead that Ezekiel revived got up on their feet, sang a hymn, and died" (whence we may infer that the future resurrectees will also die). R. Judah objects to treating vss. 1–10 as narrative of reality: "It was really only a parable [*mšl*]" (i.e., there weren't bones that really came to life, only a vision of the resurrection aimed to hearten those who die before the messianic age; for this meaning of *mšl*, cf. the Talmudic statement that "Job never existed in reality, but he was only a parable" — a fictive character serving to teach a lesson [*b. Baba Batra* 15a]). However, the "realist" view prevails in the ensuing discussion, which revolves around the question: who were resurrected?

Early Christian sources mention a different Jewish reading of the vision closer to what we should judge to be the correct reading — as a metaphor for the restoration of Israel. This reading, they say, is typically Jewish, as opposed to the prevailing Christian resurrectionist (= the prevailing Talmudic!) one (C. H. Kraeling, *The Synagogue, The Excavations at Dura-Europos: Final Report*, VIII/1 [New Haven: Yale University Press, 1956], p. 179 n. 689). The Ezekiel paintings of the synagogue at Dura-Europos (on the upper Euphrates, near ancient Mari; third century C.E.) include scenes of the four winds (in the form of winged Psyches) entering dead bodies, and next to them an assembly of standing men in an attitude of praising (cf. R. Eliezer's view, cited above). But there is no way of telling whether the artist meant to convey a parabolic/metaphoric vision or a reality (cf. Kraeling, op. cit., 185–94). Thus the dominant trend of the earliest interpretations of our passage is furthest from its original meaning as we today understand it.

A clear attestation of the metaphoric interpretation of the vision is in Rashi's commentary to R. Judah's view in the Talmud, that vss. 1–10 are "really a parable (*mšl*)." Rashi takes R. Judah's *mšl* to mean "metaphor" (wrongly I believe, with all respect), thus: "[Ezekiel] gave them a figure [*hyh mrmz lhm*] for the exile: like a dead man who revives, so Israel will return from exile." In his Ezekiel commentary (on vs. 11), Rashi again offers the metaphoric interpretation of vss. 1–10 as a possible one. However, he reads the opening of the graves in vs. 12 literally as a description of resurrection.

Kimḥi comes closer to the modern view. He asserts that the revival of the bones was in vision only: "these things didn't really happen." Ambiguity exists only in the referents of the revived bones and the disinterred. One possibility is the resurrection: "He showed him this (i.e., the revival of the bones) to demonstrate to him that he will eventually resurrect the Israelite dead at the time of the final Restoration (*yšwʿh*), so that they may experience the Restoration"; conformably the opening of the graves is to be taken literally. But Kimḥi allows another possibility: "He showed him this matter as a metaphor for Israel's exodus from their exile, in which they are like dry bones"; conformably, the graves, too, are metaphors for "the gentile lands of exile."

The resurrectionist interpretation, so needful for its solace, recommended this passage for liturgical purposes. In the Synagogue it is read as the prophetic lesson (*hafṭarah*) for the sabbath included in Passover week—the festival celebrating the liberation from Egyptian bondage. In the services of the Church it was specially associated with Baptism at Lent and Easter (Cooke, p. 398). Both communions thus found it appropriate for celebrating redemption and new life.

XLV. Reuniting the Two Kingdoms of Israel and Judah (37:15–28)

37 [15]The word of YHWH came to me: [16][a]And you,[a] man, take for you one[a] stick
and write on it "[Belonging] to Judah and to the Israelites associated with him."
Then take one[b] stick and write on it "[Belonging] to Joseph—Ephraim's stick—
and all the house of Israel associated with him." [17]Join them together, one to one,
for you, as one stick, so that they become one in your hand. [18]And when your
fellow countrymen say to you, "Do tell us what meaning these have for you,"
[19]speak to them: Thus said Lord YHWH: See, I am going to take the stick of
Joseph—which is in Ephraim's hand—and the tribes of Israel who are associated
with him, and [c]join them /to it/ with the stick of Judah,[c] and I will turn them into
one stick, so that they shall be one in [d]my hand.[d]

[20]And let the sticks on which you write be in your hand before their eyes.

[21]And speak to them: Thus said Lord YHWH: See, I am going to take the
Israelites from among the nations where they have gone, and gather them from
all sides, and bring them to their soil. [22]I will turn them into one nation in the
land, in the mountains of Israel, and one king shall serve for all of them [e]as king.[e]
They shall no more be two nations, nor again be divided into two kingdoms
[e]any more.[e]

[23]They shall no more be polluted by their idols and by their loathsome things
and by all their transgressions. But I will deliver them from all their [f]dwelling
places[f] in which they have sinned, and I will purify them, and they shall be my
people and I will be their God.

[24] My servant David [g][shall be] king[g] over them, and one shepherd shall be for
all of them; and they shall follow my rules, and my laws—they shall carefully
observe them. [25]So they shall dwell on the land that I gave to my servant, to Jacob,
in which your[h] ancestors dwelt; they shall dwell on it, they and their children,

[a(–a)] Not in G.
[b] G "(a) second"; S "another."
[c–c] G S "put them on (S with) the tribe (S stick) of Judah"—as from *wntty 'wtm ʿl* (= *'t* "with") *ʿṣ yhwdh.*
[d–d] G "the hand of Judah"; V "in his [i.e., Judah's] hand."
[e–e] Not in G S.
[f–f] G "iniquities"; Symmachus "turnings-away"—as from *mšwbh* "backturning."
[g–g] G "chief"; S "shall reign (*nmlk*)."
[h] G S "their."

and their children's children, eternally. And David my servant [shall be] their chief eternally. [26]I will make for them a covenant of well-being, an eternal covenant it shall be with them; [a]and I will set them, and make them numerous;[a] and I will set my sanctuary in their midst eternally. [27]My tabernacle shall be over them, and I will be their God and they shall be my people. [28]And the nations shall know that I YHWH sanctify Israel, by my sanctuary's being in their midst eternally.

COMMENT

37:16. *And you.* Usually a mark of continuation, this address sometimes appears at the very start of an oracle (see comment to 7:2 [I, 145]). Here it alerts one to a relation of this prophecy to the preceding one (see Structure and Themes). No such alert is effected by G, which lacks the opening "and you."

take for you. The reflexive nuance of the postpositive *lk* "for you" (found often in commands to perform symbolic acts: 4:1, 3, 9; 5:1 [twice]; 12:3) focuses attention on the actor: at the initial stage, the action concerns him alone; he must concentrate on executing it as ordered (Joüon-Muraoka, § 133 d, esp. n. 2). Here the subjective isolation of the actor is underlined by the query of the onlookers about ". . . what meaning these have for you" (vs. 18).

one stick. G "(a) stick" (*rhabdos*); this sense of *ʿeṣ* (usually "tree" or "wood") is rare, but attested; e.g., "a couple of sticks" (I Kings 17:12); "a stick of cedar" (Lev 14:4; Rashi glosses by *maqqel* "rod, stick"—cf. Milgrom, *Leviticus*, AB, p. 835). In Hos 4:12 *ʿṣ* || *mql*; both terms serve for a stick in natural or finished state. The choice of *ʿṣ* seems to have been dictated by its ambiguity, symbolizing both king and kingdom (see vs. 22 and comment, and Structure and Themes).

"One" (*ʾḥd*) is a key term throughout this prophecy of reunification (eleven occurrences)—lost in G (see text note) and in modern translations of our verse (e.g., "a stick . . . another stick" in *RSV*, NJPS).

T translates *ʿṣ* by *lwḥʾ* "tablet," possibly influenced by the analogous command to Isaiah (Isa 8:1), "Take for you a large tablet (*lwḥ*) and write on it . . ." G. R. Driver suggested that *ʿṣ* here refers to a hinged writing board (a diptych; see G. R. Driver, *JThS* 22 [1971], 549–50). Now while it is surely easier to write on a tablet or a diptych, the former does not associate with king or kingdom, and the latter in essence (di- "two") contradicts the emphasis on oneness in this prophecy.

With regard to the practicality of the command: a staff donated by Ramses II to the god Amun was inscribed over most of its length with the name and epithets of the king, and a dedication to the god (W. C. Hayes, *The Scepter of Egypt*, II [Cambridge, Mass.: Harvard University Press, 1959], p. 342).

"*[Belonging] to Judah and to the Israelites associated with him.*" The prepositional *l-* "to" is modeled on the customary indication of the owner on stamp seals; e.g., *lyʾznyhw ʿbd hmlk* "[Belonging] to Yaazanyahu servant of the king." See *ANEP*[2], ##276–78, for this and other examples. In Lev 16:8 the destination of sacrificial animals is determined by lots inscribed *lyhwh* "of YHWH" and *lʿzʾzl* "of Azazel" (Milgrom, *Leviticus 1–16*, AB, p. 1020). The inscription personifies the southern kingdom and its population, mainly claiming descent from (the tribe of) Judah but, with other Israelite elements mixed in (e.g., Simeonites, Calebites, and, more recently, refugees from the collapsed northern kingdom).

Then take. The sequence of the normal imperative form *qḥ* followed by the rare form *wlqḥ* (in which the first radical is kept; again in Exod 29:1; Prov 20:16) is paralleled in I Kings 17:10–11 *qḥy . . . wlqḥy.* In both passages G renders the short form by an imperative, the long form by a future, indicating that its underlying Hebrew text did not show the same word twice (as those suppose who, invoking G, emend the long form out of existence in both passages—so *BHS*).

Joseph—Ephraim's stick. The proper rival of Judah was Joseph (see the contest for the richest blessing in Gen 49, and for the primogeniture in I Chron 5:1–2). But historically the tribe of Joseph consisted of a junior tribe, Ephraim, and a senior one, Manasseh. The secession of the bulk of the tribes from the Davidic kingdom after Solomon's death was led by the Ephraimite Jeroboam (I Kings 11:26), and betokened the leadership of his tribe in the new northern kingdom (usually called Israel, as throughout the Book of Kings). After the Assyrian annexation of the peripheral territories of the kingdom (731), the remaining heartland—the area of the tribes of Manasseh and Ephraim—was called Ephraim. This designation appears (alongside "Israel") frequently in Hosea (e.g., 4:17; 5:3; 11:8), and occurs in Isaiah (e.g., 7:17; 11:13) and Jeremiah (e.g., 31:18, 20 [17, 19]) as well. Here "Ephraim's stick" seems to be a gloss, defining "Joseph" as the later-named kingdom of Ephraim. A similar gloss appears in vs. 19, where "stick" is implicitly construed—too narrowly—as scepter (see there), as it is probably in this gloss also.

all the house of Israel. A greater aggregation than the "Israelites" associated with Judah, reflecting the relative sizes of the two kingdoms.

17. *Join* (qrb) *them together, one to one.* The language evokes 37:7b: "the bones came together (*wtqrbw*) bone to proper (lit. "its") bone." The second vowel of the imperative piʿel *qarab, a* instead of normal *e*, recurs in Ps 55:10 *pallag* "divide."

become one in your hand. Lit. "ones" (*ʾḥdym*), elsewhere meaning "a few" (e.g., Gen 29:20: seven years that seemed "a few days"), but here a paradoxical expression meaning perhaps "a composite one" = a one made out of two ones. Contrast the parallel final clause of vs. 19: "so that they shall be one *ʾḥd* in my (= God's) hand"; what God joins together is a seamless unity, unlike the human product. The prophet is to hold the two sticks in one hand and (we may suppose, on the basis of vs. 20) brandish them in the sight of the people, rousing their curiosity ("Why doesn't he take a single long stick instead of joining two short ones?" [Eliezer]).

G. R. Driver (1938, pp. 182–83) made a notable attempt to overcome the paradoxical *lʾḥdym* on the strength of G's "by binding them" (occurring before the final result clause; G has no positional equivalent for MT *lʾḥdym*). G, he proposed, reflects a piʿel verb *lʾḥdm* "to unite them," otherwise unattested in Biblical Hebrew (but newly coined in modern Hebrew). Rearranging the latter part of the verse, he arrives at a reading: ". . . for you, to unite them, and they will become one stick in your hand" (my corrected rendering of his reconstructed Hebrew). But G is most likely no more than an explanatory rendering of MT's unusual wording, in the spirit of MenbSh's gloss to it: "they being bound together." (The Arabic version that Driver cites in support of his emendation is merely a translation of G [Cornill, 67ff.].)

18. *Do tell us.* See comment to 24:19.

19. *which is in Ephraim's hand.* An explanatory phrase that, like its mate in vs. 16, breaks the sequence "Joseph and the tribes of Israel associated with him." "Stick" is here understood narrowly as scepter (held in hand) — a symbol of kingship. The royal scepter of the nation Joseph is in the possession of the leading tribe, Ephraim.

and join . . . to it . . . the stick of Judah. The sense of vs. 19b$^{\alpha}$ comes through: to the stick of Joseph I will join the stick of Judah; but the text can hardly be in order. Kimḥi's gloss only underscores the problems: I will put [= join] them (*'wtm*) — i.e., the tribes of Israel, with him (*'lyw*) — i.e., the tribe of Ephraim, with (*'t*) the stick of Judah. Problematic are: the mixture of tribes and stick; the juxtaposition of two different prepositions (*'l-* and *'t*) expressing "with"; the involvement of Ephraim as a separate entity. Moreover, the object pronoun "them" (*'wtm*) mistakenly identifies the object of the verb "put/join" as the immediately preceding "tribes of Israel" (merely part of the title of Joseph's stick) when it is rather "the stick of Judah" at the end of the clause. The versions simplify (see text note c–c), but show the same mistake: G "I will put them on (*'l?*) the tribe of Judah"; S: "I will put them with (*'l? 't?*) the stick of Judah"; = V, cf. the *New Jerusalem Bible:* "shall join them to the stick of Judah."

Abarbanel stated the problem clearly: "Properly the text should have read: 'I will put with/upon it (*'lyw;* namely, the stick of Joseph) *'t* (the direct-object marker) the stick of Judah'; the word *'wtm* has no function here." Most moderns would agree; e.g., *RSV:* "and I will join with it [*NAB:* it to] the stick of Judah." This posits an original reading *wntty 'lyw 't 'ṣ yhwdh* (so NJPS: "and I will place the stick of Judah [a]upon it[a] [[a–a]meaning of Heb. uncertain]"; similarly *NRSV*). The present MT is conflated, showing both *'wtm* — produced by a mistaken decision as to the object of the verb — and the presumedly original *'lyw.*

be one in my hand. In a miraculous act of my power ("my hand"). Apparently this phrase was misunderstood as an allusion to a scepter in God's hand, whence the gloss in the first part of this verse locating Joseph's stick "in Ephraim's hand" — i.e., as a scepter.

The readings of G and V (see text note d–d) reflect the view of the sticks as scepters. They belong to the history of interpretation, anticipating in vs. 19 what is to be revealed only in vs. 22 — the restored monopoly on kingship of the Judahite Davidides.

20. The visual, concrete union of the sticks promises realization of the verbal message; on Ezekiel's symbolic acts, see I, 126.

21–22. Vs. 21 picks up the account of restoration where vss. 12 and 14 left it: God himself will restore the people to their soil; for the language, cf. 34:13; 36:24. Then the new political arrangement (vs. 22) with a divinely appointed human leader is described nonfiguratively, with just enough repetition of key terms to show that it is a decoding of the symbolism; see Structure and Themes. The two stages of national rehabilitation repeat the sequence of 34:11–24 — God ingathers and settles the people in the land, then appoints a human ruler over them.

22. *I will turn them into one nation . . . one king.* This verse decodes "I will turn them into one stick" (end of vs. 19), showing that "stick" is a complex symbol referring to king as well as to nation.

one nation in the land. "The land" unqualified is the land of Israel, as in 20:40, hence G "my land" is not preferable. All the less since the phrase occurs in II Sam 7:23 (but with a different sense: a nation unique on earth).

the mountains of Israel. The entire land is meant; see comment to 34:13–14.

The parallelism of "one nation—one king" / "two nations—two kingdoms" supports the authenticity of the term "king" against G's translation "chief" (*archon*), by which it normally renders Hebrew *naśi'* (as in vs. 25).

In vs. 22b the K *yhyh* (singular, Q *yhyw* plural) looks like a scribal error influenced by *yhyh* four words before.

23. Pollution through transgressions (14:11) and idols (22:4; 23:30) and the pairing of idols and loathsome things (20:7; cf. Deut 29:16; II Kings 23:24) are Ezekielian commonplaces.

I will deliver them from all their dwelling places in which they have sinned. The connection of idols and dwelling places evokes 6:6, 14, alluding to idolatry in the land of Israel; hence Kara's reference to "Bethel and Dan, where the calf-idols were installed, by which the Israelites sinned." However, the context indicates an exilic location, favoring Abarbanel's view: "Their dwelling places were in the lands where they sojourned and they sinned there, as our master Moses said; 'there you shall worship other gods,' etc. (Deut 28:36, 64 [one might adduce Ezek 14:3ff.; 20:39, in support]). And because they were sullied and defiled by their sins he goes on to say, 'and I will purify you.'" Such attempts at wresting sense from this sentence are unconvincing. The difficulty is highlighted by comparison with Zech 8:7f.: "I will deliver my people from the lands of east and . . . west, and I will bring them home to dwell in Jerusalem . . ." Promise of deliverance from a place leads to promise of return to home; but in our passage the return home is already behind us (vs. 21). And if the point here is deliverance from sin, why not say so instead of intruding *mošᵉbotehem* "their dwelling places" into the sentence?

G obviates the difficulties by translating the problematic noun "iniquities." More helpful in accounting for the origin of the problem is Symmachus's "turnings-away"—a Hexaplaric rendition of *mᵉšubot-* "defections" in Jer 2:19 and 14:7. Comparing with Ezek 36:29, "I will deliver you from all your impurities," makes it all but certain that the reading here should be *mšwb(w)tyhm* "(I will deliver them from all) their defections," a promise to cancel guilt and its baneful consequences. On the endowment of "defection" with baleful power, see comment to 36:29. The erroneous reading replaced the Jeremianic word (nine occurrences in Jeremiah) with a priestly term (e.g., Exod 35:3; Lev 3:17) attested in Ezekiel (6:6, 14). It is another sign of Jeremianic influence.

24. *My servant David.* For the epithet, see comment to 34:23; for the theme, see Structure and Themes.

and they shall follow my rules . . . laws. This echoes 36:27b, only there obedience results from God's infusing his spirit into the people. Here association with the new David — one king, one shepherd — recalls 34:6: the indictment of the "bad shepherds" for leading the people astray. There is just a suggestion that as the past misleaders are held responsible for the apostasy of the people, so the future good shepherd will be credited with the people's obedience to God's law.

25. "You find careful observance of God's laws juxtaposed to settling the land, implying that . . . because the people observe them they are not exiled. The same appears in Lev 26 [vss. 1, 5]: 'If you follow my laws . . . you will dwell secure in your land'" (Kara). The same juxtaposition occurs in Ezek 36:27–28.

your ancestors. A lapse for "their ancestors" (see text note), perhaps influenced by such phrases as "the land that I gave to your ancestors" (36:28; cf. 20:42; 47:14). The expected form *'bwt(yh)m* occurs only in reproofs (2:3; 5:10; 20:4, 24).

26. *a covenant of well-being.* See at 34:25.

I will set them. Another inconstruable occurrence of *ntn* "set, put, give," beside 17:22; 34:26. Kara and Ehrlich [Hebrew] guessed that it is the start of some such an expression as "set them supreme over all nations" (cf. Deut 26:19). Perles (*JQR* n.s. 2 [1910–11], 121) regarded the omission in G of this and the next two words (see text note) as primary, and conjectured that MT came about in two stages: (1) "I will make them numerous" was inserted, under the influence of 36:10, 11. (2) Later a second insertion was made before it — *wntty m* (*m* being an abbreviation for *mqdšy*) — directing the reader to skip the first insertion and go straight to *wntty mqdšy* "I will set my sanctuary." Copyists mistakenly joined the *m* to the preceding verb (as though it were an object suffix) and the result is MT. Ingenious.

27. *My tabernacle* (mškny) *shall be over them.* Ezekiel spiritualizes the antique priestly term for the desert Tabernacle. In the promise of Lev 26:11 (whose wording resounds in this new promise), "I will set my tabernacle (*mškny*) in their midst" refers to the material tent-sanctuary, God's dwelling amidst Israel (Exod 25:8; 29:44f.). Here that promise is couched in contemporary terms by the preceding sentence: "I will set my sanctuary (*mqdšy*) in their midst eternally" (end of vs. 26). The antique term was freed for a new meaning. Now the tent-sanctuary of the priestly writings was closely associated with the divine cloud that covered it by day, appearing as fire by night (Exod 40:34–38, abbreviated from Num 9:15–23). In Isa 4:5f. the cloud evolves into the image of a protective cover (like a tent) over Zion:

YHWH will create over the whole shrine of Mount Zion
and over its whole place of assembly
a cloud by day and smoke,
and the glow of flaming fire by night.
Indeed over all Glory there shall be a canopy (*ḥuppa*);
It shall be a pavilion (*sukka*) for shade by day from heat
and for shelter and protection against streaming rain.

Ezekiel reconnects the Isaianic "canopy" with its origin, the priestly desert *miš-kan*, but sublimates the latter in the light of the former: God's *miškan* is no longer "amidst" the people (*btwkm*), it is now a protective tent "over them" (*ʿlyhm*). The original meaning "place of [God's] (in)dwelling" charges Ezekiel's novel usage with the sense of divine presence, so that his spiritual *miškan* amounts to a sheltering divine presence—a mere step away from the post-biblical concept of the Shekinah.

The versions miss the point by ignoring the difference between "in their midst" and "over them" (T gets it halfway right: "I will cause my Shekinah to abide among them").

STRUCTURE AND THEMES

After the revelation-event formula (vs. 1) the prophet is ordered to enact a symbol with two sticks labeled "Judah" and "Joseph" which he is to hold together to form one long stick (vss. 16–17). The people will ask what meaning this has for him (vs. 18), and he is to answer in two stages: (1) In metaphoric language: God is about to unite the sticks of Judah and Joseph—in so saying the prophet is to present the sticks to the sight of the people (vss. 19–20). (2) The metaphor is to be explained: God is not only going to ingather Israel's dispersed (vs. 21; cf. 34:11; 36:24), he will reconstitute them as a single kingdom with a single king, so to be forever (vs. 22). This flows into a recapitulation of the entire range of restorative acts, spread through chs. 34 and 36:

vs. 23: Israel shall be purged and delivered from sin/pollution = 36:25, 29a
YHWH their God Israel his people = 36:28 [cf. 34:24a$^{\alpha}$]
vs. 24: one shepherd-king, my servant David = 34:23 [minus "king"]
they shall follow my laws = 36:27

From vs. 25 to the end each restored condition is said to be eternal, a new emphasis.

vs. 25: they shall dwell in their ancestral land = 36:28a
my servant David, their chief = 34:24a$^{\beta}$
a covenant of well-being = 34:25
they shall be numerous = 36:10f., 37f.

The climax is reached in vs. 26b$^{\beta}$–28 in which God's sanctuary and his sheltering presence are promised to the people forever. An expanded recognition formula closes the passage.

One cannot miss the deliberate slowness of the movement, retarded by repetitions and tiny steps (e.g., the two stages of decoding the symbolic act; the repeated "eternally"; the recap of blessings). The prophecy lingers on the bright future, savors it repeatedly. In this it recalls the deliberate pace of the previous vision of the dry bones. A further point of contact between the two parts of ch. 37 is the motif of unification of the separated, the coming together (*qrb*) of sticks (*ʿṣym*) and bones (*ʿṣmwt;* vss. 7, 17; note the assonance).

The choice of *ʿṣ* for the sense "stick" instead of the more common *šebeṭ*, *maṭṭe*, or *maqqel* may be due to its many connotations in Ezekiel's usage. He has used trees as figures for kings, dynasties, and kingdoms (chs. 17, 31), and for human beings innocent and guilty (21:1–10). The suggestion of "scepter" is also strongly present. By this choice the prophet achieved a riddling effect that suited his rhetorical purpose (to arouse the curiosity of the audience).

This prophecy states, explicitly and uniquely in the book, that the population of the former northern kingdom of Israel will be restored to its land. But the viewpoint is of a Jerusalemite advocate of the line of David. The hope of the Davidic kings to regain their lost northern realm is evinced by Josiah's reform activity in Samaria, then an Assyrian province (II Kings 23:15–20). Clearly Josiah ignored the Assyrian domination and regarded the land of Samaria as YHWH's land, destined to be subject once again to a Davidide. As for the deported population of the northern kingdom, Jeremiah expressly foretold their return (Jer 30; 31). Here, as in much else in the restoration prophecies, Ezekiel follows the path of his great homeland contemporary. A realistic basis for this expectation is not given; nor is there a sign that either prophet was in touch with north Israelites.

Names in eighth-century B.C.E. documents from Gozan, Calah, and elsewhere in Assyria bearing *-yahu* endings may confirm the deportations to remote areas of the empire as reported in the Bible (see A. Malamat, *EJ*, s.v. "Exile, Assyrian," for details). But if colonies of north Israelites existed, we have no evidence that they and the Judahites who followed them into exile over a century later ever were in contact (C. Gordon conjectures that the earlier deportees merged with the later ones; *EI* 3 [1954], 104f.). In our present ignorance, it seems most likely that the prophecies of Jeremiah and Ezekiel about the return of the north Israelites to their land are expressions of the ideal unity of the two kingdoms. In prophetic circles, the staunch defenders of national traditions, this ideal survived the political schism of centuries, and was to be realized in the promised rectification of all wrongs in the future.

As in 34:23f., "my servant David" is named here as the future single shepherd-king of the reunited kingdom. This is the ultimate exaltation of the founder of the uncommonly long-lived Judahite dynasty (some four hundred years). G. von Rad (in *Old Testament Theology*, I [Edinburgh and London: Oliver and Boyd, 1962], p. 345) showed how the editor-author of the Book of Kings measures all the kings of Judah

> against the picture of the one perfect king whom he knows, namely David. David walked before Jahweh "with integrity of heart and uprightness" (I Kings 9:4); David's heart was "wholly true to Jahweh" (I Kings 11:4); he did according to what "pleased Jahweh and kept his statutes and commandments" (I Kings 11:38); "he followed Jahweh with his whole heart, doing only what pleased Jahweh" (I Kings 14:8; see also I Kings 3:3; 8:17; 11:33; 15:3, 5, 11; II Kings 14:3; 16:2; 18:3; 22:2).

That writer "had a picture of the perfect anointed unremittingly present to his mind" (ibid.); implicit in his condemnation of the subsequent Davidic monarchs is the vision of a messianic king (p. 344). Isa 11:1ff. explicity identifies the perfect king of the future as "a shoot from the stock of Jesse" (David's father). Jeremiah 23:5 calls him "a righteous (or: legitimate) sprout" that God "will raise up for

David." The ultimate in adoration of David is his revival in the figure of the future ideal king. This occurs in Hos 3:5 ("Afterwards, the Israelites will turn and seek YHWH their God and David their king"), Jer 30:9 ("They shall serve YHWH their God and David their king whom I will raise up for them"), and in our Ezekiel passages. Just what this means is not altogether clear. Kimḥi offers the two obvious possibilities: "The King Messiah will be named David, for he will be of David's line; alternatively, this is an allusion to resurrection [i.e., the founder of the line will be revived]." Both interpretations seem too clear-cut; the text requires no more than "a new David" who is not the old one resurrected or merely one of David's line, but something in between: a future king who will be the moral (and physical?) duplicate of the David idealized by late biblical writers.

The climactic summary of future blessing in vss. 23ff. is closely related to the covenant blessings in Lev 26:2–13 (as are the promises of restoration in Ezek 34 and 36). The divergences reflect the different horizons of each document: Leviticus looks to the situation of Israel as a settled premonarchic society; Ezekiel, to a post-exilic ideal end-time.

While Leviticus promises victory in war to the obedient people, Ezekiel makes no mention of it. The restored community will not have to wage war, being under God's protection (on fortified cities, 36:35, see comment there).

Leviticus makes no mention of a king, Ezekiel does.

Leviticus locates God's presence in a tent-shrine (*miškan*), Ezekiel, in a temple (*miqdaš*). Ezekiel utilizes *miškan* in a new sense ("sheltering presence"), approaching post-biblical Shekinah.

How the collapse of the kingdom and the burning of the Temple undermined national self-confidence is reflected in the emphasis laid on the permanence of the new arrangements of the future restoration. "No more" will evils occur; the rectifications will be "eternal."

The conclusion to the prophecies of restoration prepares the way for the "constitution" of the new Israel in the sequel. The sudden mention of the temple-sanctuary (*mqdšy*, vs. 26b$^{\beta}$) presages the extensive description of the future building, its personnel and its rites, the duties of the chief, and the settlement of the restored tribes that will be set out in chs. 40–48. Before that, however, comes the final worldwide vindication of God through the crushing of Gog and his horde on the mountains of Israel (chs. 38–39).